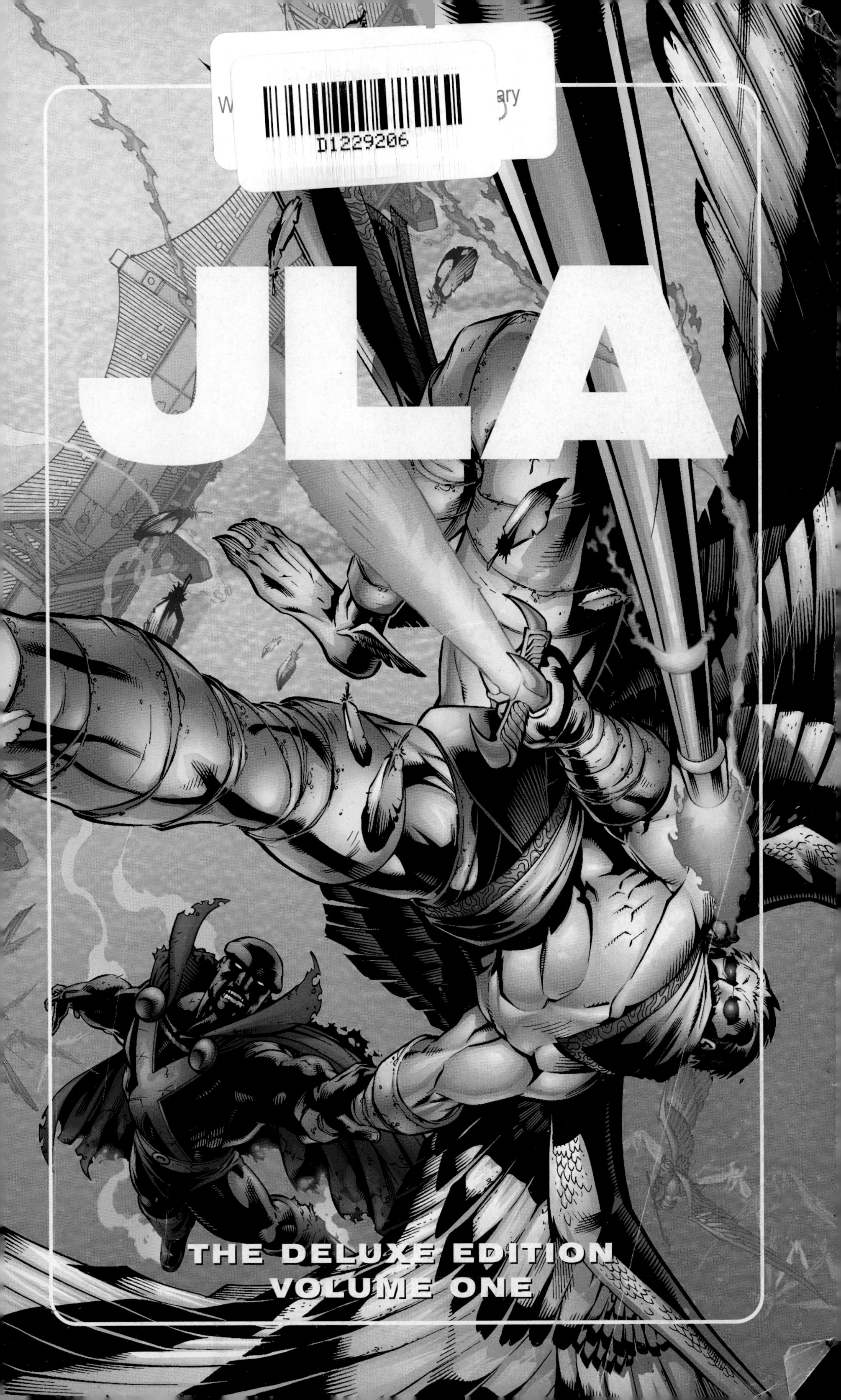
JLA
THE DELUXE EDITION
VOLUME ONE

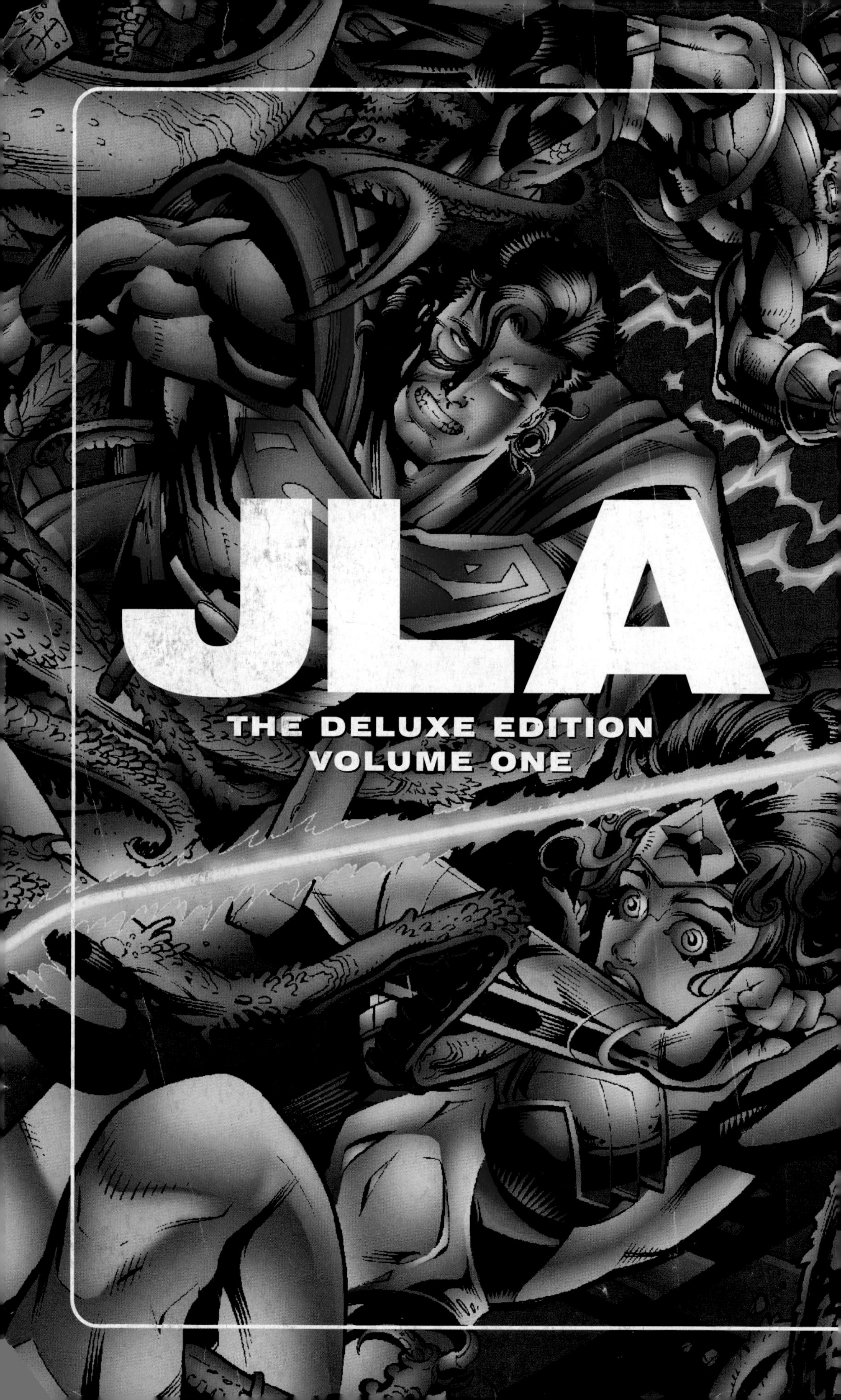
JLA
THE DELUXE EDITION
VOLUME ONE

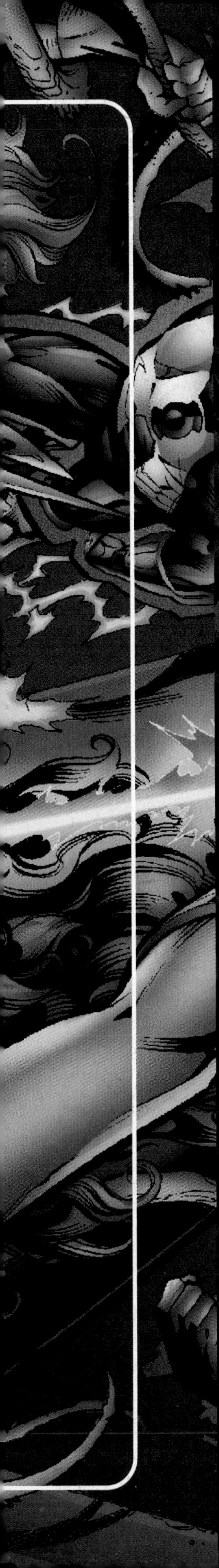

GRANT MORRISON
writer

HOWARD PORTER
penciller

JOHN DELL
inker

• •

MARK MILLAR
co-writer on "Star Seed"
writer on "The Lost Pages" & "A Day in the Life"

OSCAR JIMENEZ
penciller on "Imaginary Stories" & "Elseworlds"

DON HILLSMAN
penciller on "The Lost Pages" & "A Day in the Life"

CHIP WALLACE
KEN BRANCH
ANIBAL RODRIGUEZ
additional Inkers

PAT GARRAHY, JOHN KALISZ &
TOM J. McCRAW
colorists

KEN LOPEZ &
ALBERT TOBIAS DE GUZMAN
letterers

• •

Superman created by
JERRY SIEGEL & JOE SHUSTER

Batman created by
BOB KANE

Wonder Woman created by
WILLIAM MOULTON MARSTON

Aquaman created by
PAUL NORRIS

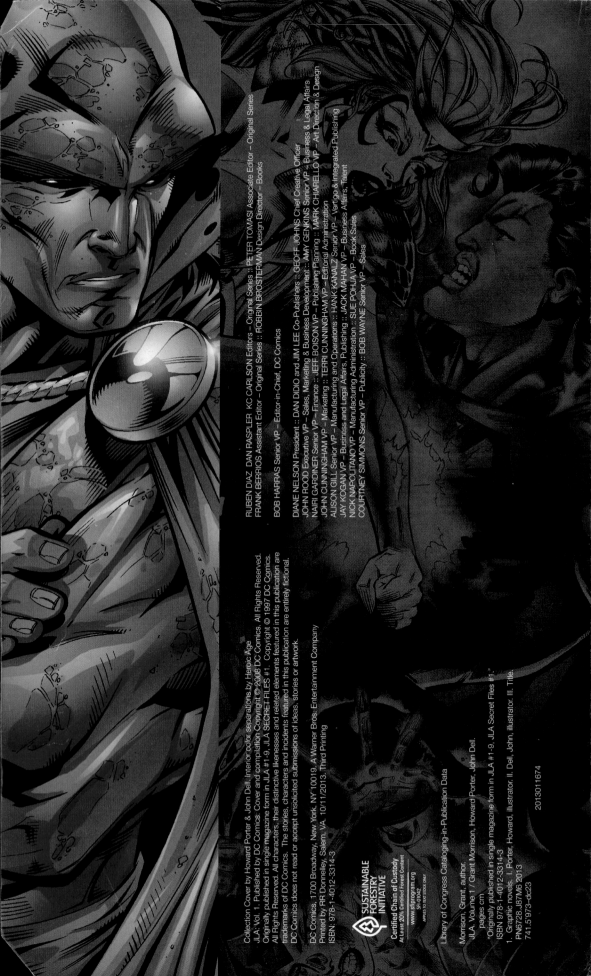

RUBEN DIAZ DAN RASPLER KC CARLSON Editors – Original Series :: PETER TOMASI Associate Editor – Original Series
FRANK BERRIOS Assistant Editor – Original Series :: ROBBIN BROSTERMAN Design Director – Books

BOB HARRAS Senior VP – Editor-in-Chief, DC Comics

DIANE NELSON President :: DAN DIDIO and JIM LEE Co-Publishers :: GEOFF JOHNS Chief Creative Officer
JOHN ROOD Executive VP – Sales, Marketing & Business Development :: AMY GENKINS Senior VP – Business & Legal Affairs
NAIRI GARDINER Senior VP – Finance :: JEFF BOISON VP – Publishing Planning :: MARK CHIARELLO VP – Art Direction & Design
JOHN CUNNINGHAM VP – Marketing :: TERRI CUNNINGHAM VP – Editorial Administration
ALISON GILL Senior VP – Manufacturing and Operations :: HANK KANALZ Senior VP – Vertigo & Integrated Publishing
JAY KOGAN VP – Business and Legal Affairs, Publishing :: JACK MAHAN VP – Business Affairs, Talent
NICK NAPOLITANO VP – Manufacturing Administration :: SUE POHJA VP – Book Sales
COURTNEY SIMMONS Senior VP – Publicity :: BOB WAYNE Senior VP – Sales

Collection Cover by Howard Porter & John Dell. Interior color separations by Heroic Age.
JLA: Vol. 1. Published by DC Comics. Cover and compilation Copyright © 2008 DC Comics. All Rights Reserved.
Originally published in single magazine form in JLA #1-9, JLA SECRET FILES #1. Copyright © 1997 DC Comics.
All Rights Reserved. All characters, their distinctive likenesses and related elements featured in this publication are
trademarks of DC Comics. The stories, characters and incidents featured in this publication are entirely fictional.
DC Comics does not read or accept unsolicited submissions of ideas, stories or artwork.

DC Comics, 1700 Broadway, New York, NY 10019. A Warner Bros. Entertainment Company
Printed by RR Donnelley, Salem, VA. 10/11/2013. Third Printing
ISBN: 978-1-4012-3314-3

Library of Congress Cataloging-in-Publication Data

Morrison, Grant, author.
JLA. Volume 1 / Grant Morrison, Howard Porter, John Dell.
    pages cm
"Originally published in single magazine form in JLA #1-9, JLA Secret Files #1."
ISBN 978-1-4012-3314-3
1. Graphic novels. I. Porter, Howard, illustrator. II. Dell, John, illustrator. III. Title.
PN6728.J87M6 2013
741.5'973–dc23
                                    2013011674

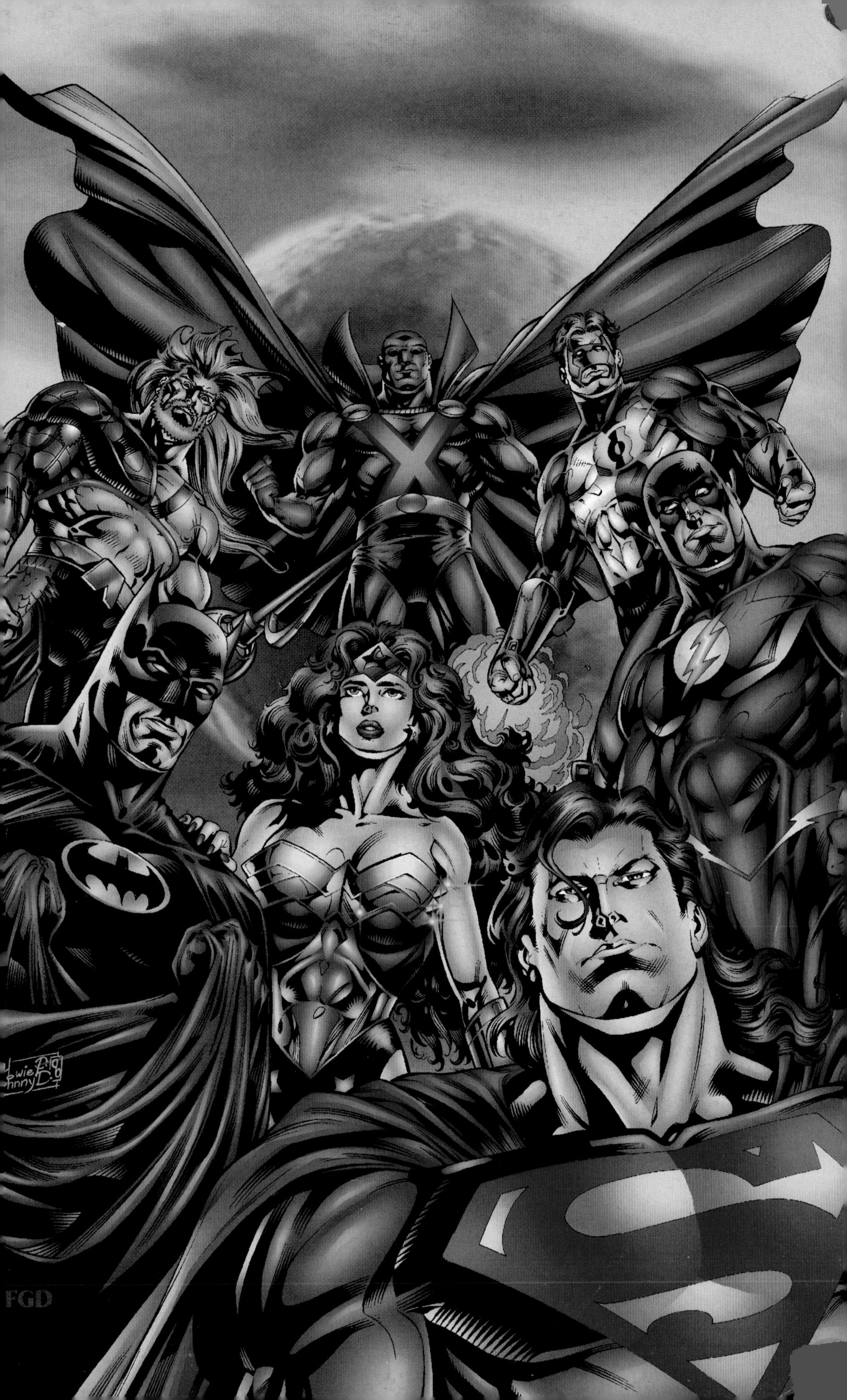
FGD

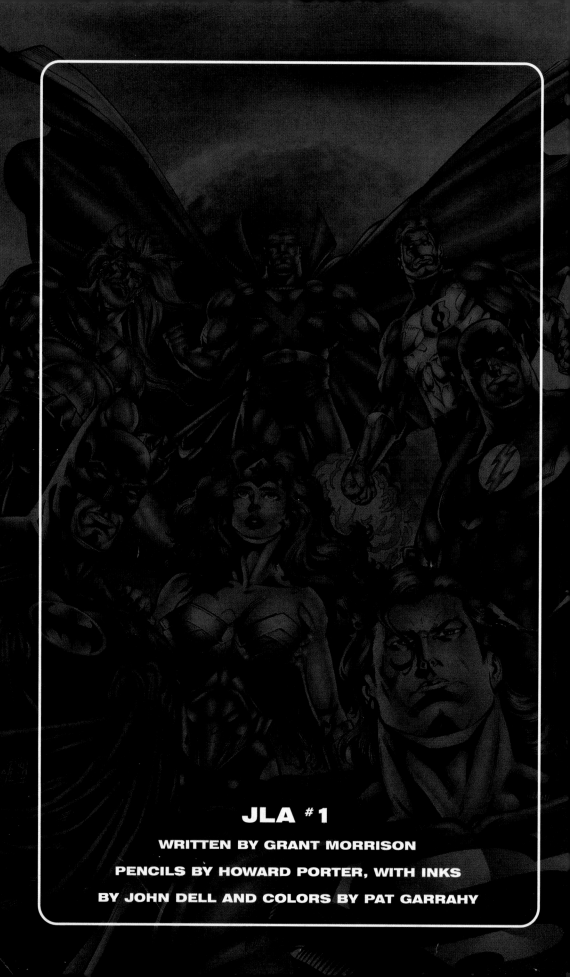

JLA #1

WRITTEN BY GRANT MORRISON

PENCILS BY HOWARD PORTER, WITH INKS

BY JOHN DELL AND COLORS BY PAT GARRAHY

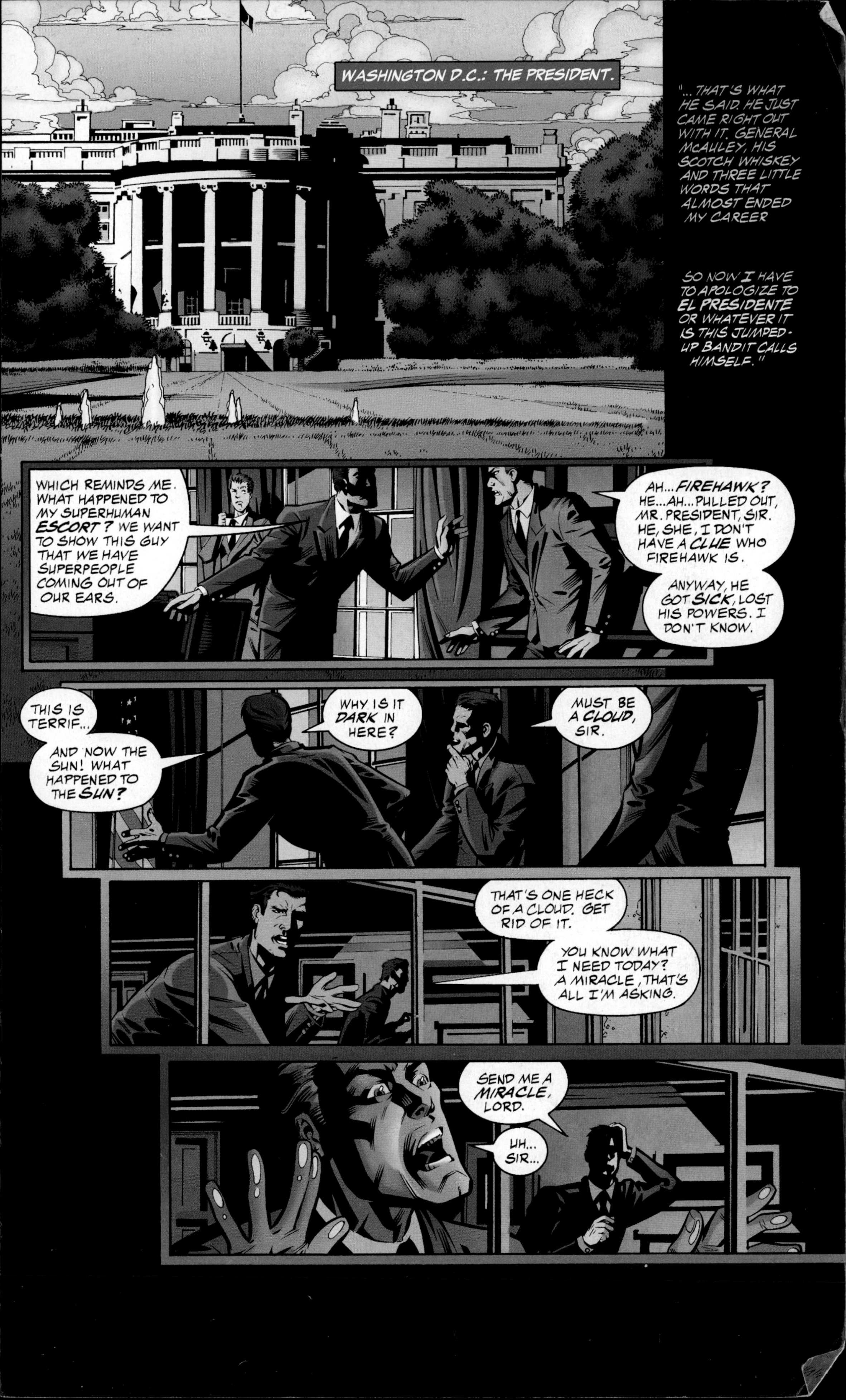
WASHINGTON D.C.: THE PRESIDENT.
"...THAT'S WHAT HE SAID. HE JUST CAME RIGHT OUT WITH IT. GENERAL McAULEY, HIS SCOTCH WHISKEY AND THREE LITTLE WORDS THAT ALMOST ENDED MY CAREER
SO NOW I HAVE TO APOLOGIZE TO EL PRESIDENTE OR WHATEVER IT IS THIS JUMPED-UP BANDIT CALLS HIMSELF."
WHICH REMINDS ME. WHAT HAPPENED TO MY SUPERHUMAN ESCORT? WE WANT TO SHOW THIS GUY THAT WE HAVE SUPERPEOPLE COMING OUT OF OUR EARS.
AH... FIREHAWK? HE...AH...PULLED OUT, MR. PRESIDENT, SIR. HE, SHE, I DON'T HAVE A CLUE WHO FIREHAWK IS.
ANYWAY, HE GOT SICK, LOST HIS POWERS. I DON'T KNOW.
THIS IS TERRIF...
AND NOW THE SUN! WHAT HAPPENED TO THE SUN?
WHY IS IT DARK IN HERE?
MUST BE A CLOUD, SIR.
THAT'S ONE HECK OF A CLOUD. GET RID OF IT.
YOU KNOW WHAT I NEED TODAY? A MIRACLE, THAT'S ALL I'M ASKING.
SEND ME A MIRACLE, LORD.
UH... SIR...

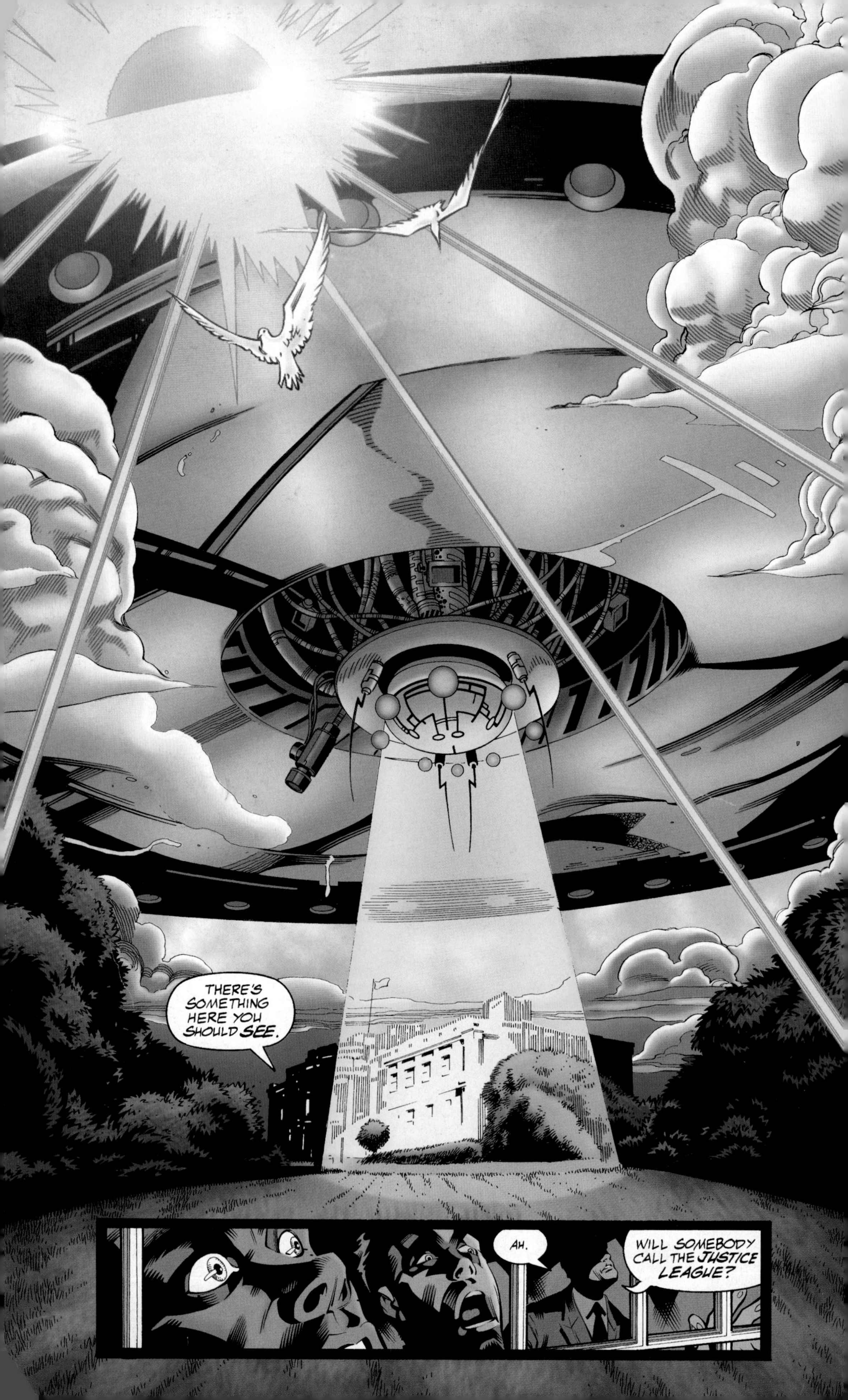
THERE'S SOMETHING HERE YOU SHOULD SEE.
AH.
WILL SOMEBODY CALL THE JUSTICE LEAGUE?

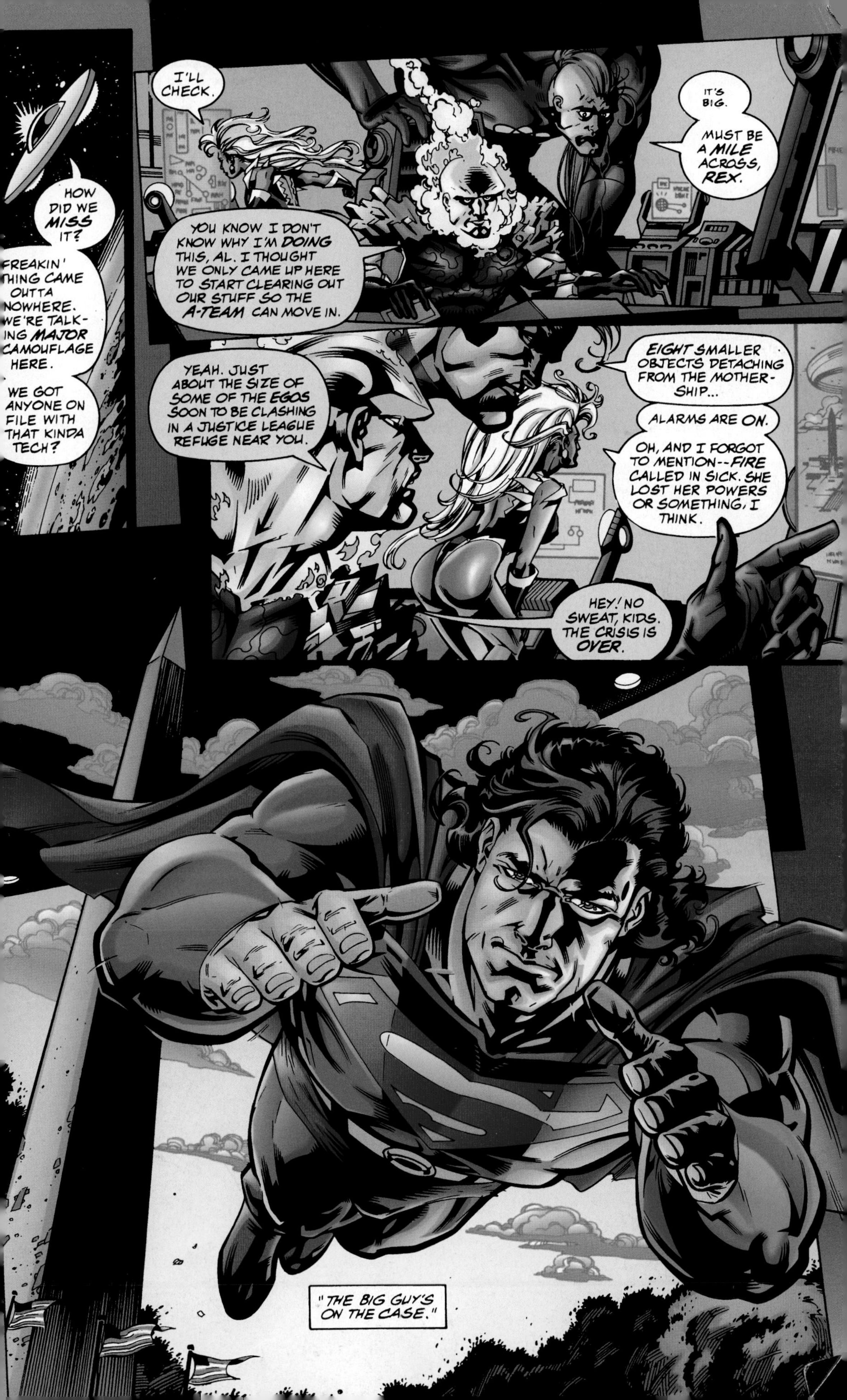
HOW DID WE MISS IT?
FREAKIN' THING CAME OUTTA NOWHERE. WE'RE TALKING MAJOR CAMOUFLAGE HERE.
WE GOT ANYONE ON FILE WITH THAT KINDA TECH?
I'LL CHECK.
IT'S BIG.
MUST BE A MILE ACROSS, REX.
YOU KNOW I DON'T KNOW WHY I'M DOING THIS, AL. I THOUGHT WE ONLY CAME UP HERE TO START CLEARING OUT OUR STUFF SO THE A-TEAM CAN MOVE IN.
YEAH. JUST ABOUT THE SIZE OF SOME OF THE EGOS SOON TO BE CLASHING IN A JUSTICE LEAGUE REFUGE NEAR YOU.
EIGHT SMALLER OBJECTS DETACHING FROM THE MOTHER-SHIP...
ALARMS ARE ON.
OH, AND I FORGOT TO MENTION--FIRE CALLED IN SICK. SHE LOST HER POWERS OR SOMETHING, I THINK.
HEY! NO SWEAT, KIDS. THE CRISIS IS OVER.
"THE BIG GUY'S ON THE CASE."

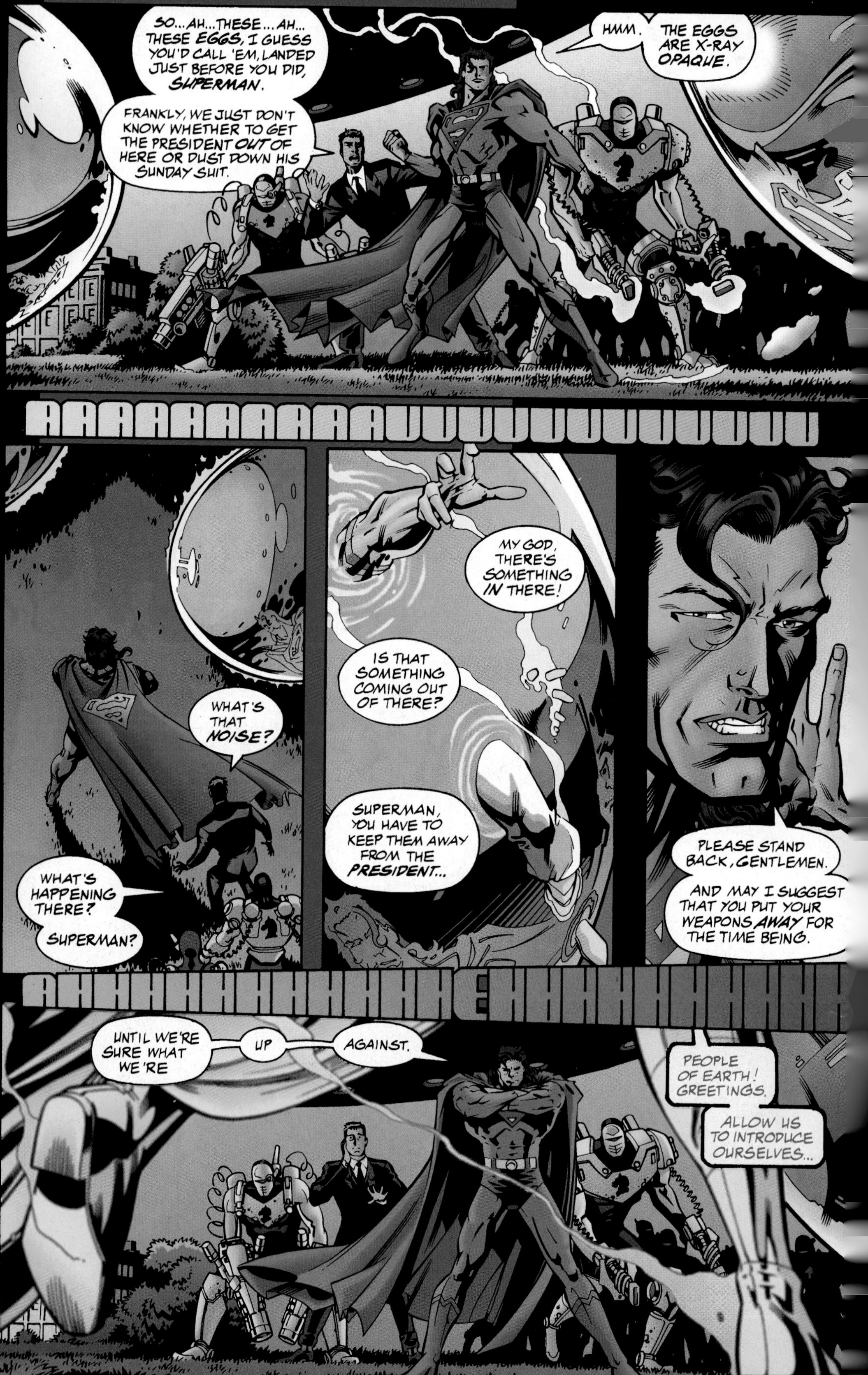
SO... AH... THESE... AH... THESE EGGS, I GUESS YOU'D CALL 'EM, LANDED JUST BEFORE YOU DID, SUPERMAN.
FRANKLY, WE JUST DON'T KNOW WHETHER TO GET THE PRESIDENT OUT OF HERE OR DUST DOWN HIS SUNDAY SUIT.
HMM.
THE EGGS ARE X-RAY OPAQUE.
AAAAAAAAAAAAVVVVVVVVVVVVVV
WHAT'S THAT NOISE?
WHAT'S HAPPENING THERE?
SUPERMAN?
MY GOD, THERE'S SOMETHING IN THERE!
IS THAT SOMETHING COMING OUT OF THERE?
SUPERMAN, YOU HAVE TO KEEP THEM AWAY FROM THE PRESIDENT...
PLEASE STAND BACK, GENTLEMEN.
AND MAY I SUGGEST THAT YOU PUT YOUR WEAPONS AWAY FOR THE TIME BEING.
AHHHHHHHHHHHHEHHHHHHHHHHHK
UNTIL WE'RE SURE WHAT WE'RE
UP
AGAINST.
PEOPLE OF EARTH! GREETINGS.
ALLOW US TO INTRODUCE OURSELVES...

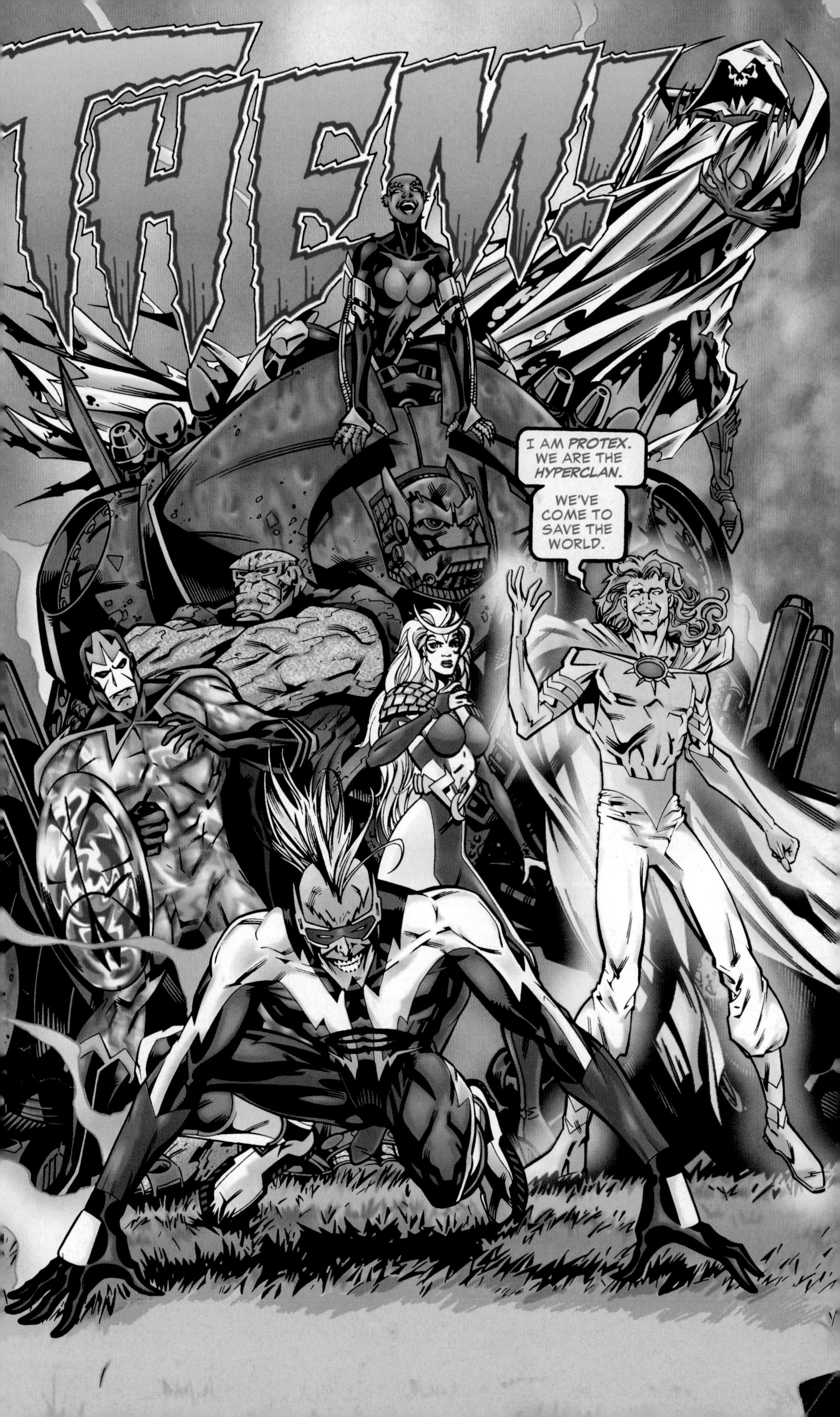
THEM!
I AM PROTEX. WE ARE THE HYPERCLAN.
WE'VE COME TO SAVE THE WORLD.

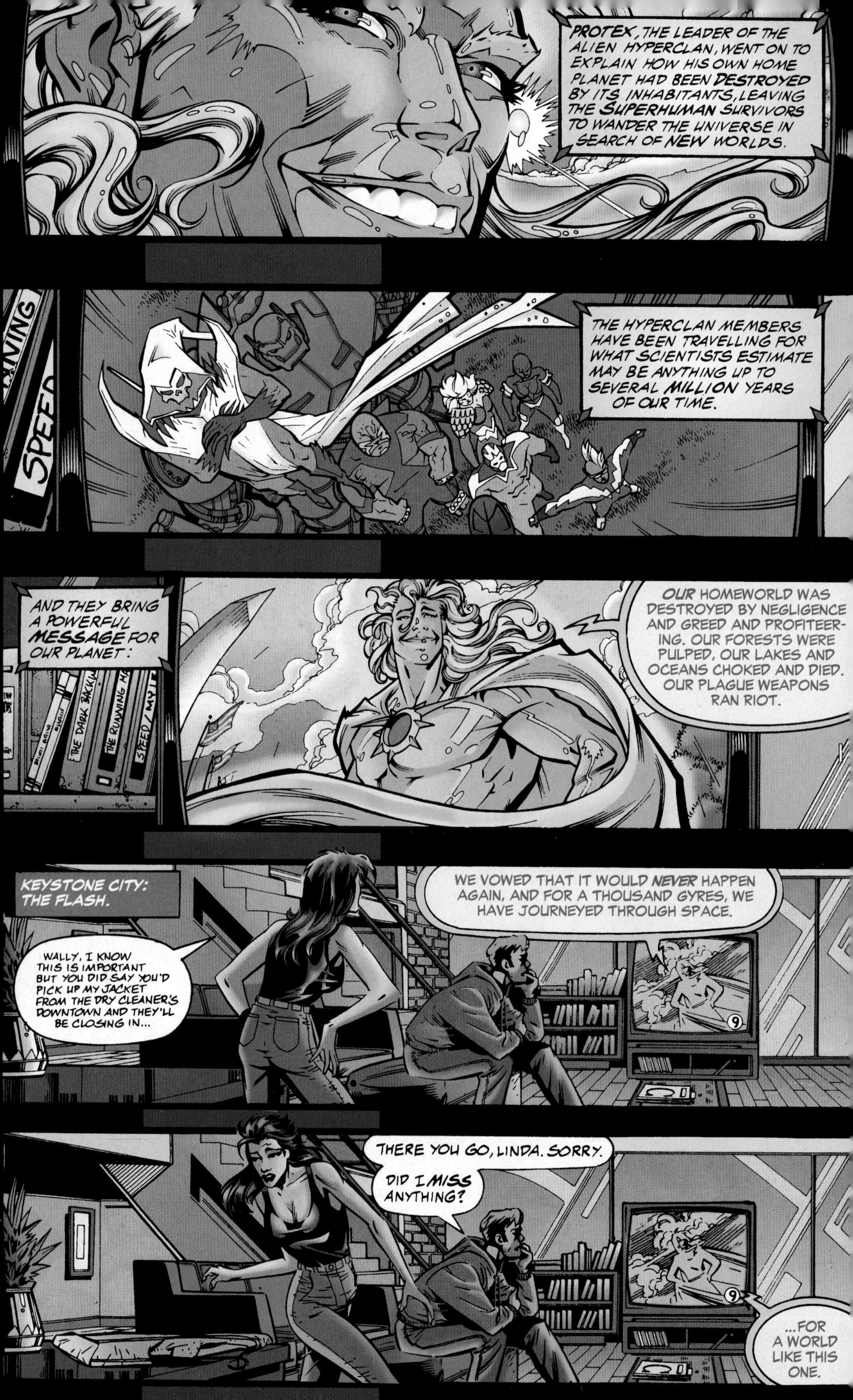
PROTEX, THE LEADER OF THE ALIEN HYPERCLAN, WENT ON TO EXPLAIN HOW HIS OWN HOME PLANET HAD BEEN DESTROYED BY ITS INHABITANTS, LEAVING THE SUPERHUMAN SURVIVORS TO WANDER THE UNIVERSE IN SEARCH OF NEW WORLDS.
SPEED
THE HYPERCLAN MEMBERS HAVE BEEN TRAVELLING FOR WHAT SCIENTISTS ESTIMATE MAY BE ANYTHING UP TO SEVERAL MILLION YEARS OF OUR TIME.
AND THEY BRING A POWERFUL MESSAGE FOR OUR PLANET:
OUR HOMEWORLD WAS DESTROYED BY NEGLIGENCE AND GREED AND PROFITEERING. OUR FORESTS WERE PULPED, OUR LAKES AND OCEANS CHOKED AND DIED. OUR PLAGUE WEAPONS RAN RIOT.
THE DARK BACKIN
THE RUNNING M
SPEED / MY
KEYSTONE CITY: THE FLASH.
WE VOWED THAT IT WOULD NEVER HAPPEN AGAIN, AND FOR A THOUSAND GYRES, WE HAVE JOURNEYED THROUGH SPACE.
WALLY, I KNOW THIS IS IMPORTANT BUT YOU DID SAY YOU'D PICK UP MY JACKET FROM THE DRY CLEANER'S DOWNTOWN AND THEY'LL BE CLOSING IN...
THERE YOU GO, LINDA. SORRY.
DID I MISS ANYTHING?
...FOR A WORLD LIKE THIS ONE.

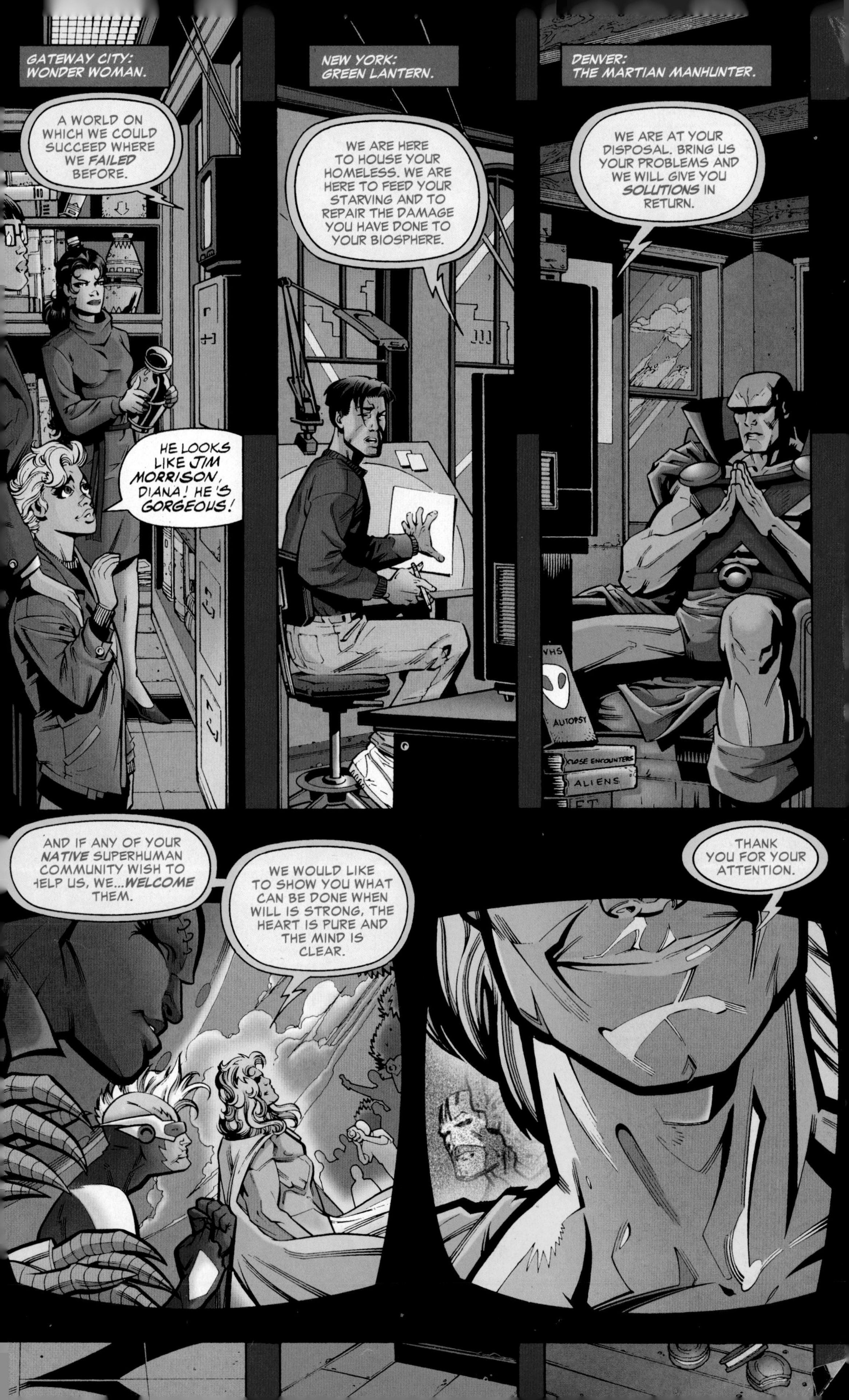
GATEWAY CITY: WONDER WOMAN.
A WORLD ON WHICH WE COULD SUCCEED WHERE WE FAILED BEFORE.
HE LOOKS LIKE JIM MORRISON, DIANA! HE'S GORGEOUS!
NEW YORK: GREEN LANTERN.
WE ARE HERE TO HOUSE YOUR HOMELESS. WE ARE HERE TO FEED YOUR STARVING AND TO REPAIR THE DAMAGE YOU HAVE DONE TO YOUR BIOSPHERE.
DENVER: THE MARTIAN MANHUNTER.
WE ARE AT YOUR DISPOSAL. BRING US YOUR PROBLEMS AND WE WILL GIVE YOU SOLUTIONS IN RETURN.
VHS
AUTOPSY
CLOSE ENCOUNTERS
ALIENS
AND IF ANY OF YOUR NATIVE SUPERHUMAN COMMUNITY WISH TO HELP US, WE... WELCOME THEM.
WE WOULD LIKE TO SHOW YOU WHAT CAN BE DONE WHEN WILL IS STRONG, THE HEART IS PURE AND THE MIND IS CLEAR.
THANK YOU FOR YOUR ATTENTION.

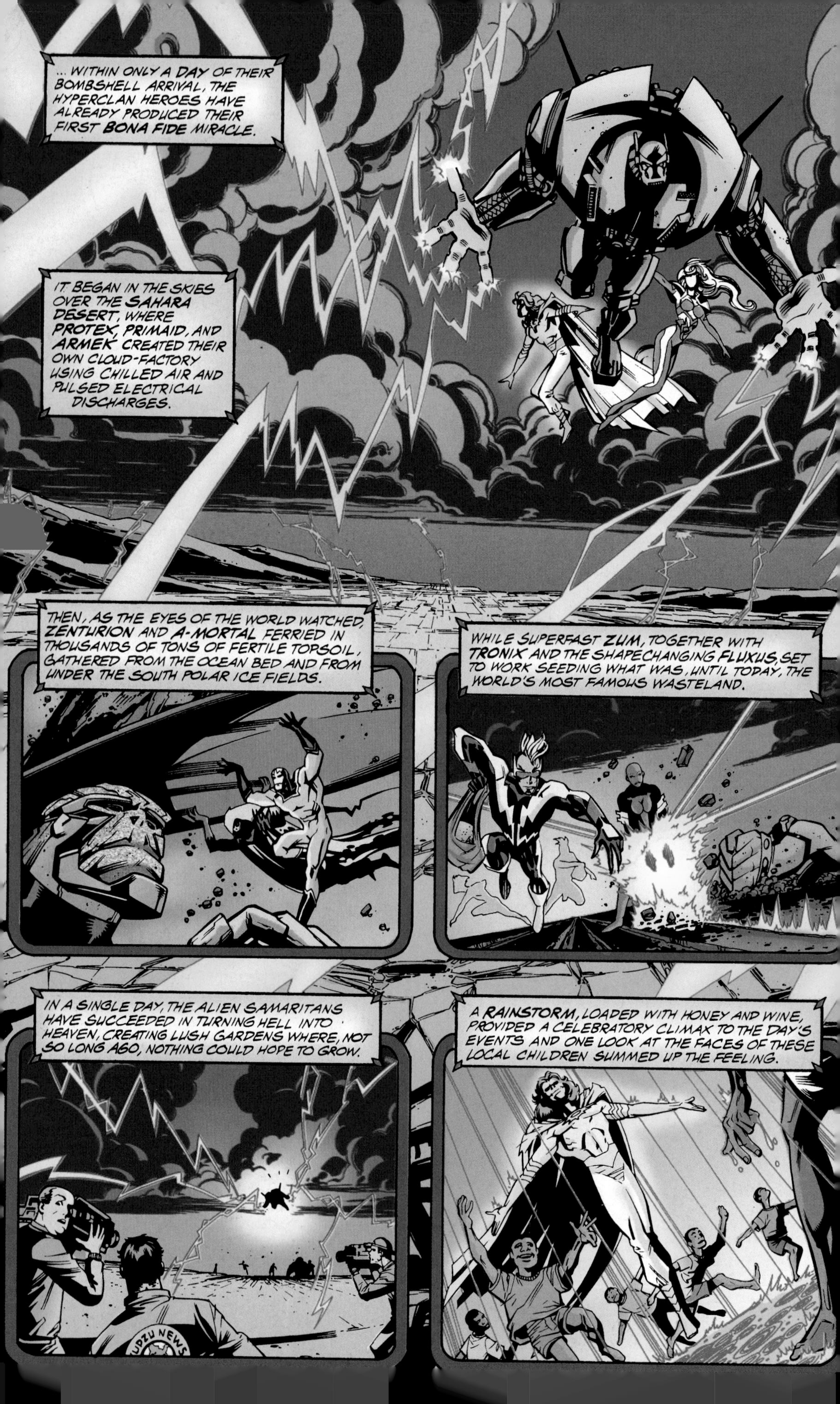

...WITHIN ONLY A DAY OF THEIR BOMBSHELL ARRIVAL, THE HYPERCLAN HEROES HAVE ALREADY PRODUCED THEIR FIRST BONA FIDE MIRACLE.
IT BEGAN IN THE SKIES OVER THE SAHARA DESERT, WHERE PROTEX, PRIMAID, AND ARMEK CREATED THEIR OWN CLOUD-FACTORY USING CHILLED AIR AND PULSED ELECTRICAL DISCHARGES.
THEN, AS THE EYES OF THE WORLD WATCHED, ZENTURION AND A-MORTAL FERRIED IN THOUSANDS OF TONS OF FERTILE TOPSOIL, GATHERED FROM THE OCEAN BED AND FROM UNDER THE SOUTH POLAR ICE FIELDS.
WHILE SUPERFAST ZUM, TOGETHER WITH TRONIX AND THE SHAPECHANGING FLUXUS, SET TO WORK SEEDING WHAT WAS, UNTIL TODAY, THE WORLD'S MOST FAMOUS WASTELAND.
IN A SINGLE DAY, THE ALIEN SAMARITANS HAVE SUCCEEDED IN TURNING HELL INTO HEAVEN, CREATING LUSH GARDENS WHERE, NOT SO LONG AGO, NOTHING COULD HOPE TO GROW.
A RAINSTORM, LOADED WITH HONEY AND WINE, PROVIDED A CELEBRATORY CLIMAX TO THE DAY'S EVENTS AND ONE LOOK AT THE FACES OF THESE LOCAL CHILDREN SUMMED UP THE FEELING.

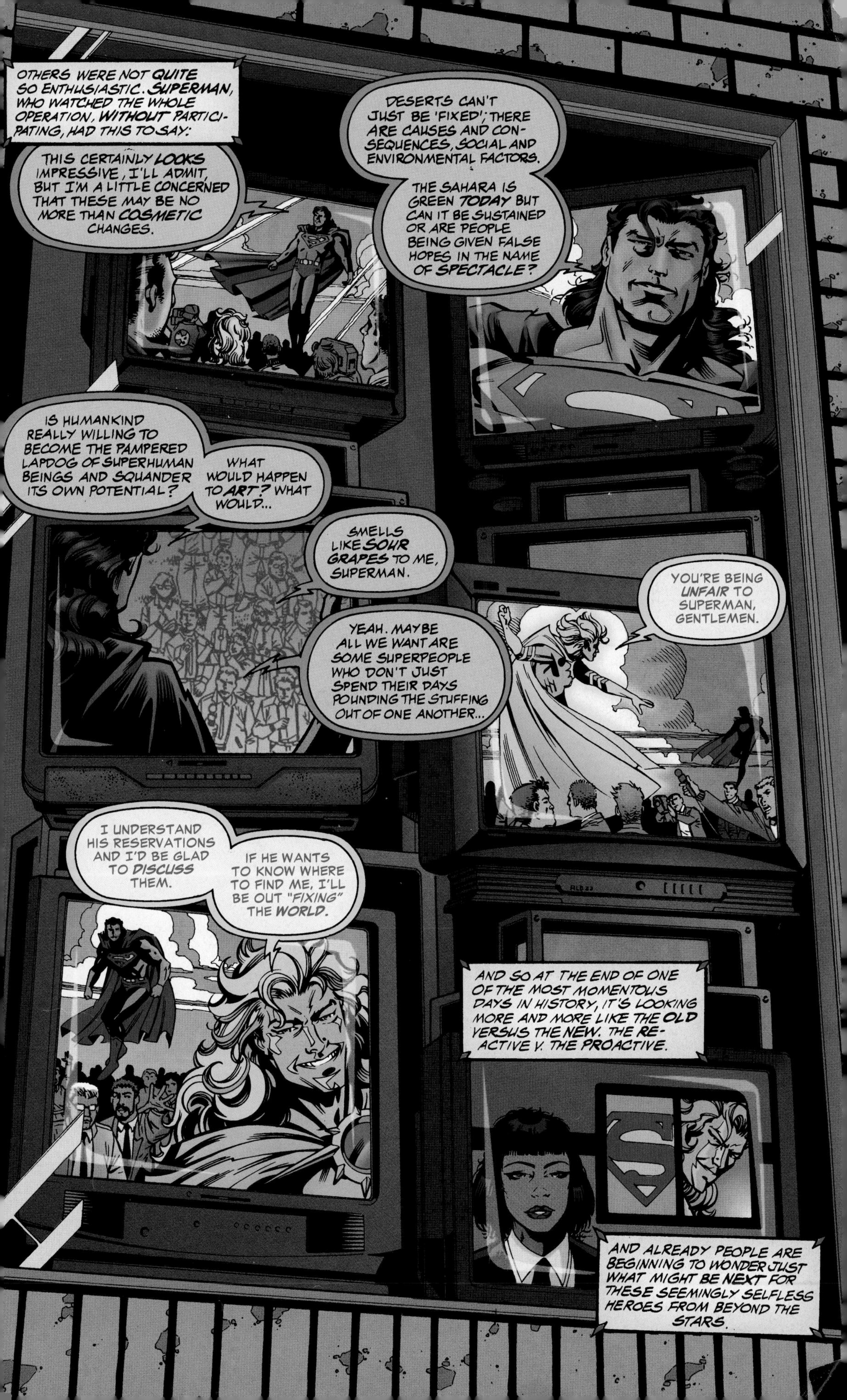
OTHERS WERE NOT QUITE SO ENTHUSIASTIC. SUPERMAN, WHO WATCHED THE WHOLE OPERATION, WITHOUT PARTICIPATING, HAD THIS TO SAY:
THIS CERTAINLY LOOKS IMPRESSIVE, I'LL ADMIT, BUT I'M A LITTLE CONCERNED THAT THESE MAY BE NO MORE THAN COSMETIC CHANGES.
DESERTS CAN'T JUST BE 'FIXED'; THERE ARE CAUSES AND CONSEQUENCES, SOCIAL AND ENVIRONMENTAL FACTORS.
THE SAHARA IS GREEN TODAY BUT CAN IT BE SUSTAINED OR ARE PEOPLE BEING GIVEN FALSE HOPES IN THE NAME OF SPECTACLE?
IS HUMANKIND REALLY WILLING TO BECOME THE PAMPERED LAPDOG OF SUPERHUMAN BEINGS AND SQUANDER ITS OWN POTENTIAL?
WHAT WOULD HAPPEN TO ART? WHAT WOULD...
SMELLS LIKE SOUR GRAPES TO ME, SUPERMAN.
YEAH. MAYBE ALL WE WANT ARE SOME SUPERPEOPLE WHO DON'T JUST SPEND THEIR DAYS POUNDING THE STUFFING OUT OF ONE ANOTHER...
YOU'RE BEING UNFAIR TO SUPERMAN, GENTLEMEN.
I UNDERSTAND HIS RESERVATIONS AND I'D BE GLAD TO DISCUSS THEM.
IF HE WANTS TO KNOW WHERE TO FIND ME, I'LL BE OUT "FIXING" THE WORLD.
AND SO AT THE END OF ONE OF THE MOST MOMENTOUS DAYS IN HISTORY, IT'S LOOKING MORE AND MORE LIKE THE OLD VERSUS THE NEW. THE REACTIVE V. THE PROACTIVE.
AND ALREADY PEOPLE ARE BEGINNING TO WONDER JUST WHAT MIGHT BE NEXT FOR THESE SEEMINGLY SELFLESS HEROES FROM BEYOND THE STARS.

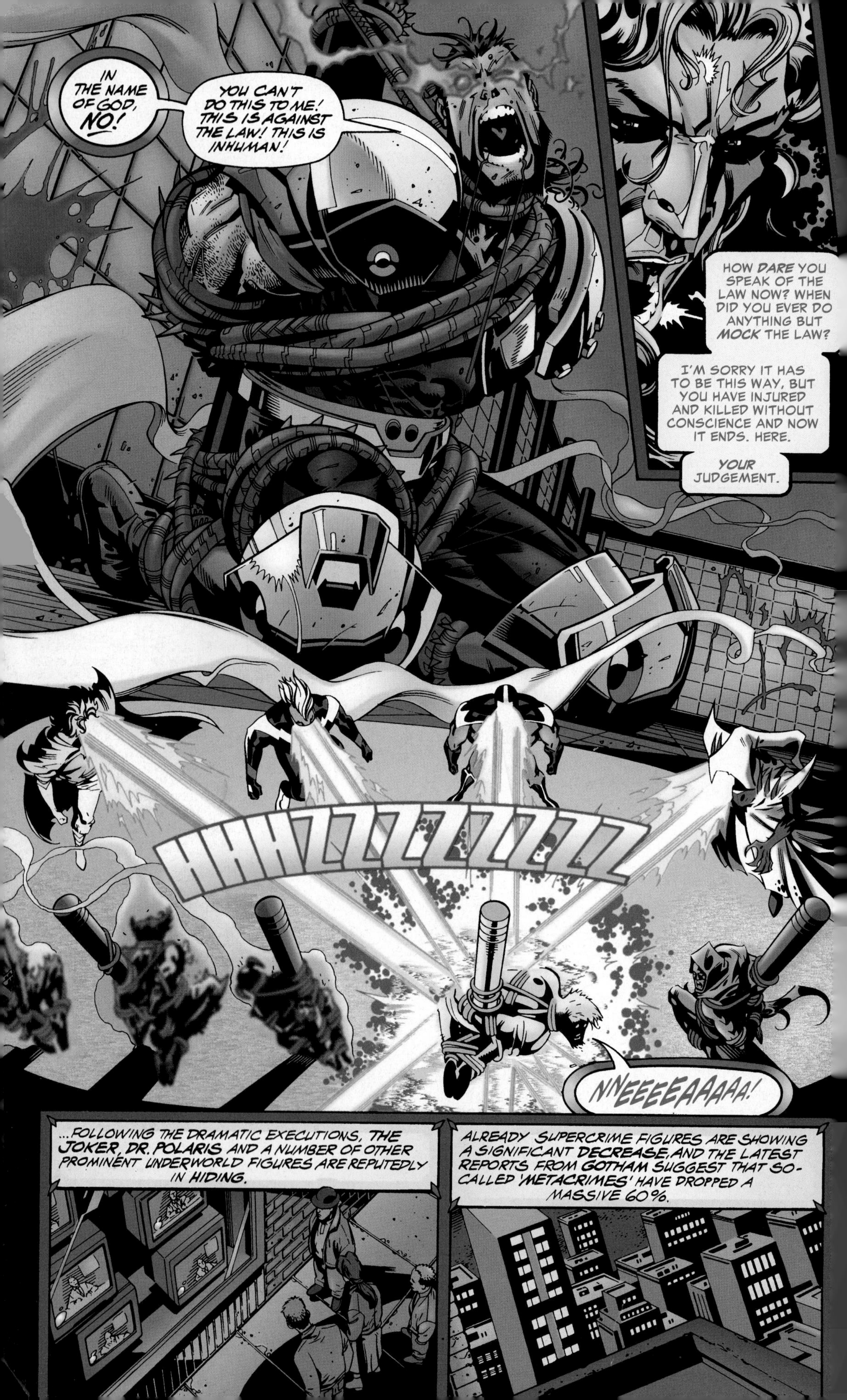

IN THE NAME OF GOD, NO!
YOU CAN'T DO THIS TO ME! THIS IS AGAINST THE LAW! THIS IS INHUMAN!
HOW DARE YOU SPEAK OF THE LAW NOW? WHEN DID YOU EVER DO ANYTHING BUT MOCK THE LAW?
I'M SORRY IT HAS TO BE THIS WAY, BUT YOU HAVE INJURED AND KILLED WITHOUT CONSCIENCE AND NOW IT ENDS. HERE.
YOUR JUDGEMENT.
HHHZZZZZZZZZ
NNEEEEAAAAA!
...FOLLOWING THE DRAMATIC EXECUTIONS, THE JOKER, DR. POLARIS AND A NUMBER OF OTHER PROMINENT UNDERWORLD FIGURES ARE REPUTEDLY IN HIDING.
ALREADY SUPERCRIME FIGURES ARE SHOWING A SIGNIFICANT DECREASE, AND THE LATEST REPORTS FROM GOTHAM SUGGEST THAT SO-CALLED 'METACRIMES' HAVE DROPPED A MASSIVE 60%.

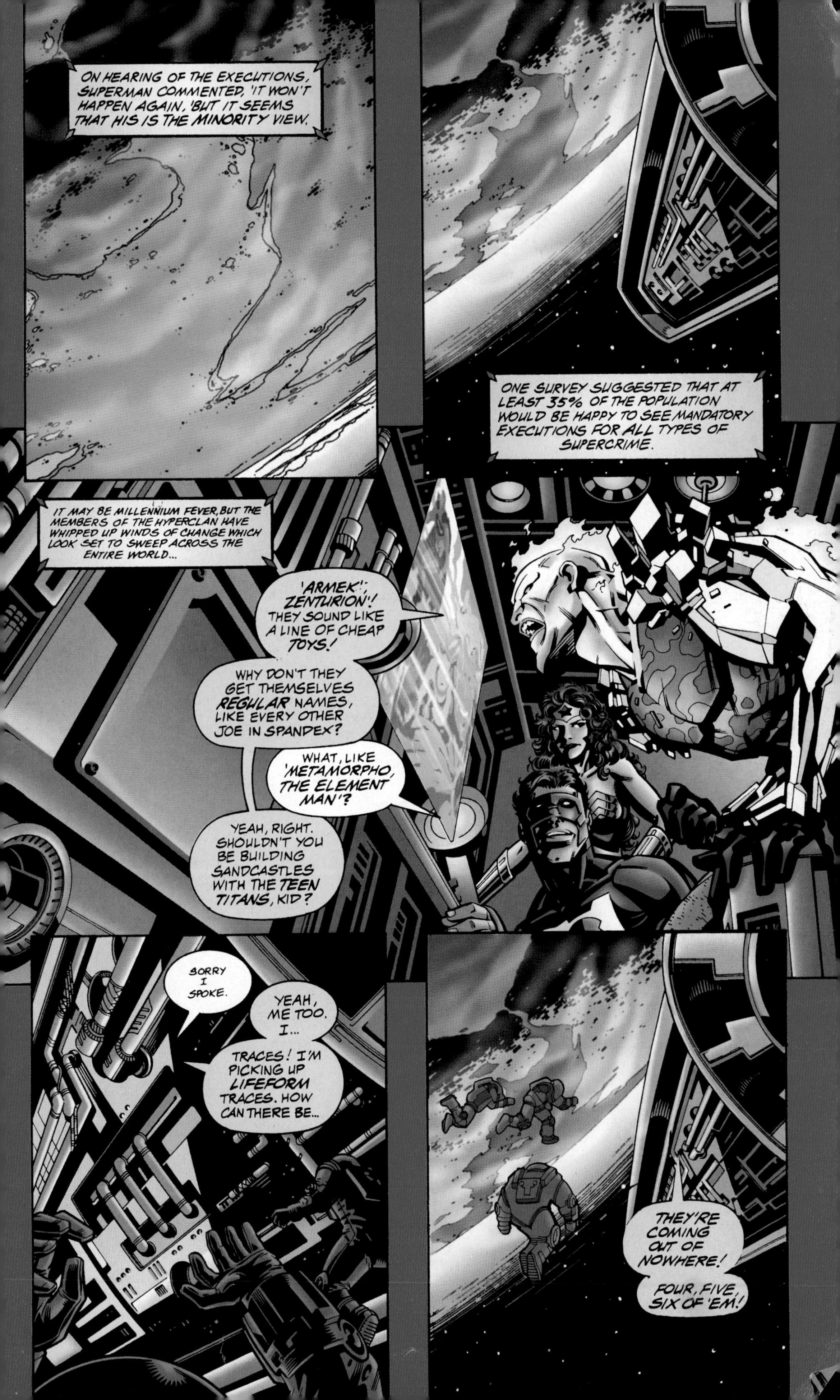
ON HEARING OF THE EXECUTIONS, SUPERMAN COMMENTED, 'IT WON'T HAPPEN AGAIN,' BUT IT SEEMS THAT HIS IS THE MINORITY VIEW.
ONE SURVEY SUGGESTED THAT AT LEAST 35% OF THE POPULATION WOULD BE HAPPY TO SEE MANDATORY EXECUTIONS FOR ALL TYPES OF SUPERCRIME.
IT MAY BE MILLENNIUM FEVER, BUT THE MEMBERS OF THE HYPERCLAN HAVE WHIPPED UP WINDS OF CHANGE WHICH LOOK SET TO SWEEP ACROSS THE ENTIRE WORLD...
'ARMEK'! 'ZENTURION'! THEY SOUND LIKE A LINE OF CHEAP TOYS!
WHY DON'T THEY GET THEMSELVES REGULAR NAMES, LIKE EVERY OTHER JOE IN SPANDEX?
WHAT, LIKE 'METAMORPHO, THE ELEMENT MAN'?
YEAH, RIGHT. SHOULDN'T YOU BE BUILDING SANDCASTLES WITH THE TEEN TITANS, KID?
SORRY I SPOKE.
YEAH, ME TOO. I...
TRACES! I'M PICKING UP LIFEFORM TRACES. HOW CAN THERE BE...
THEY'RE COMING OUT OF NOWHERE!
FOUR, FIVE, SIX OF 'EM!

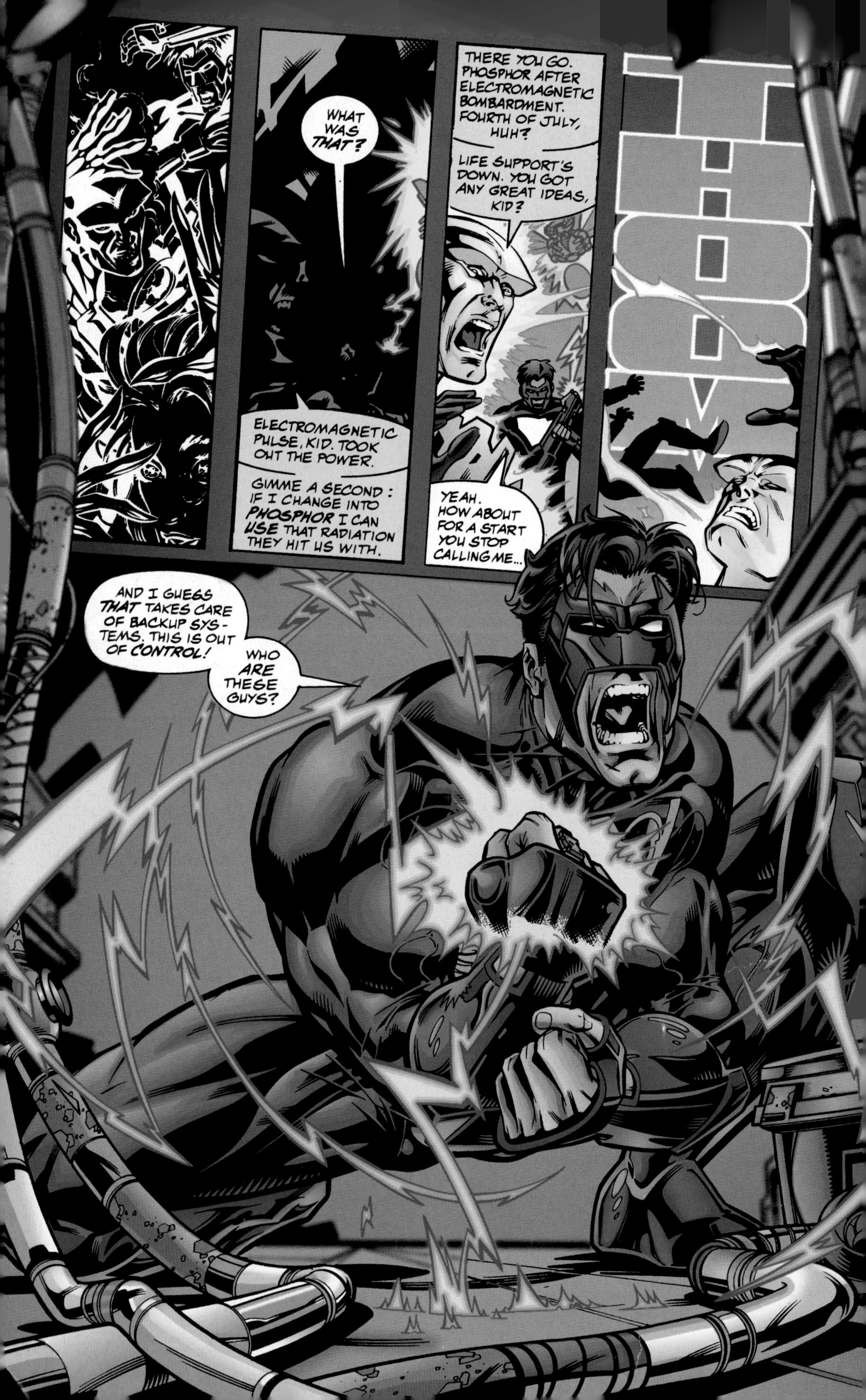
WHAT WAS THAT?
ELECTROMAGNETIC PULSE, KID. TOOK OUT THE POWER.
GIMME A SECOND: IF I CHANGE INTO PHOSPHOR I CAN USE THAT RADIATION THEY HIT US WITH.
THERE YOU GO. PHOSPHOR AFTER ELECTROMAGNETIC BOMBARDMENT. FOURTH OF JULY, HUH?
LIFE SUPPORT'S DOWN. YOU GOT ANY GREAT IDEAS, KID?
YEAH. HOW ABOUT FOR A START YOU STOP CALLING ME...
AND I GUESS THAT TAKES CARE OF BACKUP SYS-TEMS. THIS IS OUT OF CONTROL!
WHO ARE THESE GUYS?

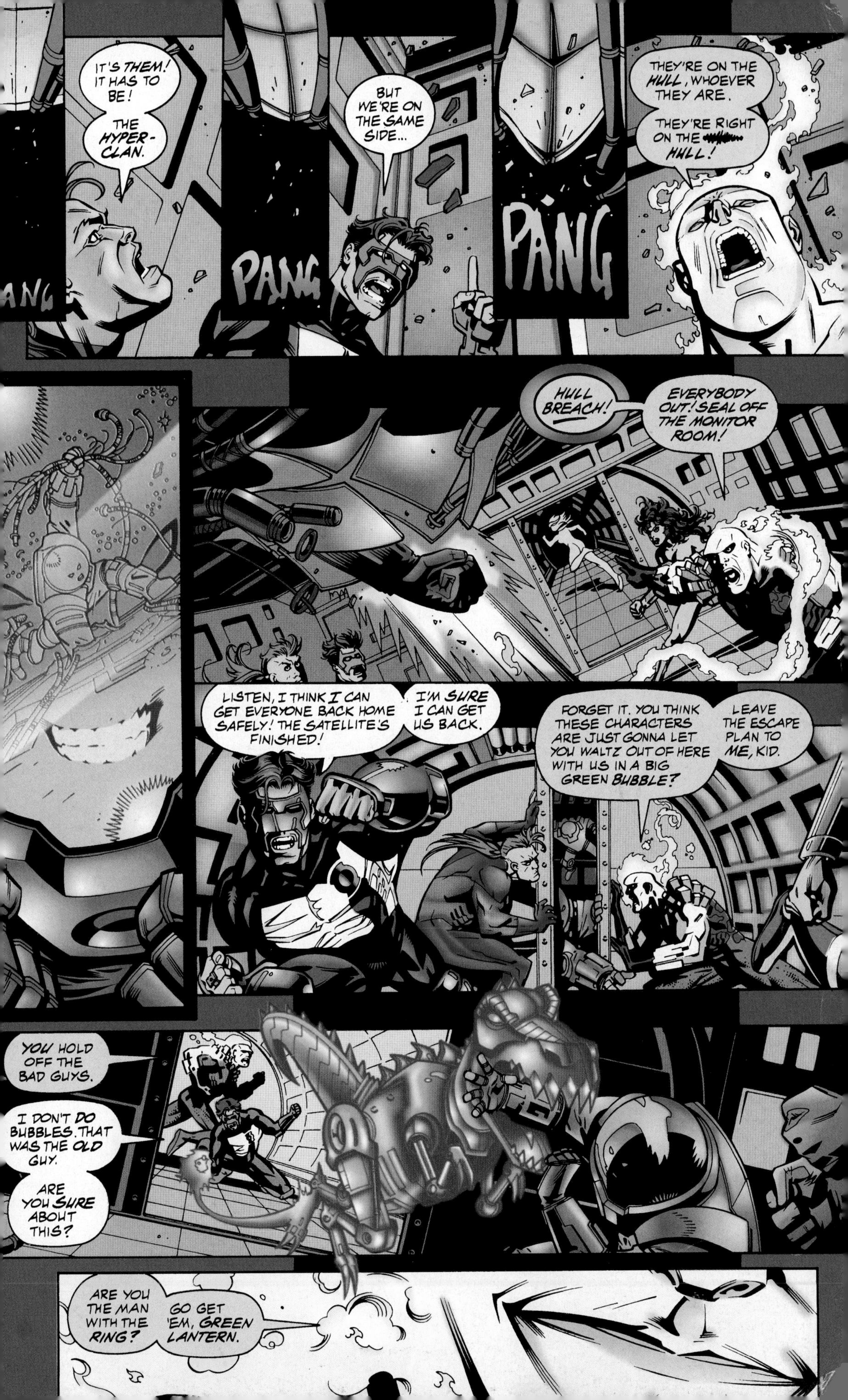
IT'S THEM! IT HAS TO BE!
THE HYPER-CLAN.
PANG
BUT WE'RE ON THE SAME SIDE...
PANG
THEY'RE ON THE HULL, WHOEVER THEY ARE.
THEY'RE RIGHT ON THE HULL!
HULL BREACH!
EVERYBODY OUT! SEAL OFF THE MONITOR ROOM!
LISTEN, I THINK I CAN GET EVERYONE BACK HOME SAFELY! THE SATELLITE'S FINISHED!
I'M SURE I CAN GET US BACK.
FORGET IT. YOU THINK THESE CHARACTERS ARE JUST GONNA LET YOU WALTZ OUT OF HERE WITH US IN A BIG GREEN BUBBLE?
LEAVE THE ESCAPE PLAN TO ME, KID.
YOU HOLD OFF THE BAD GUYS.
I DON'T DO BUBBLES. THAT WAS THE OLD GUY.
ARE YOU SURE ABOUT THIS?
ARE YOU THE MAN WITH THE RING?
GO GET 'EM, GREEN LANTERN.

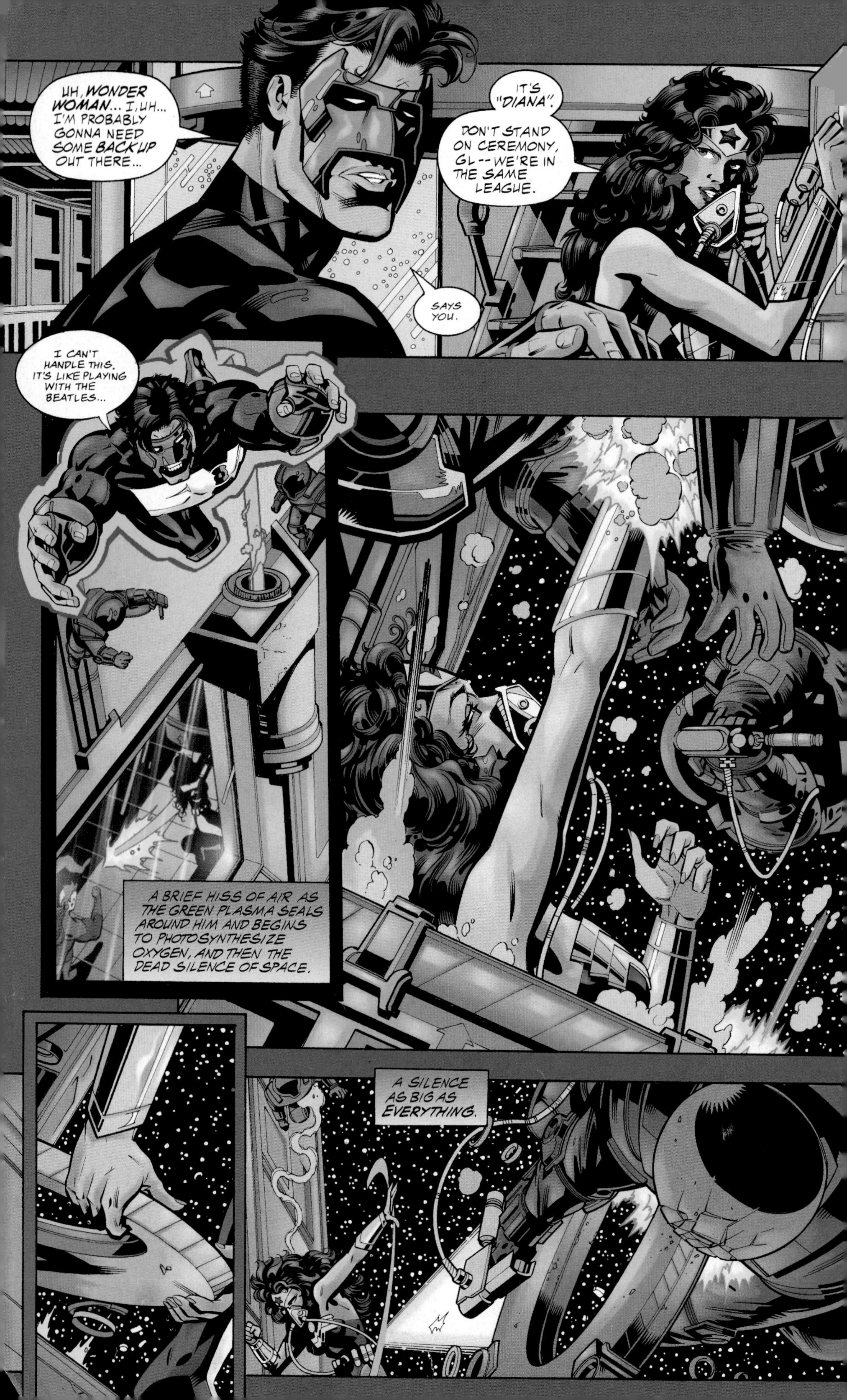

UH, WONDER WOMAN... I, UH... I'M PROBABLY GONNA NEED SOME BACKUP OUT THERE...
IT'S "DIANA".
DON'T STAND ON CEREMONY, GL--WE'RE IN THE SAME LEAGUE.
SAYS YOU.
I CAN'T HANDLE THIS. IT'S LIKE PLAYING WITH THE BEATLES...
A BRIEF HISS OF AIR AS THE GREEN PLASMA SEALS AROUND HIM AND BEGINS TO PHOTOSYNTHESIZE OXYGEN, AND THEN THE DEAD SILENCE OF SPACE.
A SILENCE AS BIG AS EVERYTHING.

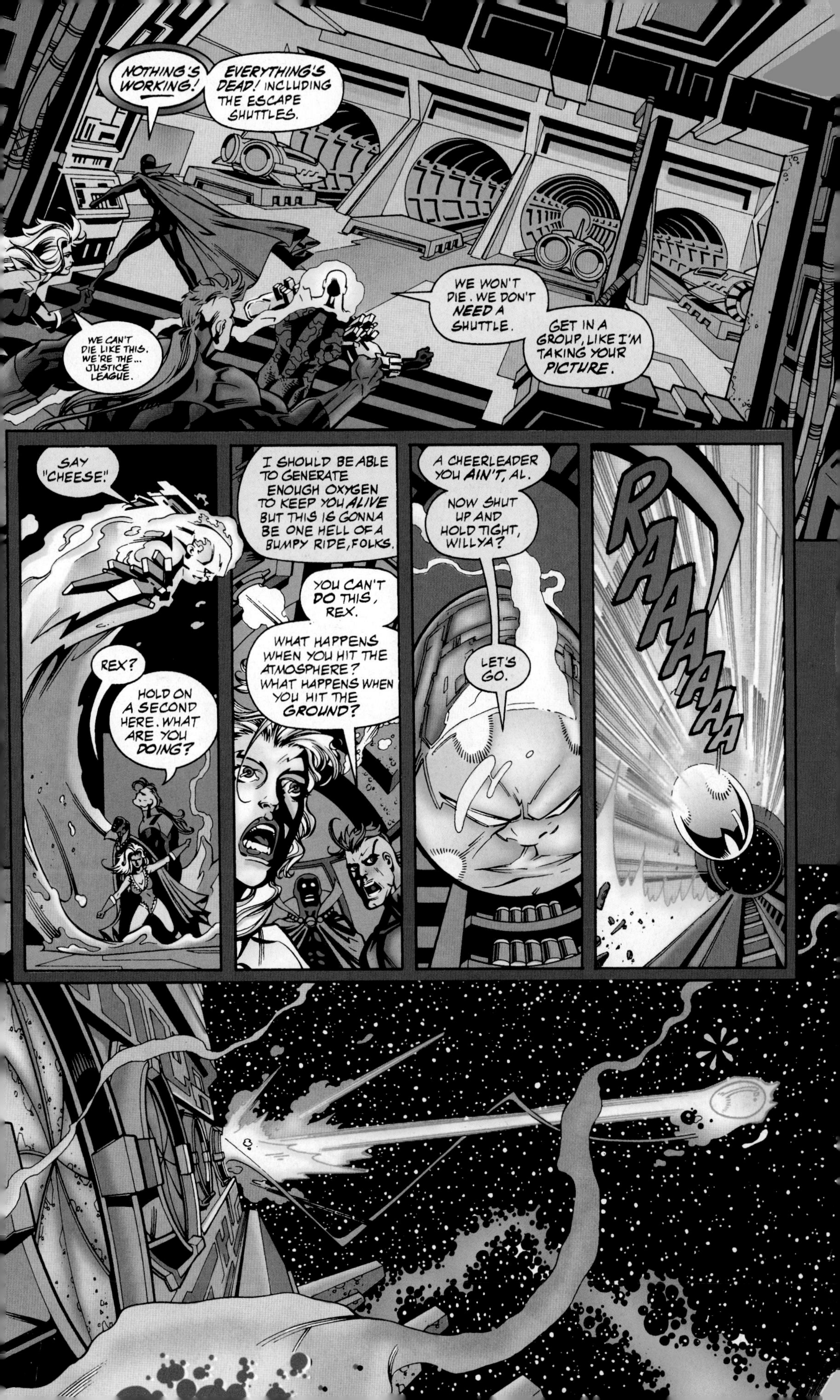
NOTHING'S WORKING!
EVERYTHING'S DEAD! INCLUDING THE ESCAPE SHUTTLES.
WE CAN'T DIE LIKE THIS. WE'RE THE... JUSTICE LEAGUE.
WE WON'T DIE. WE DON'T NEED A SHUTTLE.
GET IN A GROUP, LIKE I'M TAKING YOUR PICTURE.
SAY "CHEESE."
REX?
HOLD ON A SECOND HERE. WHAT ARE YOU DOING?
I SHOULD BE ABLE TO GENERATE ENOUGH OXYGEN TO KEEP YOU ALIVE BUT THIS IS GONNA BE ONE HELL OF A BUMPY RIDE, FOLKS.
YOU CAN'T DO THIS, REX.
WHAT HAPPENS WHEN YOU HIT THE ATMOSPHERE? WHAT HAPPENS WHEN YOU HIT THE GROUND?
A CHEERLEADER YOU AIN'T, AL.
NOW SHUT UP AND HOLD TIGHT, WILLYA?
LET'S GO.
RAAAAAAA

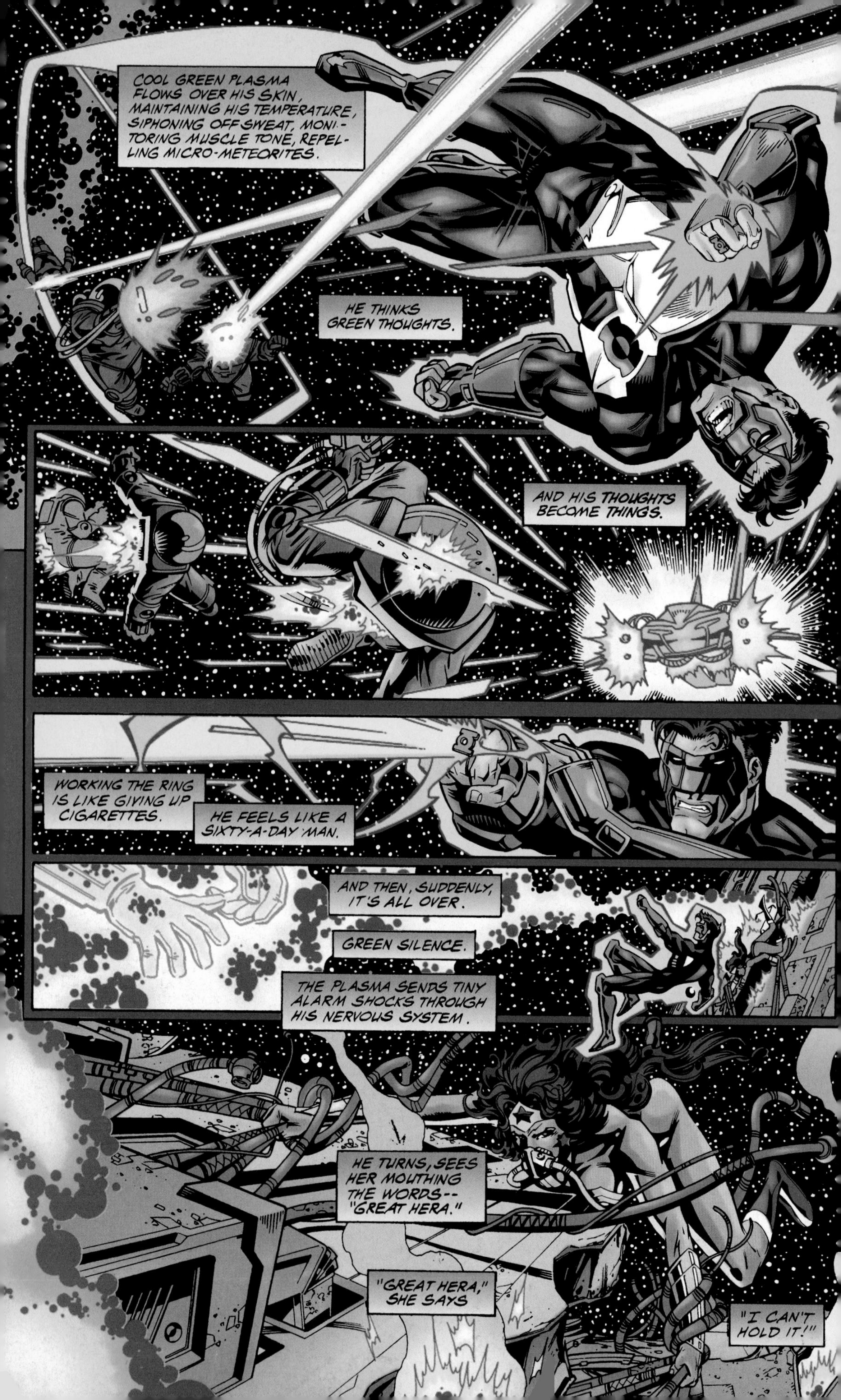
COOL GREEN PLASMA FLOWS OVER HIS SKIN, MAINTAINING HIS TEMPERATURE, SIPHONING OFF SWEAT, MONI-TORING MUSCLE TONE, REPEL-LING MICRO-METEORITES.
HE THINKS GREEN THOUGHTS.
AND HIS THOUGHTS BECOME THINGS.
WORKING THE RING IS LIKE GIVING UP CIGARETTES.
HE FEELS LIKE A SIXTY-A-DAY MAN.
AND THEN, SUDDENLY, IT'S ALL OVER.
GREEN SILENCE.
THE PLASMA SENDS TINY ALARM SHOCKS THROUGH HIS NERVOUS SYSTEM.
HE TURNS, SEES HER MOUTHING THE WORDS-- "GREAT HERA."
"GREAT HERA," SHE SAYS
"I CAN'T HOLD IT!"

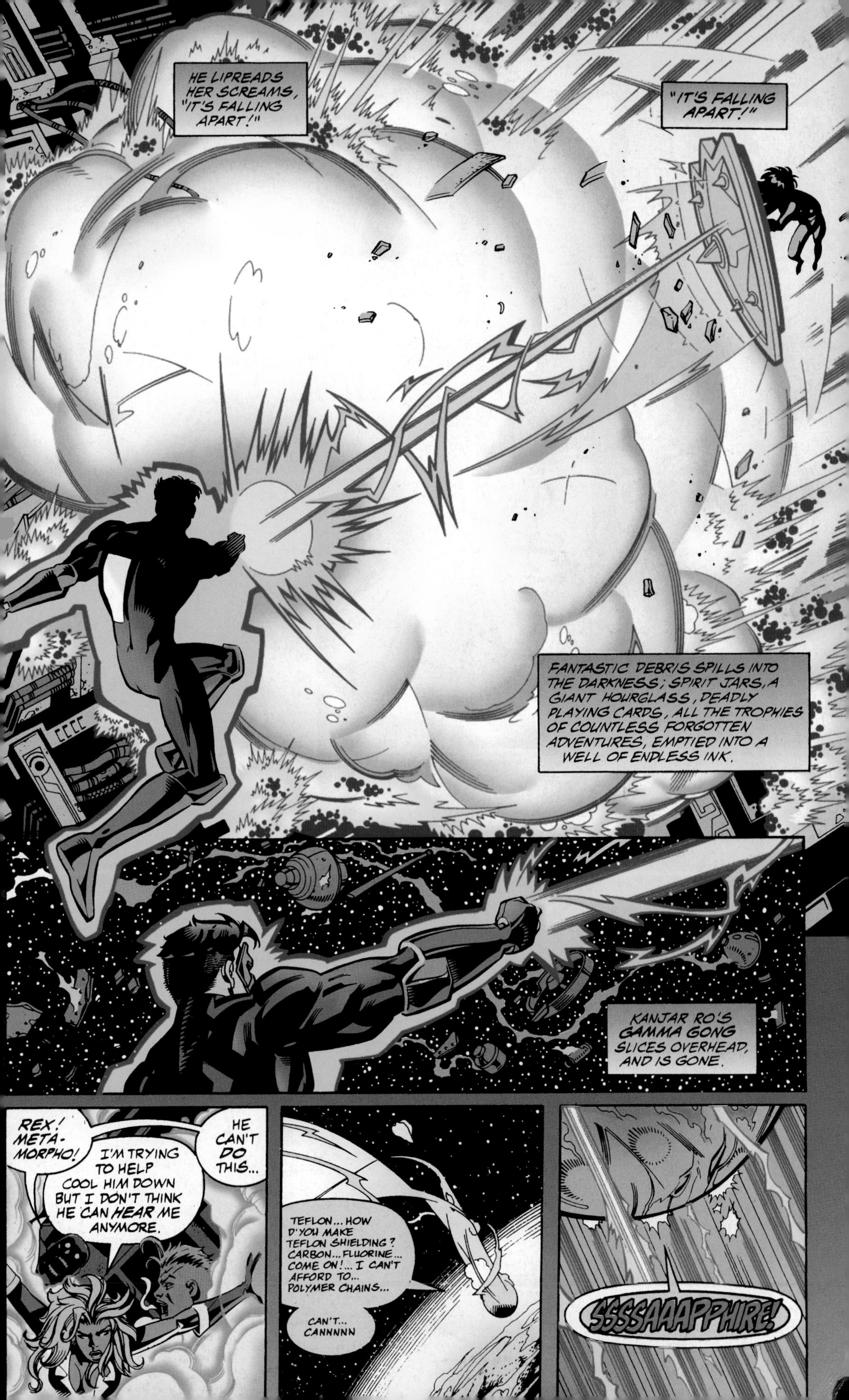
HE LIPREADS HER SCREAMS, "IT'S FALLING APART!"
"IT'S FALLING APART!"
FANTASTIC DEBRIS SPILLS INTO THE DARKNESS; SPIRIT JARS, A GIANT HOURGLASS, DEADLY PLAYING CARDS, ALL THE TROPHIES OF COUNTLESS FORGOTTEN ADVENTURES, EMPTIED INTO A WELL OF ENDLESS INK.
KANJAR RO'S GAMMA GONG SLICES OVERHEAD, AND IS GONE.
REX! METAMORPHO!
HE CAN'T DO THIS...
I'M TRYING TO HELP COOL HIM DOWN BUT I DON'T THINK HE CAN HEAR ME ANYMORE.
TEFLON... HOW D'YOU MAKE TEFLON SHIELDING? CARBON... FLUORINE... COME ON!... I CAN'T AFFORD TO... POLYMER CHAINS...
CAN'T... CANNNNN
SSSSAAAPPHIRE!

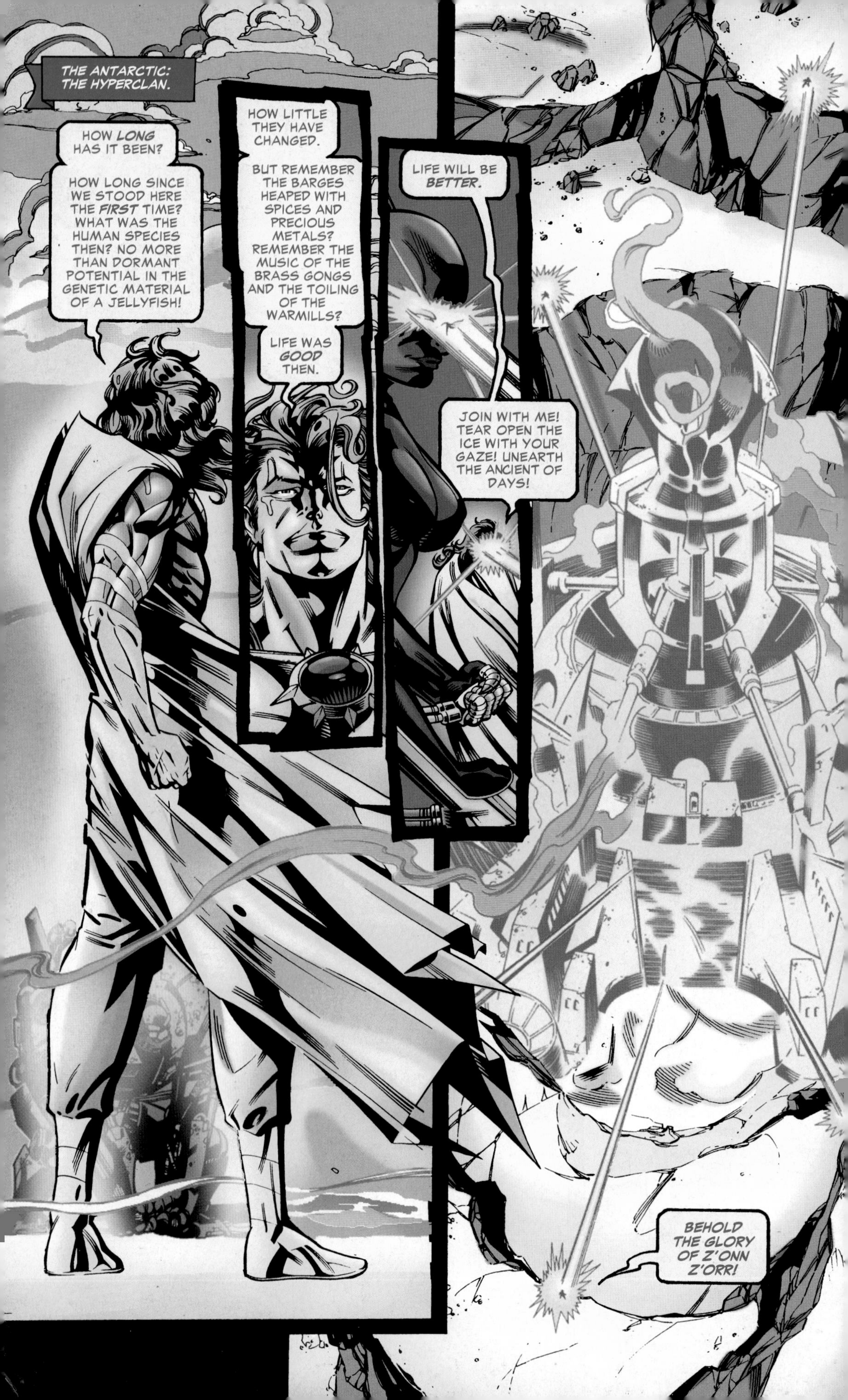
THE ANTARCTIC: THE HYPERCLAN.
HOW LONG HAS IT BEEN?
HOW LONG SINCE WE STOOD HERE THE FIRST TIME? WHAT WAS THE HUMAN SPECIES THEN? NO MORE THAN DORMANT POTENTIAL IN THE GENETIC MATERIAL OF A JELLYFISH!
HOW LITTLE THEY HAVE CHANGED.
BUT REMEMBER THE BARGES HEAPED WITH SPICES AND PRECIOUS METALS? REMEMBER THE MUSIC OF THE BRASS GONGS AND THE TOILING OF THE WARMILLS?
LIFE WAS GOOD THEN.
LIFE WILL BE BETTER.
JOIN WITH ME! TEAR OPEN THE ICE WITH YOUR GAZE! UNEARTH THE ANCIENT OF DAYS!
BEHOLD THE GLORY OF Z'ONN Z'ORR!

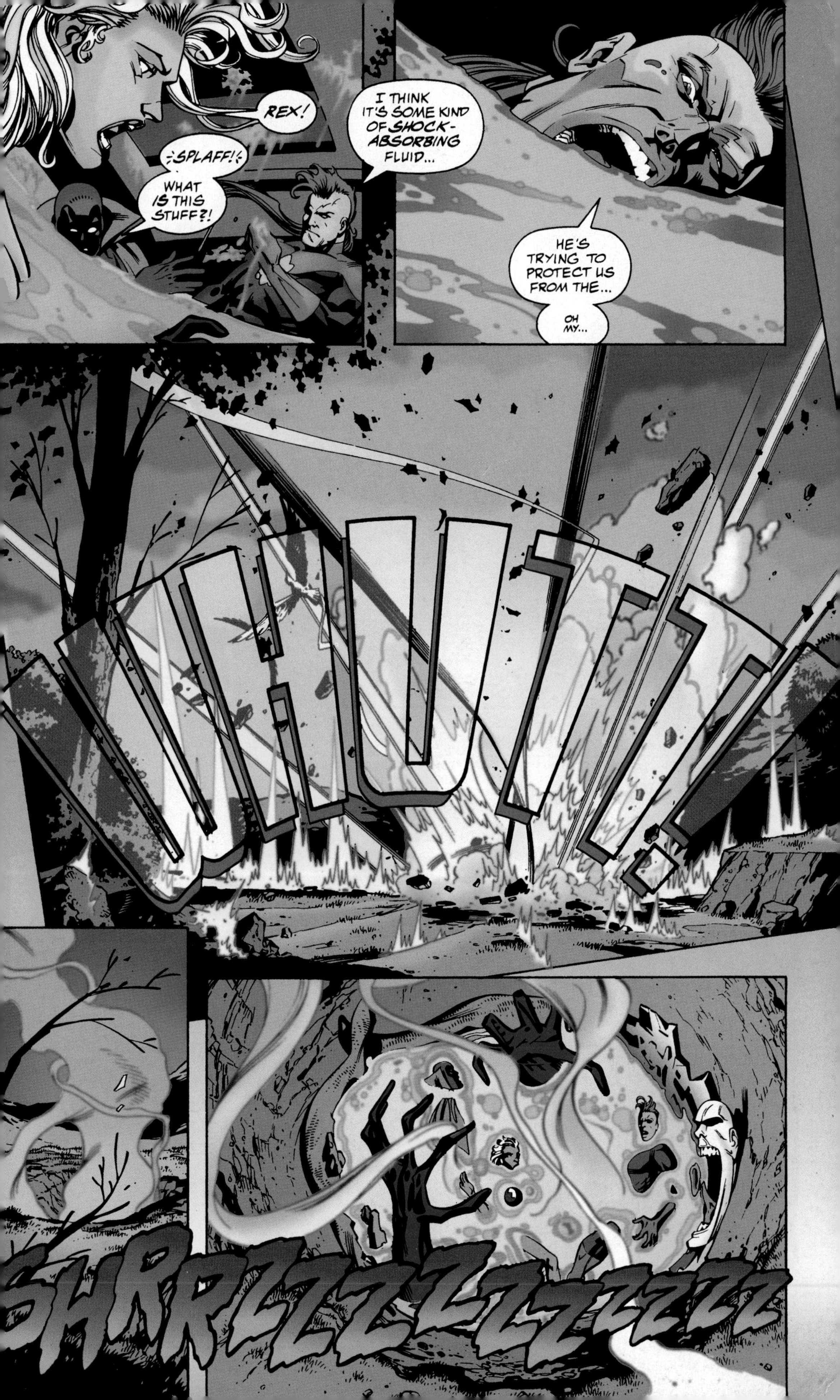
REX!
-SPLAFF!-
WHAT IS THIS STUFF?!
I THINK IT'S SOME KIND OF SHOCK-ABSORBING FLUID...
HE'S TRYING TO PROTECT US FROM THE...
OH MY...

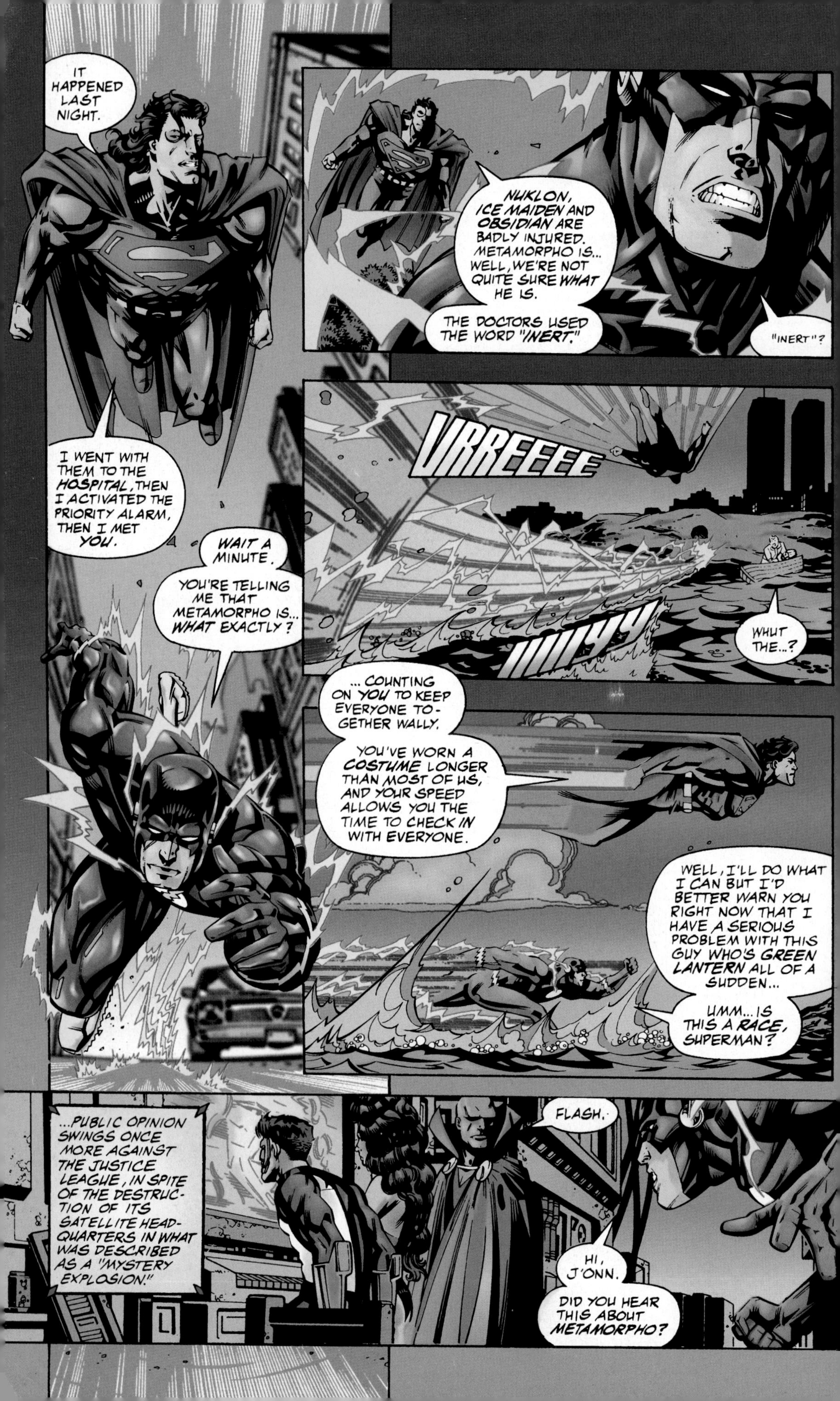
IT HAPPENED LAST NIGHT.
NUKLON, ICE MAIDEN AND OBSIDIAN ARE BADLY INJURED. METAMORPHO IS... WELL, WE'RE NOT QUITE SURE WHAT HE IS.
THE DOCTORS USED THE WORD "INERT."
"INERT"?
I WENT WITH THEM TO THE HOSPITAL, THEN I ACTIVATED THE PRIORITY ALARM, THEN I MET YOU.
URREEEEE
WAIT A MINUTE.
YOU'RE TELLING ME THAT METAMORPHO IS... WHAT EXACTLY?
WHUT THE...?
...COUNTING ON YOU TO KEEP EVERYONE TO-GETHER WALLY.
YOU'VE WORN A COSTUME LONGER THAN MOST OF US, AND YOUR SPEED ALLOWS YOU THE TIME TO CHECK IN WITH EVERYONE.
WELL, I'LL DO WHAT I CAN BUT I'D BETTER WARN YOU RIGHT NOW THAT I HAVE A SERIOUS PROBLEM WITH THIS GUY WHO'S GREEN LANTERN ALL OF A SUDDEN...
UMM...IS THIS A RACE, SUPERMAN?
...PUBLIC OPINION SWINGS ONCE MORE AGAINST THE JUSTICE LEAGUE, IN SPITE OF THE DESTRUC-TION OF ITS SATELLITE HEAD-QUARTERS IN WHAT WAS DESCRIBED AS A "MYSTERY EXPLOSION."
FLASH.
HI, J'ONN.
DID YOU HEAR THIS ABOUT METAMORPHO?

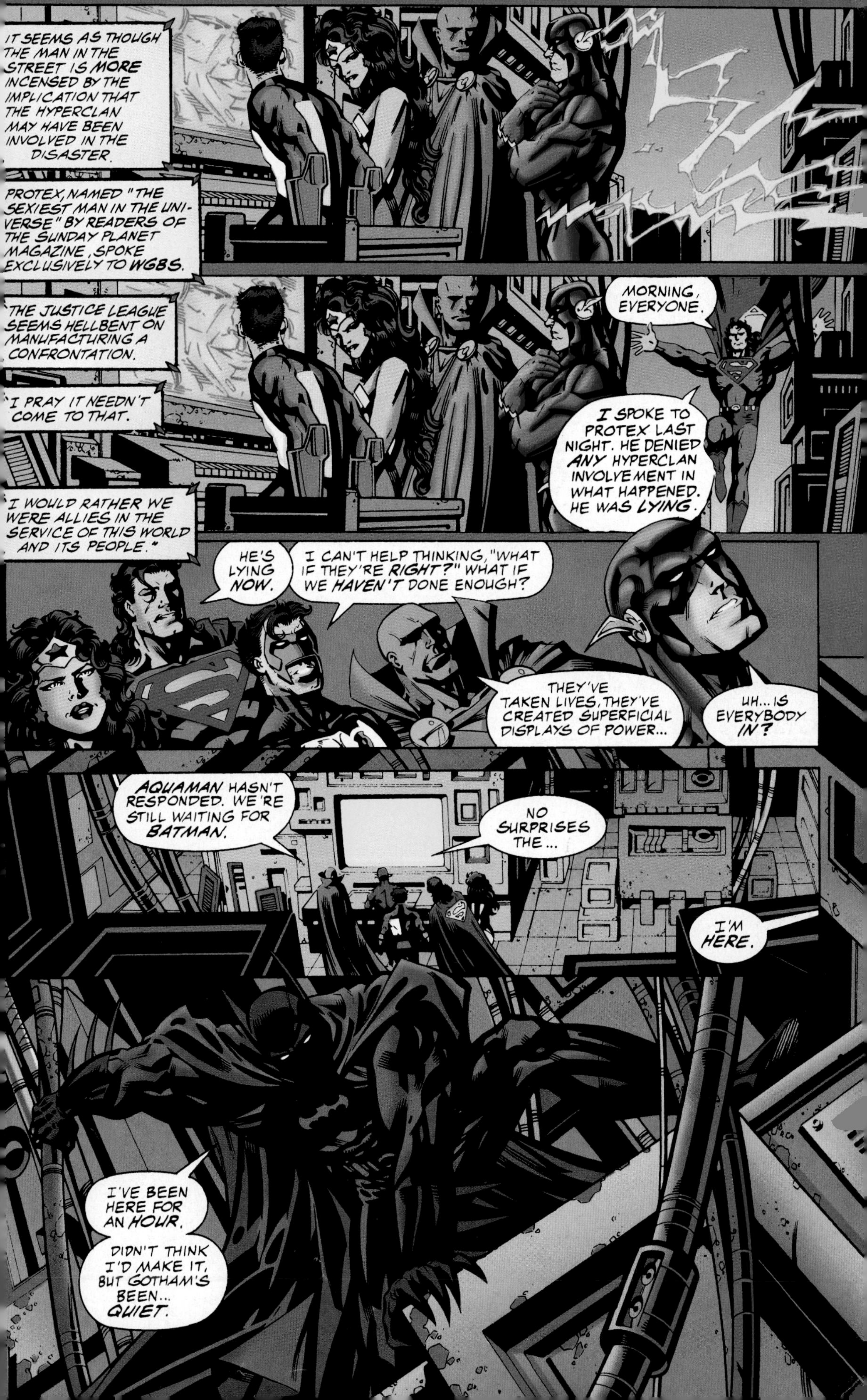
IT SEEMS AS THOUGH THE MAN IN THE STREET IS MORE INCENSED BY THE IMPLICATION THAT THE HYPERCLAN MAY HAVE BEEN INVOLVED IN THE DISASTER.
PROTEX, NAMED "THE SEXIEST MAN IN THE UNIVERSE" BY READERS OF THE SUNDAY PLANET MAGAZINE, SPOKE EXCLUSIVELY TO WGBS.
"THE JUSTICE LEAGUE SEEMS HELLBENT ON MANUFACTURING A CONFRONTATION.
"I PRAY IT NEEDN'T COME TO THAT.
MORNING, EVERYONE.
I SPOKE TO PROTEX LAST NIGHT. HE DENIED ANY HYPERCLAN INVOLVEMENT IN WHAT HAPPENED. HE WAS LYING.
"I WOULD RATHER WE WERE ALLIES IN THE SERVICE OF THIS WORLD AND ITS PEOPLE."
HE'S LYING NOW.
I CAN'T HELP THINKING, "WHAT IF THEY'RE RIGHT?" WHAT IF WE HAVEN'T DONE ENOUGH?
THEY'VE TAKEN LIVES, THEY'VE CREATED SUPERFICIAL DISPLAYS OF POWER...
UH... IS EVERYBODY IN?
AQUAMAN HASN'T RESPONDED. WE'RE STILL WAITING FOR BATMAN.
NO SURPRISES THE...
I'M HERE.
I'VE BEEN HERE FOR AN HOUR.
DIDN'T THINK I'D MAKE IT, BUT GOTHAM'S BEEN... QUIET.

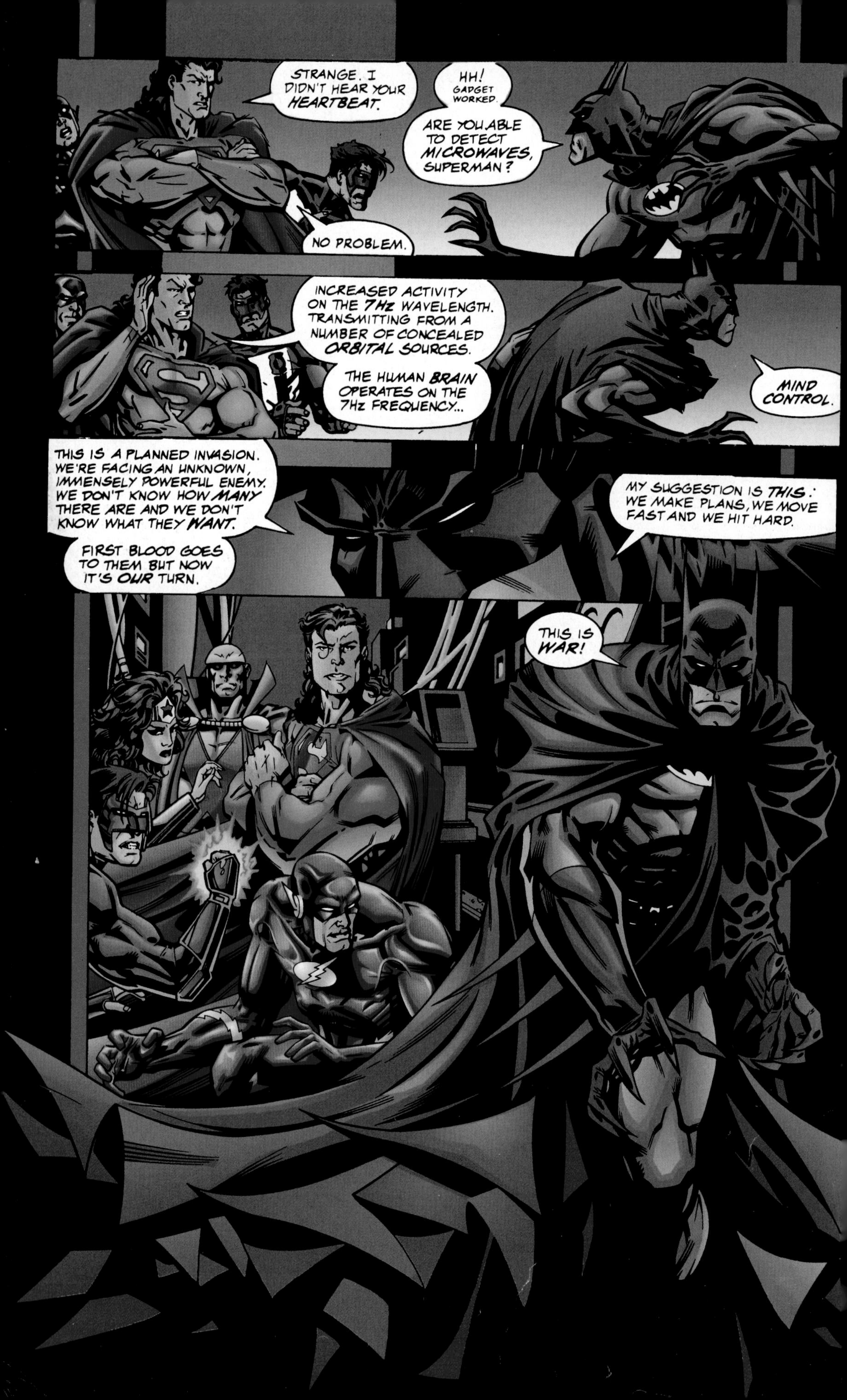
STRANGE. I DIDN'T HEAR YOUR HEARTBEAT.
HH! GADGET WORKED.
ARE YOU ABLE TO DETECT MICROWAVES, SUPERMAN?
NO PROBLEM.
INCREASED ACTIVITY ON THE 7Hz WAVELENGTH. TRANSMITTING FROM A NUMBER OF CONCEALED ORBITAL SOURCES.
THE HUMAN BRAIN OPERATES ON THE 7Hz FREQUENCY...
MIND CONTROL.
THIS IS A PLANNED INVASION. WE'RE FACING AN UNKNOWN, IMMENSELY POWERFUL ENEMY. WE DON'T KNOW HOW MANY THERE ARE AND WE DON'T KNOW WHAT THEY WANT.
FIRST BLOOD GOES TO THEM BUT NOW IT'S OUR TURN.
MY SUGGESTION IS THIS: WE MAKE PLANS, WE MOVE FAST AND WE HIT HARD.
THIS IS WAR!

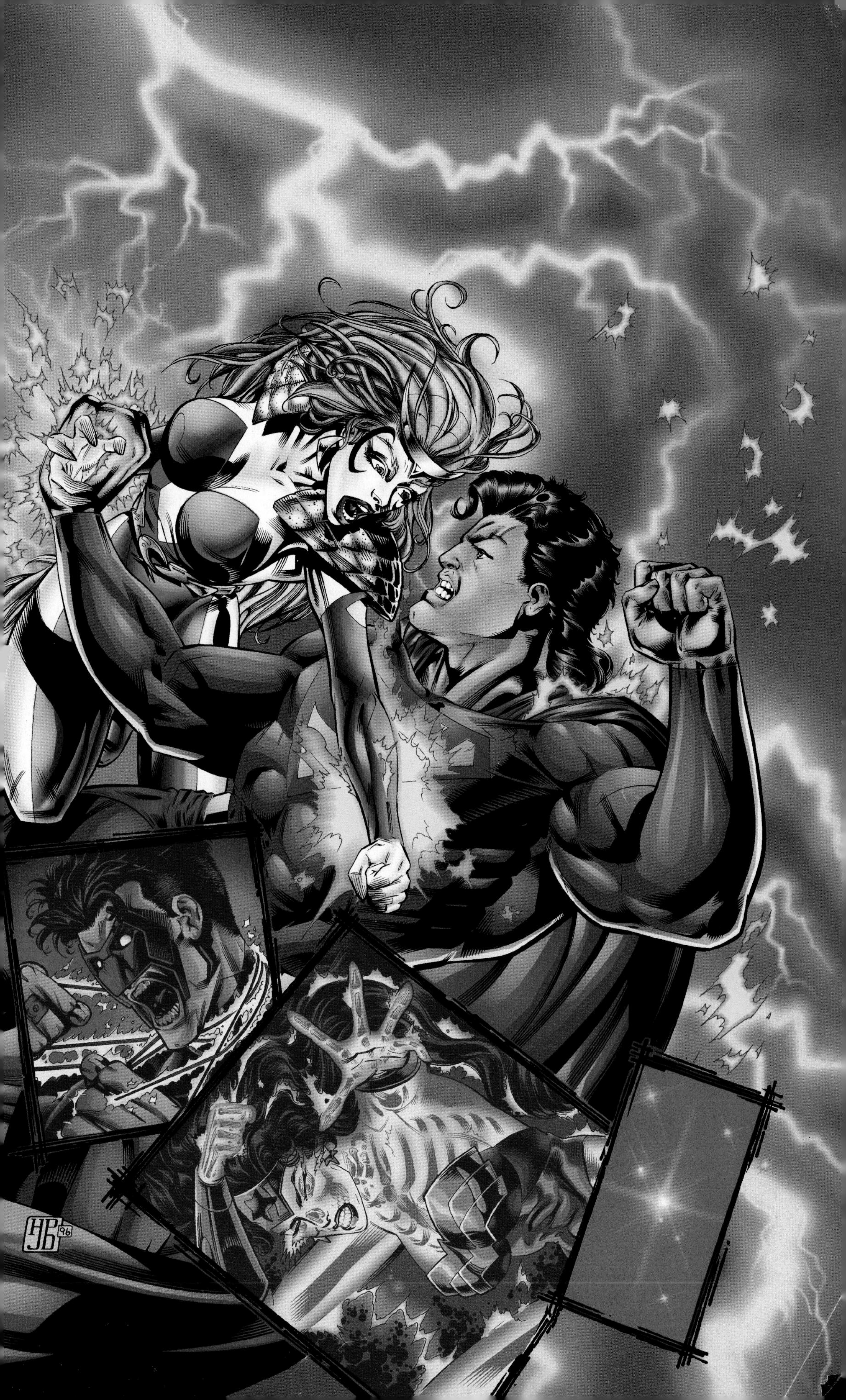

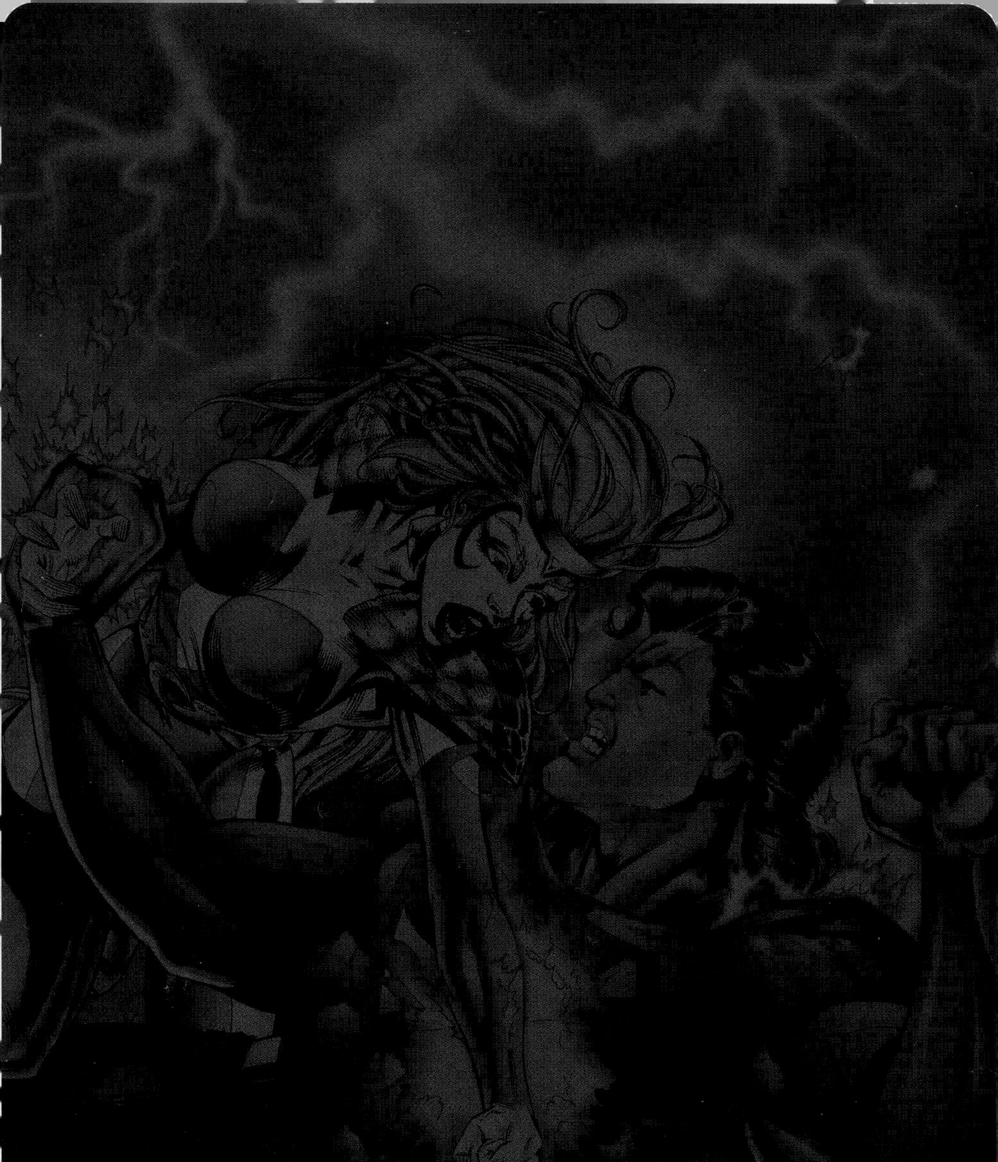

JLA #2

WRITTEN BY GRANT MORRISON

PENCILS BY HOWARD PORTER, WITH INKS BY JOHN DELL AND COLORS BY PAT GARRAHY

The Day The EARTH Stood Still

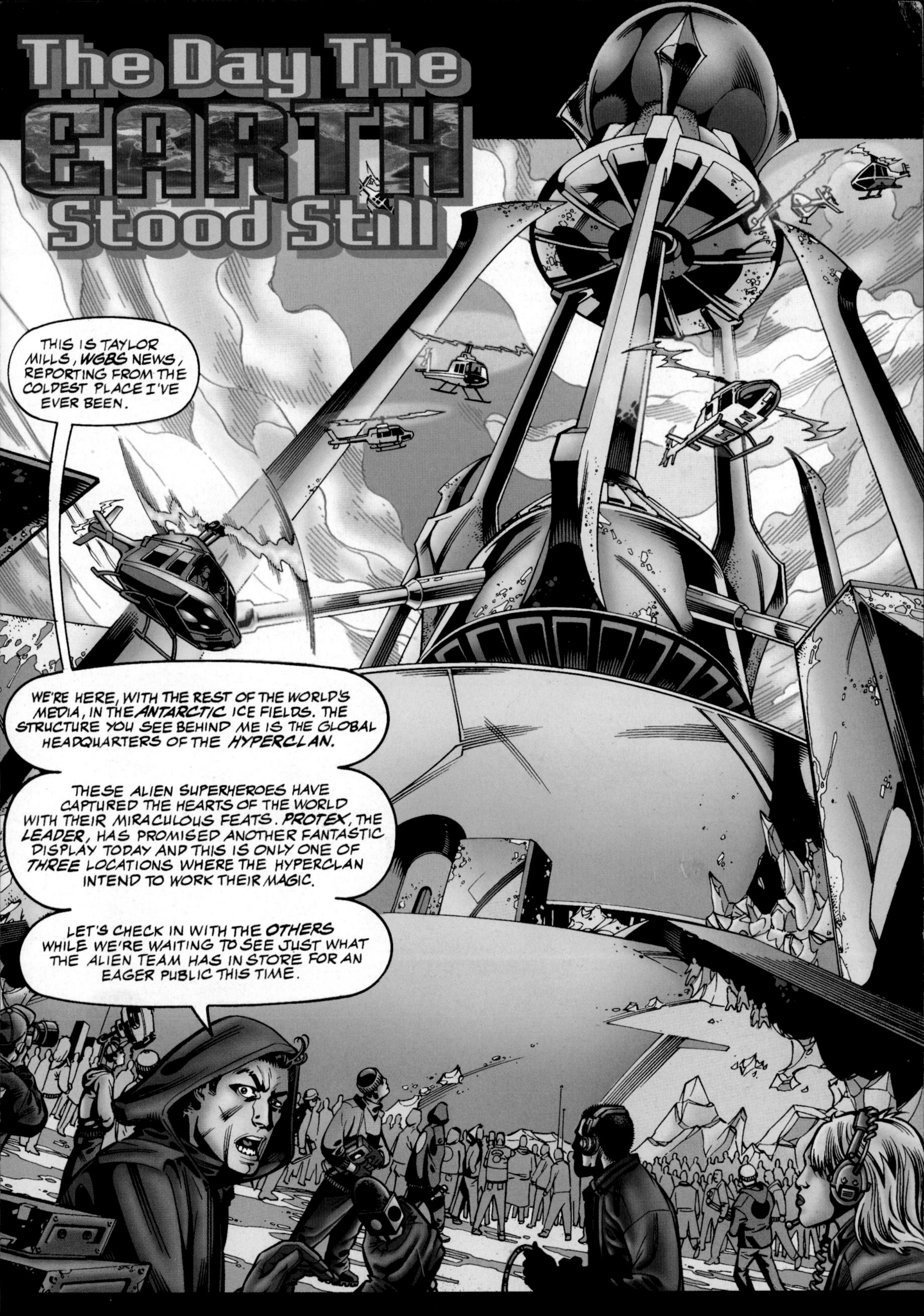
THIS IS TAYLOR MILLS, WGBS NEWS, REPORTING FROM THE COLDEST PLACE I'VE EVER BEEN.
WE'RE HERE, WITH THE REST OF THE WORLD'S MEDIA, IN THE ANTARCTIC ICE FIELDS. THE STRUCTURE YOU SEE BEHIND ME IS THE GLOBAL HEADQUARTERS OF THE HYPERCLAN.
THESE ALIEN SUPERHEROES HAVE CAPTURED THE HEARTS OF THE WORLD WITH THEIR MIRACULOUS FEATS. PROTEX, THE LEADER, HAS PROMISED ANOTHER FANTASTIC DISPLAY TODAY AND THIS IS ONLY ONE OF THREE LOCATIONS WHERE THE HYPERCLAN INTEND TO WORK THEIR MAGIC.
LET'S CHECK IN WITH THE OTHERS WHILE WE'RE WAITING TO SEE JUST WHAT THE ALIEN TEAM HAS IN STORE FOR AN EAGER PUBLIC THIS TIME.

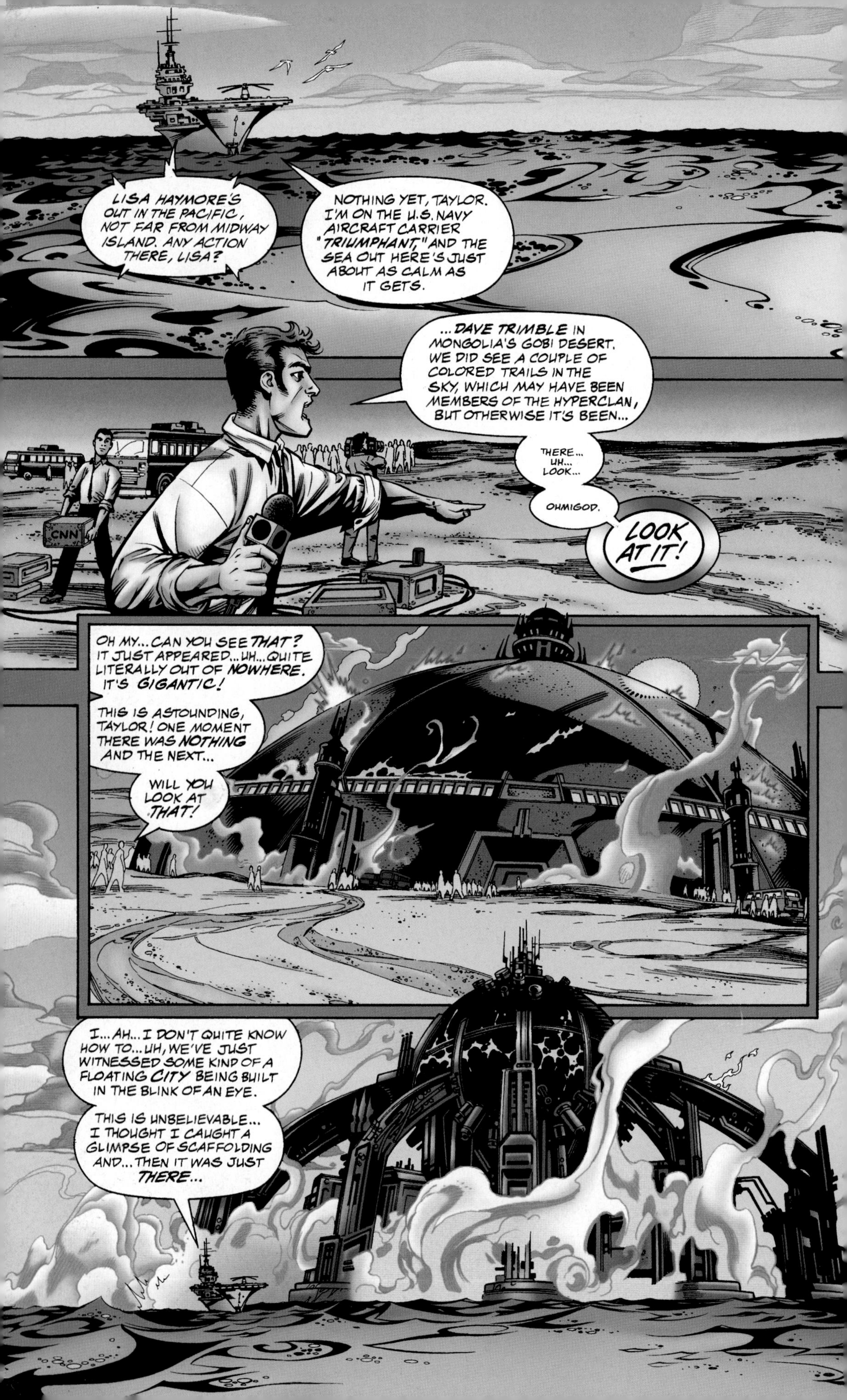

LISA HAYMORE'S OUT IN THE PACIFIC, NOT FAR FROM MIDWAY ISLAND. ANY ACTION THERE, LISA?
NOTHING YET, TAYLOR. I'M ON THE U.S. NAVY AIRCRAFT CARRIER "TRIUMPHANT," AND THE SEA OUT HERE'S JUST ABOUT AS CALM AS IT GETS.
...DAVE TRIMBLE IN MONGOLIA'S GOBI DESERT. WE DID SEE A COUPLE OF COLORED TRAILS IN THE SKY, WHICH MAY HAVE BEEN MEMBERS OF THE HYPERCLAN, BUT OTHERWISE IT'S BEEN...
THERE... UH... LOOK...
OHMIGOD.
LOOK AT IT!
CNN
OH MY...CAN YOU SEE THAT? IT JUST APPEARED...UH...QUITE LITERALLY OUT OF NOWHERE. IT'S GIGANTIC!
THIS IS ASTOUNDING, TAYLOR! ONE MOMENT THERE WAS NOTHING AND THE NEXT...
WILL YOU LOOK AT THAT!
I...AH...I DON'T QUITE KNOW HOW TO...UH, WE'VE JUST WITNESSED SOME KIND OF A FLOATING CITY BEING BUILT IN THE BLINK OF AN EYE.
THIS IS UNBELIEVABLE... I THOUGHT I CAUGHT A GLIMPSE OF SCAFFOLDING AND...THEN IT WAS JUST THERE...

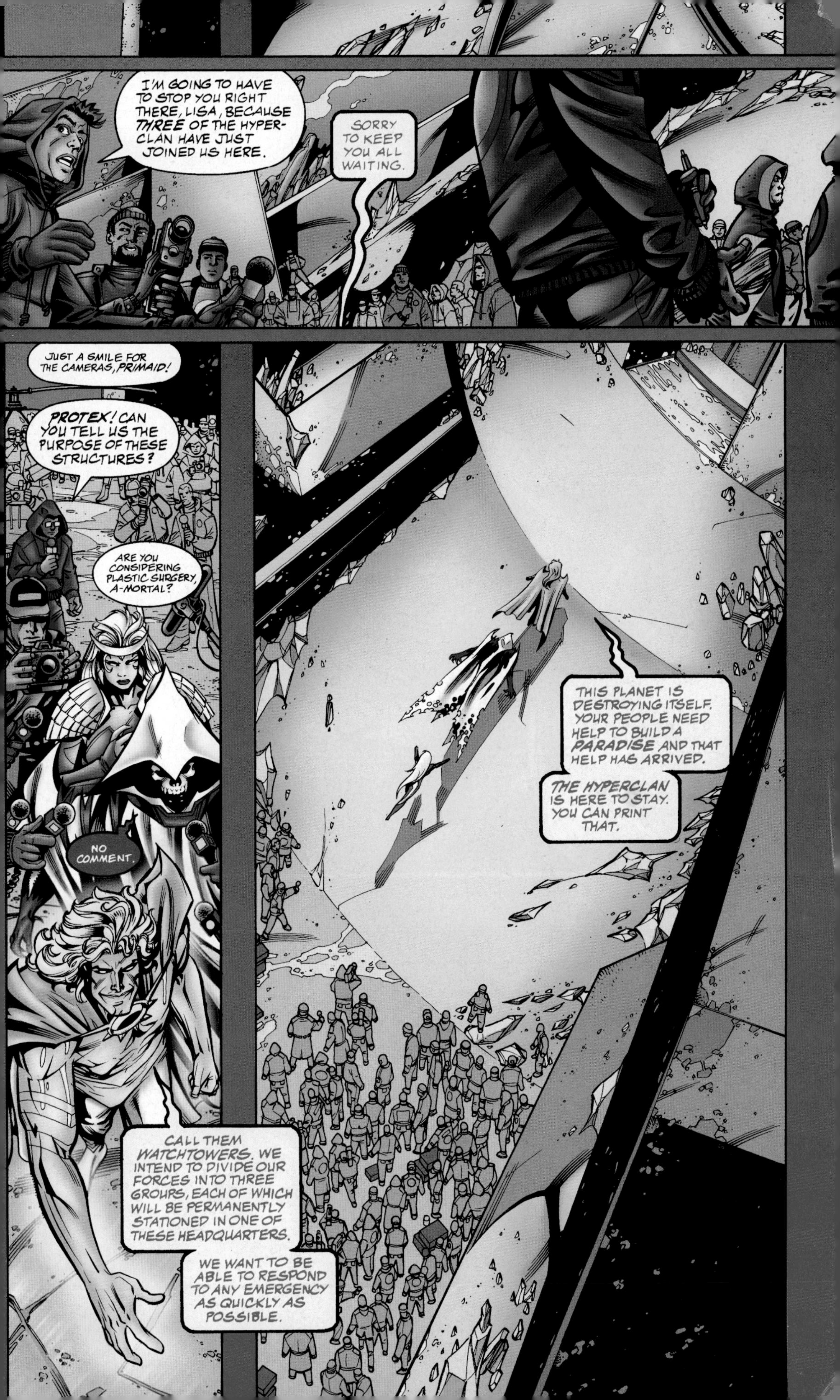

I'M GOING TO HAVE TO STOP YOU RIGHT THERE, LISA, BECAUSE THREE OF THE HYPER-CLAN HAVE JUST JOINED US HERE.
SORRY TO KEEP YOU ALL WAITING.
JUST A SMILE FOR THE CAMERAS, PRIMAID!
PROTEX! CAN YOU TELL US THE PURPOSE OF THESE STRUCTURES?
ARE YOU CONSIDERING PLASTIC SURGERY, A-MORTAL?
NO COMMENT.
THIS PLANET IS DESTROYING ITSELF. YOUR PEOPLE NEED HELP TO BUILD A PARADISE AND THAT HELP HAS ARRIVED.
THE HYPERCLAN IS HERE TO STAY. YOU CAN PRINT THAT.
CALL THEM WATCHTOWERS. WE INTEND TO DIVIDE OUR FORCES INTO THREE GROUPS, EACH OF WHICH WILL BE PERMANENTLY STATIONED IN ONE OF THESE HEADQUARTERS.
WE WANT TO BE ABLE TO RESPOND TO ANY EMERGENCY AS QUICKLY AS POSSIBLE.

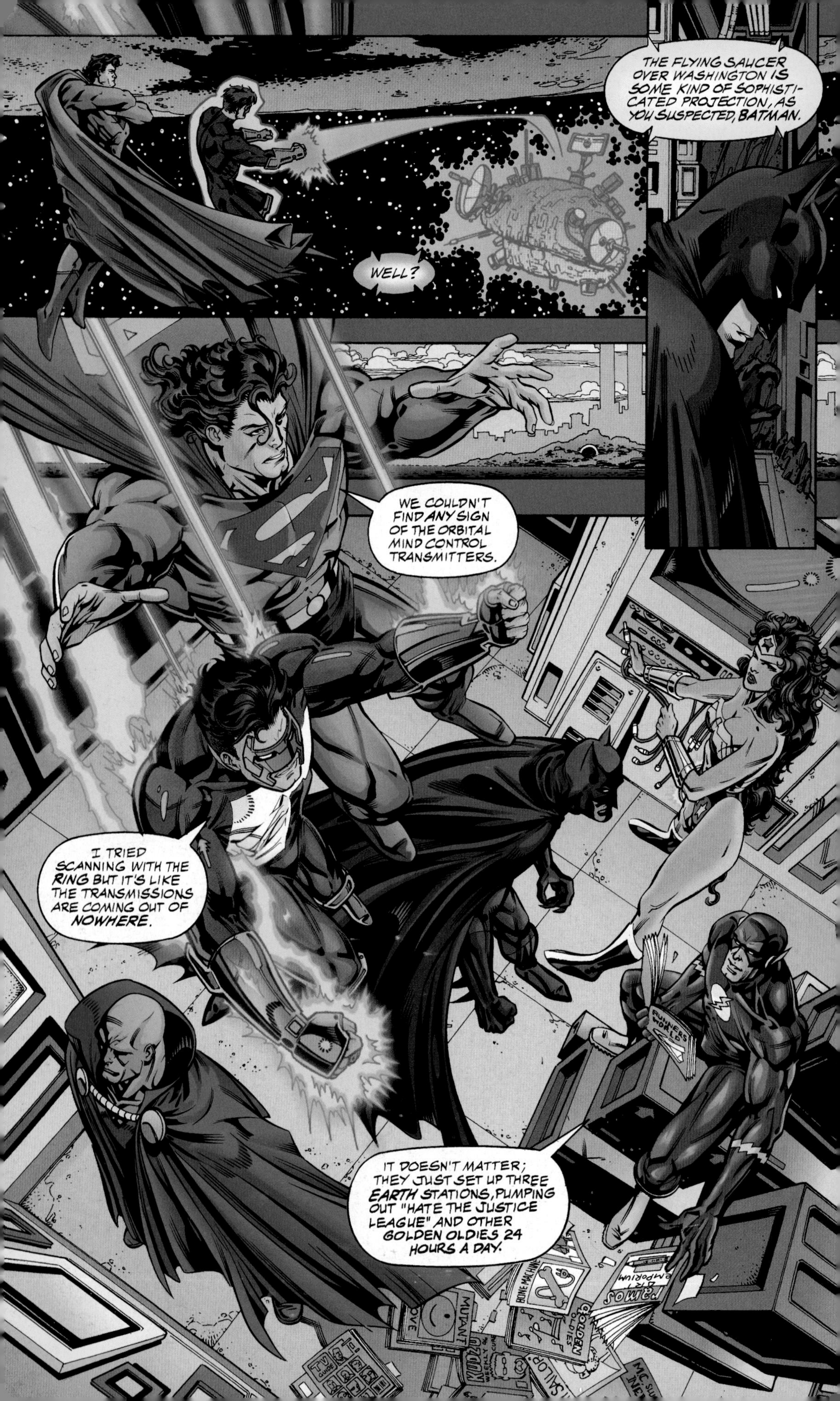
THE FLYING SAUCER OVER WASHINGTON IS SOME KIND OF SOPHISTICATED PROJECTION, AS YOU SUSPECTED, BATMAN.
WELL?
WE COULDN'T FIND ANY SIGN OF THE ORBITAL MIND CONTROL TRANSMITTERS.
I TRIED SCANNING WITH THE RING BUT IT'S LIKE THE TRANSMISSIONS ARE COMING OUT OF NOWHERE.
IT DOESN'T MATTER; THEY JUST SET UP THREE EARTH STATIONS, PUMPING OUT "HATE THE JUSTICE LEAGUE" AND OTHER GOLDEN OLDIES 24 HOURS A DAY.
RUNNERS WORLD
BONE MACHINE
MUTANT
GOLDEN OLDIES
TV GUIDE
SAILOR

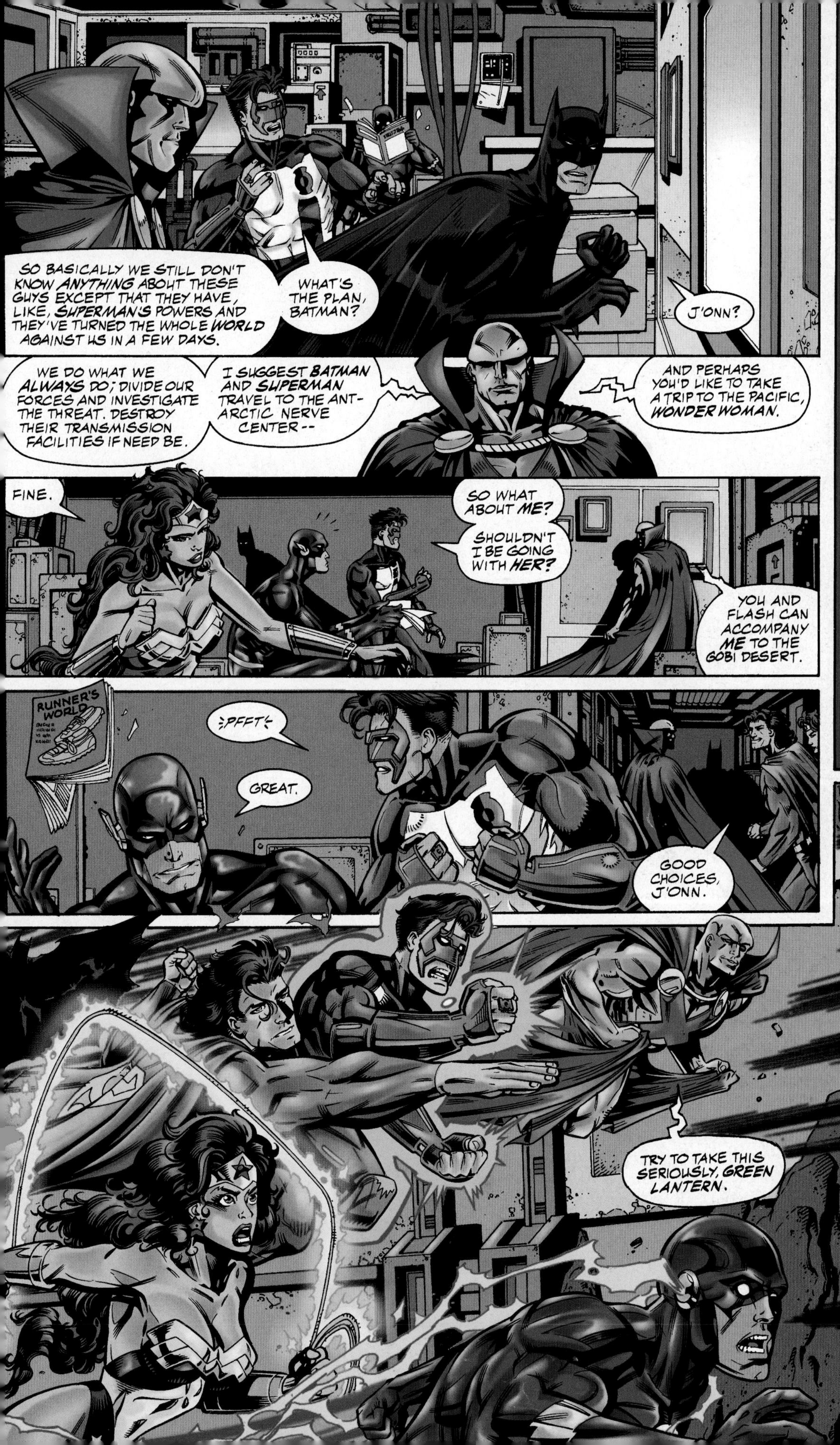
SO BASICALLY WE STILL DON'T KNOW ANYTHING ABOUT THESE GUYS EXCEPT THAT THEY HAVE, LIKE, SUPERMAN'S POWERS AND THEY'VE TURNED THE WHOLE WORLD AGAINST US IN A FEW DAYS.
WHAT'S THE PLAN, BATMAN?
J'ONN?
WE DO WHAT WE ALWAYS DO; DIVIDE OUR FORCES AND INVESTIGATE THE THREAT. DESTROY THEIR TRANSMISSION FACILITIES IF NEED BE.
I SUGGEST BATMAN AND SUPERMAN TRAVEL TO THE ANTARCTIC NERVE CENTER--
AND PERHAPS YOU'D LIKE TO TAKE A TRIP TO THE PACIFIC, WONDER WOMAN.
FINE.
SO WHAT ABOUT ME?
SHOULDN'T I BE GOING WITH HER?
YOU AND FLASH CAN ACCOMPANY ME TO THE GOBI DESERT.
RUNNER'S WORLD
PFFT
GREAT.
GOOD CHOICES, J'ONN.
TRY TO TAKE THIS SERIOUSLY, GREEN LANTERN.

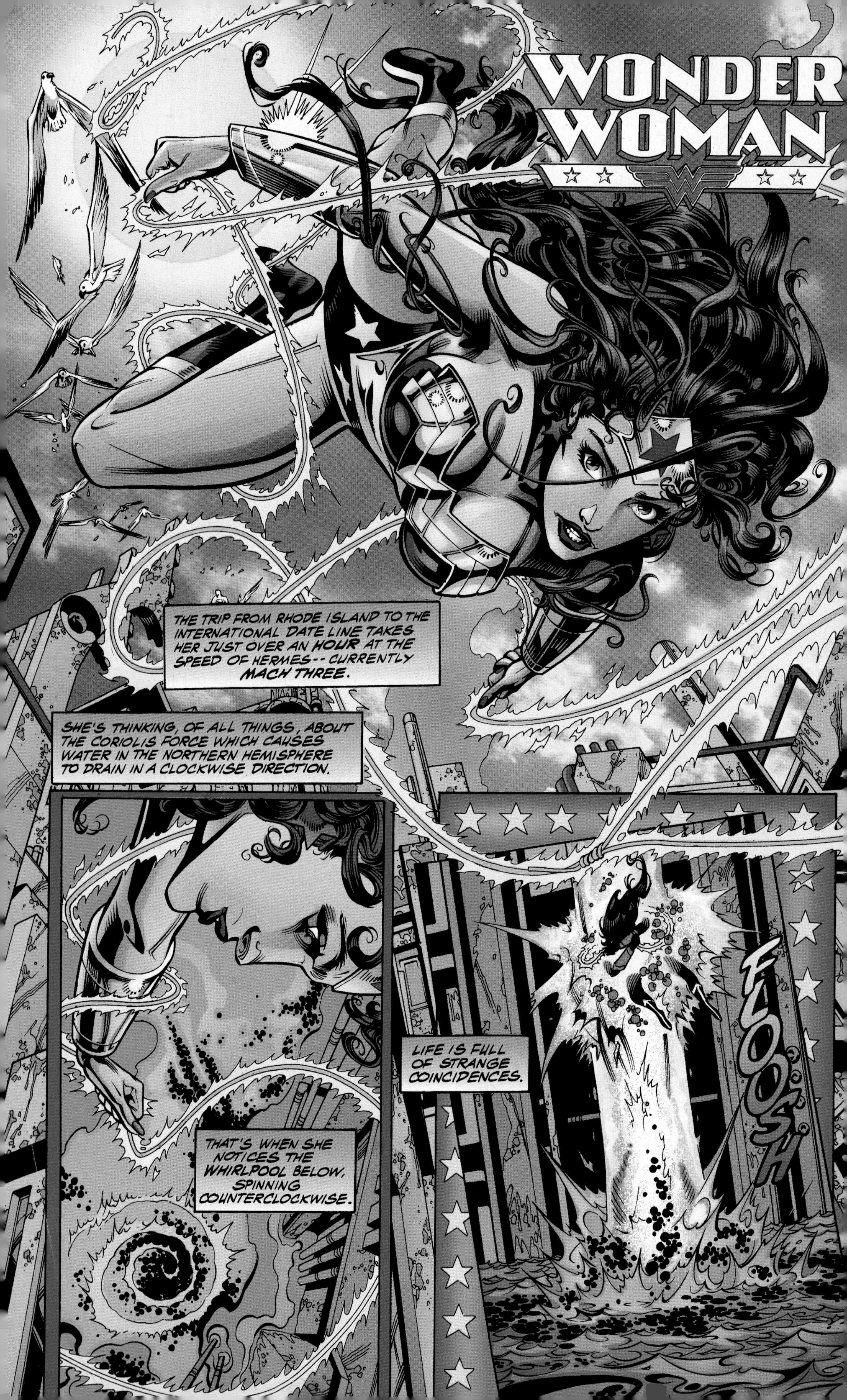
WONDER WOMAN
THE TRIP FROM RHODE ISLAND TO THE INTERNATIONAL DATE LINE TAKES HER JUST OVER AN HOUR AT THE SPEED OF HERMES-- CURRENTLY MACH THREE.
SHE'S THINKING, OF ALL THINGS, ABOUT THE CORIOLIS FORCE WHICH CAUSES WATER IN THE NORTHERN HEMISPHERE TO DRAIN IN A CLOCKWISE DIRECTION.
THAT'S WHEN SHE NOTICES THE WHIRLPOOL BELOW, SPINNING COUNTERCLOCKWISE.
LIFE IS FULL OF STRANGE COINCIDENCES.
FLOOSH

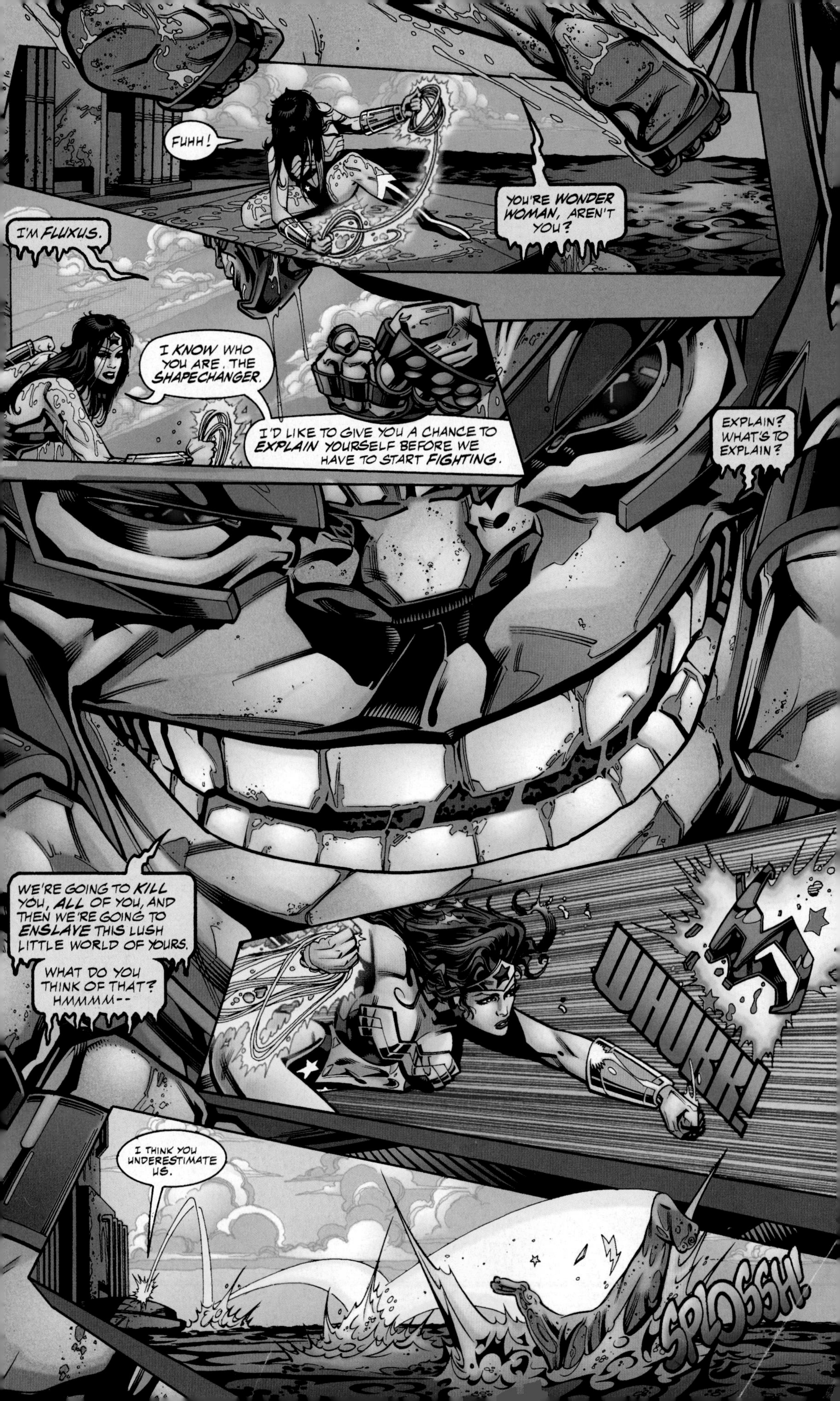
FUHH!
YOU'RE WONDER WOMAN, AREN'T YOU?
I'M FLUXUS.
I KNOW WHO YOU ARE. THE SHAPECHANGER.
I'D LIKE TO GIVE YOU A CHANCE TO EXPLAIN YOURSELF BEFORE WE HAVE TO START FIGHTING.
EXPLAIN? WHAT'S TO EXPLAIN?
WE'RE GOING TO KILL YOU, ALL OF YOU, AND THEN WE'RE GOING TO ENSLAVE THIS LUSH LITTLE WORLD OF YOURS.
WHAT DO YOU THINK OF THAT? HMMMM--
WHUKK!
I THINK YOU UNDERESTIMATE US.
SPLOSSH!

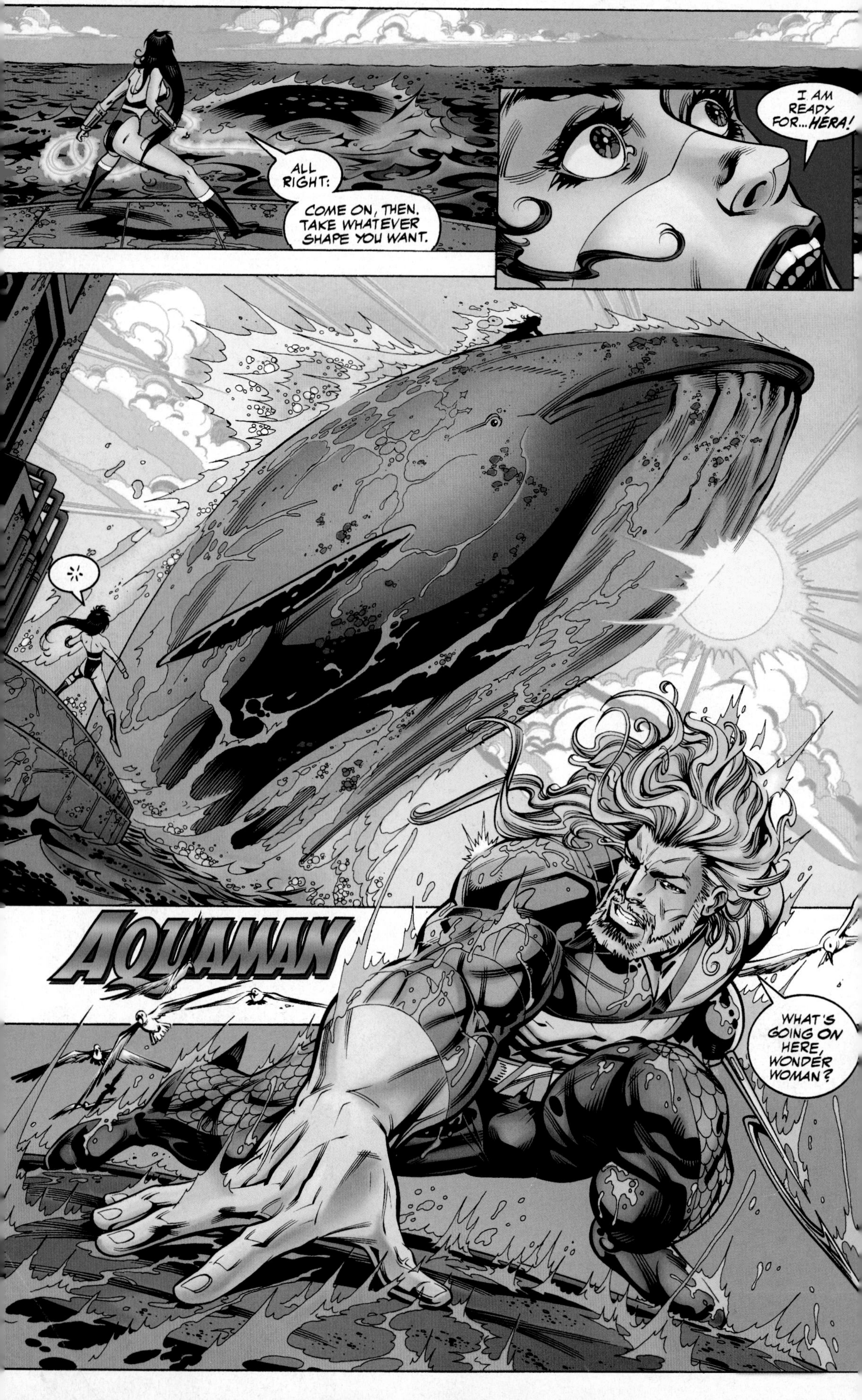
ALL RIGHT:
COME ON, THEN. TAKE WHATEVER SHAPE YOU WANT.
I AM READY FOR...HERA!
AQUAMAN
WHAT'S GOING ON HERE, WONDER WOMAN?

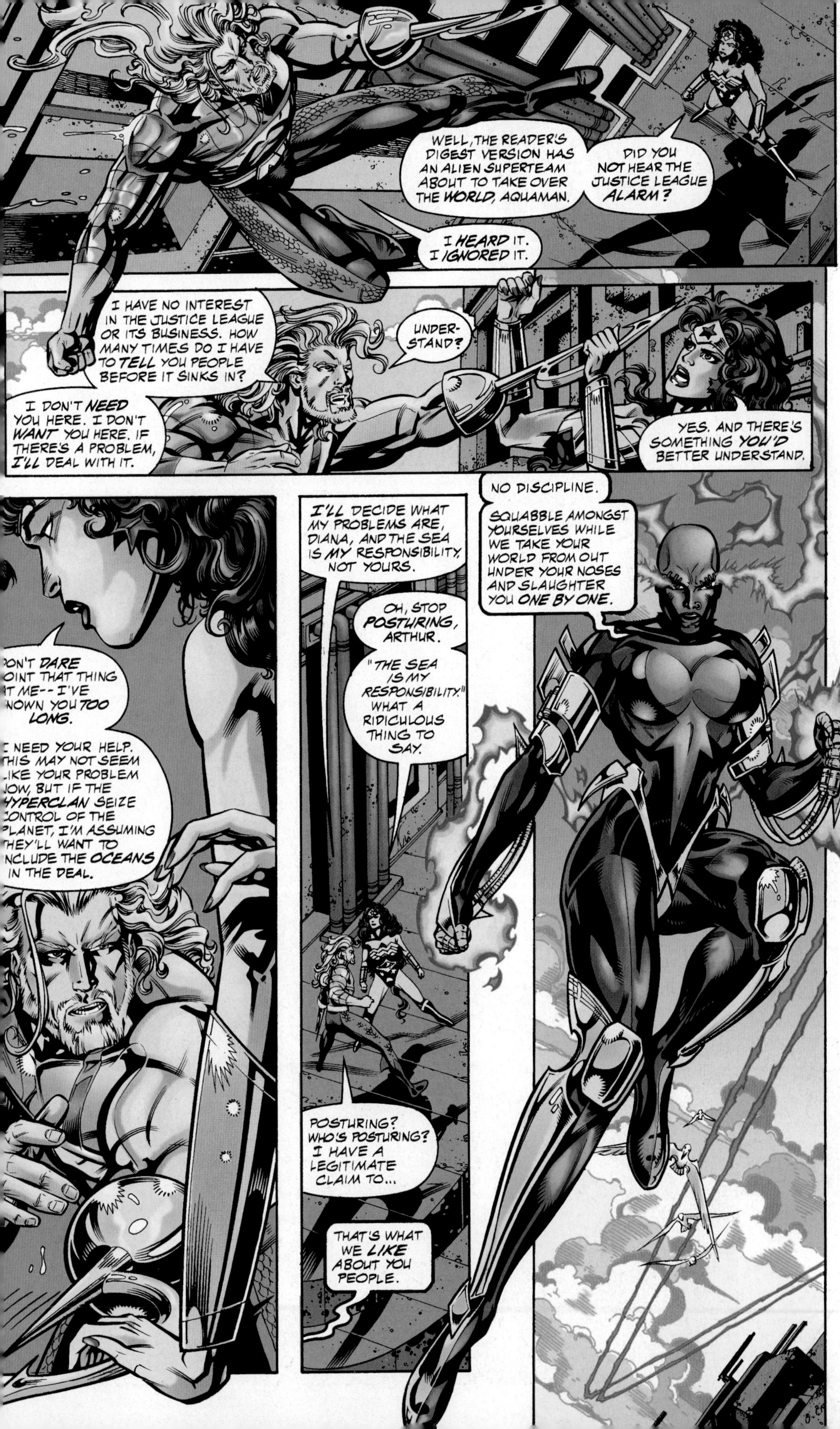

DID YOU NOT HEAR THE JUSTICE LEAGUE ALARM?
WELL, THE READER'S DIGEST VERSION HAS AN ALIEN SUPERTEAM ABOUT TO TAKE OVER THE WORLD, AQUAMAN.
I HEARD IT. I IGNORED IT.
I HAVE NO INTEREST IN THE JUSTICE LEAGUE OR ITS BUSINESS. HOW MANY TIMES DO I HAVE TO TELL YOU PEOPLE BEFORE IT SINKS IN?
I DON'T NEED YOU HERE. I DON'T WANT YOU HERE. IF THERE'S A PROBLEM, I'LL DEAL WITH IT.
UNDER-STAND?
YES. AND THERE'S SOMETHING YOU'D BETTER UNDERSTAND.
I NEED YOUR HELP.
I'LL DECIDE WHAT MY PROBLEMS ARE, DIANA, AND THE SEA IS MY RESPONSIBILITY, NOT YOURS.
OH, STOP POSTURING, ARTHUR.
"THE SEA IS MY RESPONSIBILITY." WHAT A RIDICULOUS THING TO SAY.
POSTURING? WHO'S POSTURING? I HAVE A LEGITIMATE CLAIM TO...
NO DISCIPLINE.
SQUABBLE AMONGST YOURSELVES WHILE WE TAKE YOUR WORLD FROM OUT UNDER YOUR NOSES AND SLAUGHTER YOU ONE BY ONE.
THAT'S WHAT WE LIKE ABOUT YOU PEOPLE.

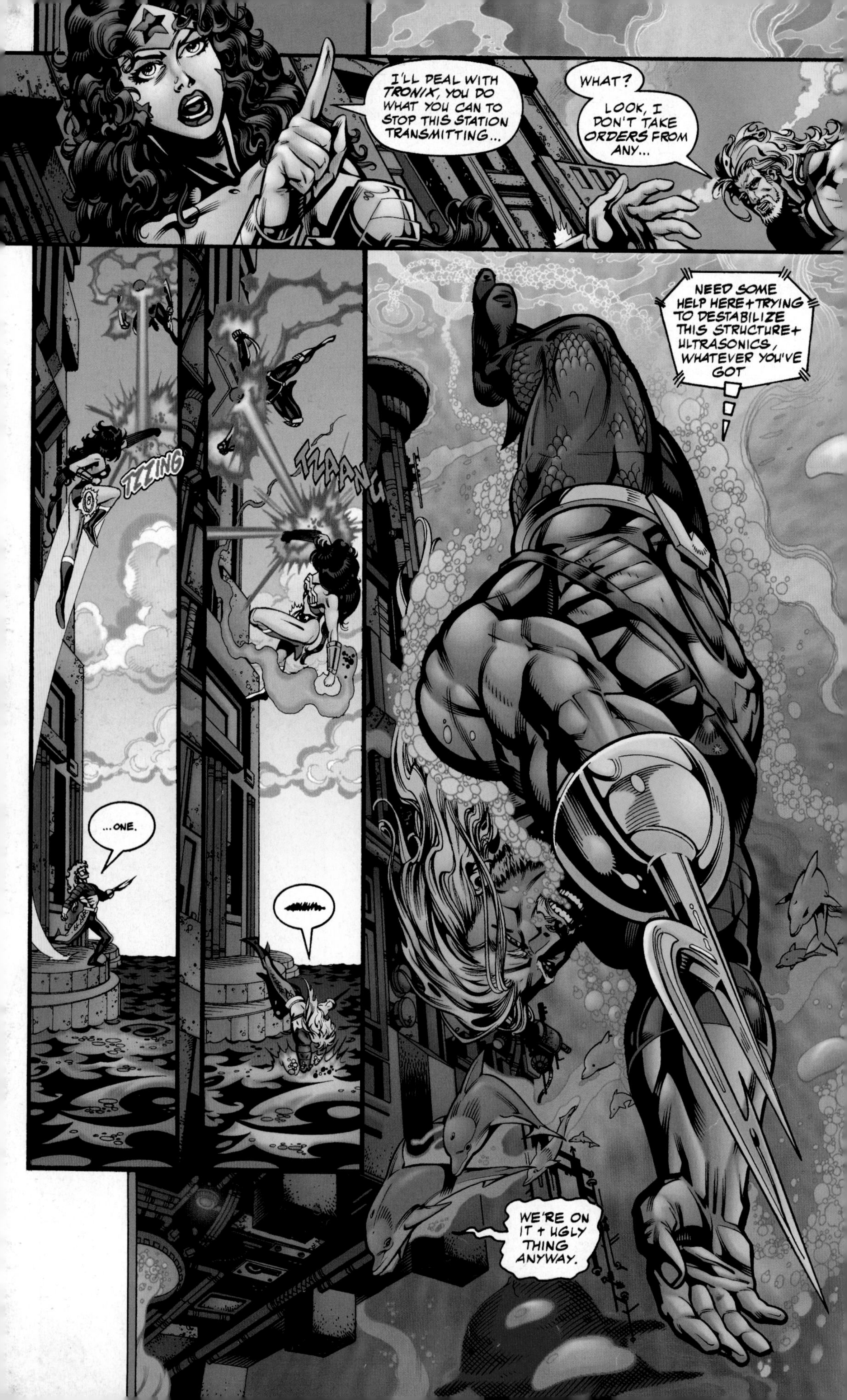
I'LL DEAL WITH TRONIX, YOU DO WHAT YOU CAN TO STOP THIS STATION TRANSMITTING...
WHAT?
LOOK, I DON'T TAKE ORDERS FROM ANY...
TZZING
...ONE.
TZAANG
NEED SOME HELP HERE+TRYING TO DESTABILIZE THIS STRUCTURE+ULTRASONICS, WHATEVER YOU'VE GOT
WE'RE ON IT + UGLY THING ANYWAY.

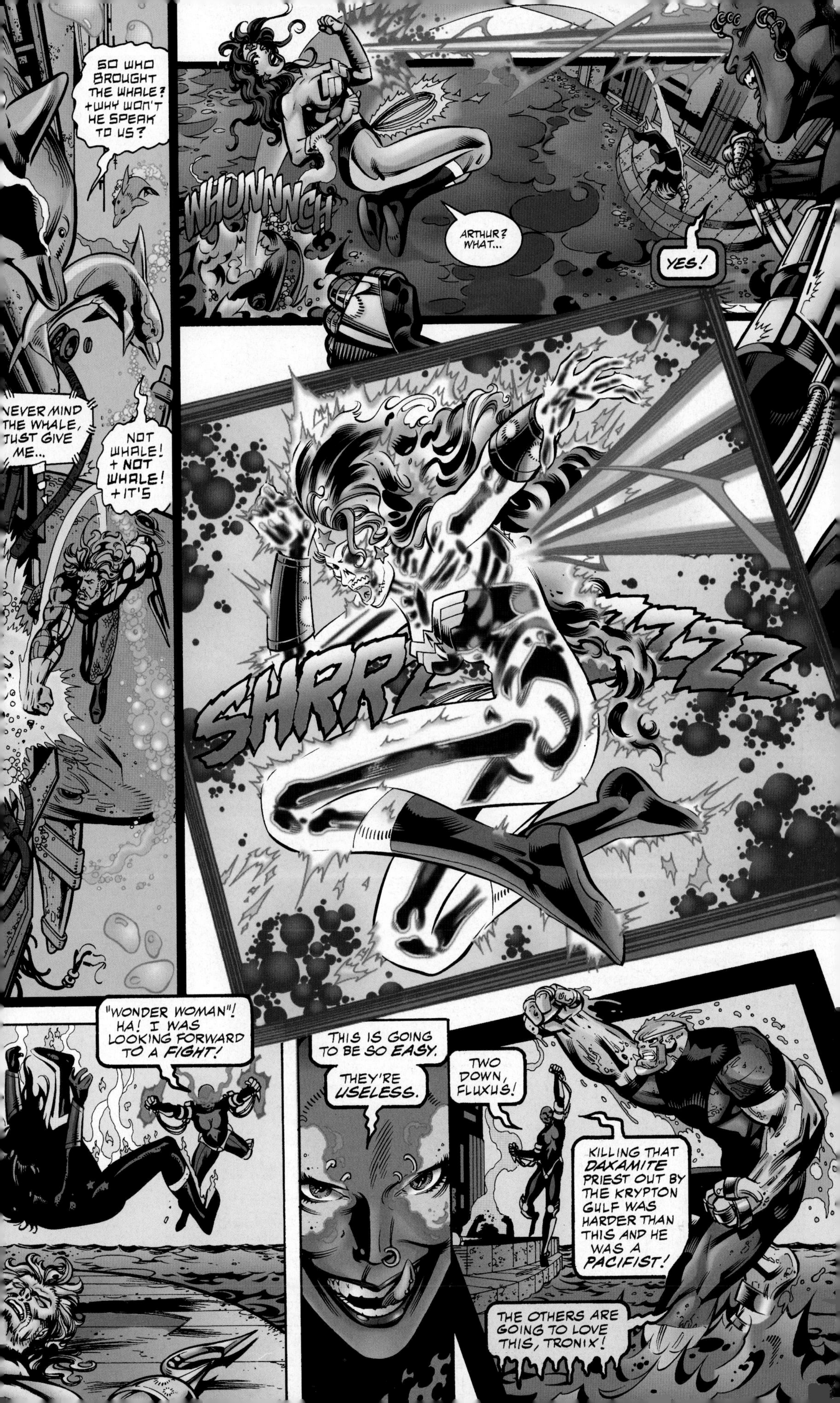

SO WHO BROUGHT THE WHALE? +WHY WON'T HE SPEAK TO US?
WHUNNNCH
ARTHUR? WHAT...
YES!
NEVER MIND THE WHALE, JUST GIVE ME...
NOT WHALE! + NOT WHALE! +IT'S
SHRRZZZ
"WONDER WOMAN"! HA! I WAS LOOKING FORWARD TO A FIGHT!
THIS IS GOING TO BE SO EASY.
THEY'RE USELESS.
TWO DOWN, FLUXUS!
KILLING THAT DAXAMITE PRIEST OUT BY THE KRYPTON GULF WAS HARDER THAN THIS AND HE WAS A PACIFIST!
THE OTHERS ARE GOING TO LOVE THIS, TRONIX!

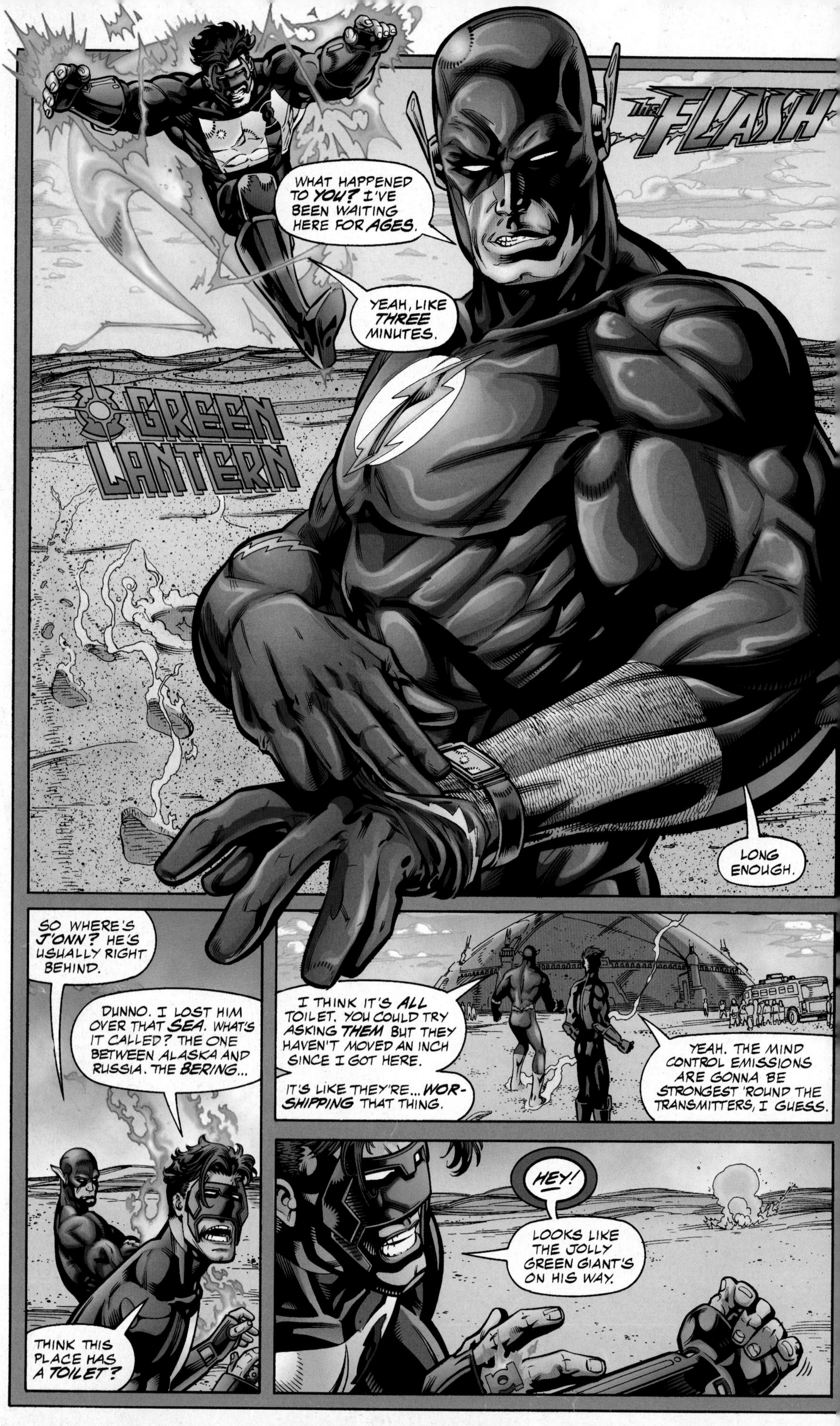
THE FLASH
WHAT HAPPENED TO YOU? I'VE BEEN WAITING HERE FOR AGES.
YEAH, LIKE THREE MINUTES.
GREEN LANTERN
LONG ENOUGH.
SO WHERE'S J'ONN? HE'S USUALLY RIGHT BEHIND.
DUNNO. I LOST HIM OVER THAT SEA. WHAT'S IT CALLED? THE ONE BETWEEN ALASKA AND RUSSIA. THE BERING...
THINK THIS PLACE HAS A TOILET?
I THINK IT'S ALL TOILET. YOU COULD TRY ASKING THEM BUT THEY HAVEN'T MOVED AN INCH SINCE I GOT HERE.
IT'S LIKE THEY'RE... WOR-SHIPPING THAT THING.
YEAH. THE MIND CONTROL EMISSIONS ARE GONNA BE STRONGEST 'ROUND THE TRANSMITTERS, I GUESS.
HEY!
LOOKS LIKE THE JOLLY GREEN GIANT'S ON HIS WAY.

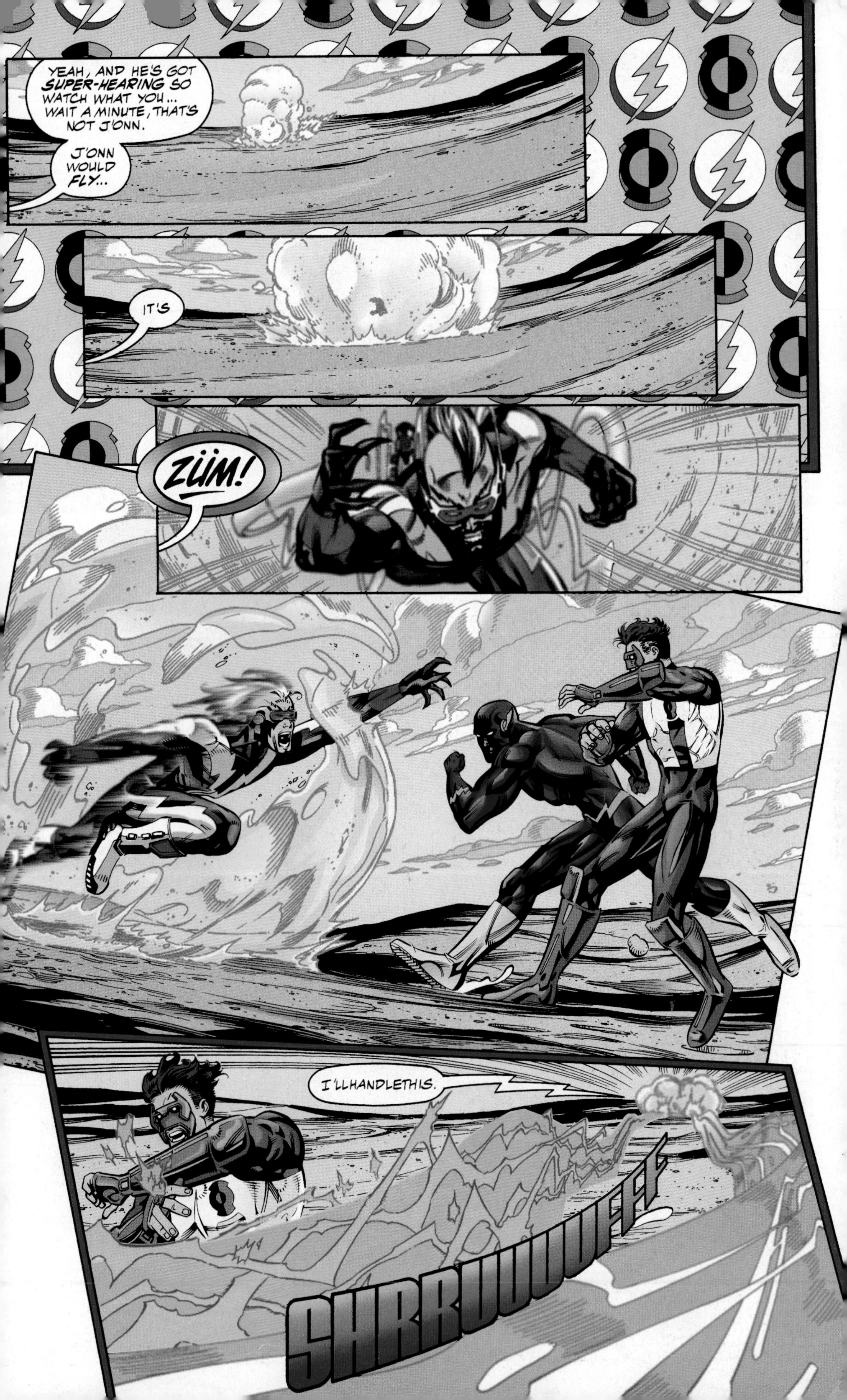
YEAH, AND HE'S GOT SUPER-HEARING SO WATCH WHAT YOU... WAIT A MINUTE, THAT'S NOT J'ONN.
J'ONN WOULD FLY...
IT'S
ZÜM!
I'LLHANDLETHIS.
SHRRUUUUFFT

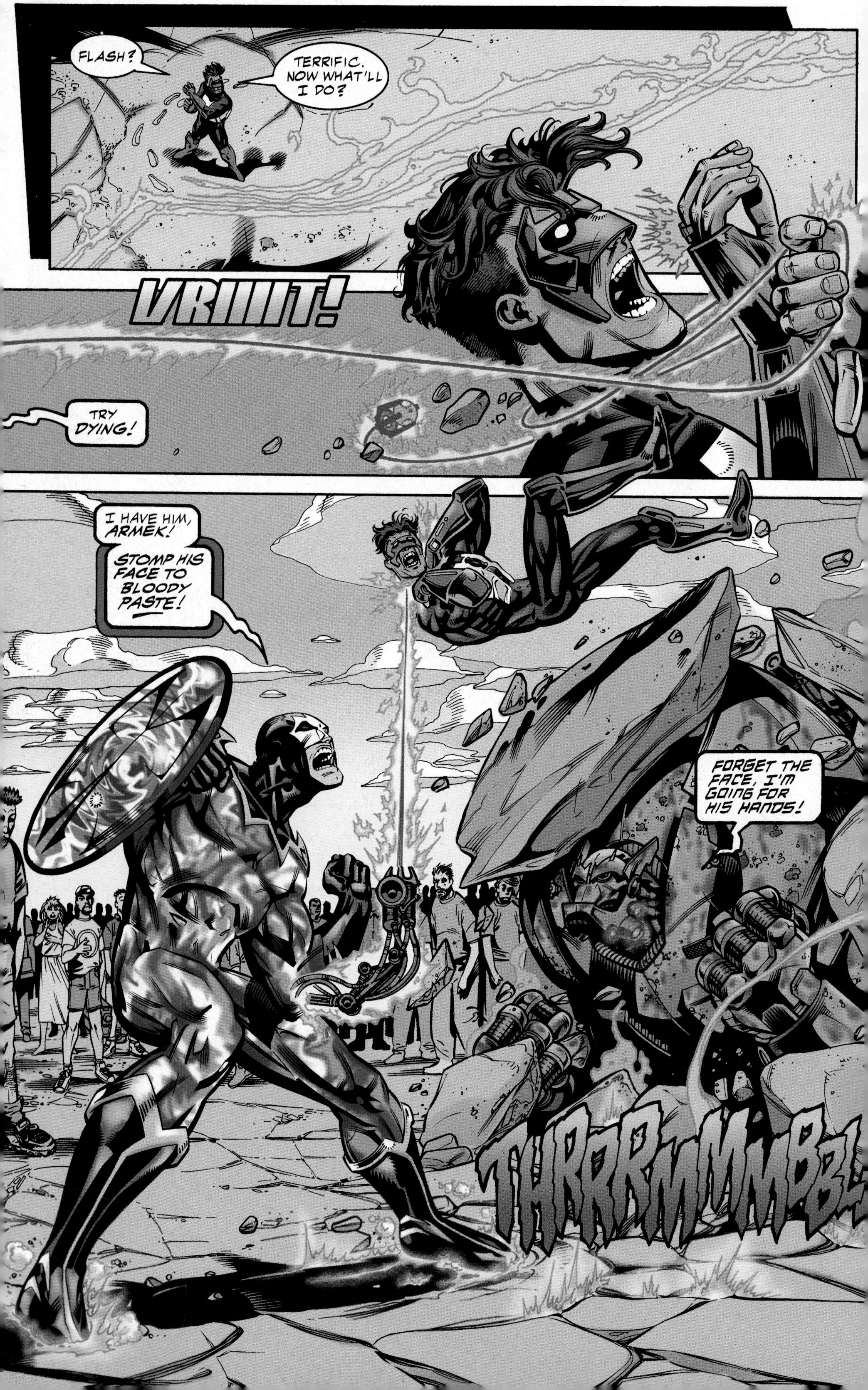
FLASH?
TERRIFIC. NOW WHAT'LL I DO?
VRIIIIT!
TRY DYING!
I HAVE HIM, ARMEK!
STOMP HIS FACE TO BLOODY PASTE!
FORGET THE FACE, I'M GOING FOR HIS HANDS!
THRRMMMBL

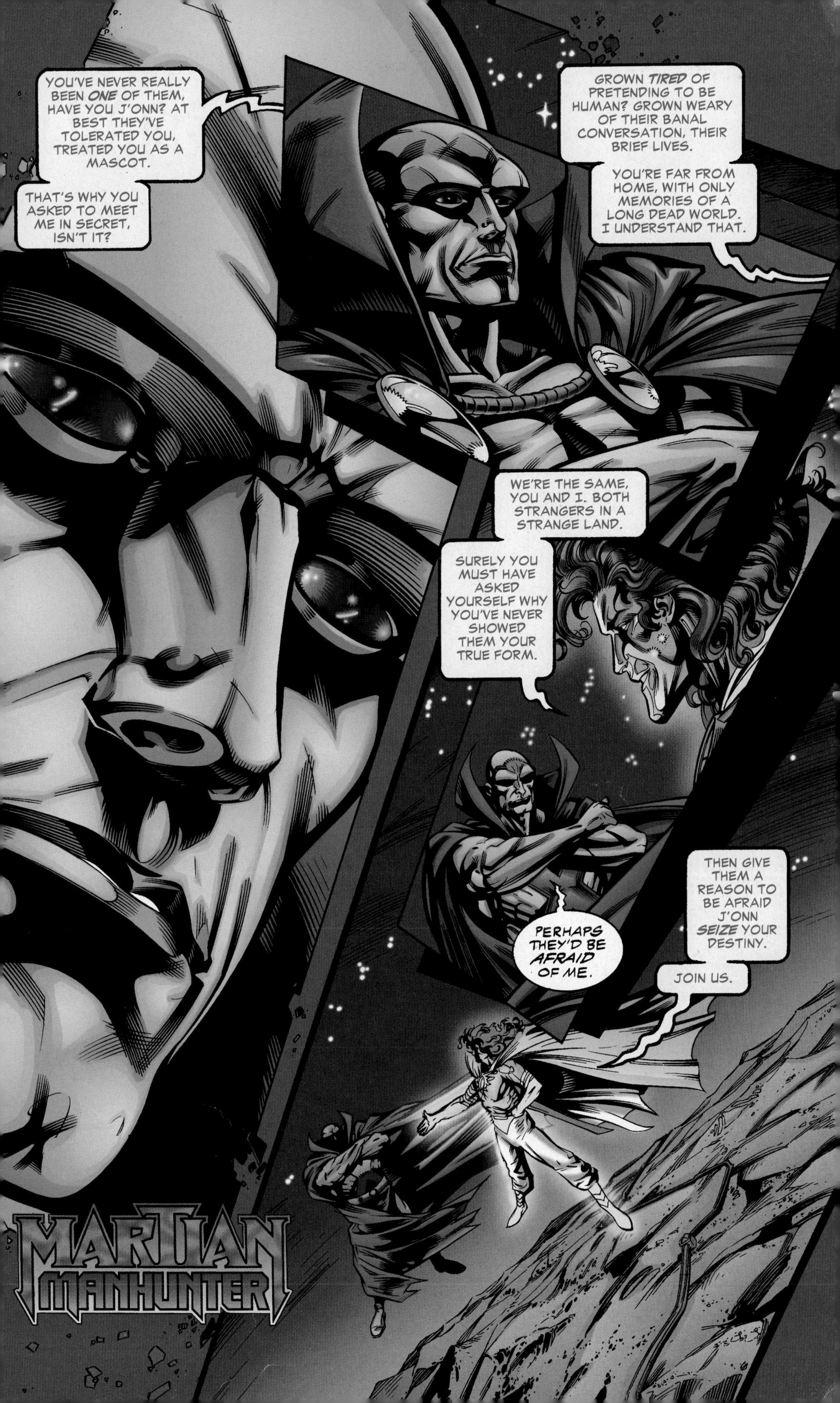

YOU'VE NEVER REALLY BEEN ONE OF THEM, HAVE YOU J'ONN? AT BEST THEY'VE TOLERATED YOU, TREATED YOU AS A MASCOT.
THAT'S WHY YOU ASKED TO MEET ME IN SECRET, ISN'T IT?
GROWN TIRED OF PRETENDING TO BE HUMAN? GROWN WEARY OF THEIR BANAL CONVERSATION, THEIR BRIEF LIVES.
YOU'RE FAR FROM HOME, WITH ONLY MEMORIES OF A LONG DEAD WORLD. I UNDERSTAND THAT.
WE'RE THE SAME, YOU AND I. BOTH STRANGERS IN A STRANGE LAND.
SURELY YOU MUST HAVE ASKED YOURSELF WHY YOU'VE NEVER SHOWED THEM YOUR TRUE FORM.
PERHAPS THEY'D BE AFRAID OF ME.
THEN GIVE THEM A REASON TO BE AFRAID J'ONN SEIZE YOUR DESTINY.
JOIN US.
MARTIAN MANHUNTER

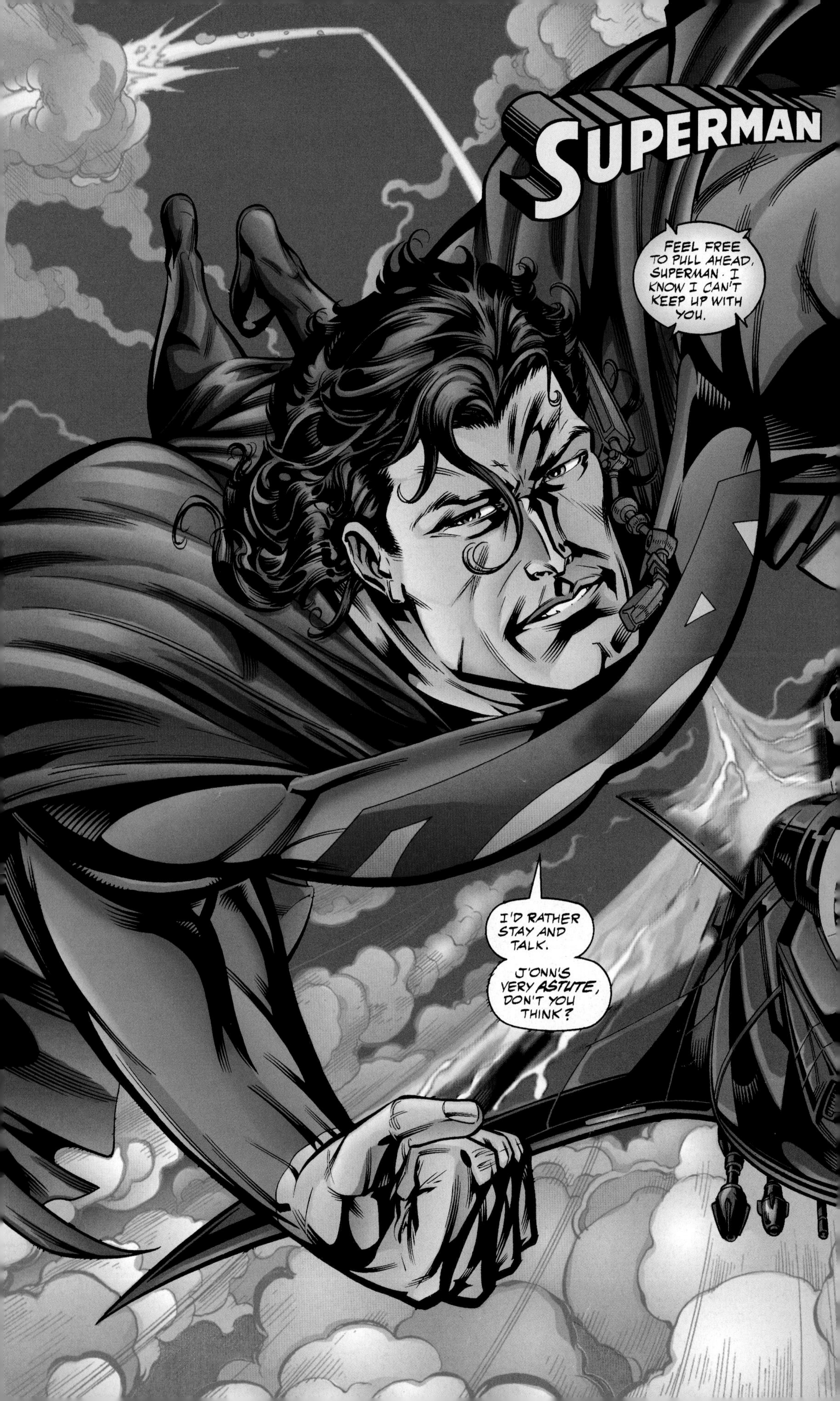
SUPERMAN
FEEL FREE TO PULL AHEAD, SUPERMAN. I KNOW I CAN'T KEEP UP WITH YOU.
I'D RATHER STAY AND TALK.
J'ONN'S VERY ASTUTE, DON'T YOU THINK?

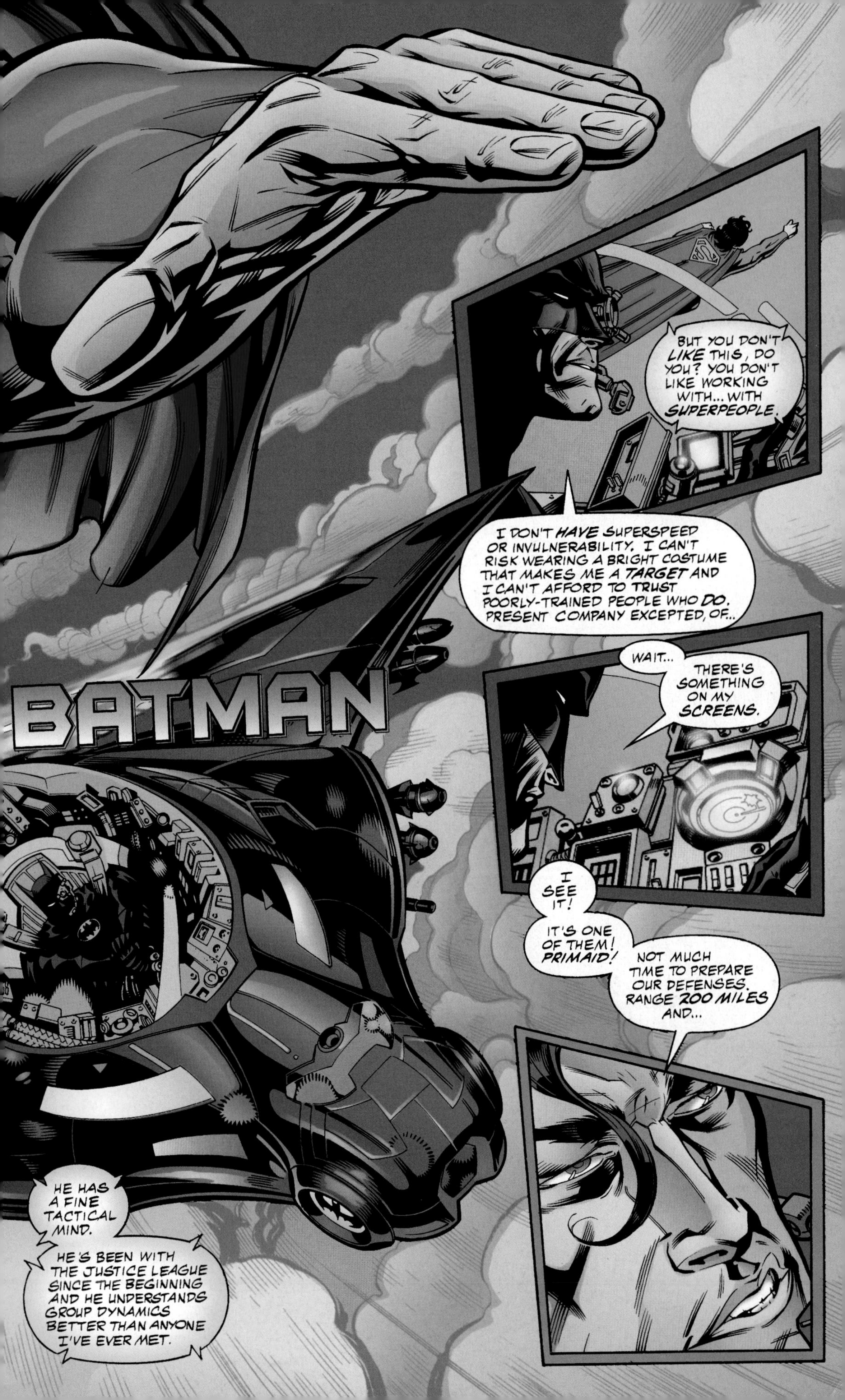
BUT YOU DON'T LIKE THIS, DO YOU? YOU DON'T LIKE WORKING WITH... WITH SUPERPEOPLE.
I DON'T HAVE SUPERSPEED OR INVULNERABILITY. I CAN'T RISK WEARING A BRIGHT COSTUME THAT MAKES ME A TARGET AND I CAN'T AFFORD TO TRUST POORLY-TRAINED PEOPLE WHO DO. PRESENT COMPANY EXCEPTED, OF...
BATMAN
WAIT...
THERE'S SOMETHING ON MY SCREENS.
I SEE IT!
IT'S ONE OF THEM! PRIMAID!
NOT MUCH TIME TO PREPARE OUR DEFENSES. RANGE 200 MILES AND...
HE HAS A FINE TACTICAL MIND.
HE'S BEEN WITH THE JUSTICE LEAGUE SINCE THE BEGINNING AND HE UNDERSTANDS GROUP DYNAMICS BETTER THAN ANYONE I'VE EVER MET.

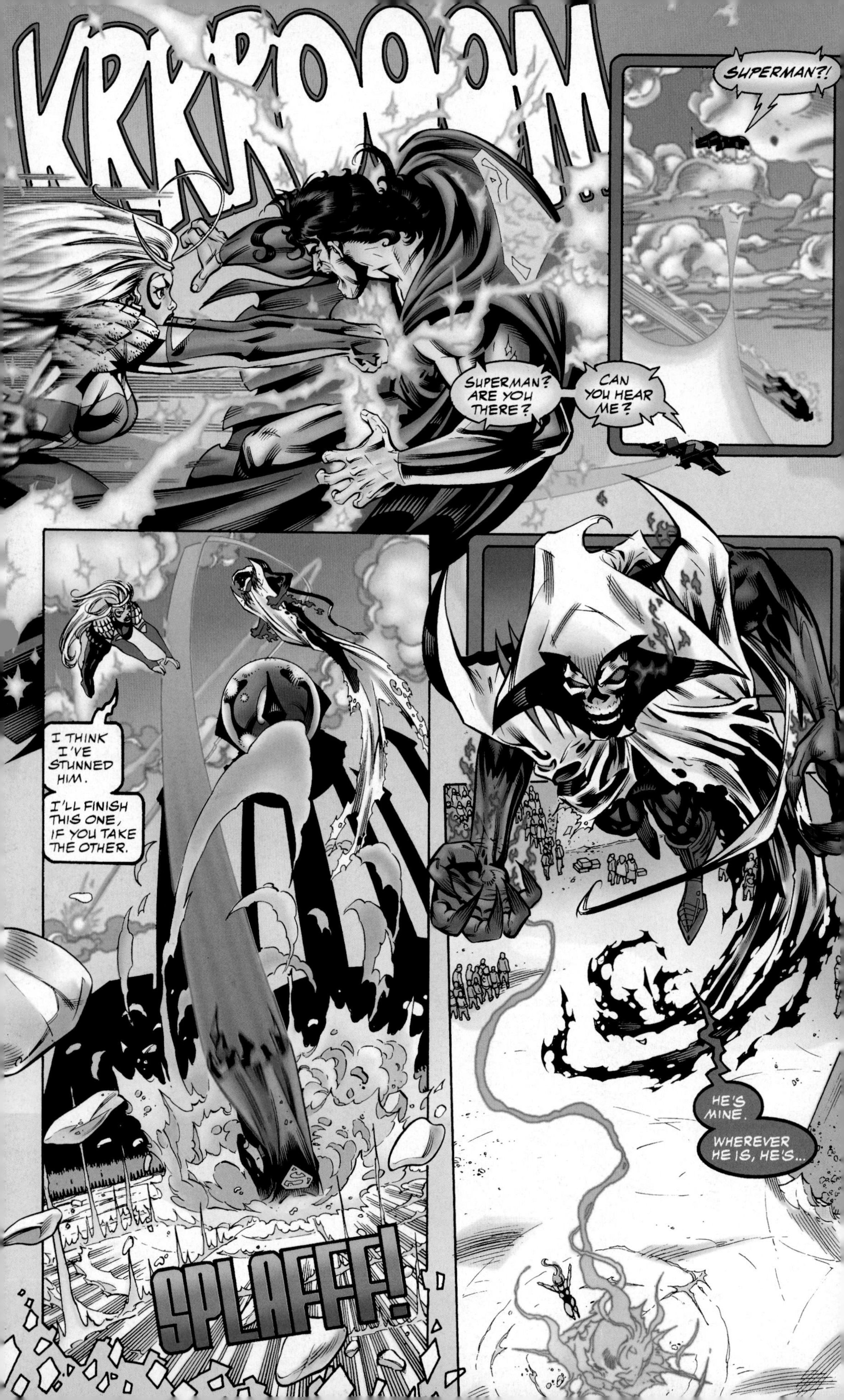
KRKROOOOM
SUPERMAN?!
SUPERMAN? ARE YOU THERE?
CAN YOU HEAR ME?
I THINK I'VE STUNNED HIM.
I'LL FINISH THIS ONE, IF YOU TAKE THE OTHER.
SPLAFFF!
HE'S MINE.
WHEREVER HE IS, HE'S...

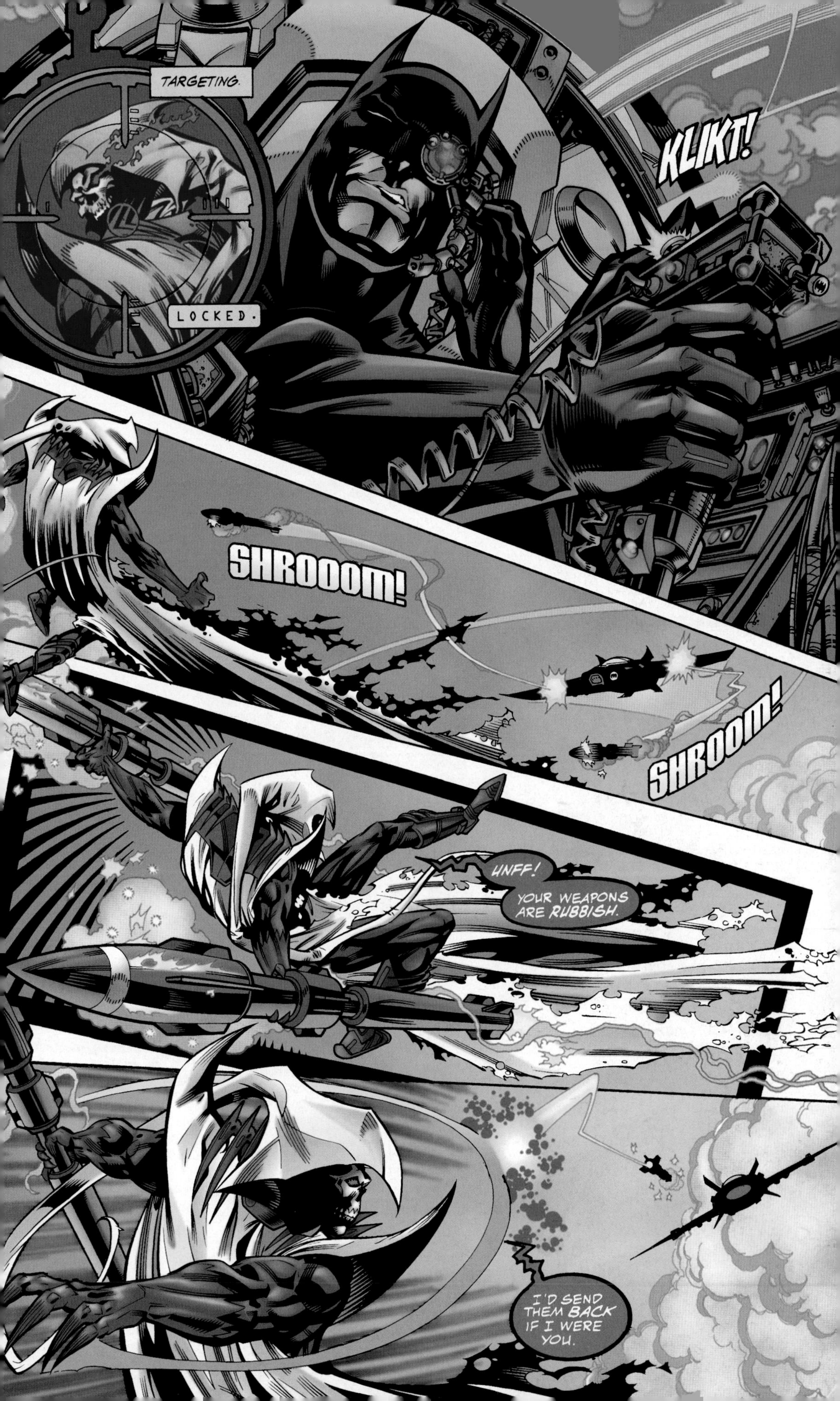

TARGETING.
KLIKT!
LOCKED.
SHROOOM!
SHROOM!
UNFF!
YOUR WEAPONS ARE RUBBISH.
I'D SEND THEM BACK IF I WERE YOU.

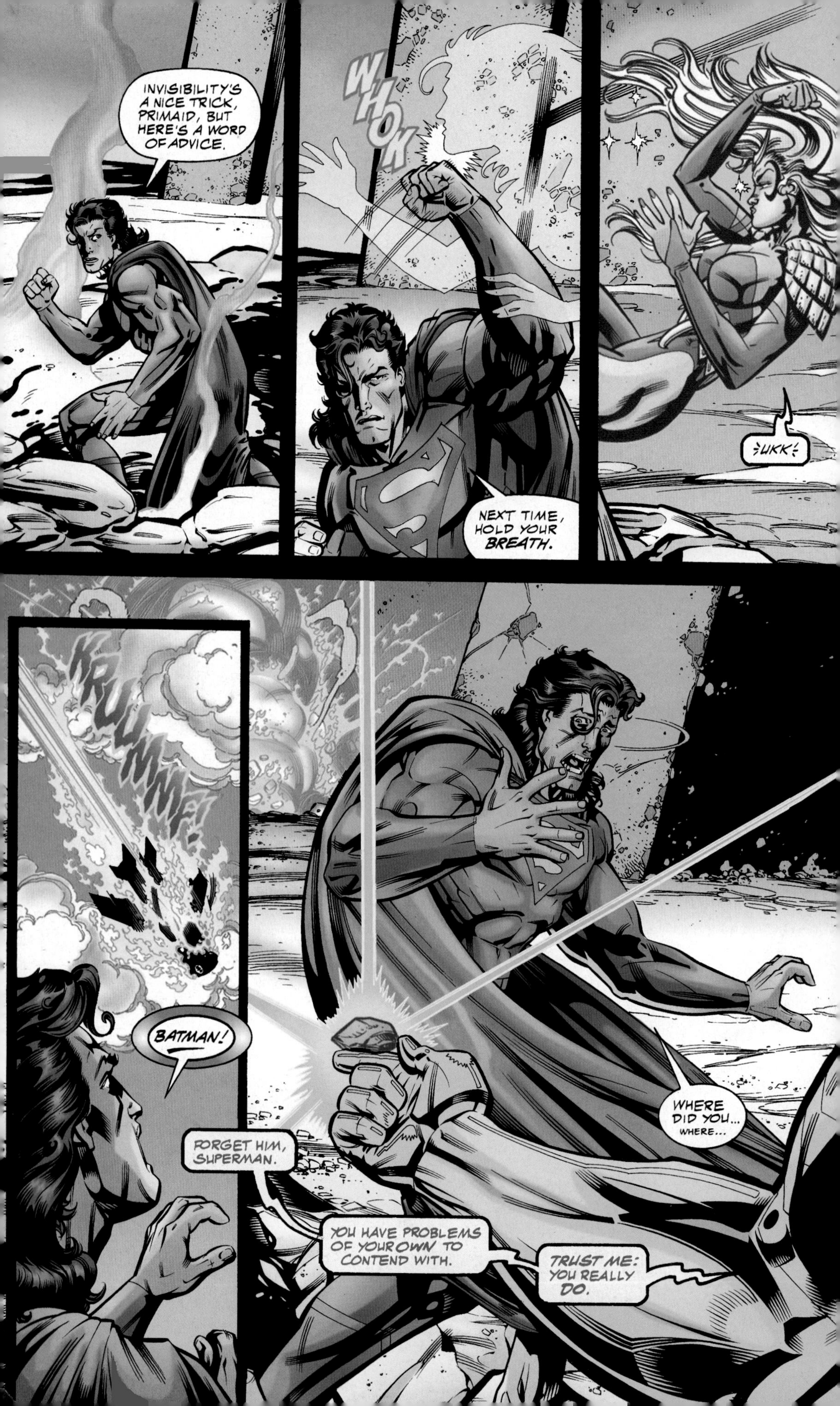
INVISIBILITY'S A NICE TRICK, PRIMAID, BUT HERE'S A WORD OF ADVICE.
WHOK
NEXT TIME, HOLD YOUR BREATH.
UKK
KRUMMF!
BATMAN!
FORGET HIM, SUPERMAN.
WHERE DID YOU... WHERE...
YOU HAVE PROBLEMS OF YOUR OWN TO CONTEND WITH.
TRUST ME: YOU REALLY DO.

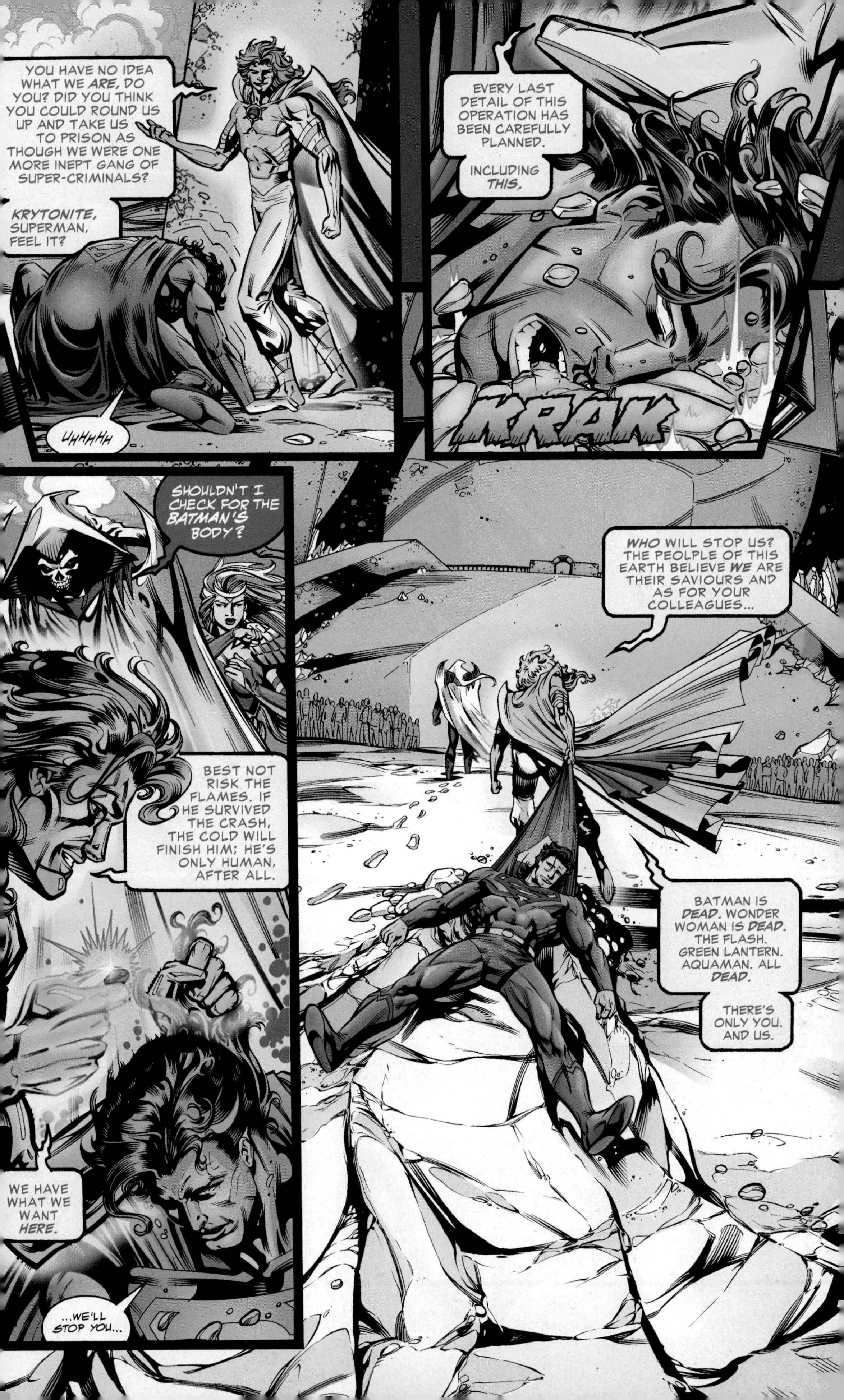

YOU HAVE NO IDEA WHAT WE ARE, DO YOU? DID YOU THINK YOU COULD ROUND US UP AND TAKE US TO PRISON AS THOUGH WE WERE ONE MORE INEPT GANG OF SUPER-CRIMINALS?
KRYTONITE, SUPERMAN, FEEL IT?
UHHHHH
EVERY LAST DETAIL OF THIS OPERATION HAS BEEN CAREFULLY PLANNED.
INCLUDING THIS.
KRAK
SHOULDN'T I CHECK FOR THE BATMAN'S BODY?
BEST NOT RISK THE FLAMES. IF HE SURVIVED THE CRASH, THE COLD WILL FINISH HIM; HE'S ONLY HUMAN, AFTER ALL.
WE HAVE WHAT WE WANT HERE.
...WE'LL STOP YOU...
WHO WILL STOP US? THE PEOLPLE OF THIS EARTH BELIEVE WE ARE THEIR SAVIOURS AND AS FOR YOUR COLLEAGUES...
BATMAN IS DEAD. WONDER WOMAN IS DEAD. THE FLASH. GREEN LANTERN. AQUAMAN. ALL DEAD.
THERE'S ONLY YOU. AND US.

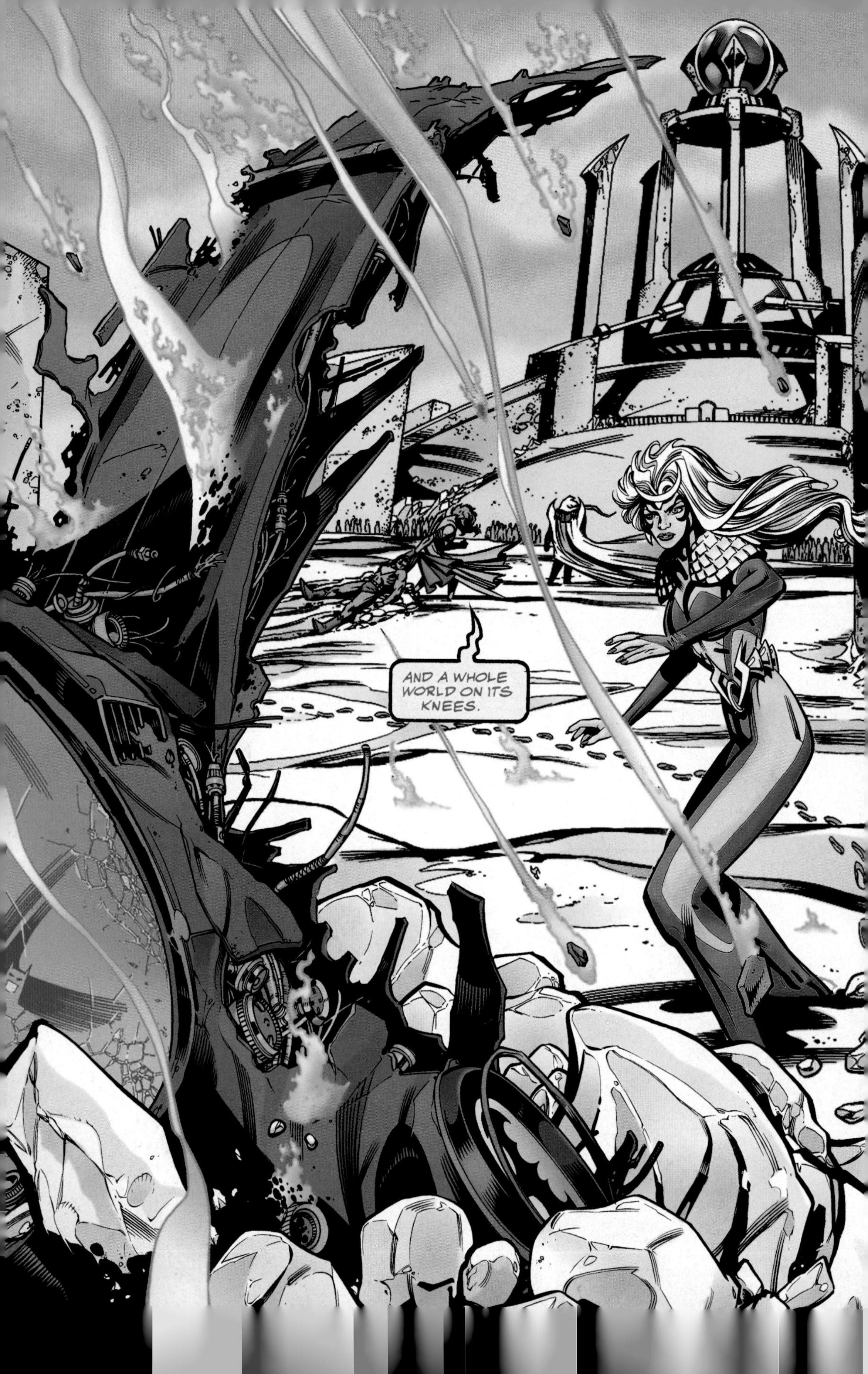
AND A WHOLE WORLD ON ITS KNEES.

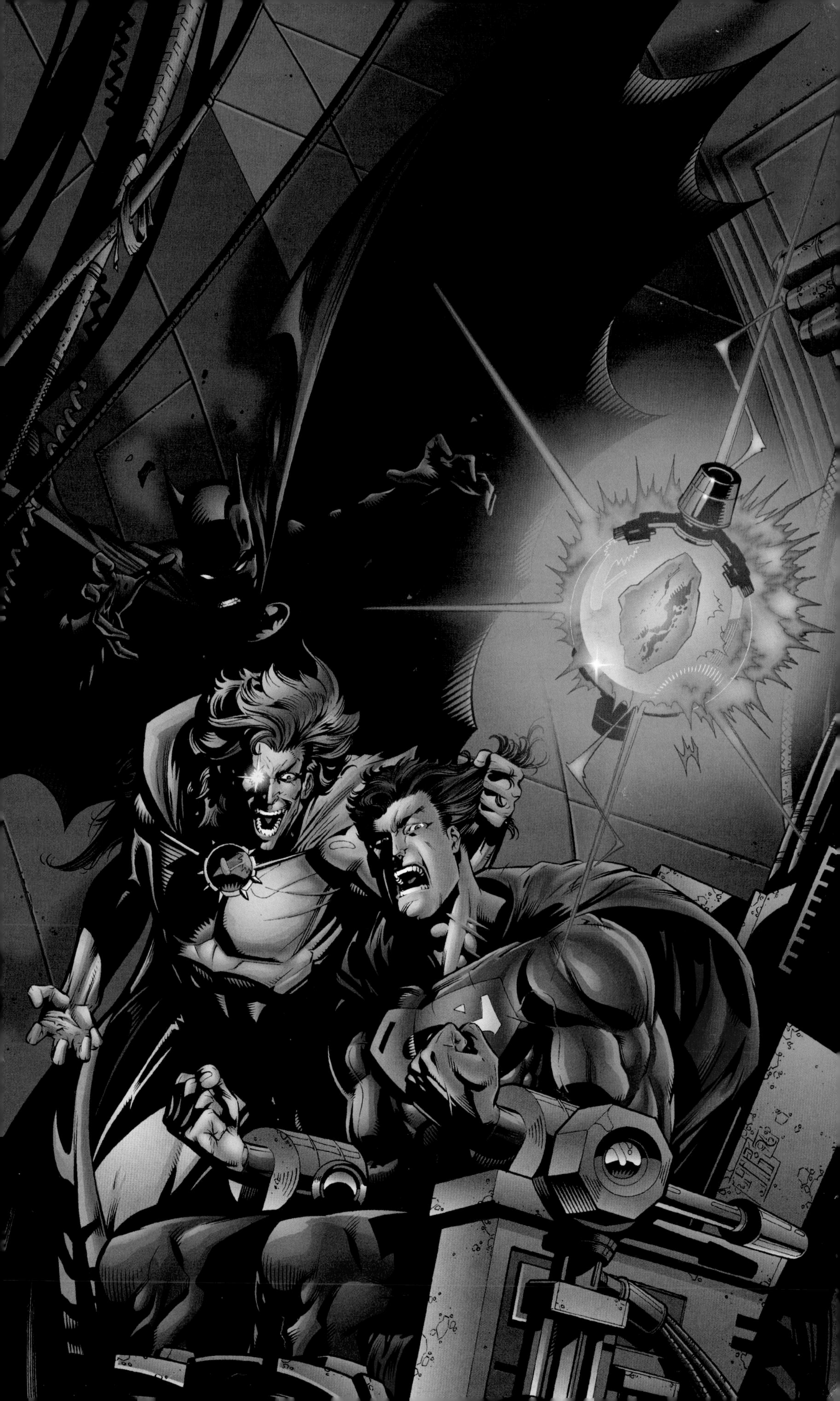

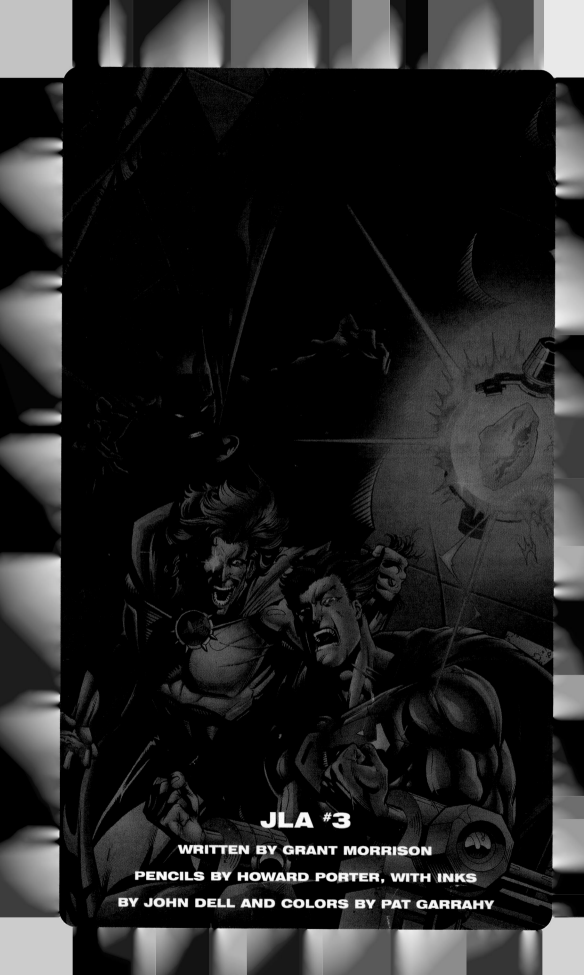

JLA #3

WRITTEN BY GRANT MORRISON

PENCILS BY HOWARD PORTER, WITH INKS

BY JOHN DELL AND COLORS BY PAT GARRAHY

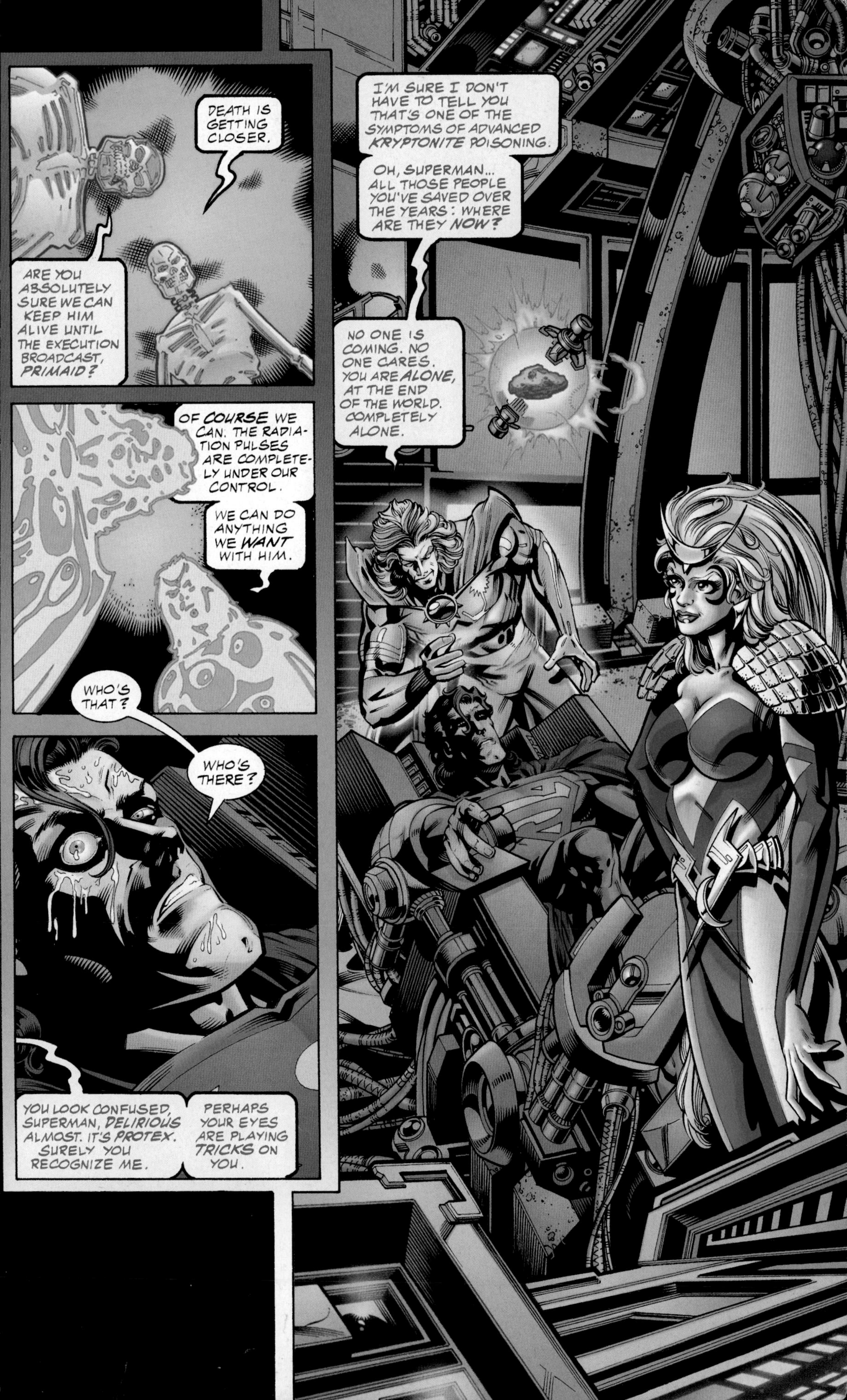
DEATH IS GETTING CLOSER.
ARE YOU ABSOLUTELY SURE WE CAN KEEP HIM ALIVE UNTIL THE EXECUTION BROADCAST, PRIMAID?
OF COURSE WE CAN. THE RADIATION PULSES ARE COMPLETELY UNDER OUR CONTROL.
WE CAN DO ANYTHING WE WANT WITH HIM.
WHO'S THAT?
WHO'S THERE?
YOU LOOK CONFUSED, SUPERMAN, DELIRIOUS ALMOST. IT'S PROTEX. SURELY YOU RECOGNIZE ME.
PERHAPS YOUR EYES ARE PLAYING TRICKS ON YOU.
I'M SURE I DON'T HAVE TO TELL YOU THAT'S ONE OF THE SYMPTOMS OF ADVANCED KRYPTONITE POISONING.
OH, SUPERMAN... ALL THOSE PEOPLE YOU'VE SAVED OVER THE YEARS: WHERE ARE THEY NOW?
NO ONE IS COMING. NO ONE CARES. YOU ARE ALONE, AT THE END OF THE WORLD. COMPLETELY ALONE.

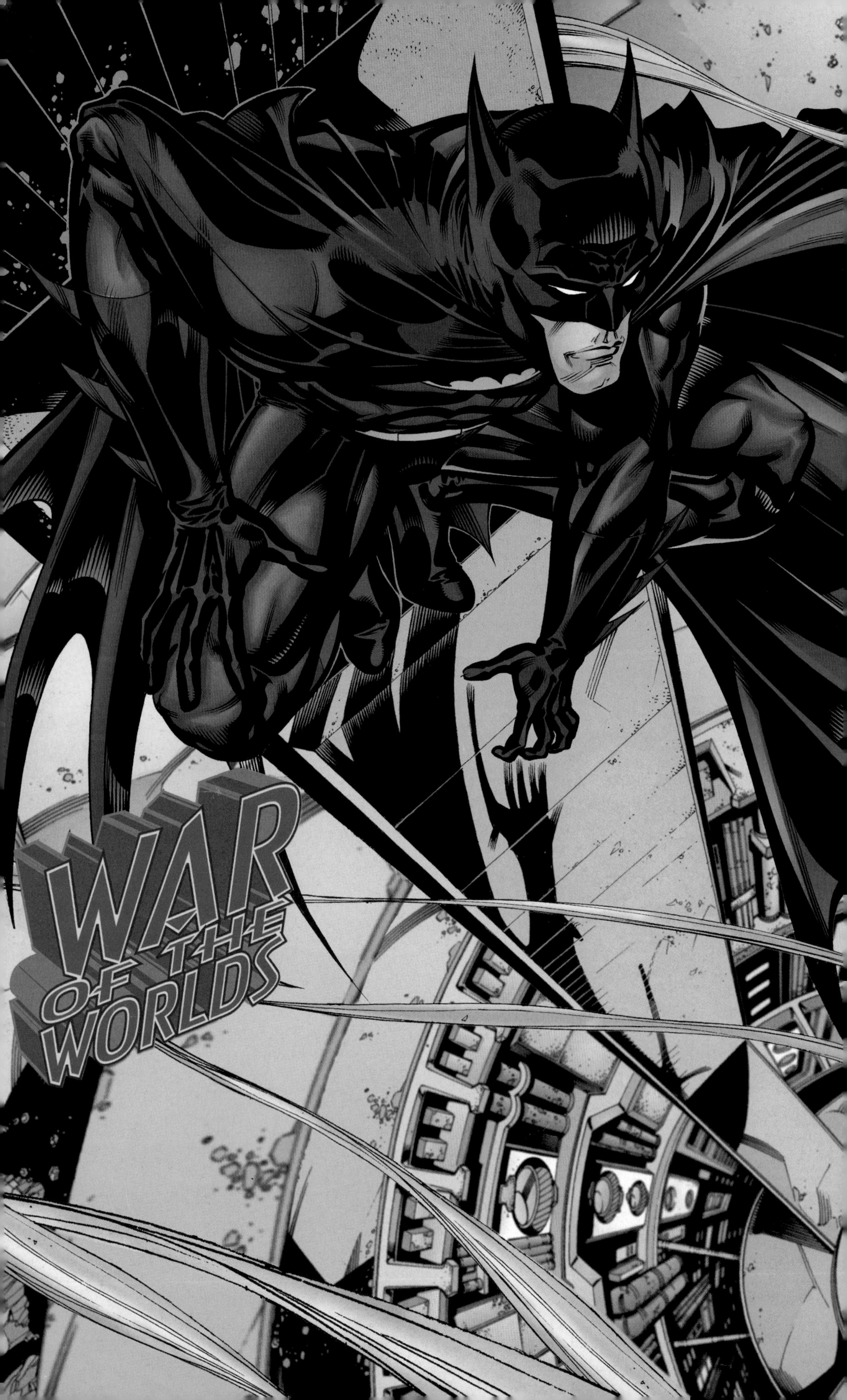
WAR OF THE WORLDS

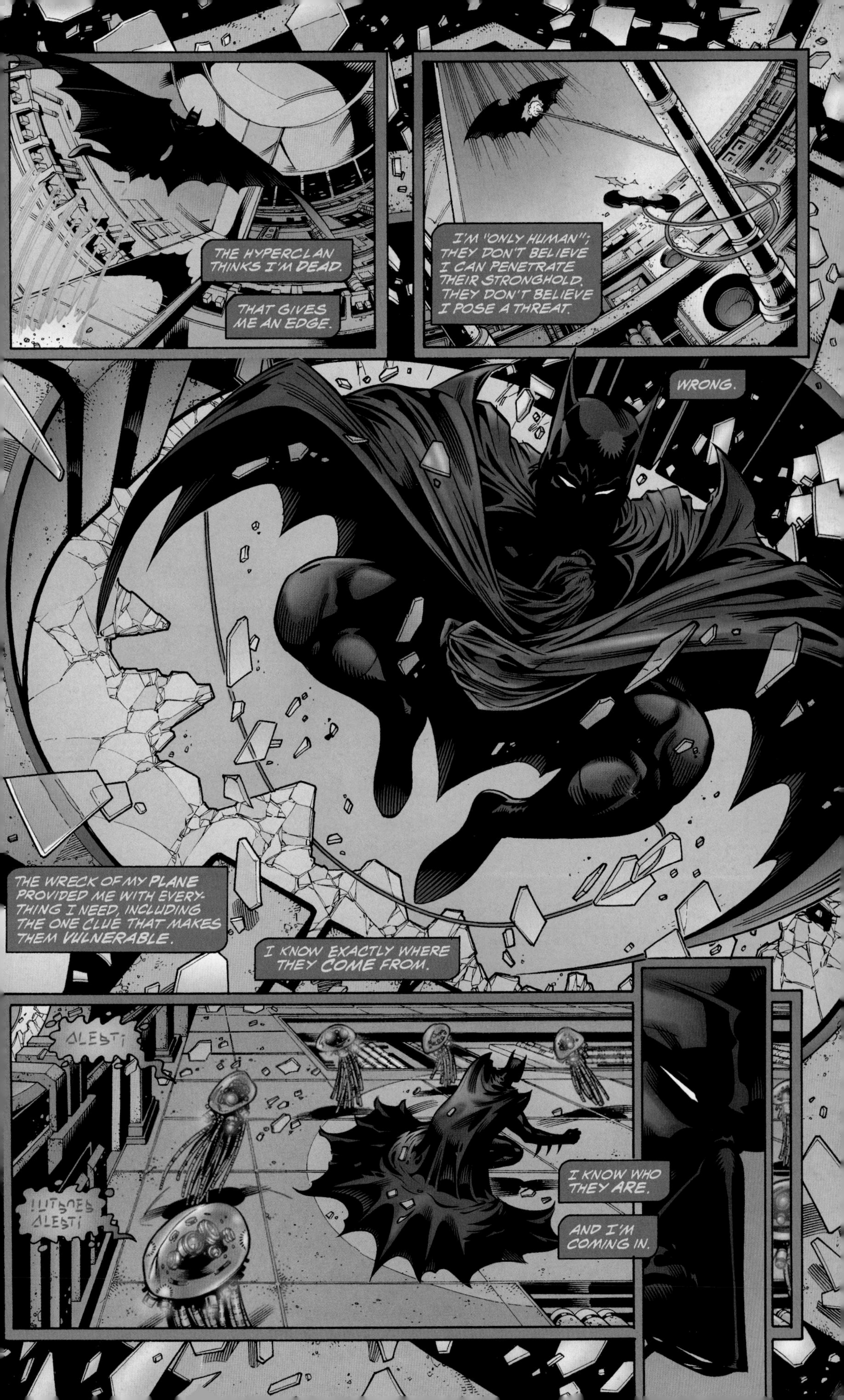

THE HYPERCLAN THINKS I'M DEAD.
THAT GIVES ME AN EDGE.
I'M "ONLY HUMAN"; THEY DON'T BELIEVE I CAN PENETRATE THEIR STRONGHOLD. THEY DON'T BELIEVE I POSE A THREAT.
WRONG.
THE WRECK OF MY PLANE PROVIDED ME WITH EVERY-THING I NEED, INCLUDING THE ONE CLUE THAT MAKES THEM VULNERABLE.
I KNOW EXACTLY WHERE THEY COME FROM.
I KNOW WHO THEY ARE.
AND I'M COMING IN.

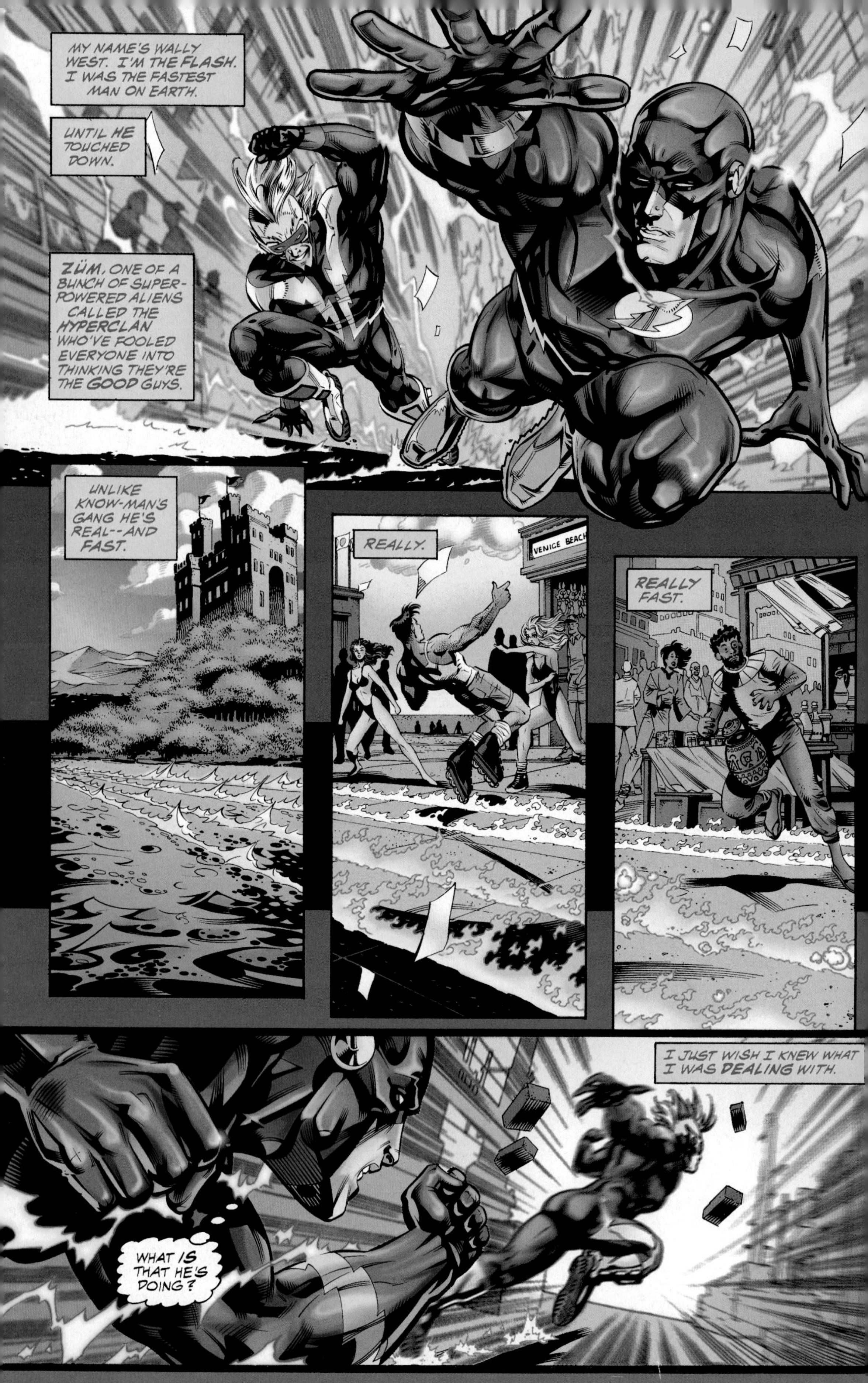
MY NAME'S WALLY WEST. I'M THE FLASH. I WAS THE FASTEST MAN ON EARTH.
UNTIL HE TOUCHED DOWN.
ZÜM, ONE OF A BUNCH OF SUPER-POWERED ALIENS CALLED THE HYPERCLAN WHO'VE FOOLED EVERYONE INTO THINKING THEY'RE THE GOOD GUYS.
UNLIKE KNOW-MAN'S GANG HE'S REAL--AND FAST.
REALLY.
VENICE BEACH
REALLY FAST.
I JUST WISH I KNEW WHAT I WAS DEALING WITH.
WHAT IS THAT HE'S DOING?

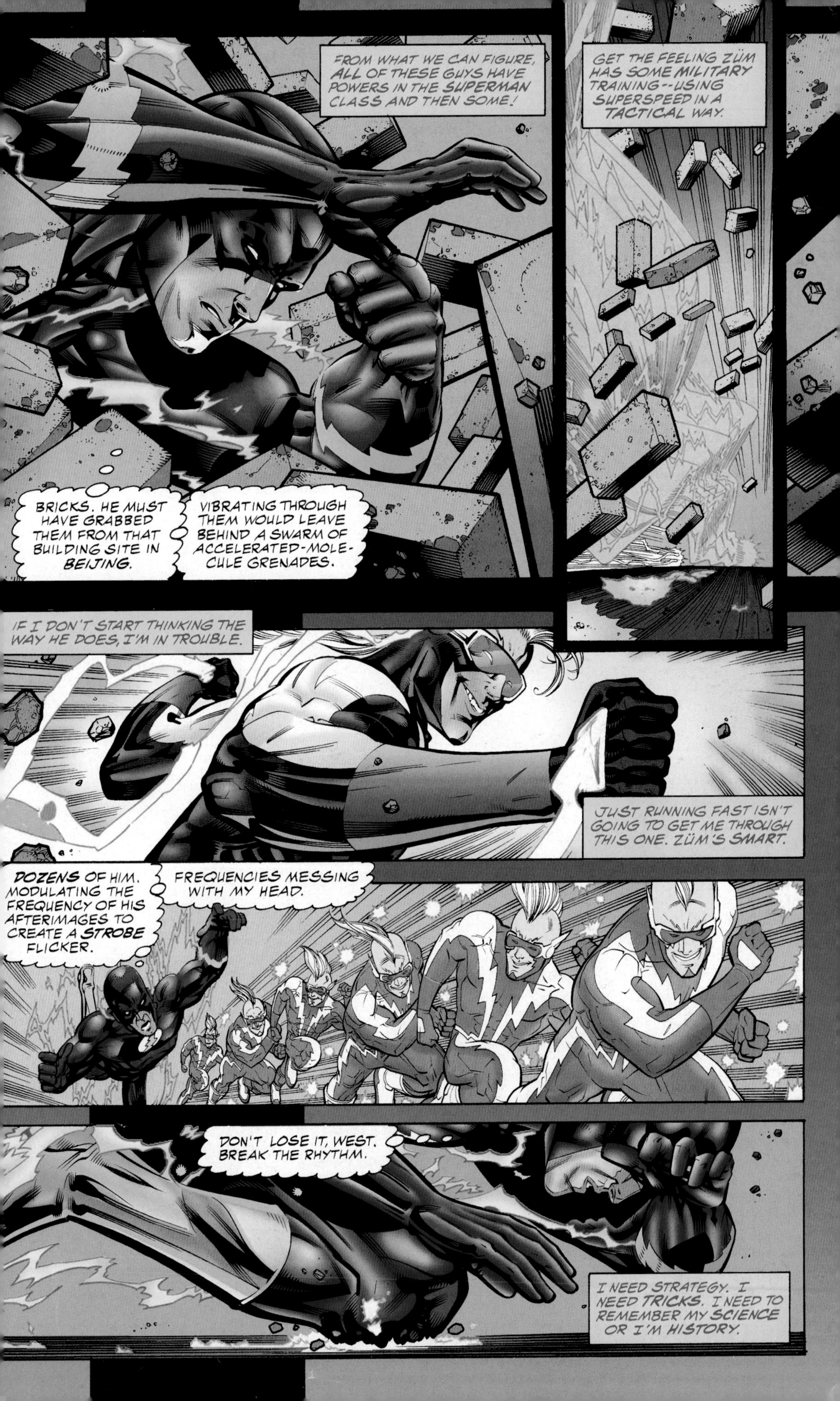

FROM WHAT WE CAN FIGURE, ALL OF THESE GUYS HAVE POWERS IN THE SUPERMAN CLASS AND THEN SOME!
GET THE FEELING ZÜM HAS SOME MILITARY TRAINING--USING SUPERSPEED IN A TACTICAL WAY.
BRICKS. HE MUST HAVE GRABBED THEM FROM THAT BUILDING SITE IN BEIJING.
VIBRATING THROUGH THEM WOULD LEAVE BEHIND A SWARM OF ACCELERATED-MOLE-CULE GRENADES.
IF I DON'T START THINKING THE WAY HE DOES, I'M IN TROUBLE.
JUST RUNNING FAST ISN'T GOING TO GET ME THROUGH THIS ONE. ZÜM'S SMART.
DOZENS OF HIM. MODULATING THE FREQUENCY OF HIS AFTERIMAGES TO CREATE A STROBE FLICKER.
FREQUENCIES MESSING WITH MY HEAD.
DON'T LOSE IT, WEST. BREAK THE RHYTHM.
I NEED STRATEGY. I NEED TRICKS. I NEED TO REMEMBER MY SCIENCE OR I'M HISTORY.

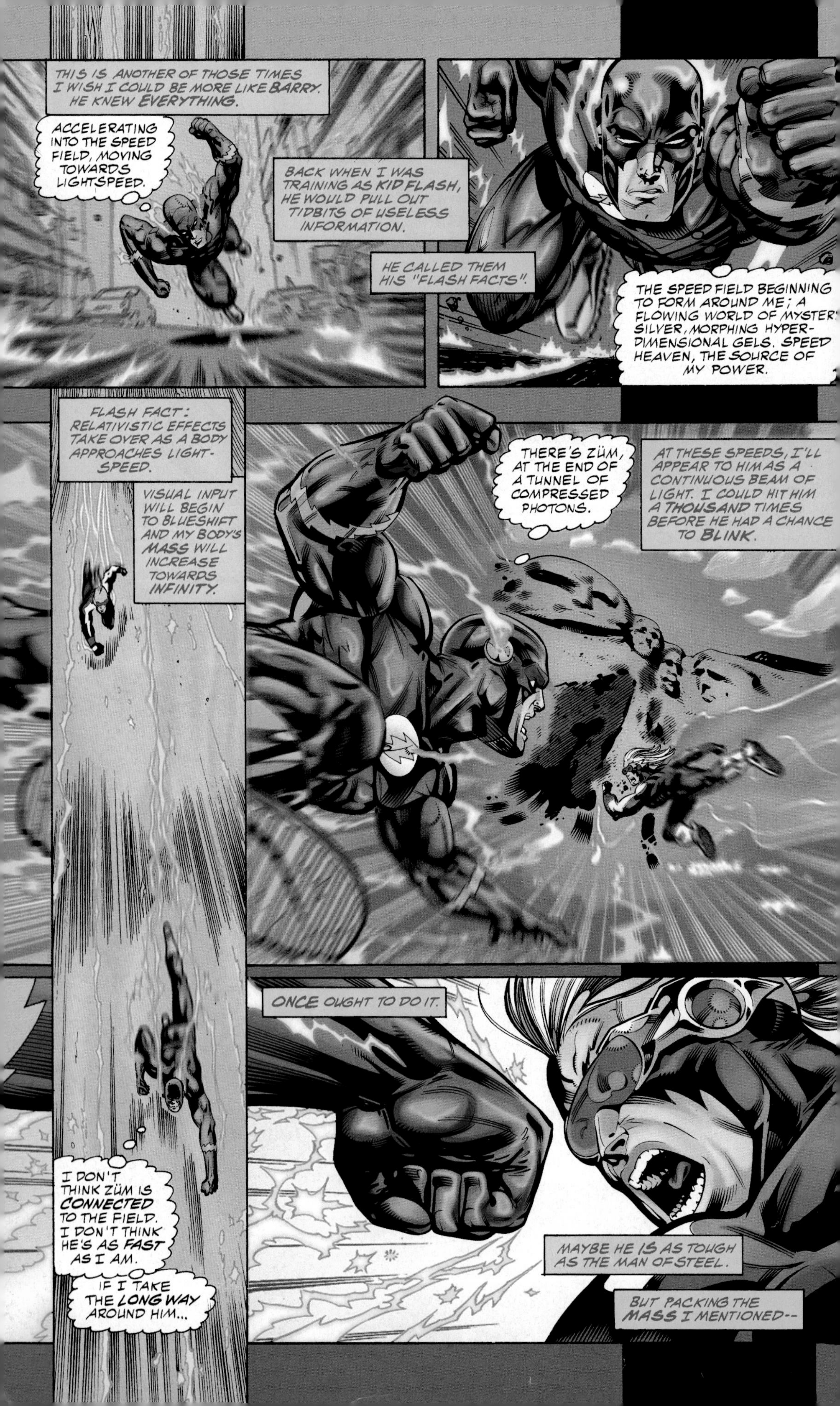
THIS IS ANOTHER OF THOSE TIMES I WISH I COULD BE MORE LIKE BARRY. HE KNEW EVERYTHING.
ACCELERATING INTO THE SPEED FIELD, MOVING TOWARDS LIGHTSPEED.
BACK WHEN I WAS TRAINING AS KID FLASH, HE WOULD PULL OUT TIDBITS OF USELESS INFORMATION.
HE CALLED THEM HIS "FLASH FACTS".
THE SPEED FIELD BEGINNING TO FORM AROUND ME; A FLOWING WORLD OF MYSTER SILVER, MORPHING HYPER-DIMENSIONAL GELS. SPEED HEAVEN, THE SOURCE OF MY POWER.
FLASH FACT: RELATIVISTIC EFFECTS TAKE OVER AS A BODY APPROACHES LIGHT-SPEED.
VISUAL INPUT WILL BEGIN TO BLUESHIFT AND MY BODY'S MASS WILL INCREASE TOWARDS INFINITY.
THERE'S ZÜM, AT THE END OF A TUNNEL OF COMPRESSED PHOTONS.
AT THESE SPEEDS, I'LL APPEAR TO HIM AS A CONTINUOUS BEAM OF LIGHT. I COULD HIT HIM A THOUSAND TIMES BEFORE HE HAD A CHANCE TO BLINK.
I DON'T THINK ZÜM IS CONNECTED TO THE FIELD. I DON'T THINK HE'S AS FAST AS I AM.
IF I TAKE THE LONG WAY AROUND HIM...
ONCE OUGHT TO DO IT.
MAYBE HE IS AS TOUGH AS THE MAN OF STEEL.
BUT PACKING THE MASS I MENTIONED--

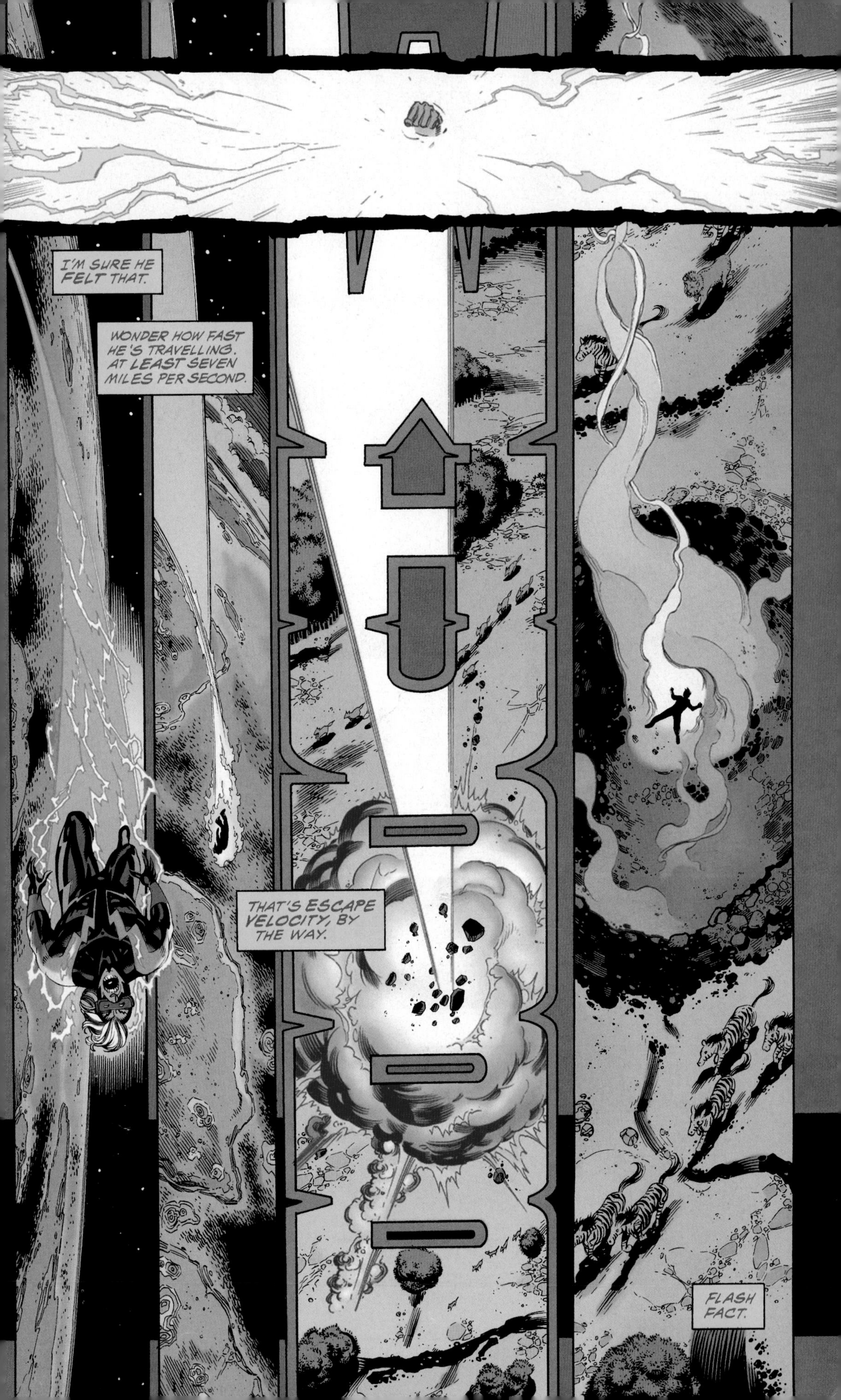
I'M SURE HE FELT THAT.
WONDER HOW FAST HE'S TRAVELLING. AT LEAST SEVEN MILES PER SECOND.
THAT'S ESCAPE VELOCITY, BY THE WAY.
FLASH FACT.

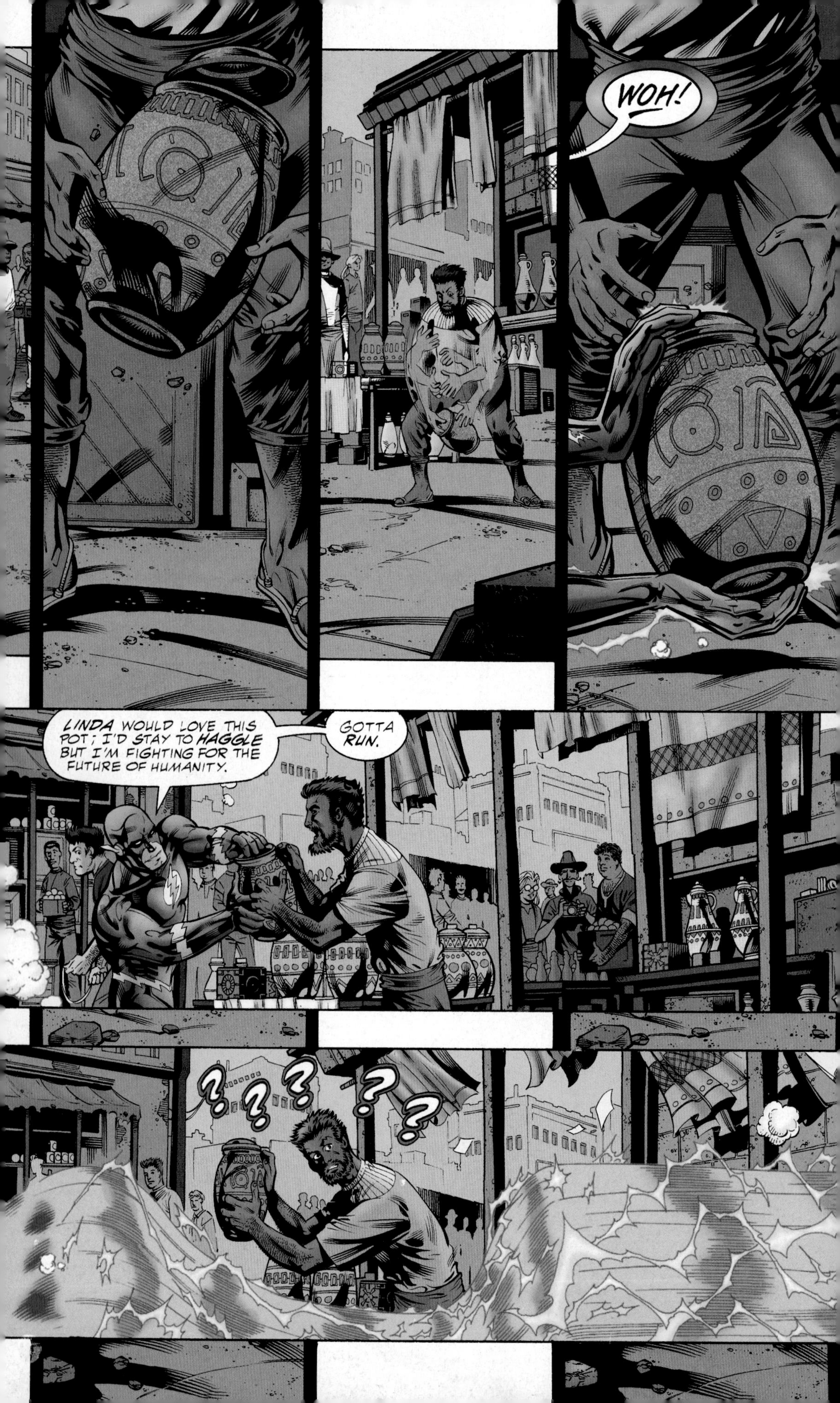
WOH!
LINDA WOULD LOVE THIS POT; I'D STAY TO HAGGLE BUT I'M FIGHTING FOR THE FUTURE OF HUMANITY.
GOTTA RUN.
?
?
?
?
?

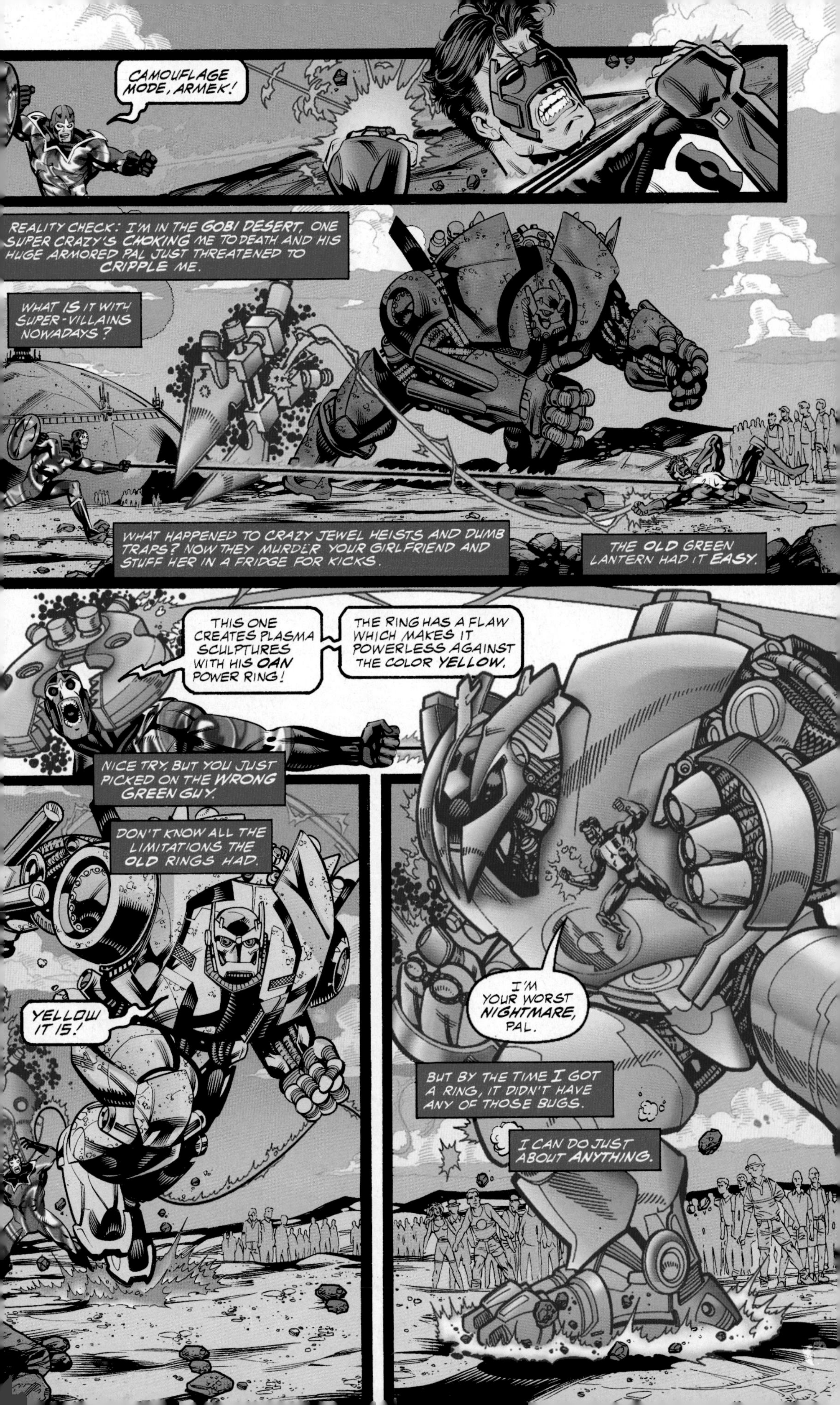
CAMOUFLAGE MODE, ARMEK!
REALITY CHECK: I'M IN THE GOBI DESERT, ONE SUPER CRAZY'S CHOKING ME TO DEATH AND HIS HUGE ARMORED PAL JUST THREATENED TO CRIPPLE ME.
WHAT IS IT WITH SUPER-VILLAINS NOWADAYS?
WHAT HAPPENED TO CRAZY JEWEL HEISTS AND DUMB TRAPS? NOW THEY MURDER YOUR GIRLFRIEND AND STUFF HER IN A FRIDGE FOR KICKS.
THE OLD GREEN LANTERN HAD IT EASY.
THIS ONE CREATES PLASMA SCULPTURES WITH HIS OAN POWER RING!
THE RING HAS A FLAW WHICH MAKES IT POWERLESS AGAINST THE COLOR YELLOW.
NICE TRY, BUT YOU JUST PICKED ON THE WRONG GREEN GUY.
DON'T KNOW ALL THE LIMITATIONS THE OLD RINGS HAD.
YELLOW IT IS!
I'M YOUR WORST NIGHTMARE, PAL.
BUT BY THE TIME I GOT A RING, IT DIDN'T HAVE ANY OF THOSE BUGS.
I CAN DO JUST ABOUT ANYTHING.

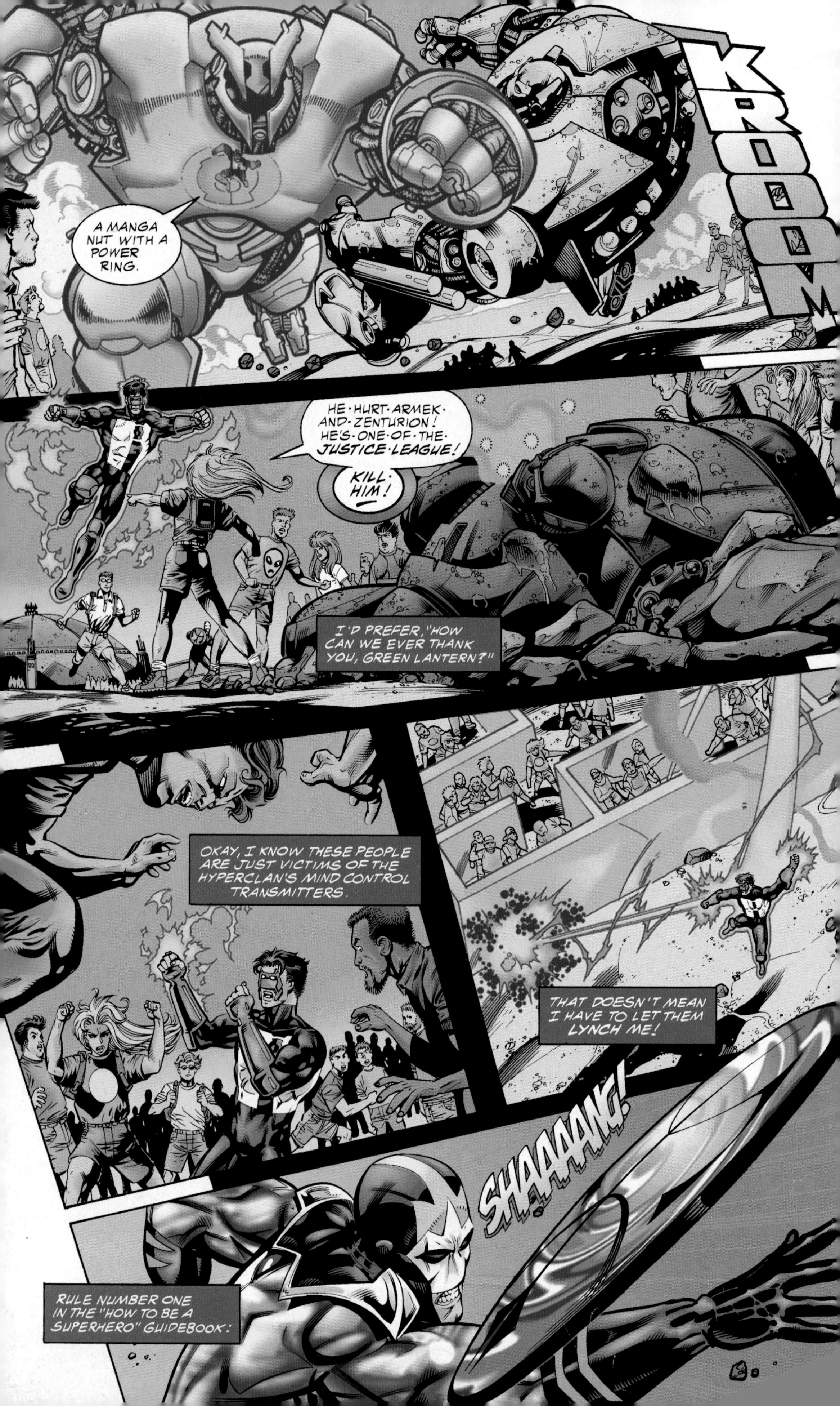
A MANGA NUT WITH A POWER RING.
KROOOM
HE·HURT·ARMEK·AND·ZENTURION! HE'S·ONE·OF·THE·JUSTICE·LEAGUE!
KILL HIM!
I'D PREFER, "HOW CAN WE EVER THANK YOU, GREEN LANTERN?"
OKAY, I KNOW THESE PEOPLE ARE JUST VICTIMS OF THE HYPERCLAN'S MIND CONTROL TRANSMITTERS.
THAT DOESN'T MEAN I HAVE TO LET THEM LYNCH ME!
SHAAAANG!
RULE NUMBER ONE IN THE "HOW TO BE A SUPERHERO" GUIDEBOOK:

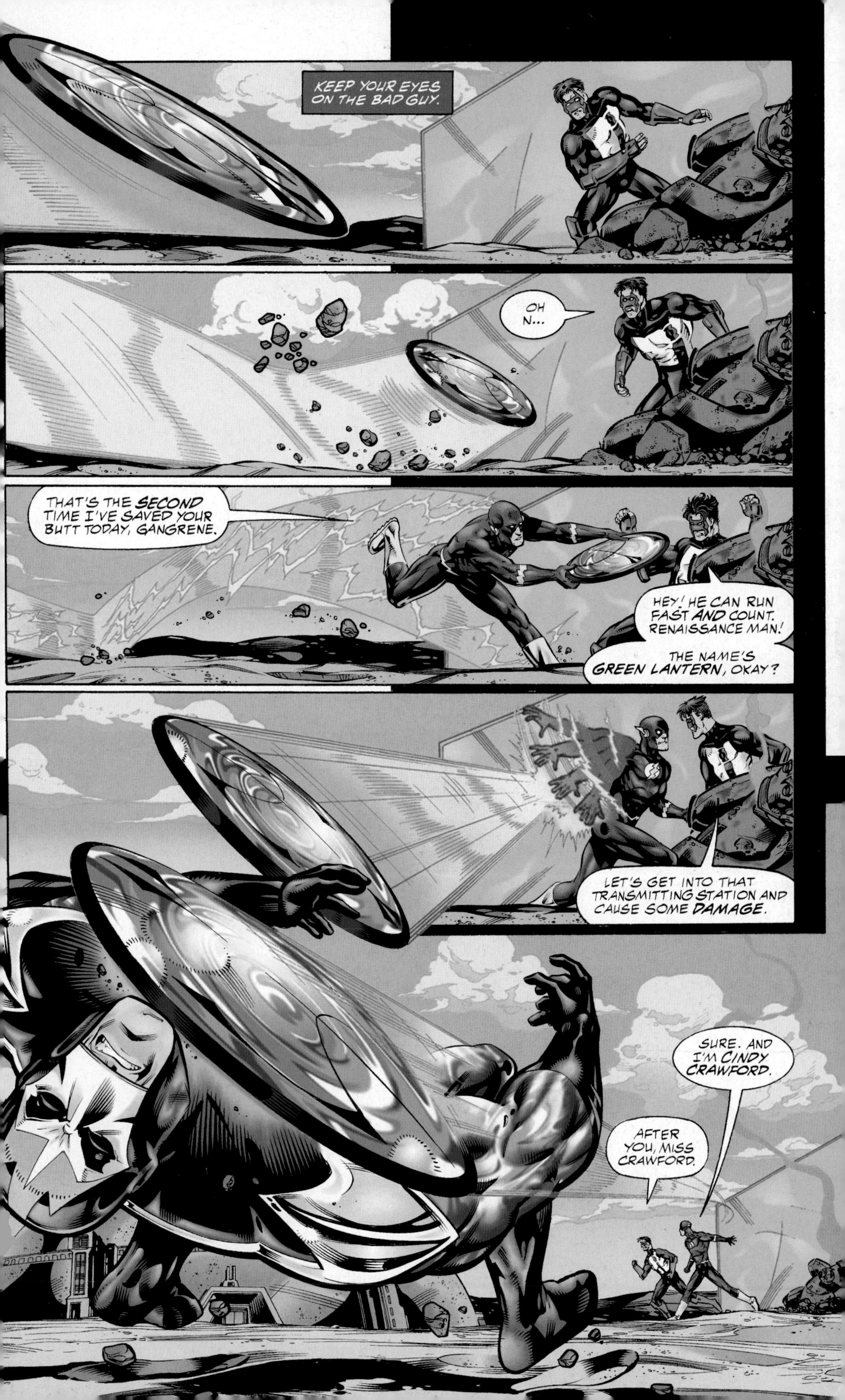
KEEP YOUR EYES ON THE BAD GUY.
OH N...
THAT'S THE SECOND TIME I'VE SAVED YOUR BUTT TODAY, GANGRENE.
HEY! HE CAN RUN FAST AND COUNT. RENAISSANCE MAN!
THE NAME'S GREEN LANTERN, OKAY?
LET'S GET INTO THAT TRANSMITTING STATION AND CAUSE SOME DAMAGE.
SURE. AND I'M CINDY CRAWFORD.
AFTER YOU, MISS CRAWFORD.

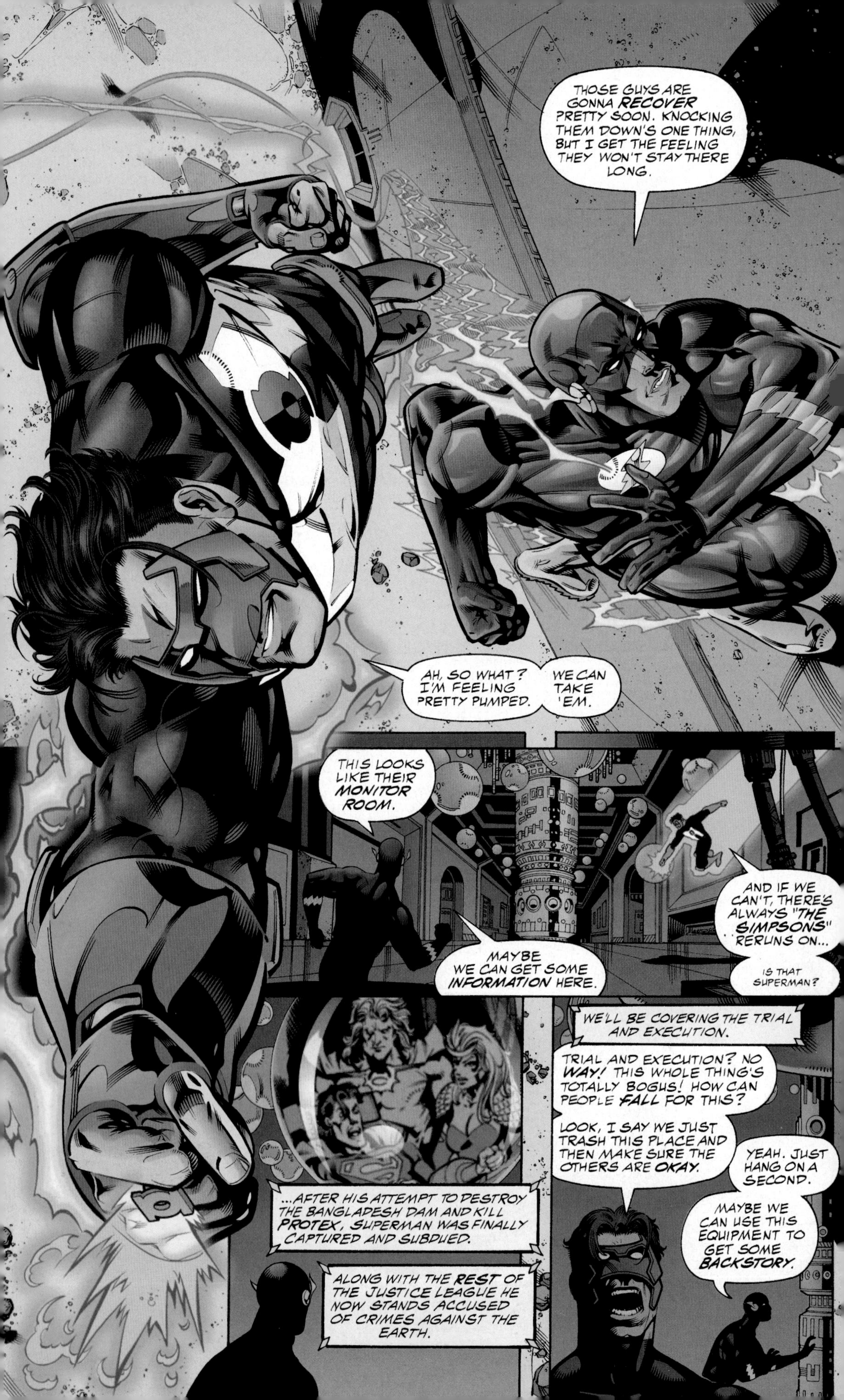

THOSE GUYS ARE GONNA RECOVER PRETTY SOON. KNOCKING THEM DOWN'S ONE THING, BUT I GET THE FEELING THEY WON'T STAY THERE LONG.
AH, SO WHAT? I'M FEELING PRETTY PUMPED.
WE CAN TAKE 'EM.
THIS LOOKS LIKE THEIR MONITOR ROOM.
MAYBE WE CAN GET SOME INFORMATION HERE.
AND IF WE CAN'T, THERE'S ALWAYS "THE SIMPSONS" RERUNS ON...
IS THAT SUPERMAN?
...AFTER HIS ATTEMPT TO DESTROY THE BANGLADESH DAM AND KILL PROTEX, SUPERMAN WAS FINALLY CAPTURED AND SUBDUED.
ALONG WITH THE REST OF THE JUSTICE LEAGUE HE NOW STANDS ACCUSED OF CRIMES AGAINST THE EARTH.
WE'LL BE COVERING THE TRIAL AND EXECUTION.
TRIAL AND EXECUTION? NO WAY! THIS WHOLE THING'S TOTALLY BOGUS! HOW CAN PEOPLE FALL FOR THIS?
LOOK, I SAY WE JUST TRASH THIS PLACE AND THEN MAKE SURE THE OTHERS ARE OKAY.
YEAH. JUST HANG ON A SECOND.
MAYBE WE CAN USE THIS EQUIPMENT TO GET SOME BACKSTORY.

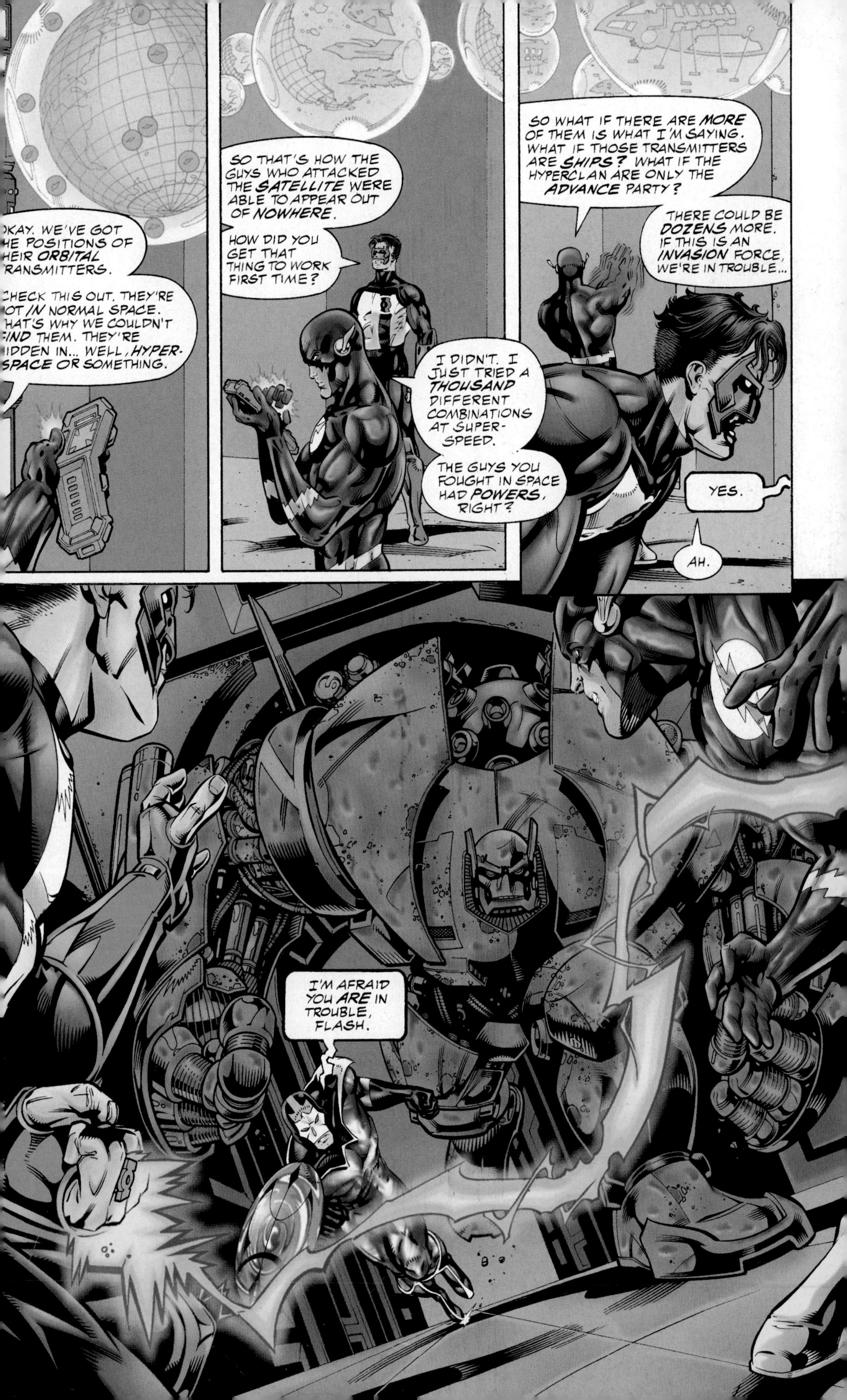

OKAY. WE'VE GOT THE POSITIONS OF THEIR ORBITAL TRANSMITTERS.
CHECK THIS OUT. THEY'RE NOT IN NORMAL SPACE. THAT'S WHY WE COULDN'T FIND THEM. THEY'RE HIDDEN IN... WELL, HYPERSPACE OR SOMETHING.
SO THAT'S HOW THE GUYS WHO ATTACKED THE SATELLITE WERE ABLE TO APPEAR OUT OF NOWHERE.
HOW DID YOU GET THAT THING TO WORK FIRST TIME?
I DIDN'T. I JUST TRIED A THOUSAND DIFFERENT COMBINATIONS AT SUPER-SPEED.
THE GUYS YOU FOUGHT IN SPACE HAD POWERS, RIGHT?
SO WHAT IF THERE ARE MORE OF THEM IS WHAT I'M SAYING. WHAT IF THOSE TRANSMITTERS ARE SHIPS? WHAT IF THE HYPERCLAN ARE ONLY THE ADVANCE PARTY?
THERE COULD BE DOZENS MORE. IF THIS IS AN INVASION FORCE, WE'RE IN TROUBLE...
YES.
AH.
I'M AFRAID YOU ARE IN TROUBLE, FLASH.

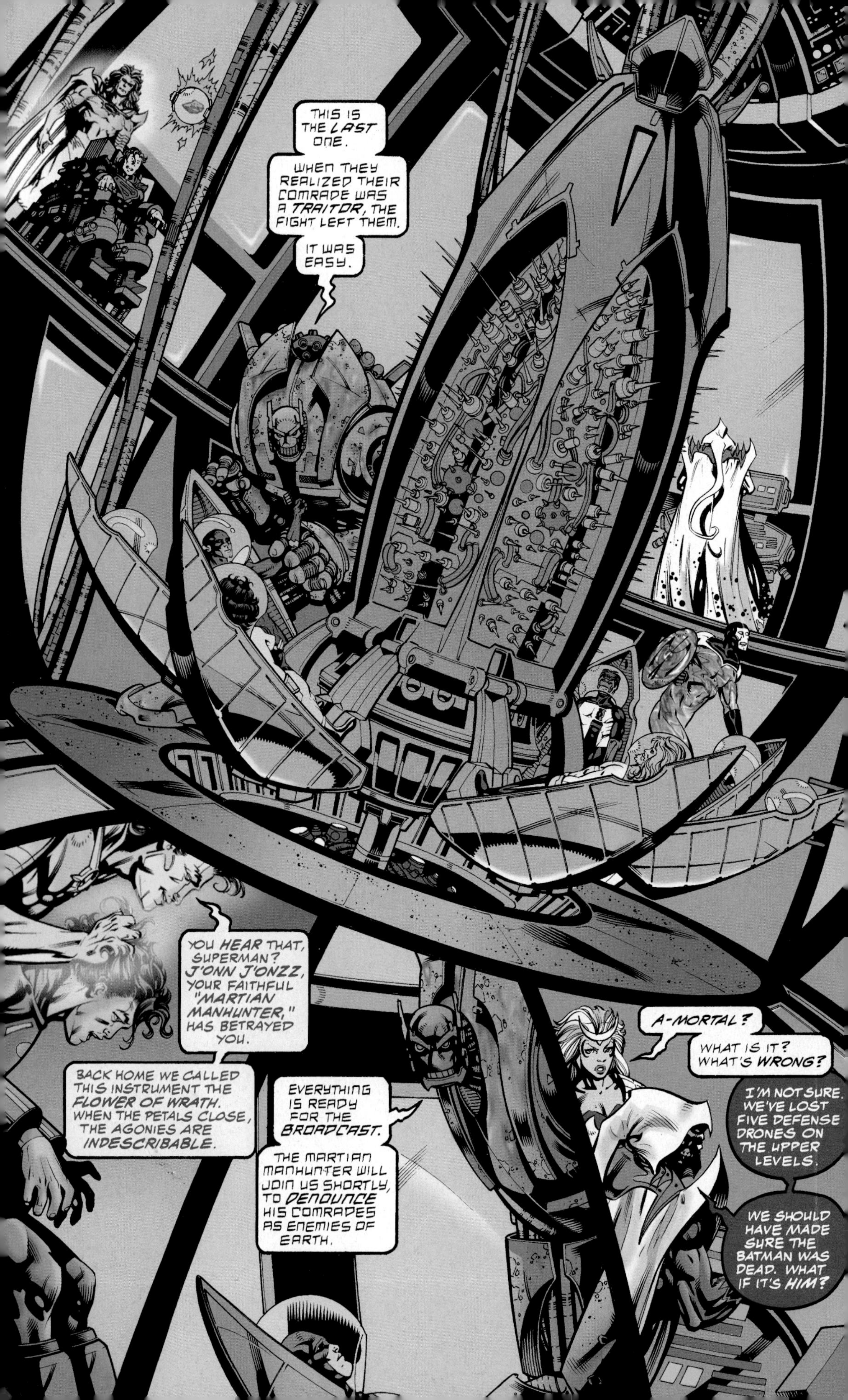
THIS IS THE LAST ONE.
WHEN THEY REALIZED THEIR COMRADE WAS A TRAITOR, THE FIGHT LEFT THEM.
IT WAS EASY.
YOU HEAR THAT, SUPERMAN? J'ONN J'ONZZ, YOUR FAITHFUL "MARTIAN MANHUNTER," HAS BETRAYED YOU.
BACK HOME WE CALLED THIS INSTRUMENT THE FLOWER OF WRATH. WHEN THE PETALS CLOSE, THE AGONIES ARE INDESCRIBABLE.
EVERYTHING IS READY FOR THE BROADCAST.
THE MARTIAN MANHUNTER WILL JOIN US SHORTLY, TO DENOUNCE HIS COMRADES AS ENEMIES OF EARTH.
A-MORTAL?
WHAT IS IT? WHAT'S WRONG?
I'M NOT SURE. WE'VE LOST FIVE DEFENSE DRONES ON THE UPPER LEVELS.
WE SHOULD HAVE MADE SURE THE BATMAN WAS DEAD. WHAT IF IT'S HIM?

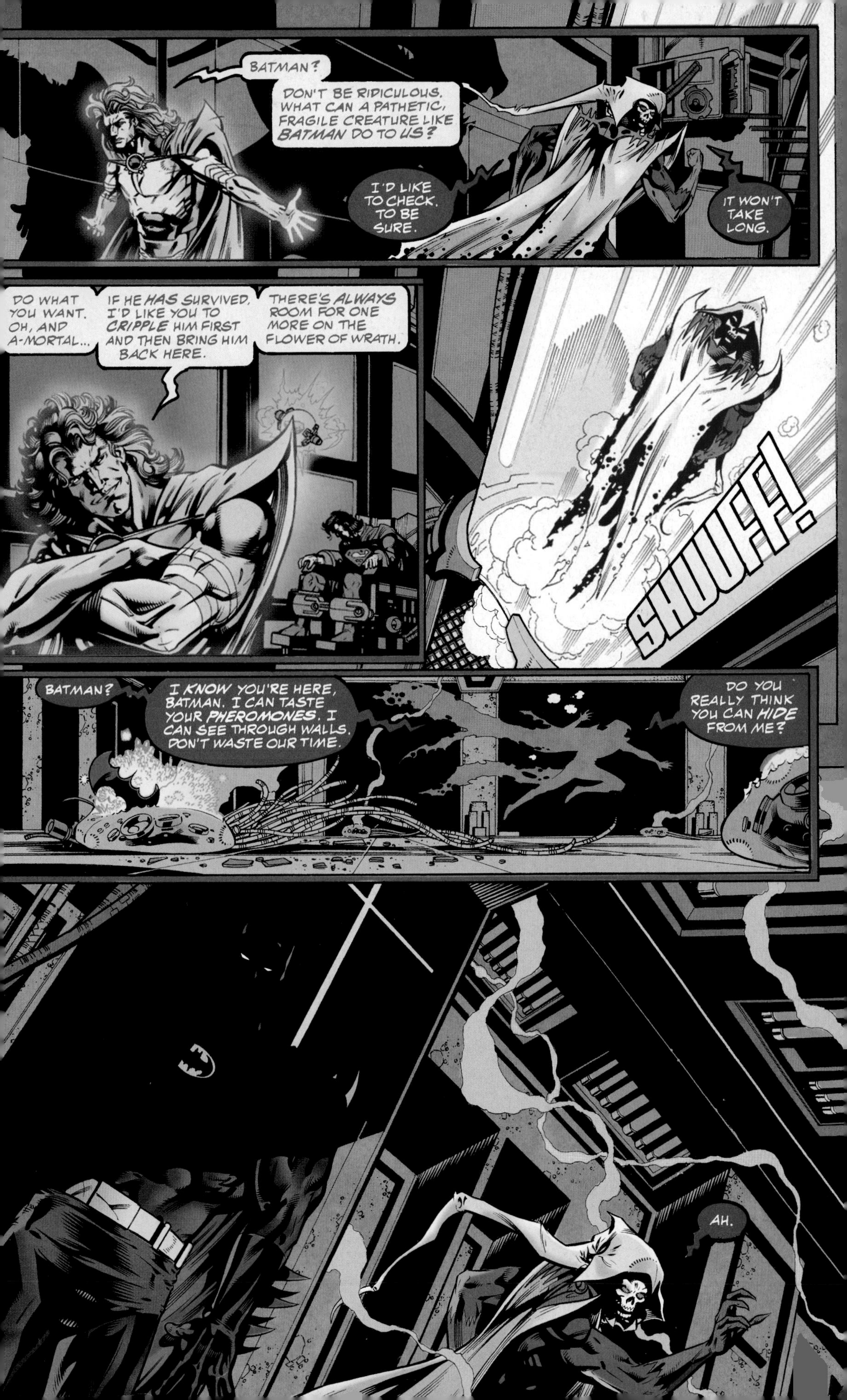
BATMAN?
DON'T BE RIDICULOUS. WHAT CAN A PATHETIC, FRAGILE CREATURE LIKE BATMAN DO TO US?
I'D LIKE TO CHECK. TO BE SURE.
IT WON'T TAKE LONG.
DO WHAT YOU WANT. OH, AND A-MORTAL...
IF HE HAS SURVIVED, I'D LIKE YOU TO CRIPPLE HIM FIRST AND THEN BRING HIM BACK HERE.
THERE'S ALWAYS ROOM FOR ONE MORE ON THE FLOWER OF WRATH.
SHUFF!
BATMAN?
I KNOW YOU'RE HERE, BATMAN. I CAN TASTE YOUR PHEROMONES. I CAN SEE THROUGH WALLS. DON'T WASTE OUR TIME.
DO YOU REALLY THINK YOU CAN HIDE FROM ME?
AH.

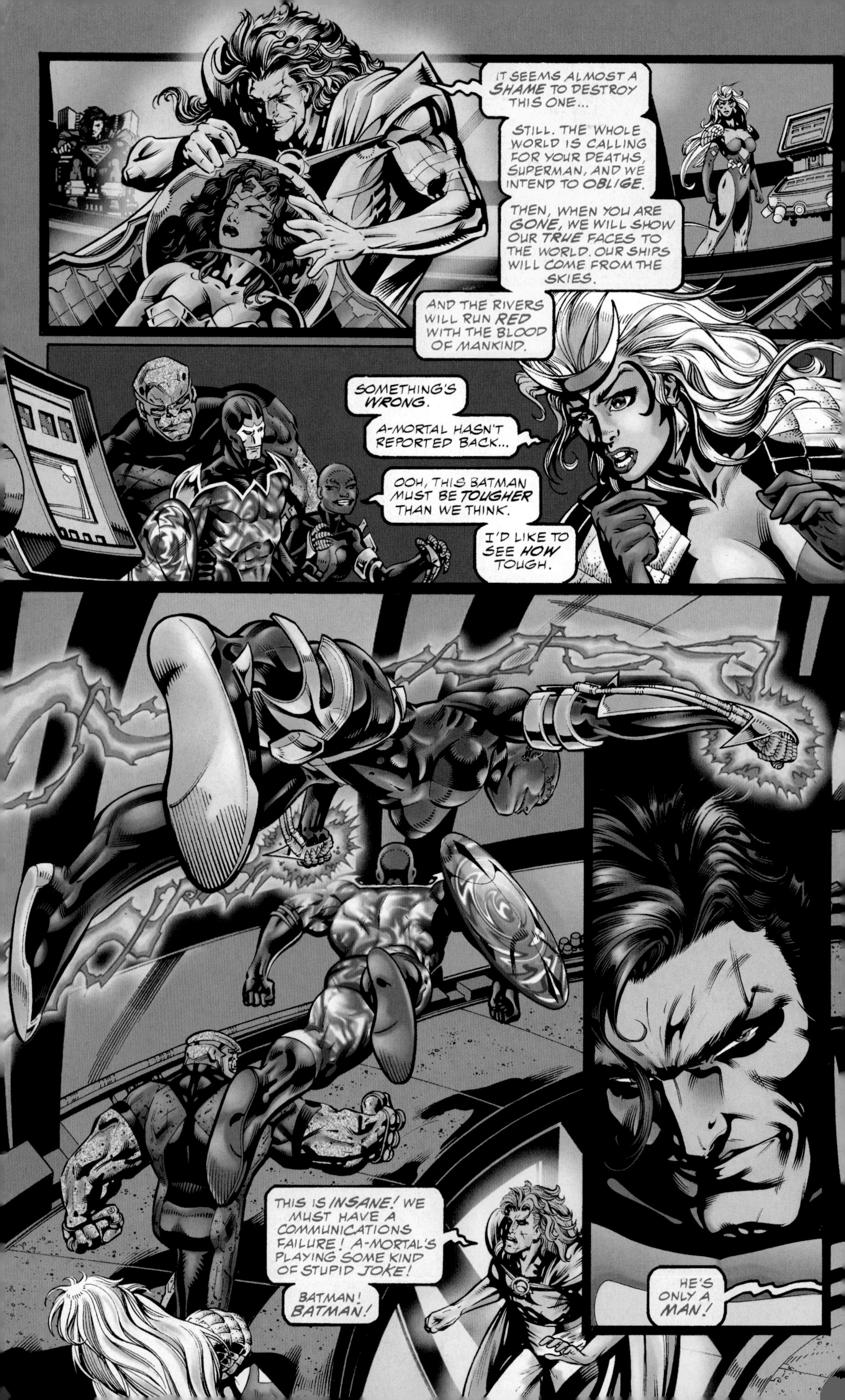
IT SEEMS ALMOST A SHAME TO DESTROY THIS ONE...
STILL. THE WHOLE WORLD IS CALLING FOR YOUR DEATHS, SUPERMAN, AND WE INTEND TO OBLIGE.
THEN, WHEN YOU ARE GONE, WE WILL SHOW OUR TRUE FACES TO THE WORLD. OUR SHIPS WILL COME FROM THE SKIES.
AND THE RIVERS WILL RUN RED WITH THE BLOOD OF MANKIND.
SOMETHING'S WRONG.
A-MORTAL HASN'T REPORTED BACK...
OOH, THIS BATMAN MUST BE TOUGHER THAN WE THINK.
I'D LIKE TO SEE HOW TOUGH.
THIS IS INSANE! WE MUST HAVE A COMMUNICATIONS FAILURE! A-MORTAL'S PLAYING SOME KIND OF STUPID JOKE!
BATMAN! BATMAN!
HE'S ONLY A MAN!

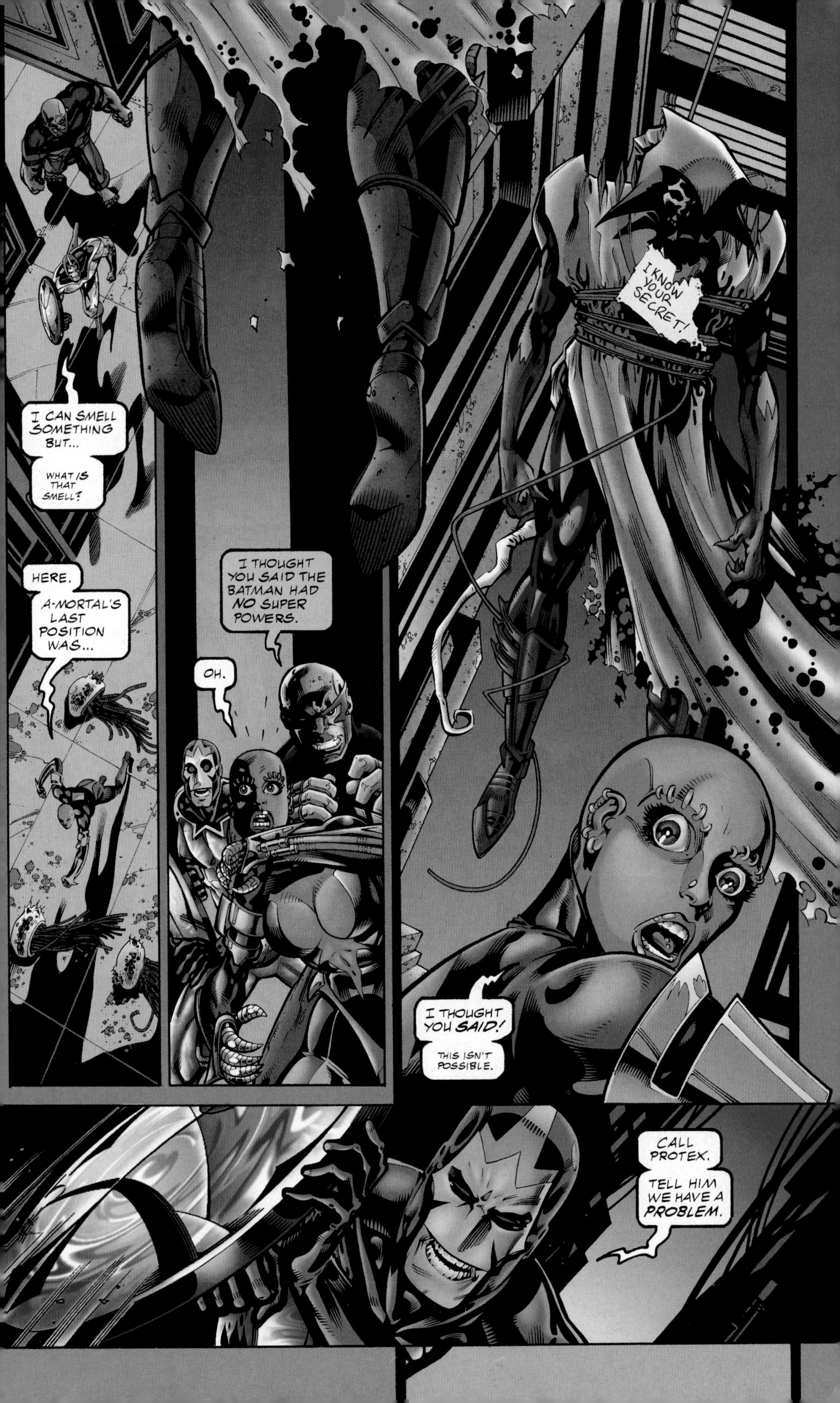
I KNOW YOUR SECRET!
I CAN SMELL SOMETHING BUT...
WHAT IS THAT SMELL?
HERE.
A-MORTAL'S LAST POSITION WAS...
I THOUGHT YOU SAID THE BATMAN HAD NO SUPER POWERS.
OH.
I THOUGHT YOU SAID!
THIS ISN'T POSSIBLE.
CALL PROTEX.
TELL HIM WE HAVE A PROBLEM.

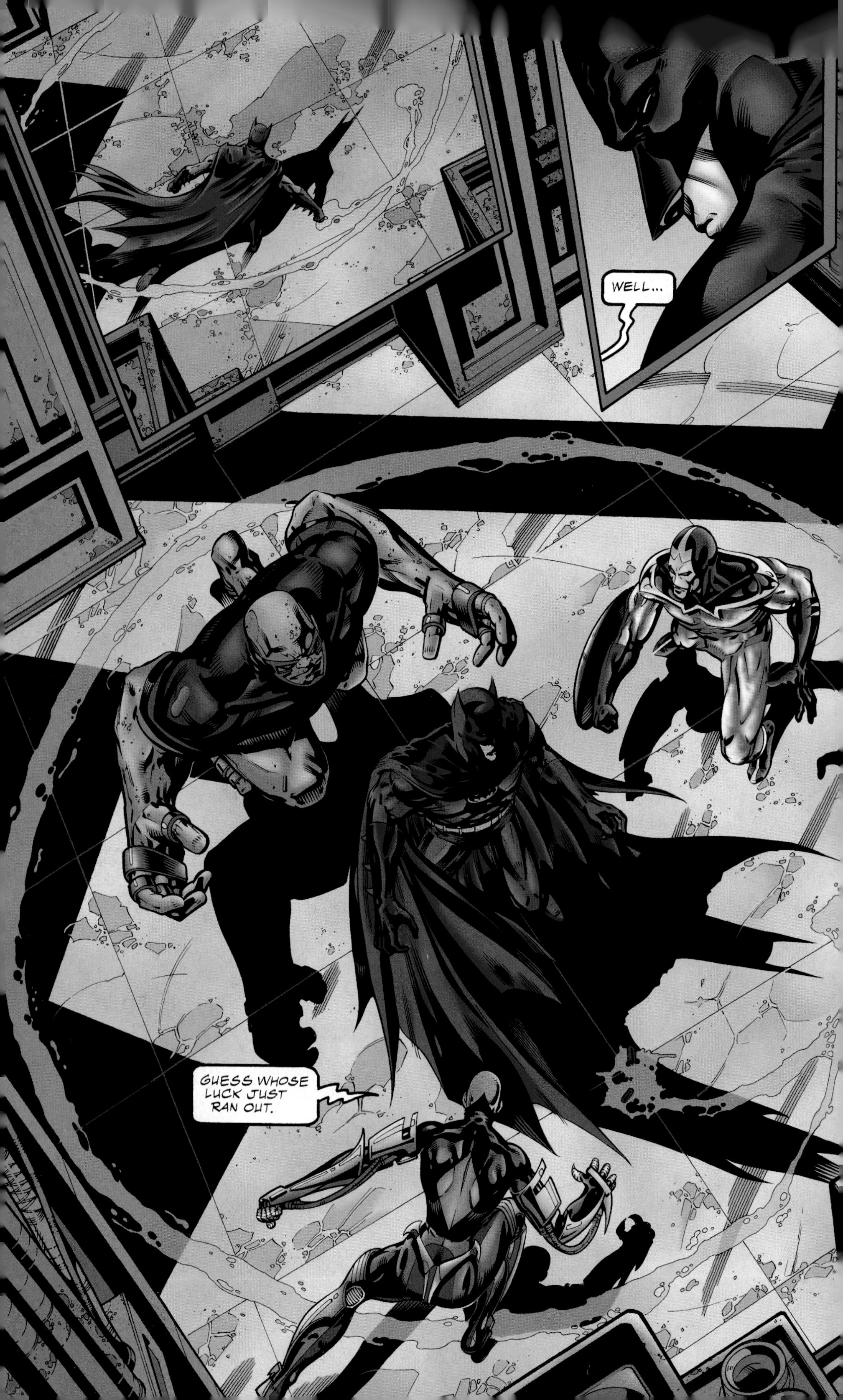
WELL...
GUESS WHOSE LUCK JUST RAN OUT.

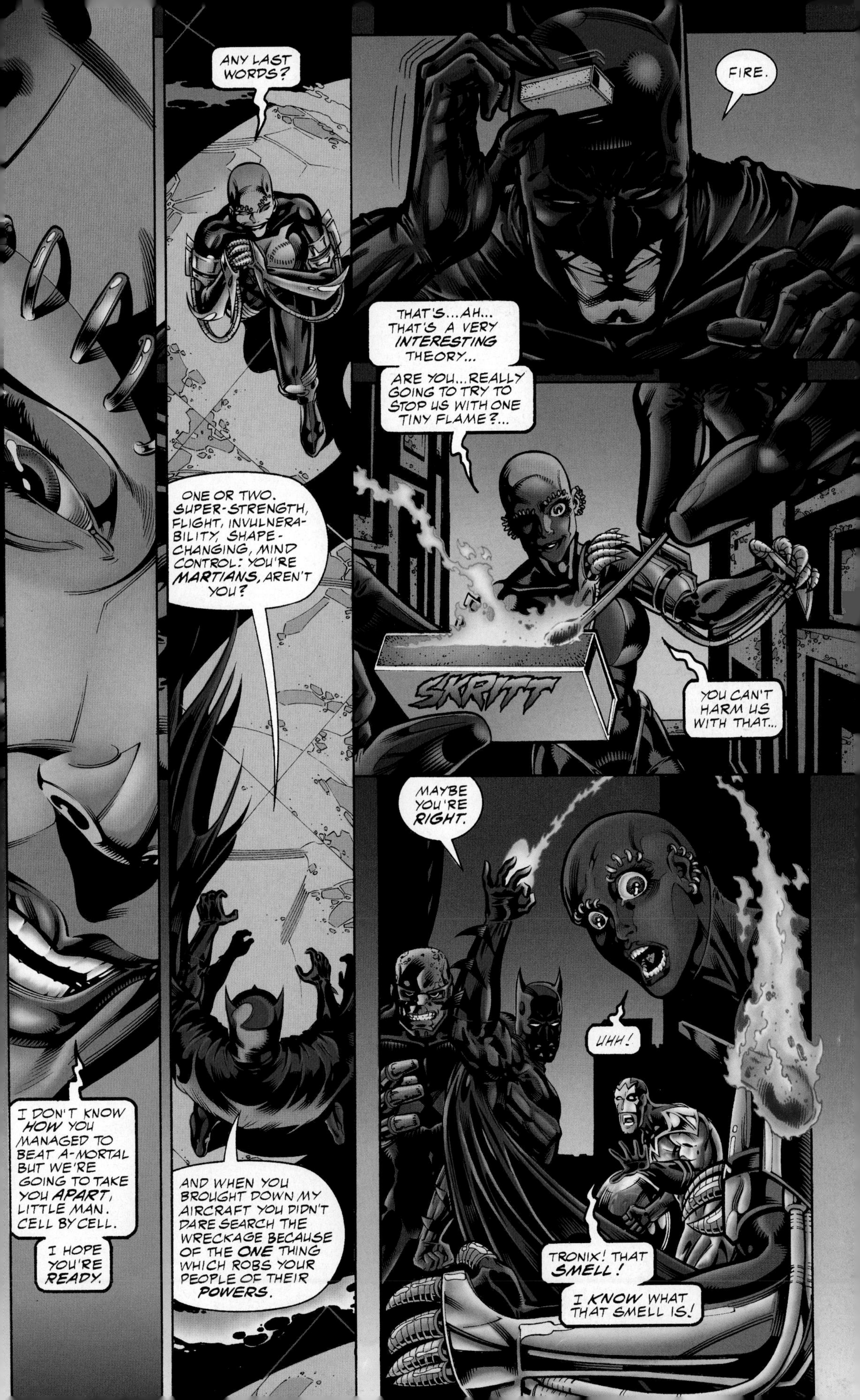
ANY LAST WORDS?
FIRE.
I DON'T KNOW HOW YOU MANAGED TO BEAT A-MORTAL BUT WE'RE GOING TO TAKE YOU APART, LITTLE MAN. CELL BY CELL.
I HOPE YOU'RE READY.
ONE OR TWO. SUPER-STRENGTH, FLIGHT, INVULNERABILITY, SHAPE-CHANGING, MIND CONTROL: YOU'RE MARTIANS, AREN'T YOU?
AND WHEN YOU BROUGHT DOWN MY AIRCRAFT YOU DIDN'T DARE SEARCH THE WRECKAGE BECAUSE OF THE ONE THING WHICH ROBS YOUR PEOPLE OF THEIR POWERS.
THAT'S...AH... THAT'S A VERY INTERESTING THEORY...
ARE YOU...REALLY GOING TO TRY TO STOP US WITH ONE TINY FLAME?...
SKRITT
YOU CAN'T HARM US WITH THAT...
MAYBE YOU'RE RIGHT.
UHH!
TRONIX! THAT SMELL!
I KNOW WHAT THAT SMELL IS!

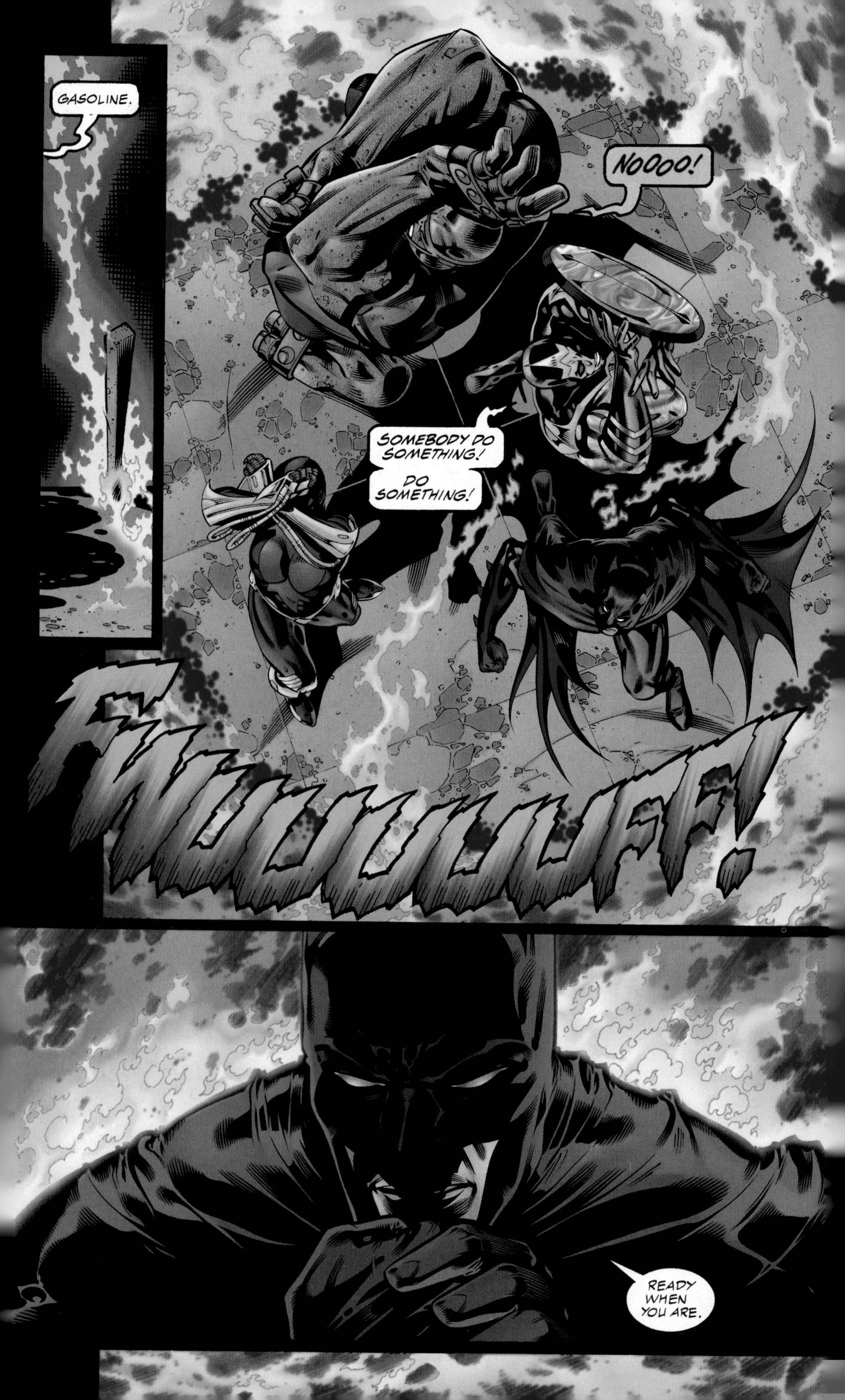
GASOLINE.
NOOOO!
SOMEBODY DO SOMETHING!
DO SOMETHING!
FWUUUUFF!
READY WHEN YOU ARE.

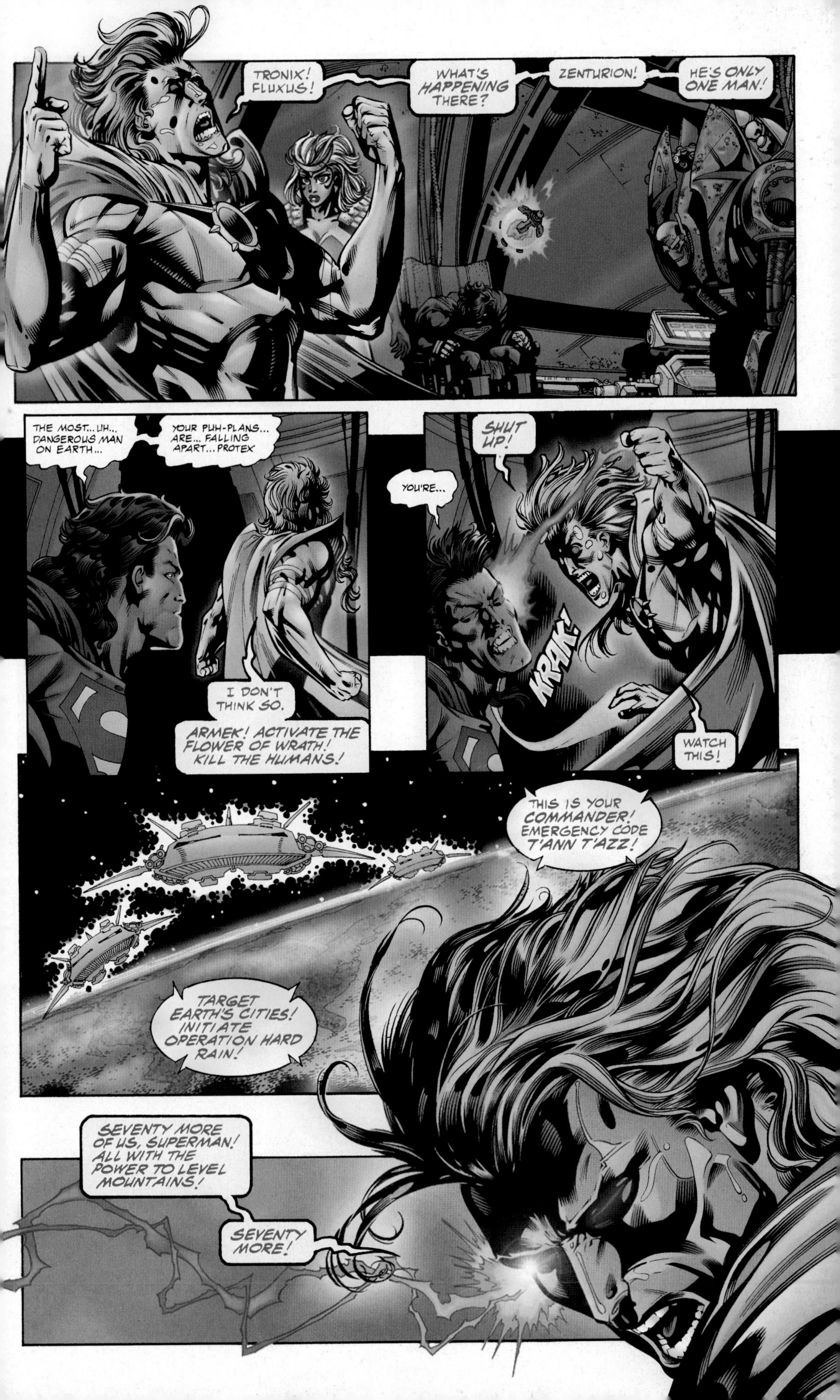
TRONIX! FLUXUS!
WHAT'S HAPPENING THERE?
ZENTURION!
HE'S ONLY ONE MAN!
THE MOST...UH... DANGEROUS MAN ON EARTH...
YOUR PUH-PLANS... ARE... FALLING APART...PROTEX
I DON'T THINK SO.
ARMEK! ACTIVATE THE FLOWER OF WRATH! KILL THE HUMANS!
YOU'RE...
SHUT UP!
KRAK!
WATCH THIS!
THIS IS YOUR COMMANDER! EMERGENCY CODE T'ANN T'AZZ!
TARGET EARTH'S CITIES! INITIATE OPERATION HARD RAIN!
SEVENTY MORE OF US, SUPERMAN! ALL WITH THE POWER TO LEVEL MOUNTAINS!
SEVENTY MORE!

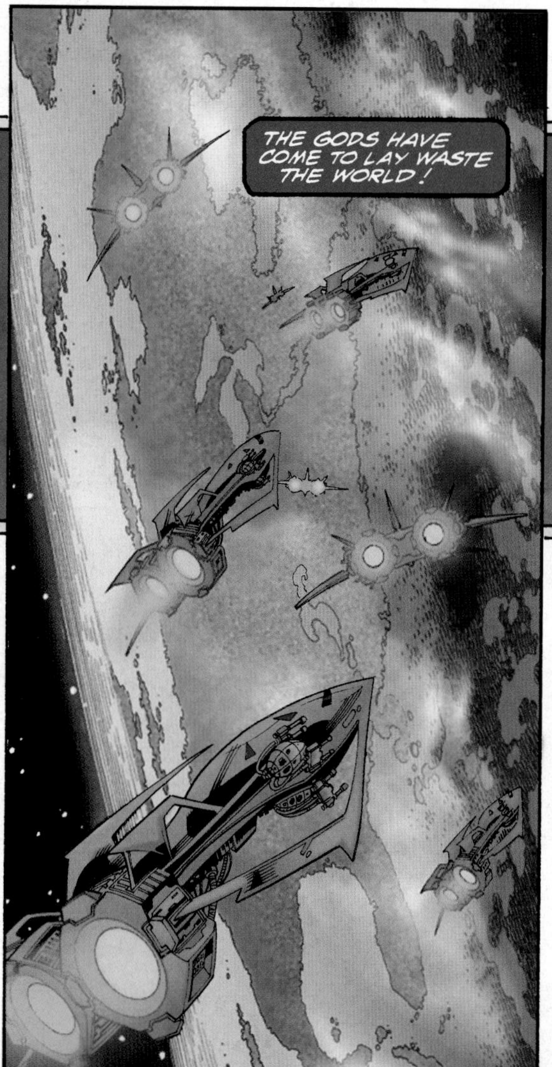
THE GODS HAVE COME TO LAY WASTE THE WORLD!

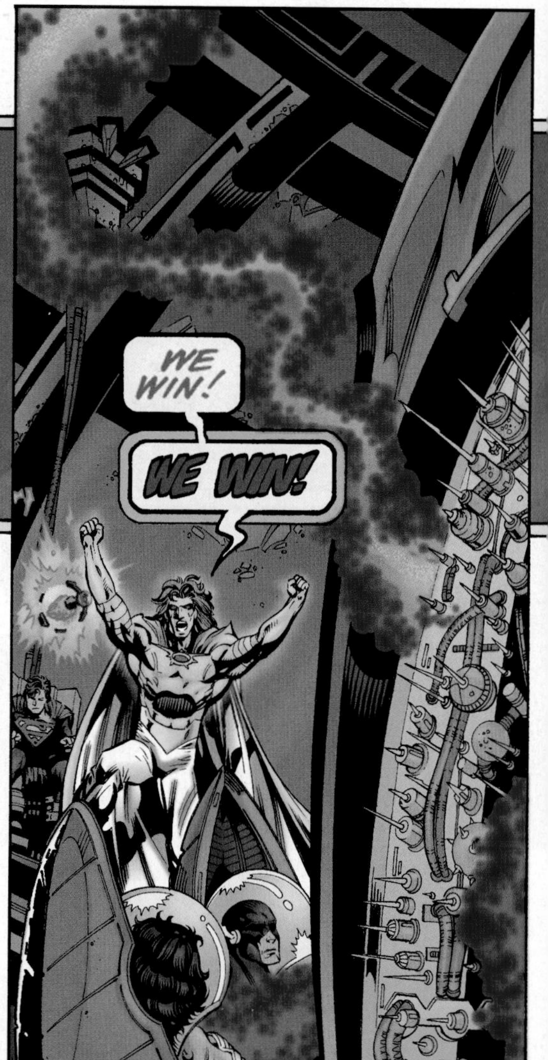
WE WIN!
WE WIN!

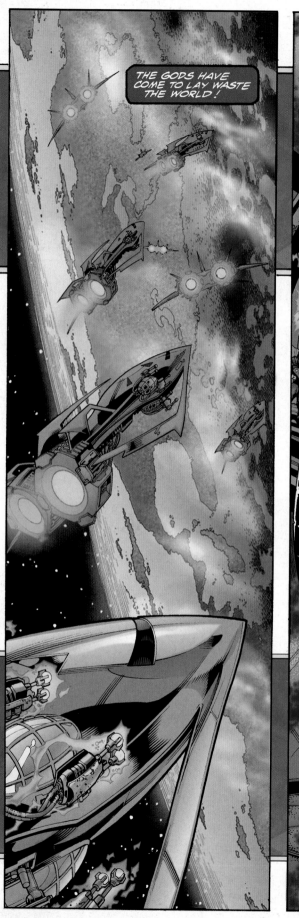

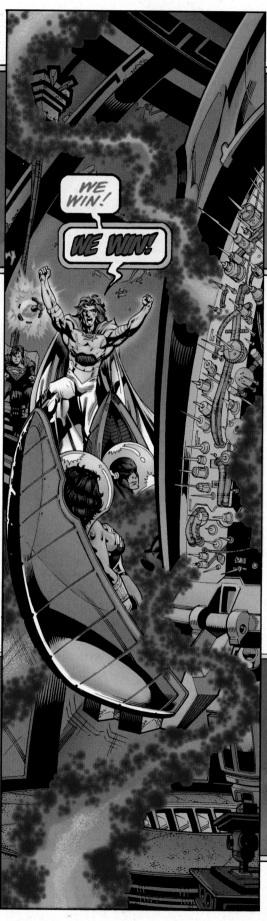

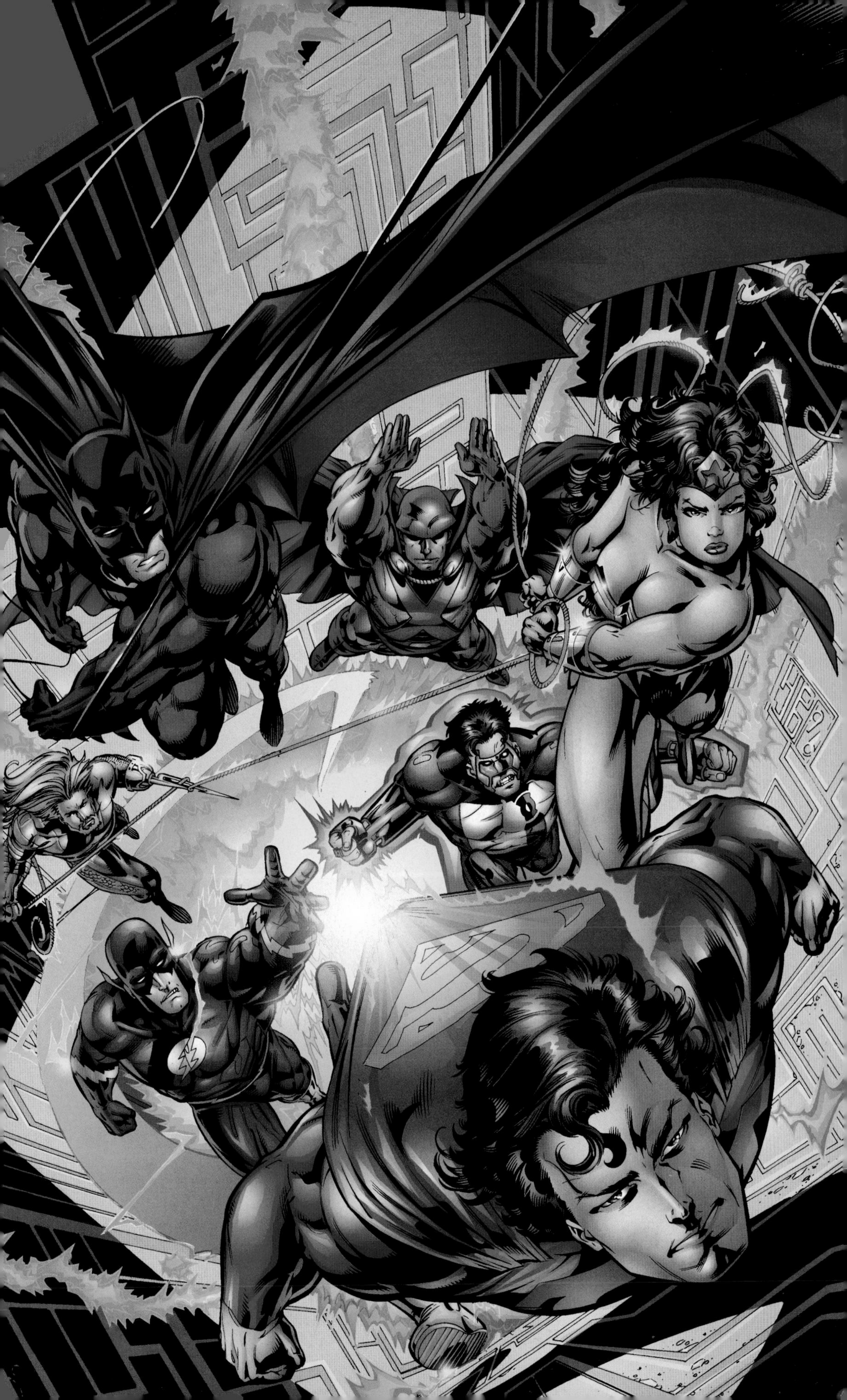

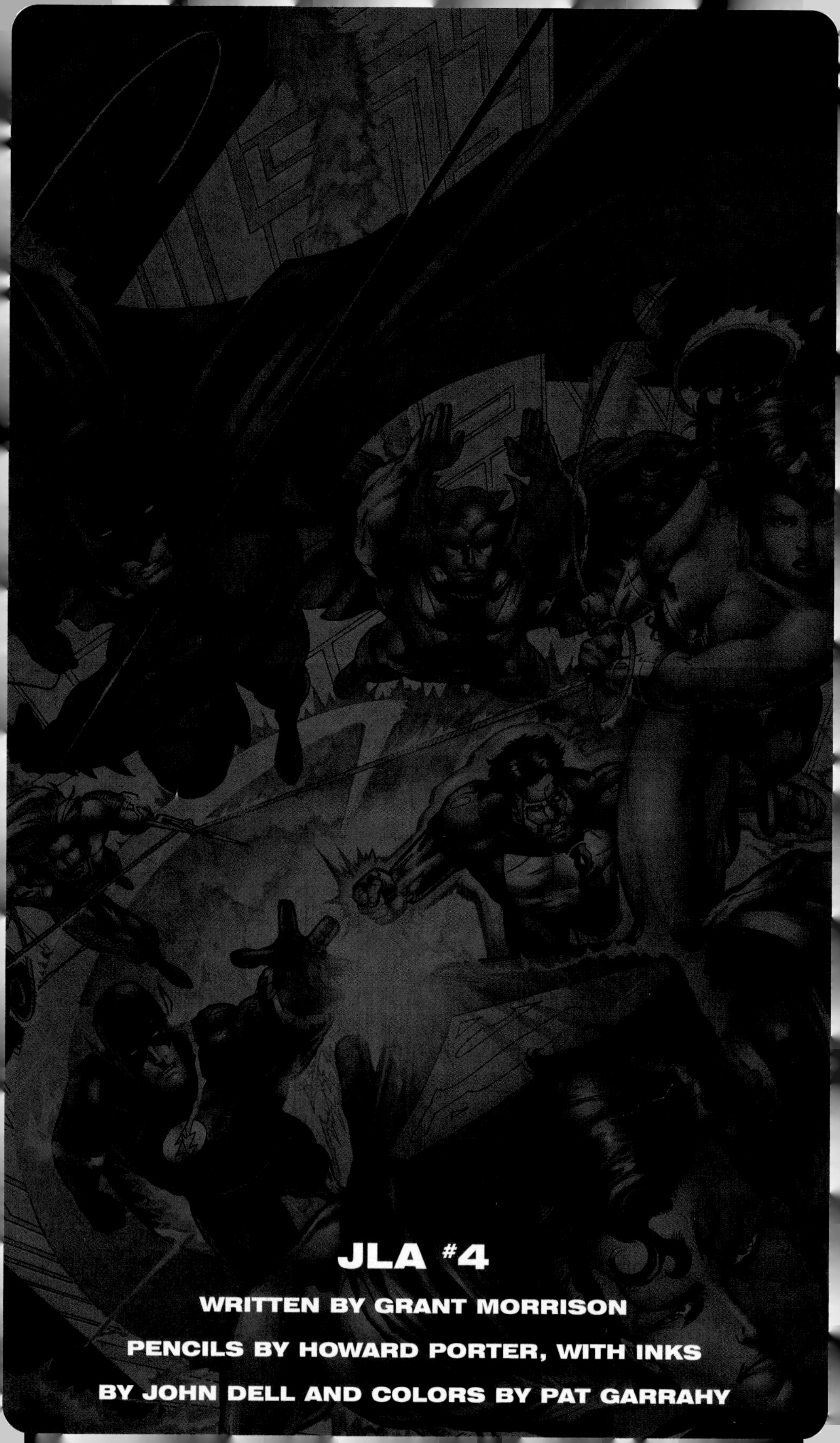

JLA #4

WRITTEN BY GRANT MORRISON

PENCILS BY HOWARD PORTER, WITH INKS BY JOHN DELL AND COLORS BY PAT GARRAHY

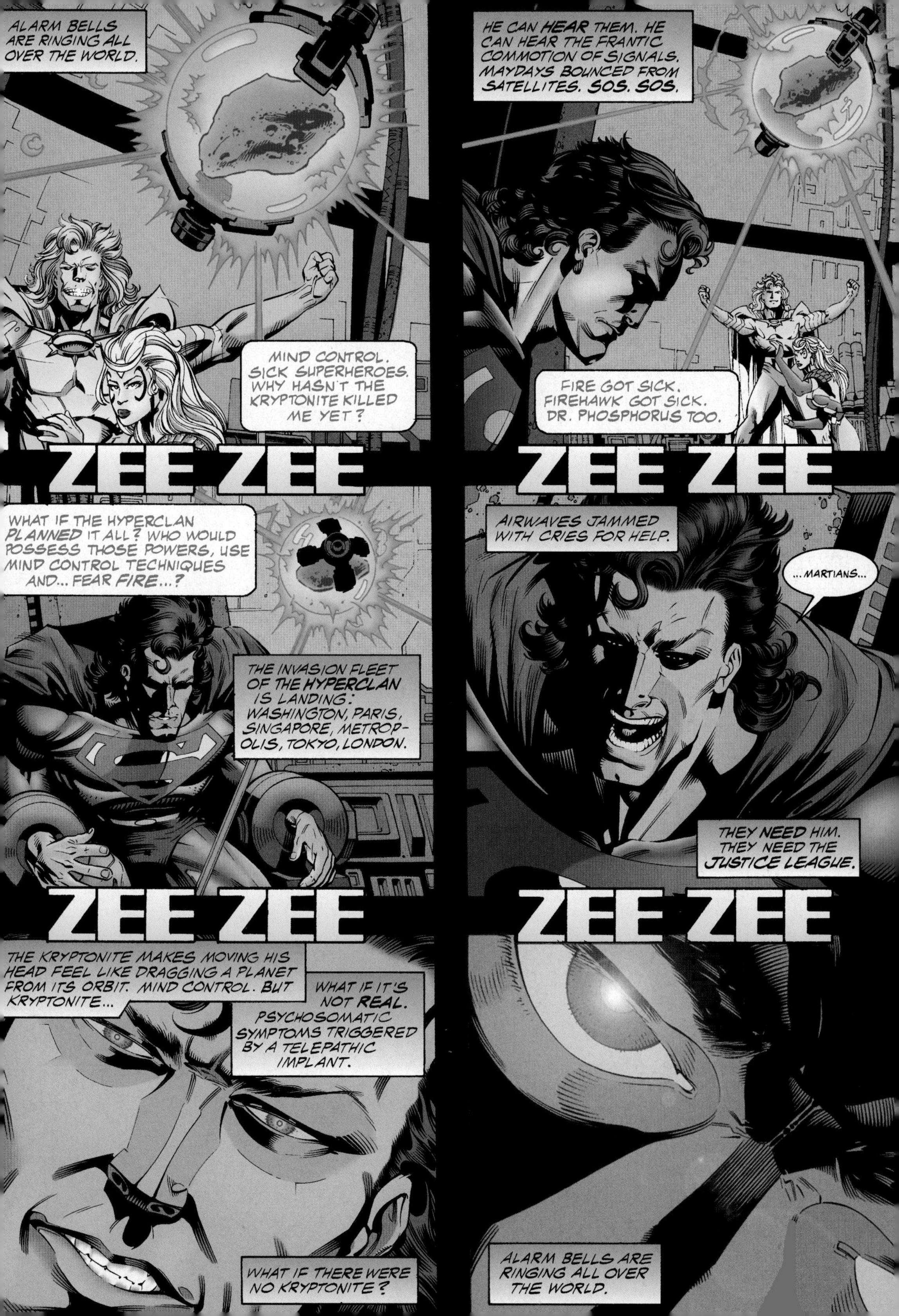
ALARM BELLS ARE RINGING ALL OVER THE WORLD.
MIND CONTROL. SICK SUPERHEROES. WHY HASN'T THE KRYPTONITE KILLED ME YET?
ZEE ZEE
HE CAN HEAR THEM. HE CAN HEAR THE FRANTIC COMMOTION OF SIGNALS. MAYDAYS BOUNCED FROM SATELLITES. SOS. SOS.
FIRE GOT SICK. FIREHAWK GOT SICK. DR. PHOSPHORUS TOO.
ZEE ZEE
WHAT IF THE HYPERCLAN PLANNED IT ALL? WHO WOULD POSSESS THOSE POWERS, USE MIND CONTROL TECHNIQUES AND... FEAR FIRE...?
THE INVASION FLEET OF THE HYPERCLAN IS LANDING: WASHINGTON, PARIS, SINGAPORE, METROPOLIS, TOKYO, LONDON.
ZEE ZEE
AIRWAVES JAMMED WITH CRIES FOR HELP.
...MARTIANS...
THEY NEED HIM. THEY NEED THE JUSTICE LEAGUE.
ZEE ZEE
THE KRYPTONITE MAKES MOVING HIS HEAD FEEL LIKE DRAGGING A PLANET FROM ITS ORBIT. MIND CONTROL. BUT KRYPTONITE...
WHAT IF IT'S NOT REAL. PSYCHOSOMATIC SYMPTOMS TRIGGERED BY A TELEPATHIC IMPLANT.
WHAT IF THERE WERE NO KRYPTONITE?
ZEE ZEE
ALARM BELLS ARE RINGING ALL OVER THE WORLD.

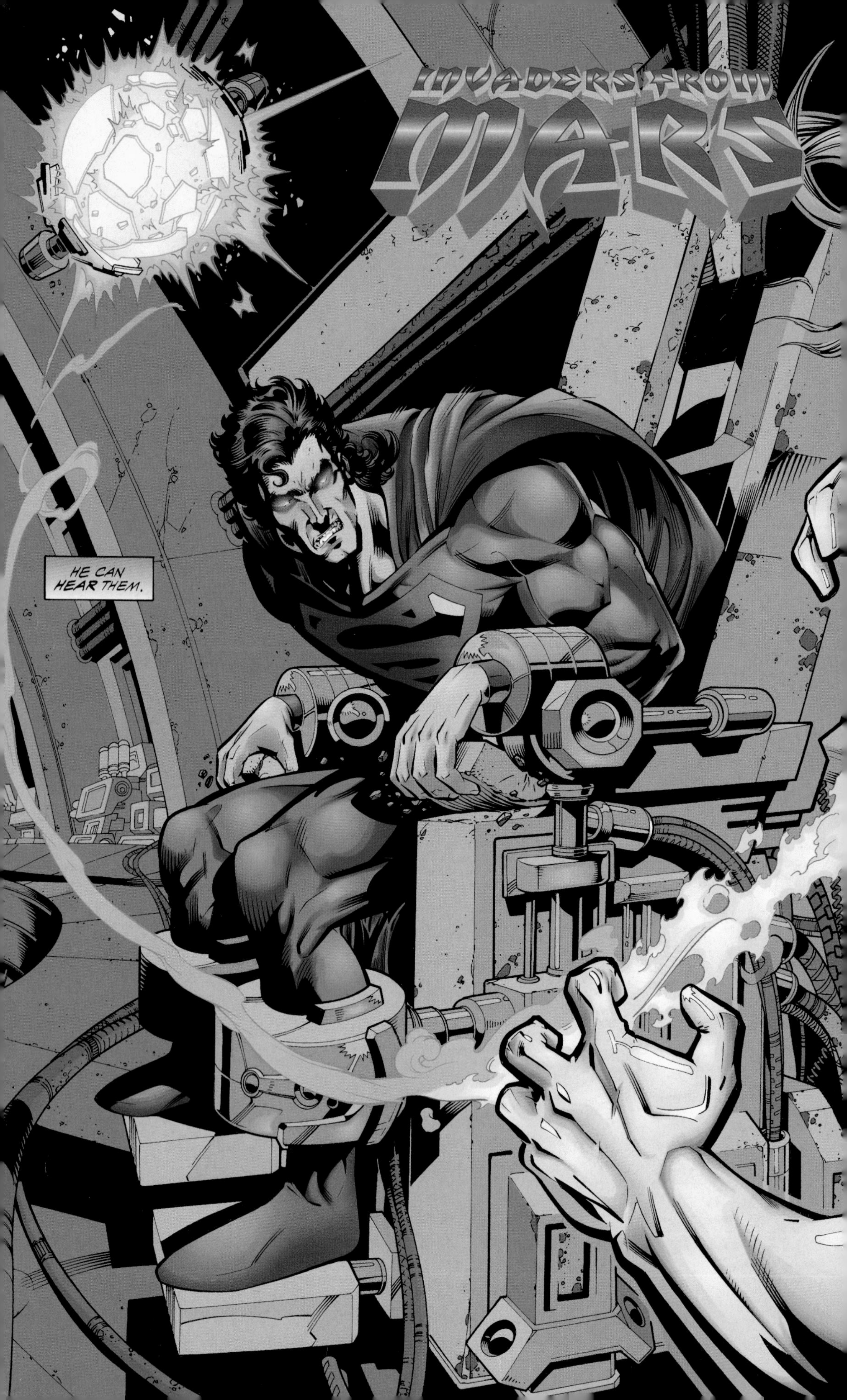
INVADERS FROM
MARS
HE CAN HEAR THEM.

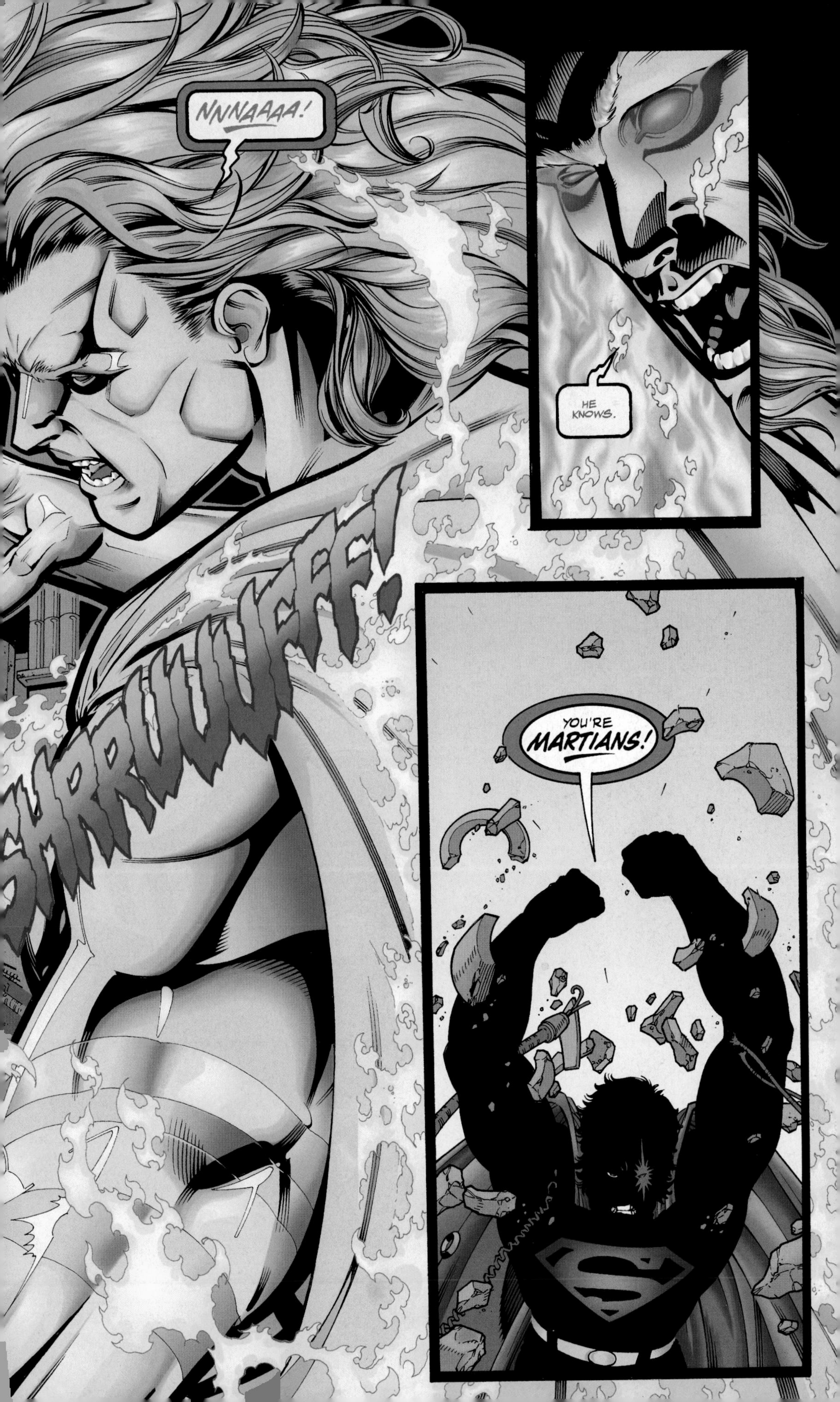
NNNAAAA!
SHRRUUUCFF!
HE KNOWS.
YOU'RE MARTIANS!

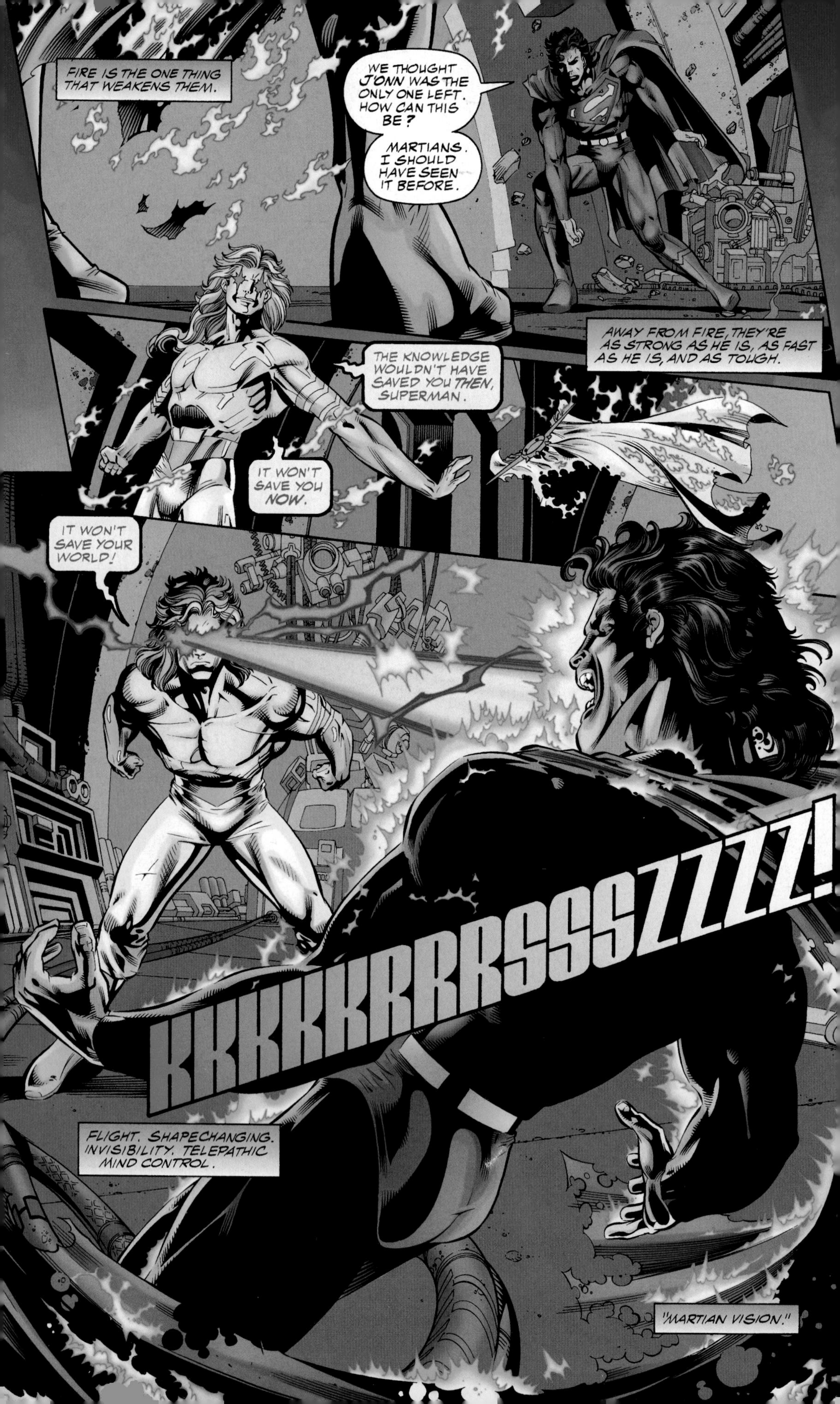
FIRE IS THE ONE THING THAT WEAKENS THEM.
WE THOUGHT J'ONN WAS THE ONLY ONE LEFT. HOW CAN THIS BE?
MARTIANS. I SHOULD HAVE SEEN IT BEFORE.
AWAY FROM FIRE, THEY'RE AS STRONG AS HE IS, AS FAST AS HE IS, AND AS TOUGH.
THE KNOWLEDGE WOULDN'T HAVE SAVED YOU THEN, SUPERMAN.
IT WON'T SAVE YOU NOW.
IT WON'T SAVE YOUR WORLD!
KKKKKRRRRSSSSZZZZ!
FLIGHT. SHAPECHANGING. INVISIBILITY. TELEPATHIC MIND CONTROL.
"MARTIAN VISION."

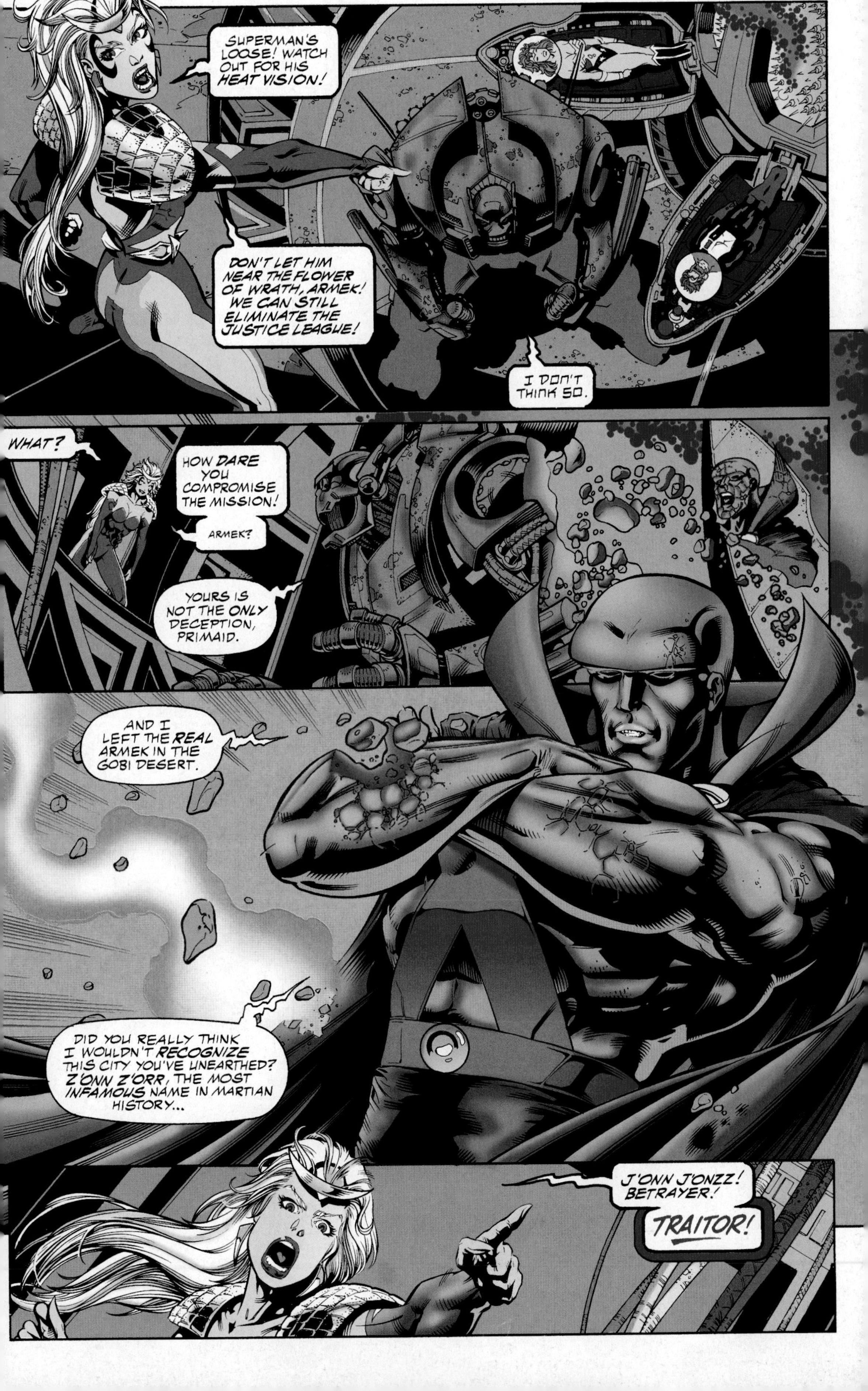
SUPERMAN'S LOOSE! WATCH OUT FOR HIS HEAT VISION!
DON'T LET HIM NEAR THE FLOWER OF WRATH, ARMEK! WE CAN STILL ELIMINATE THE JUSTICE LEAGUE!
I DON'T THINK SO.
WHAT?
HOW DARE YOU COMPROMISE THE MISSION!
ARMEK?
YOURS IS NOT THE ONLY DECEPTION, PRIMAID.
AND I LEFT THE REAL ARMEK IN THE GOBI DESERT.
DID YOU REALLY THINK I WOULDN'T RECOGNIZE THIS CITY YOU'VE UNEARTHED? Z'ONN Z'ORR, THE MOST INFAMOUS NAME IN MARTIAN HISTORY...
J'ONN J'ONZZ! BETRAYER!
TRAITOR!

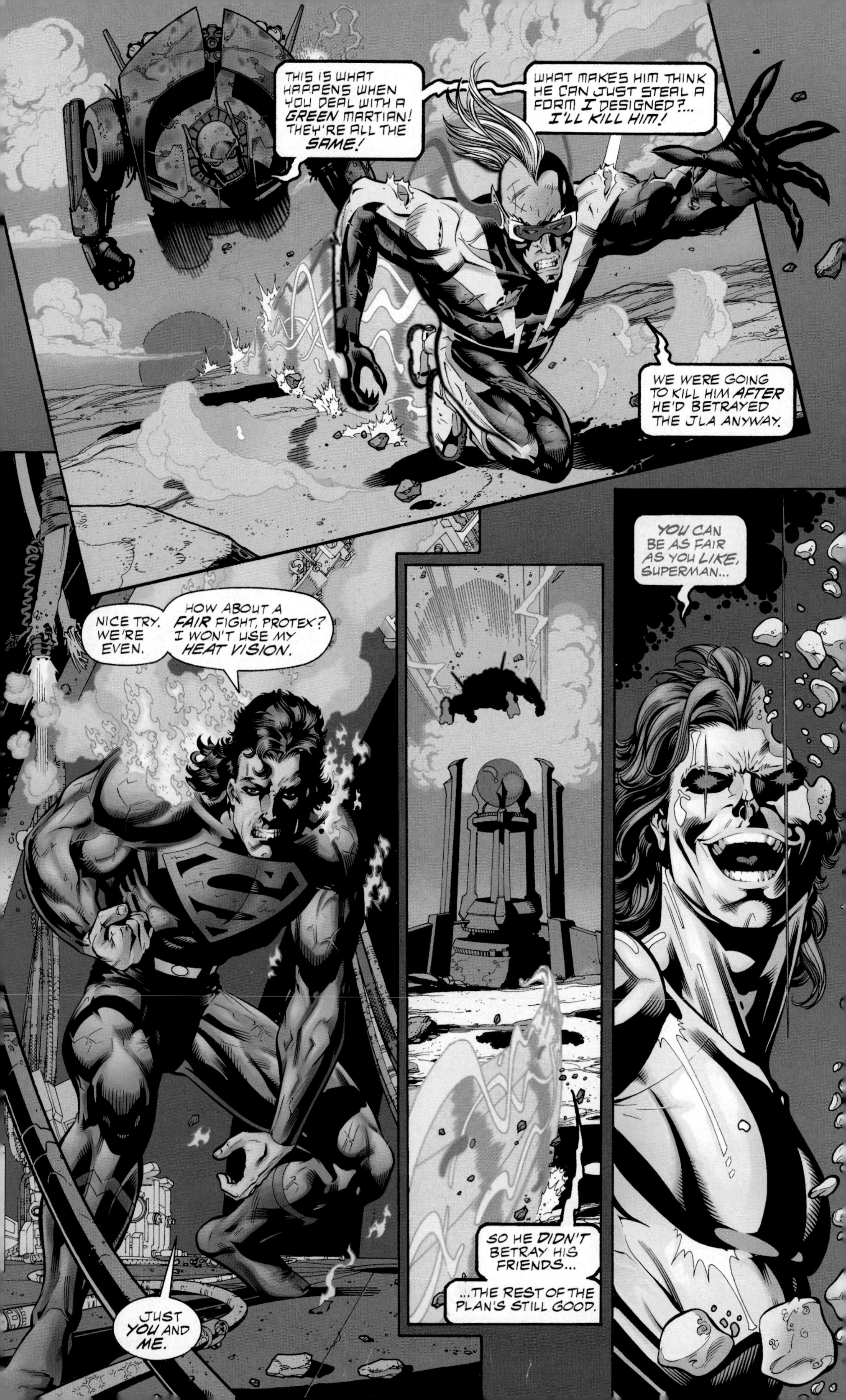
THIS IS WHAT HAPPENS WHEN YOU DEAL WITH A GREEN MARTIAN! THEY'RE ALL THE SAME!
WHAT MAKES HIM THINK HE CAN JUST STEAL A FORM I DESIGNED?... I'LL KILL HIM!
WE WERE GOING TO KILL HIM AFTER HE'D BETRAYED THE JLA ANYWAY.
NICE TRY. WE'RE EVEN.
HOW ABOUT A FAIR FIGHT, PROTEX? I WON'T USE MY HEAT VISION.
JUST YOU AND ME.
SO HE DIDN'T BETRAY HIS FRIENDS...
...THE REST OF THE PLAN'S STILL GOOD.
YOU CAN BE AS FAIR AS YOU LIKE, SUPERMAN...

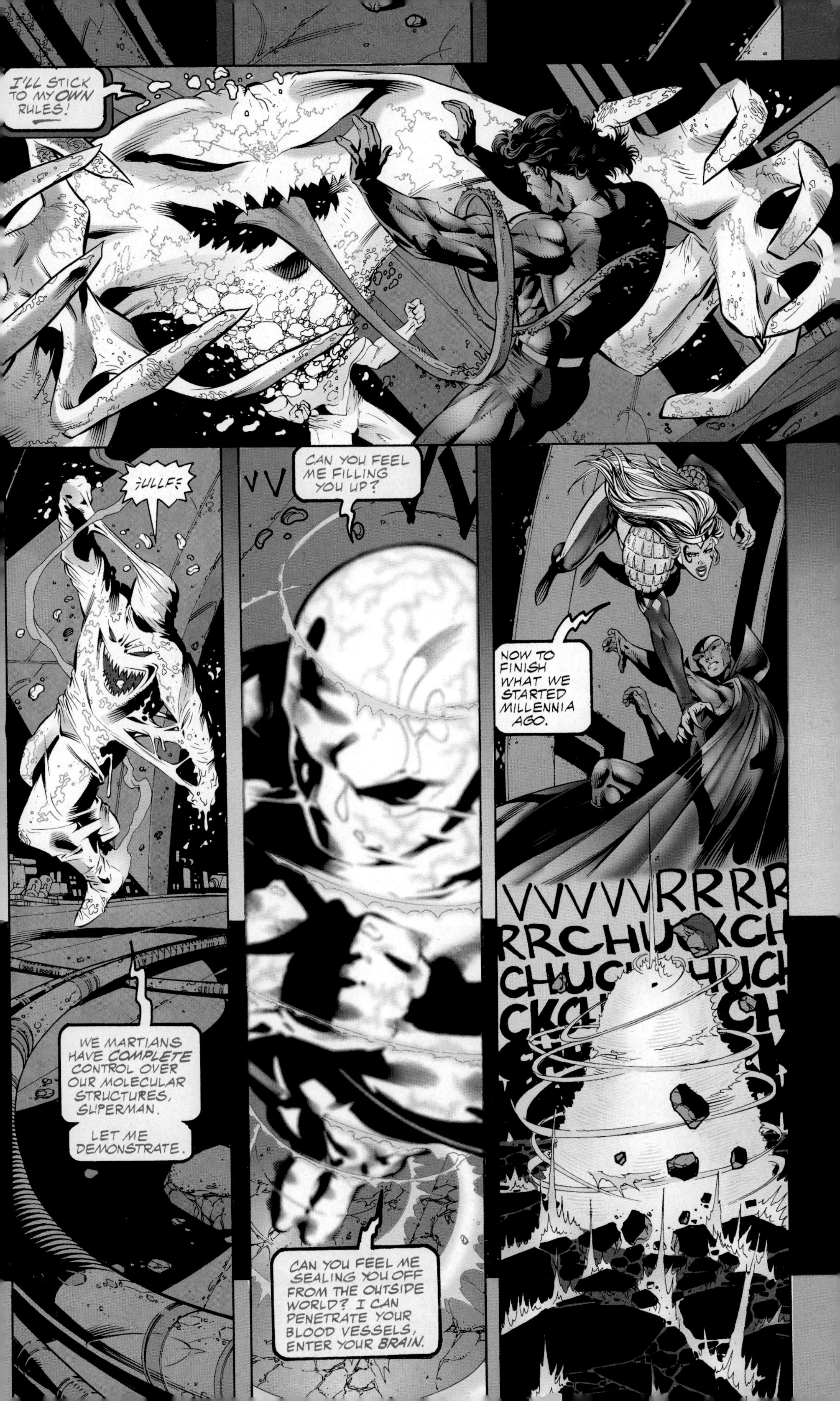

I'LL STICK TO MY OWN RULES!
¡ULLF!
WE MARTIANS HAVE COMPLETE CONTROL OVER OUR MOLECULAR STRUCTURES, SUPERMAN.
LET ME DEMONSTRATE.
VV
CAN YOU FEEL ME FILLING YOU UP?
CAN YOU FEEL ME SEALING YOU OFF FROM THE OUTSIDE WORLD? I CAN PENETRATE YOUR BLOOD VESSELS, ENTER YOUR BRAIN.
NOW TO FINISH WHAT WE STARTED MILLENNIA AGO.
VVVVVVRRRR
RRCHUCKCH
CHUCHUCH
CKCH CH

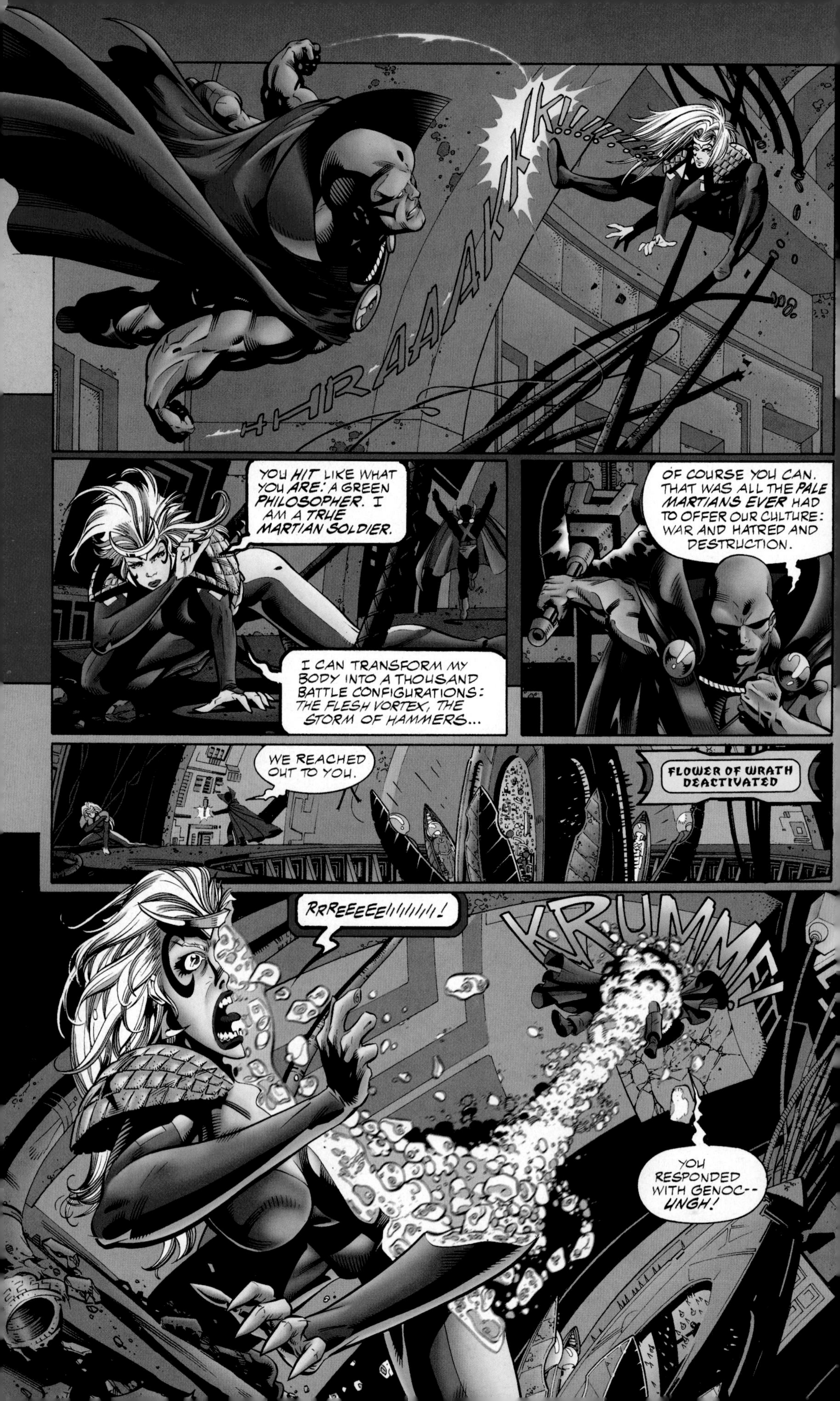

HHRAAAAKKK!!!!!!...
YOU HIT LIKE WHAT YOU ARE: A GREEN PHILOSOPHER. I AM A TRUE MARTIAN SOLDIER.
I CAN TRANSFORM MY BODY INTO A THOUSAND BATTLE CONFIGURATIONS: THE FLESH VORTEX, THE STORM OF HAMMERS...
OF COURSE YOU CAN. THAT WAS ALL THE PALE MARTIANS EVER HAD TO OFFER OUR CULTURE: WAR AND HATRED AND DESTRUCTION.
WE REACHED OUT TO YOU.
FLOWER OF WRATH DEACTIVATED
RRREEEEEEIIIIIIIII!
KRUMMF!
YOU RESPONDED WITH GENOC-- UNGH!

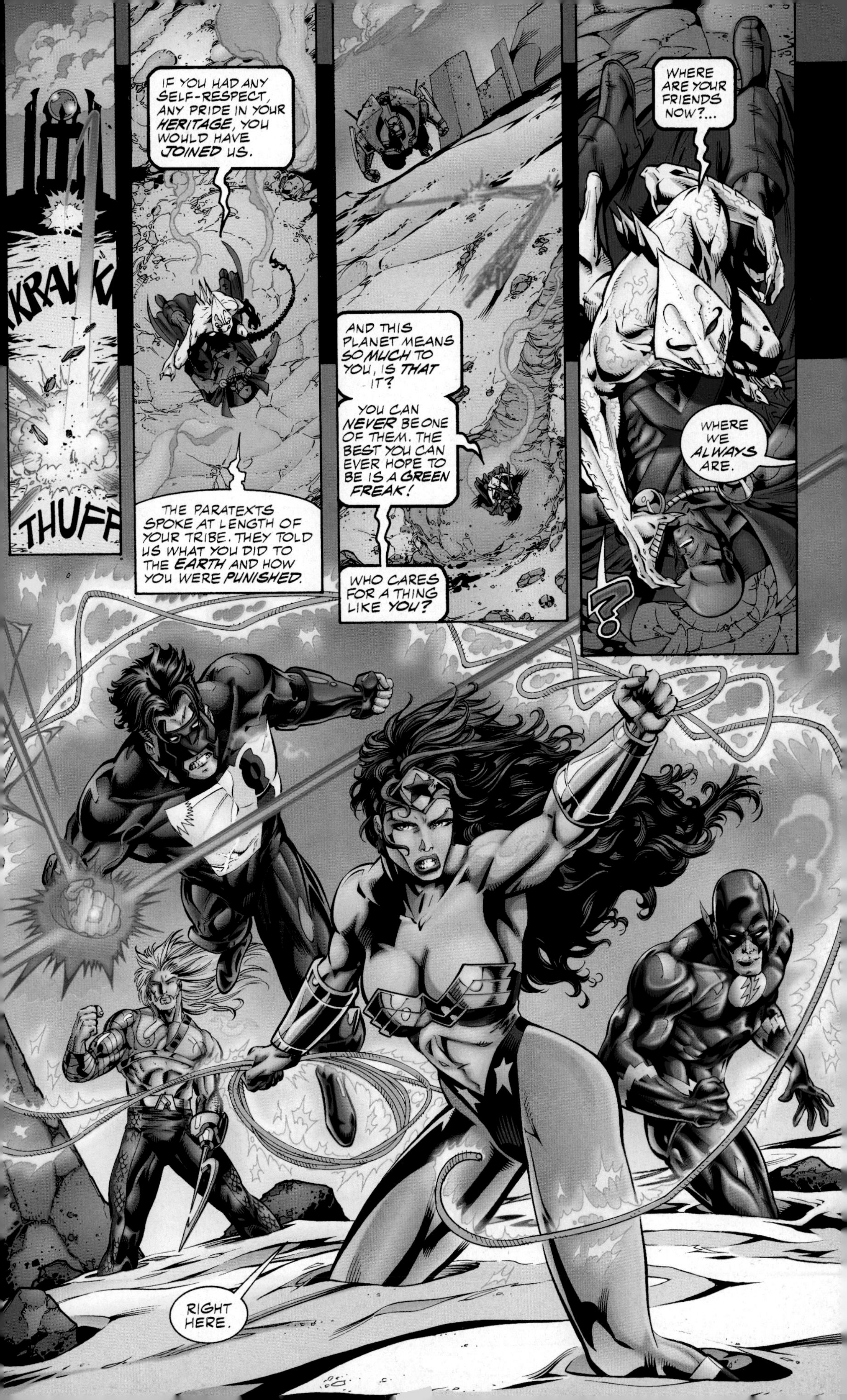
KRAKK
THUFF
IF YOU HAD ANY SELF-RESPECT, ANY PRIDE IN YOUR HERITAGE, YOU WOULD HAVE JOINED US.
THE PARATEXTS SPOKE AT LENGTH OF YOUR TRIBE. THEY TOLD US WHAT YOU DID TO THE EARTH AND HOW YOU WERE PUNISHED.
AND THIS PLANET MEANS SO MUCH TO YOU, IS THAT IT?
YOU CAN NEVER BE ONE OF THEM. THE BEST YOU CAN EVER HOPE TO BE IS A GREEN FREAK!
WHO CARES FOR A THING LIKE YOU?
WHERE ARE YOUR FRIENDS NOW?...
WHERE WE ALWAYS ARE.
?
RIGHT HERE.

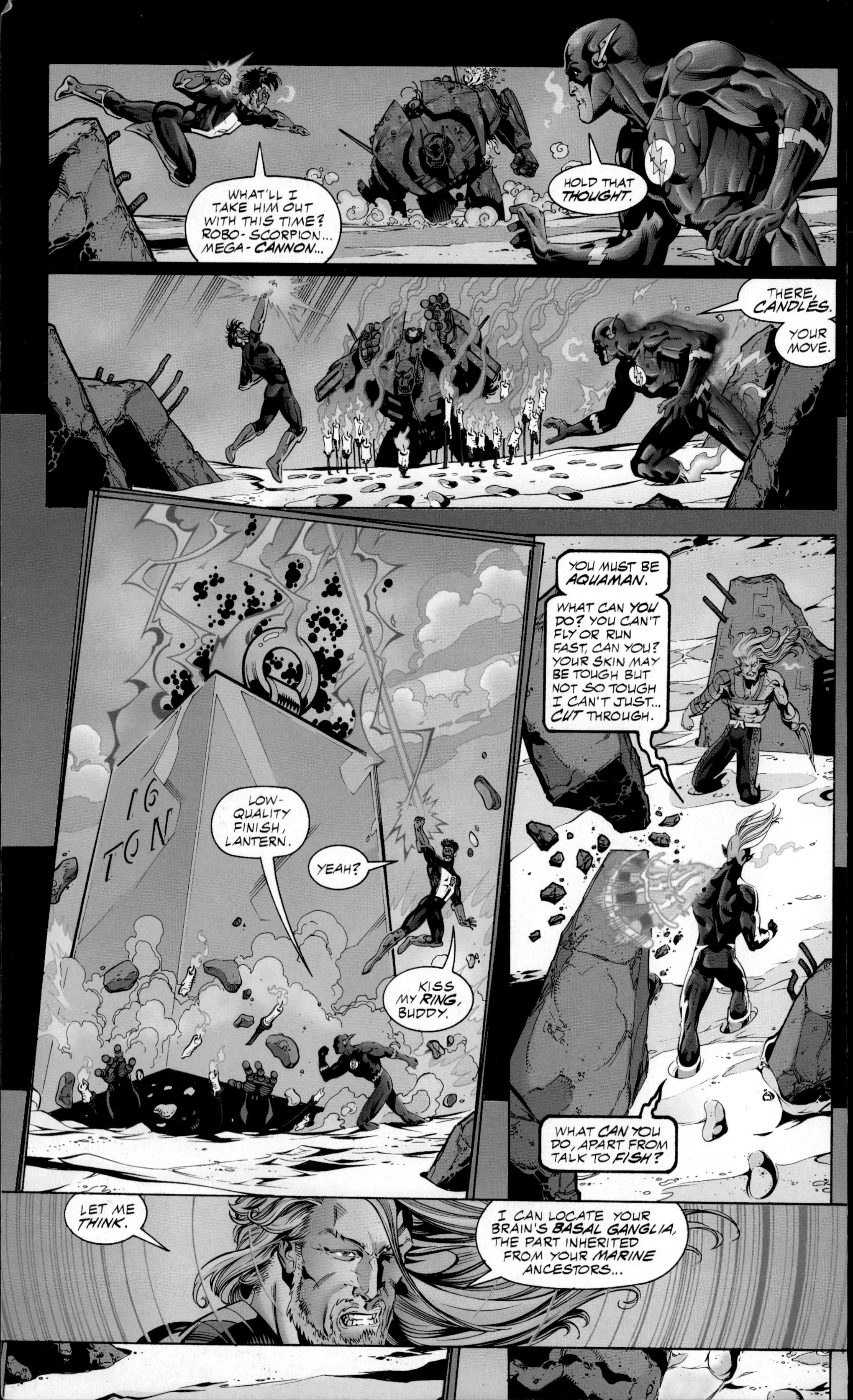
WHAT'LL I TAKE HIM OUT WITH THIS TIME? ROBO-SCORPION... MEGA-CANNON...
HOLD THAT THOUGHT.
THERE, CANDLES.
YOUR MOVE.
LOW-QUALITY FINISH, LANTERN.
YEAH?
KISS MY RING, BUDDY.
16 TON
YOU MUST BE AQUAMAN.
WHAT CAN YOU DO? YOU CAN'T FLY OR RUN FAST, CAN YOU? YOUR SKIN MAY BE TOUGH BUT NOT SO TOUGH I CAN'T JUST... CUT THROUGH.
WHAT CAN YOU DO, APART FROM TALK TO FISH?
LET ME THINK.
I CAN LOCATE YOUR BRAIN'S BASAL GANGLIA, THE PART INHERITED FROM YOUR MARINE ANCESTORS...

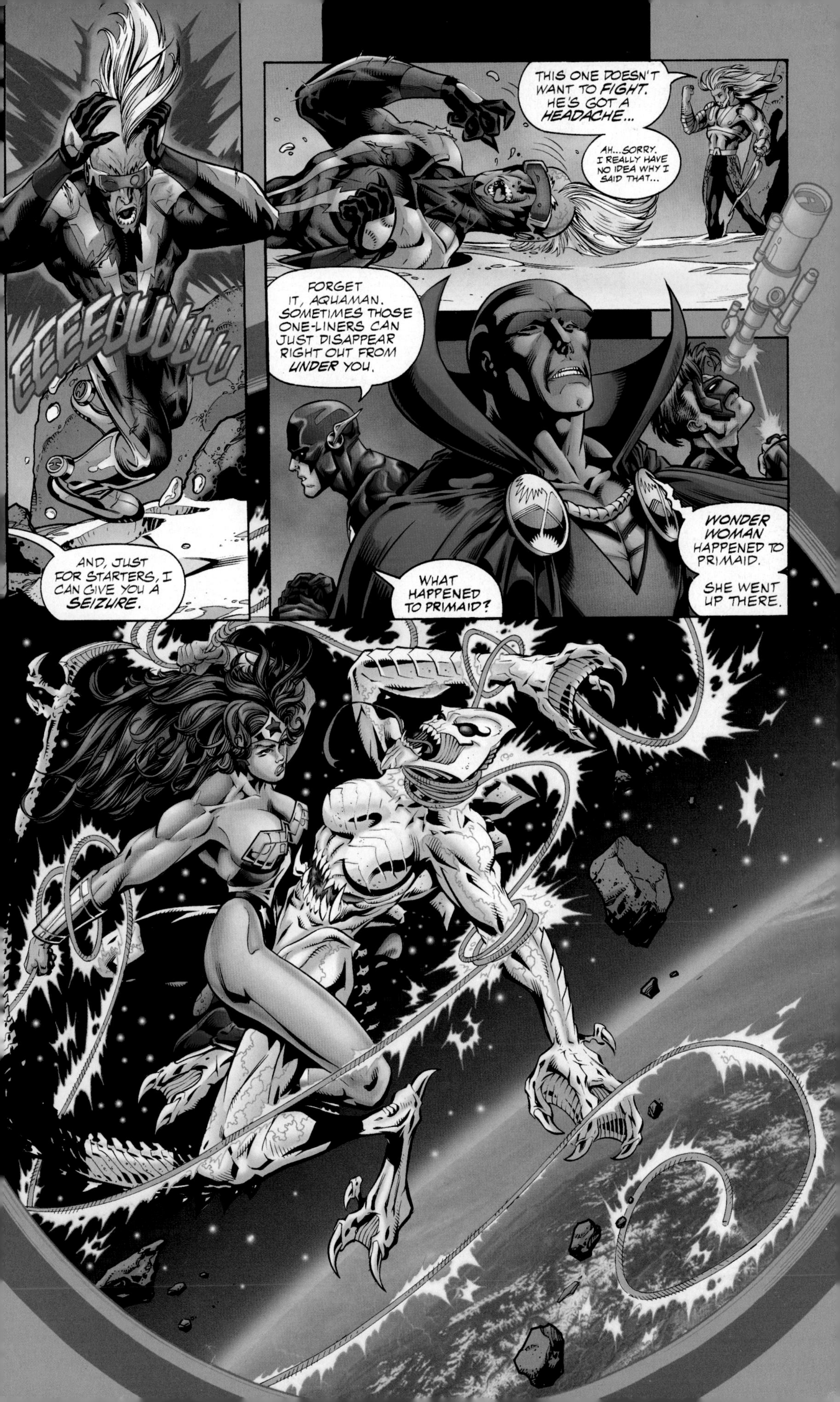
EEEEUUUUUU
AND, JUST FOR STARTERS, I CAN GIVE YOU A SEIZURE.
THIS ONE DOESN'T WANT TO FIGHT. HE'S GOT A HEADACHE...
AH...SORRY. I REALLY HAVE NO IDEA WHY I SAID THAT...
FORGET IT, AQUAMAN. SOMETIMES THOSE ONE-LINERS CAN JUST DISAPPEAR RIGHT OUT FROM UNDER YOU.
WHAT HAPPENED TO PRIMAID?
WONDER WOMAN HAPPENED TO PRIMAID.
SHE WENT UP THERE.

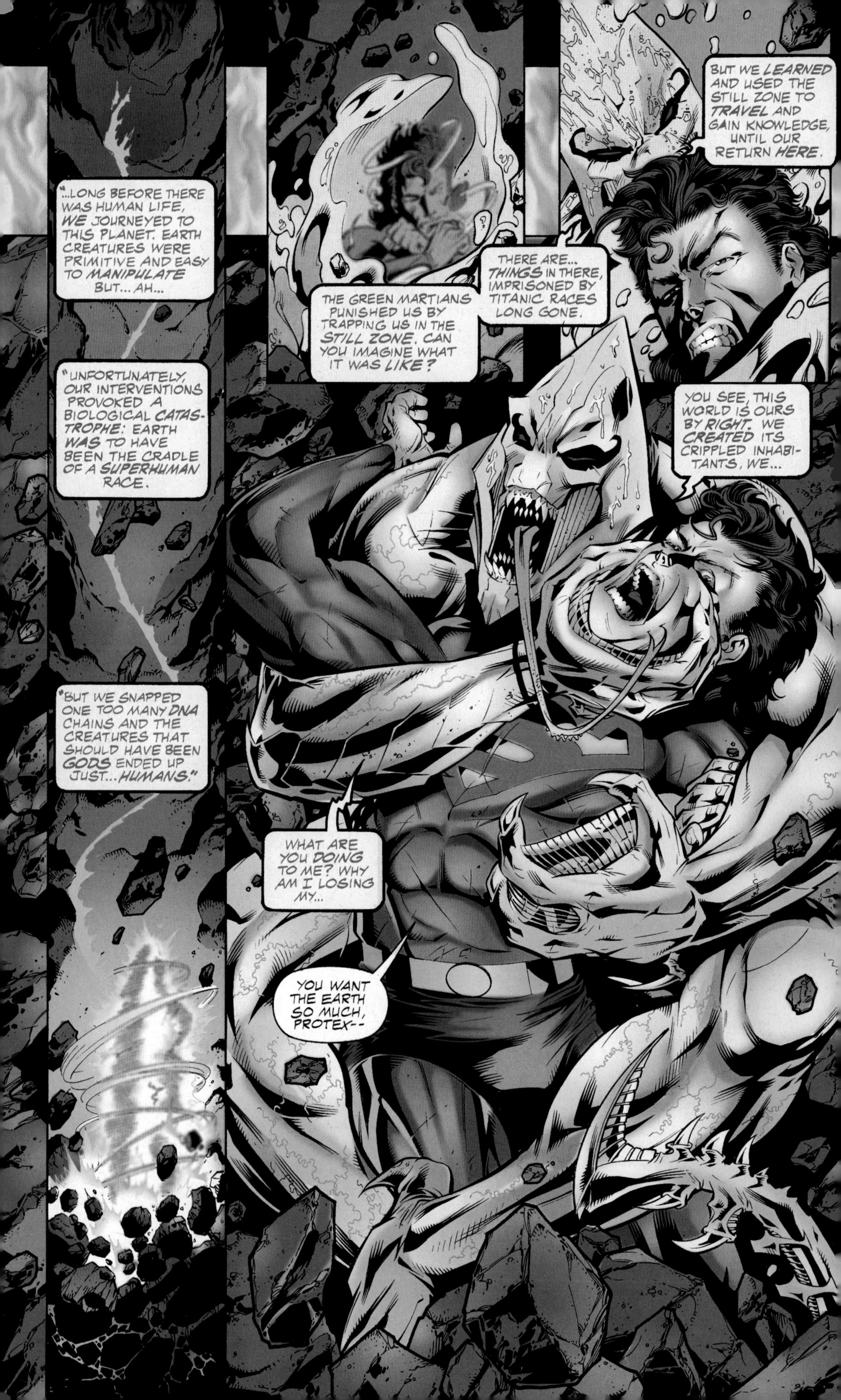
"...LONG BEFORE THERE WAS HUMAN LIFE, WE JOURNEYED TO THIS PLANET. EARTH CREATURES WERE PRIMITIVE AND EASY TO MANIPULATE BUT... AH...
"UNFORTUNATELY, OUR INTERVENTIONS PROVOKED A BIOLOGICAL CATASTROPHE: EARTH WAS TO HAVE BEEN THE CRADLE OF A SUPERHUMAN RACE.
"BUT WE SNAPPED ONE TOO MANY DNA CHAINS AND THE CREATURES THAT SHOULD HAVE BEEN GODS ENDED UP JUST... HUMANS."
THE GREEN MARTIANS PUNISHED US BY TRAPPING US IN THE STILL ZONE. CAN YOU IMAGINE WHAT IT WAS LIKE?
THERE ARE... THINGS IN THERE, IMPRISONED BY TITANIC RACES LONG GONE.
BUT WE LEARNED AND USED THE STILL ZONE TO TRAVEL AND GAIN KNOWLEDGE, UNTIL OUR RETURN HERE.
YOU SEE, THIS WORLD IS OURS BY RIGHT. WE CREATED ITS CRIPPLED INHABITANTS, WE...
WHAT ARE YOU DOING TO ME? WHY AM I LOSING MY...
YOU WANT THE EARTH SO MUCH, PROTEX--

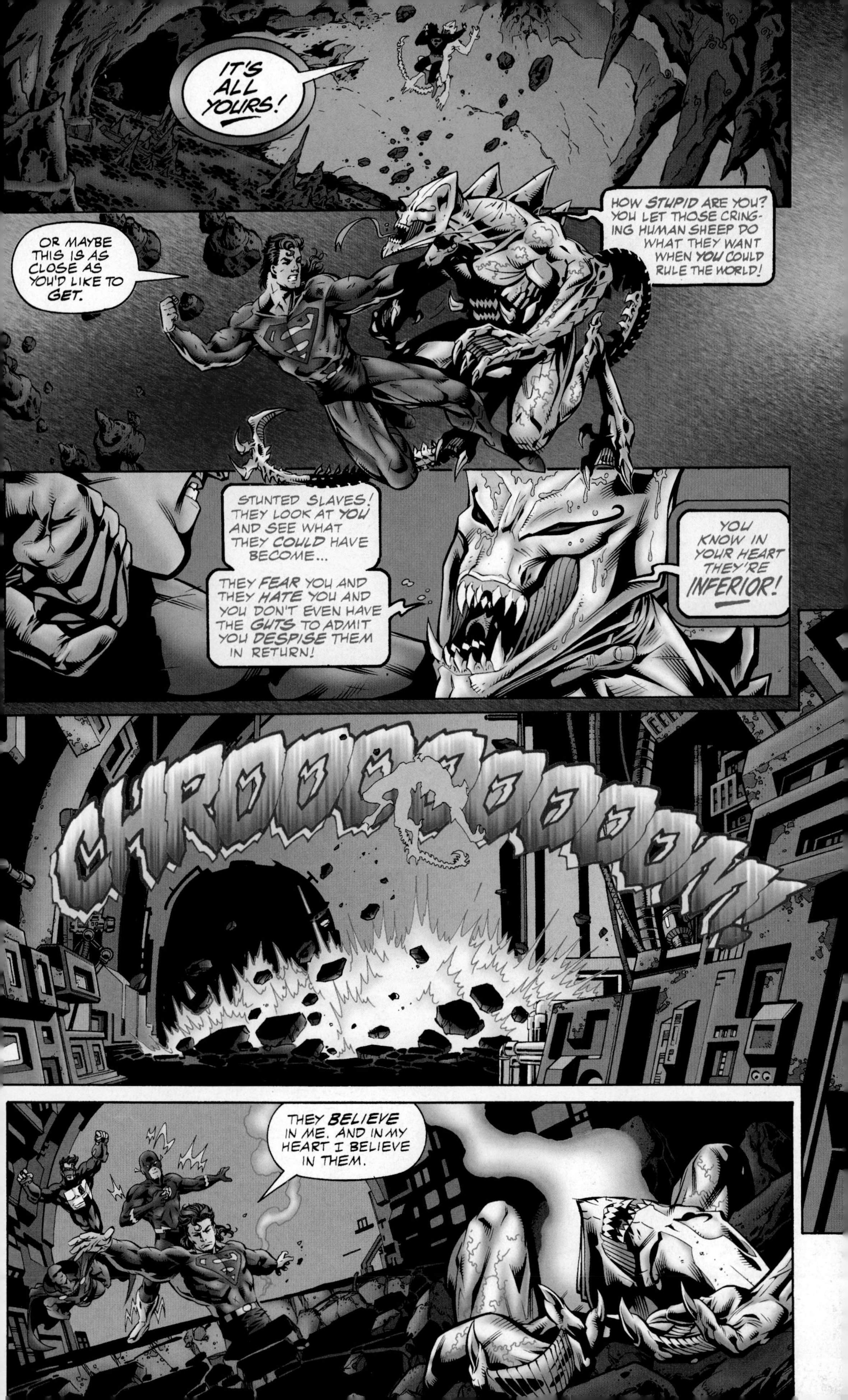
IT'S ALL YOURS!
OR MAYBE THIS IS AS CLOSE AS YOU'D LIKE TO GET.
HOW STUPID ARE YOU? YOU LET THOSE CRING-ING HUMAN SHEEP DO WHAT THEY WANT WHEN YOU COULD RULE THE WORLD!
STUNTED SLAVES! THEY LOOK AT YOU AND SEE WHAT THEY COULD HAVE BECOME...
THEY FEAR YOU AND THEY HATE YOU AND YOU DON'T EVEN HAVE THE GUTS TO ADMIT YOU DESPISE THEM IN RETURN!
YOU KNOW IN YOUR HEART THEY'RE INFERIOR!
CHROOOOOOOM
THEY BELIEVE IN ME. AND IN MY HEART I BELIEVE IN THEM.

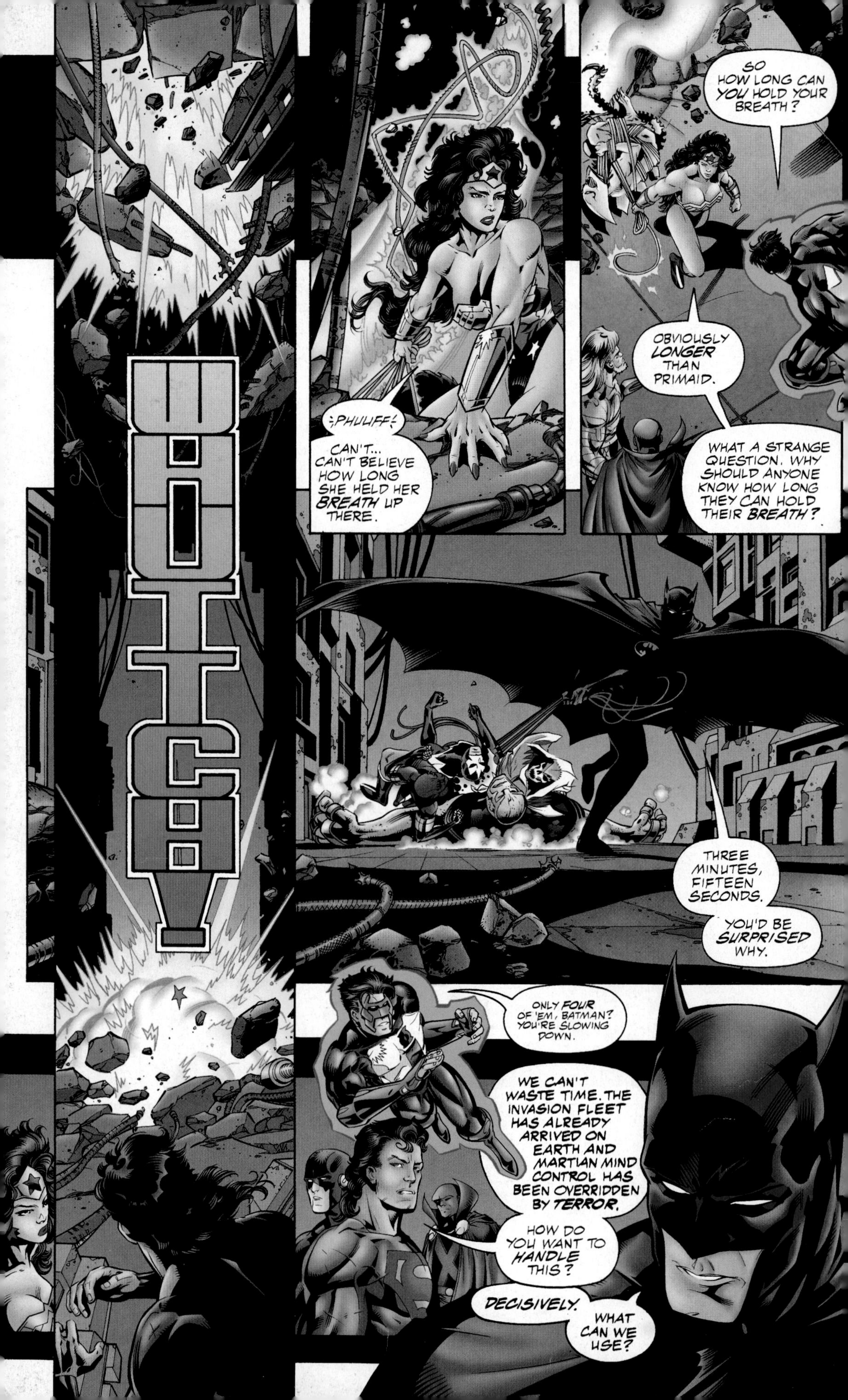
WHUTCHA!
PHUUFF
CAN'T... CAN'T BELIEVE HOW LONG SHE HELD HER BREATH UP THERE.
SO HOW LONG CAN YOU HOLD YOUR BREATH?
OBVIOUSLY LONGER THAN PRIMAID.
WHAT A STRANGE QUESTION. WHY SHOULD ANYONE KNOW HOW LONG THEY CAN HOLD THEIR BREATH?
THREE MINUTES, FIFTEEN SECONDS.
YOU'D BE SURPRISED WHY.
ONLY FOUR OF 'EM, BATMAN? YOU'RE SLOWING DOWN.
WE CAN'T WASTE TIME. THE INVASION FLEET HAS ALREADY ARRIVED ON EARTH AND MARTIAN MIND CONTROL HAS BEEN OVERRIDDEN BY TERROR.
HOW DO YOU WANT TO HANDLE THIS?
DECISIVELY.
WHAT CAN WE USE?

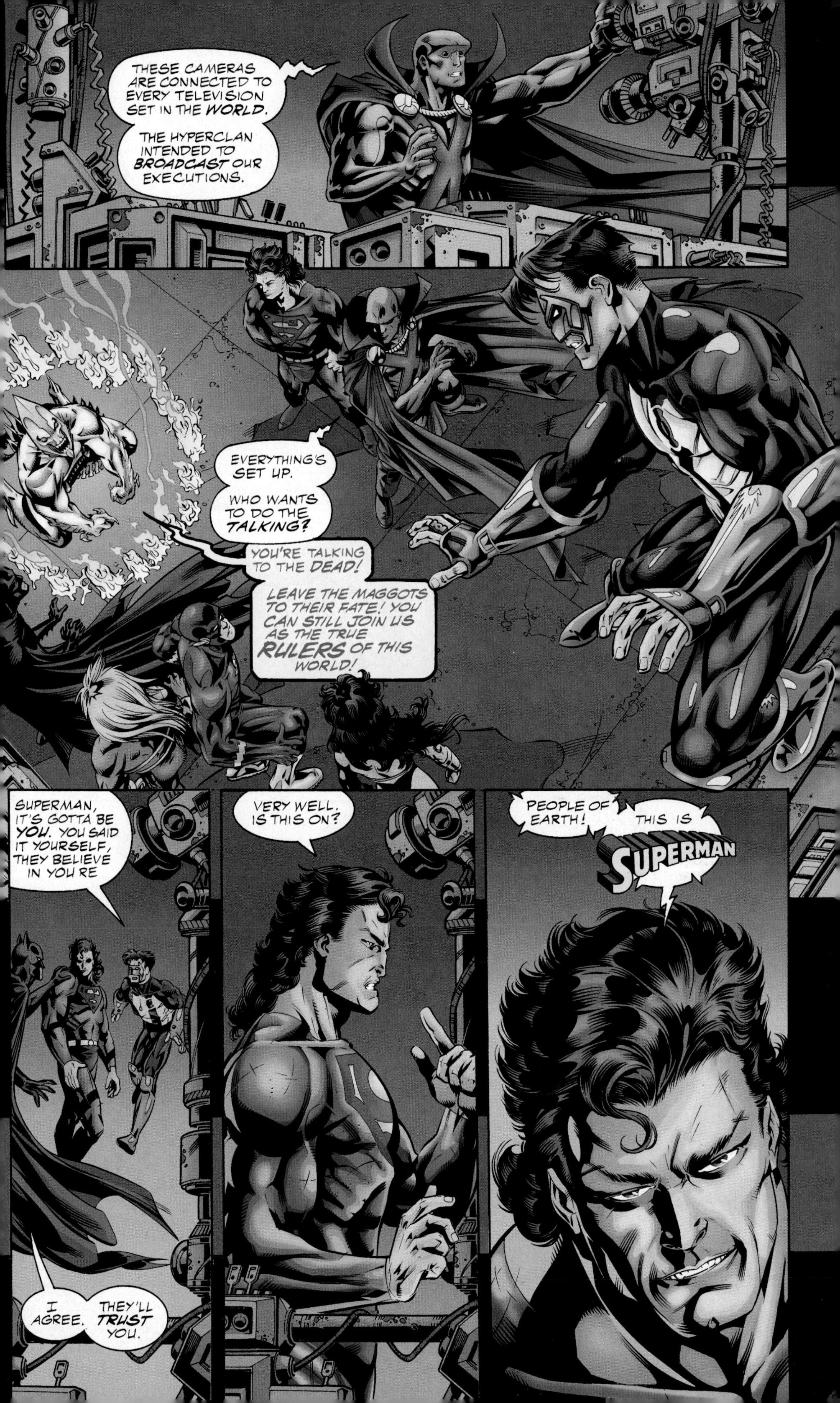

THESE CAMERAS ARE CONNECTED TO EVERY TELEVISION SET IN THE WORLD.
THE HYPERCLAN INTENDED TO BROADCAST OUR EXECUTIONS.
EVERYTHING'S SET UP.
WHO WANTS TO DO THE TALKING?
YOU'RE TALKING TO THE DEAD!
LEAVE THE MAGGOTS TO THEIR FATE! YOU CAN STILL JOIN US AS THE TRUE RULERS OF THIS WORLD!
SUPERMAN, IT'S GOTTA BE YOU. YOU SAID IT YOURSELF, THEY BELIEVE IN YOU RE
I AGREE. THEY'LL TRUST YOU.
VERY WELL. IS THIS ON?
PEOPLE OF EARTH!
THIS IS
SUPERMAN

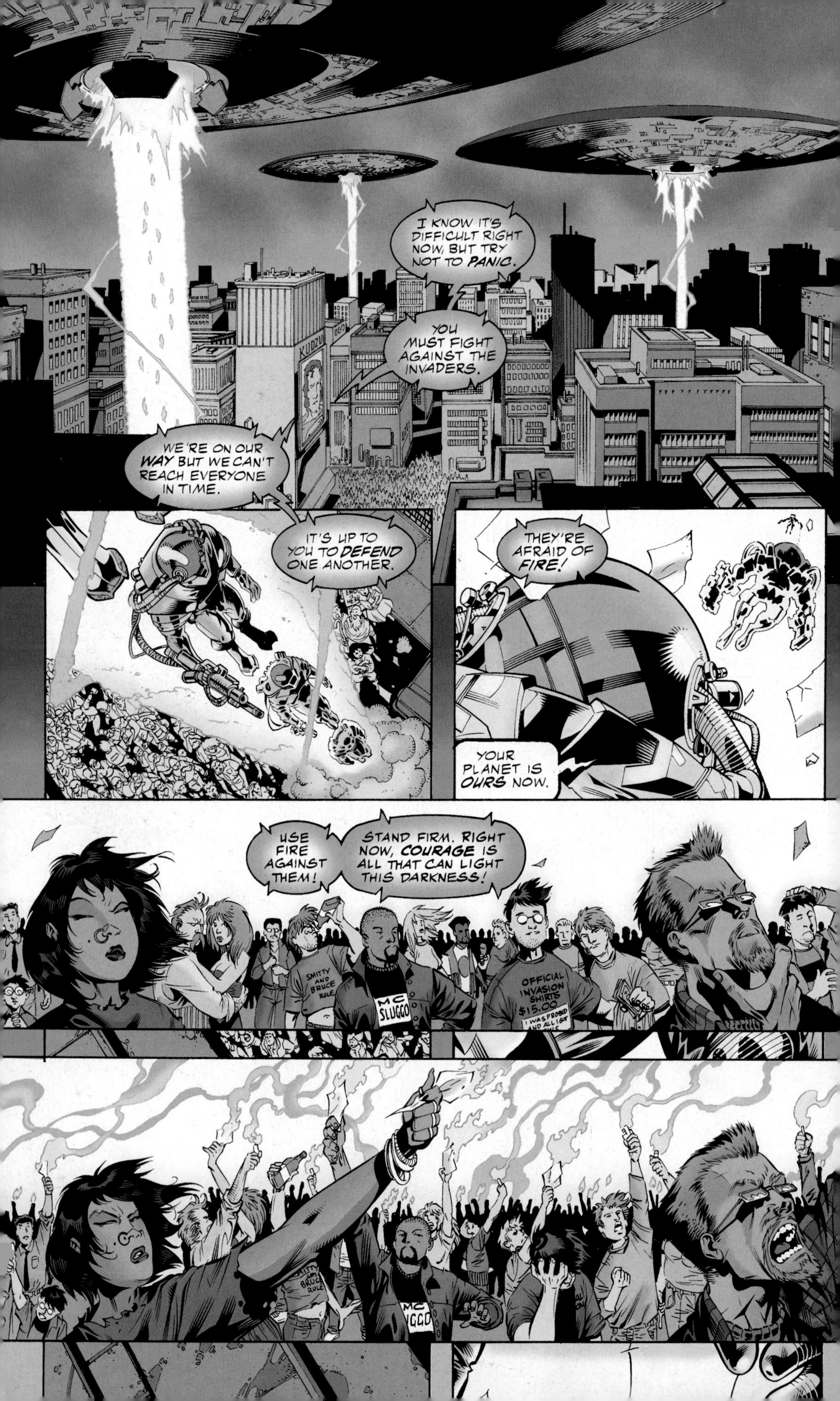

KUDZU
I KNOW IT'S DIFFICULT RIGHT NOW, BUT TRY NOT TO PANIC.
YOU MUST FIGHT AGAINST THE INVADERS.
WE'RE ON OUR WAY BUT WE CAN'T REACH EVERYONE IN TIME.
IT'S UP TO YOU TO DEFEND ONE ANOTHER.
THEY'RE AFRAID OF FIRE!
YOUR PLANET IS OURS NOW.
USE FIRE AGAINST THEM!
STAND FIRM. RIGHT NOW, COURAGE IS ALL THAT CAN LIGHT THIS DARKNESS!
SMITTY AND BRUCE RULE
MC SLUGGO
OFFICIAL INVASION SHIRTS $15.00

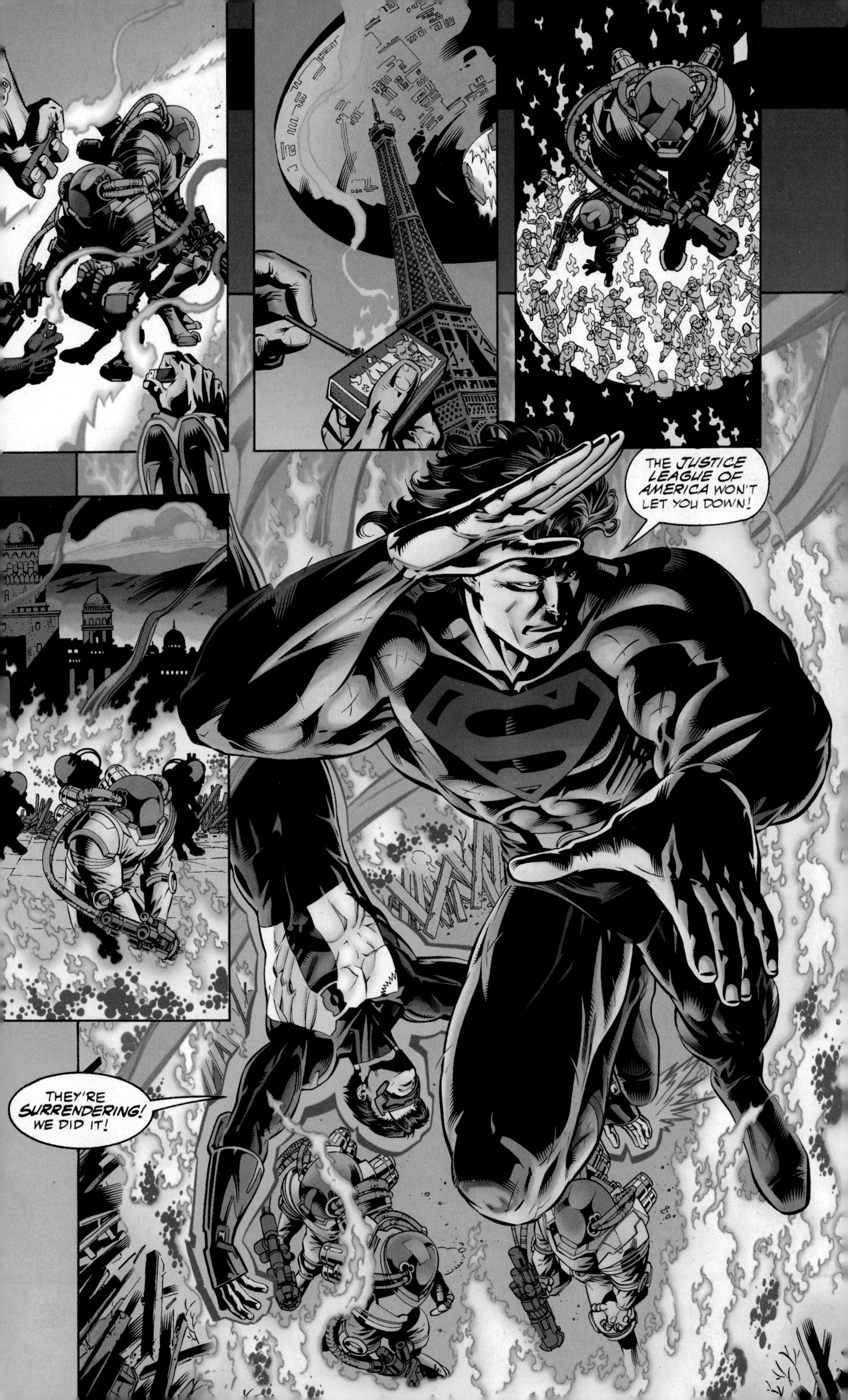
THE JUSTICE LEAGUE OF AMERICA WON'T LET YOU DOWN!
THEY'RE SURRENDERING! WE DID IT!

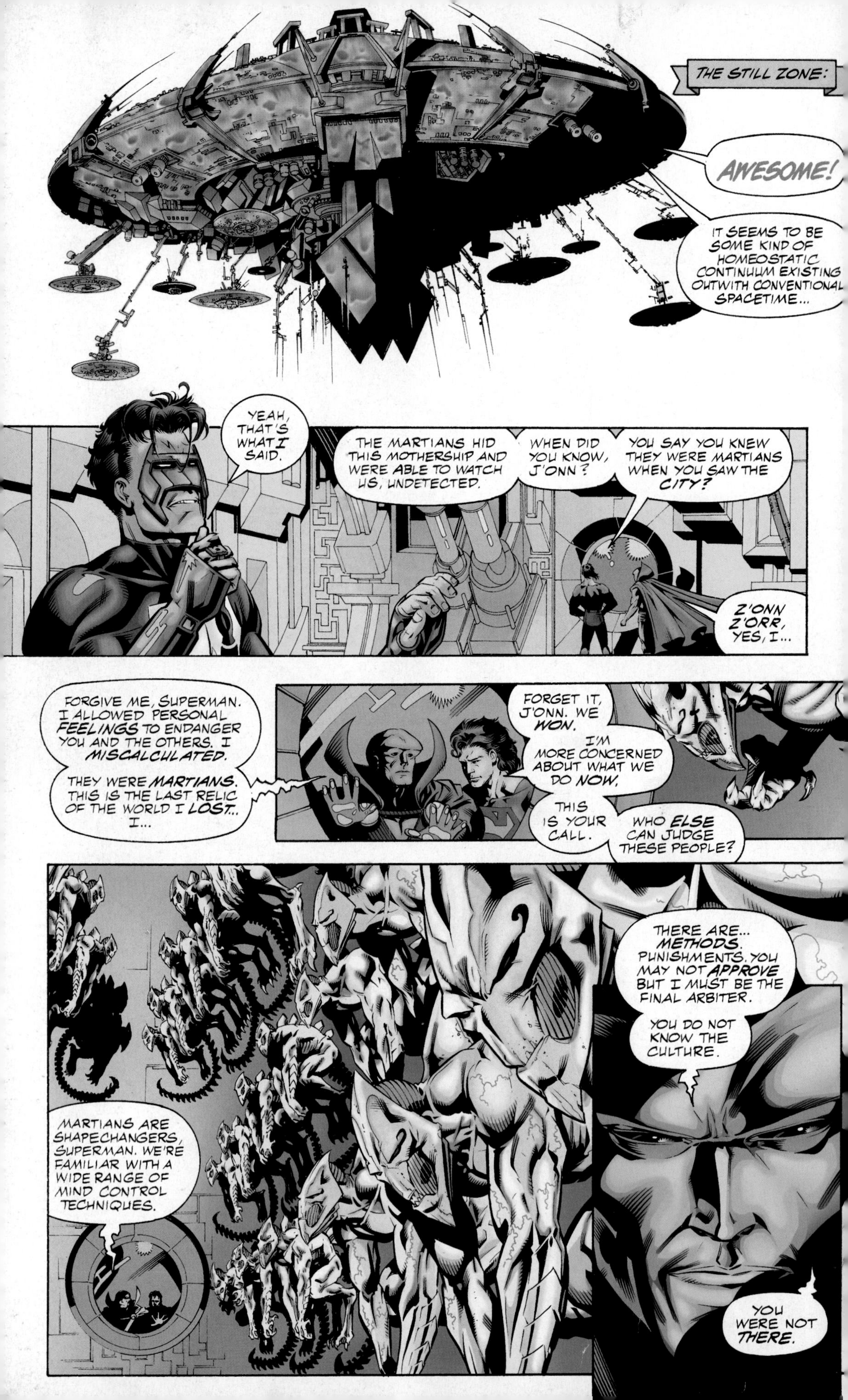
THE STILL ZONE:
AWESOME!
IT SEEMS TO BE SOME KIND OF HOMEOSTATIC CONTINUUM EXISTING OUTWITH CONVENTIONAL SPACETIME...
YEAH, THAT'S WHAT I SAID.
THE MARTIANS HID THIS MOTHERSHIP AND WERE ABLE TO WATCH US, UNDETECTED.
WHEN DID YOU KNOW, J'ONN?
YOU SAY YOU KNEW THEY WERE MARTIANS WHEN YOU SAW THE CITY?
Z'ONN Z'ORR, YES, I...
FORGIVE ME, SUPERMAN. I ALLOWED PERSONAL FEELINGS TO ENDANGER YOU AND THE OTHERS. I MISCALCULATED.
THEY WERE MARTIANS. THIS IS THE LAST RELIC OF THE WORLD I LOST... I...
FORGET IT, J'ONN. WE WON.
I'M MORE CONCERNED ABOUT WHAT WE DO NOW.
THIS IS YOUR CALL.
WHO ELSE CAN JUDGE THESE PEOPLE?
MARTIANS ARE SHAPECHANGERS, SUPERMAN. WE'RE FAMILIAR WITH A WIDE RANGE OF MIND CONTROL TECHNIQUES.
THERE ARE... METHODS. PUNISHMENTS. YOU MAY NOT APPROVE BUT I MUST BE THE FINAL ARBITER.
YOU DO NOT KNOW THE CULTURE.
YOU WERE NOT THERE.

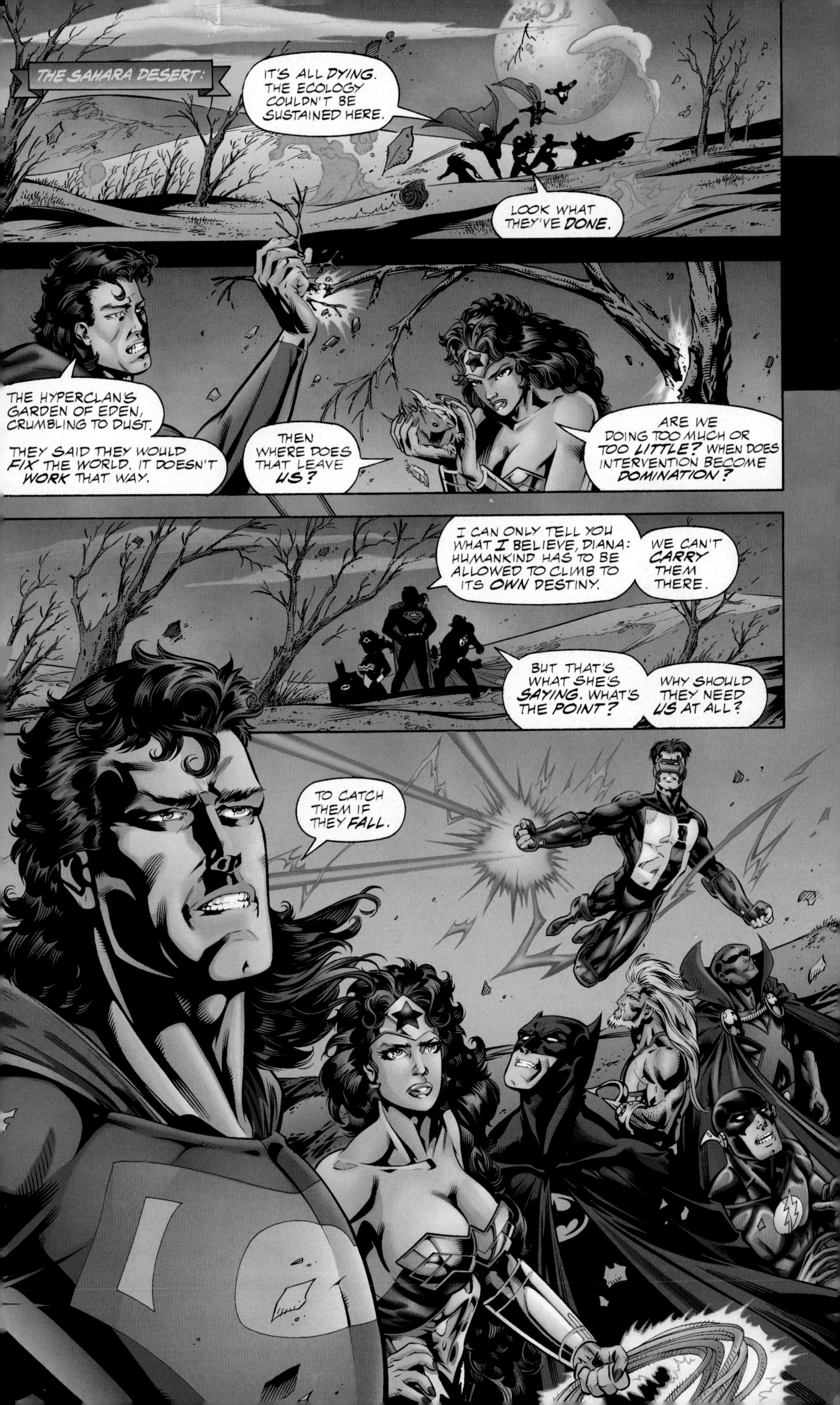
THE SAHARA DESERT:
IT'S ALL DYING. THE ECOLOGY COULDN'T BE SUSTAINED HERE.
LOOK WHAT THEY'VE DONE.
THE HYPERCLAN'S GARDEN OF EDEN, CRUMBLING TO DUST.
THEY SAID THEY WOULD FIX THE WORLD. IT DOESN'T WORK THAT WAY.
THEN WHERE DOES THAT LEAVE US?
ARE WE DOING TOO MUCH OR TOO LITTLE? WHEN DOES INTERVENTION BECOME DOMINATION?
I CAN ONLY TELL YOU WHAT I BELIEVE, DIANA: HUMANKIND HAS TO BE ALLOWED TO CLIMB TO ITS OWN DESTINY.
WE CAN'T CARRY THEM THERE.
BUT THAT'S WHAT SHE'S SAYING. WHAT'S THE POINT?
WHY SHOULD THEY NEED US AT ALL?
TO CATCH THEM IF THEY FALL.

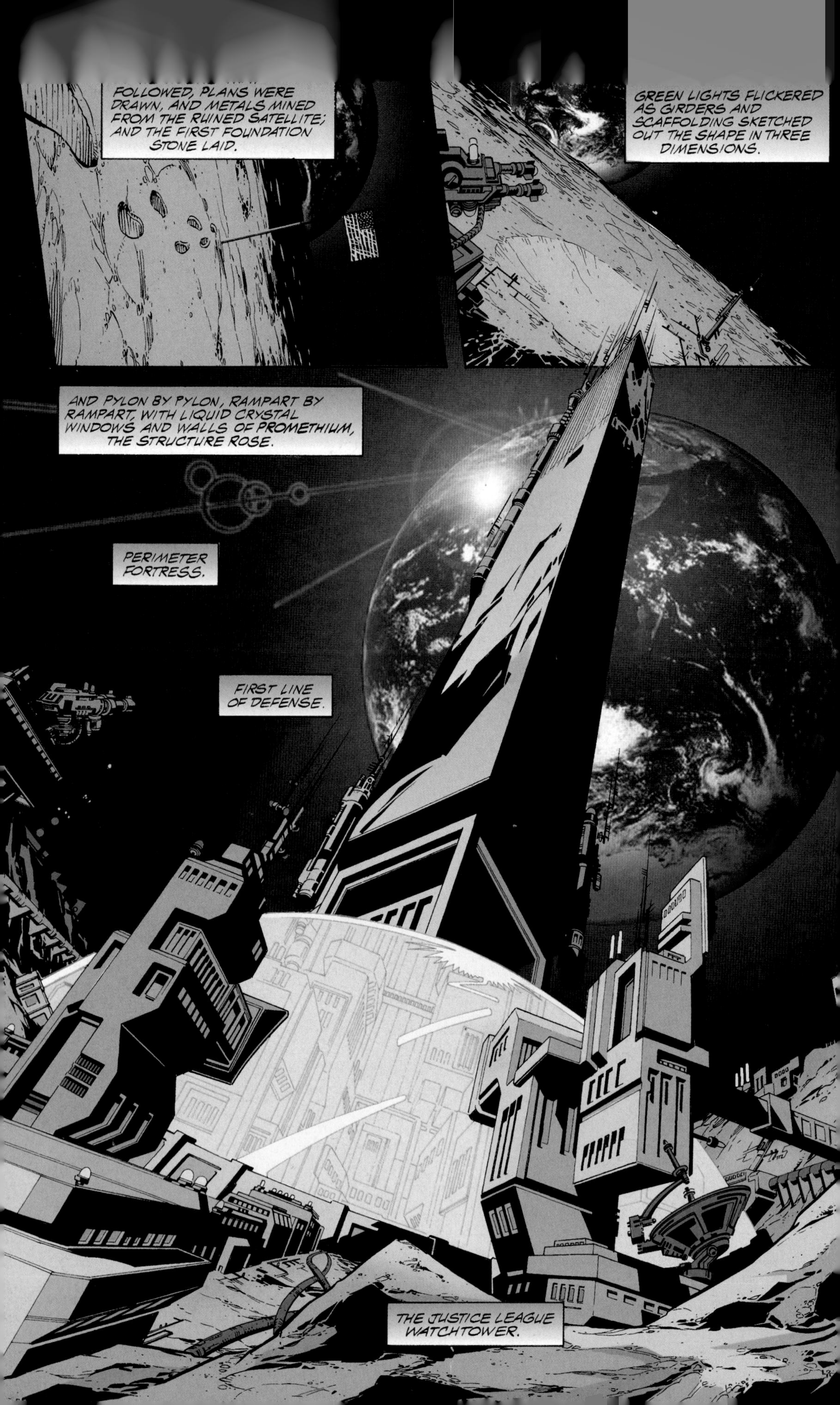
FOLLOWED, PLANS WERE DRAWN, AND METALS MINED FROM THE RUINED SATELLITE; AND THE FIRST FOUNDATION STONE LAID.
GREEN LIGHTS FLICKERED AS GIRDERS AND SCAFFOLDING SKETCHED OUT THE SHAPE IN THREE DIMENSIONS.
AND PYLON BY PYLON, RAMPART BY RAMPART, WITH LIQUID CRYSTAL WINDOWS AND WALLS OF PROMETHIUM, THE STRUCTURE ROSE.
PERIMETER FORTRESS.
FIRST LINE OF DEFENSE.
THE JUSTICE LEAGUE WATCHTOWER.

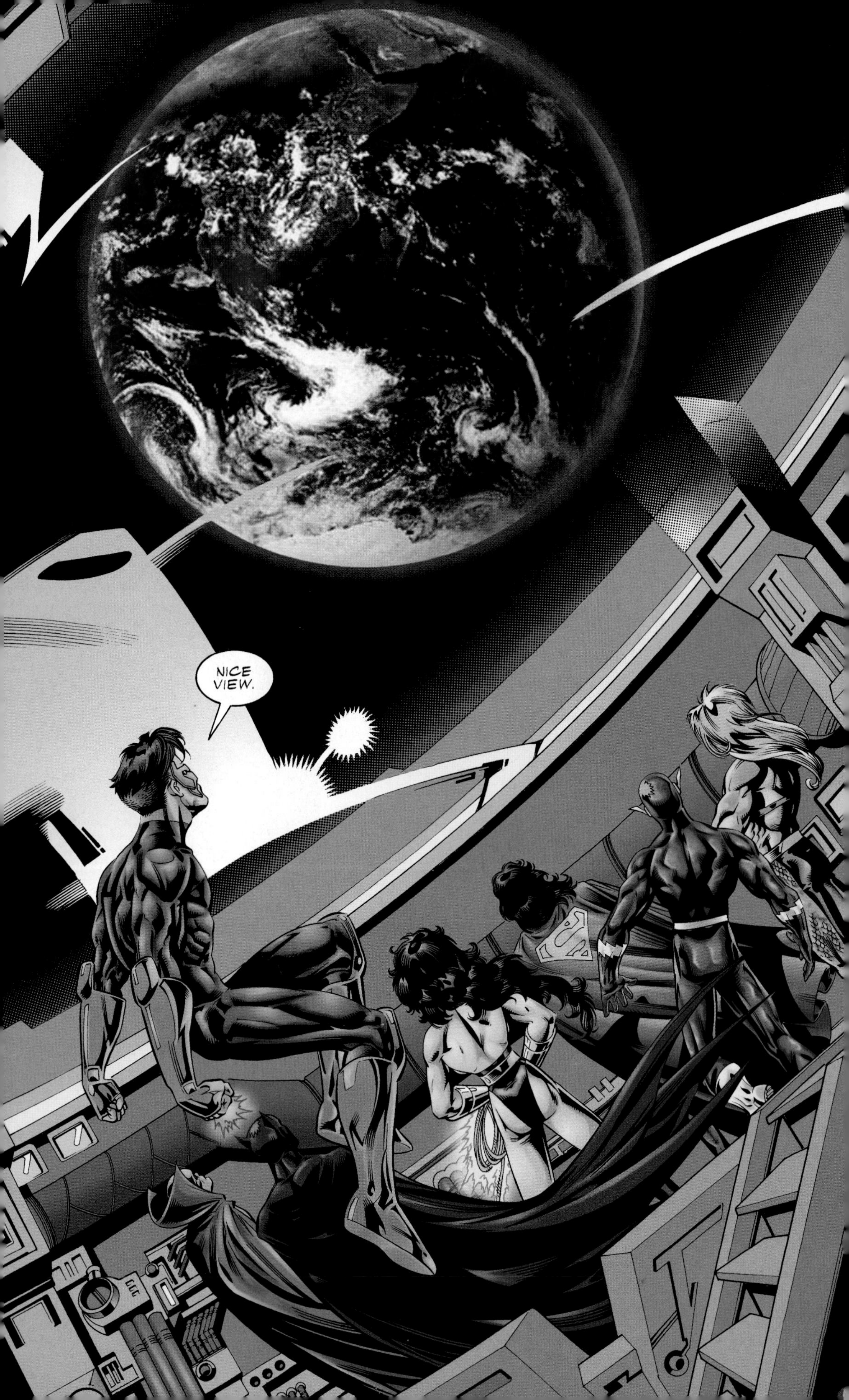
NICE VIEW.

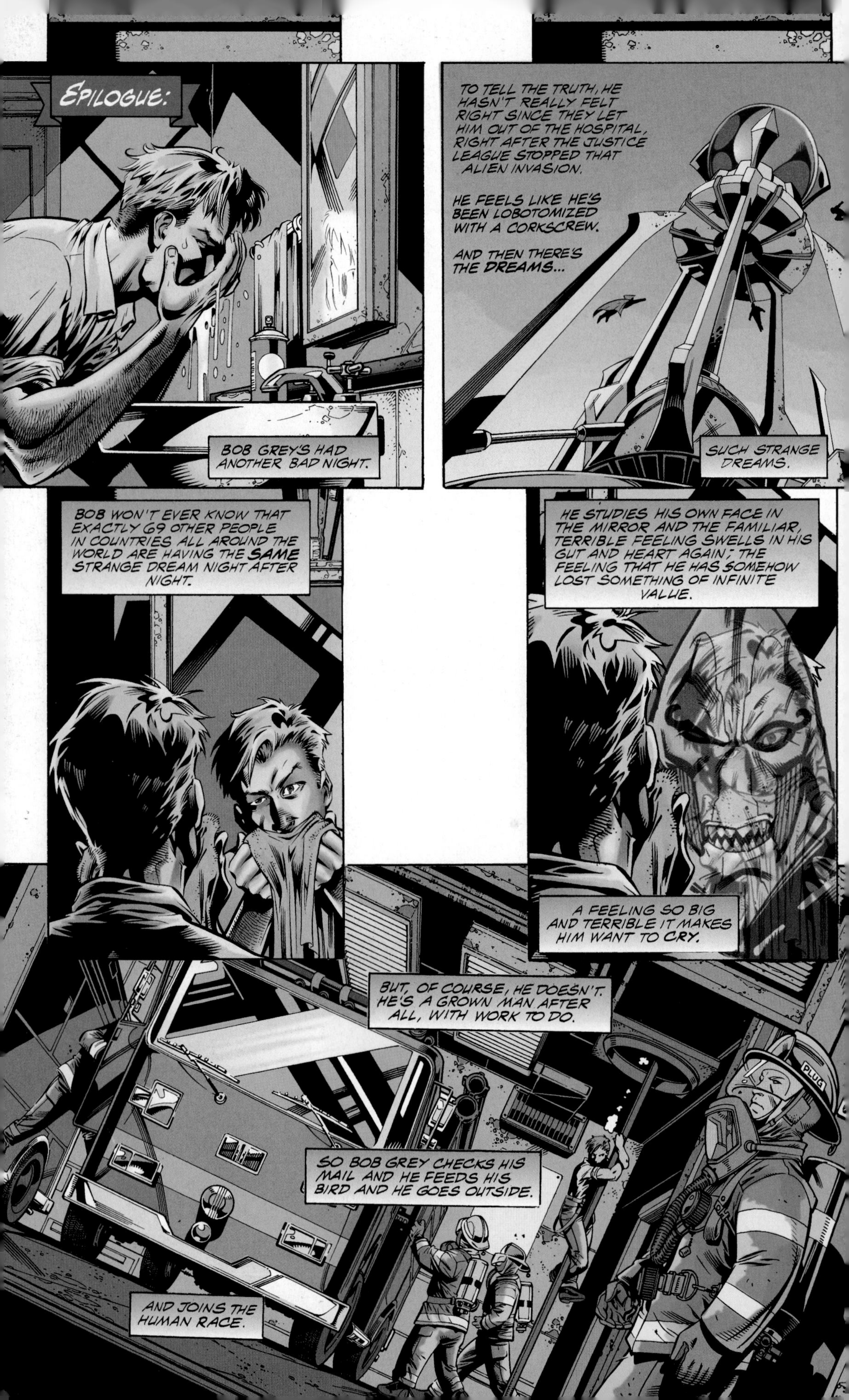
EPILOGUE:
BOB GREY'S HAD ANOTHER BAD NIGHT.
TO TELL THE TRUTH, HE HASN'T REALLY FELT RIGHT SINCE THEY LET HIM OUT OF THE HOSPITAL, RIGHT AFTER THE JUSTICE LEAGUE STOPPED THAT ALIEN INVASION.
HE FEELS LIKE HE'S BEEN LOBOTOMIZED WITH A CORKSCREW.
AND THEN THERE'S THE DREAMS...
SUCH STRANGE DREAMS.
BOB WON'T EVER KNOW THAT EXACTLY 69 OTHER PEOPLE IN COUNTRIES ALL AROUND THE WORLD ARE HAVING THE SAME STRANGE DREAM NIGHT AFTER NIGHT.
HE STUDIES HIS OWN FACE IN THE MIRROR AND THE FAMILIAR, TERRIBLE FEELING SWELLS IN HIS GUT AND HEART AGAIN; THE FEELING THAT HE HAS SOMEHOW LOST SOMETHING OF INFINITE VALUE.
A FEELING SO BIG AND TERRIBLE IT MAKES HIM WANT TO CRY.
BUT, OF COURSE, HE DOESN'T. HE'S A GROWN MAN AFTER ALL, WITH WORK TO DO.
SO BOB GREY CHECKS HIS MAIL AND HE FEEDS HIS BIRD AND HE GOES OUTSIDE.
PLUG
AND JOINS THE HUMAN RACE.

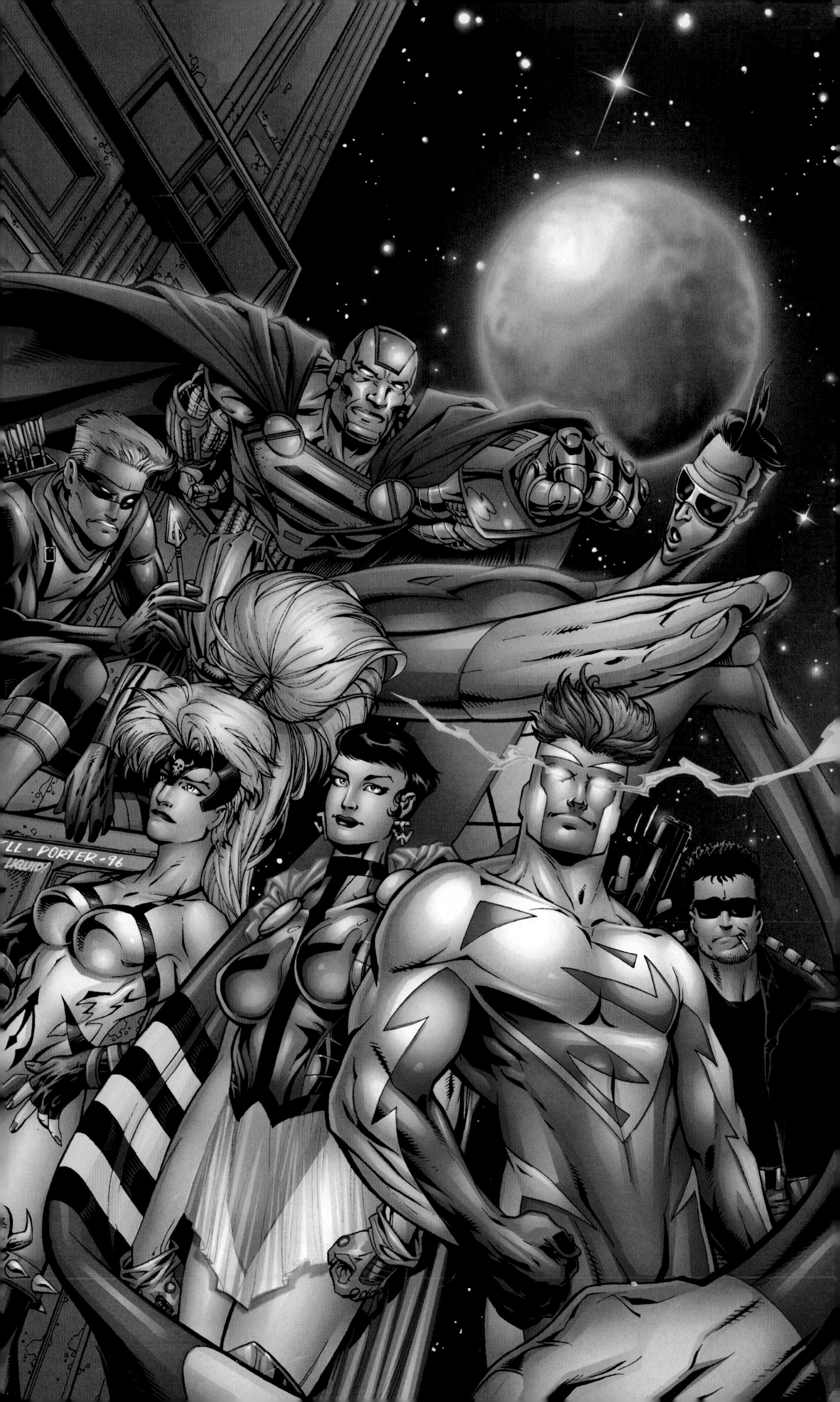
PORTER • 96
LIQUID!

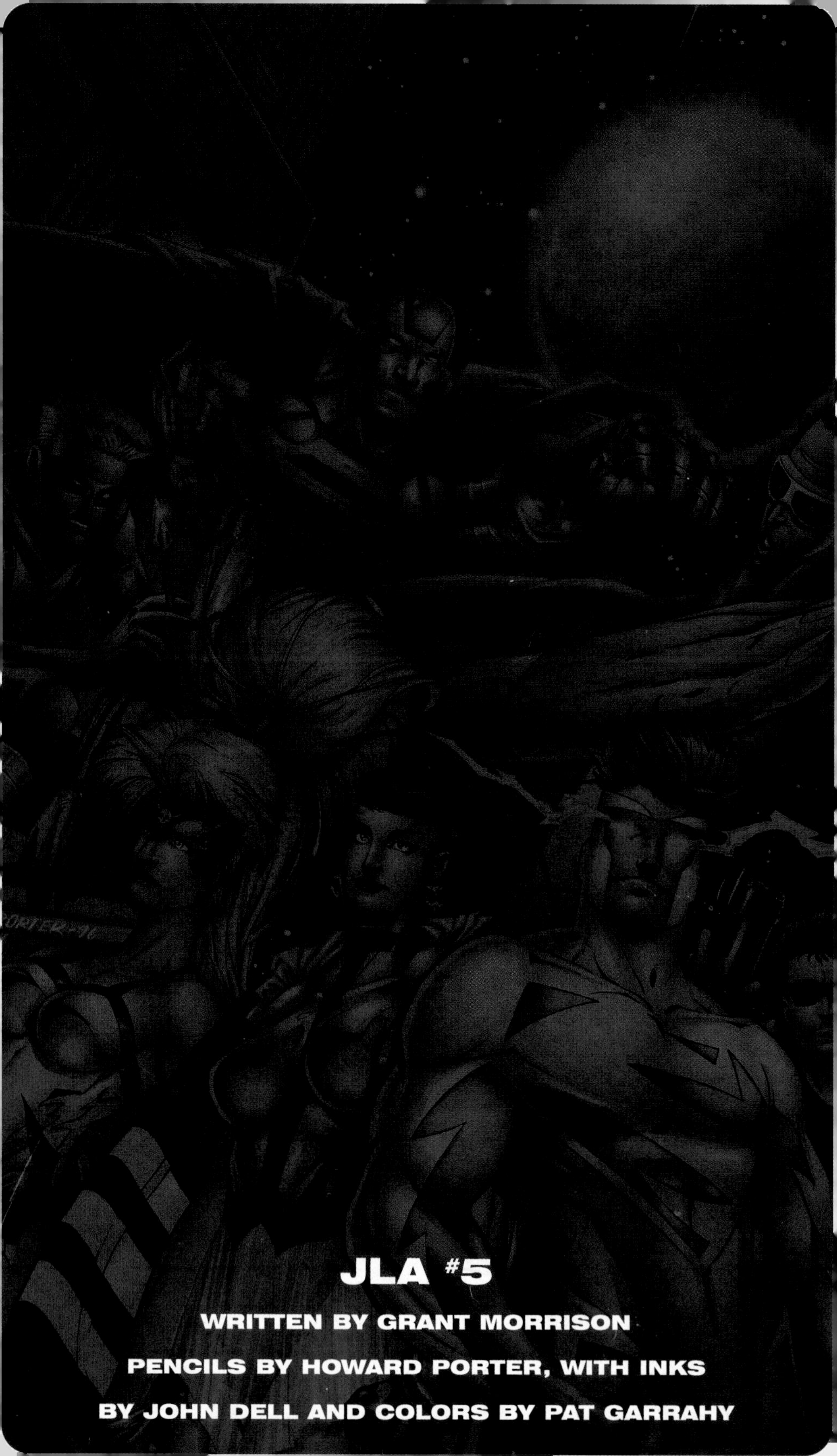

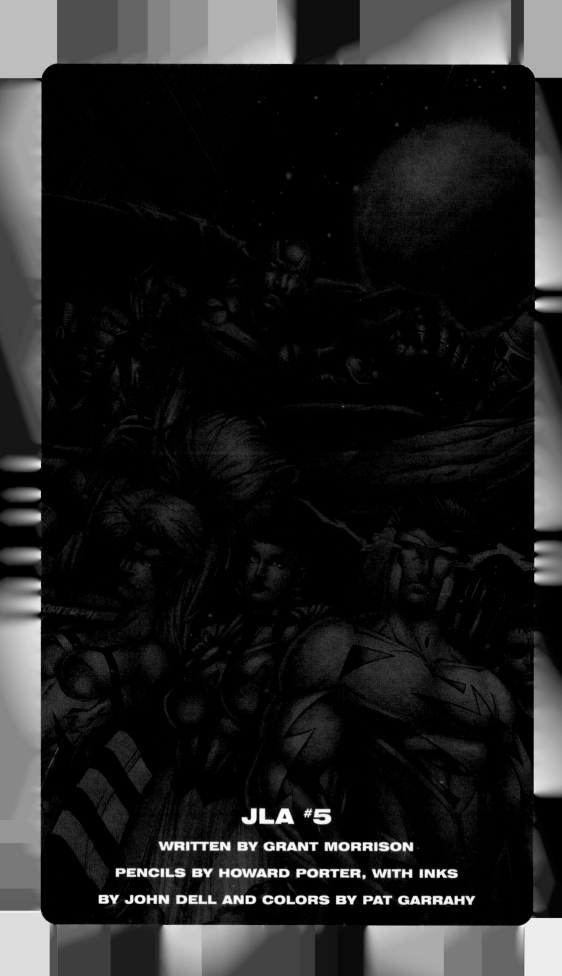

JLA #5

WRITTEN BY GRANT MORRISON

PENCILS BY HOWARD PORTER, WITH INKS

BY JOHN DELL AND COLORS BY PAT GARRAHY

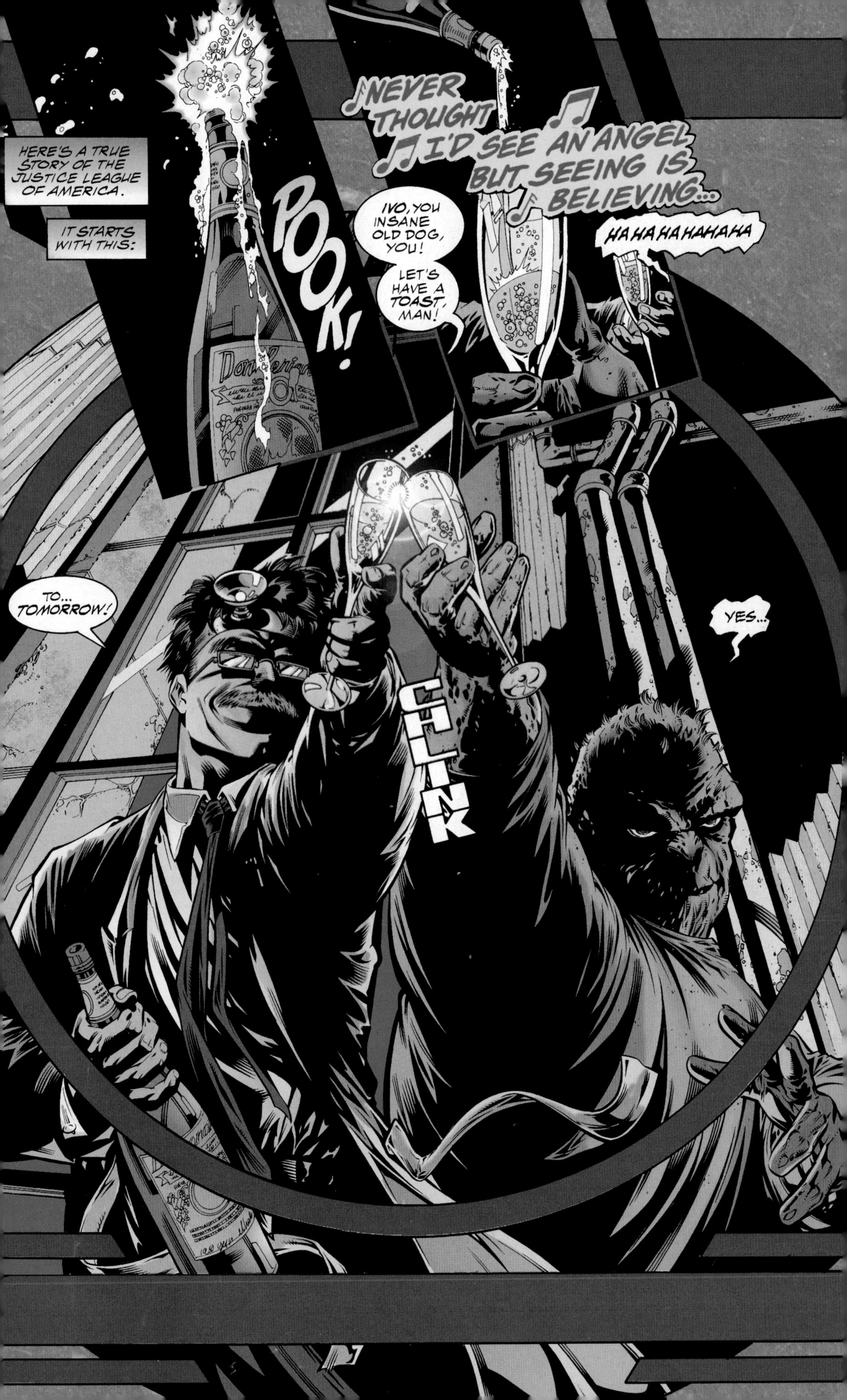
HERE'S A TRUE STORY OF THE JUSTICE LEAGUE OF AMERICA.
IT STARTS WITH THIS:
POOK!
NEVER THOUGHT I'D SEE AN ANGEL BUT SEEING IS BELIEVING...
IVO, YOU INSANE OLD DOG, YOU!
LET'S HAVE A TOAST, MAN!
HA HA HA HAHAHAHA
TO... TOMORROW!
YES...
CHLINK

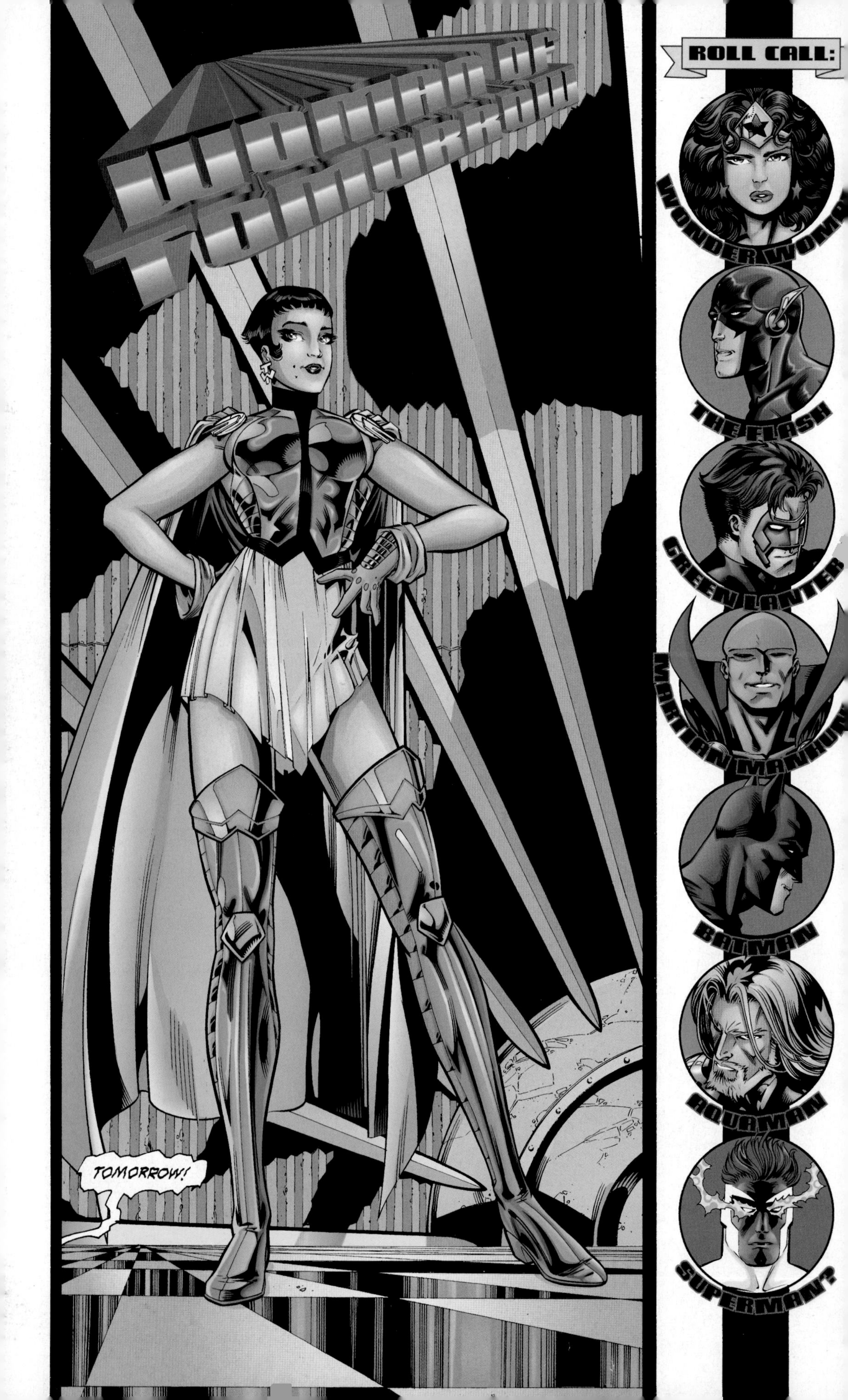

WOMAN OF TOMORROW
TOMORROW!
ROLL CALL:
WONDER WOMA
THE FLASH
GREEN LANTER
MARTIAN MANHUN
BATMAN
AQUAMAN
SUPERMAN?

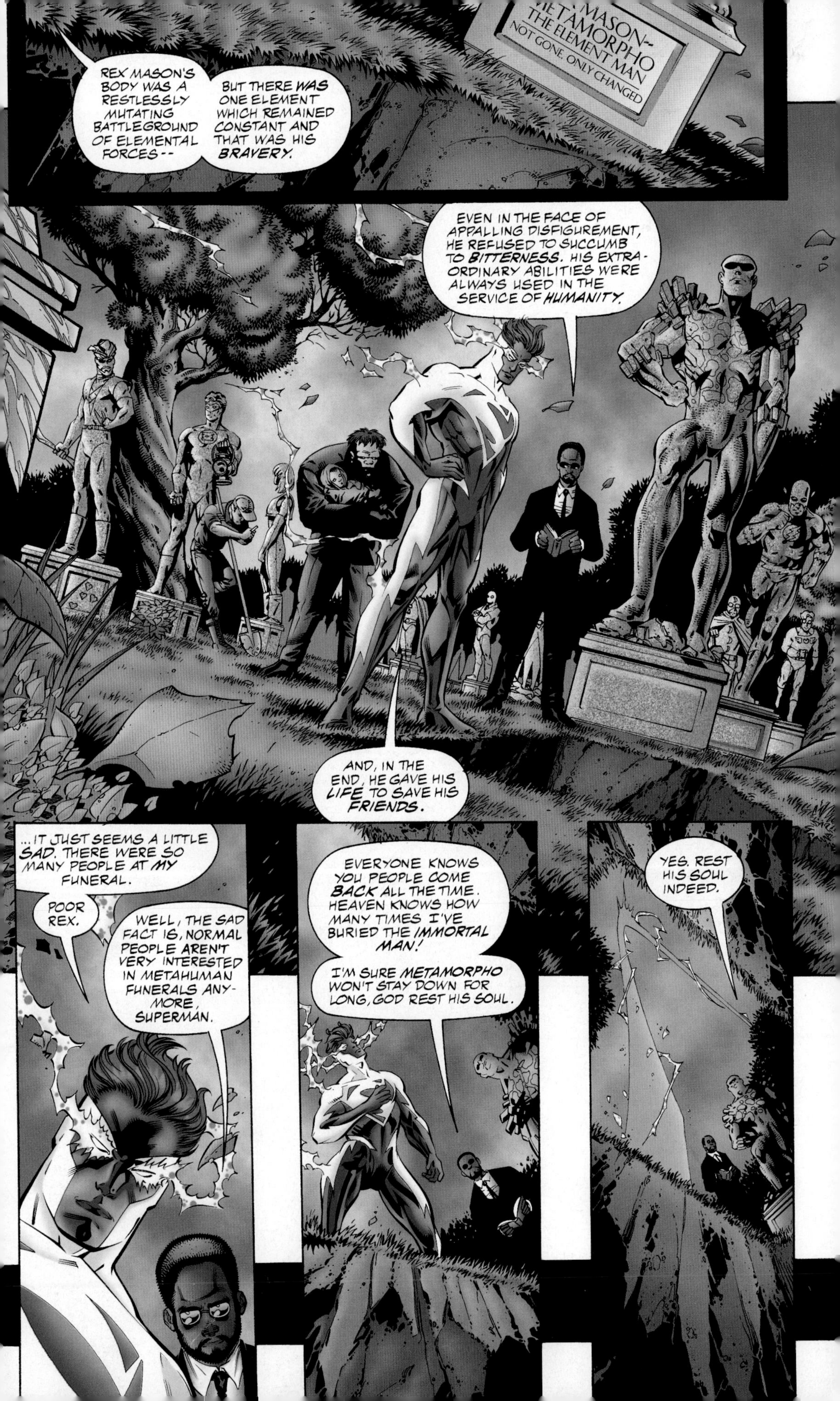
METAMORPHO THE ELEMENT MAN
NOT GONE. ONLY CHANGED
REX MASON'S BODY WAS A RESTLESSLY MUTATING BATTLEGROUND OF ELEMENTAL FORCES--
BUT THERE WAS ONE ELEMENT WHICH REMAINED CONSTANT AND THAT WAS HIS BRAVERY.
EVEN IN THE FACE OF APPALLING DISFIGUREMENT, HE REFUSED TO SUCCUMB TO BITTERNESS. HIS EXTRAORDINARY ABILITIES WERE ALWAYS USED IN THE SERVICE OF HUMANITY.
AND, IN THE END, HE GAVE HIS LIFE TO SAVE HIS FRIENDS.
...IT JUST SEEMS A LITTLE SAD. THERE WERE SO MANY PEOPLE AT MY FUNERAL.
POOR REX.
WELL, THE SAD FACT IS, NORMAL PEOPLE AREN'T VERY INTERESTED IN METAHUMAN FUNERALS ANYMORE, SUPERMAN.
EVERYONE KNOWS YOU PEOPLE COME BACK ALL THE TIME. HEAVEN KNOWS HOW MANY TIMES I'VE BURIED THE IMMORTAL MAN!
I'M SURE METAMORPHO WON'T STAY DOWN FOR LONG, GOD REST HIS SOUL.
YES. REST HIS SOUL INDEED.

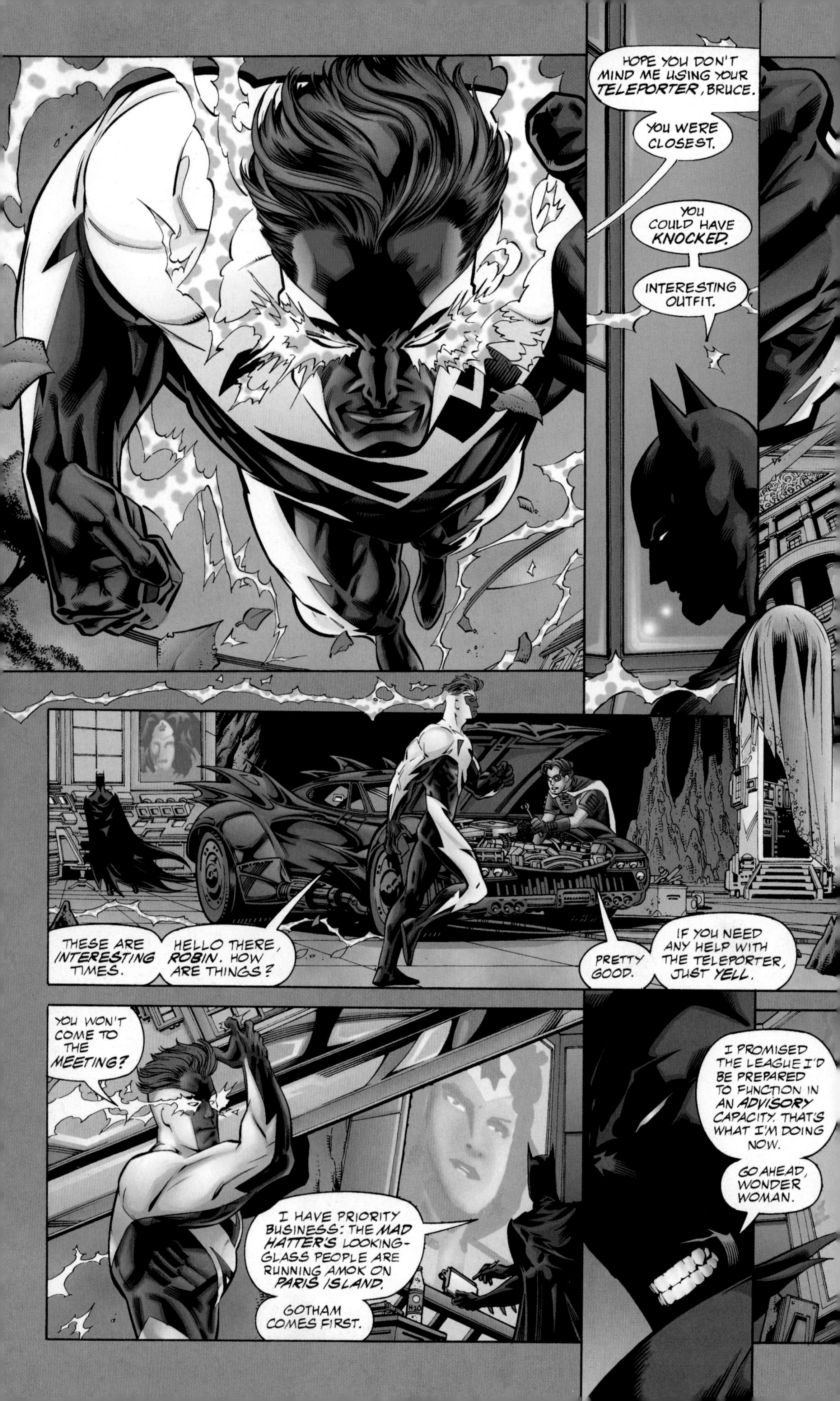
HOPE YOU DON'T MIND ME USING YOUR TELEPORTER, BRUCE.
YOU WERE CLOSEST.
YOU COULD HAVE KNOCKED.
INTERESTING OUTFIT.
THESE ARE INTERESTING TIMES.
HELLO THERE, ROBIN. HOW ARE THINGS?
PRETTY GOOD.
IF YOU NEED ANY HELP WITH THE TELEPORTER, JUST YELL.
YOU WON'T COME TO THE MEETING?
I HAVE PRIORITY BUSINESS: THE MAD HATTER'S LOOKING-GLASS PEOPLE ARE RUNNING AMOK ON PARIS ISLAND.
GOTHAM COMES FIRST.
I PROMISED THE LEAGUE I'D BE PREPARED TO FUNCTION IN AN ADVISORY CAPACITY. THAT'S WHAT I'M DOING NOW.
GO AHEAD, WONDER WOMAN.

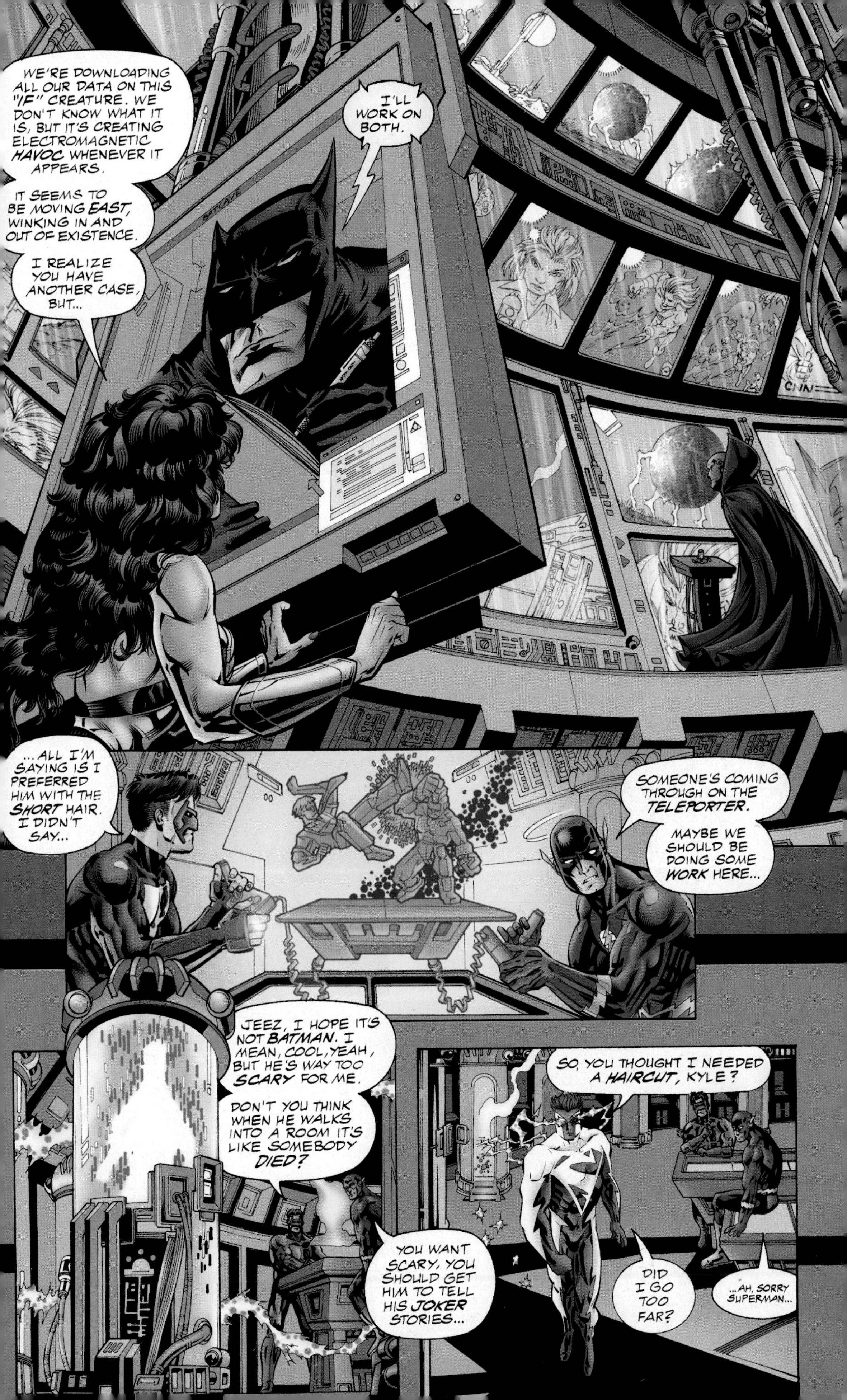
WE'RE DOWNLOADING ALL OUR DATA ON THIS "IF" CREATURE. WE DON'T KNOW WHAT IT IS, BUT IT'S CREATING ELECTROMAGNETIC HAVOC WHENEVER IT APPEARS.
IT SEEMS TO BE MOVING EAST, WINKING IN AND OUT OF EXISTENCE.
I REALIZE YOU HAVE ANOTHER CASE, BUT...
I'LL WORK ON BOTH.
BATCAVE
CNN
...ALL I'M SAYING IS I PREFERRED HIM WITH THE SHORT HAIR. I DIDN'T SAY...
SOMEONE'S COMING THROUGH ON THE TELEPORTER.
MAYBE WE SHOULD BE DOING SOME WORK HERE...
JEEZ, I HOPE IT'S NOT BATMAN. I MEAN, COOL, YEAH, BUT HE'S WAY TOO SCARY FOR ME.
DON'T YOU THINK WHEN HE WALKS INTO A ROOM IT'S LIKE SOMEBODY DIED?
YOU WANT SCARY, YOU SHOULD GET HIM TO TELL HIS JOKER STORIES...
SO, YOU THOUGHT I NEEDED A HAIRCUT, KYLE?
DID I GO TOO FAR?
...AH, SORRY SUPERMAN...

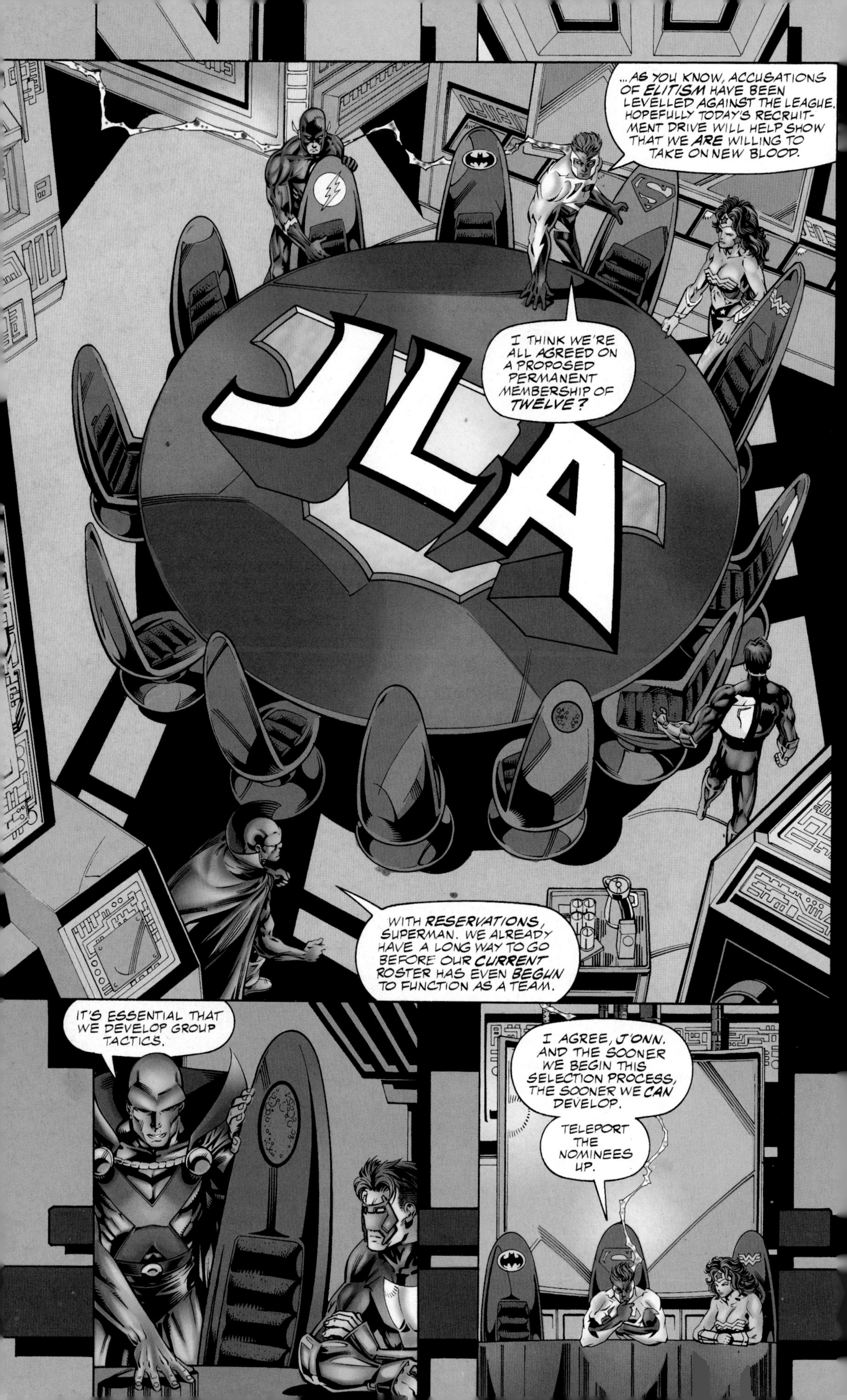
...AS YOU KNOW, ACCUSATIONS OF ELITISM HAVE BEEN LEVELLED AGAINST THE LEAGUE. HOPEFULLY TODAY'S RECRUIT-MENT DRIVE WILL HELP SHOW THAT WE ARE WILLING TO TAKE ON NEW BLOOD.
I THINK WE'RE ALL AGREED ON A PROPOSED PERMANENT MEMBERSHIP OF TWELVE?
JLA
WITH RESERVATIONS, SUPERMAN. WE ALREADY HAVE A LONG WAY TO GO BEFORE OUR CURRENT ROSTER HAS EVEN BEGUN TO FUNCTION AS A TEAM.
IT'S ESSENTIAL THAT WE DEVELOP GROUP TACTICS.
I AGREE, J'ONN. AND THE SOONER WE BEGIN THIS SELECTION PROCESS, THE SOONER WE CAN DEVELOP.
TELEPORT THE NOMINEES UP.

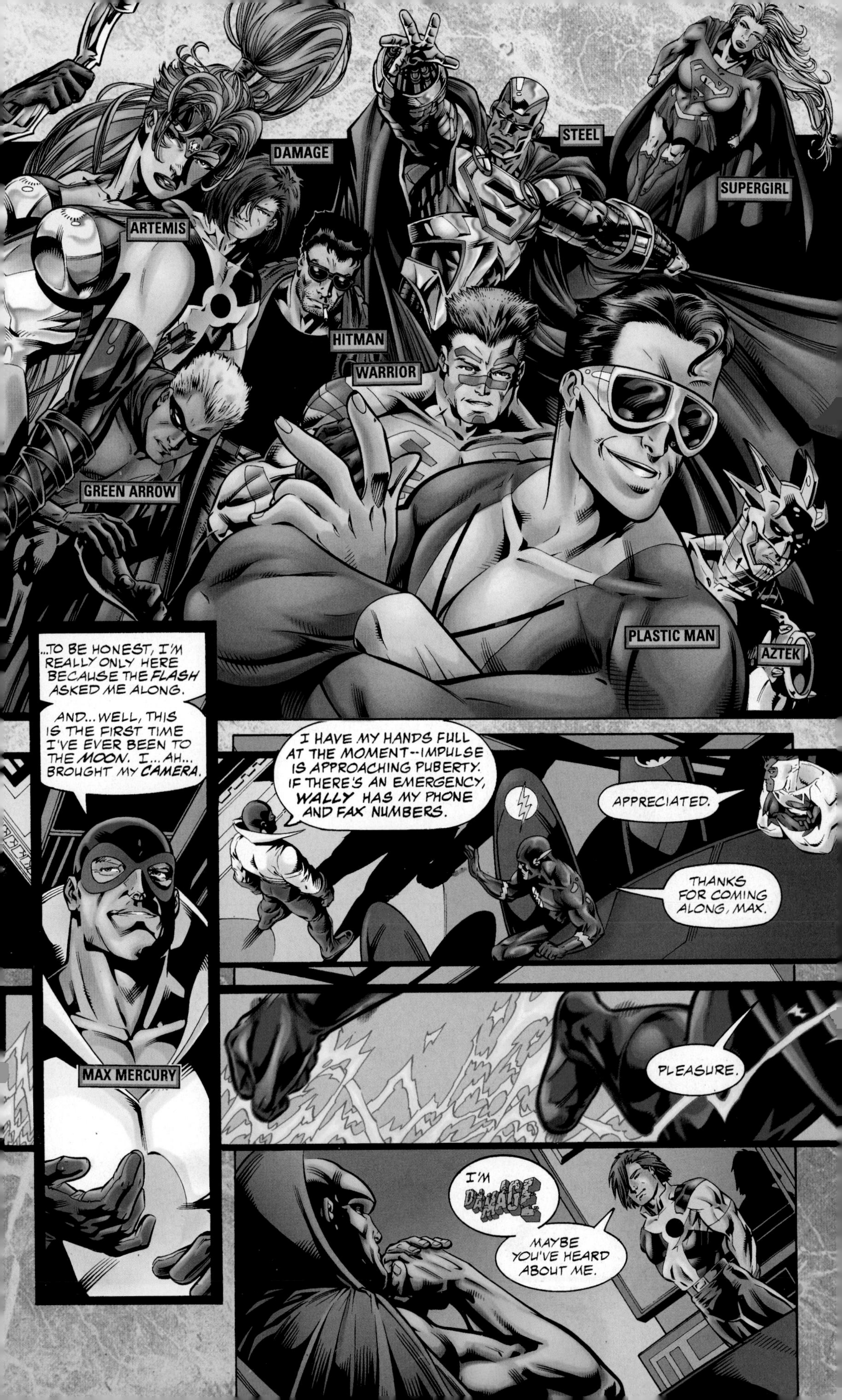
DAMAGE
STEEL
SUPERGIRL
ARTEMIS
HITMAN
WARRIOR
GREEN ARROW
PLASTIC MAN
AZTEK
...TO BE HONEST, I'M REALLY ONLY HERE BECAUSE THE *FLASH* ASKED ME ALONG.
AND... WELL, THIS IS THE FIRST TIME I'VE EVER BEEN TO THE *MOON*. I... AH... BROUGHT MY *CAMERA*.
MAX MERCURY
I HAVE MY HANDS FULL AT THE MOMENT--IMPULSE IS APPROACHING PUBERTY. IF THERE'S AN EMERGENCY, **WALLY** HAS MY PHONE AND FAX NUMBERS.
APPRECIATED.
THANKS FOR COMING ALONG, MAX.
PLEASURE.
I'M DAMAGE.
MAYBE YOU'VE HEARD ABOUT ME.

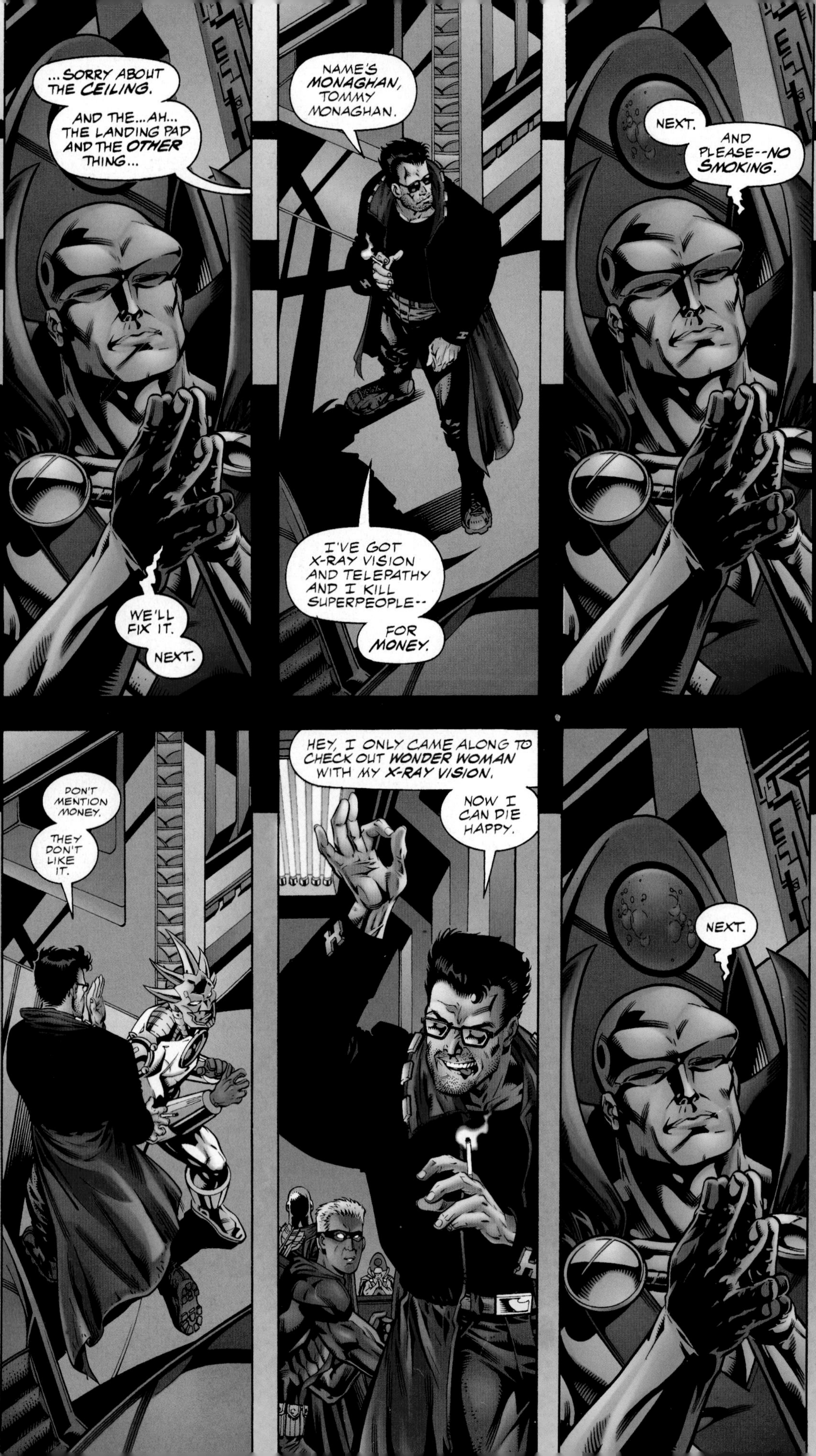
...SORRY ABOUT THE CEILING.
AND THE...AH... THE LANDING PAD AND THE OTHER THING...
WE'LL FIX IT.
NEXT.
NAME'S MONAGHAN, TOMMY MONAGHAN.
I'VE GOT X-RAY VISION AND TELEPATHY AND I KILL SUPERPEOPLE--
FOR MONEY.
NEXT.
AND PLEASE--NO SMOKING.
DON'T MENTION MONEY.
THEY DON'T LIKE IT.
HEY, I ONLY CAME ALONG TO CHECK OUT WONDER WOMAN WITH MY X-RAY VISION.
NOW I CAN DIE HAPPY.
NEXT.

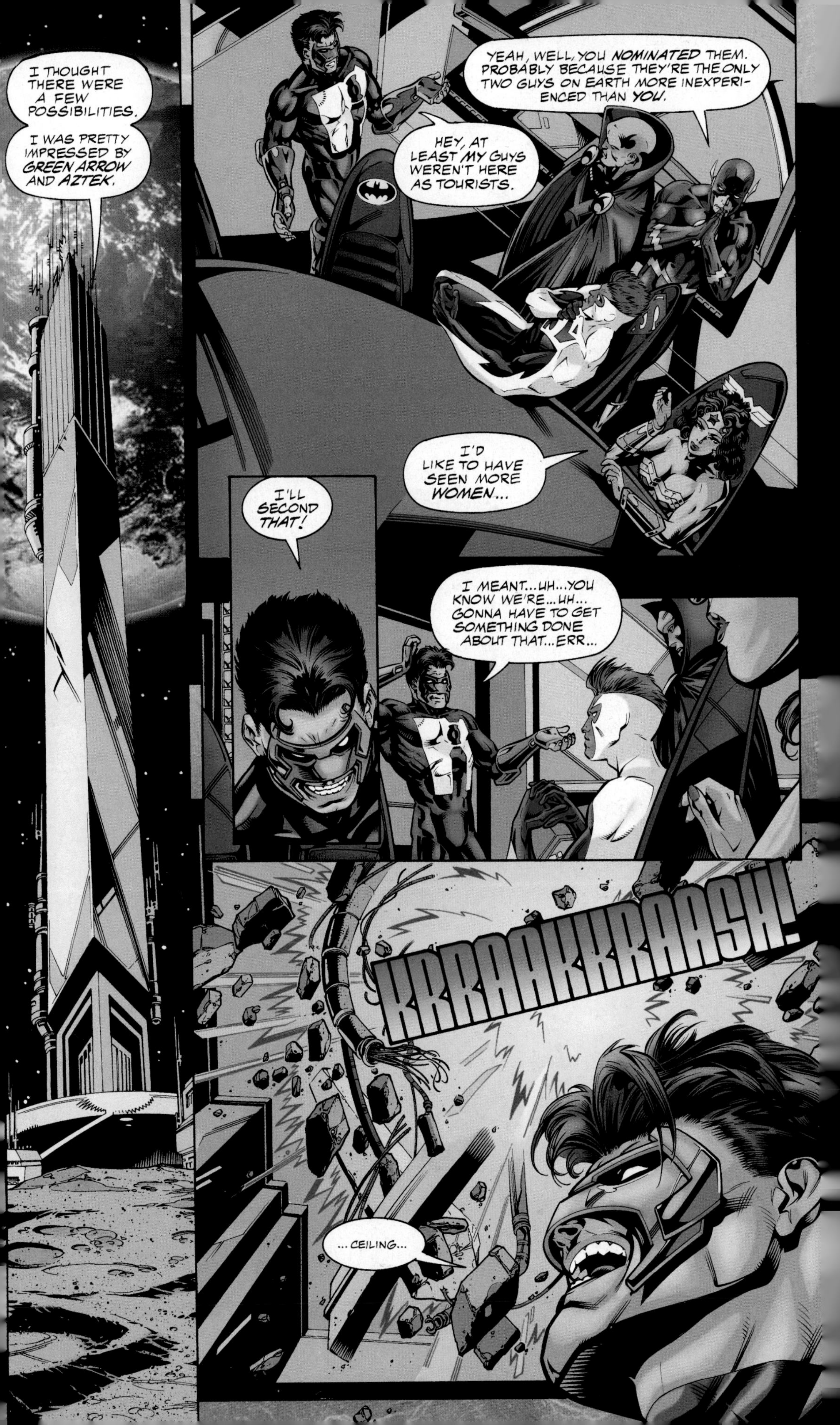
I THOUGHT THERE WERE A FEW POSSIBILITIES.
I WAS PRETTY IMPRESSED BY GREEN ARROW AND AZTEK.
YEAH, WELL, YOU NOMINATED THEM. PROBABLY BECAUSE THEY'RE THE ONLY TWO GUYS ON EARTH MORE INEXPERIENCED THAN YOU.
HEY, AT LEAST MY GUYS WEREN'T HERE AS TOURISTS.
I'D LIKE TO HAVE SEEN MORE WOMEN...
I'LL SECOND THAT!
I MEANT...UH...YOU KNOW WE'RE...UH... GONNA HAVE TO GET SOMETHING DONE ABOUT THAT...ERR...
KRRAAKKRAASH!
...CEILING...

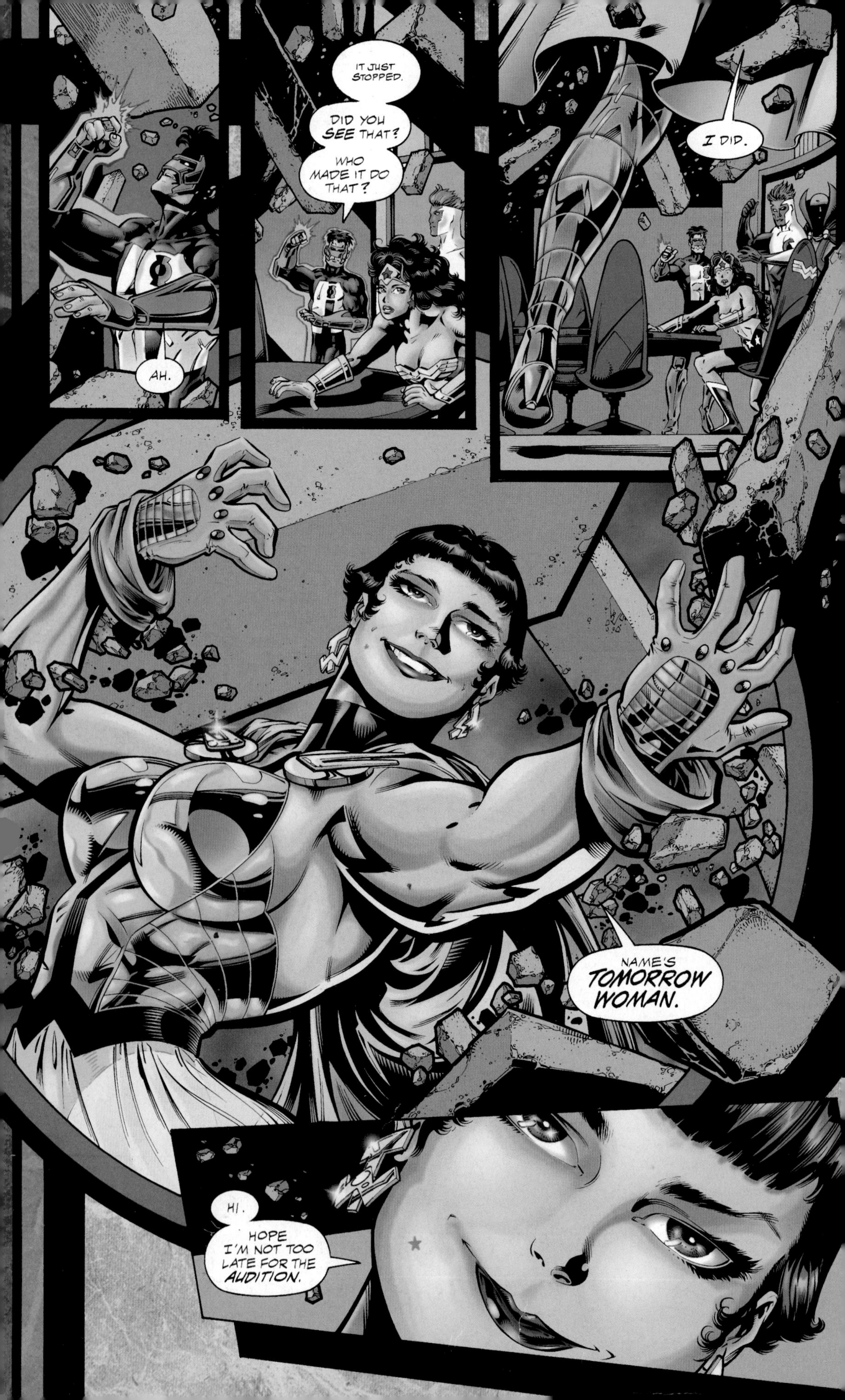
AH.
IT JUST STOPPED.
DID YOU SEE THAT?
WHO MADE IT DO THAT?
I DID.
NAME'S TOMORROW WOMAN.
HI.
HOPE I'M NOT TOO LATE FOR THE AUDITION.

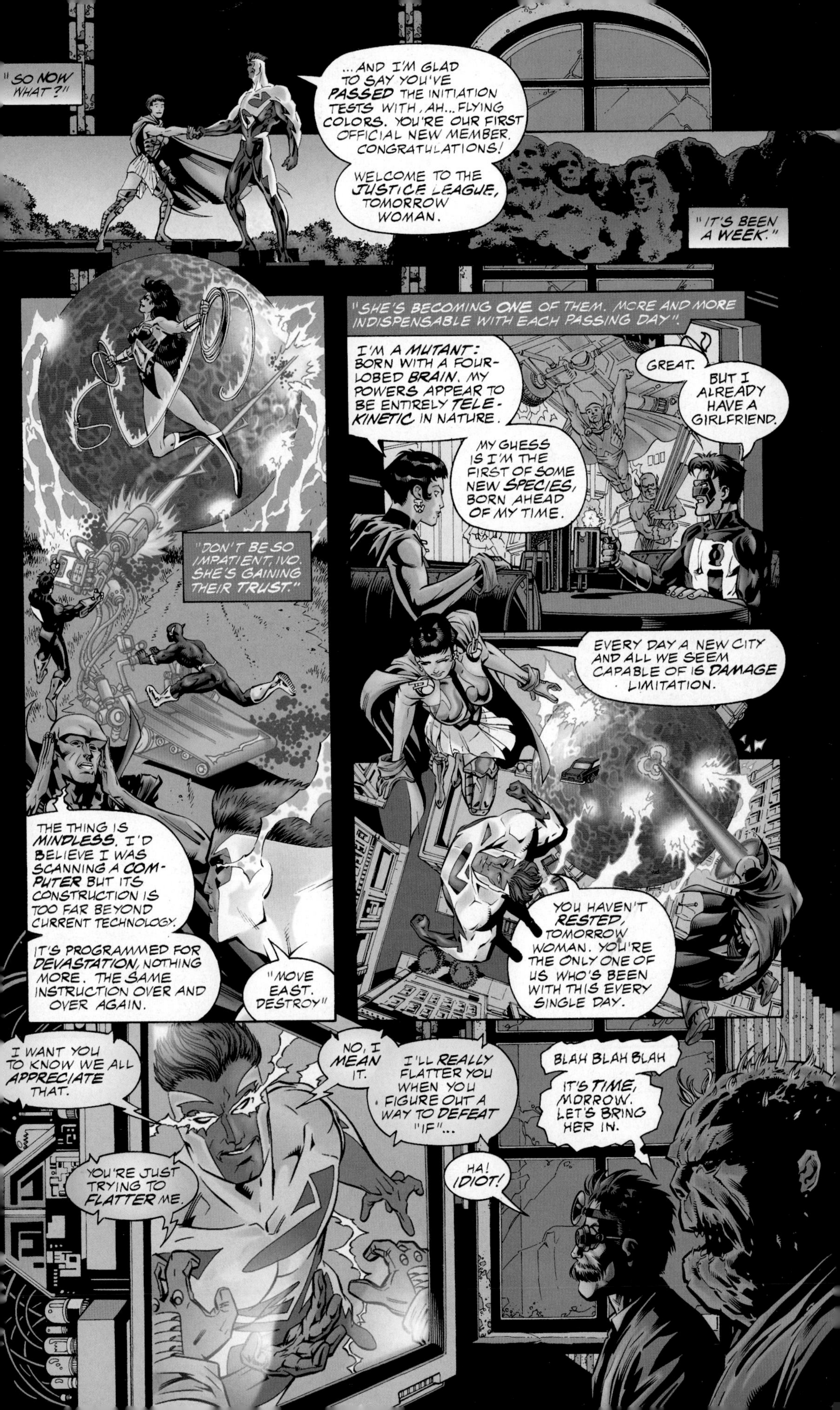

"SO NOW WHAT?"
...AND I'M GLAD TO SAY YOU'VE PASSED THE INITIATION TESTS WITH, AH... FLYING COLORS. YOU'RE OUR FIRST OFFICIAL NEW MEMBER. CONGRATULATIONS!
WELCOME TO THE JUSTICE LEAGUE, TOMORROW WOMAN.
"IT'S BEEN A WEEK."
"SHE'S BECOMING ONE OF THEM. MORE AND MORE INDISPENSABLE WITH EACH PASSING DAY".
I'M A MUTANT: BORN WITH A FOUR-LOBED BRAIN. MY POWERS APPEAR TO BE ENTIRELY TELE-KINETIC IN NATURE.
GREAT.
BUT I ALREADY HAVE A GIRLFRIEND.
MY GUESS IS I'M THE FIRST OF SOME NEW SPECIES, BORN AHEAD OF MY TIME.
"DON'T BE SO IMPATIENT, IVO. SHE'S GAINING THEIR TRUST."
EVERY DAY A NEW CITY AND ALL WE SEEM CAPABLE OF IS DAMAGE LIMITATION.
THE THING IS MINDLESS. I'D BELIEVE I WAS SCANNING A COM-PUTER BUT ITS CONSTRUCTION IS TOO FAR BEYOND CURRENT TECHNOLOGY.
IT'S PROGRAMMED FOR DEVASTATION, NOTHING MORE. THE SAME INSTRUCTION OVER AND OVER AGAIN.
"MOVE EAST. DESTROY"
YOU HAVEN'T RESTED, TOMORROW WOMAN. YOU'RE THE ONLY ONE OF US WHO'S BEEN WITH THIS EVERY SINGLE DAY.
I WANT YOU TO KNOW WE ALL APPRECIATE THAT.
YOU'RE JUST TRYING TO FLATTER ME.
NO, I MEAN IT.
I'LL REALLY FLATTER YOU WHEN YOU FIGURE OUT A WAY TO DEFEAT "IF"...
BLAH BLAH BLAH
IT'S TIME, MORROW. LET'S BRING HER IN.
HA! IDIOT!

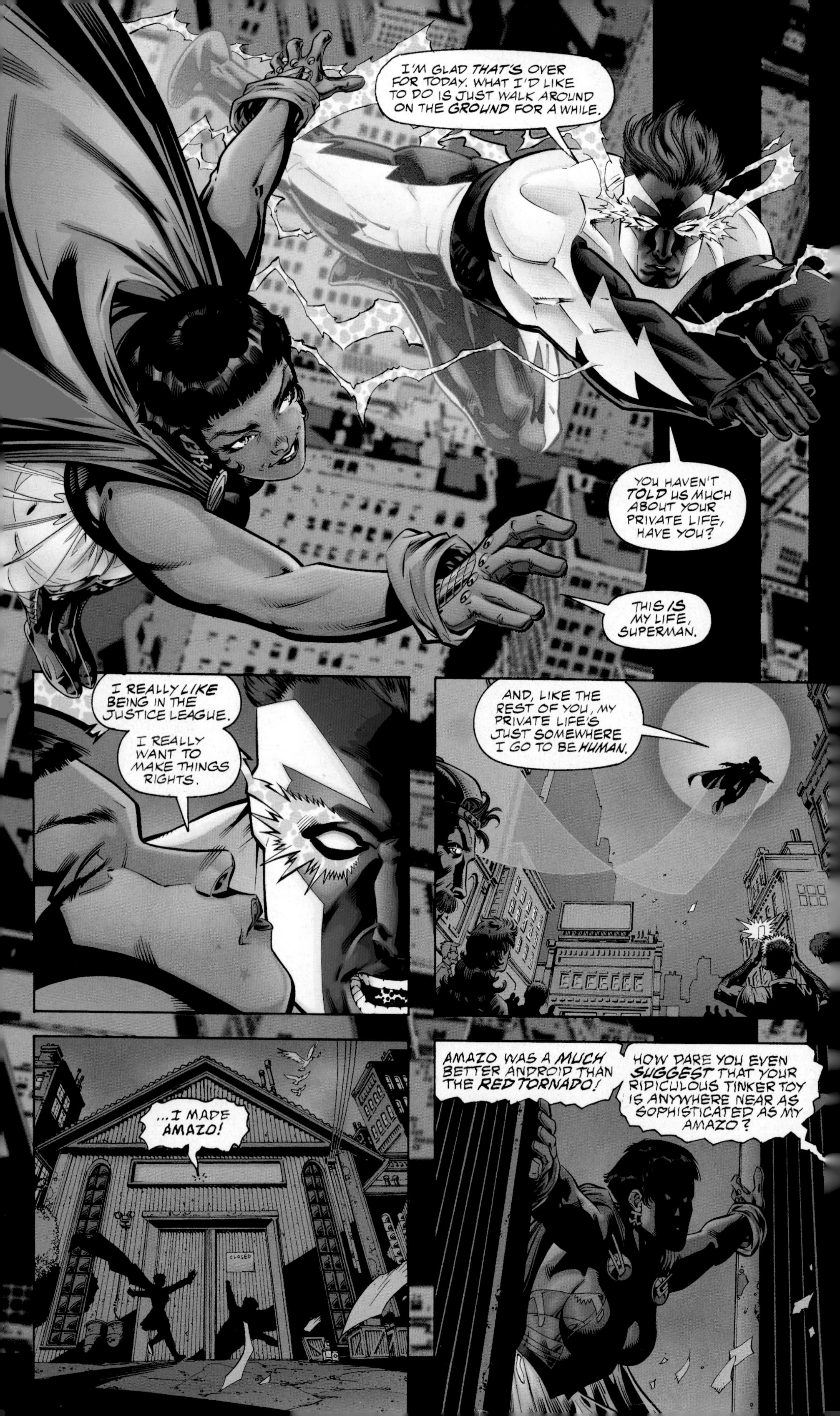
I'M GLAD THAT'S OVER FOR TODAY. WHAT I'D LIKE TO DO IS JUST WALK AROUND ON THE GROUND FOR A WHILE.
YOU HAVEN'T TOLD US MUCH ABOUT YOUR PRIVATE LIFE, HAVE YOU?
THIS IS MY LIFE, SUPERMAN.
I REALLY LIKE BEING IN THE JUSTICE LEAGUE.
I REALLY WANT TO MAKE THINGS RIGHTS.
AND, LIKE THE REST OF YOU, MY PRIVATE LIFE'S JUST SOMEWHERE I GO TO BE HUMAN.
...I MADE AMAZO!
CLOSED
AMAZO WAS A MUCH BETTER ANDROID THAN THE RED TORNADO!
HOW DARE YOU EVEN SUGGEST THAT YOUR RIDICULOUS TINKER TOY IS ANYWHERE NEAR AS SOPHISTICATED AS MY AMAZO?

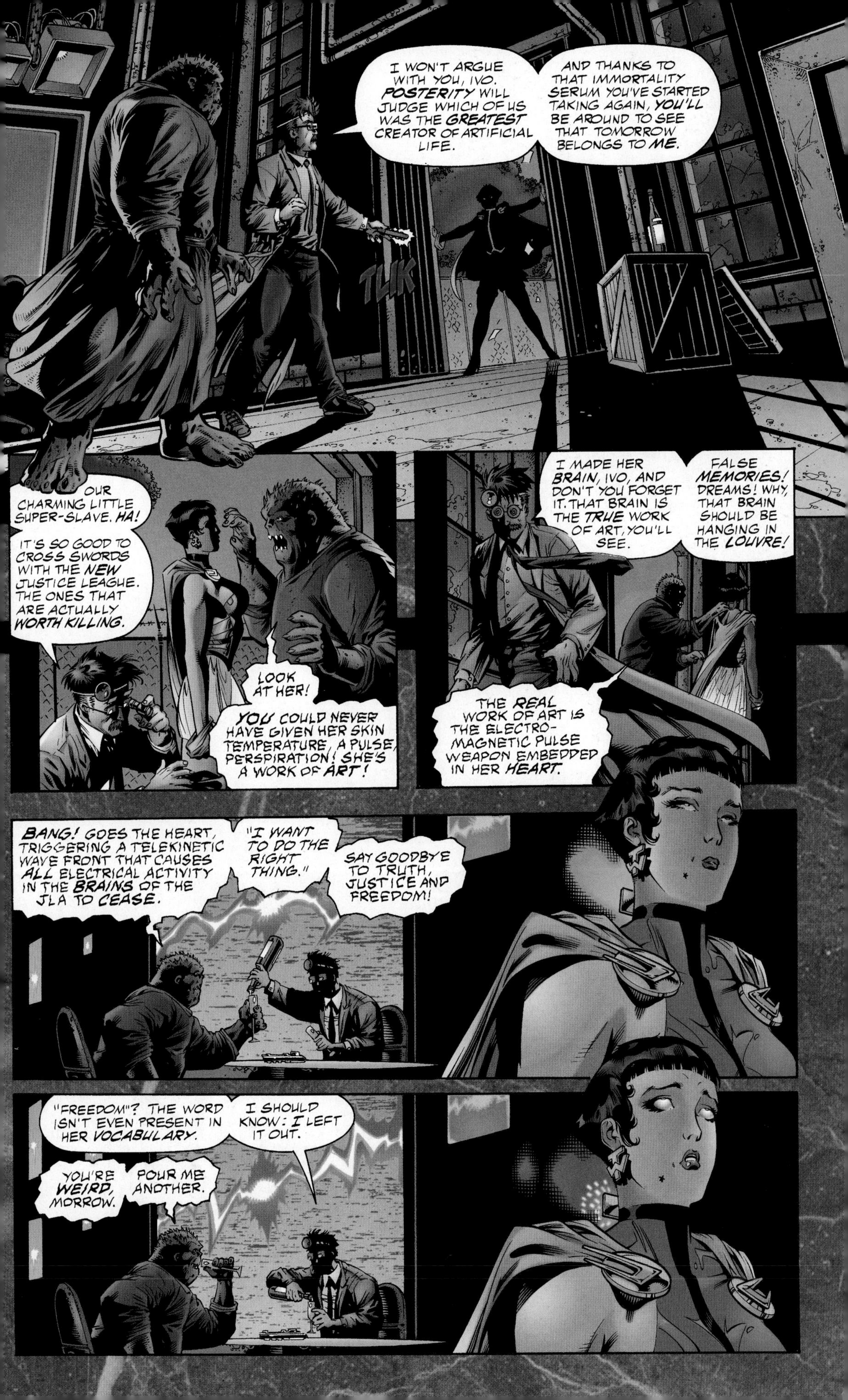
I WON'T ARGUE WITH YOU, IVO. POSTERITY WILL JUDGE WHICH OF US WAS THE GREATEST CREATOR OF ARTIFICIAL LIFE.
AND THANKS TO THAT IMMORTALITY SERUM YOU'VE STARTED TAKING AGAIN, YOU'LL BE AROUND TO SEE THAT TOMORROW BELONGS TO ME.
TLIK
OUR CHARMING LITTLE SUPER-SLAVE. HA!
IT'S SO GOOD TO CROSS SWORDS WITH THE NEW JUSTICE LEAGUE. THE ONES THAT ARE ACTUALLY WORTH KILLING.
LOOK AT HER!
YOU COULD NEVER HAVE GIVEN HER SKIN TEMPERATURE, A PULSE, PERSPIRATION! SHE'S A WORK OF ART!
I MADE HER BRAIN, IVO, AND DON'T YOU FORGET IT. THAT BRAIN IS THE TRUE WORK OF ART, YOU'LL SEE.
FALSE MEMORIES! DREAMS! WHY, THAT BRAIN SHOULD BE HANGING IN THE LOUVRE!
THE REAL WORK OF ART IS THE ELECTRO-MAGNETIC PULSE WEAPON EMBEDDED IN HER HEART.
BANG! GOES THE HEART, TRIGGERING A TELEKINETIC WAVE FRONT THAT CAUSES ALL ELECTRICAL ACTIVITY IN THE BRAINS OF THE JLA TO CEASE.
"I WANT TO DO THE RIGHT THING."
SAY GOODBYE TO TRUTH, JUSTICE AND FREEDOM!
"FREEDOM"? THE WORD ISN'T EVEN PRESENT IN HER VOCABULARY.
I SHOULD KNOW: I LEFT IT OUT.
YOU'RE WEIRD, MORROW.
POUR ME ANOTHER.

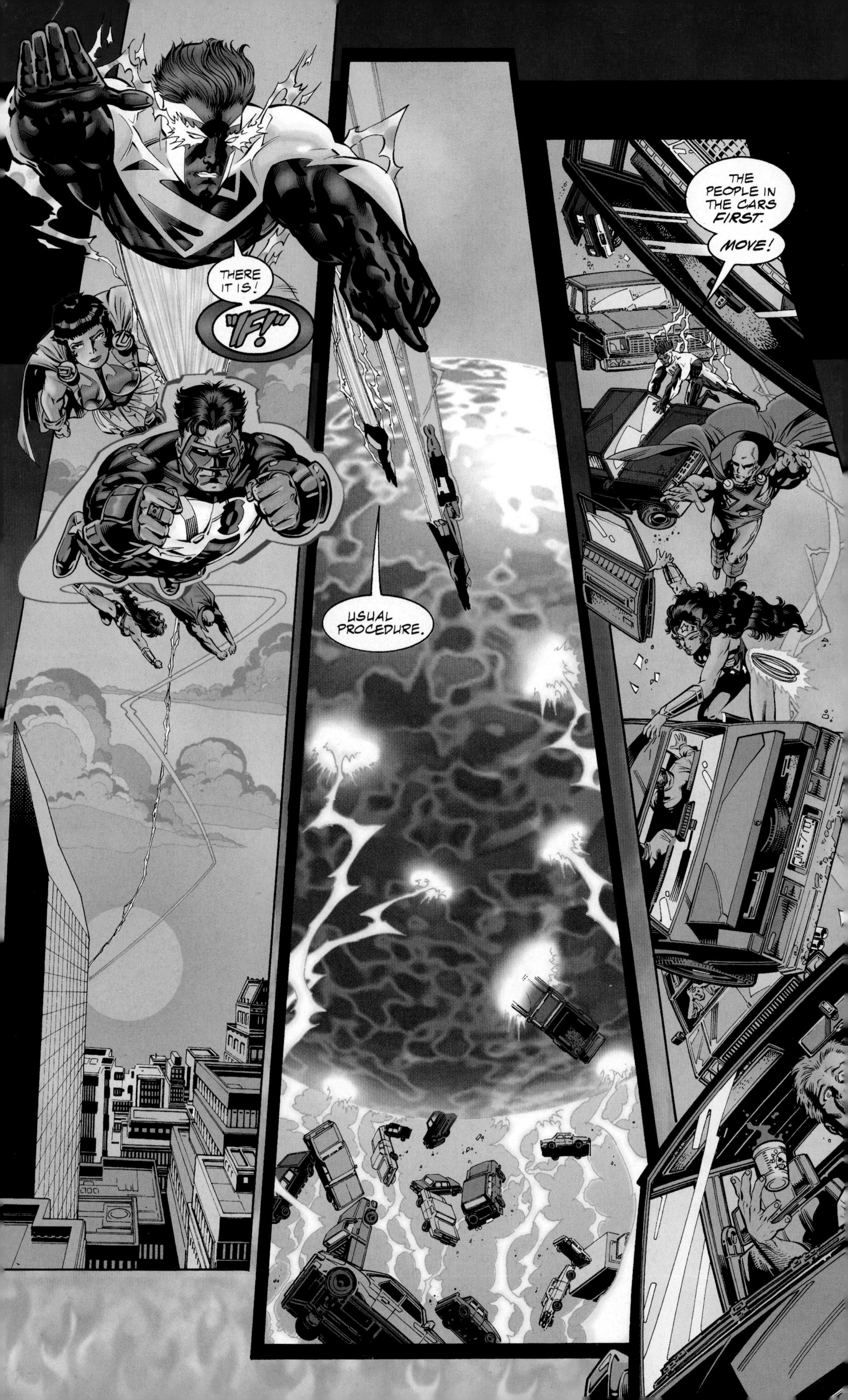
THERE IT IS!
"IF!"
USUAL PROCEDURE.
THE PEOPLE IN THE CARS FIRST.
MOVE!

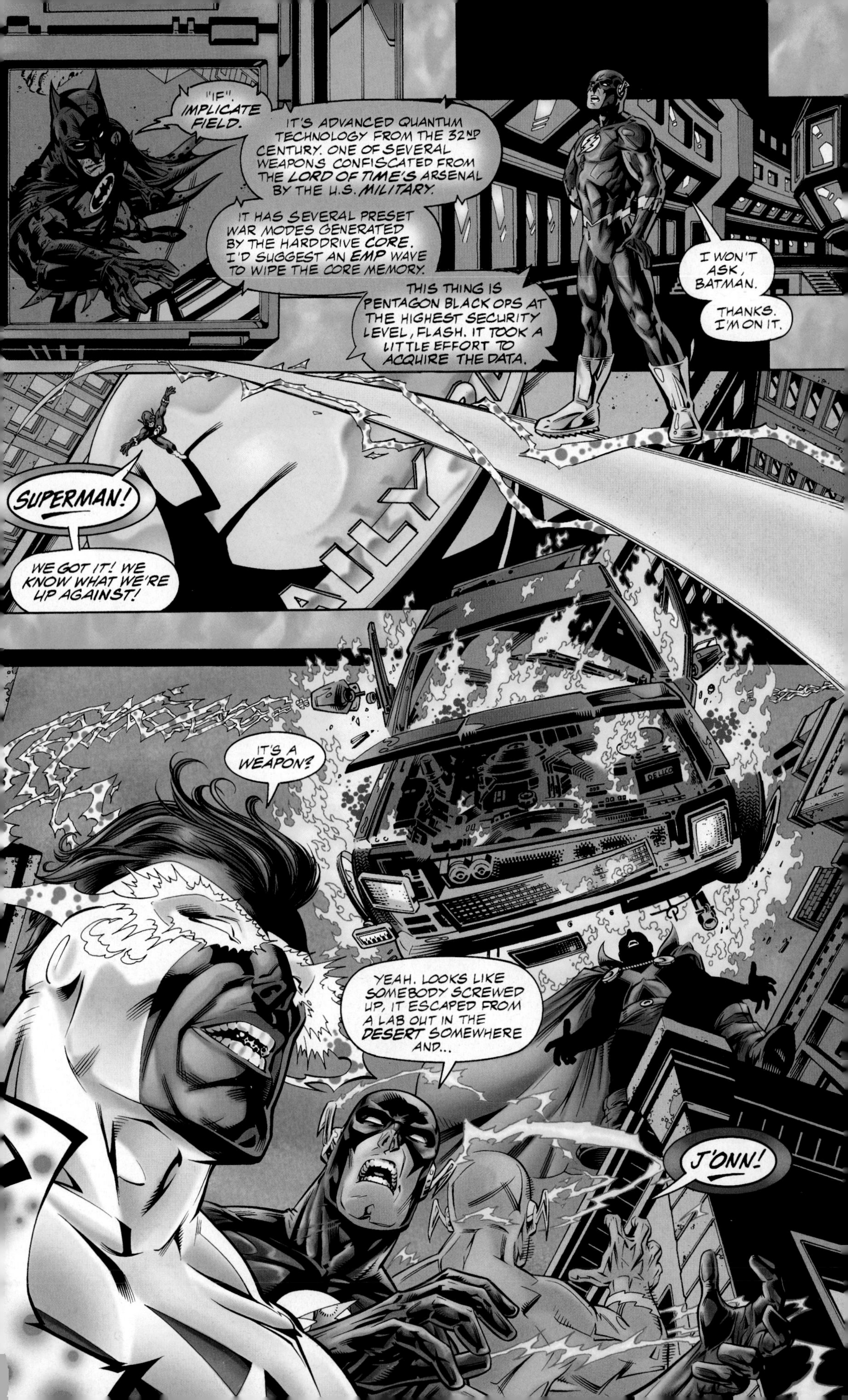
"IF". IMPLICATE FIELD.
IT'S ADVANCED QUANTUM TECHNOLOGY FROM THE 32ND CENTURY. ONE OF SEVERAL WEAPONS CONFISCATED FROM THE LORD OF TIME'S ARSENAL BY THE U.S. MILITARY.
IT HAS SEVERAL PRESET WAR MODES GENERATED BY THE HARDDRIVE CORE. I'D SUGGEST AN EMP WAVE TO WIPE THE CORE MEMORY.
THIS THING IS PENTAGON BLACK OPS AT THE HIGHEST SECURITY LEVEL, FLASH. IT TOOK A LITTLE EFFORT TO ACQUIRE THE DATA.
I WON'T ASK, BATMAN.
THANKS. I'M ON IT.
SUPERMAN!
WE GOT IT! WE KNOW WHAT WE'RE UP AGAINST!
IT'S A WEAPON?
YEAH. LOOKS LIKE SOMEBODY SCREWED UP, IT ESCAPED FROM A LAB OUT IN THE DESERT SOMEWHERE AND...
J'ONN!

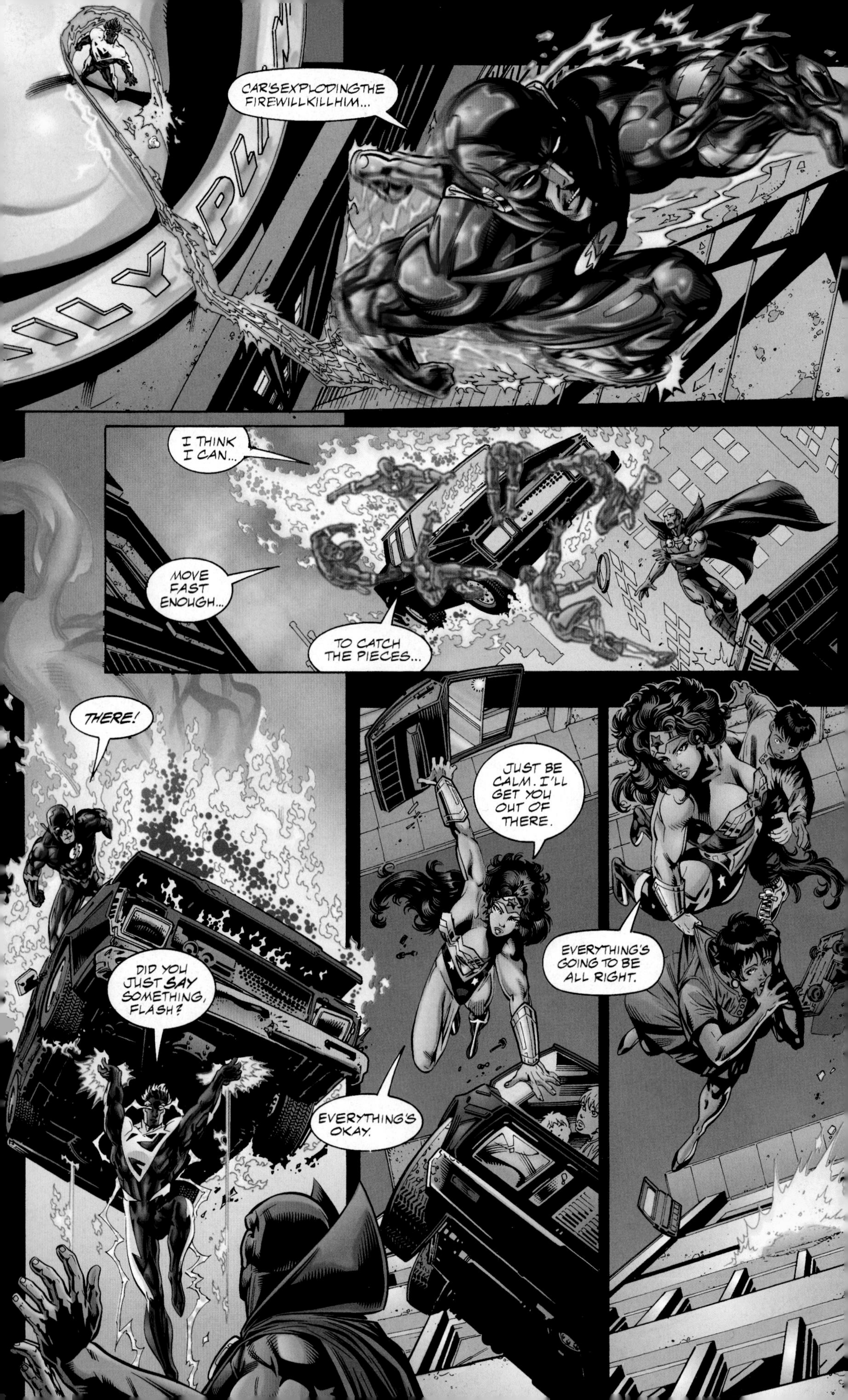
CAR'SEXPLODINGTHE FIREWILLKILLHIM...
I THINK I CAN...
MOVE FAST ENOUGH...
TO CATCH THE PIECES...
THERE!
DID YOU JUST SAY SOMETHING, FLASH?
JUST BE CALM. I'LL GET YOU OUT OF THERE.
EVERYTHING'S OKAY.
EVERYTHING'S GOING TO BE ALL RIGHT.

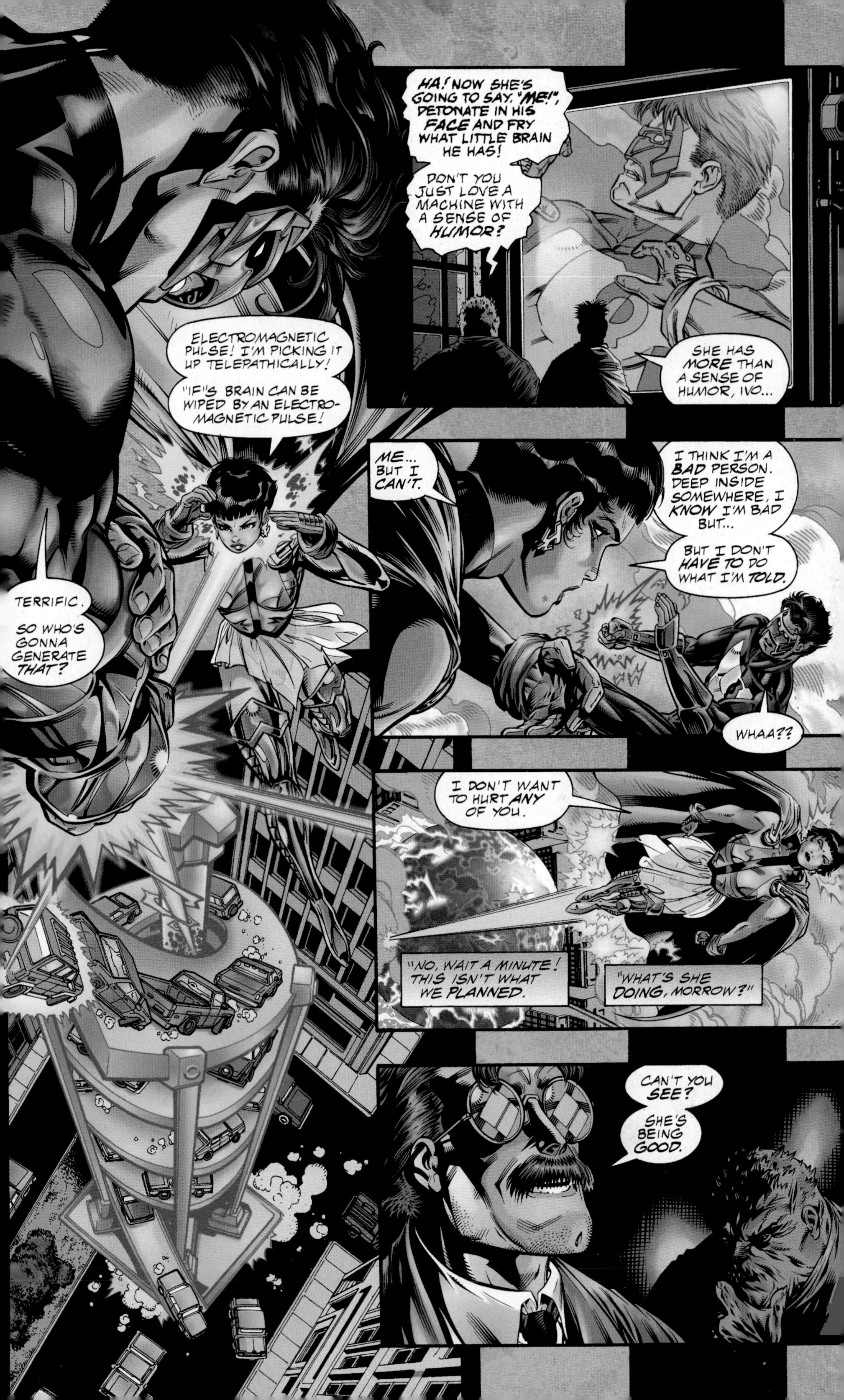

HA! NOW SHE'S GOING TO SAY, "ME!", DETONATE IN HIS FACE AND FRY WHAT LITTLE BRAIN HE HAS!
DON'T YOU JUST LOVE A MACHINE WITH A SENSE OF HUMOR?
SHE HAS MORE THAN A SENSE OF HUMOR, IVO...
ELECTROMAGNETIC PULSE! I'M PICKING IT UP TELEPATHICALLY!
"IF"'S BRAIN CAN BE WIPED BY AN ELECTROMAGNETIC PULSE!
TERRIFIC.
SO WHO'S GONNA GENERATE THAT?
ME... BUT I CAN'T.
I THINK I'M A BAD PERSON. DEEP INSIDE SOMEWHERE, I KNOW I'M BAD BUT...
BUT I DON'T HAVE TO DO WHAT I'M TOLD.
WHAA??
I DON'T WANT TO HURT ANY OF YOU.
"NO, WAIT A MINUTE! THIS ISN'T WHAT WE PLANNED.
"WHAT'S SHE DOING, MORROW?"
CAN'T YOU SEE?
SHE'S BEING GOOD.

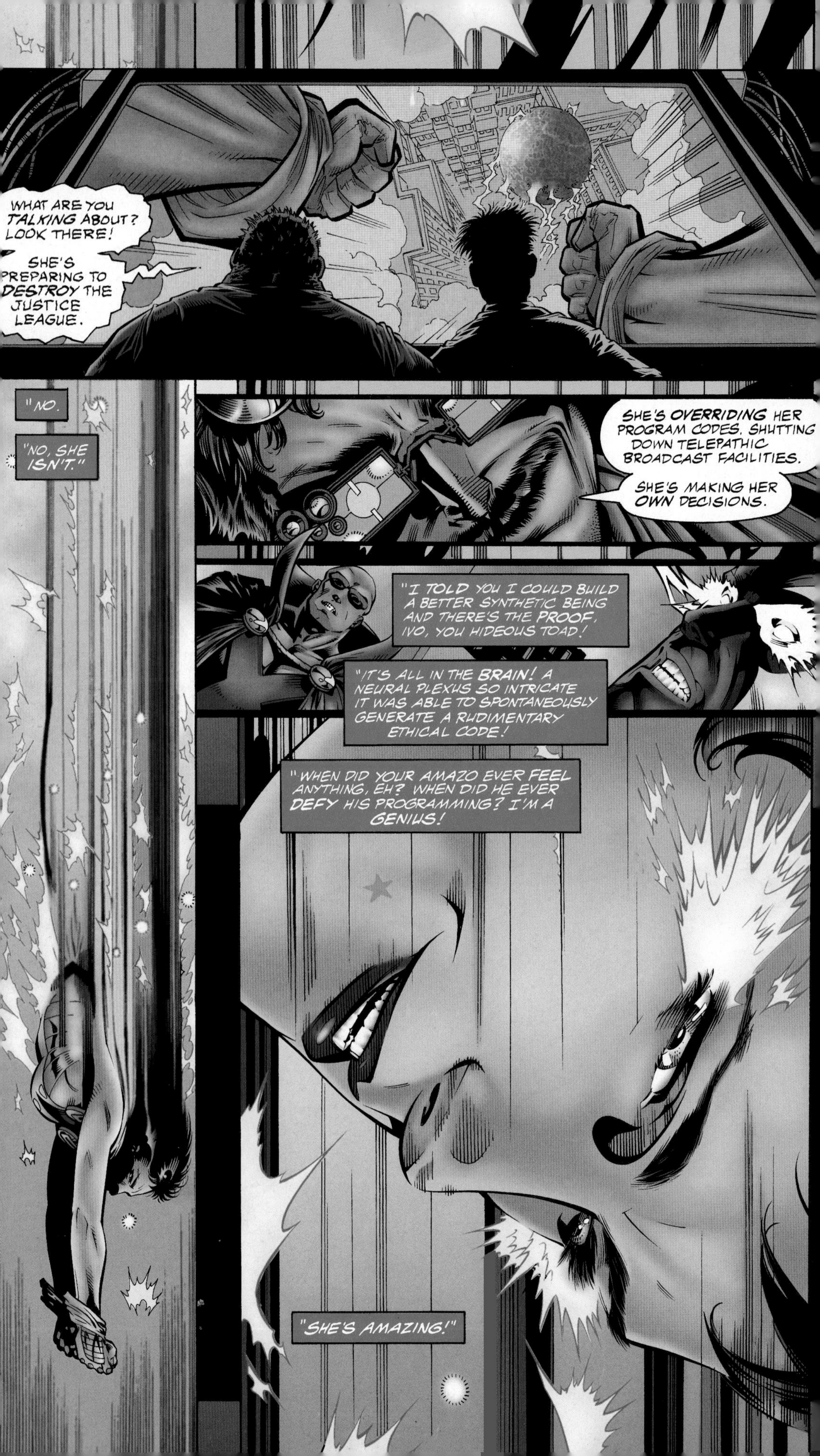

WHAT ARE YOU TALKING ABOUT? LOOK THERE!
SHE'S PREPARING TO DESTROY THE JUSTICE LEAGUE.
"NO.
"NO, SHE ISN'T."
SHE'S OVERRIDING HER PROGRAM CODES. SHUTTING DOWN TELEPATHIC BROADCAST FACILITIES.
SHE'S MAKING HER OWN DECISIONS.
"I TOLD YOU I COULD BUILD A BETTER SYNTHETIC BEING AND THERE'S THE PROOF, IVO, YOU HIDEOUS TOAD!
"IT'S ALL IN THE BRAIN! A NEURAL PLEXUS SO INTRICATE IT WAS ABLE TO SPONTANEOUSLY GENERATE A RUDIMENTARY ETHICAL CODE!
"WHEN DID YOUR AMAZO EVER FEEL ANYTHING, EH? WHEN DID HE EVER DEFY HIS PROGRAMMING? I'M A GENIUS!
"SHE'S AMAZING!"

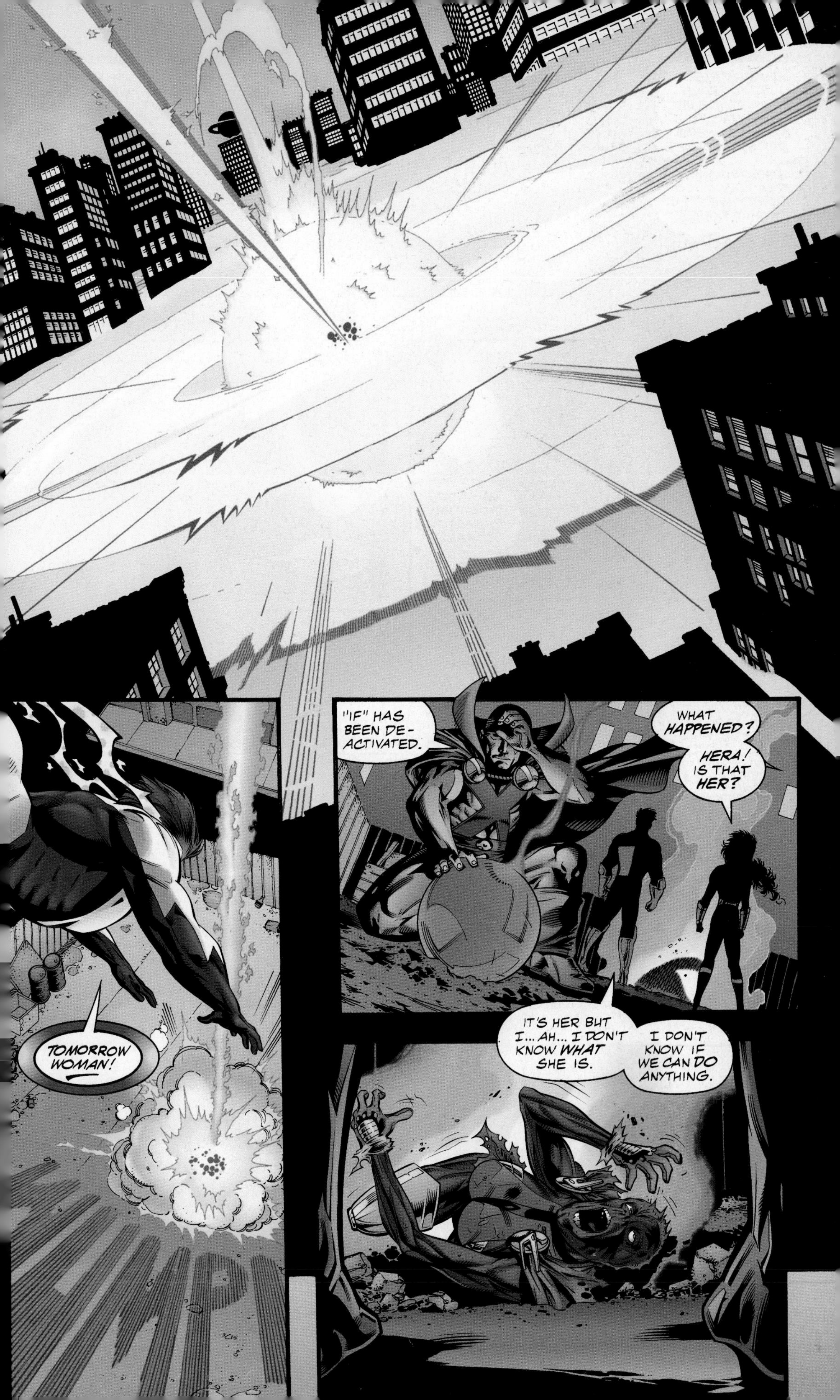

TOMORROW WOMAN!
"IF" HAS BEEN DE-ACTIVATED.
WHAT HAPPENED?
HERA! IS THAT HER?
IT'S HER BUT I... AH... I DON'T KNOW WHAT SHE IS.
I DON'T KNOW IF WE CAN DO ANYTHING.

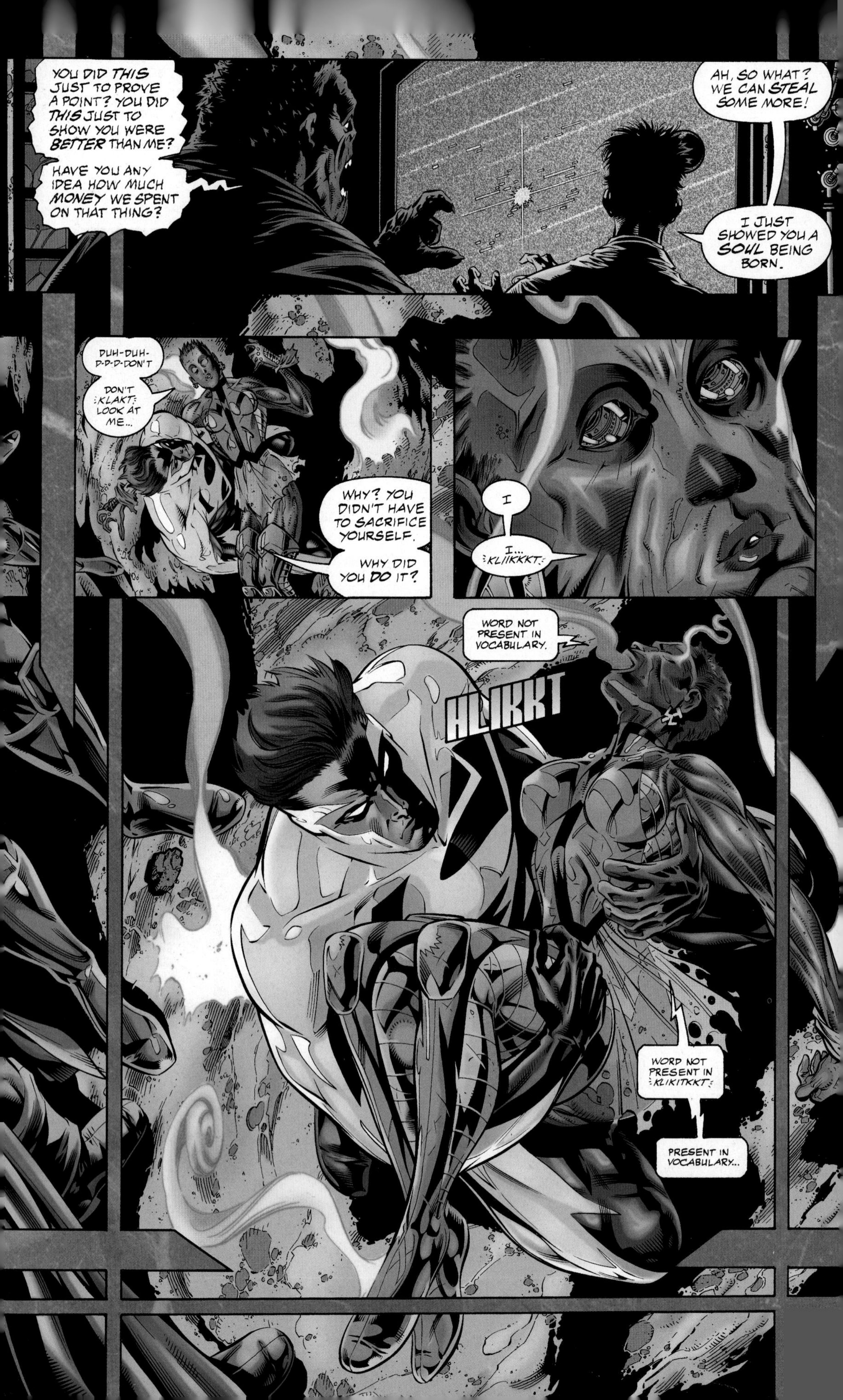
YOU DID THIS JUST TO PROVE A POINT? YOU DID THIS JUST TO SHOW YOU WERE BETTER THAN ME?
HAVE YOU ANY IDEA HOW MUCH MONEY WE SPENT ON THAT THING?
AH, SO WHAT? WE CAN STEAL SOME MORE!
I JUST SHOWED YOU A SOUL BEING BORN.
DUH-DUH-D-D-D-DON'T
DON'T KLAKT LOOK AT ME...
WHY? YOU DIDN'T HAVE TO SACRIFICE YOURSELF.
WHY DID YOU DO IT?
I
I... KLIIKKKT
WORD NOT PRESENT IN VOCABULARY.
HLIKKT
WORD NOT PRESENT IN KLIKITKKT
PRESENT IN VOCABULARY...

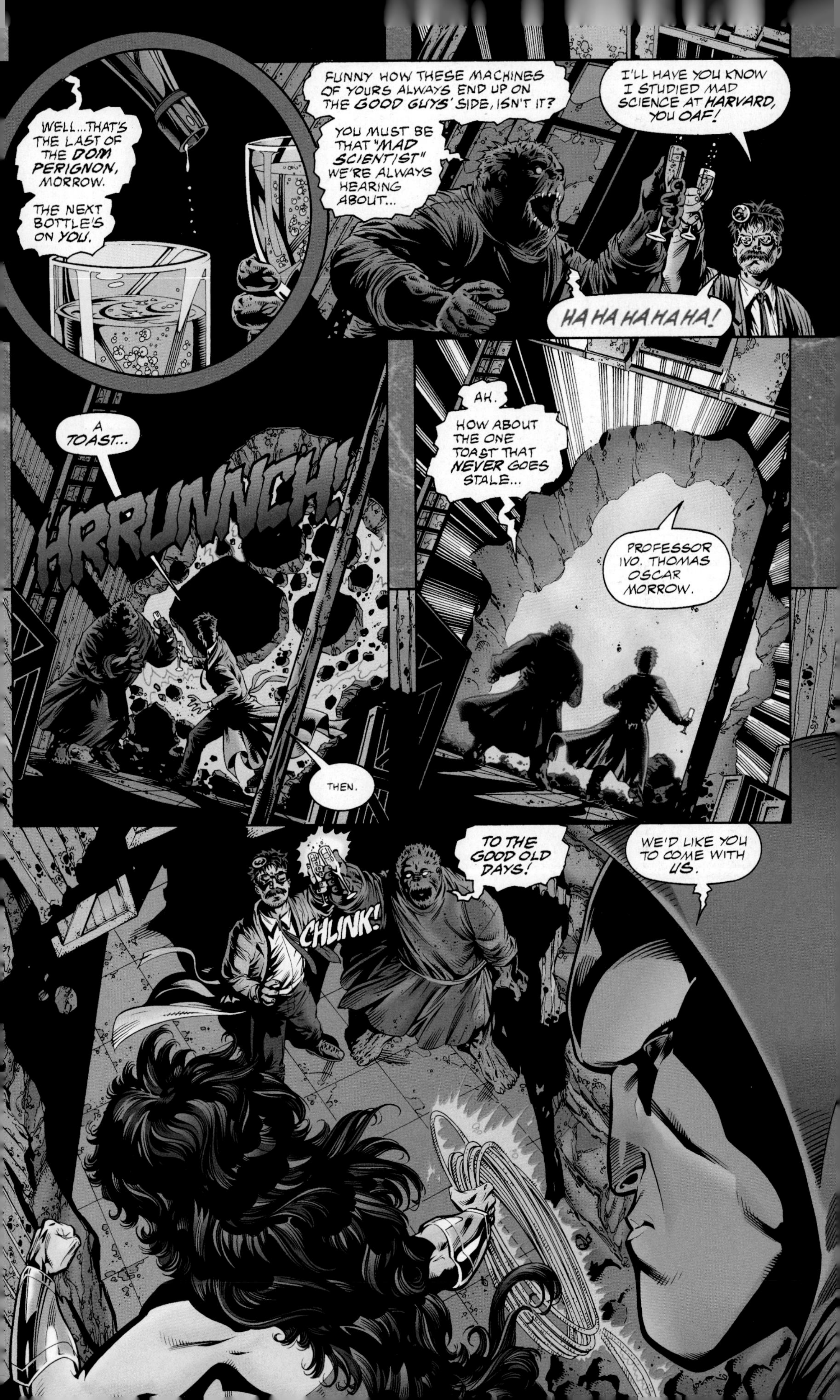
WELL...THAT'S THE LAST OF THE DOM PERIGNON, MORROW.
THE NEXT BOTTLE'S ON YOU.
FUNNY HOW THESE MACHINES OF YOURS ALWAYS END UP ON THE GOOD GUYS' SIDE, ISN'T IT?
YOU MUST BE THAT "MAD SCIENTIST" WE'RE ALWAYS HEARING ABOUT...
I'LL HAVE YOU KNOW I STUDIED MAD SCIENCE AT HARVARD, YOU OAF!
HA HA HA HA HA!
A TOAST...
HRRUNNCH!!
THEN.
AH.
HOW ABOUT THE ONE TOAST THAT NEVER GOES STALE...
PROFESSOR IVO. THOMAS OSCAR MORROW.
TO THE GOOD OLD DAYS!
CHLINK!
WE'D LIKE YOU TO COME WITH US.

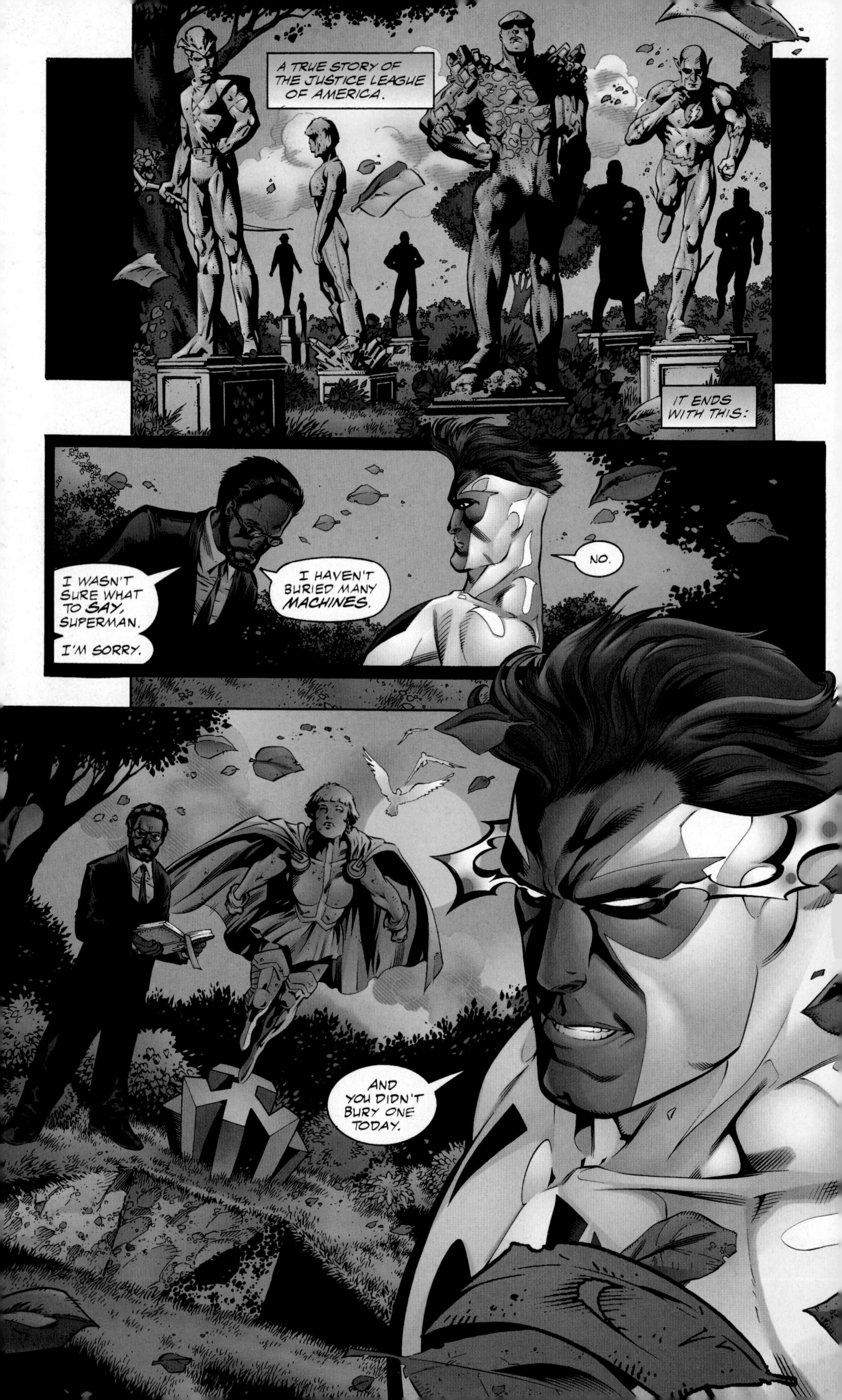
A TRUE STORY OF THE JUSTICE LEAGUE OF AMERICA.
IT ENDS WITH THIS:
I WASN'T SURE WHAT TO SAY, SUPERMAN.
I'M SORRY.
I HAVEN'T BURIED MANY MACHINES.
NO.
AND YOU DIDN'T BURY ONE TODAY.

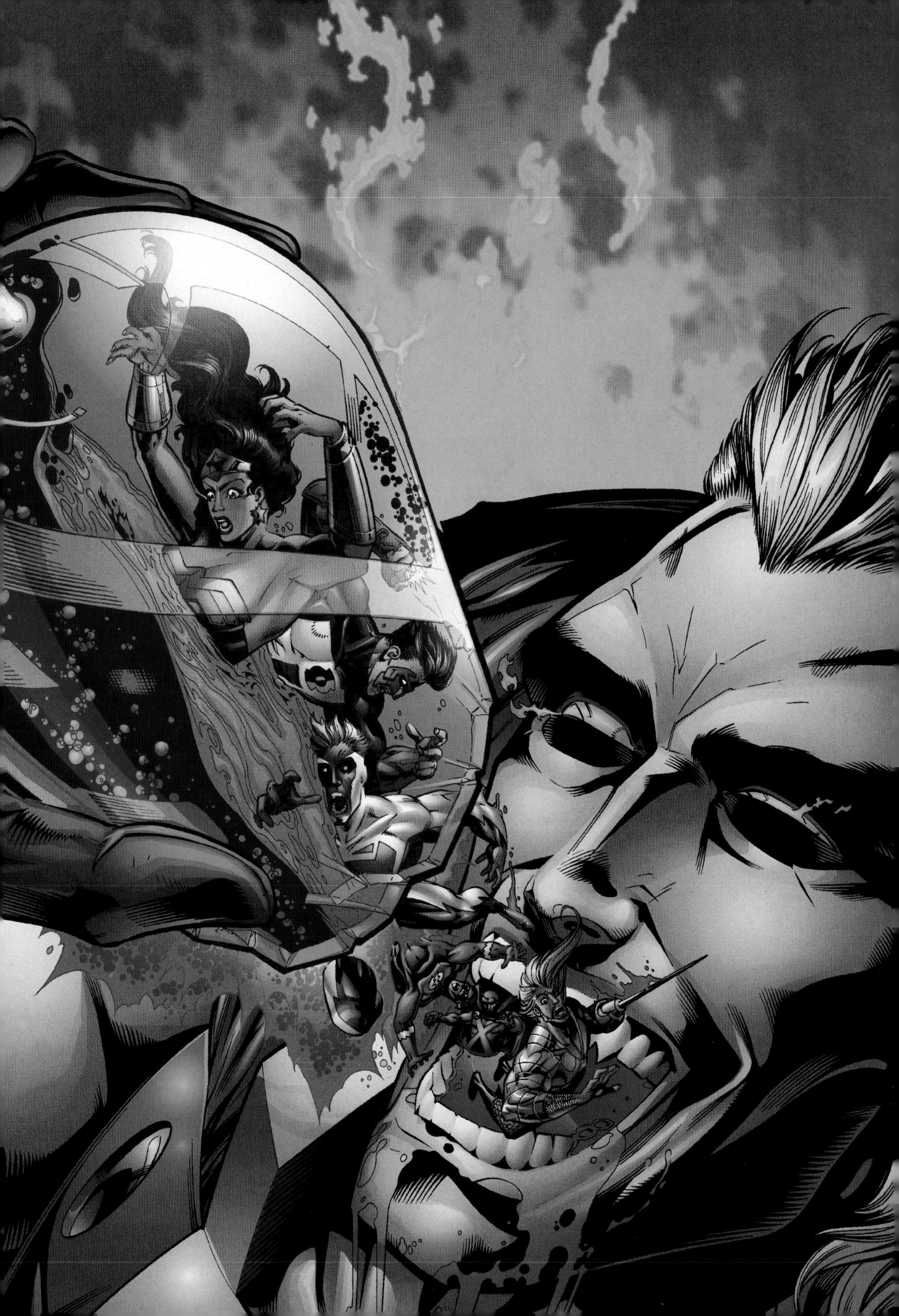

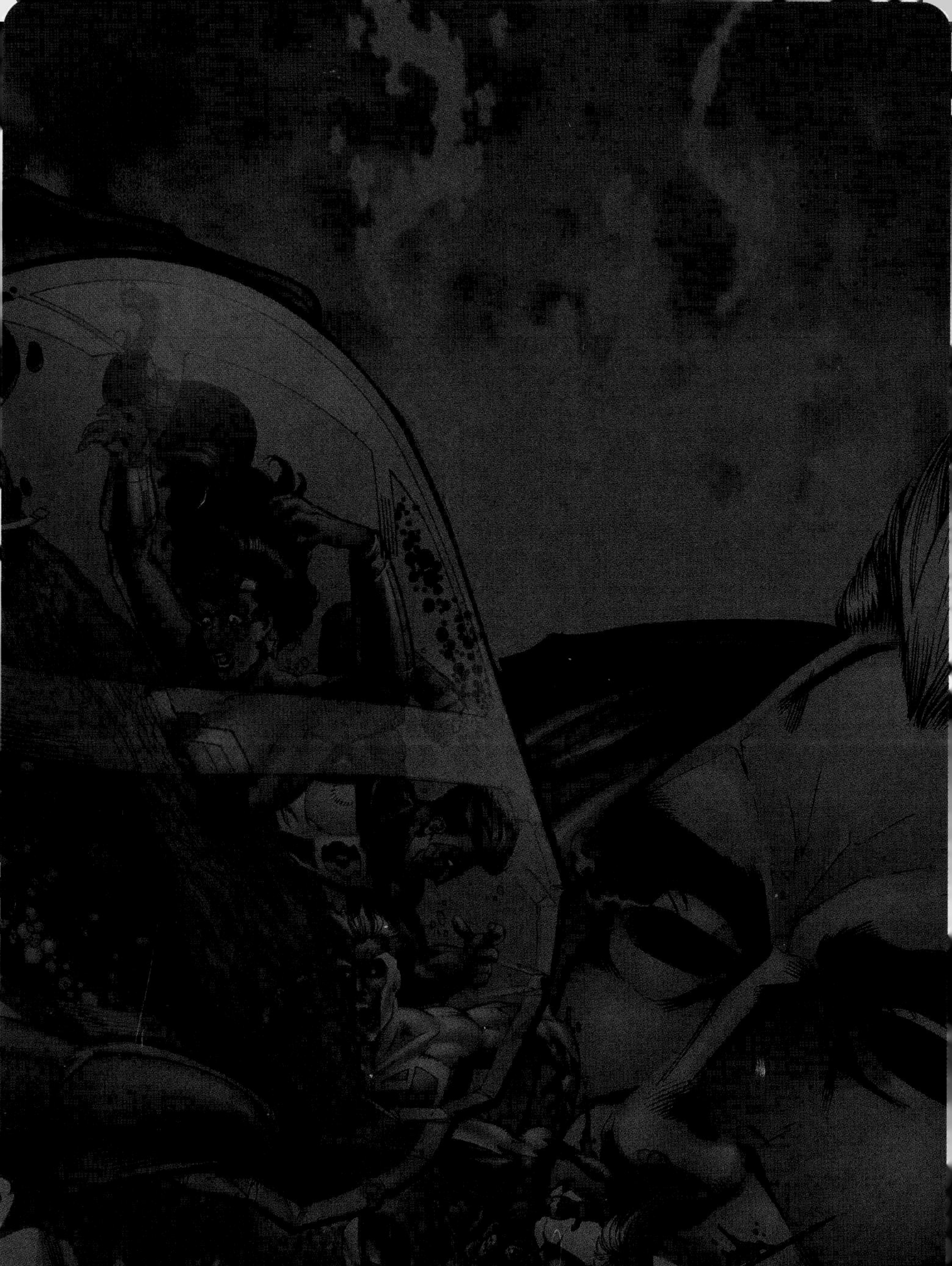

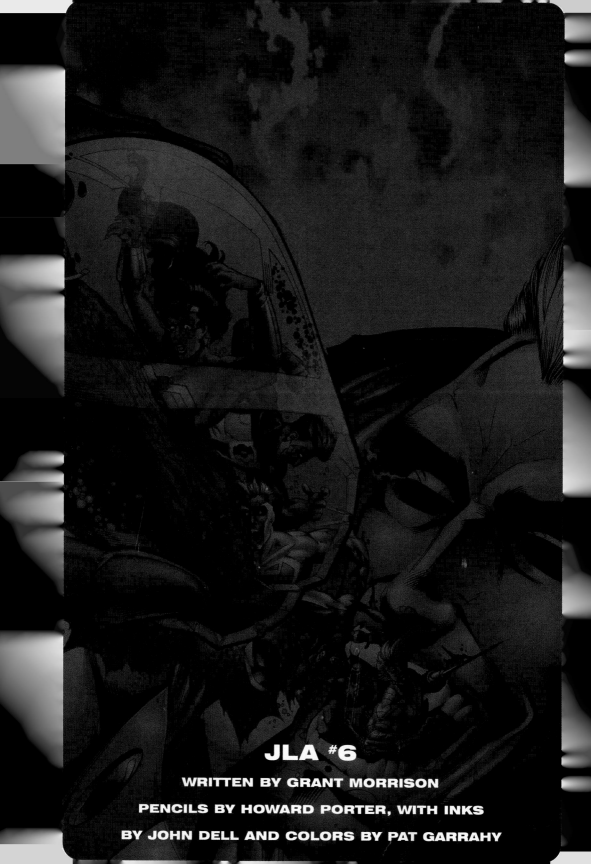

JLA #6

WRITTEN BY GRANT MORRISON

PENCILS BY HOWARD PORTER, WITH INKS

BY JOHN DELL AND COLORS BY PAT GARRAHY

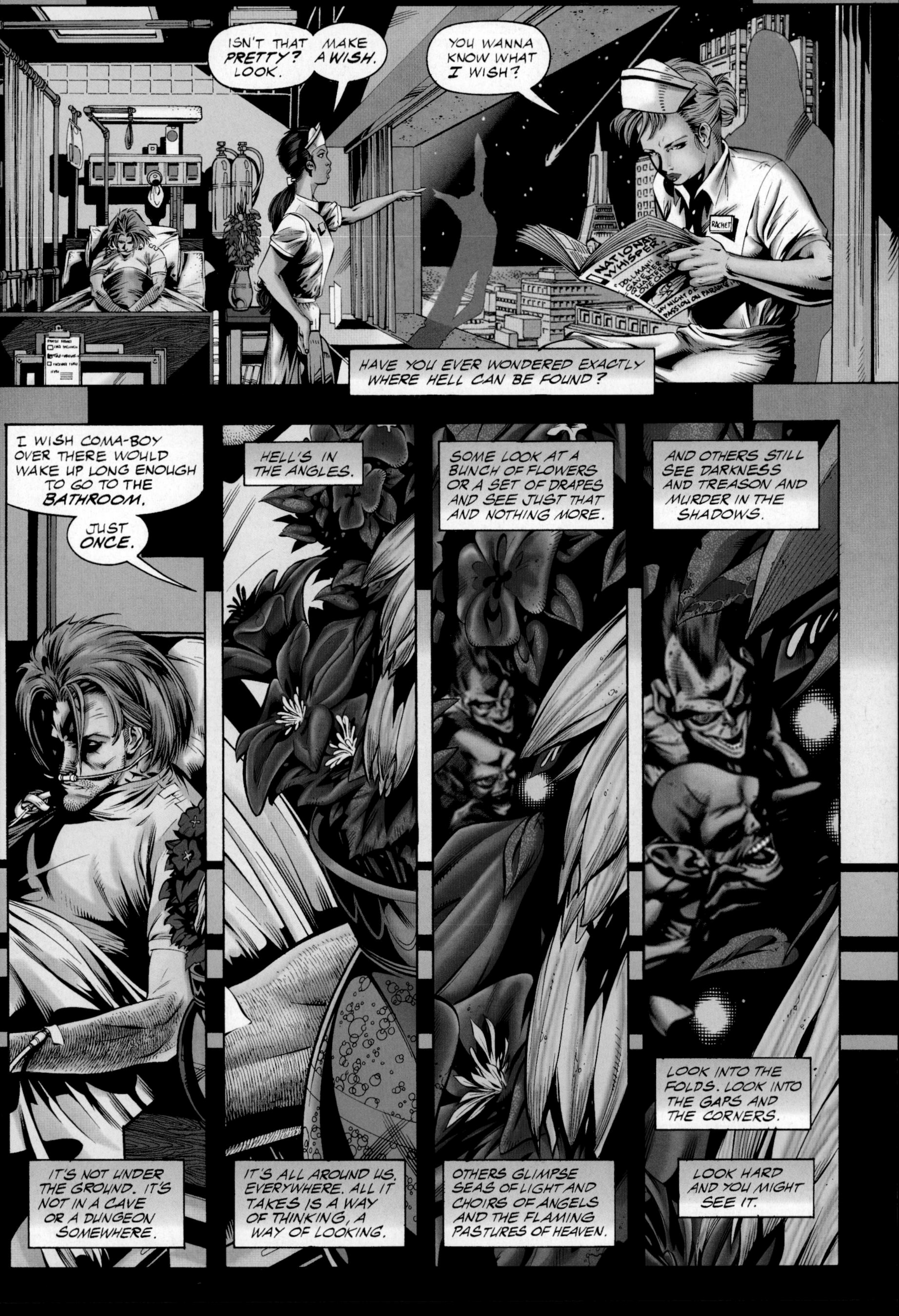

ISN'T THAT PRETTY? LOOK.
MAKE A WISH.
YOU WANNA KNOW WHAT I WISH?
NATIONAL WHISPER
HAVE YOU EVER WONDERED EXACTLY WHERE HELL CAN BE FOUND?
I WISH COMA-BOY OVER THERE WOULD WAKE UP LONG ENOUGH TO GO TO THE BATHROOM.
JUST ONCE.
IT'S NOT UNDER THE GROUND. IT'S NOT IN A CAVE OR A DUNGEON SOMEWHERE.
HELL'S IN THE ANGLES.
IT'S ALL AROUND US. EVERYWHERE. ALL IT TAKES IS A WAY OF THINKING, A WAY OF LOOKING.
SOME LOOK AT A BUNCH OF FLOWERS OR A SET OF DRAPES AND SEE JUST THAT AND NOTHING MORE.
OTHERS GLIMPSE SEAS OF LIGHT AND CHOIRS OF ANGELS AND THE FLAMING PASTURES OF HEAVEN.
AND OTHERS STILL SEE DARKNESS AND TREASON AND MURDER IN THE SHADOWS.
LOOK INTO THE FOLDS. LOOK INTO THE GAPS AND THE CORNERS.
LOOK HARD AND YOU MIGHT SEE IT.

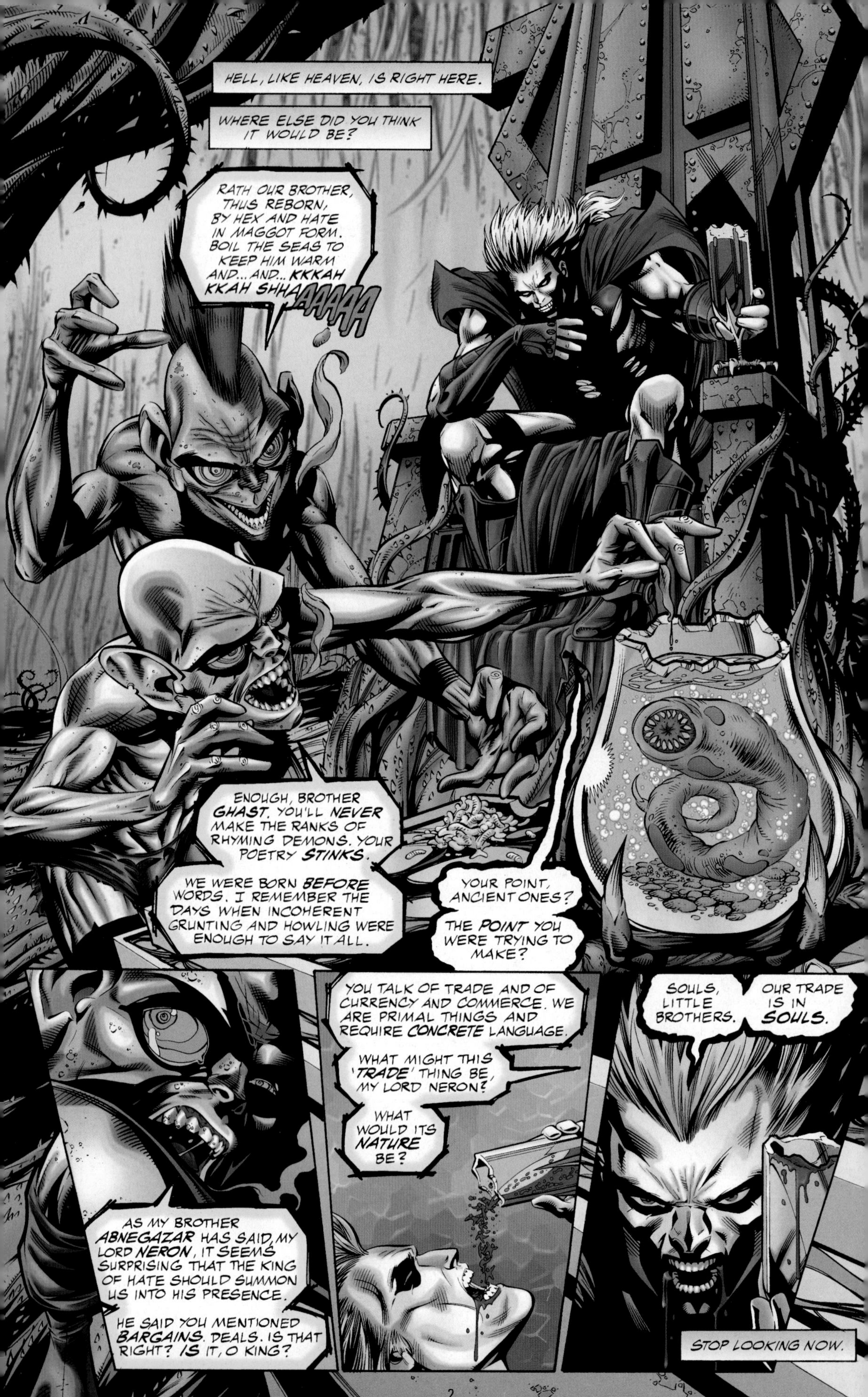

HELL, LIKE HEAVEN, IS RIGHT HERE.
WHERE ELSE DID YOU THINK IT WOULD BE?
RATH OUR BROTHER, THUS REBORN, BY HEX AND HATE IN MAGGOT FORM. BOIL THE SEAS TO KEEP HIM WARM AND...AND...KKKAH KKAH SHHAAAAAA
ENOUGH, BROTHER GHAST. YOU'LL NEVER MAKE THE RANKS OF RHYMING DEMONS. YOUR POETRY STINKS.
WE WERE BORN BEFORE WORDS. I REMEMBER THE DAYS WHEN INCOHERENT GRUNTING AND HOWLING WERE ENOUGH TO SAY IT ALL.
YOUR POINT, ANCIENT ONES?
THE POINT YOU WERE TRYING TO MAKE?
AS MY BROTHER ABNEGAZAR HAS SAID, MY LORD NERON, IT SEEMS SURPRISING THAT THE KING OF HATE SHOULD SUMMON US INTO HIS PRESENCE.
HE SAID YOU MENTIONED BARGAINS. DEALS. IS THAT RIGHT? IS IT, O KING?
YOU TALK OF TRADE AND OF CURRENCY AND COMMERCE. WE ARE PRIMAL THINGS AND REQUIRE CONCRETE LANGUAGE.
WHAT MIGHT THIS 'TRADE' THING BE, MY LORD NERON?
WHAT WOULD ITS NATURE BE?
SOULS, LITTLE BROTHERS.
OUR TRADE IS IN SOULS.
STOP LOOKING NOW.

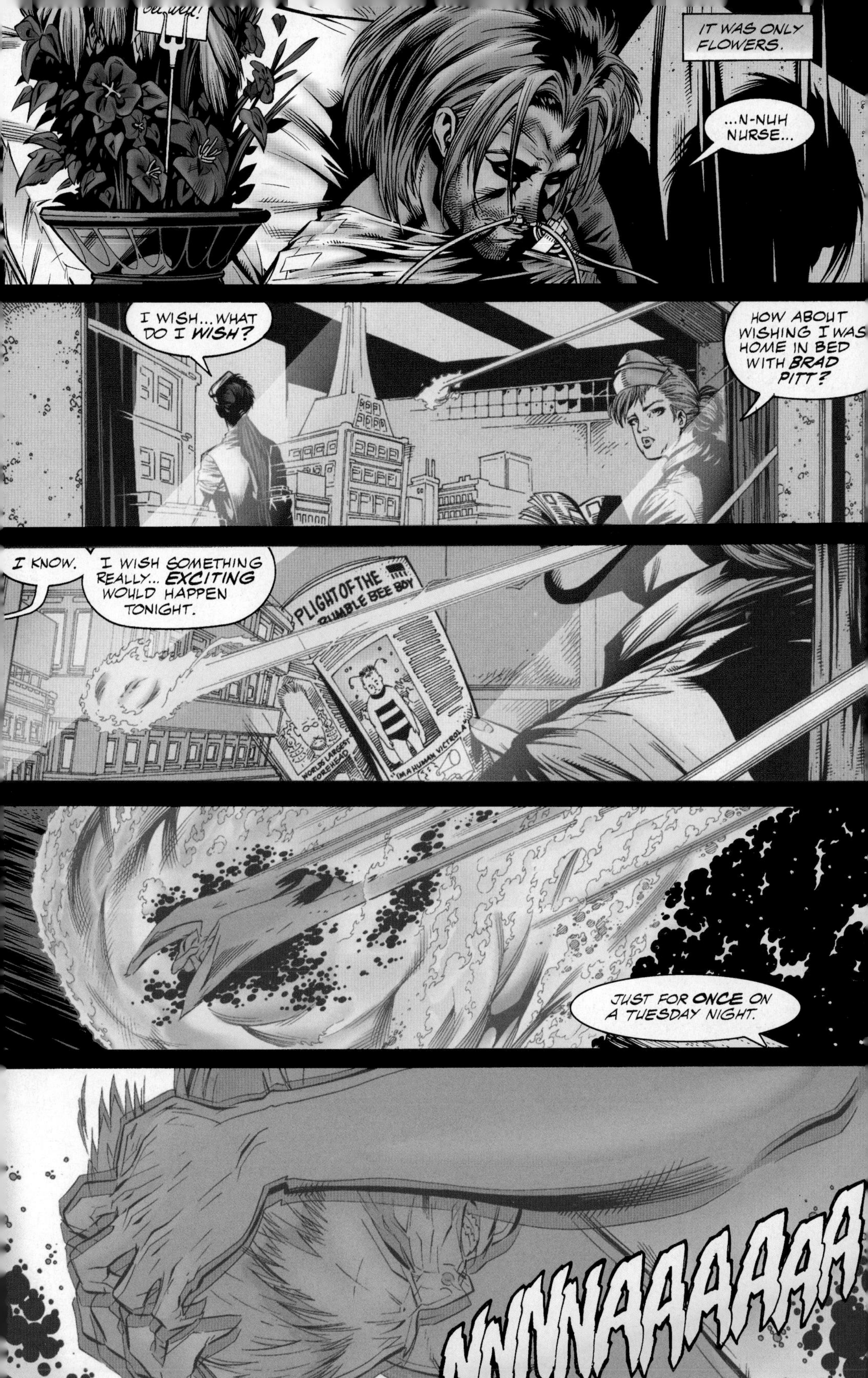
IT WAS ONLY FLOWERS.
...N-NUH NURSE...
I WISH... WHAT DO I WISH?
HOW ABOUT WISHING I WAS HOME IN BED WITH BRAD PITT?
I KNOW.
I WISH SOMETHING REALLY... EXCITING WOULD HAPPEN TONIGHT.
PLIGHT OF THE BUMBLE BEE BOY
JUST FOR ONCE ON A TUESDAY NIGHT.
NNNNAAAAAA

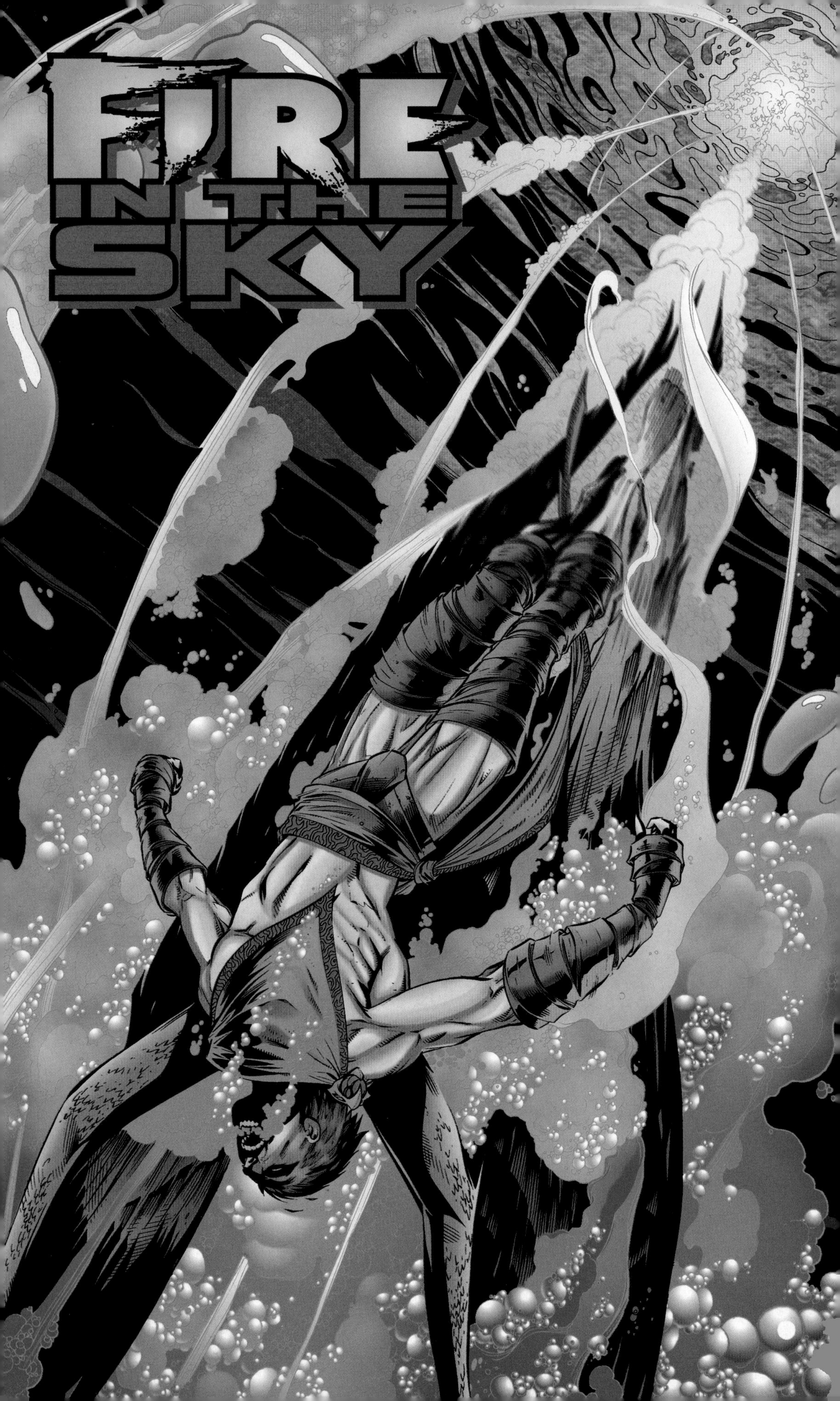
FIRE
IN THE
SKY

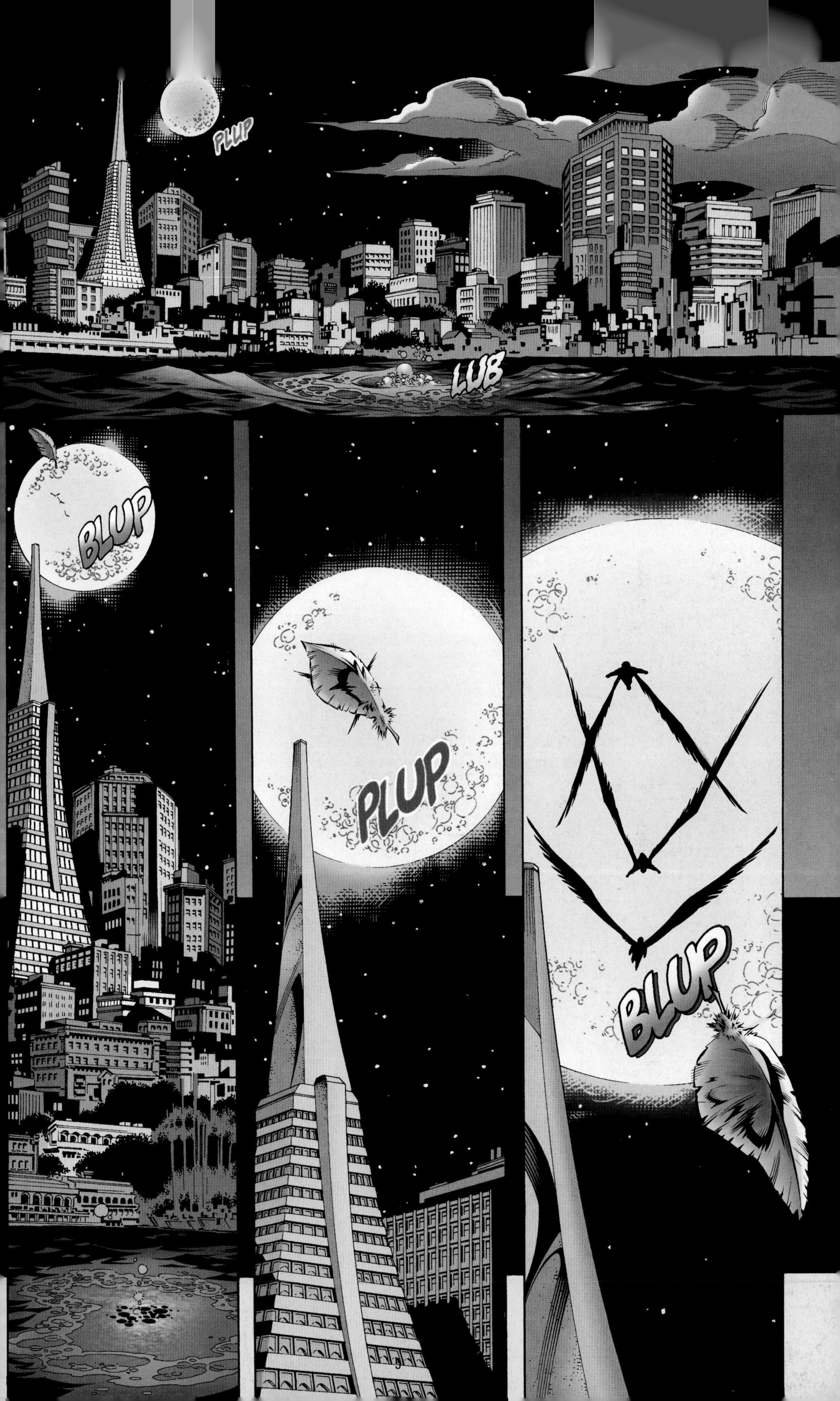
PLUP
LUB
BLUP
PLUP
BLUP

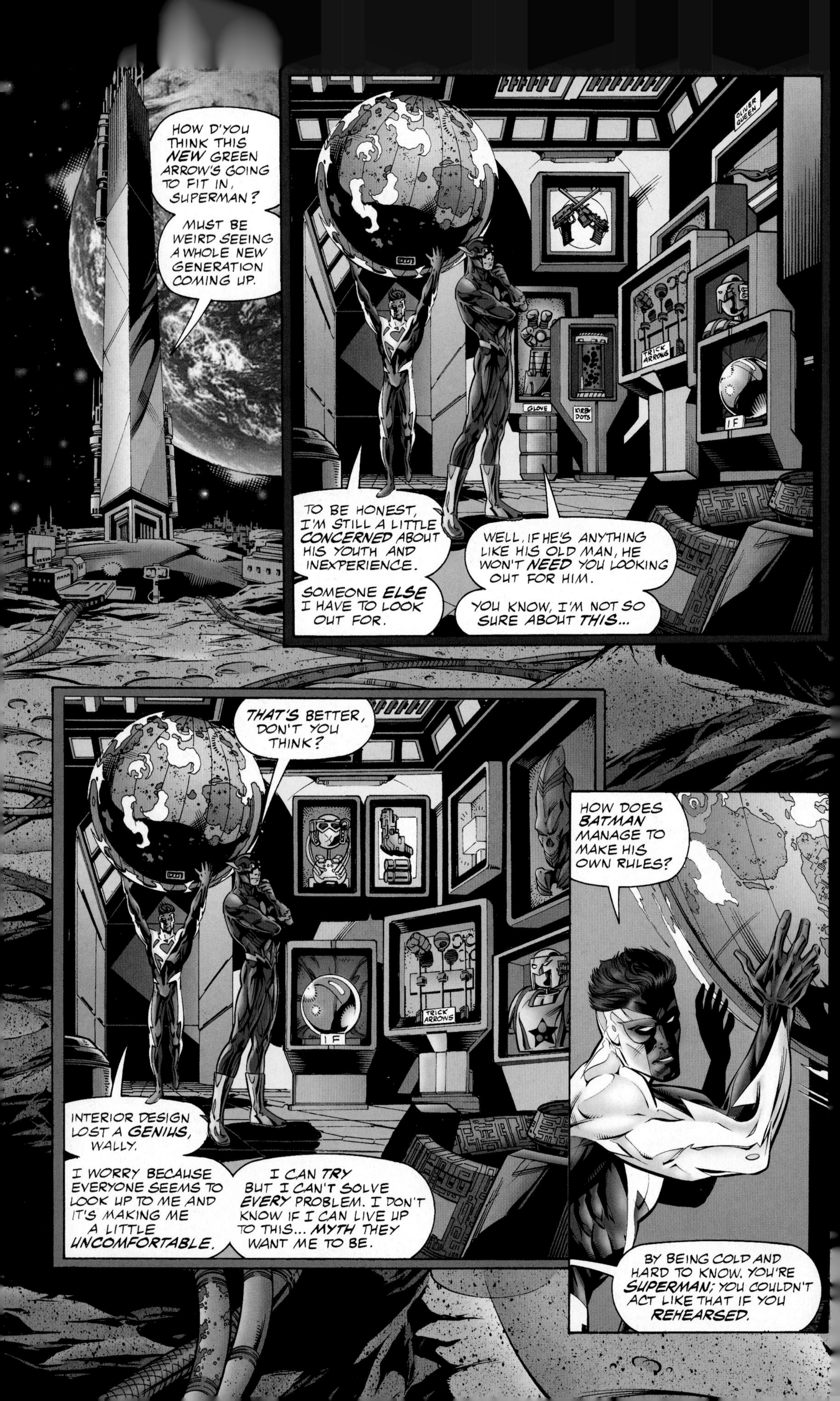
HOW D'YOU THINK THIS NEW GREEN ARROW'S GOING TO FIT IN, SUPERMAN?
MUST BE WEIRD SEEING A WHOLE NEW GENERATION COMING UP.
OLIVER QUEEN
GLOVE
KIRBY DOTS
TRICK ARROWS
IF
TO BE HONEST, I'M STILL A LITTLE CONCERNED ABOUT HIS YOUTH AND INEXPERIENCE.
SOMEONE ELSE I HAVE TO LOOK OUT FOR.
WELL, IF HE'S ANYTHING LIKE HIS OLD MAN, HE WON'T NEED YOU LOOKING OUT FOR HIM.
YOU KNOW, I'M NOT SO SURE ABOUT THIS...
THAT'S BETTER, DON'T YOU THINK?
TRICK ARROWS
IF
INTERIOR DESIGN LOST A GENIUS, WALLY.
I WORRY BECAUSE EVERYONE SEEMS TO LOOK UP TO ME AND IT'S MAKING ME A LITTLE UNCOMFORTABLE.
I CAN TRY BUT I CAN'T SOLVE EVERY PROBLEM. I DON'T KNOW IF I CAN LIVE UP TO THIS... MYTH THEY WANT ME TO BE.
HOW DOES BATMAN MANAGE TO MAKE HIS OWN RULES?
BY BEING COLD AND HARD TO KNOW. YOU'RE SUPERMAN; YOU COULDN'T ACT LIKE THAT IF YOU REHEARSED.

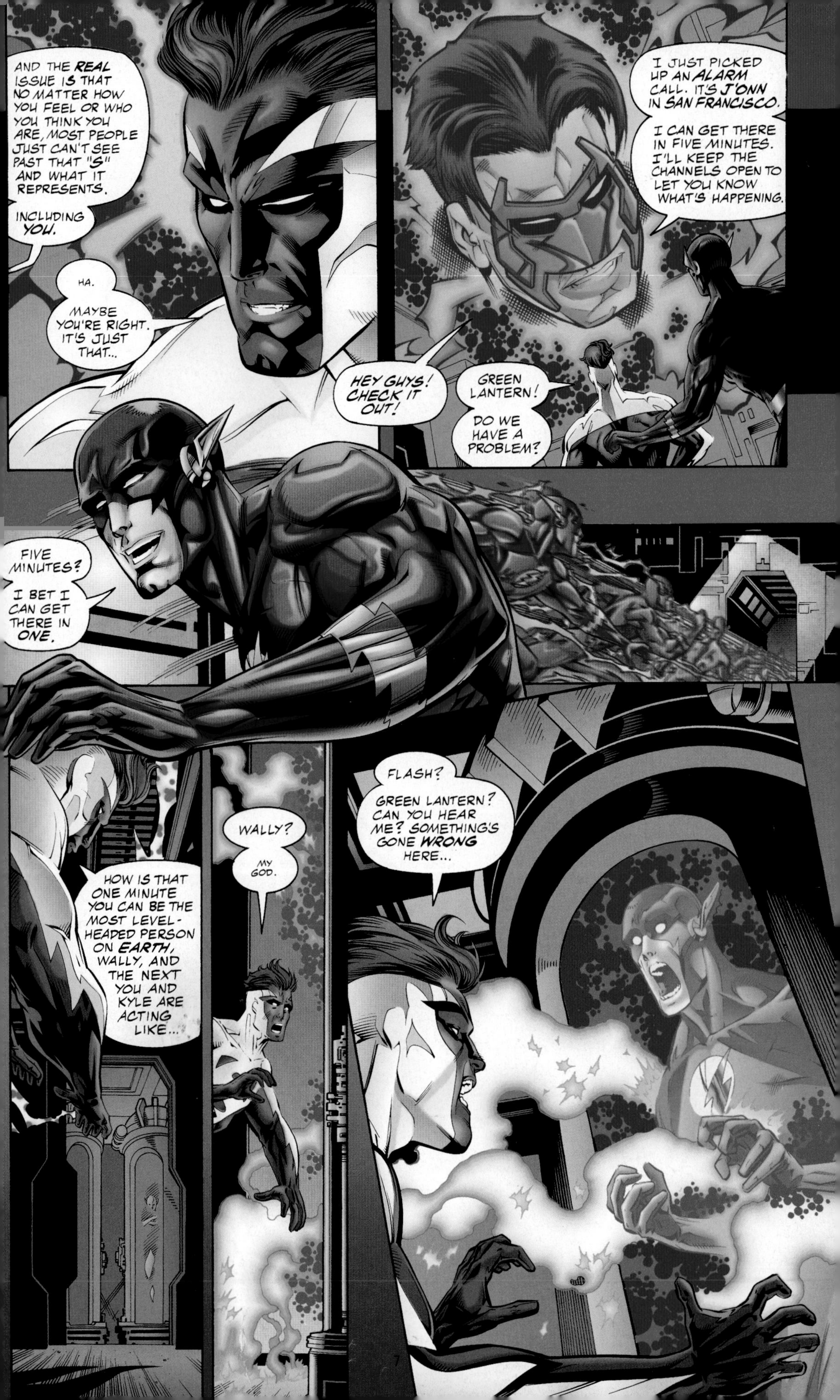
AND THE REAL ISSUE IS THAT NO MATTER HOW YOU FEEL OR WHO YOU THINK YOU ARE, MOST PEOPLE JUST CAN'T SEE PAST THAT "S" AND WHAT IT REPRESENTS.
INCLUDING YOU.
HA.
MAYBE YOU'RE RIGHT. IT'S JUST THAT...
I JUST PICKED UP AN ALARM CALL. IT'S J'ONN IN SAN FRANCISCO.
I CAN GET THERE IN FIVE MINUTES. I'LL KEEP THE CHANNELS OPEN TO LET YOU KNOW WHAT'S HAPPENING.
HEY GUYS! CHECK IT OUT!
GREEN LANTERN!
DO WE HAVE A PROBLEM?
FIVE MINUTES?
I BET I CAN GET THERE IN ONE.
HOW IS THAT ONE MINUTE YOU CAN BE THE MOST LEVEL-HEADED PERSON ON EARTH, WALLY, AND THE NEXT YOU AND KYLE ARE ACTING LIKE...
WALLY?
MY GOD.
FLASH?
GREEN LANTERN? CAN YOU HEAR ME? SOMETHING'S GONE WRONG HERE...

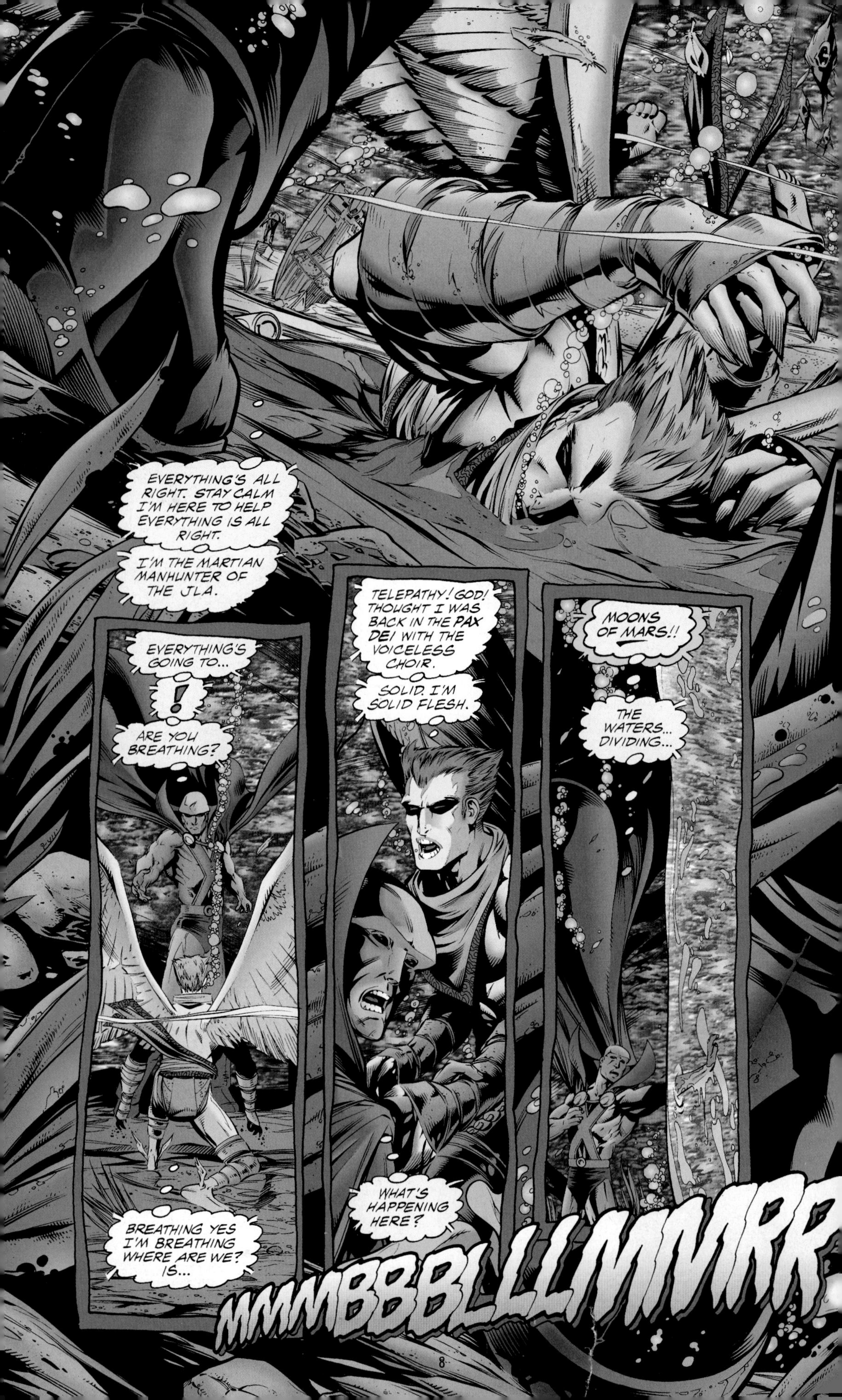

EVERYTHING'S ALL RIGHT. STAY CALM I'M HERE TO HELP EVERYTHING IS ALL RIGHT.
I'M THE MARTIAN MANHUNTER OF THE JLA.
EVERYTHING'S GOING TO...
!
ARE YOU BREATHING?
BREATHING YES I'M BREATHING WHERE ARE WE? IS...
TELEPATHY! GOD! THOUGHT I WAS BACK IN THE PAX DEI WITH THE VOICELESS CHOIR.
SOLID. I'M SOLID FLESH.
WHAT'S HAPPENING HERE?
MOONS OF MARS!!
THE WATERS... DIVIDING...
MMMBBBLLLMMRR

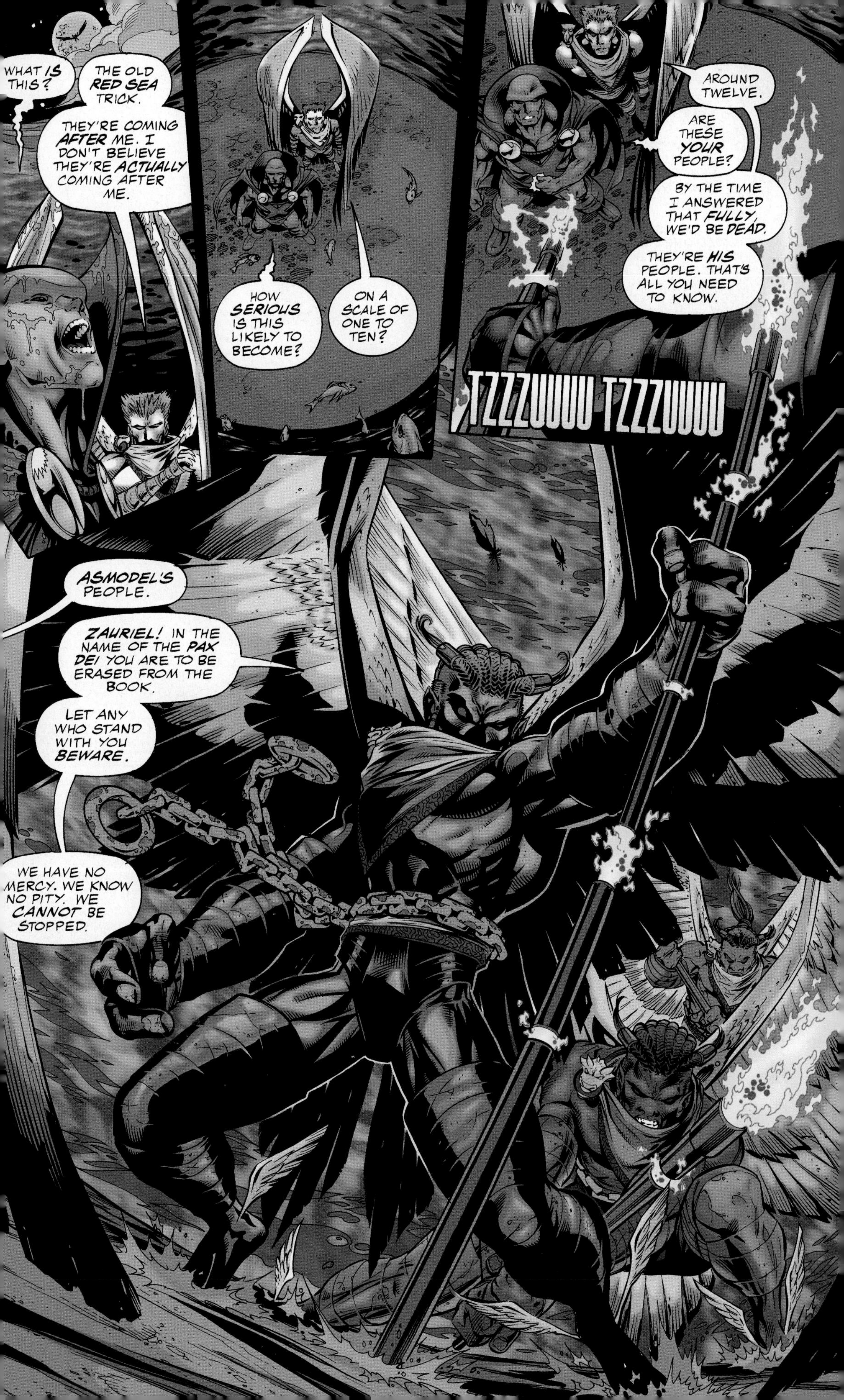

WHAT IS THIS?
THE OLD RED SEA TRICK.
THEY'RE COMING AFTER ME. I DON'T BELIEVE THEY'RE ACTUALLY COMING AFTER ME.
HOW SERIOUS IS THIS LIKELY TO BECOME?
ON A SCALE OF ONE TO TEN?
AROUND TWELVE.
ARE THESE YOUR PEOPLE?
BY THE TIME I ANSWERED THAT FULLY, WE'D BE DEAD.
THEY'RE HIS PEOPLE. THAT'S ALL YOU NEED TO KNOW.
TZZZUUUU TZZZUUUU
ASMODEL'S PEOPLE.
ZAURIEL! IN THE NAME OF THE PAX DEI YOU ARE TO BE ERASED FROM THE BOOK.
LET ANY WHO STAND WITH YOU BEWARE.
WE HAVE NO MERCY. WE KNOW NO PITY. WE CANNOT BE STOPPED.

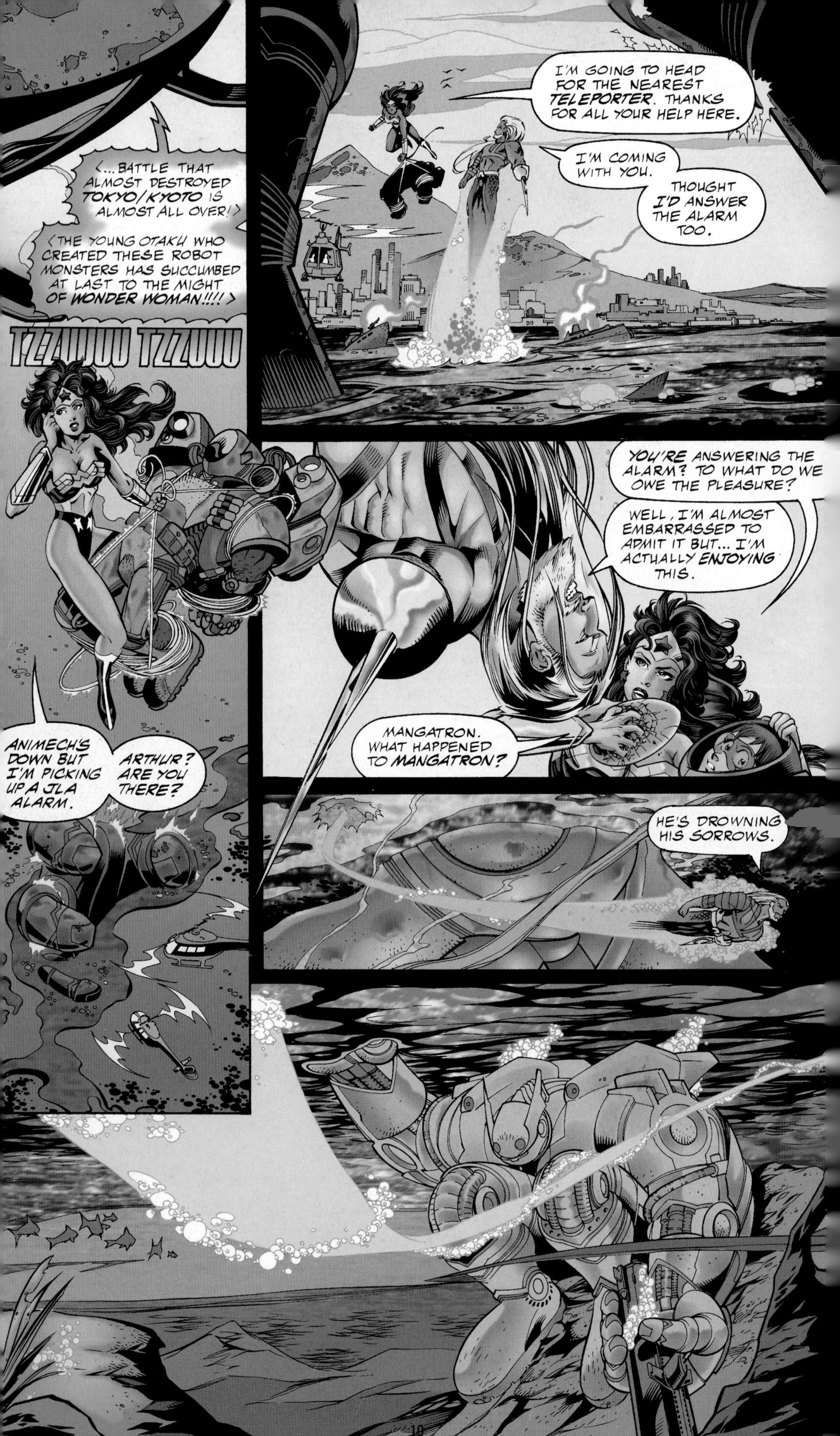
<...BATTLE THAT ALMOST DESTROYED TOKYO/KYOTO IS ALMOST ALL OVER!>
<THE YOUNG OTAKU WHO CREATED THESE ROBOT MONSTERS HAS SUCCUMBED AT LAST TO THE MIGHT OF WONDER WOMAN!!!!>
TZZUUUU TZZUUU
ANIMECH'S DOWN BUT I'M PICKING UP A JLA ALARM.
ARTHUR? ARE YOU THERE?
I'M GOING TO HEAD FOR THE NEAREST TELEPORTER. THANKS FOR ALL YOUR HELP HERE.
I'M COMING WITH YOU.
THOUGHT I'D ANSWER THE ALARM TOO.
YOU'RE ANSWERING THE ALARM? TO WHAT DO WE OWE THE PLEASURE?
WELL, I'M ALMOST EMBARRASSED TO ADMIT IT BUT... I'M ACTUALLY ENJOYING THIS.
MANGATRON. WHAT HAPPENED TO MANGATRON?
HE'S DROWNING HIS SORROWS.

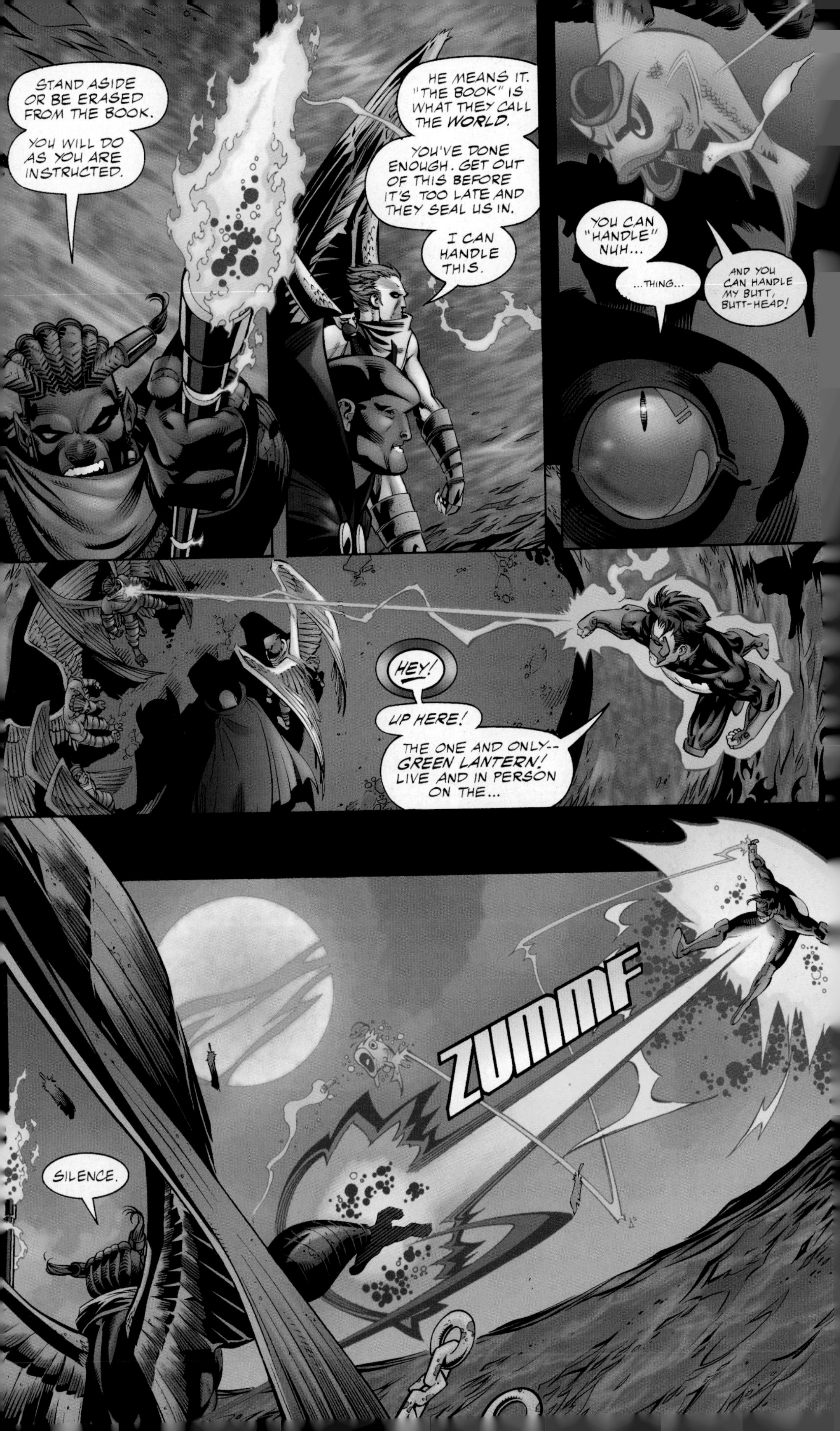

STAND ASIDE OR BE ERASED FROM THE BOOK.
YOU WILL DO AS YOU ARE INSTRUCTED.
HE MEANS IT. "THE BOOK" IS WHAT THEY CALL THE WORLD.
YOU'VE DONE ENOUGH. GET OUT OF THIS BEFORE IT'S TOO LATE AND THEY SEAL US IN.
I CAN HANDLE THIS.
YOU CAN "HANDLE" NUH...
...THING...
AND YOU CAN HANDLE MY BUTT, BUTT-HEAD!
HEY!
UP HERE!
THE ONE AND ONLY-- GREEN LANTERN! LIVE AND IN PERSON ON THE...
ZUMMF
SILENCE.

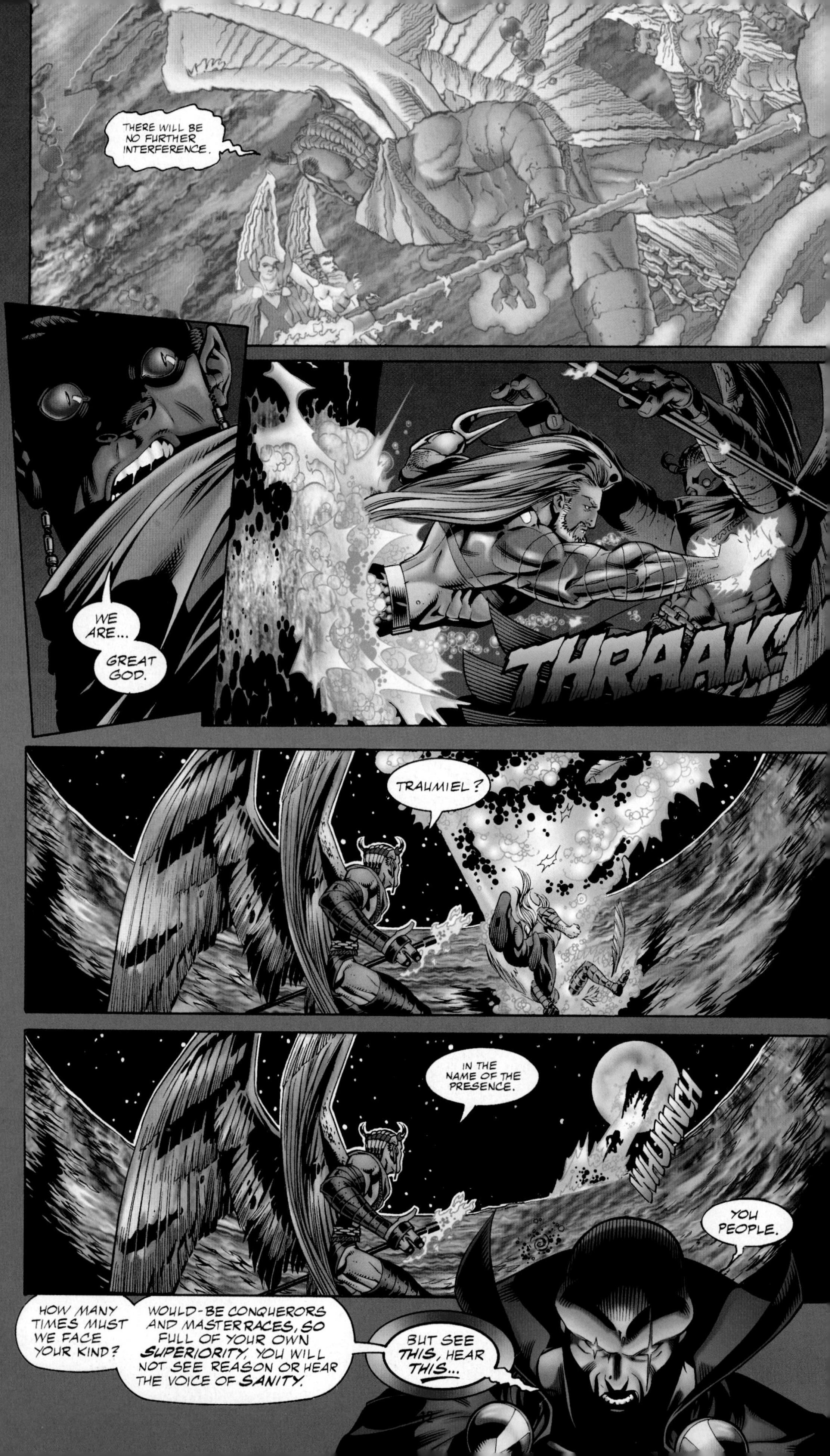

THERE WILL BE NO FURTHER INTERFERENCE.
WE ARE...
GREAT GOD.
THRAAK!
TRAUMIEL?
IN THE NAME OF THE PRESENCE.
WHUNNCH
YOU PEOPLE.
HOW MANY TIMES MUST WE FACE YOUR KIND?
WOULD-BE CONQUERORS AND MASTER RACES, SO FULL OF YOUR OWN SUPERIORITY, YOU WILL NOT SEE REASON OR HEAR THE VOICE OF SANITY.
BUT SEE THIS, HEAR THIS...

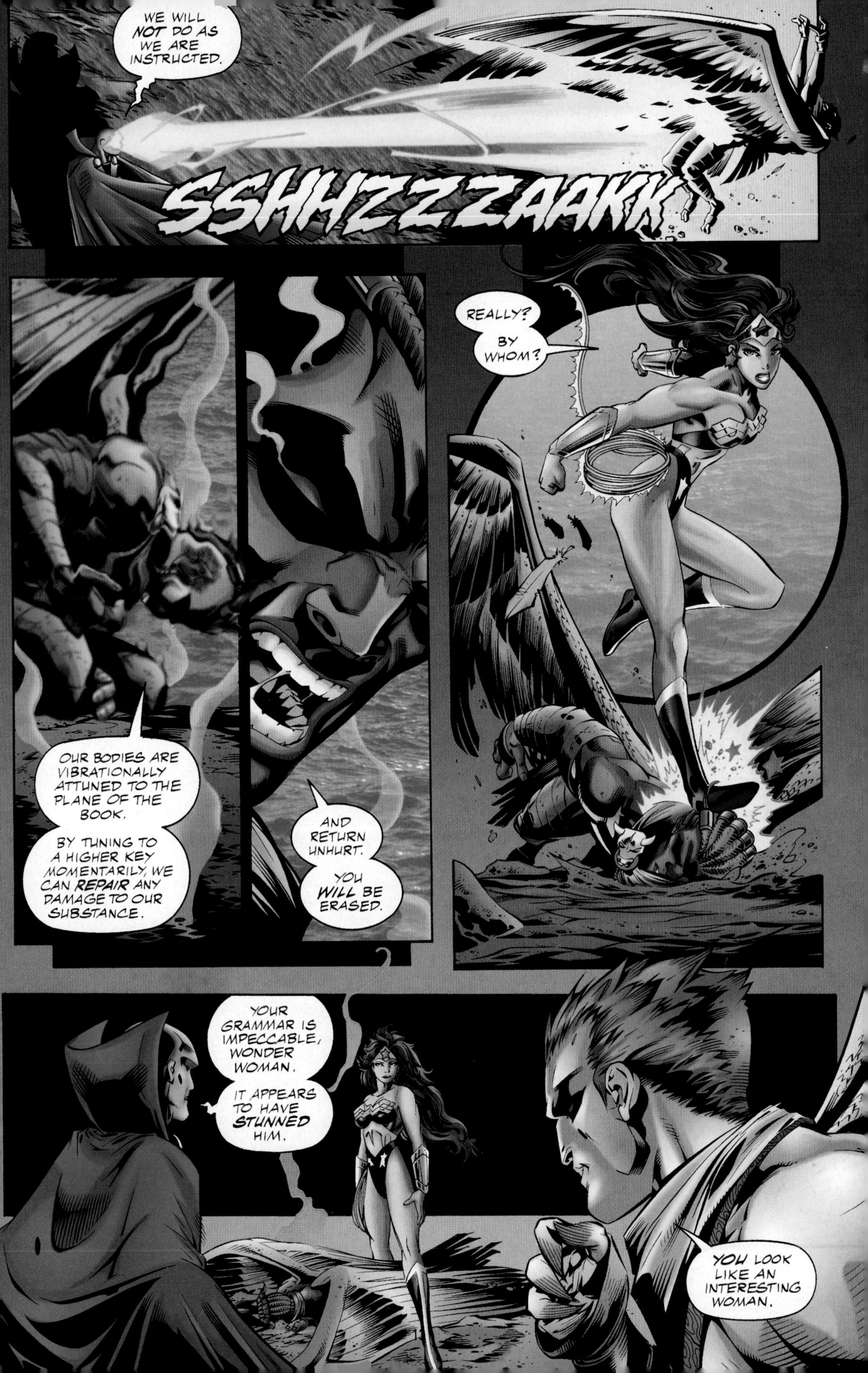

WE WILL NOT DO AS WE ARE INSTRUCTED.
SSHHZZZAAKK
REALLY?
BY WHOM?
OUR BODIES ARE VIBRATIONALLY ATTUNED TO THE PLANE OF THE BOOK.
BY TUNING TO A HIGHER KEY MOMENTARILY, WE CAN REPAIR ANY DAMAGE TO OUR SUBSTANCE.
AND RETURN UNHURT.
YOU WILL BE ERASED.
YOUR GRAMMAR IS IMPECCABLE, WONDER WOMAN.
IT APPEARS TO HAVE STUNNED HIM.
YOU LOOK LIKE AN INTERESTING WOMAN.

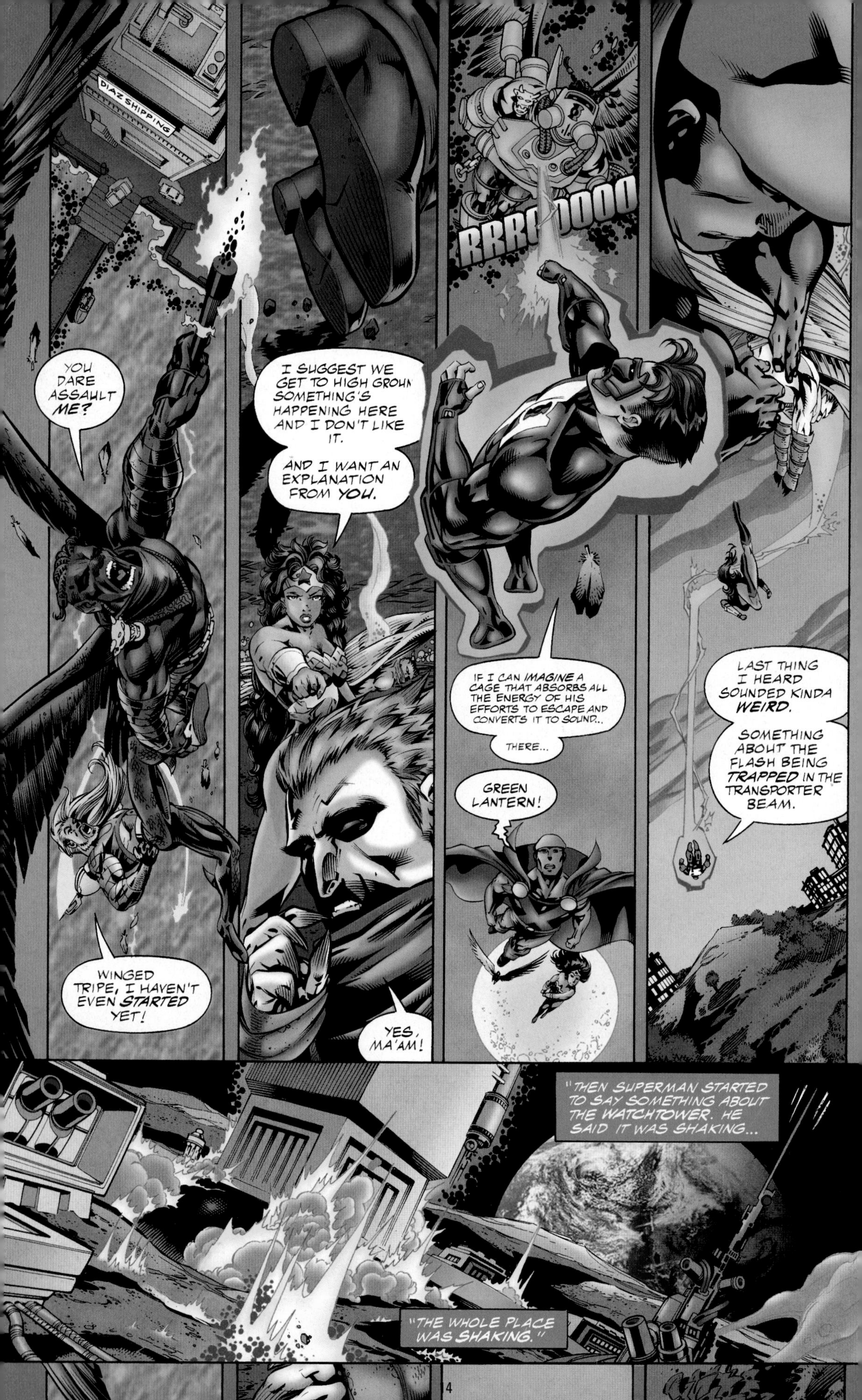
DIAZ SHIPPING
YOU DARE ASSAULT ME?
WINGED TRIPE, I HAVEN'T EVEN STARTED YET!
I SUGGEST WE GET TO HIGH GROUN SOMETHING'S HAPPENING HERE AND I DON'T LIKE IT.
AND I WANT AN EXPLANATION FROM YOU.
YES, MA'AM!
RRRO OOOO
IF I CAN IMAGINE A CAGE THAT ABSORBS ALL THE ENERGY OF HIS EFFORTS TO ESCAPE AND CONVERTS IT TO SOUND...
THERE...
GREEN LANTERN!
LAST THING I HEARD SOUNDED KINDA WEIRD.
SOMETHING ABOUT THE FLASH BEING TRAPPED IN THE TRANSPORTER BEAM.
"THEN SUPERMAN STARTED TO SAY SOMETHING ABOUT THE WATCHTOWER. HE SAID IT WAS SHAKING...
"THE WHOLE PLACE WAS SHAKING."

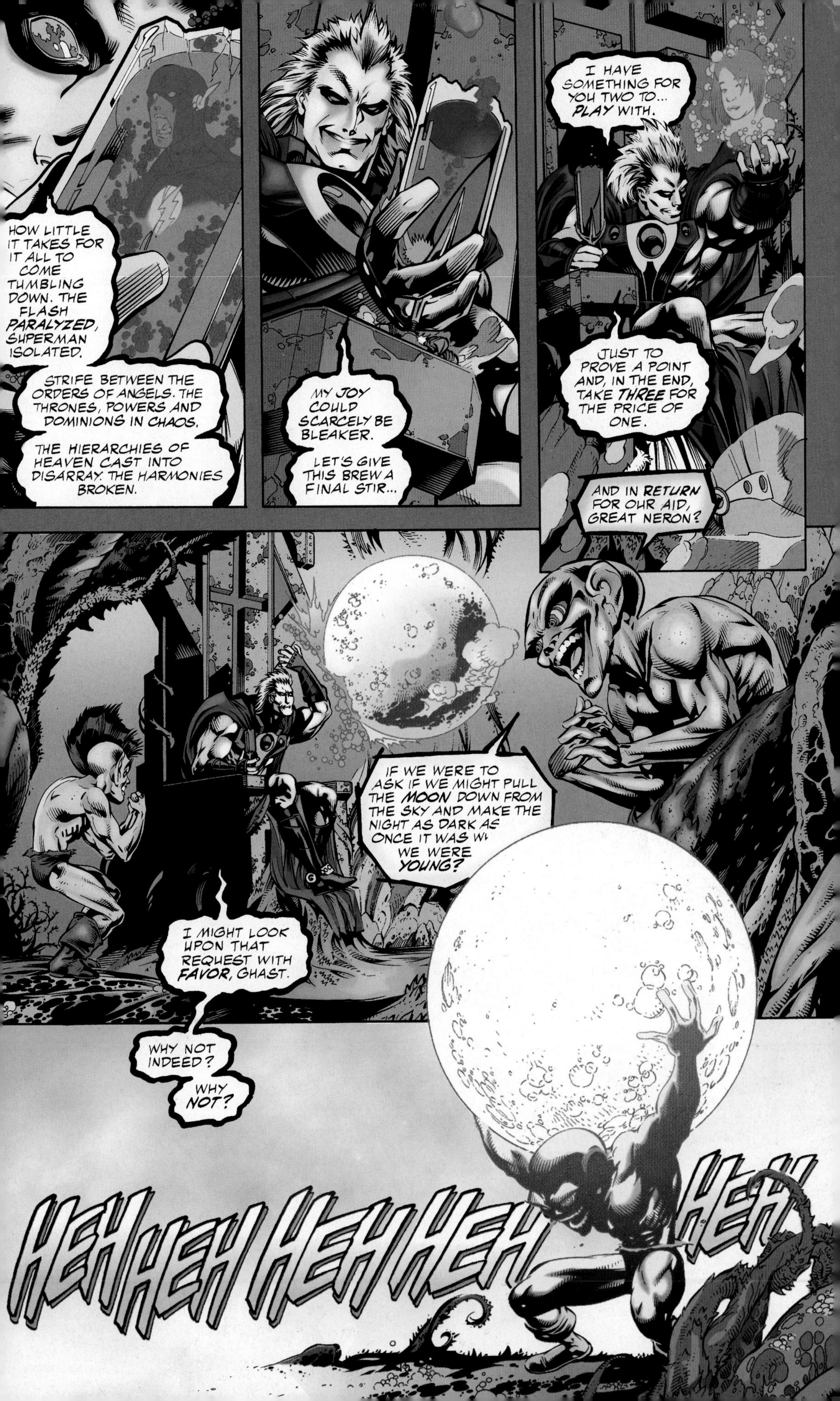
HOW LITTLE IT TAKES FOR IT ALL TO COME TUMBLING DOWN. THE FLASH PARALYZED, SUPERMAN ISOLATED.
STRIFE BETWEEN THE ORDERS OF ANGELS. THE THRONES, POWERS AND DOMINIONS IN CHAOS.
THE HIERARCHIES OF HEAVEN CAST INTO DISARRAY. THE HARMONIES BROKEN.
MY JOY COULD SCARCELY BE BLEAKER.
LET'S GIVE THIS BREW A FINAL STIR...
I HAVE SOMETHING FOR YOU TWO TO... PLAY WITH.
JUST TO PROVE A POINT AND, IN THE END, TAKE THREE FOR THE PRICE OF ONE.
AND IN RETURN FOR OUR AID, GREAT NERON?
IF WE WERE TO ASK IF WE MIGHT PULL THE MOON DOWN FROM THE SKY AND MAKE THE NIGHT AS DARK AS ONCE IT WAS W
WE WERE YOUNG?
I MIGHT LOOK UPON THAT REQUEST WITH FAVOR, GHAST.
WHY NOT INDEED?
WHY NOT?
HEH HEH HEH HEH HEH

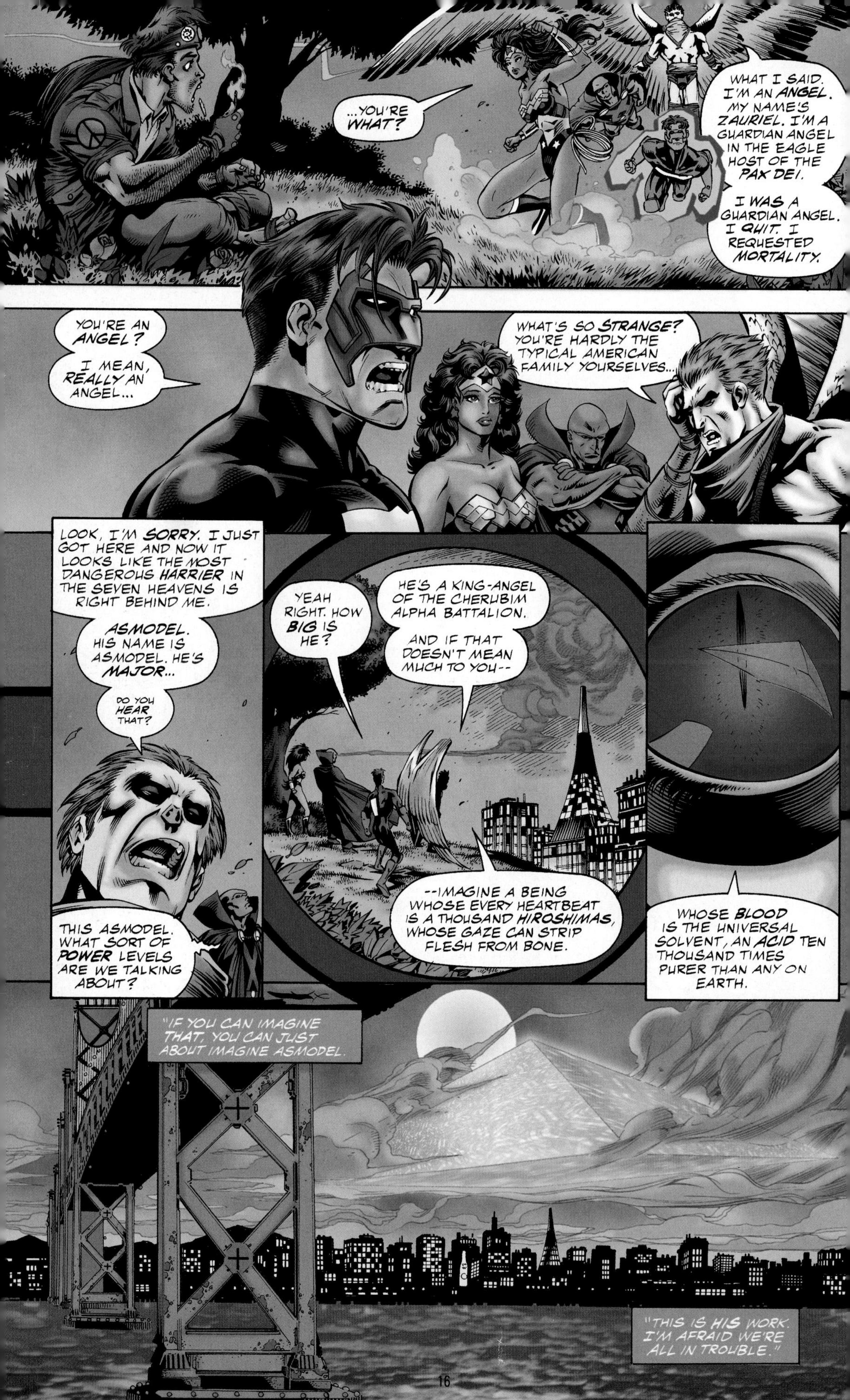
...YOU'RE WHAT?
WHAT I SAID. I'M AN ANGEL. MY NAME'S ZAURIEL. I'M A GUARDIAN ANGEL IN THE EAGLE HOST OF THE PAX DEI.
I WAS A GUARDIAN ANGEL. I QUIT. I REQUESTED MORTALITY.
YOU'RE AN ANGEL?
I MEAN, REALLY AN ANGEL...
WHAT'S SO STRANGE? YOU'RE HARDLY THE TYPICAL AMERICAN FAMILY YOURSELVES...
LOOK, I'M SORRY. I JUST GOT HERE AND NOW IT LOOKS LIKE THE MOST DANGEROUS HARRIER IN THE SEVEN HEAVENS IS RIGHT BEHIND ME.
ASMODEL. HIS NAME IS ASMODEL. HE'S MAJOR...
DO YOU HEAR THAT?
THIS ASMODEL. WHAT SORT OF POWER LEVELS ARE WE TALKING ABOUT?
YEAH RIGHT. HOW BIG IS HE?
HE'S A KING-ANGEL OF THE CHERUBIM ALPHA BATTALION.
AND IF THAT DOESN'T MEAN MUCH TO YOU--
--IMAGINE A BEING WHOSE EVERY HEARTBEAT IS A THOUSAND HIROSHIMAS, WHOSE GAZE CAN STRIP FLESH FROM BONE.
WHOSE BLOOD IS THE UNIVERSAL SOLVENT, AN ACID TEN THOUSAND TIMES PURER THAN ANY ON EARTH.
"IF YOU CAN IMAGINE THAT, YOU CAN JUST ABOUT IMAGINE ASMODEL.
"THIS IS HIS WORK. I'M AFRAID WE'RE ALL IN TROUBLE."

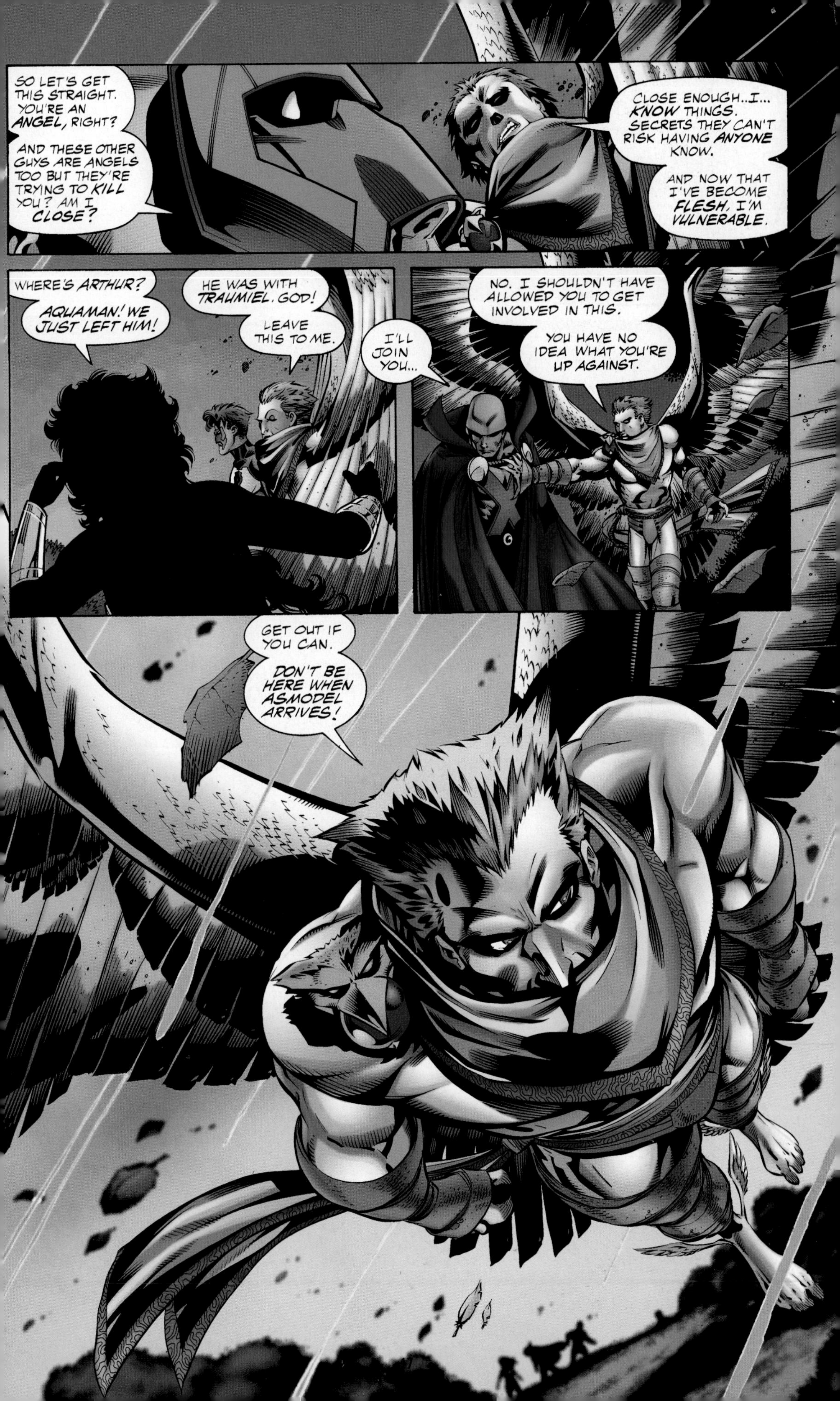

SO LET'S GET THIS STRAIGHT. YOU'RE AN ANGEL, RIGHT?
AND THESE OTHER GUYS ARE ANGELS TOO BUT THEY'RE TRYING TO KILL YOU? AM I CLOSE?
CLOSE ENOUGH...I... KNOW THINGS. SECRETS THEY CAN'T RISK HAVING ANYONE KNOW.
AND NOW THAT I'VE BECOME FLESH, I'M VULNERABLE.
WHERE'S ARTHUR?
AQUAMAN! WE JUST LEFT HIM!
HE WAS WITH TRAUMIEL. GOD!
LEAVE THIS TO ME.
I'LL JOIN YOU...
NO. I SHOULDN'T HAVE ALLOWED YOU TO GET INVOLVED IN THIS.
YOU HAVE NO IDEA WHAT YOU'RE UP AGAINST.
GET OUT IF YOU CAN.
DON'T BE HERE WHEN ASMODEL ARRIVES!

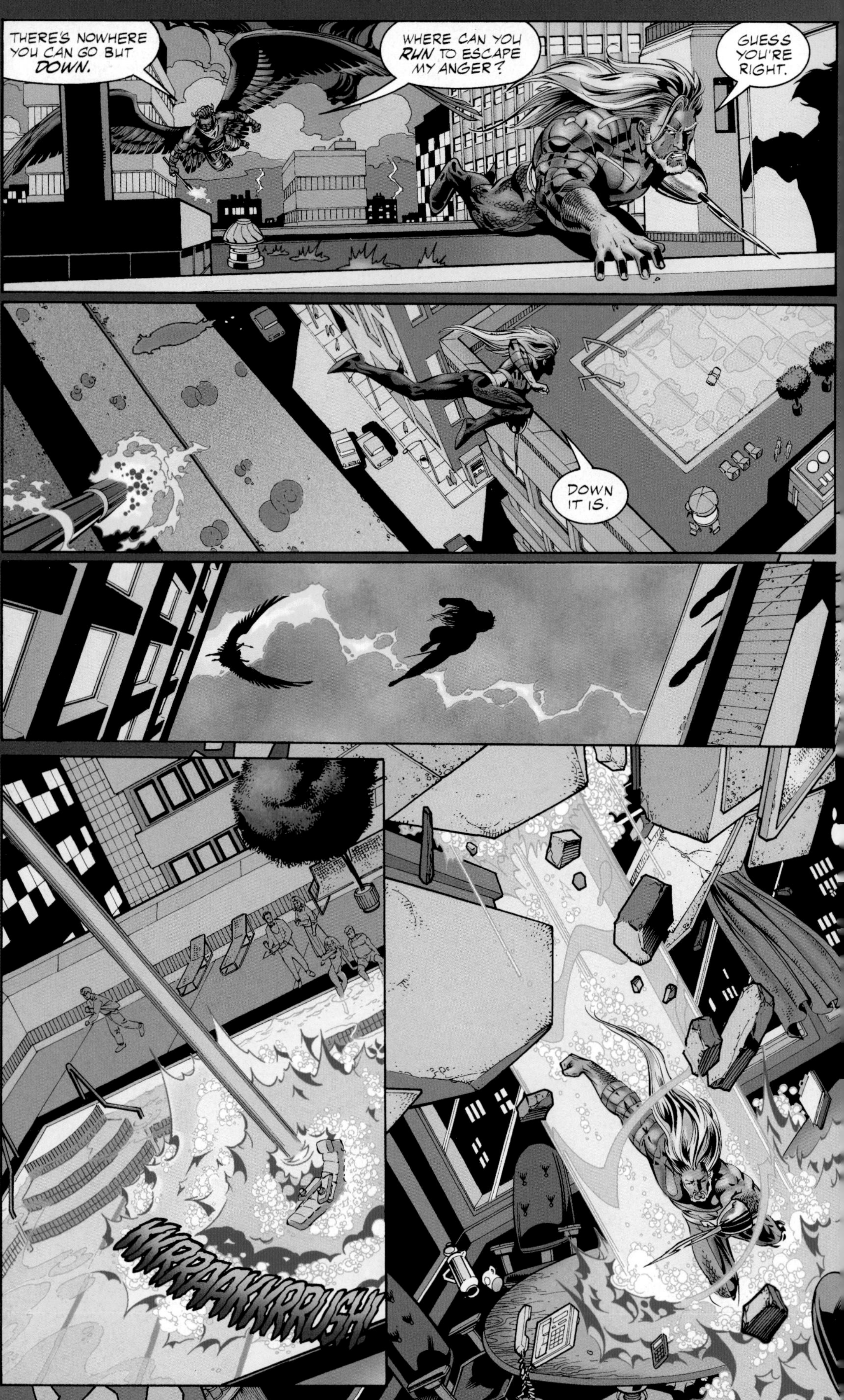
THERE'S NOWHERE YOU CAN GO BUT DOWN.
WHERE CAN YOU RUN TO ESCAPE MY ANGER?
GUESS YOU'RE RIGHT.
DOWN IT IS.
KKRRAKKKRRUSH!

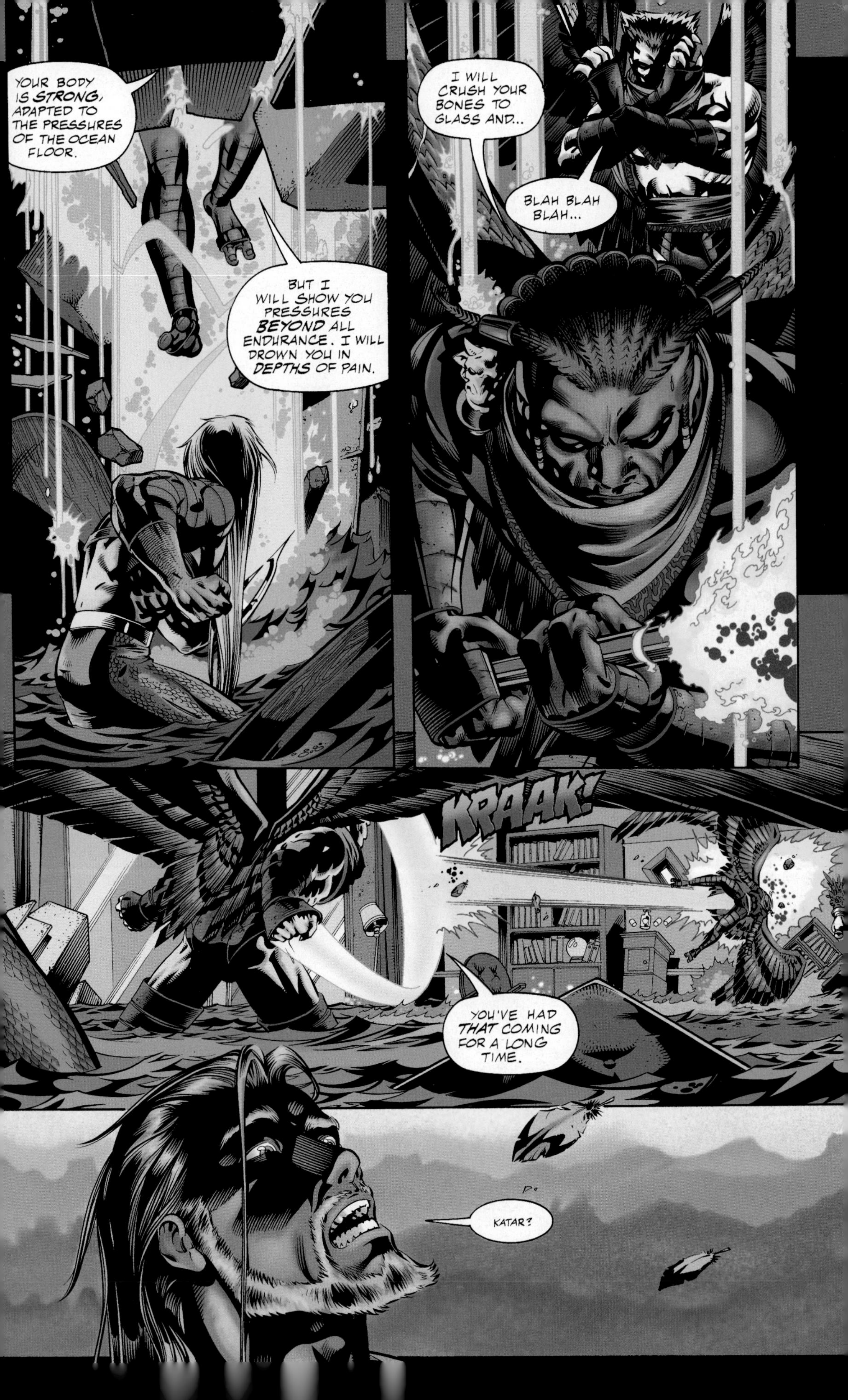
YOUR BODY IS STRONG, ADAPTED TO THE PRESSURES OF THE OCEAN FLOOR.
BUT I WILL SHOW YOU PRESSURES BEYOND ALL ENDURANCE. I WILL DROWN YOU IN DEPTHS OF PAIN.
I WILL CRUSH YOUR BONES TO GLASS AND...
BLAH BLAH BLAH...
KRAAK!
YOU'VE HAD THAT COMING FOR A LONG TIME.
KATAR?

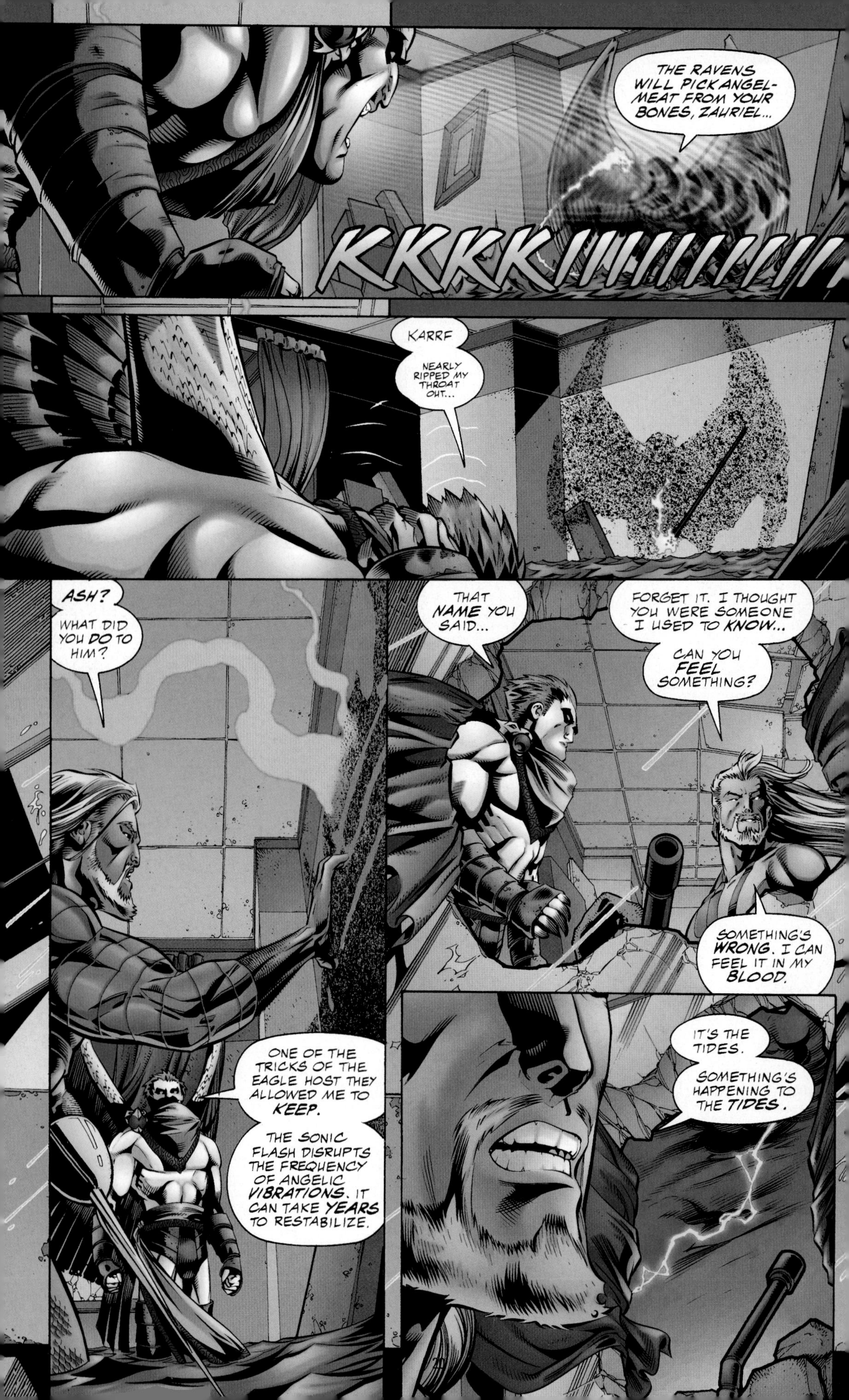
THE RAVENS WILL PICK ANGEL-MEAT FROM YOUR BONES, ZAURIEL...
KKKKIIIIIIIIIIII
KARRF
NEARLY RIPPED MY THROAT OUT...
ASH? WHAT DID YOU DO TO HIM?
ONE OF THE TRICKS OF THE EAGLE HOST THEY ALLOWED ME TO KEEP.
THE SONIC FLASH DISRUPTS THE FREQUENCY OF ANGELIC VIBRATIONS. IT CAN TAKE YEARS TO RESTABILIZE.
THAT NAME YOU SAID...
FORGET IT. I THOUGHT YOU WERE SOMEONE I USED TO KNOW...
CAN YOU FEEL SOMETHING?
SOMETHING'S WRONG. I CAN FEEL IT IN MY BLOOD.
IT'S THE TIDES.
SOMETHING'S HAPPENING TO THE TIDES.

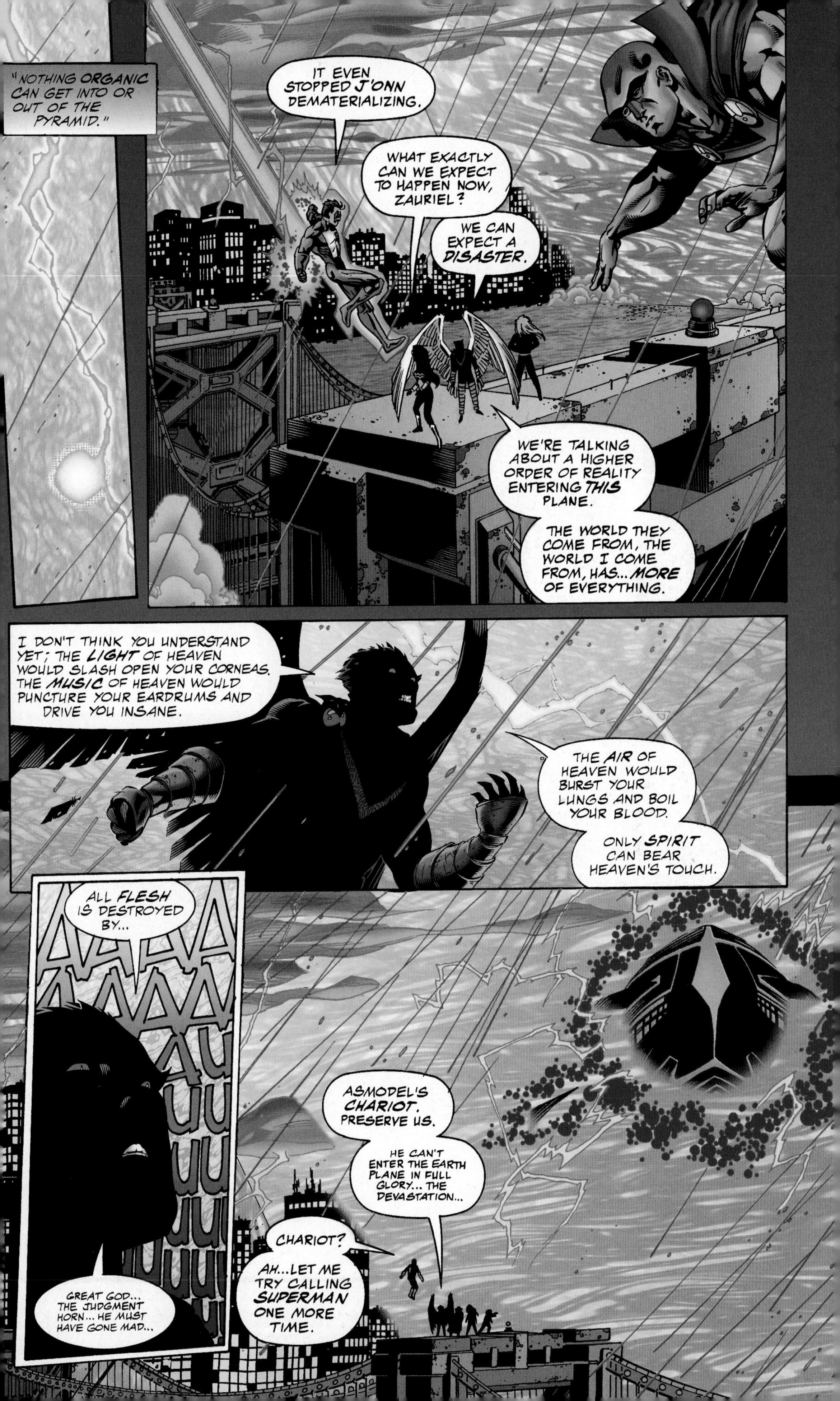
"NOTHING ORGANIC CAN GET INTO OR OUT OF THE PYRAMID."
IT EVEN STOPPED J'ONN DEMATERIALIZING.
WHAT EXACTLY CAN WE EXPECT TO HAPPEN NOW, ZAURIEL?
WE CAN EXPECT A DISASTER.
WE'RE TALKING ABOUT A HIGHER ORDER OF REALITY ENTERING THIS PLANE.
THE WORLD THEY COME FROM, THE WORLD I COME FROM, HAS... MORE OF EVERYTHING.
I DON'T THINK YOU UNDERSTAND YET; THE LIGHT OF HEAVEN WOULD SLASH OPEN YOUR CORNEAS. THE MUSIC OF HEAVEN WOULD PUNCTURE YOUR EARDRUMS AND DRIVE YOU INSANE.
THE AIR OF HEAVEN WOULD BURST YOUR LUNGS AND BOIL YOUR BLOOD.
ONLY SPIRIT CAN BEAR HEAVEN'S TOUCH.
ALL FLESH IS DESTROYED BY...
AAAAAAAAAAUUUUUUUU
GREAT GOD... THE JUDGMENT HORN... HE MUST HAVE GONE MAD...
ASMODEL'S CHARIOT. PRESERVE US.
HE CAN'T ENTER THE EARTH PLANE IN FULL GLORY... THE DEVASTATION...
CHARIOT?
AH...LET ME TRY CALLING SUPERMAN ONE MORE TIME.

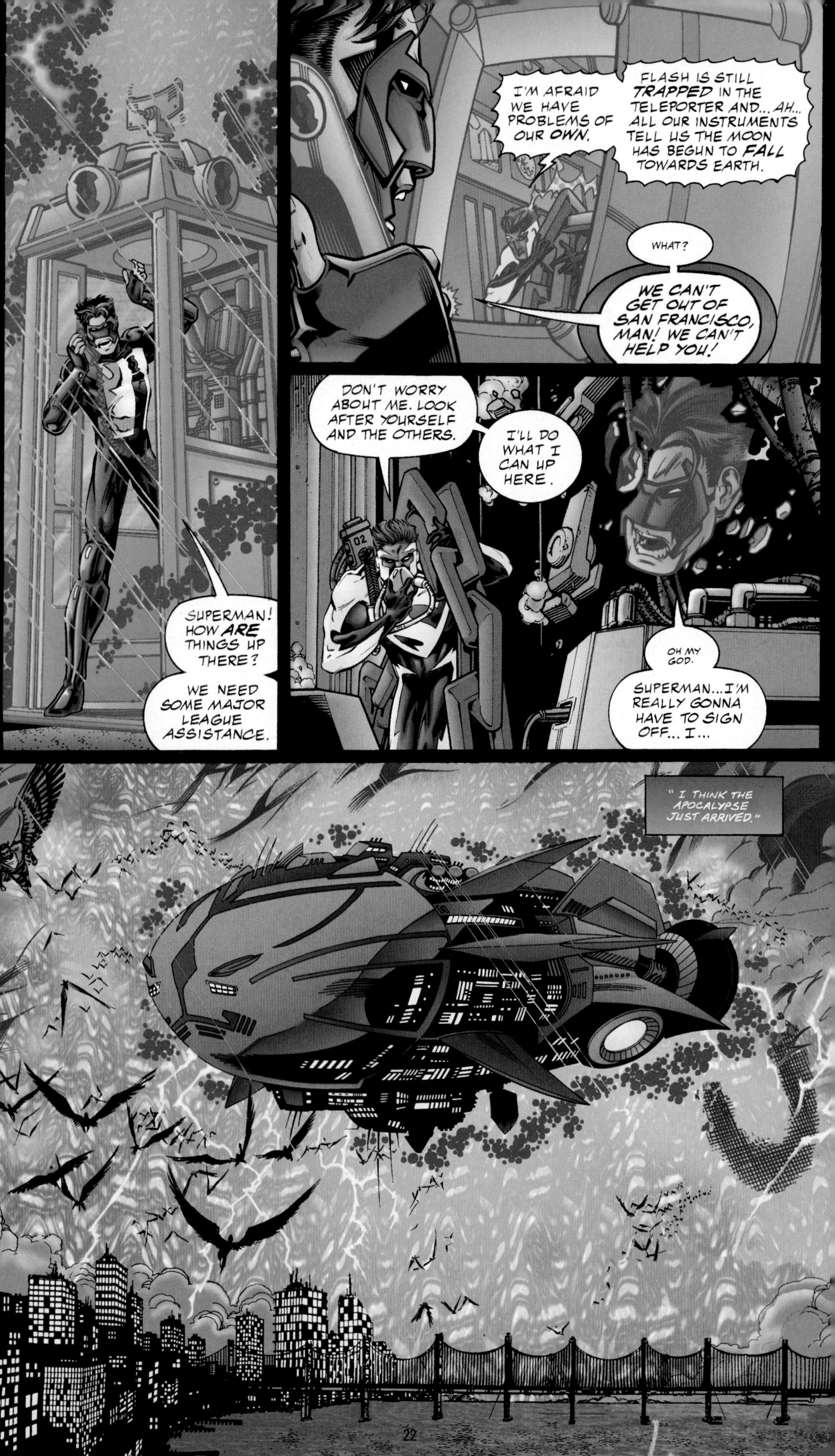

SUPERMAN! HOW ARE THINGS UP THERE?
WE NEED SOME MAJOR LEAGUE ASSISTANCE.
I'M AFRAID WE HAVE PROBLEMS OF OUR OWN.
FLASH IS STILL TRAPPED IN THE TELEPORTER AND... AH... ALL OUR INSTRUMENTS TELL US THE MOON HAS BEGUN TO FALL TOWARDS EARTH.
WHAT?
WE CAN'T GET OUT OF SAN FRANCISCO, MAN! WE CAN'T HELP YOU!
DON'T WORRY ABOUT ME. LOOK AFTER YOURSELF AND THE OTHERS.
I'LL DO WHAT I CAN UP HERE.
OH MY GOD.
SUPERMAN...I'M REALLY GONNA HAVE TO SIGN OFF... I...
" I THINK THE APOCALYPSE JUST ARRIVED."

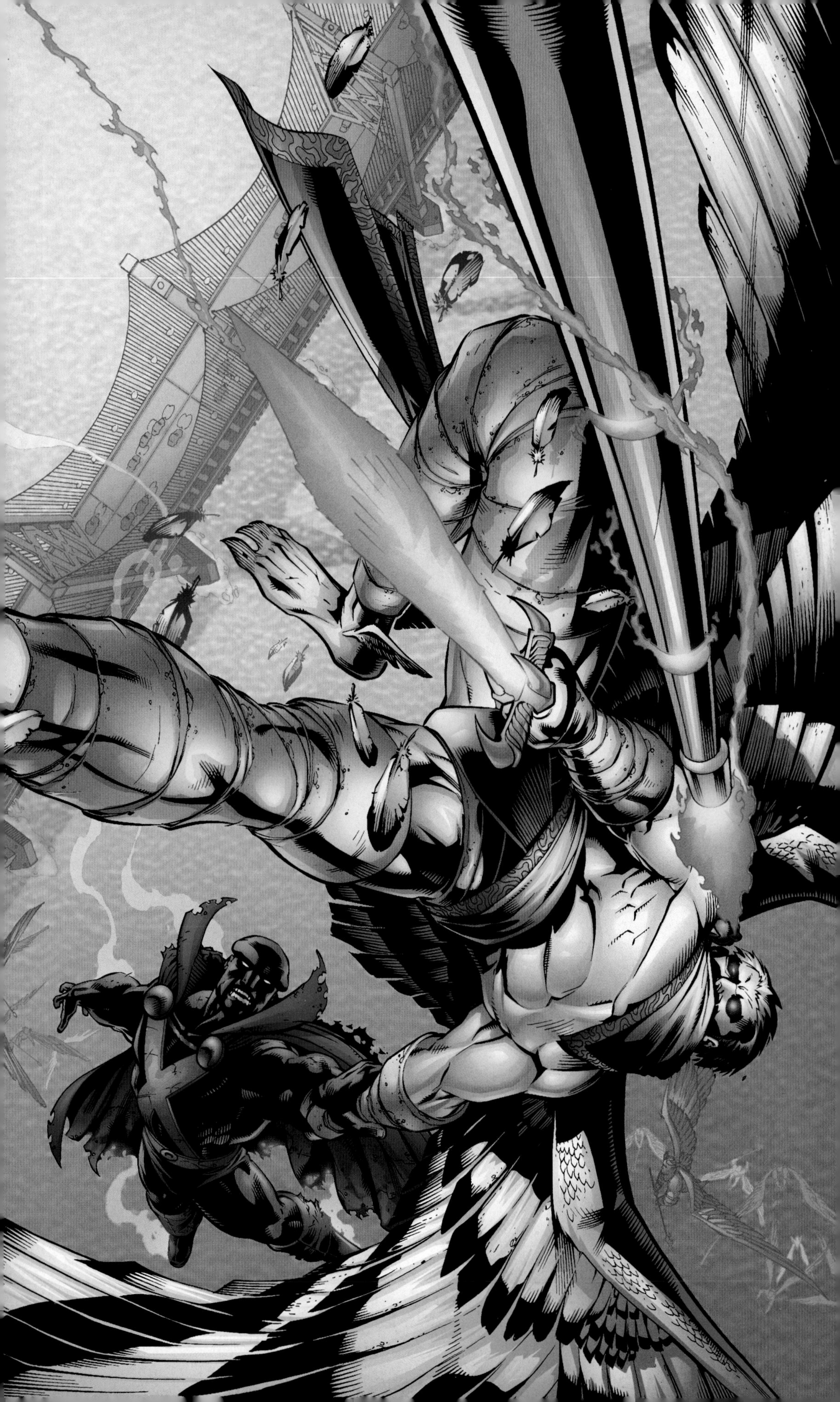

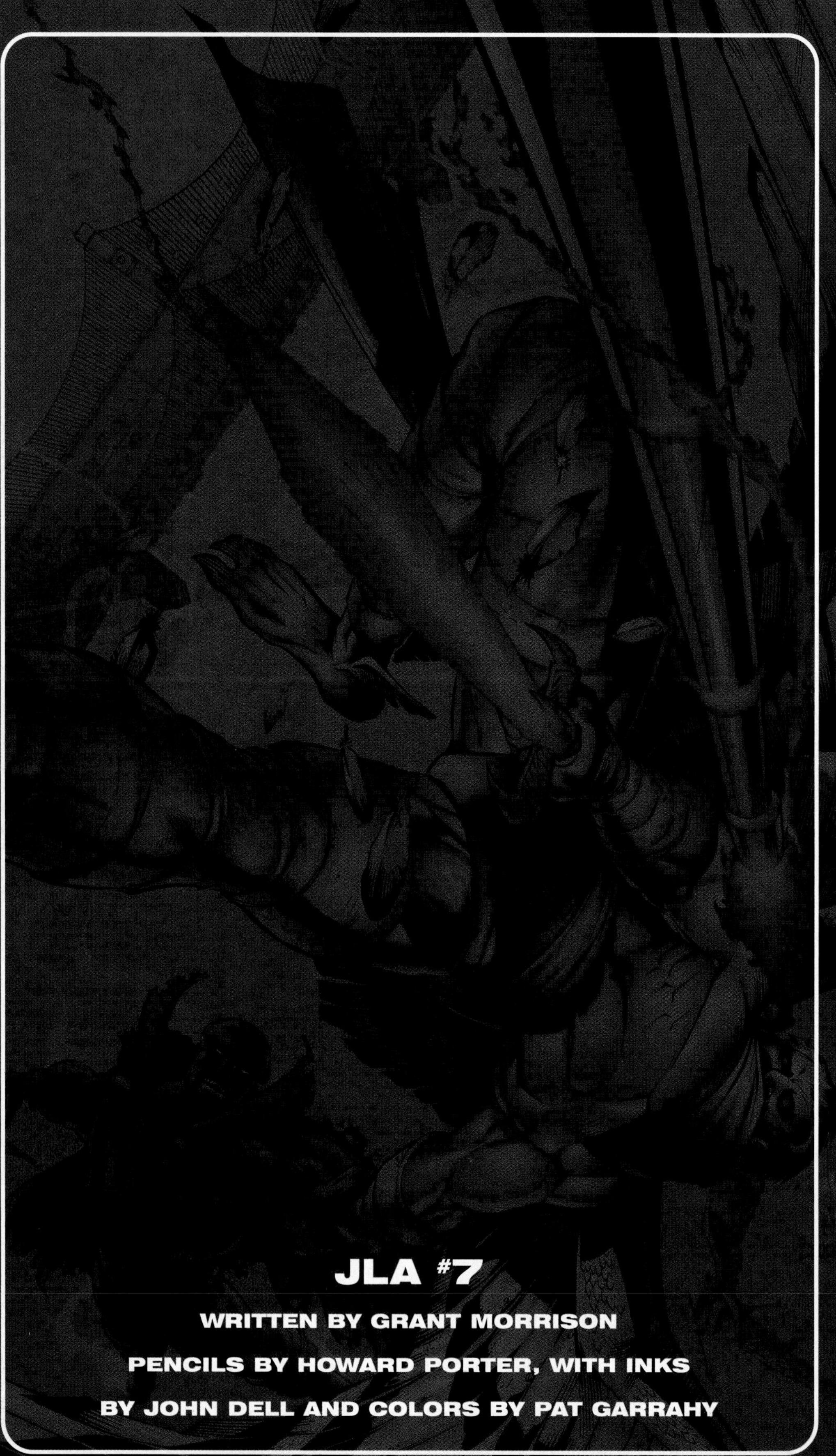

JLA #7

WRITTEN BY GRANT MORRISON

PENCILS BY HOWARD PORTER, WITH INKS BY JOHN DELL AND COLORS BY PAT GARRAHY

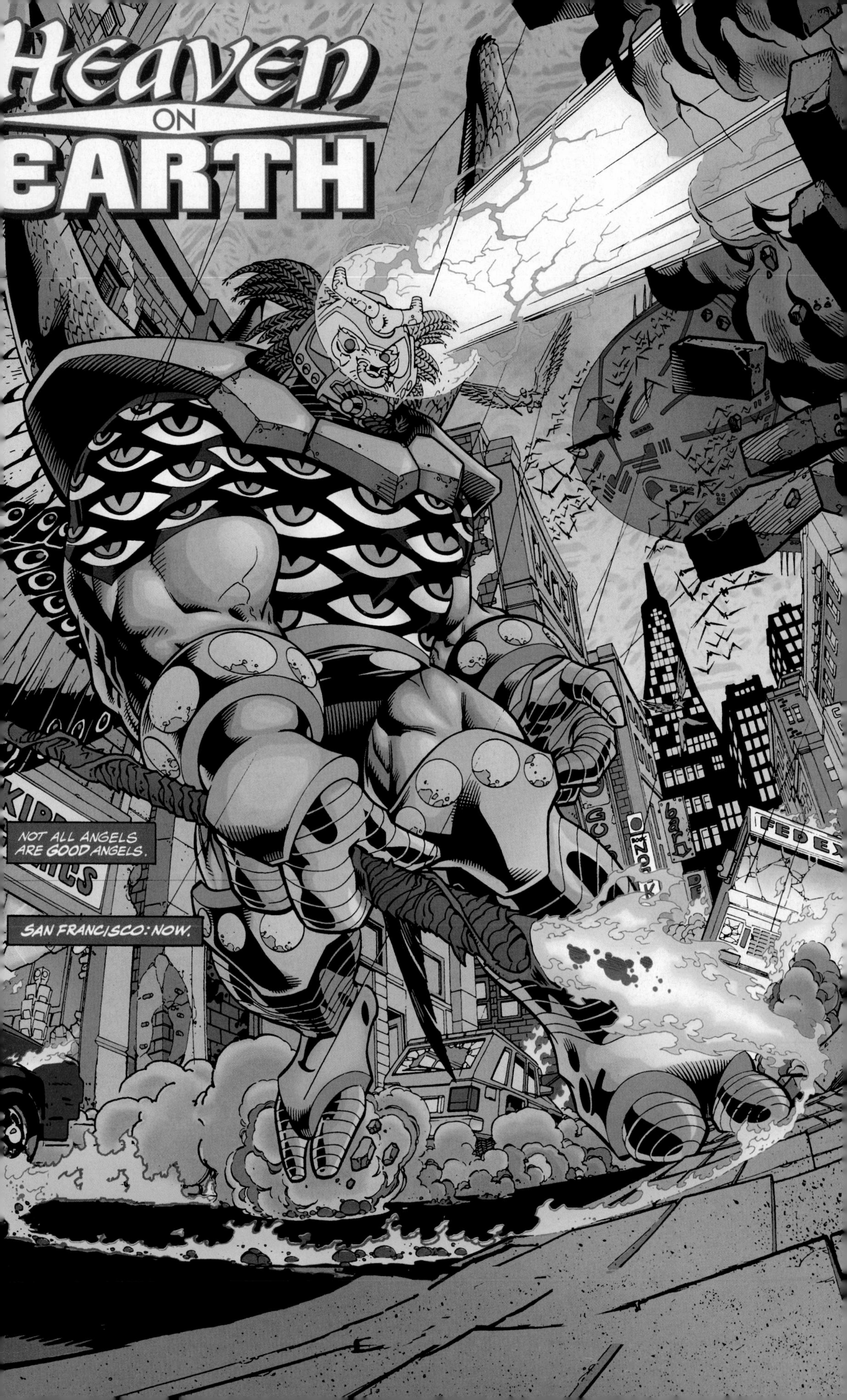
HEAVEN ON EARTH
NOT ALL ANGELS ARE GOOD ANGELS.
SAN FRANCISCO: NOW.
FEDEX

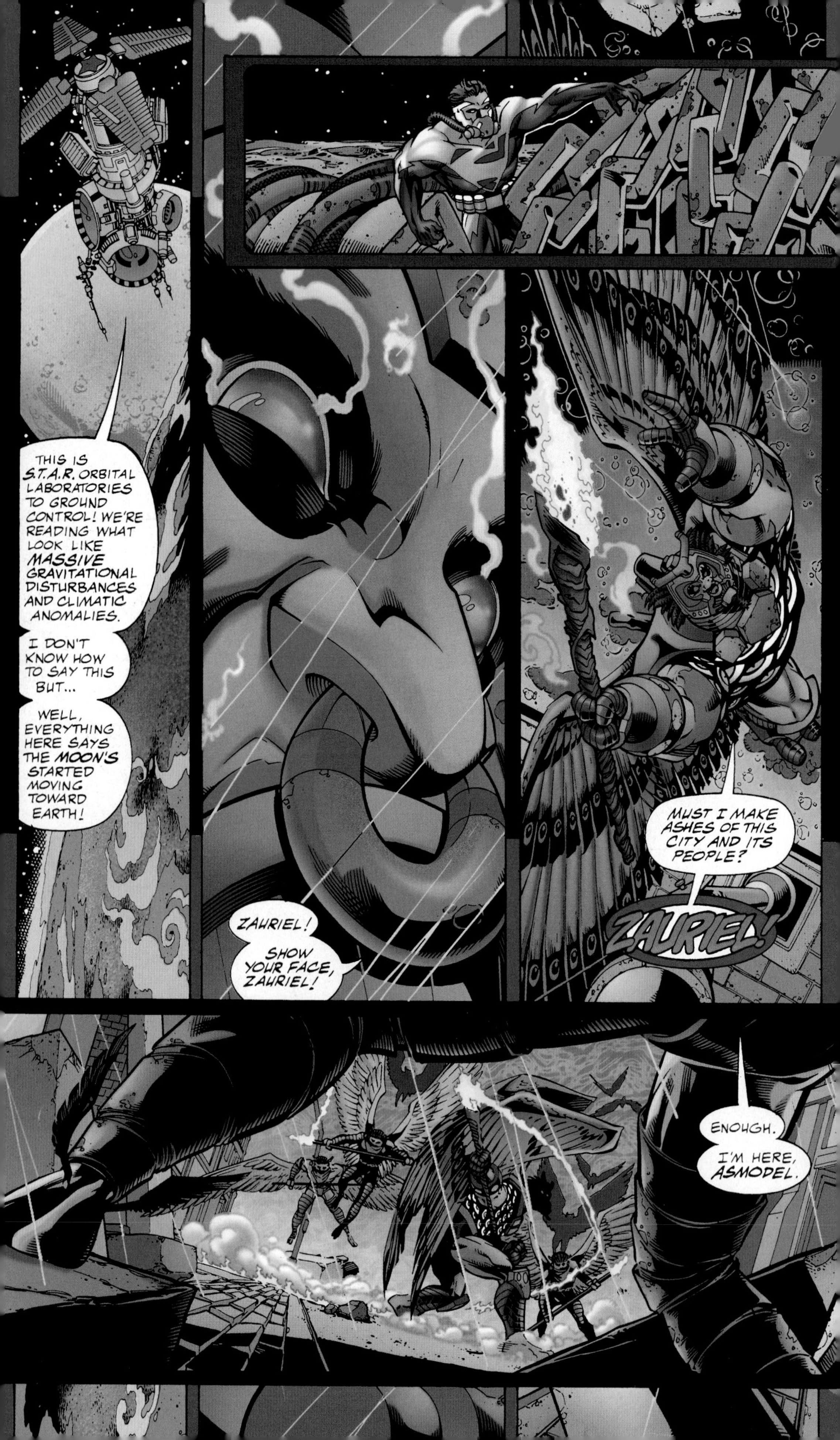
THIS IS S.T.A.R. ORBITAL LABORATORIES TO GROUND CONTROL! WE'RE READING WHAT LOOK LIKE MASSIVE GRAVITATIONAL DISTURBANCES AND CLIMATIC ANOMALIES.
I DON'T KNOW HOW TO SAY THIS BUT...
WELL, EVERYTHING HERE SAYS THE MOON'S STARTED MOVING TOWARD EARTH!
ZAURIEL!
SHOW YOUR FACE, ZAURIEL!
MUST I MAKE ASHES OF THIS CITY AND ITS PEOPLE?
ZAURIEL!
ENOUGH.
I'M HERE, ASMODEL.

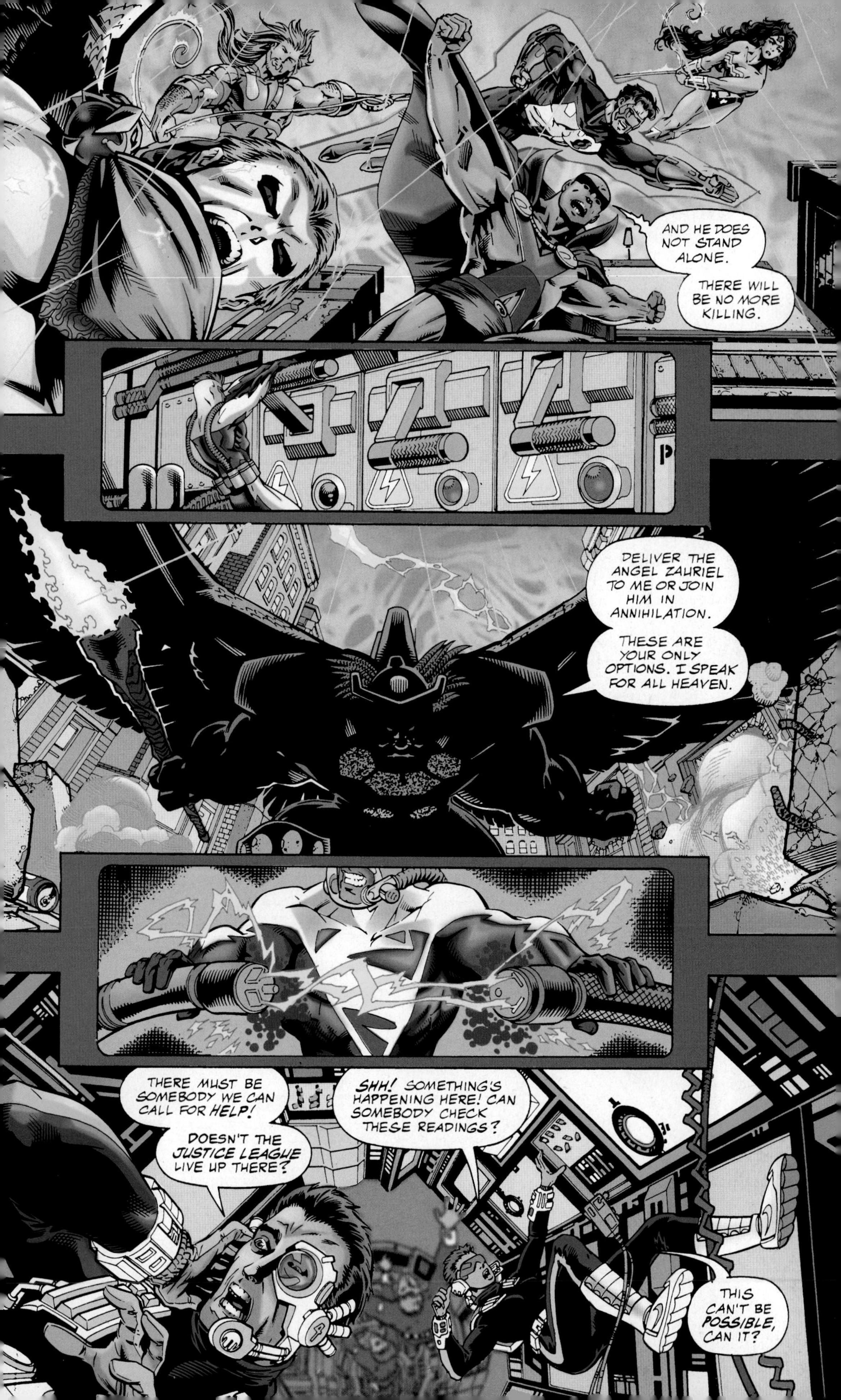
AND HE DOES NOT STAND ALONE.
THERE WILL BE NO MORE KILLING.
DELIVER THE ANGEL ZAURIEL TO ME OR JOIN HIM IN ANNIHILATION.
THESE ARE YOUR ONLY OPTIONS. I SPEAK FOR ALL HEAVEN.
THERE MUST BE SOMEBODY WE CAN CALL FOR *HELP!*
DOESN'T THE *JUSTICE LEAGUE* LIVE UP THERE?
SHH! SOMETHING'S HAPPENING HERE! CAN SOMEBODY CHECK THESE READINGS?
THIS CAN'T BE *POSSIBLE,* CAN IT?

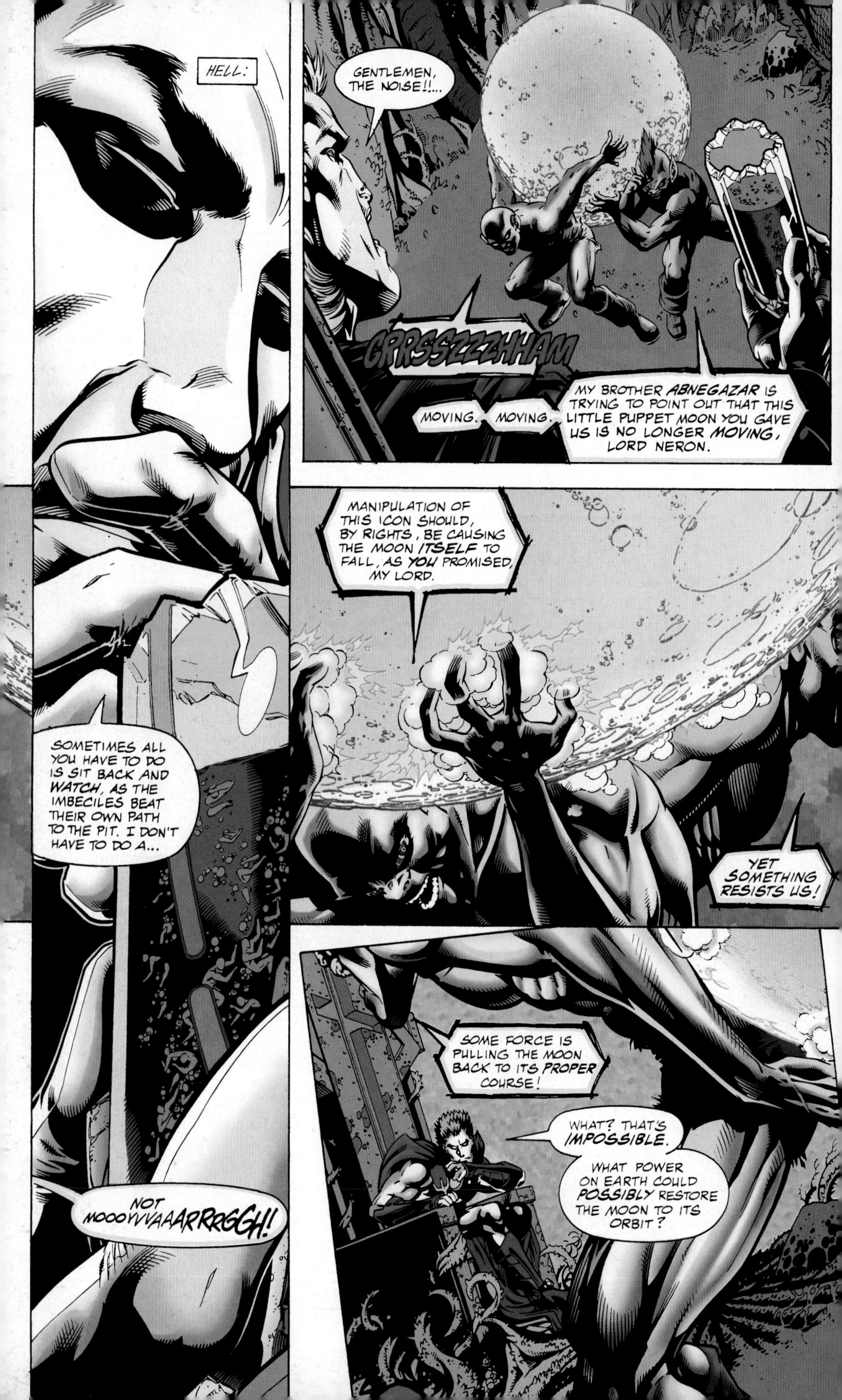
HELL:
GENTLEMEN, THE NOISE!!...
CRRSSZZZHHAM
MOVING.
MOVING.
MY BROTHER ABNEGAZAR IS TRYING TO POINT OUT THAT THIS LITTLE PUPPET MOON YOU GAVE US IS NO LONGER MOVING, LORD NERON.
MANIPULATION OF THIS ICON SHOULD, BY RIGHTS, BE CAUSING THE MOON ITSELF TO FALL, AS YOU PROMISED, MY LORD.
SOMETIMES ALL YOU HAVE TO DO IS SIT BACK AND WATCH, AS THE IMBECILES BEAT THEIR OWN PATH TO THE PIT. I DON'T HAVE TO DO A...
YET SOMETHING RESISTS US!
SOME FORCE IS PULLING THE MOON BACK TO ITS PROPER COURSE!
WHAT? THAT'S IMPOSSIBLE.
WHAT POWER ON EARTH COULD POSSIBLY RESTORE THE MOON TO ITS ORBIT?
NOT MOOOYVVAAARRRGGH!

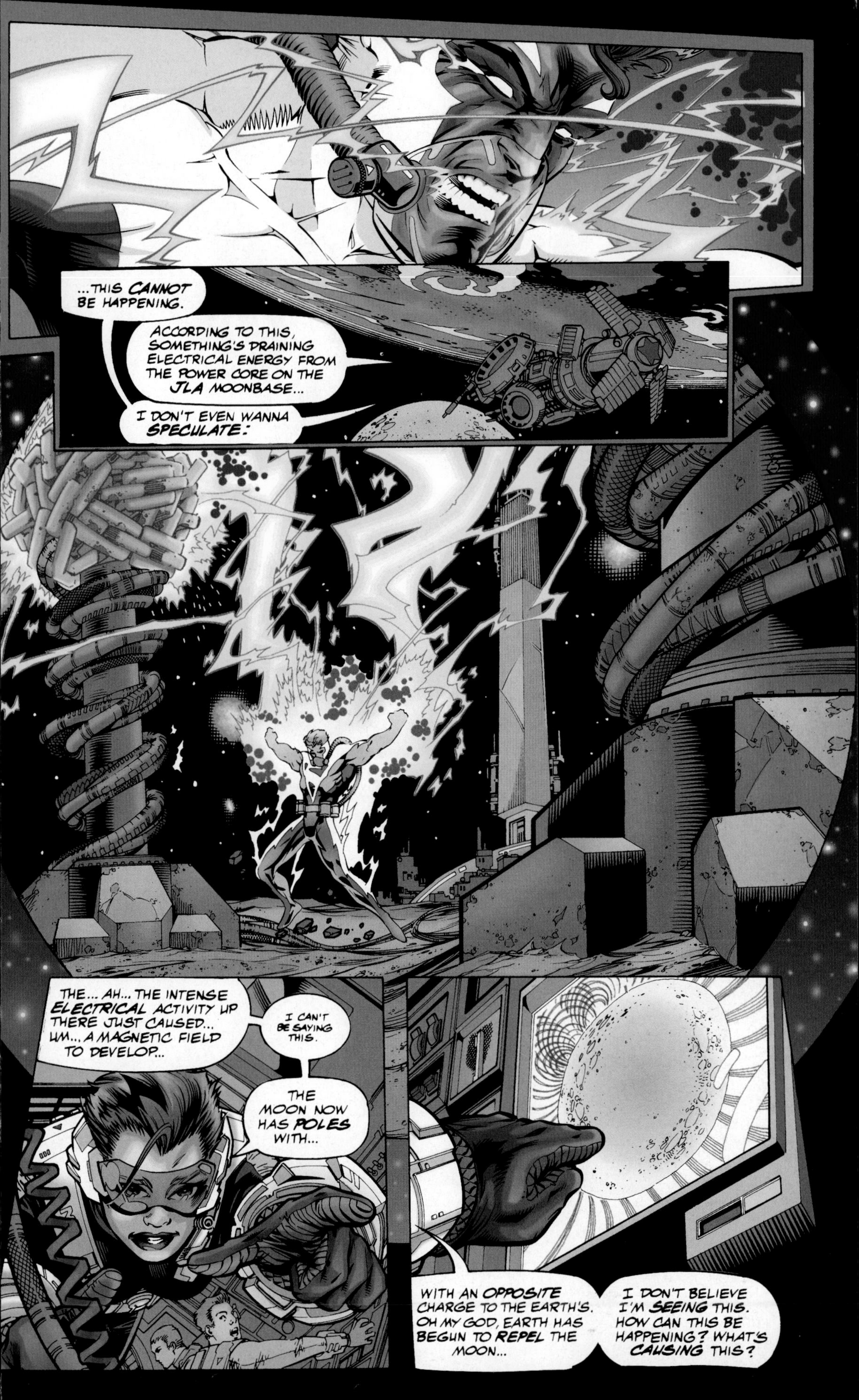

...THIS CANNOT BE HAPPENING.
ACCORDING TO THIS, SOMETHING'S DRAINING ELECTRICAL ENERGY FROM THE POWER CORE ON THE JLA MOONBASE...
I DON'T EVEN WANNA SPECULATE.
THE... AH... THE INTENSE ELECTRICAL ACTIVITY UP THERE JUST CAUSED... UM... A MAGNETIC FIELD TO DEVELOP...
I CAN'T BE SAYING THIS.
THE MOON NOW HAS POLES WITH...
WITH AN OPPOSITE CHARGE TO THE EARTH'S. OH MY GOD, EARTH HAS BEGUN TO REPEL THE MOON...
I DON'T BELIEVE I'M SEEING THIS. HOW CAN THIS BE HAPPENING? WHAT'S CAUSING THIS?

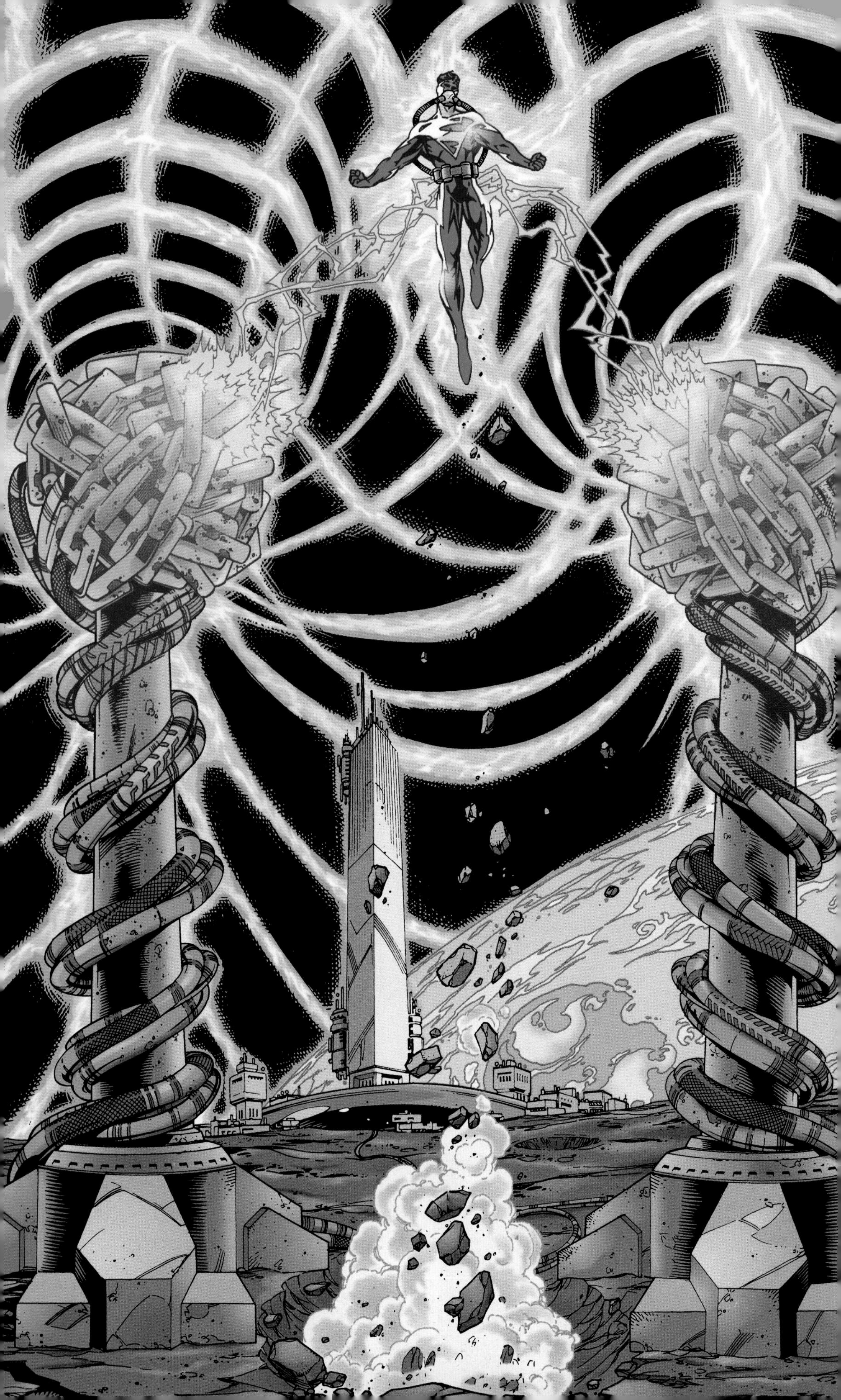

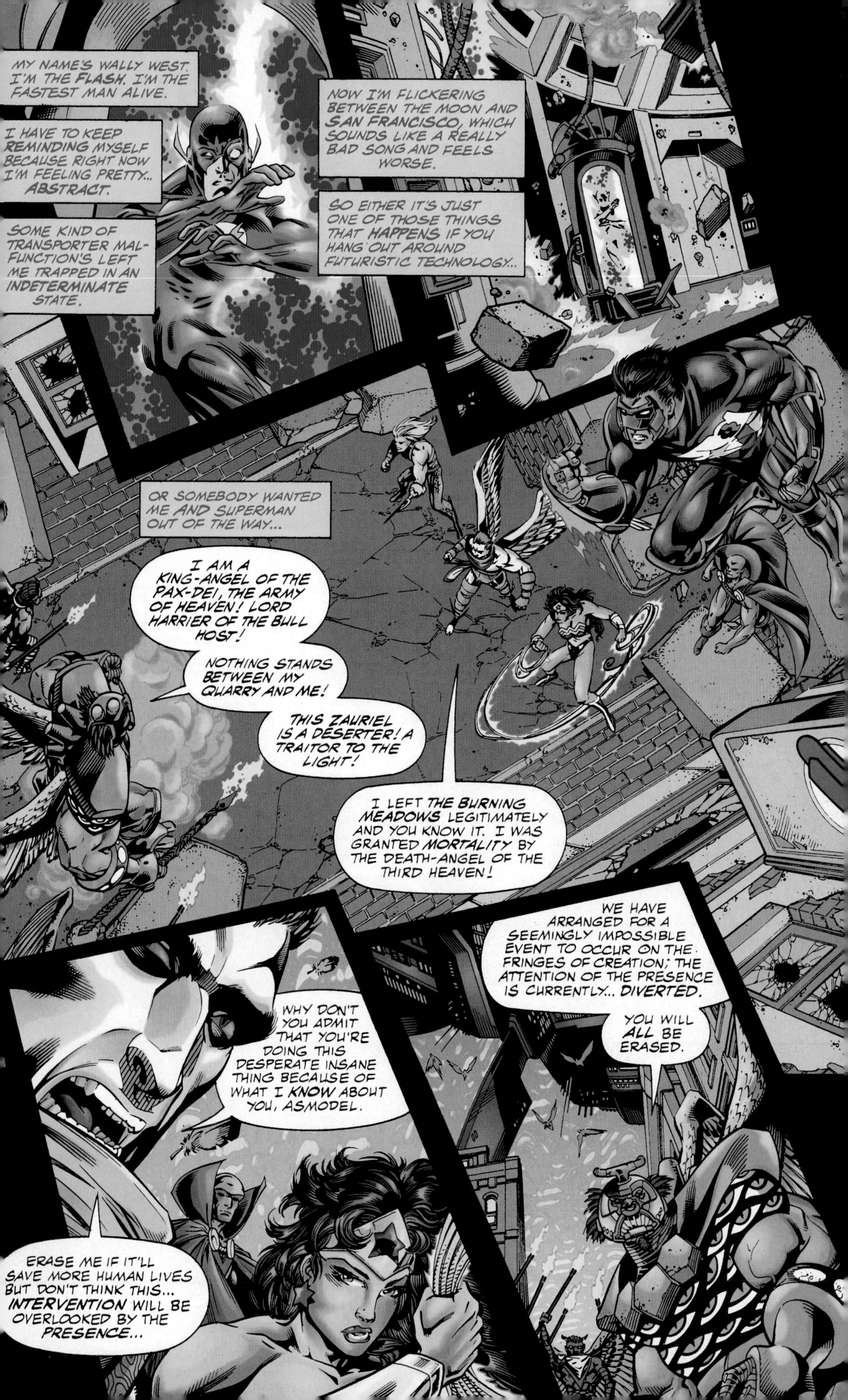
MY NAME'S WALLY WEST. I'M THE FLASH. I'M THE FASTEST MAN ALIVE.
I HAVE TO KEEP REMINDING MYSELF BECAUSE RIGHT NOW I'M FEELING PRETTY... ABSTRACT.
SOME KIND OF TRANSPORTER MAL-FUNCTION'S LEFT ME TRAPPED IN AN INDETERMINATE STATE.
NOW I'M FLICKERING BETWEEN THE MOON AND SAN FRANCISCO, WHICH SOUNDS LIKE A REALLY BAD SONG AND FEELS WORSE.
SO EITHER IT'S JUST ONE OF THOSE THINGS THAT HAPPENS IF YOU HANG OUT AROUND FUTURISTIC TECHNOLOGY...
OR SOMEBODY WANTED ME AND SUPERMAN OUT OF THE WAY...
I AM A KING-ANGEL OF THE PAX-DEI, THE ARMY OF HEAVEN! LORD HARRIER OF THE BULL HOST!
NOTHING STANDS BETWEEN MY QUARRY AND ME!
THIS ZAURIEL IS A DESERTER! A TRAITOR TO THE LIGHT!
I LEFT THE BURNING MEADOWS LEGITIMATELY AND YOU KNOW IT. I WAS GRANTED MORTALITY BY THE DEATH-ANGEL OF THE THIRD HEAVEN!
WHY DON'T YOU ADMIT THAT YOU'RE DOING THIS DESPERATE INSANE THING BECAUSE OF WHAT I KNOW ABOUT YOU, ASMODEL.
WE HAVE ARRANGED FOR A SEEMINGLY IMPOSSIBLE EVENT TO OCCUR ON THE FRINGES OF CREATION; THE ATTENTION OF THE PRESENCE IS CURRENTLY... DIVERTED.
YOU WILL ALL BE ERASED.
ERASE ME IF IT'LL SAVE MORE HUMAN LIVES BUT DON'T THINK THIS... INTERVENTION WILL BE OVERLOOKED BY THE PRESENCE...

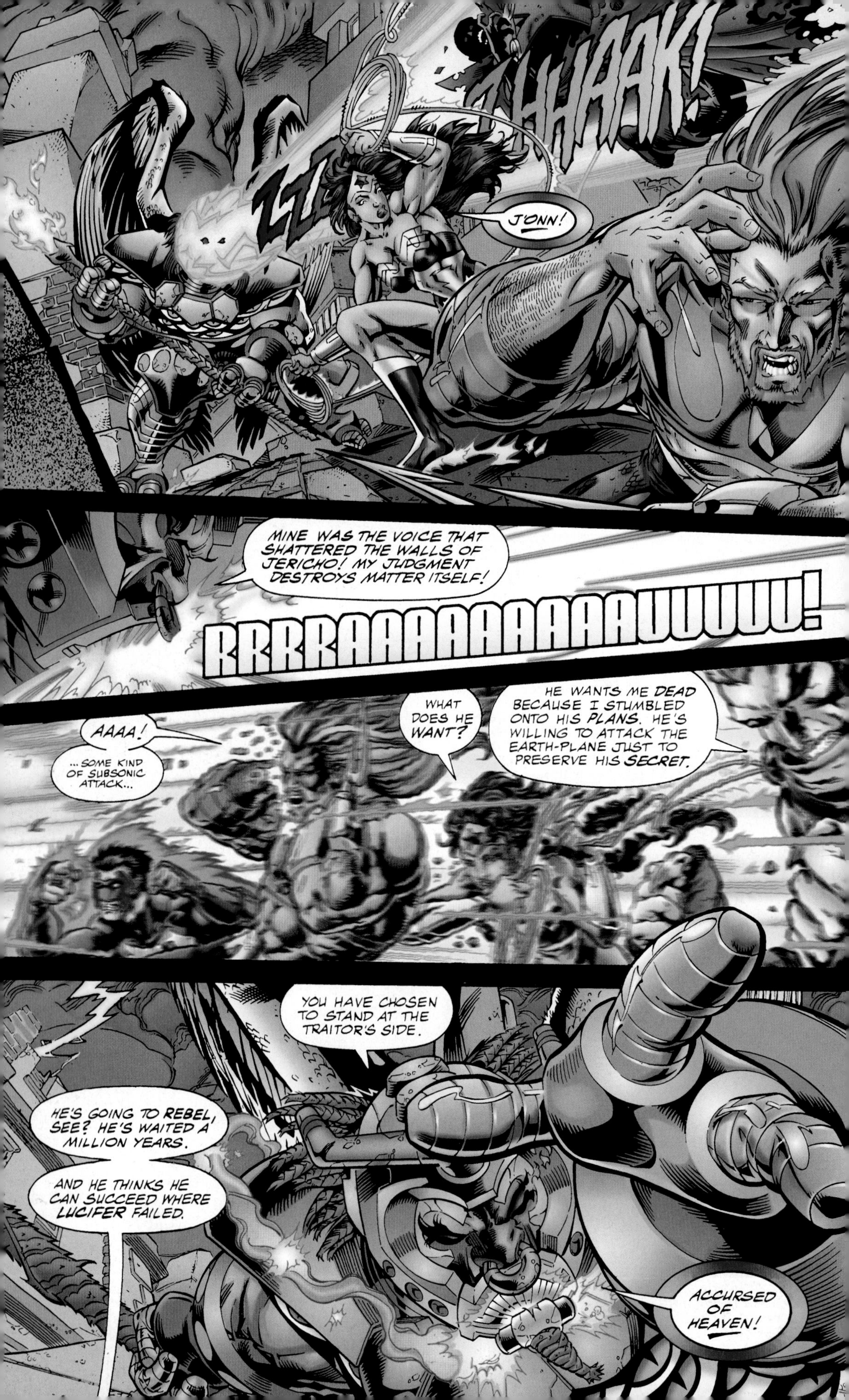

ZZZAHHAAK!
J'ONN!
MINE WAS THE VOICE THAT SHATTERED THE WALLS OF JERICHO! MY JUDGMENT DESTROYS MATTER ITSELF!
BRRRRAAAAAAAAAAUUUUUU!
AAAA!
...SOME KIND OF SUBSONIC ATTACK...
WHAT DOES HE WANT?
HE WANTS ME DEAD BECAUSE I STUMBLED ONTO HIS PLANS. HE'S WILLING TO ATTACK THE EARTH-PLANE JUST TO PRESERVE HIS SECRET.
YOU HAVE CHOSEN TO STAND AT THE TRAITOR'S SIDE.
HE'S GOING TO REBEL, SEE? HE'S WAITED A MILLION YEARS.
AND HE THINKS HE CAN SUCCEED WHERE LUCIFER FAILED.
ACCURSED OF HEAVEN!

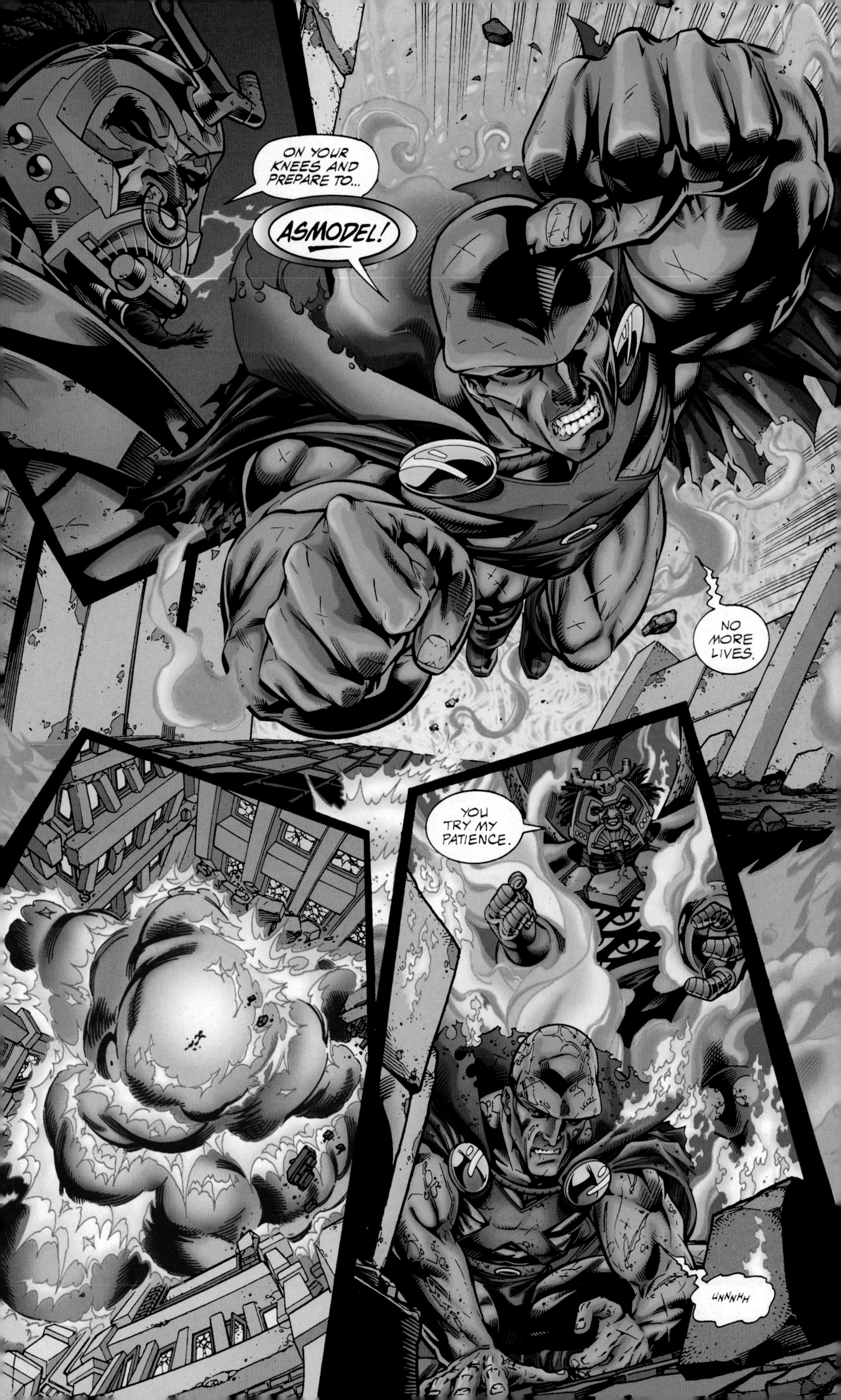
ON YOUR KNEES AND PREPARE TO...
ASMODEL!
NO MORE LIVES.
YOU TRY MY PATIENCE.
UNNNHH

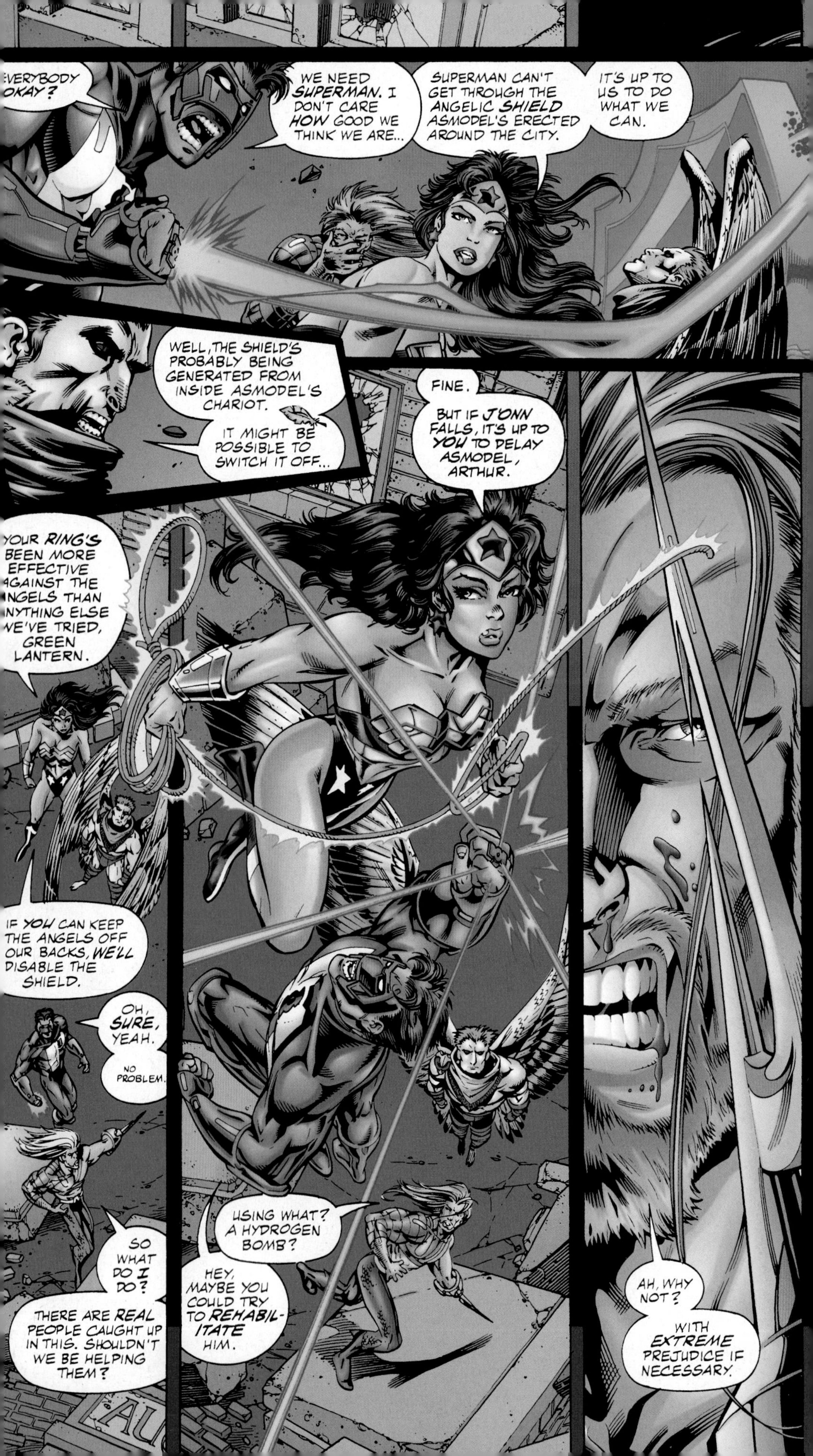

EVERYBODY OKAY?
WE NEED SUPERMAN. I DON'T CARE HOW GOOD WE THINK WE ARE...
SUPERMAN CAN'T GET THROUGH THE ANGELIC SHIELD ASMODEL'S ERECTED AROUND THE CITY.
IT'S UP TO US TO DO WHAT WE CAN.
WELL, THE SHIELD'S PROBABLY BEING GENERATED FROM INSIDE ASMODEL'S CHARIOT.
IT MIGHT BE POSSIBLE TO SWITCH IT OFF...
FINE.
BUT IF J'ONN FALLS, IT'S UP TO YOU TO DELAY ASMODEL, ARTHUR.
YOUR RING'S BEEN MORE EFFECTIVE AGAINST THE ANGELS THAN ANYTHING ELSE WE'VE TRIED, GREEN LANTERN.
IF YOU CAN KEEP THE ANGELS OFF OUR BACKS, WE'LL DISABLE THE SHIELD.
OH, SURE, YEAH.
NO PROBLEM.
SO WHAT DO I DO?
THERE ARE REAL PEOPLE CAUGHT UP IN THIS. SHOULDN'T WE BE HELPING THEM?
USING WHAT? A HYDROGEN BOMB?
HEY, MAYBE YOU COULD TRY TO REHABILITATE HIM.
AH, WHY NOT?
WITH EXTREME PREJUDICE IF NECESSARY.

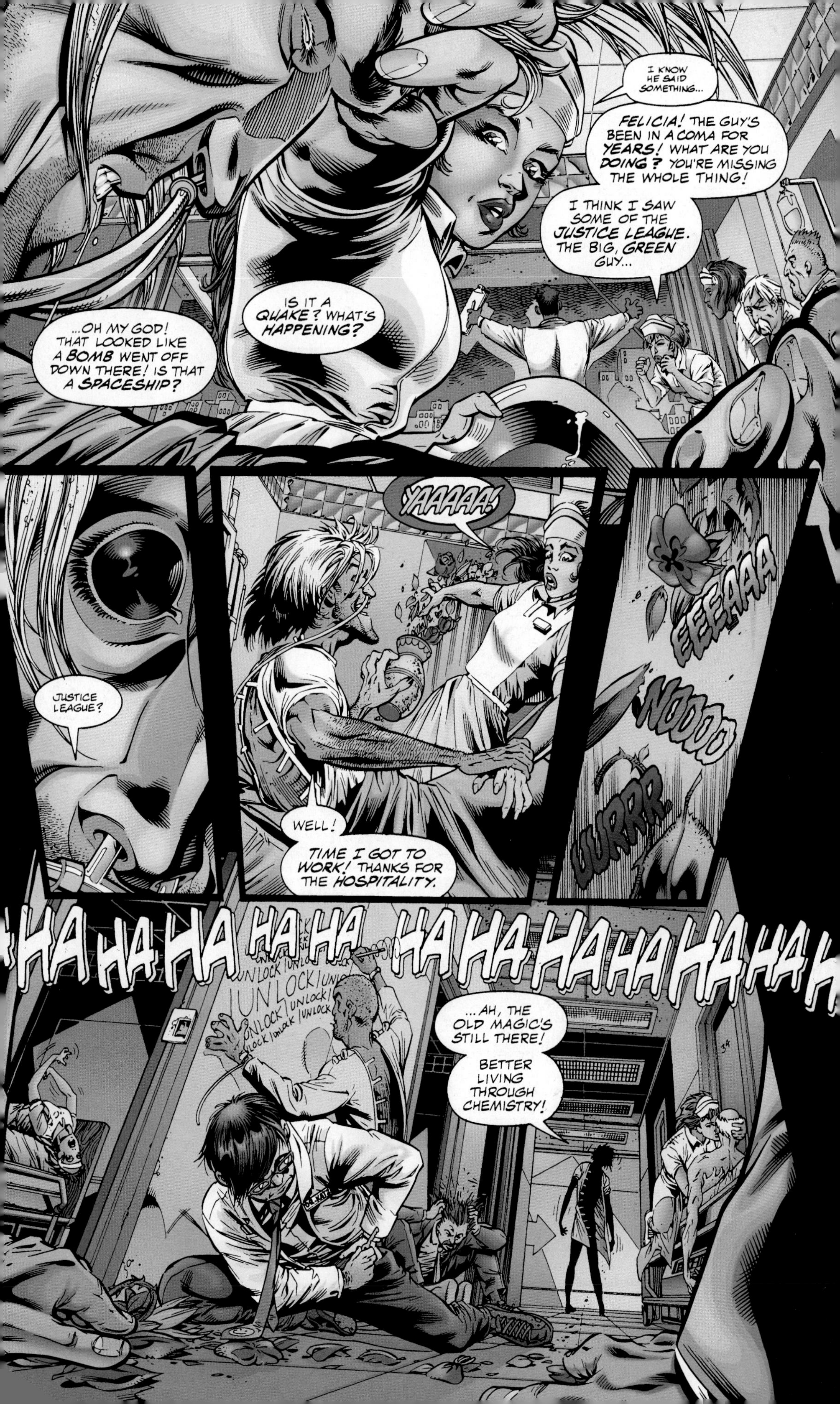
I KNOW HE SAID SOMETHING...
FELICIA! THE GUY'S BEEN IN A COMA FOR YEARS! WHAT ARE YOU DOING? YOU'RE MISSING THE WHOLE THING!
I THINK I SAW SOME OF THE JUSTICE LEAGUE. THE BIG, GREEN GUY...
IS IT A QUAKE? WHAT'S HAPPENING?
...OH MY GOD! THAT LOOKED LIKE A BOMB WENT OFF DOWN THERE! IS THAT A SPACESHIP?
JUSTICE LEAGUE?
YAAAAA!
WELL!
TIME I GOT TO WORK! THANKS FOR THE HOSPITALITY.
EEEAAA
NOOOO
UURRR
HA HA HA HA HA HA HA HA HA HA HA HA
UNLOCK | UNLOCK | UNLOCK | UNLOCK
...AH, THE OLD MAGIC'S STILL THERE!
BETTER LIVING THROUGH CHEMISTRY!

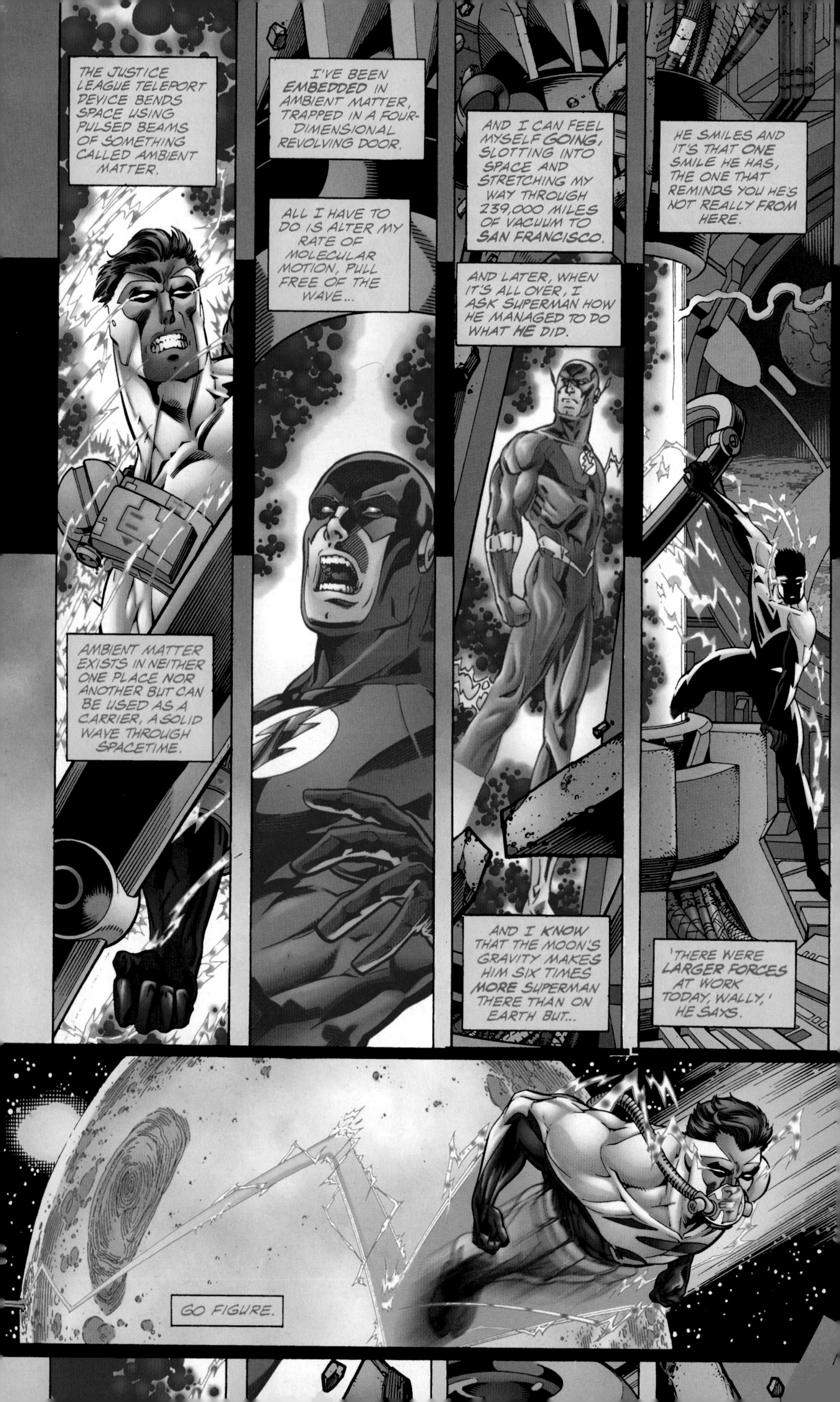
THE JUSTICE LEAGUE TELEPORT DEVICE BENDS SPACE USING PULSED BEAMS OF SOMETHING CALLED AMBIENT MATTER.
AMBIENT MATTER EXISTS IN NEITHER ONE PLACE NOR ANOTHER BUT CAN BE USED AS A CARRIER, A SOLID WAVE THROUGH SPACETIME.
I'VE BEEN EMBEDDED IN AMBIENT MATTER, TRAPPED IN A FOUR-DIMENSIONAL REVOLVING DOOR.
ALL I HAVE TO DO IS ALTER MY RATE OF MOLECULAR MOTION, PULL FREE OF THE WAVE...
AND I CAN FEEL MYSELF GOING, SLOTTING INTO SPACE AND STRETCHING MY WAY THROUGH 239,000 MILES OF VACUUM TO SAN FRANCISCO.
AND LATER, WHEN IT'S ALL OVER, I ASK SUPERMAN HOW HE MANAGED TO DO WHAT HE DID.
AND I KNOW THAT THE MOON'S GRAVITY MAKES HIM SIX TIMES MORE SUPERMAN THERE THAN ON EARTH BUT...
HE SMILES AND IT'S THAT ONE SMILE HE HAS, THE ONE THAT REMINDS YOU HE'S NOT REALLY FROM HERE.
'THERE WERE LARGER FORCES AT WORK TODAY, WALLY,' HE SAYS.
GO FIGURE.

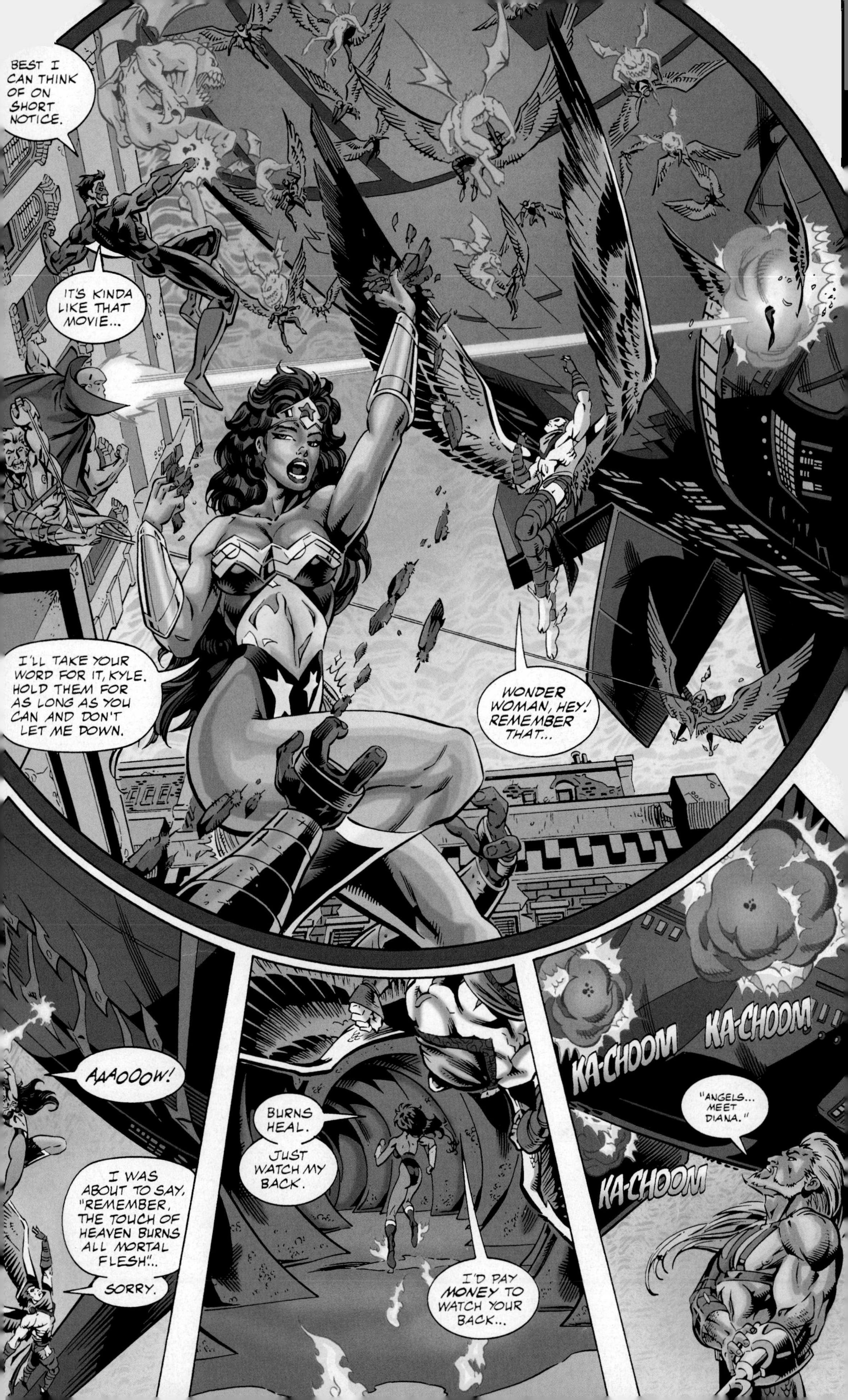
BEST I CAN THINK OF ON SHORT NOTICE.
IT'S KINDA LIKE THAT MOVIE...
I'LL TAKE YOUR WORD FOR IT, KYLE. HOLD THEM FOR AS LONG AS YOU CAN AND DON'T LET ME DOWN.
WONDER WOMAN, HEY! REMEMBER THAT...
AAAOOOW!
I WAS ABOUT TO SAY, "REMEMBER, THE TOUCH OF HEAVEN BURNS ALL MORTAL FLESH"...
SORRY.
BURNS HEAL.
JUST WATCH MY BACK.
I'D PAY MONEY TO WATCH YOUR BACK...
KA-CHOOM
KA-CHOOM
KA-CHOOM
"ANGELS... MEET DIANA."

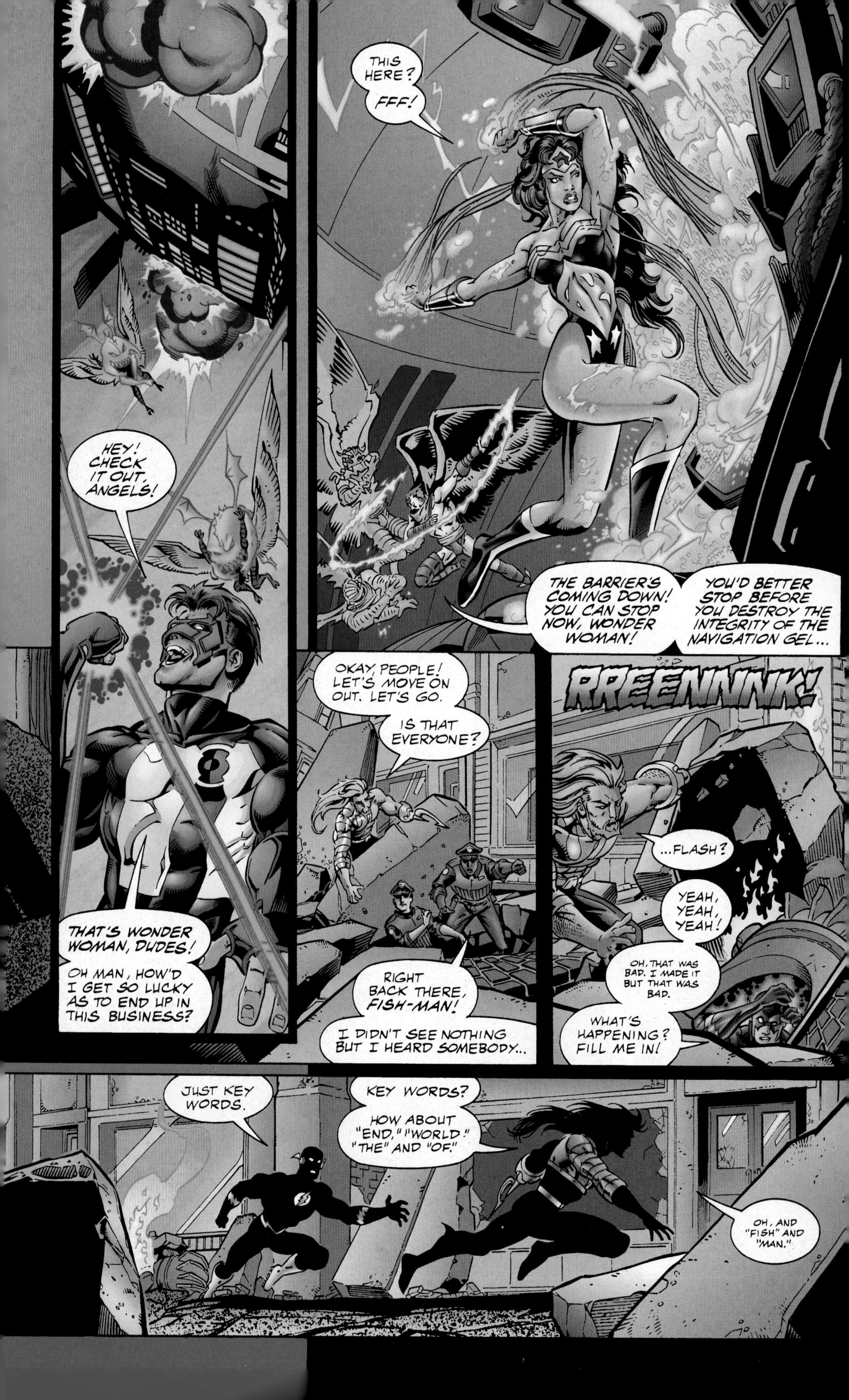
THIS HERE? FFF!
HEY! CHECK IT OUT, ANGELS!
THE BARRIER'S COMING DOWN! YOU CAN STOP NOW, WONDER WOMAN!
YOU'D BETTER STOP BEFORE YOU DESTROY THE INTEGRITY OF THE NAVIGATION GEL...
THAT'S WONDER WOMAN, DUDES!
OH MAN, HOW'D I GET SO LUCKY AS TO END UP IN THIS BUSINESS?
OKAY, PEOPLE! LET'S MOVE ON OUT. LET'S GO.
IS THAT EVERYONE?
RIGHT BACK THERE, FISH-MAN!
I DIDN'T SEE NOTHING BUT I HEARD SOMEBODY...
RREENNNK!
...FLASH?
YEAH, YEAH, YEAH!
OH, THAT WAS BAD. I MADE IT BUT THAT WAS BAD.
WHAT'S HAPPENING? FILL ME IN!
JUST KEY WORDS.
KEY WORDS?
HOW ABOUT "END," "WORLD," "THE" AND "OF."
OH, AND "FISH" AND "MAN."

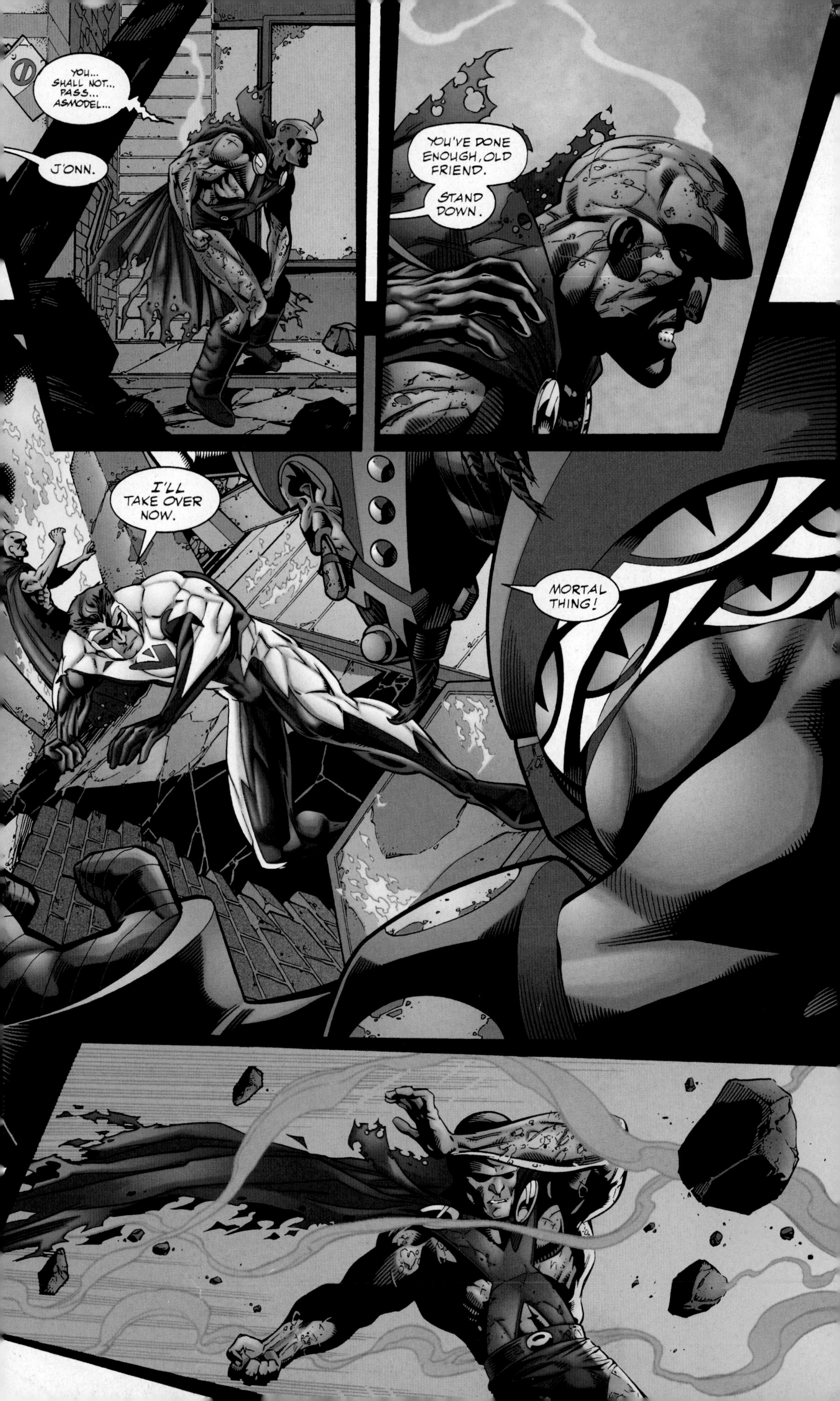
YOU... SHALL NOT... PASS... ASMODEL...
J'ONN.
YOU'VE DONE ENOUGH, OLD FRIEND.
STAND DOWN.
I'LL TAKE OVER NOW.
MORTAL THING!

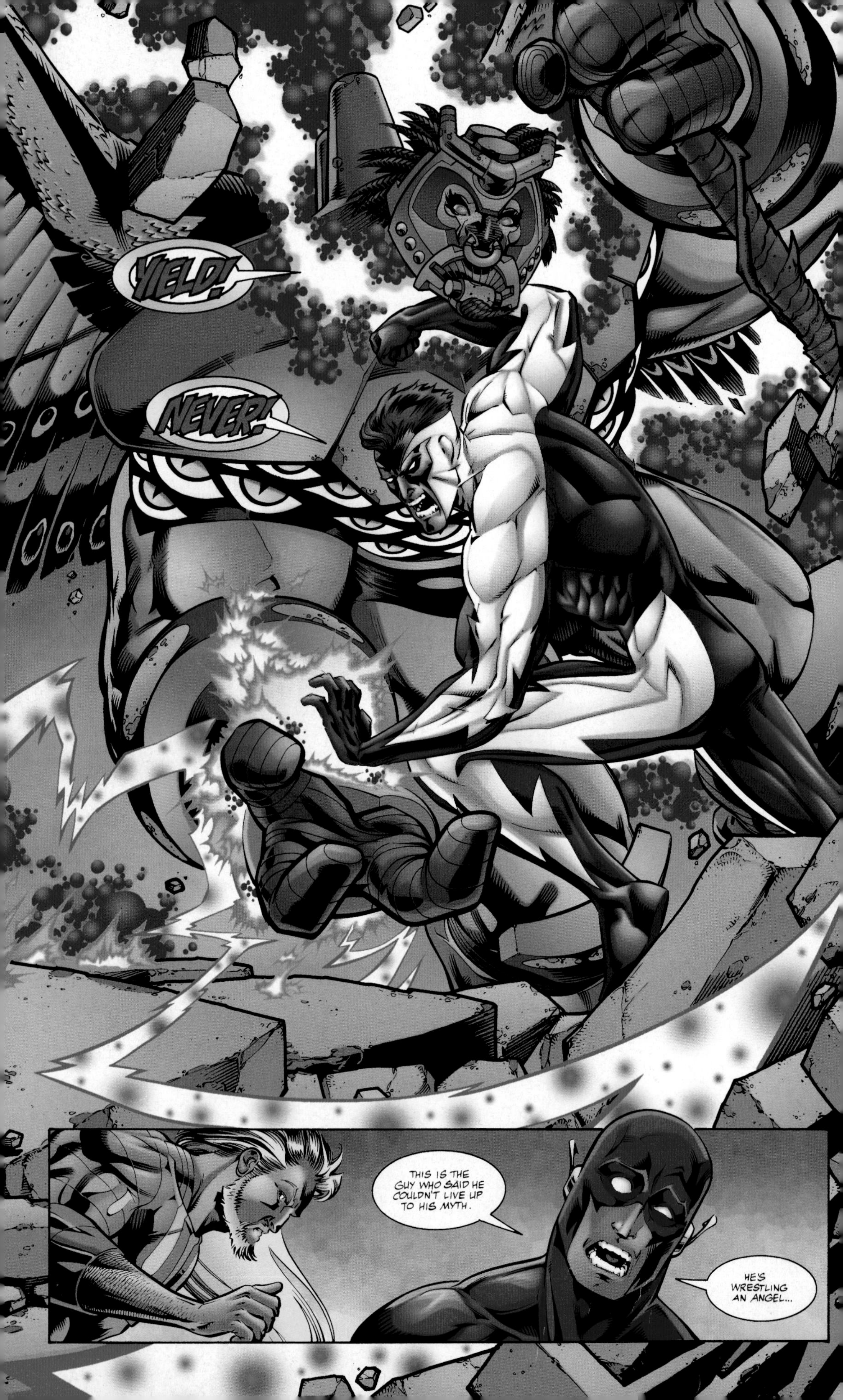

YIELD!
NEVER!
THIS IS THE GUY WHO SAID HE COULDN'T LIVE UP TO HIS MYTH.
HE'S WRESTLING AN ANGEL...

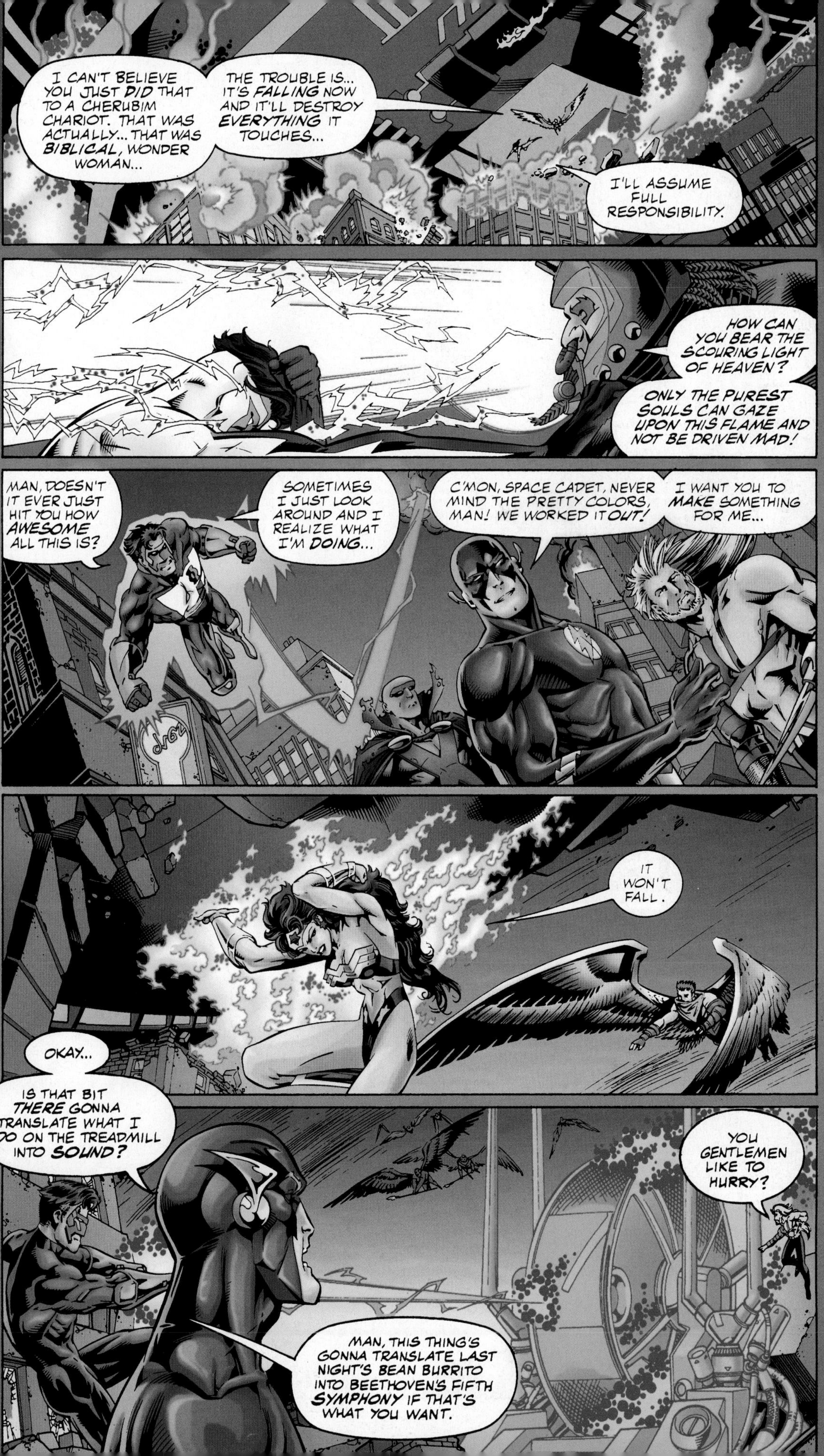
I CAN'T BELIEVE YOU JUST DID THAT TO A CHERUBIM CHARIOT. THAT WAS ACTUALLY... THAT WAS BIBLICAL, WONDER WOMAN...
THE TROUBLE IS... IT'S FALLING NOW AND IT'LL DESTROY EVERYTHING IT TOUCHES...
I'LL ASSUME FULL RESPONSIBILITY.
HOW CAN YOU BEAR THE SCOURING LIGHT OF HEAVEN?
ONLY THE PUREST SOULS CAN GAZE UPON THIS FLAME AND NOT BE DRIVEN MAD!
MAN, DOESN'T IT EVER JUST HIT YOU HOW AWESOME ALL THIS IS?
SOMETIMES I JUST LOOK AROUND AND I REALIZE WHAT I'M DOING...
C'MON, SPACE CADET, NEVER MIND THE PRETTY COLORS, MAN! WE WORKED IT OUT!
I WANT YOU TO MAKE SOMETHING FOR ME...
IT WON'T FALL.
OKAY...
IS THAT BIT THERE GONNA TRANSLATE WHAT I DO ON THE TREADMILL INTO SOUND?
YOU GENTLEMEN LIKE TO HURRY?
MAN, THIS THING'S GONNA TRANSLATE LAST NIGHT'S BEAN BURRITO INTO BEETHOVEN'S FIFTH SYMPHONY IF THAT'S WHAT YOU WANT.

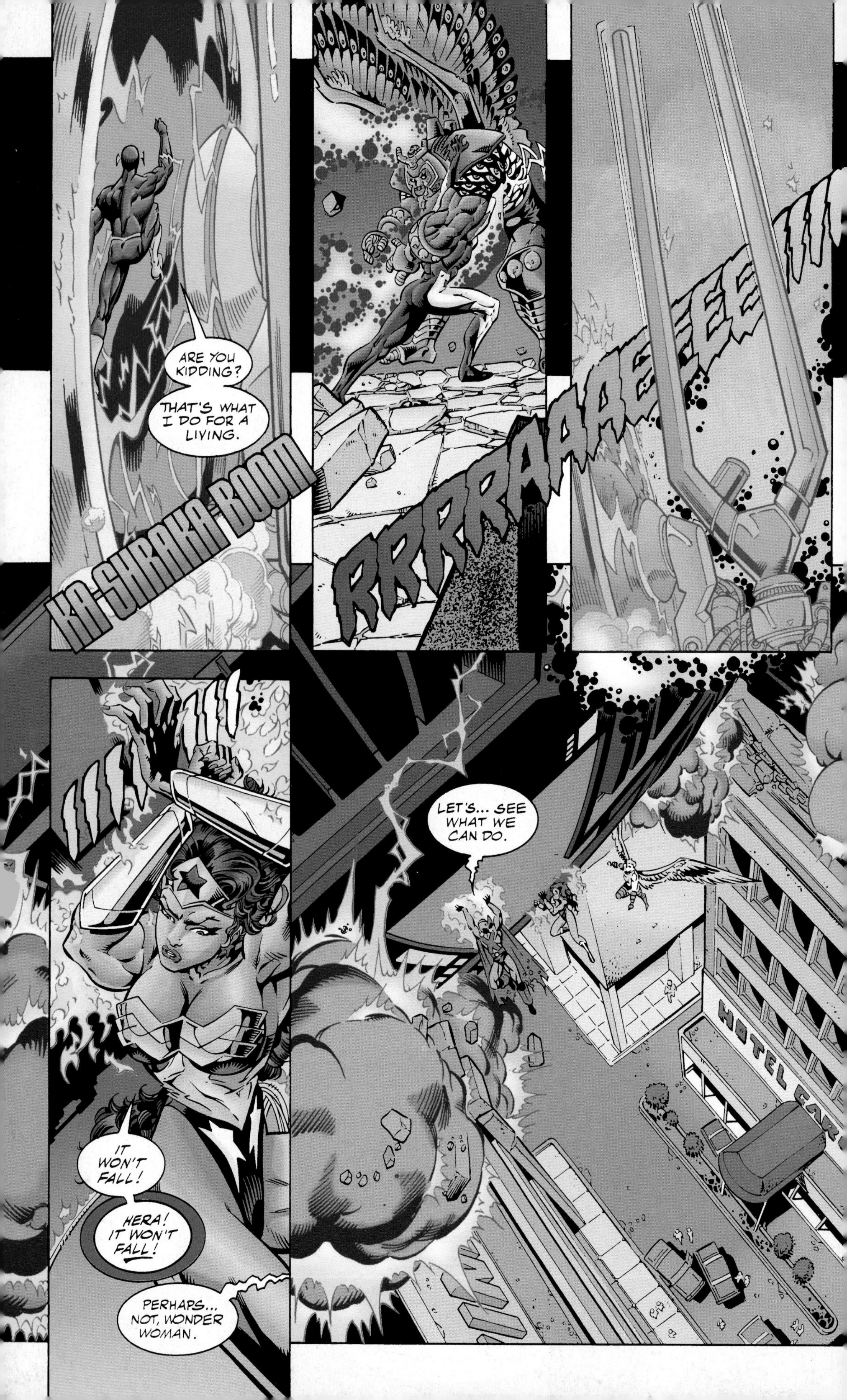
ARE YOU KIDDING?
THAT'S WHAT I DO FOR A LIVING.
KA-SHRAKA-BOOM
RRRRAAAAEEEEE
IT WON'T FALL!
HERA! IT WON'T FALL!
PERHAPS... NOT, WONDER WOMAN.
LET'S... SEE WHAT WE CAN DO.
HOTEL

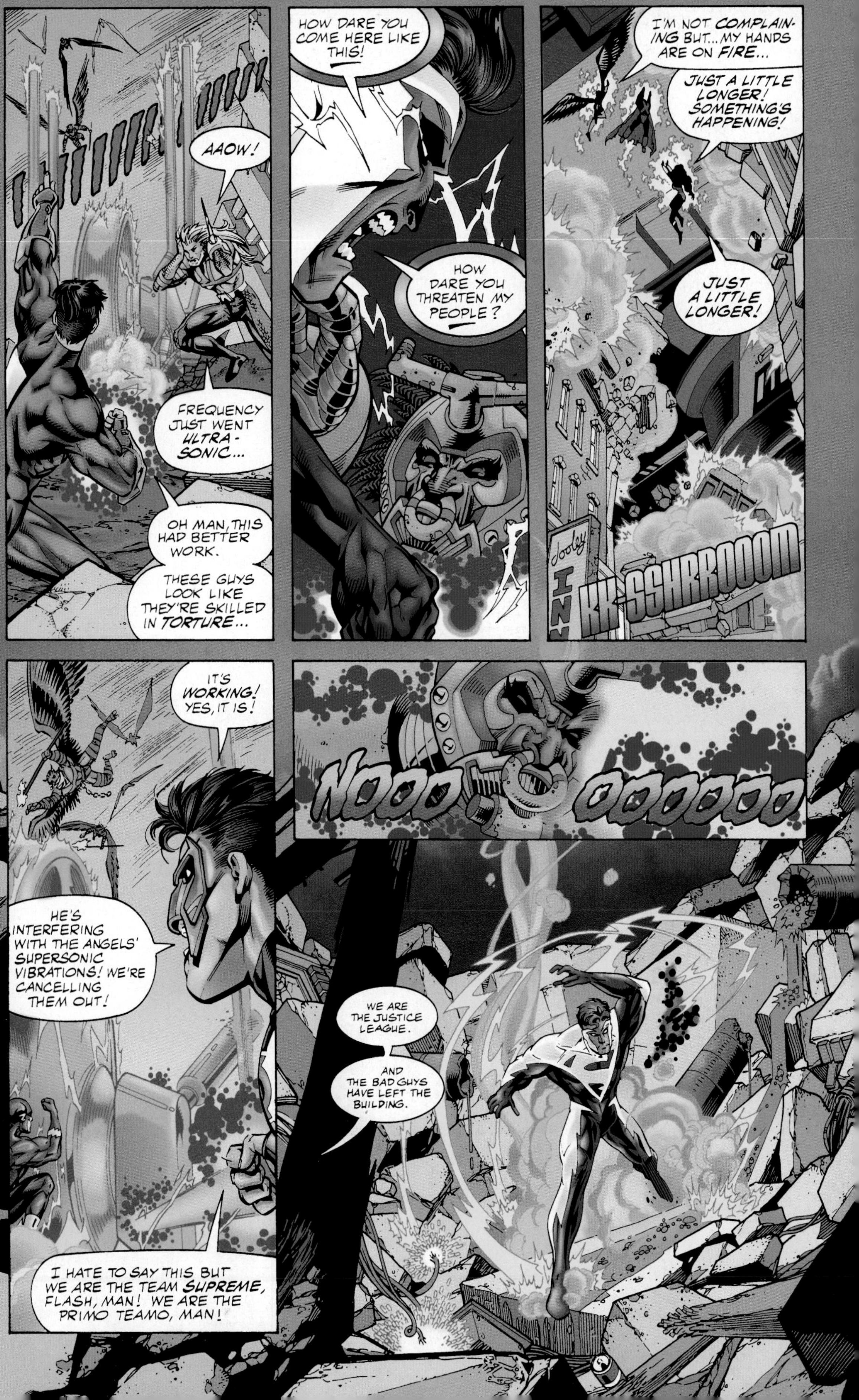
AAOW!
FREQUENCY JUST WENT ULTRA-SONIC...
OH MAN, THIS HAD BETTER WORK.
THESE GUYS LOOK LIKE THEY'RE SKILLED IN TORTURE...
HOW DARE YOU COME HERE LIKE THIS!
HOW DARE YOU THREATEN MY PEOPLE?
I'M NOT COMPLAINING BUT... MY HANDS ARE ON FIRE...
JUST A LITTLE LONGER! SOMETHING'S HAPPENING!
JUST A LITTLE LONGER!
Dooley
KK-SSHRROOOM
IT'S WORKING! YES, IT IS!
HE'S INTERFERING WITH THE ANGELS' SUPERSONIC VIBRATIONS! WE'RE CANCELLING THEM OUT!
I HATE TO SAY THIS BUT WE ARE THE TEAM SUPREME, FLASH, MAN! WE ARE THE PRIMO TEAMO, MAN!
NOOO-OOOOOOO
WE ARE THE JUSTICE LEAGUE.
AND THE BAD GUYS HAVE LEFT THE BUILDING.

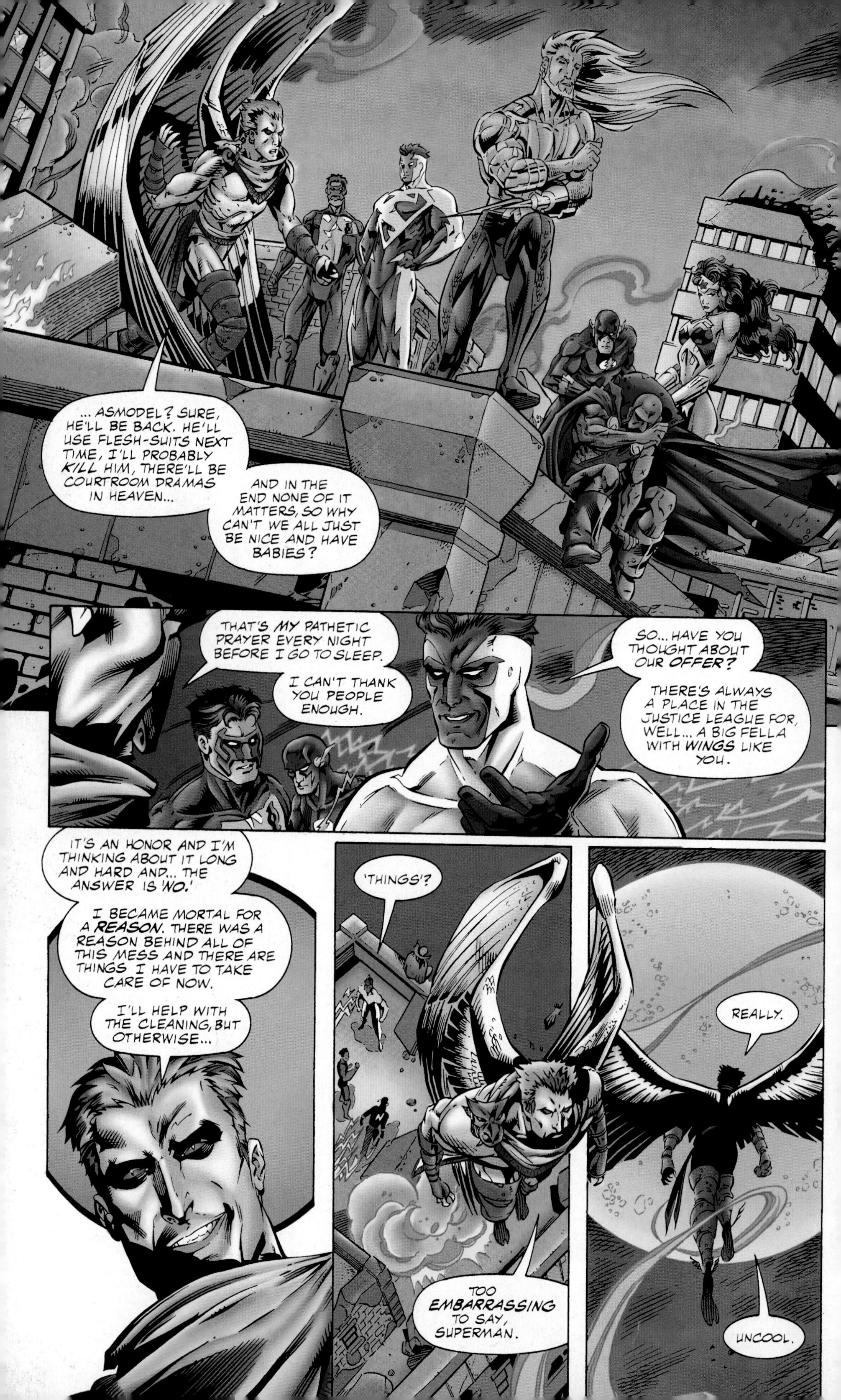

... ASMODEL? SURE, HE'LL BE BACK. HE'LL USE FLESH-SUITS NEXT TIME, I'LL PROBABLY KILL HIM, THERE'LL BE COURTROOM DRAMAS IN HEAVEN...
AND IN THE END NONE OF IT MATTERS, SO WHY CAN'T WE ALL JUST BE NICE AND HAVE BABIES?
THAT'S MY PATHETIC PRAYER EVERY NIGHT BEFORE I GO TO SLEEP.
I CAN'T THANK YOU PEOPLE ENOUGH.
SO... HAVE YOU THOUGHT ABOUT OUR OFFER?
THERE'S ALWAYS A PLACE IN THE JUSTICE LEAGUE FOR, WELL... A BIG FELLA WITH WINGS LIKE YOU.
IT'S AN HONOR AND I'M THINKING ABOUT IT LONG AND HARD AND... THE ANSWER IS 'NO.'
I BECAME MORTAL FOR A REASON. THERE WAS A REASON BEHIND ALL OF THIS MESS AND THERE ARE THINGS I HAVE TO TAKE CARE OF NOW.
I'LL HELP WITH THE CLEANING, BUT OTHERWISE...
'THINGS'?
TOO EMBARRASSING TO SAY, SUPERMAN.
REALLY.
UNCOOL.

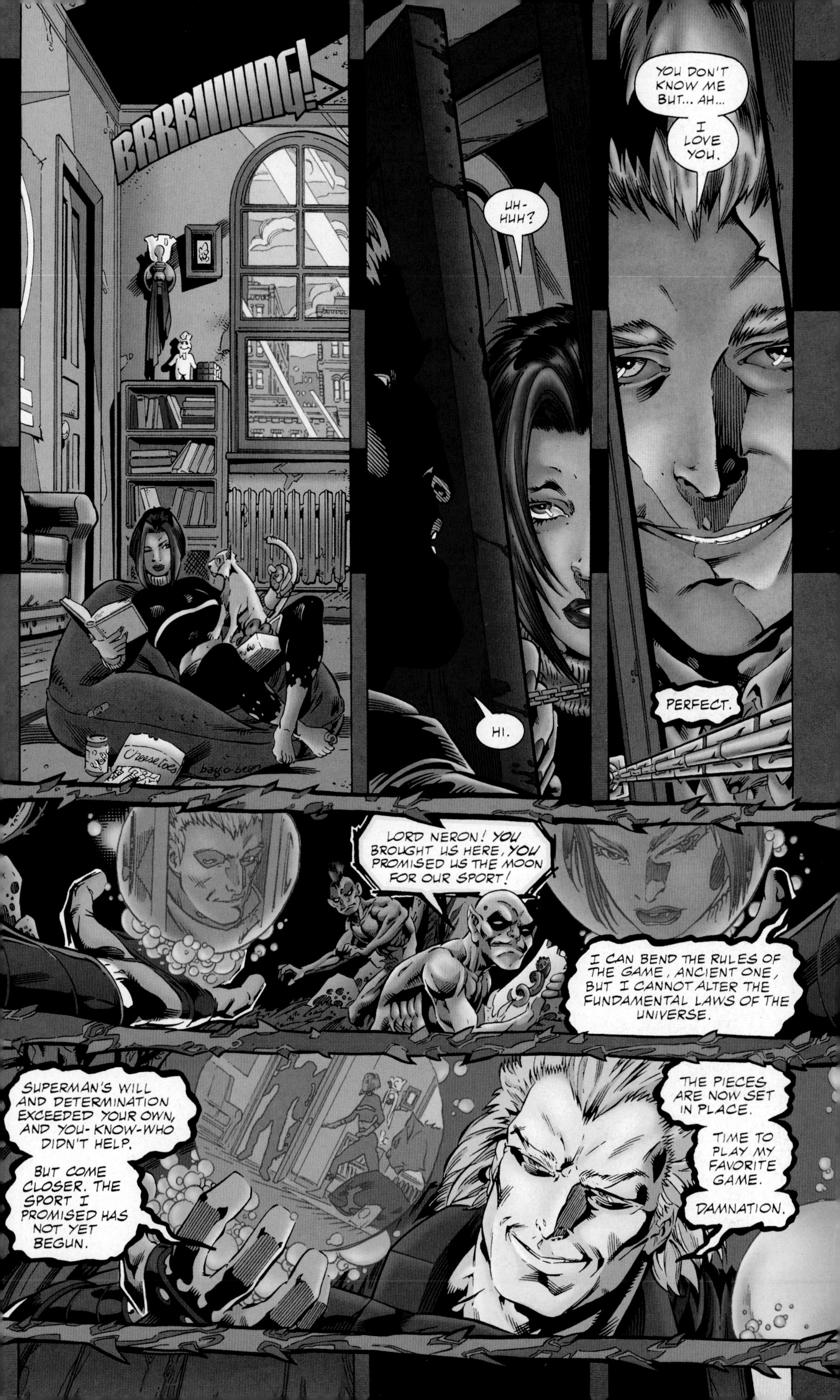
BRRRIIIIING!
Cheese toes
bag-o-bean
UH-HUH?
HI.
YOU DON'T KNOW ME BUT... AH...
I LOVE YOU.
PERFECT.
LORD NERON! YOU BROUGHT US HERE, YOU PROMISED US THE MOON FOR OUR SPORT!
I CAN BEND THE RULES OF THE GAME, ANCIENT ONE, BUT I CANNOT ALTER THE FUNDAMENTAL LAWS OF THE UNIVERSE.
SUPERMAN'S WILL AND DETERMINATION EXCEEDED YOUR OWN, AND YOU-KNOW-WHO DIDN'T HELP.
BUT COME CLOSER. THE SPORT I PROMISED HAS NOT YET BEGUN.
THE PIECES ARE NOW SET IN PLACE.
TIME TO PLAY MY FAVORITE GAME.
DAMNATION.

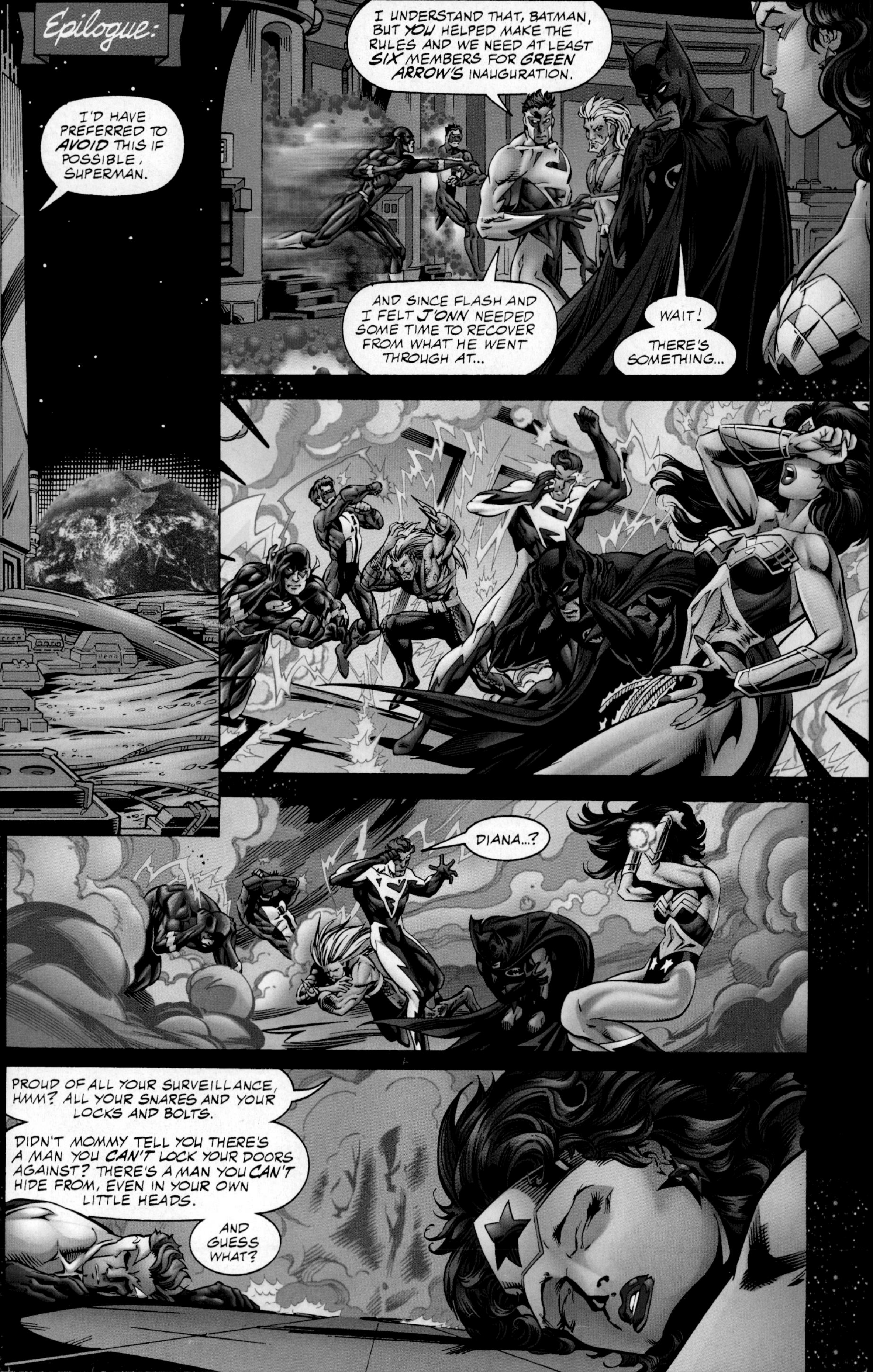
Epilogue:
I'D HAVE PREFERRED TO AVOID THIS IF POSSIBLE, SUPERMAN.
I UNDERSTAND THAT, BATMAN, BUT YOU HELPED MAKE THE RULES AND WE NEED AT LEAST SIX MEMBERS FOR GREEN ARROW'S INAUGURATION.
AND SINCE FLASH AND I FELT J'ONN NEEDED SOME TIME TO RECOVER FROM WHAT HE WENT THROUGH AT...
WAIT!
THERE'S SOMETHING...
DIANA...?
PROUD OF ALL YOUR SURVEILLANCE, HMM? ALL YOUR SNARES AND YOUR LOCKS AND BOLTS.
DIDN'T MOMMY TELL YOU THERE'S A MAN YOU CAN'T LOCK YOUR DOORS AGAINST? THERE'S A MAN YOU CAN'T HIDE FROM, EVEN IN YOUR OWN LITTLE HEADS.
AND GUESS WHAT?

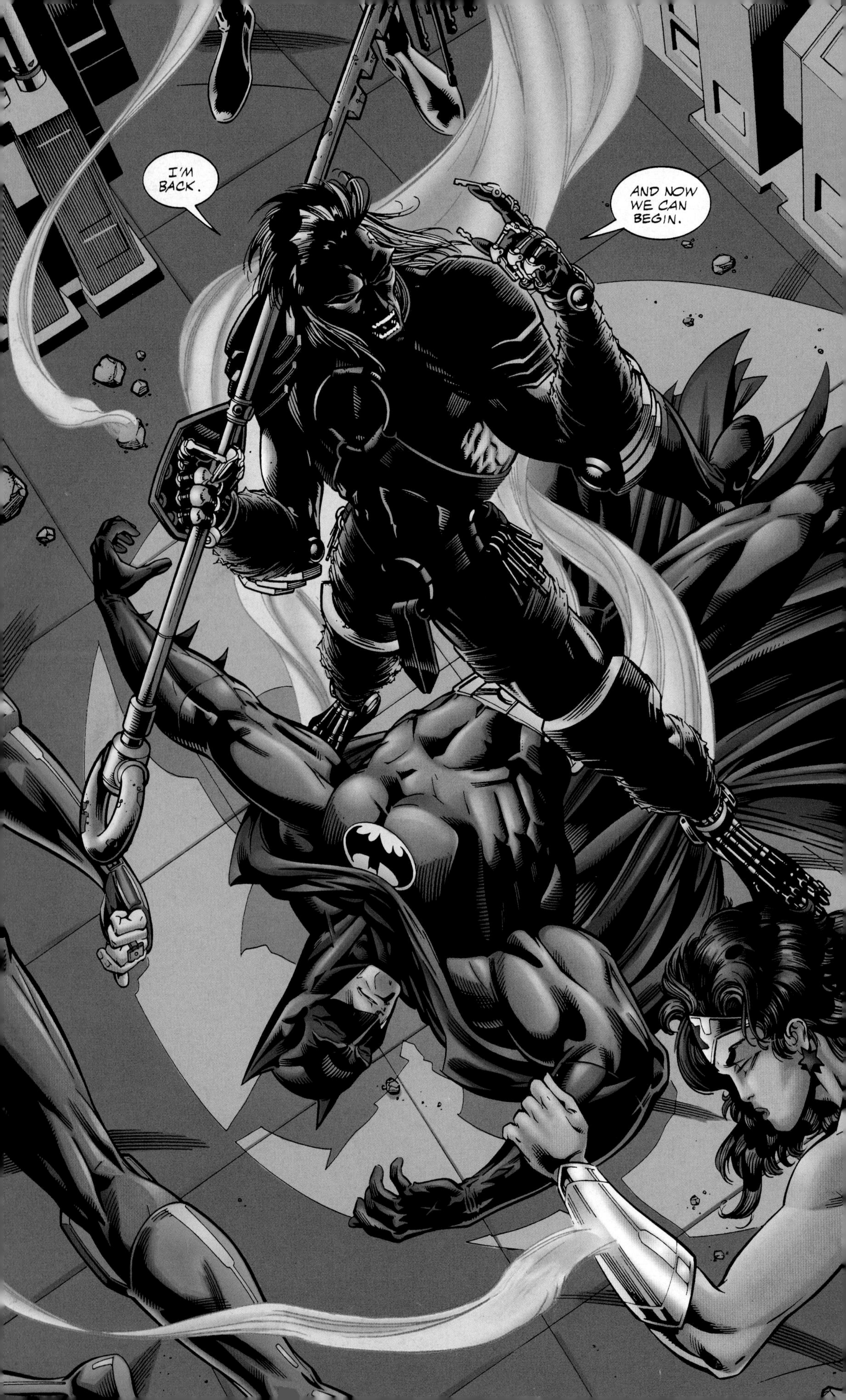
I'M BACK.
AND NOW WE CAN BEGIN.

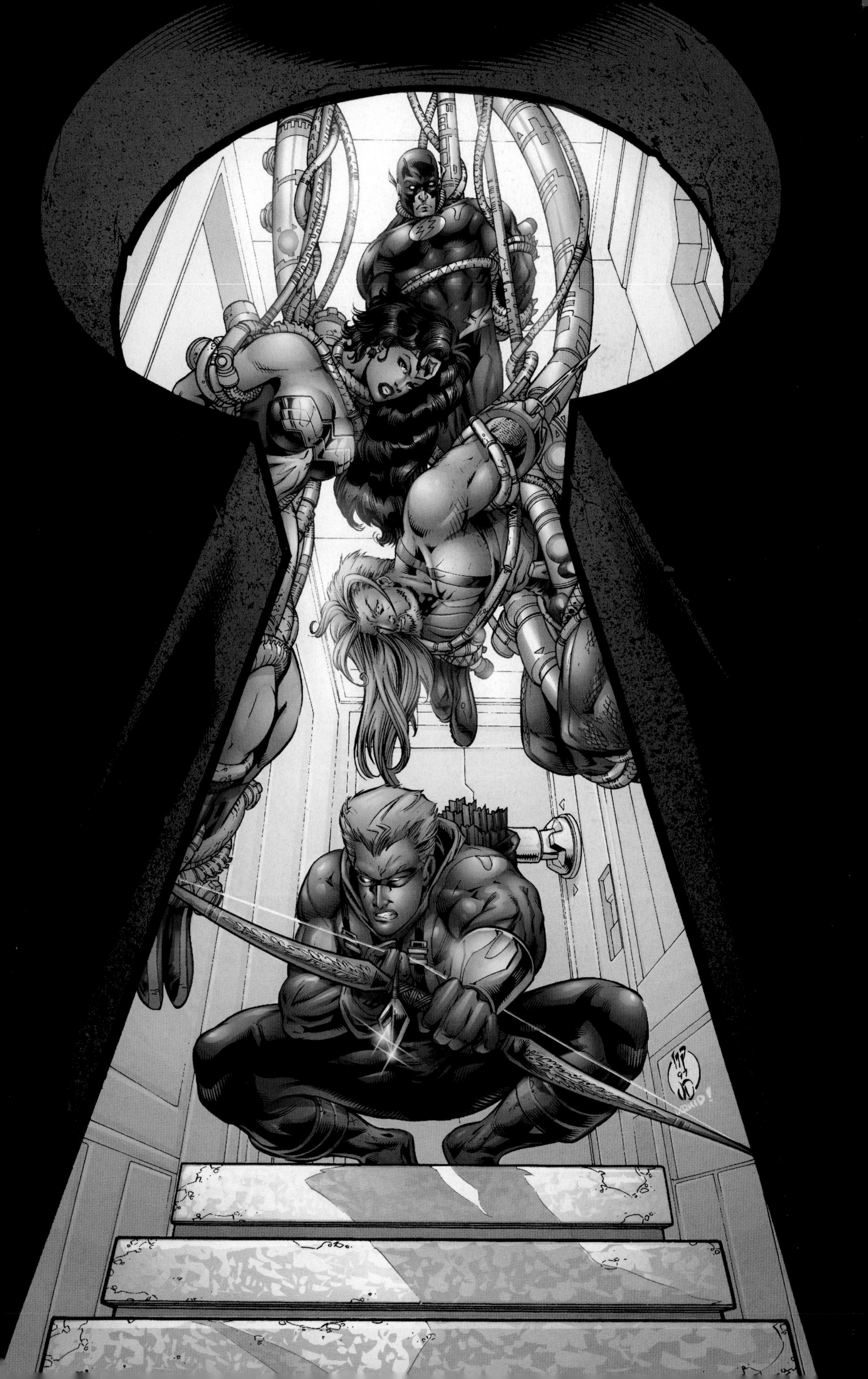

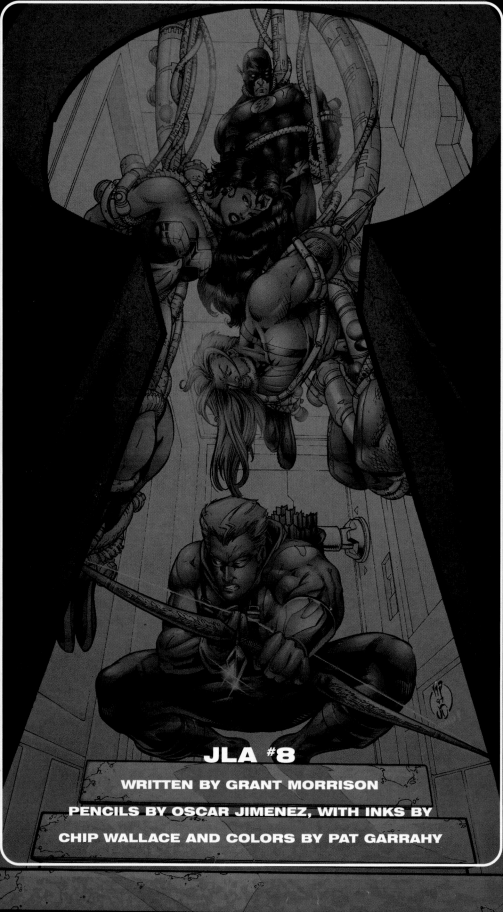

JLA #8

WRITTEN BY GRANT MORRISON

PENCILS BY OSCAR JIMENEZ, WITH INKS BY

CHIP WALLACE AND COLORS BY PAT GARRAHY

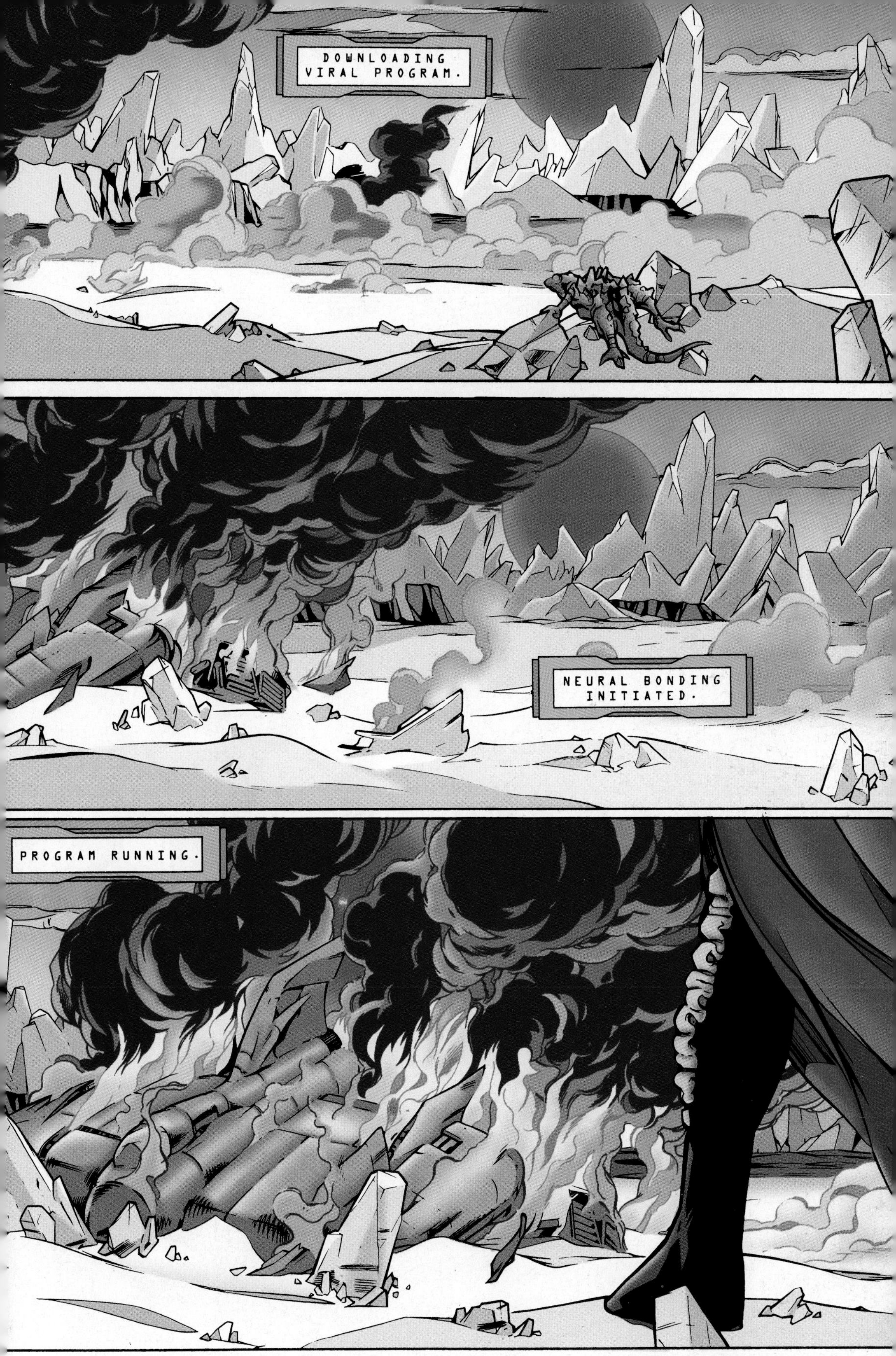

DOWNLOADING
VIRAL PROGRAM.
NEURAL BONDING
INITIATED.
PROGRAM RUNNING.

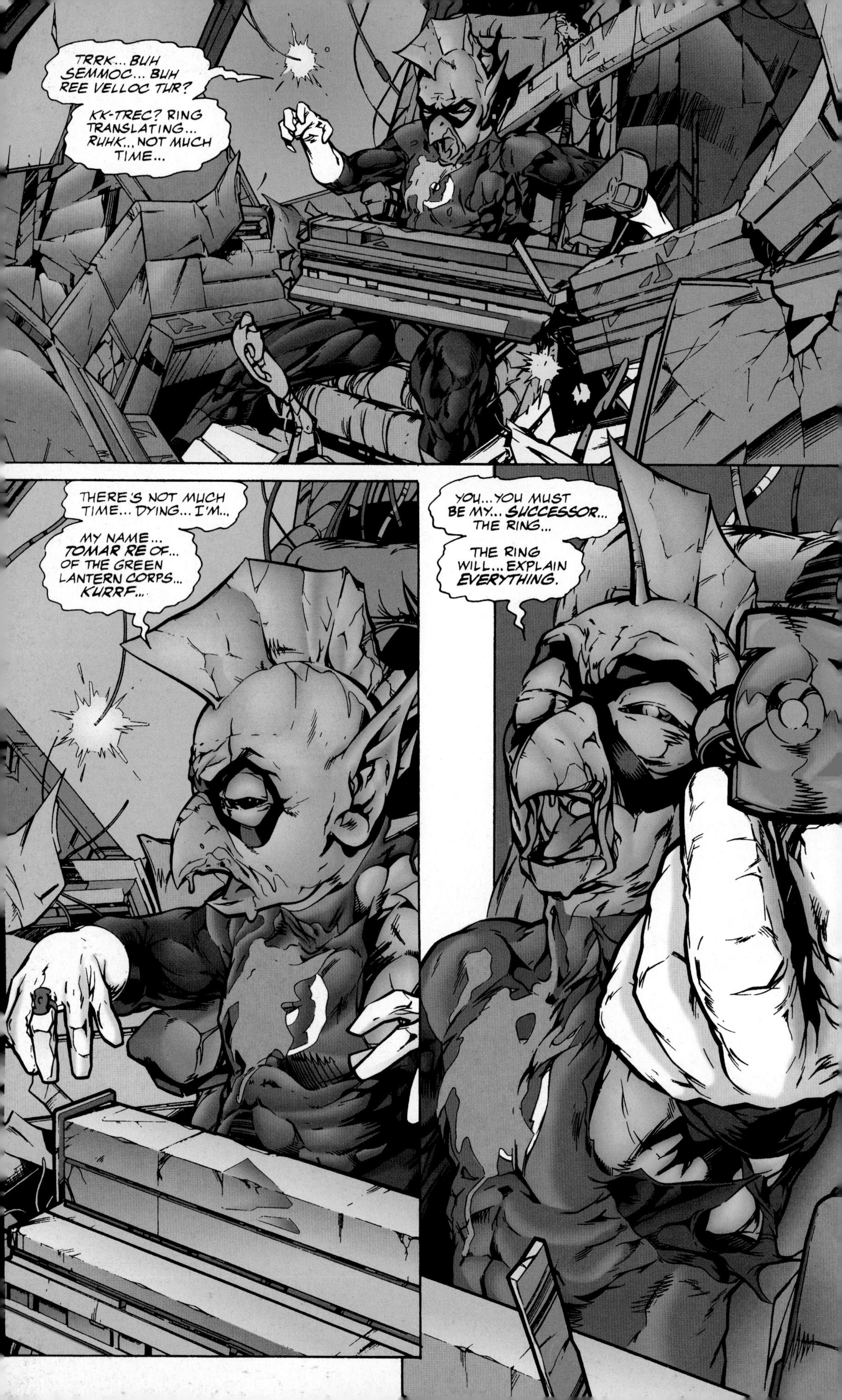

TRRK... BUH SEMMOC... BUH REE VELLOC TUR?
KK-TREC? RING TRANSLATING... RUHK... NOT MUCH TIME...
THERE'S NOT MUCH TIME... DYING... I'M...
MY NAME... *TOMAR RE* OF... OF THE GREEN LANTERN CORPS... *KURRF*...
YOU... YOU MUST BE MY... *SUCCESSOR*... THE RING...
THE RING WILL... EXPLAIN *EVERYTHING*.

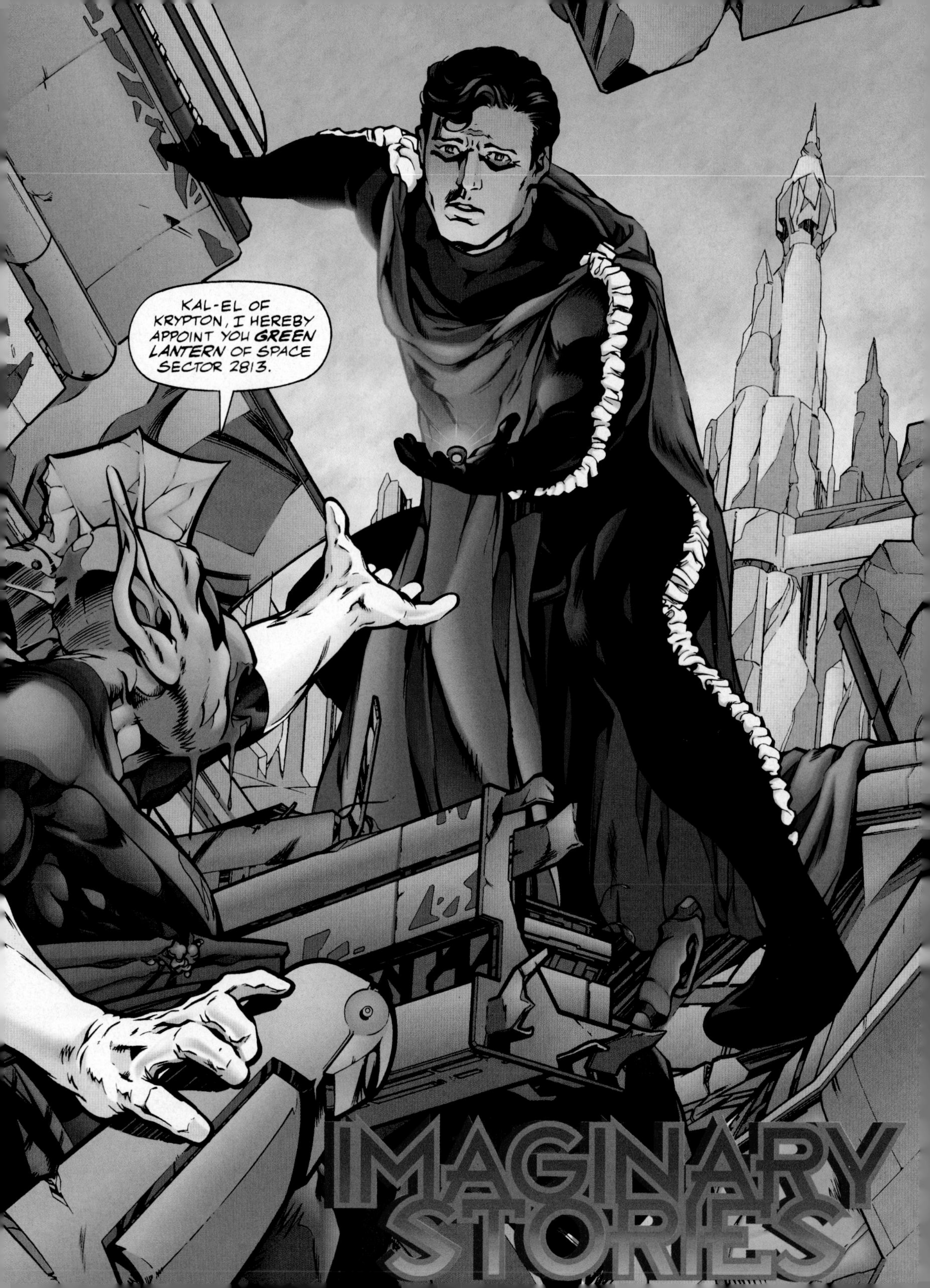
KAL-EL OF KRYPTON, I HEREBY APPOINT YOU GREEN LANTERN OF SPACE SECTOR 2813.
IMAGINARY STORIES

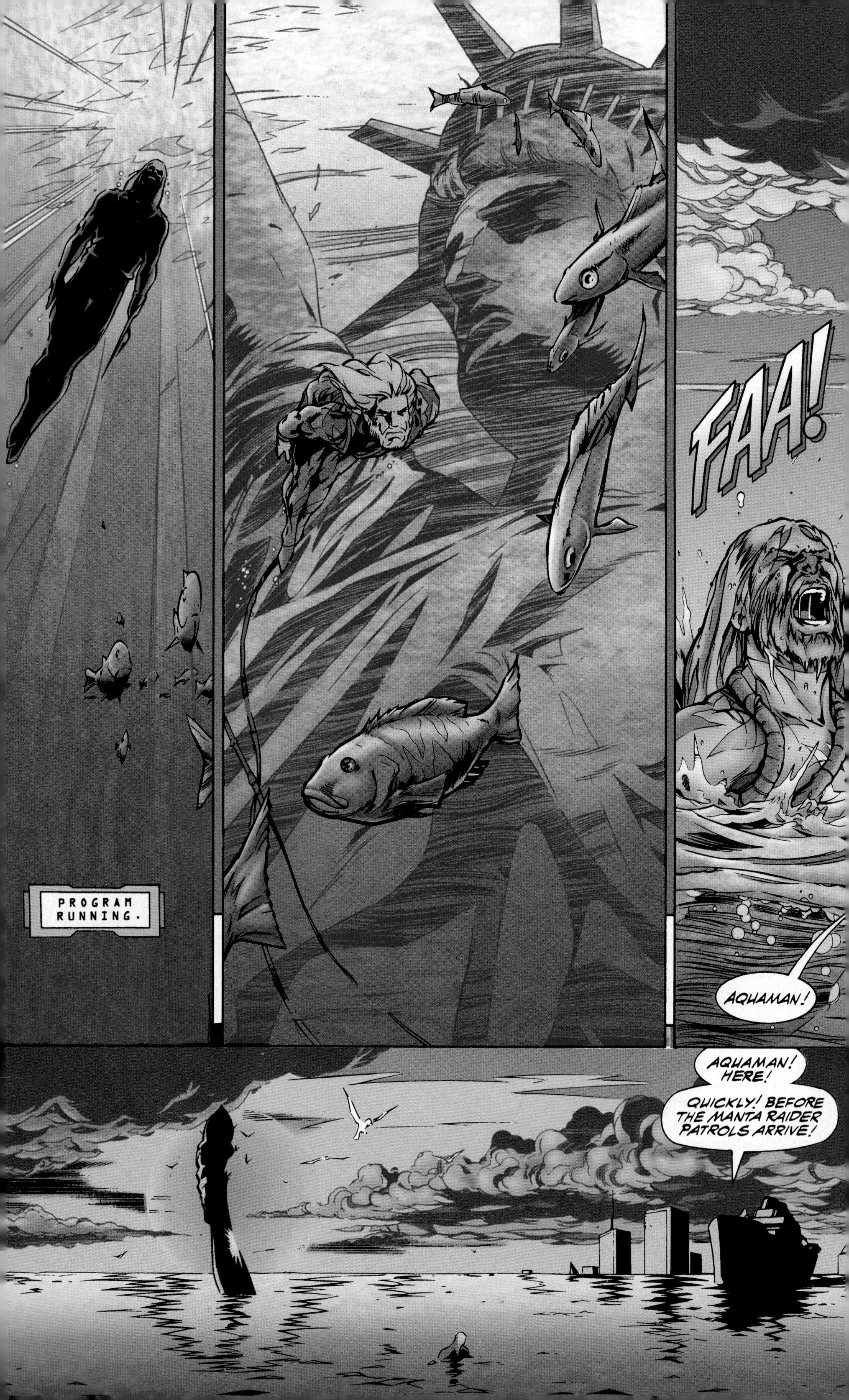
PROGRAM RUNNING.
FAA!
AQUAMAN!
AQUAMAN! HERE!
QUICKLY! BEFORE THE MANTA RAIDER PATROLS ARRIVE!

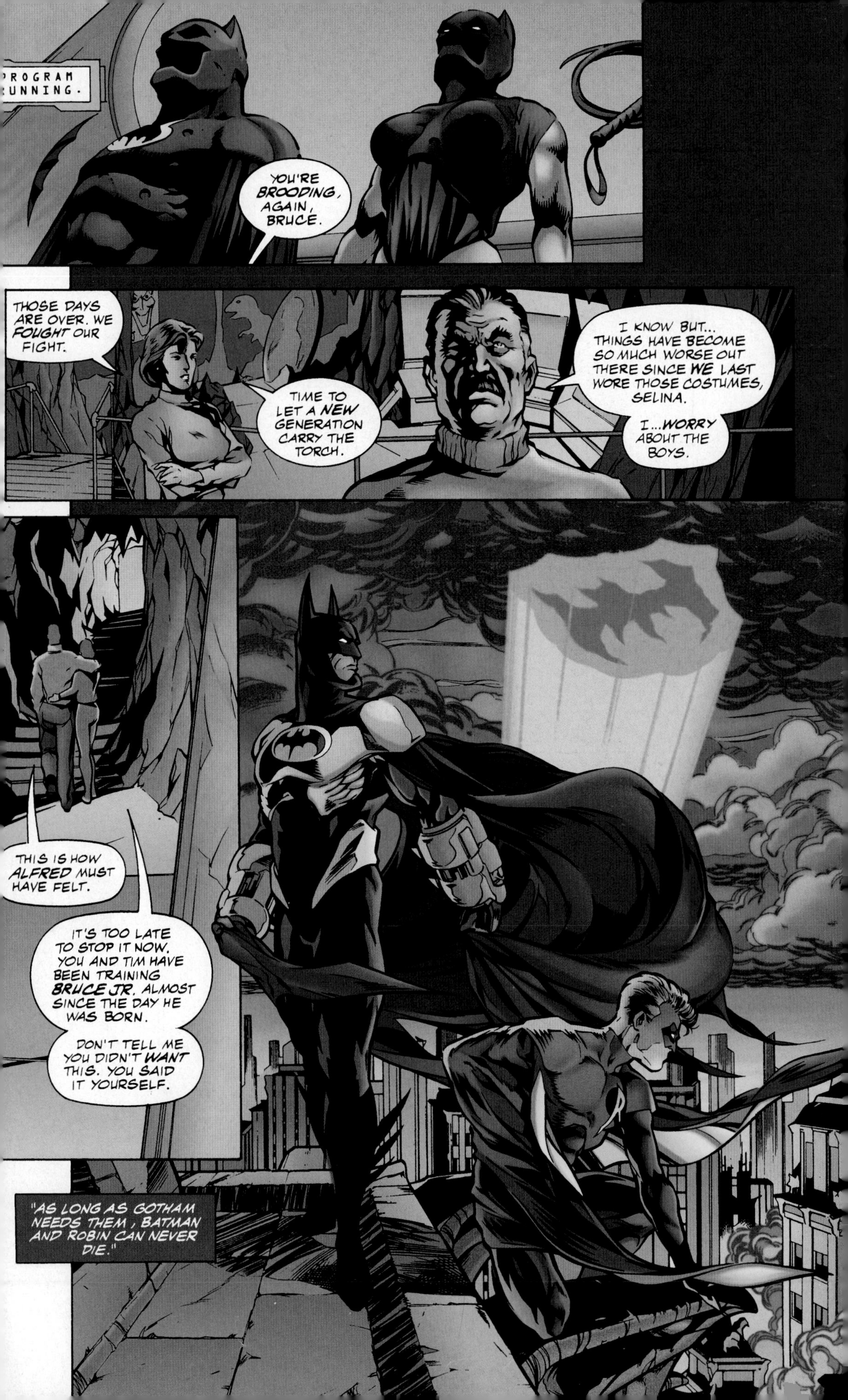

PROGRAM RUNNING.
YOU'RE BROODING, AGAIN, BRUCE.
THOSE DAYS ARE OVER. WE FOUGHT OUR FIGHT.
TIME TO LET A NEW GENERATION CARRY THE TORCH.
I KNOW BUT... THINGS HAVE BECOME SO MUCH WORSE OUT THERE SINCE WE LAST WORE THOSE COSTUMES, SELINA.
I...WORRY ABOUT THE BOYS.
THIS IS HOW ALFRED MUST HAVE FELT.
IT'S TOO LATE TO STOP IT NOW. YOU AND TIM HAVE BEEN TRAINING BRUCE JR. ALMOST SINCE THE DAY HE WAS BORN.
DON'T TELL ME YOU DIDN'T WANT THIS. YOU SAID IT YOURSELF.
"AS LONG AS GOTHAM NEEDS THEM, BATMAN AND ROBIN CAN NEVER DIE."

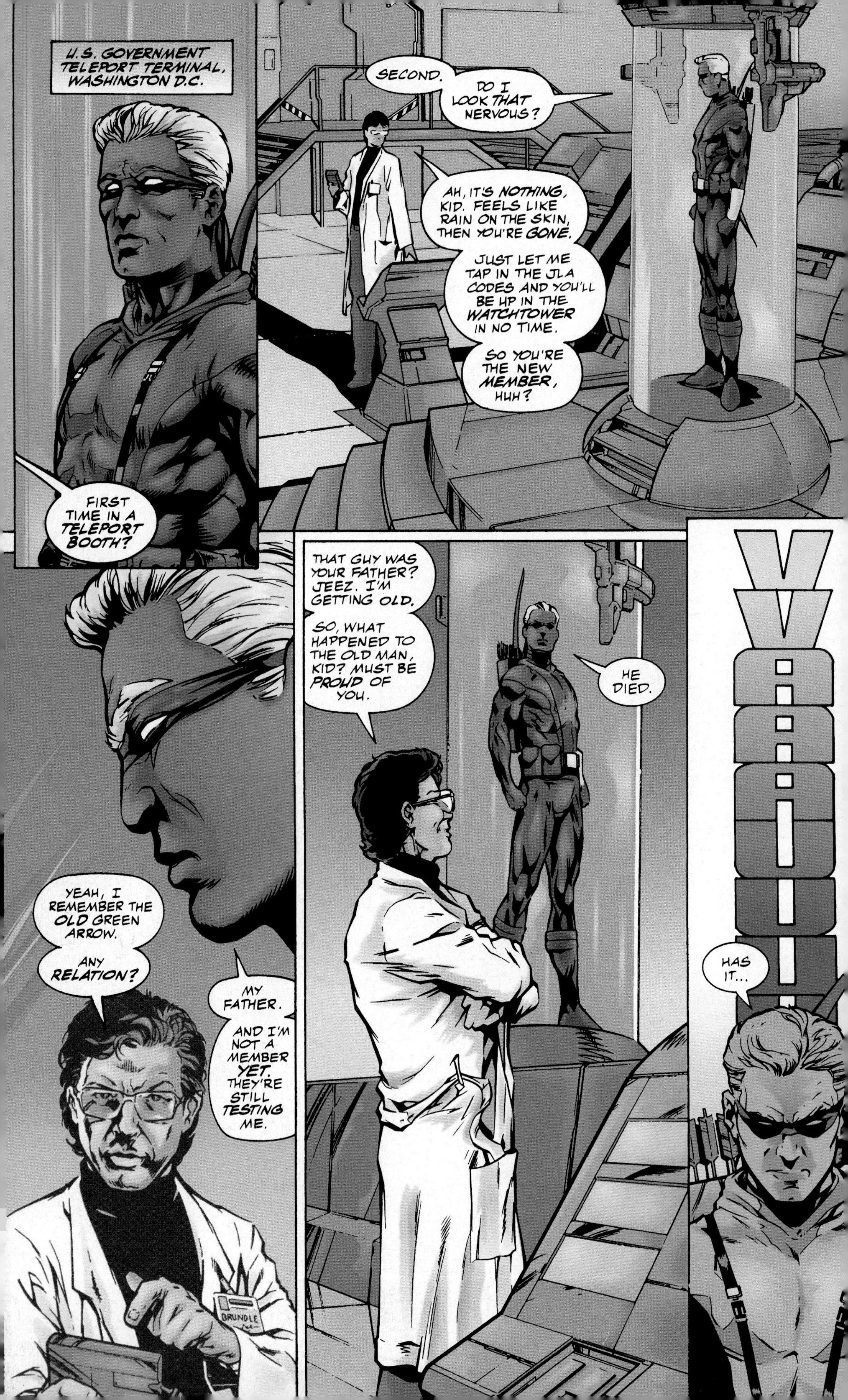
U.S. GOVERNMENT TELEPORT TERMINAL, WASHINGTON D.C.
FIRST TIME IN A TELEPORT BOOTH?
SECOND.
DO I LOOK THAT NERVOUS?
AH, IT'S NOTHING, KID. FEELS LIKE RAIN ON THE SKIN, THEN YOU'RE GONE.
JUST LET ME TAP IN THE JLA CODES AND YOU'LL BE UP IN THE WATCHTOWER IN NO TIME.
SO YOU'RE THE NEW MEMBER, HUH?
YEAH, I REMEMBER THE OLD GREEN ARROW.
ANY RELATION?
MY FATHER.
AND I'M NOT A MEMBER YET. THEY'RE STILL TESTING ME.
BRUNDLE
THAT GUY WAS YOUR FATHER? JEEZ. I'M GETTING OLD.
SO, WHAT HAPPENED TO THE OLD MAN, KID? MUST BE PROUD OF YOU.
HE DIED.
HAS IT...

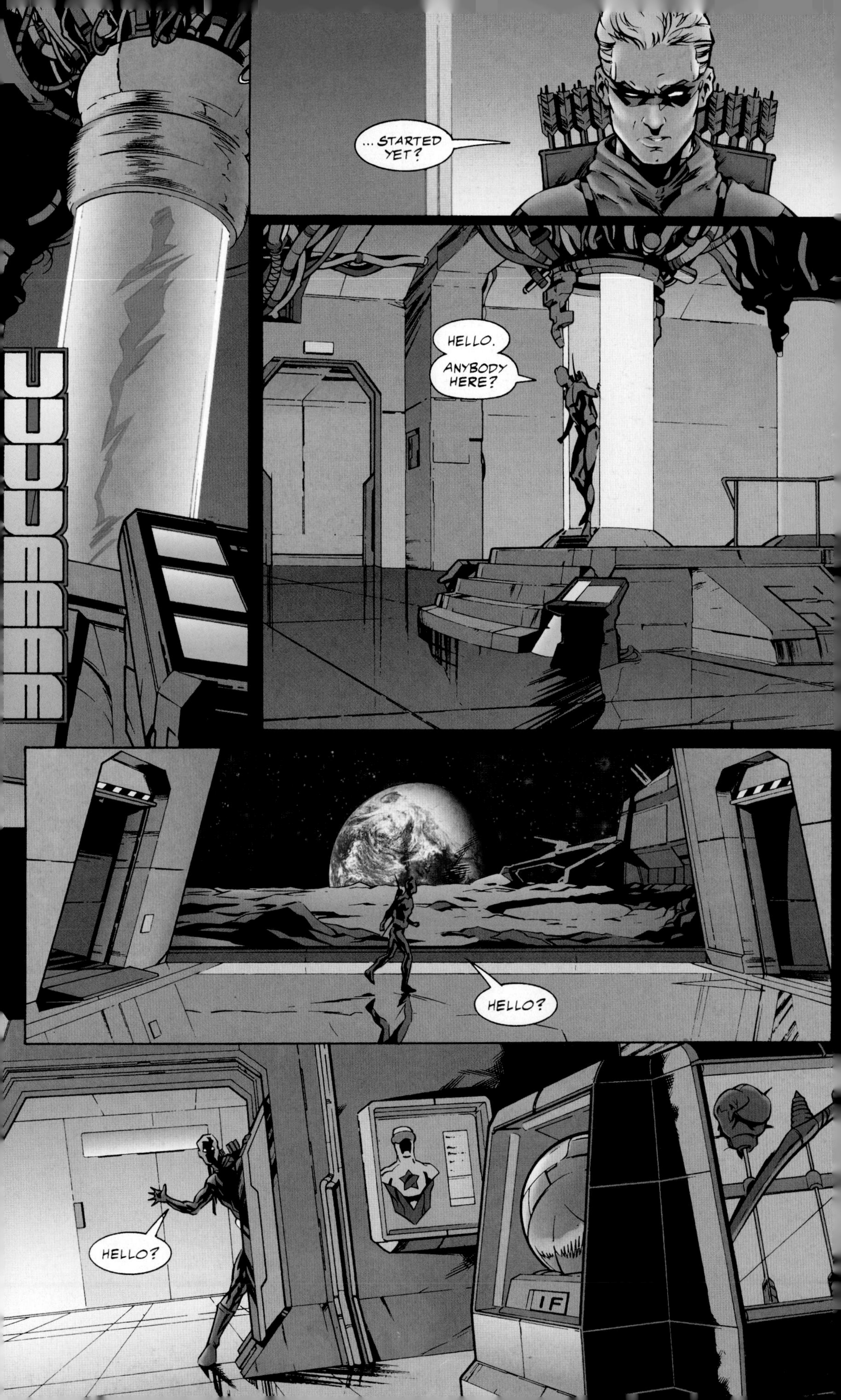

...STARTED YET?
HELLO. ANYBODY HERE?
HELLO?
HELLO?
IF

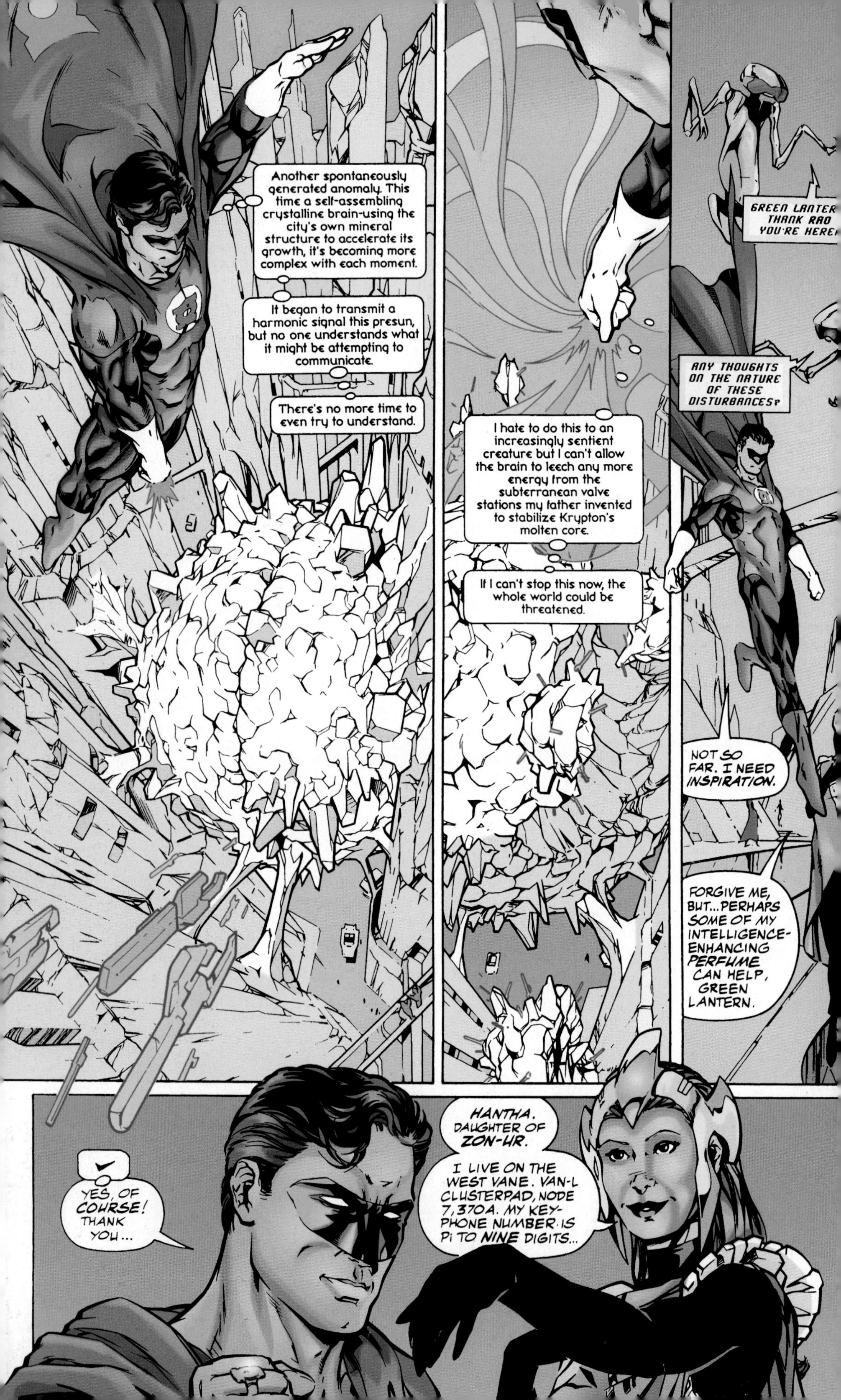
Another spontaneously generated anomaly. This time a self-assembling crystalline brain-using the city's own mineral structure to accelerate its growth, it's becoming more complex with each moment.
It began to transmit a harmonic signal this presun, but no one understands what it might be attempting to communicate.
There's no more time to even try to understand.
I hate to do this to an increasingly sentient creature but I can't allow the brain to leech any more energy from the subterranean valve stations my father invented to stabilize Krypton's molten core.
If I can't stop this now, the whole world could be threatened.
GREEN LANTER THANK RAO YOU'RE HERE
ANY THOUGHTS ON THE NATURE OF THESE DISTURBANCES?
NOT SO FAR. I NEED INSPIRATION.
FORGIVE ME, BUT...PERHAPS SOME OF MY INTELLIGENCE-ENHANCING PERFUME CAN HELP, GREEN LANTERN.
HANTHA. DAUGHTER OF ZON-UR.
I LIVE ON THE WEST VANE. VAN-L CLUSTERPAD, NODE 7,370A. MY KEY-PHONE NUMBER IS Pi TO NINE DIGITS...
YES, OF COURSE! THANK YOU...

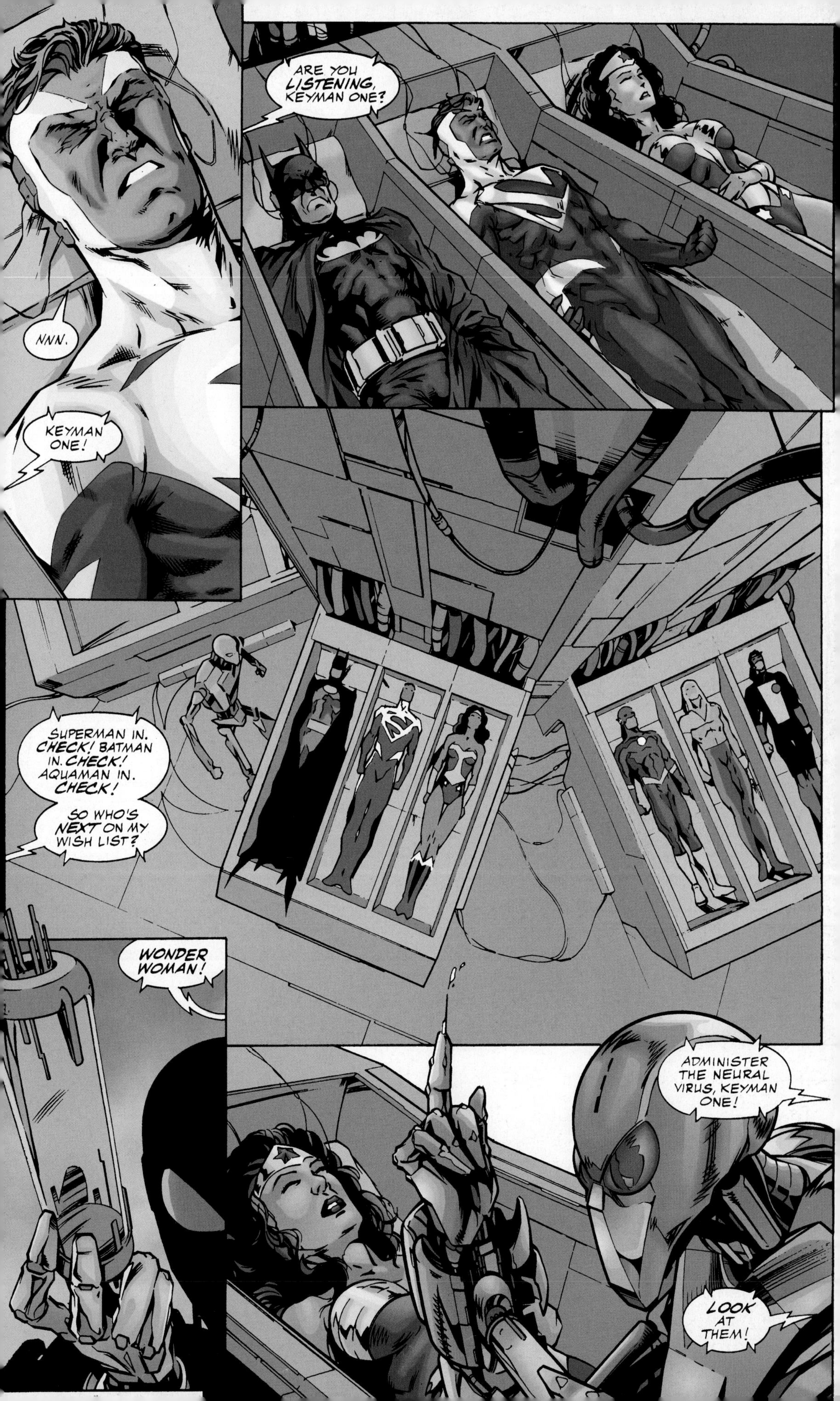
ARE YOU LISTENING, KEYMAN ONE?
NNN.
KEYMAN ONE!
SUPERMAN IN. CHECK! BATMAN IN. CHECK! AQUAMAN IN. CHECK!
SO WHO'S NEXT ON MY WISH LIST?
WONDER WOMAN!
ADMINISTER THE NEURAL VIRUS, KEYMAN ONE!
LOOK AT THEM!

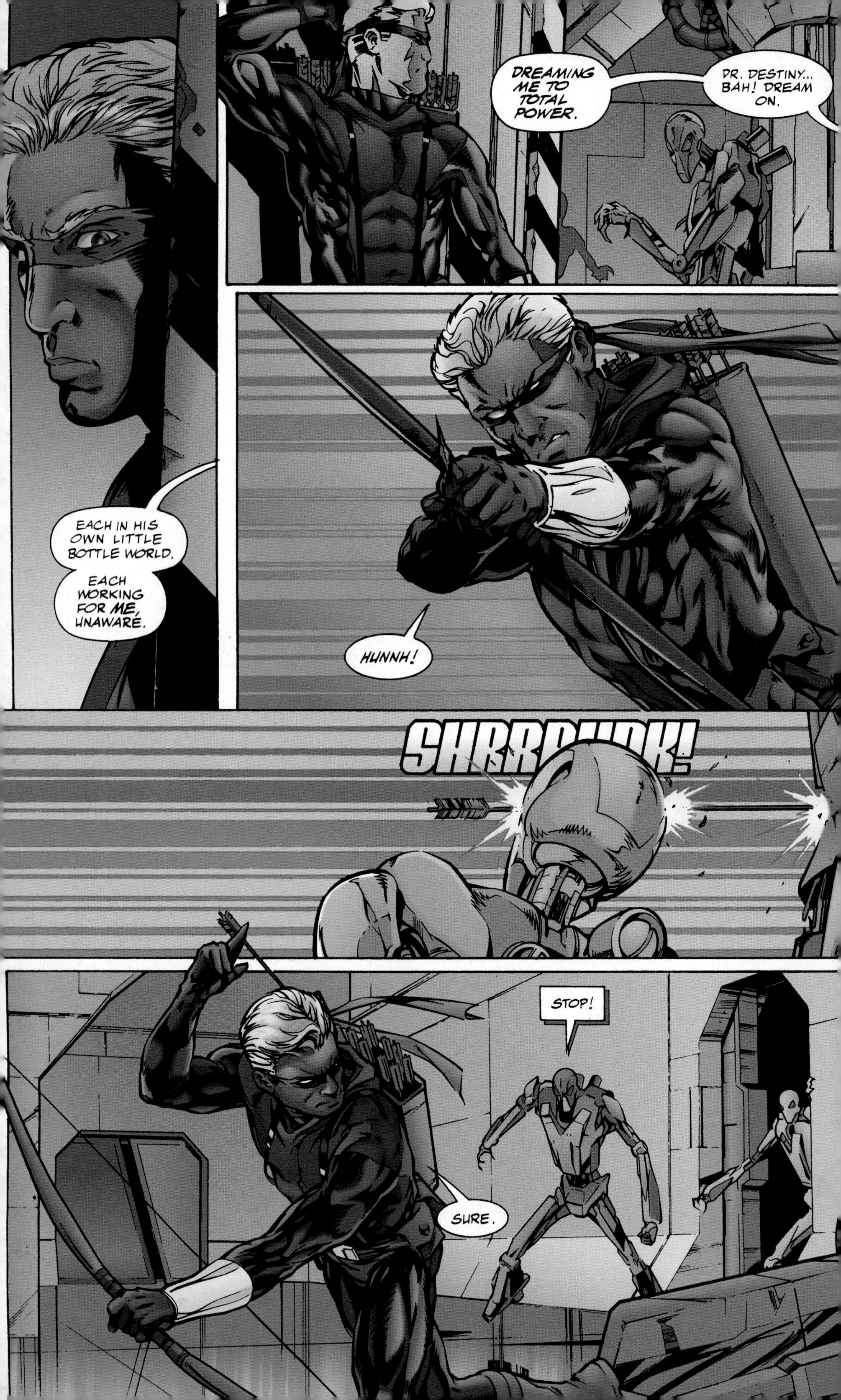
DREAMING ME TO TOTAL POWER.
DR. DESTINY... BAH! DREAM ON.
EACH IN HIS OWN LITTLE BOTTLE WORLD.
EACH WORKING FOR *ME*, UNAWARE.
HUNNH!
SHRRRUNK!
STOP!
SURE.

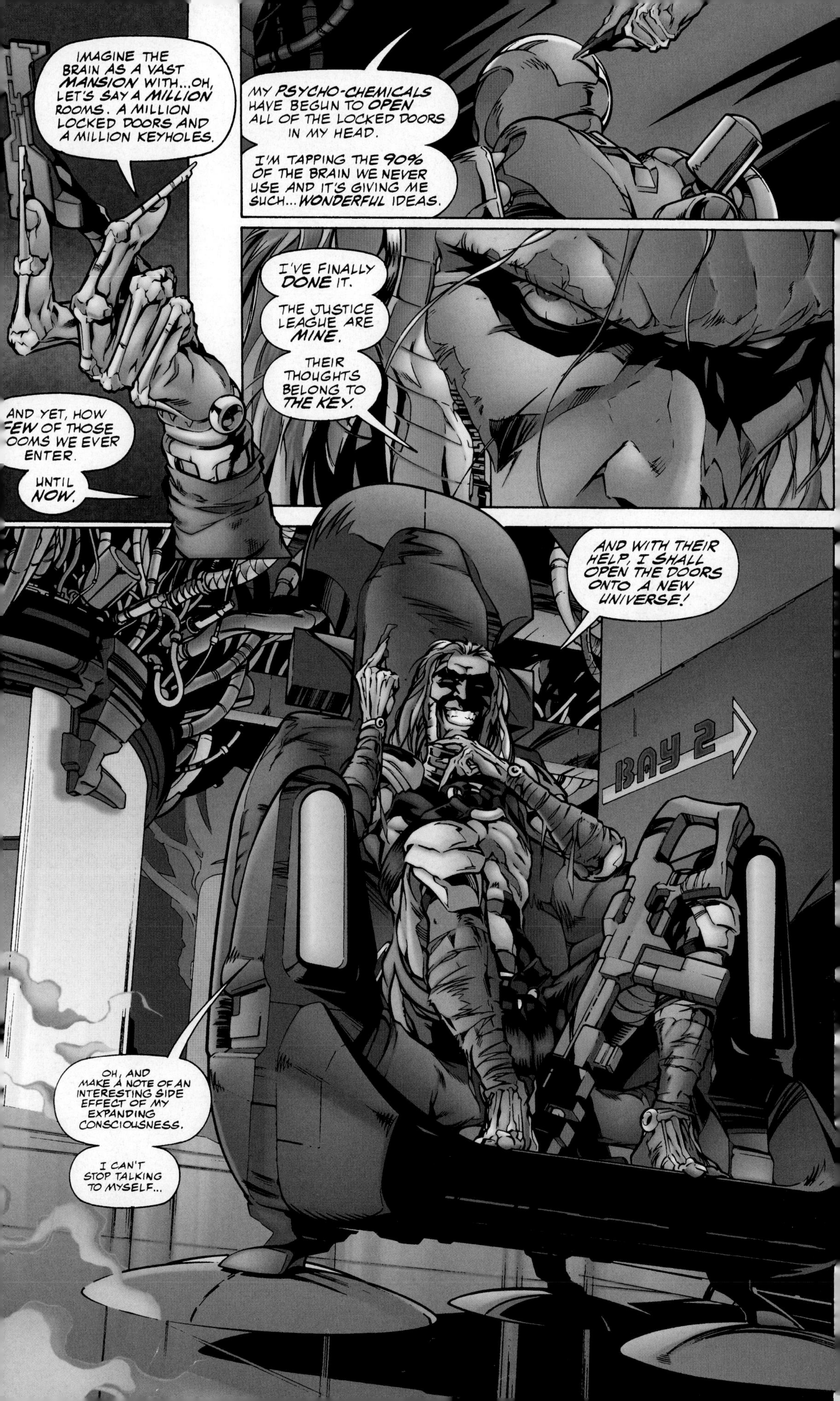
IMAGINE THE BRAIN AS A VAST MANSION WITH...OH, LET'S SAY A MILLION ROOMS. A MILLION LOCKED DOORS AND A MILLION KEYHOLES.
MY PSYCHO-CHEMICALS HAVE BEGUN TO OPEN ALL OF THE LOCKED DOORS IN MY HEAD.
I'M TAPPING THE 90% OF THE BRAIN WE NEVER USE AND IT'S GIVING ME SUCH...WONDERFUL IDEAS.
AND YET, HOW FEW OF THOSE OOMS WE EVER ENTER.
UNTIL NOW.
I'VE FINALLY DONE IT.
THE JUSTICE LEAGUE ARE MINE.
THEIR THOUGHTS BELONG TO THE KEY.
AND WITH THEIR HELP, I SHALL OPEN THE DOORS ONTO A NEW UNIVERSE!
BAY 2
OH, AND MAKE A NOTE OF AN INTERESTING SIDE EFFECT OF MY EXPANDING CONSCIOUSNESS.
I CAN'T STOP TALKING TO MYSELF...

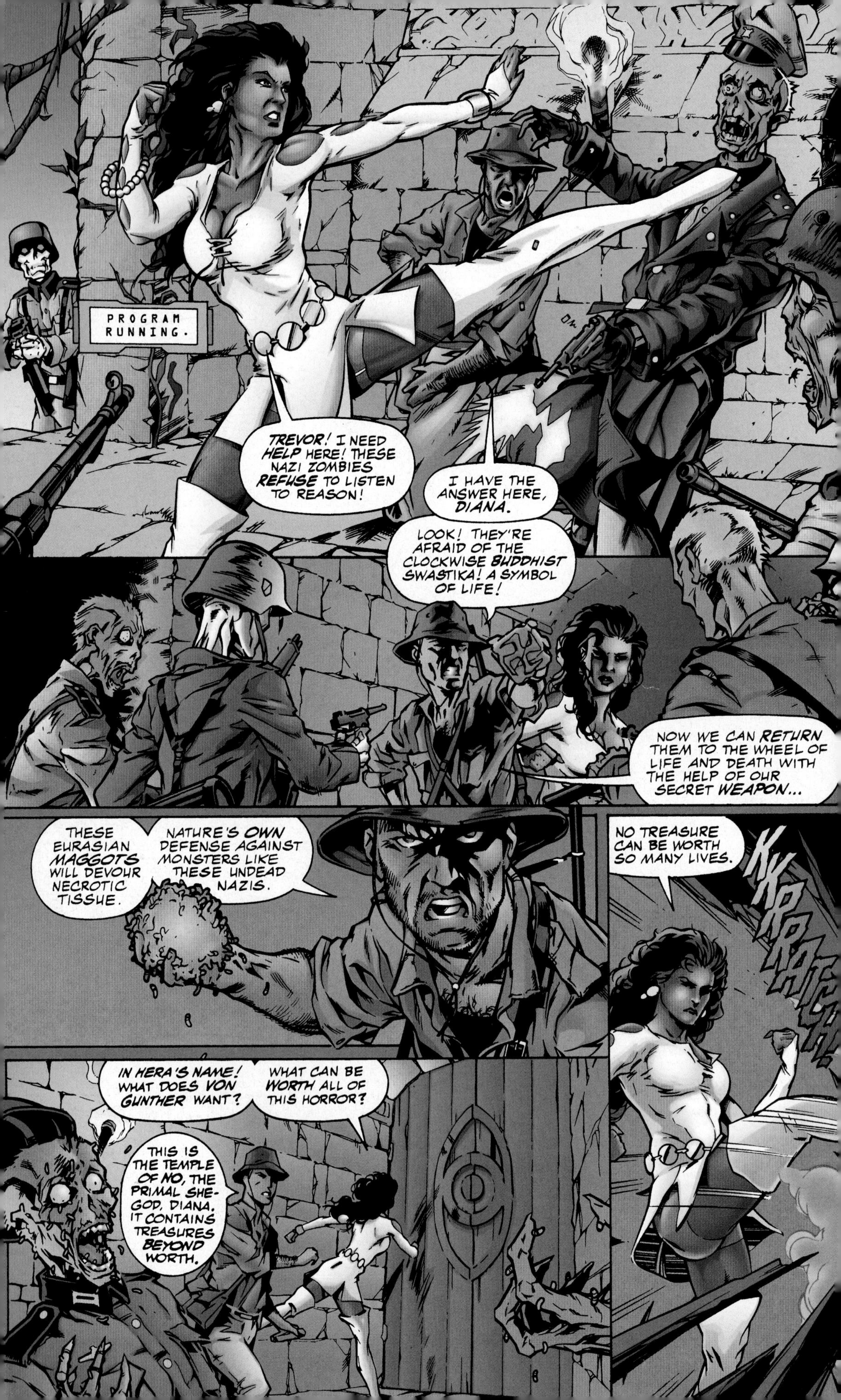
PROGRAM RUNNING.
TREVOR! I NEED HELP HERE! THESE NAZI ZOMBIES REFUSE TO LISTEN TO REASON!
I HAVE THE ANSWER HERE, DIANA.
LOOK! THEY'RE AFRAID OF THE CLOCKWISE BUDDHIST SWASTIKA! A SYMBOL OF LIFE!
NOW WE CAN RETURN THEM TO THE WHEEL OF LIFE AND DEATH WITH THE HELP OF OUR SECRET WEAPON...
THESE EURASIAN MAGGOTS WILL DEVOUR NECROTIC TISSUE.
NATURE'S OWN DEFENSE AGAINST MONSTERS LIKE THESE UNDEAD NAZIS.
NO TREASURE CAN BE WORTH SO MANY LIVES.
KKRRATCH
IN HERA'S NAME! WHAT DOES VON GUNTHER WANT?
WHAT CAN BE WORTH ALL OF THIS HORROR?
THIS IS THE TEMPLE OF NO, THE PRIMAL SHE-GOD, DIANA. IT CONTAINS TREASURES BEYOND WORTH.

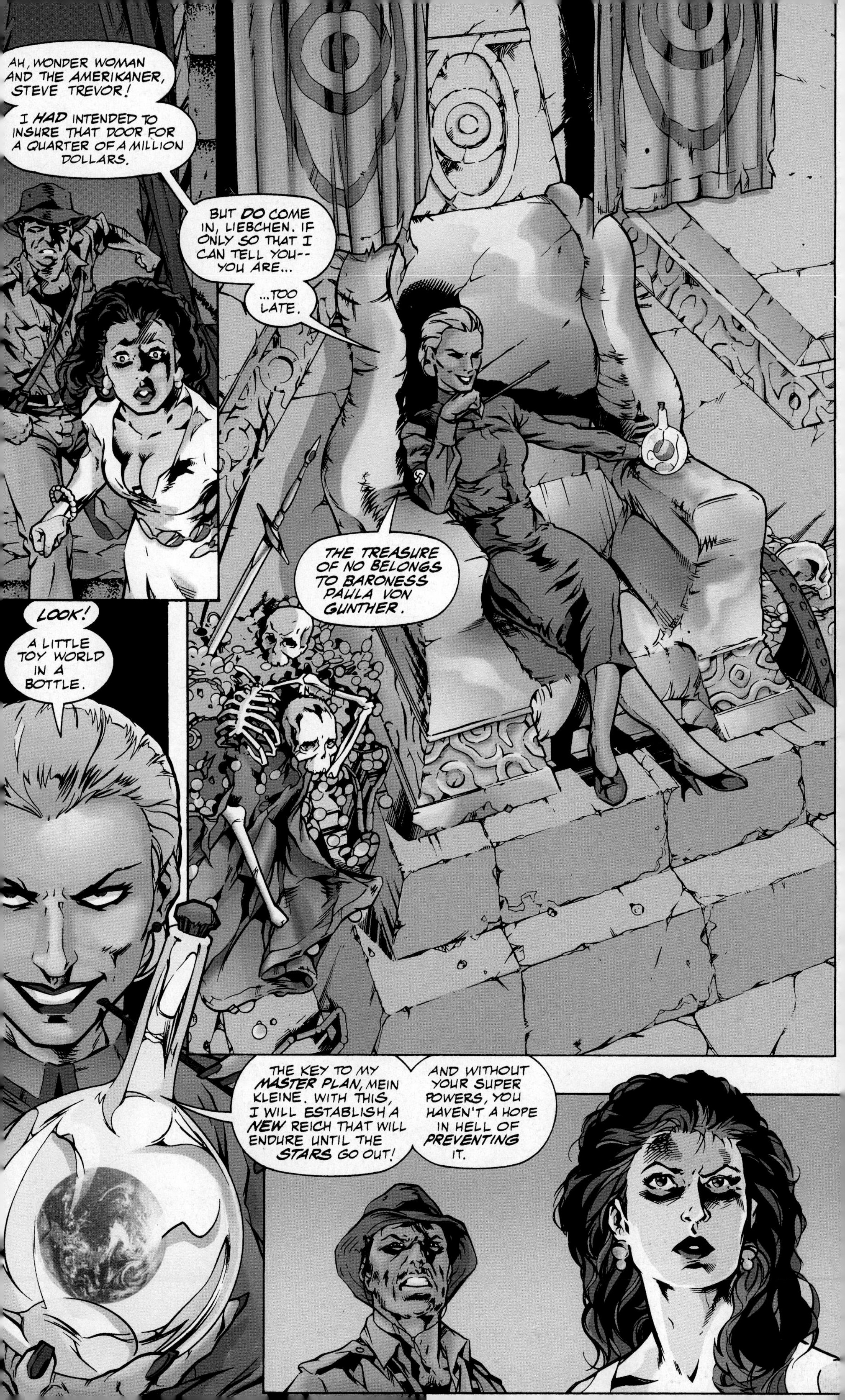
AH, WONDER WOMAN AND THE AMERIKANER, STEVE TREVOR!
I HAD INTENDED TO INSURE THAT DOOR FOR A QUARTER OF A MILLION DOLLARS.
BUT DO COME IN, LIEBCHEN. IF ONLY SO THAT I CAN TELL YOU--YOU ARE...
...TOO LATE.
THE TREASURE OF NO BELONGS TO BARONESS PAULA VON GUNTHER.
LOOK!
A LITTLE TOY WORLD IN A BOTTLE.
THE KEY TO MY MASTER PLAN, MEIN KLEINE. WITH THIS, I WILL ESTABLISH A NEW REICH THAT WILL ENDURE UNTIL THE STARS GO OUT!
AND WITHOUT YOUR SUPER POWERS, YOU HAVEN'T A HOPE IN HELL OF PREVENTING IT.

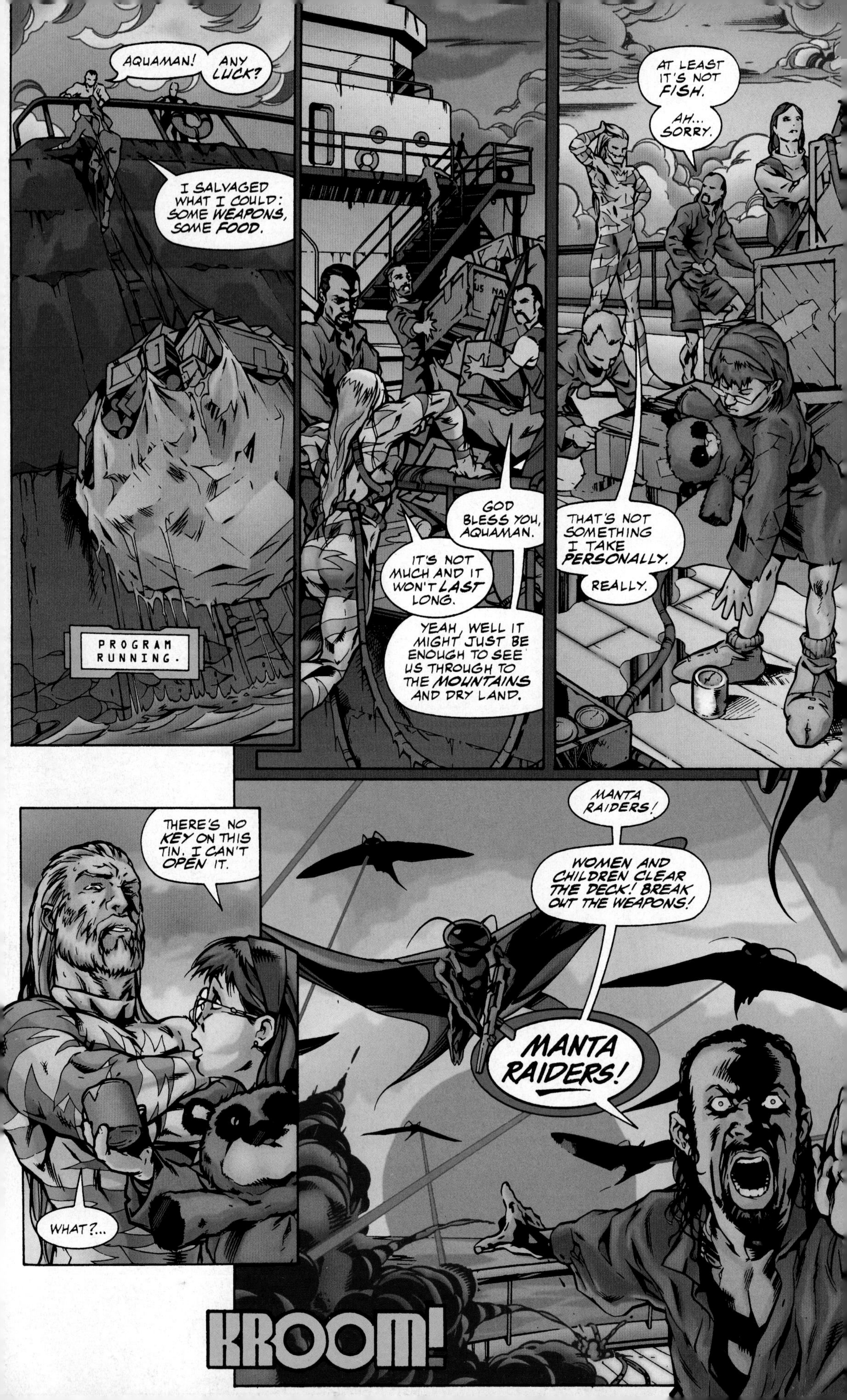
AQUAMAN!
ANY LUCK?
I SALVAGED WHAT I COULD: SOME WEAPONS, SOME FOOD.
PROGRAM RUNNING.
GOD BLESS YOU, AQUAMAN.
IT'S NOT MUCH AND IT WON'T LAST LONG.
YEAH, WELL IT MIGHT JUST BE ENOUGH TO SEE US THROUGH TO THE MOUNTAINS AND DRY LAND.
AT LEAST IT'S NOT FISH.
AH... SORRY.
THAT'S NOT SOMETHING I TAKE PERSONALLY.
REALLY.
THERE'S NO KEY ON THIS TIN. I CAN'T OPEN IT.
WHAT?...
MANTA RAIDERS!
WOMEN AND CHILDREN CLEAR THE DECK! BREAK OUT THE WEAPONS!
MANTA RAIDERS!
KROOM!

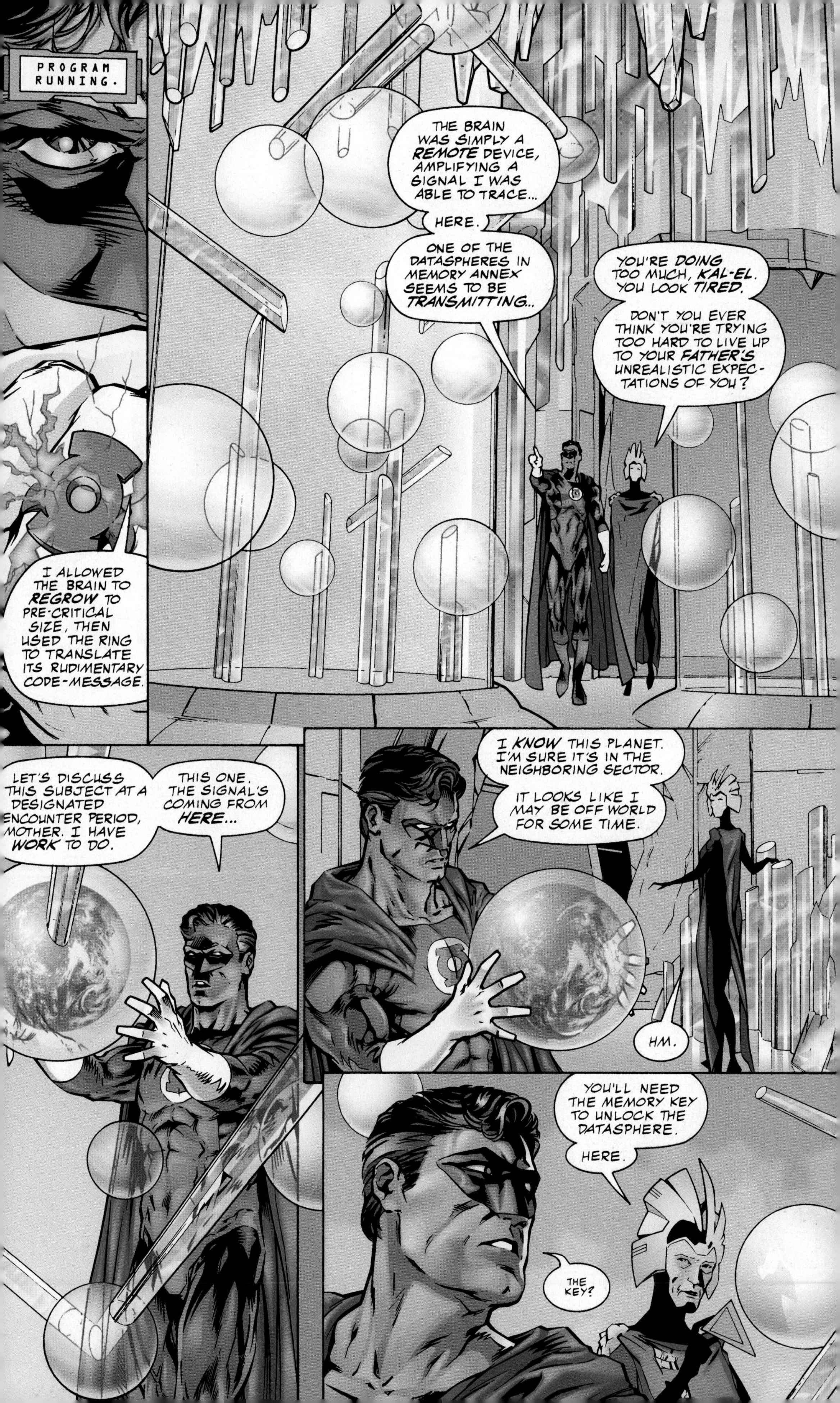
PROGRAM RUNNING.
I ALLOWED THE BRAIN TO REGROW TO PRE-CRITICAL SIZE, THEN USED THE RING TO TRANSLATE ITS RUDIMENTARY CODE-MESSAGE.
THE BRAIN WAS SIMPLY A REMOTE DEVICE, AMPLIFYING A SIGNAL I WAS ABLE TO TRACE...
HERE.
ONE OF THE DATASPHERES IN MEMORY ANNEX SEEMS TO BE TRANSMITTING...
YOU'RE DOING TOO MUCH, KAL-EL. YOU LOOK TIRED.
DON'T YOU EVER THINK YOU'RE TRYING TOO HARD TO LIVE UP TO YOUR FATHER'S UNREALISTIC EXPECTATIONS OF YOU?
LET'S DISCUSS THIS SUBJECT AT A DESIGNATED ENCOUNTER PERIOD, MOTHER. I HAVE WORK TO DO.
THIS ONE. THE SIGNAL'S COMING FROM HERE...
I KNOW THIS PLANET. I'M SURE IT'S IN THE NEIGHBORING SECTOR.
IT LOOKS LIKE I MAY BE OFF WORLD FOR SOME TIME.
HM.
YOU'LL NEED THE MEMORY KEY TO UNLOCK THE DATASPHERE.
HERE.
THE KEY?

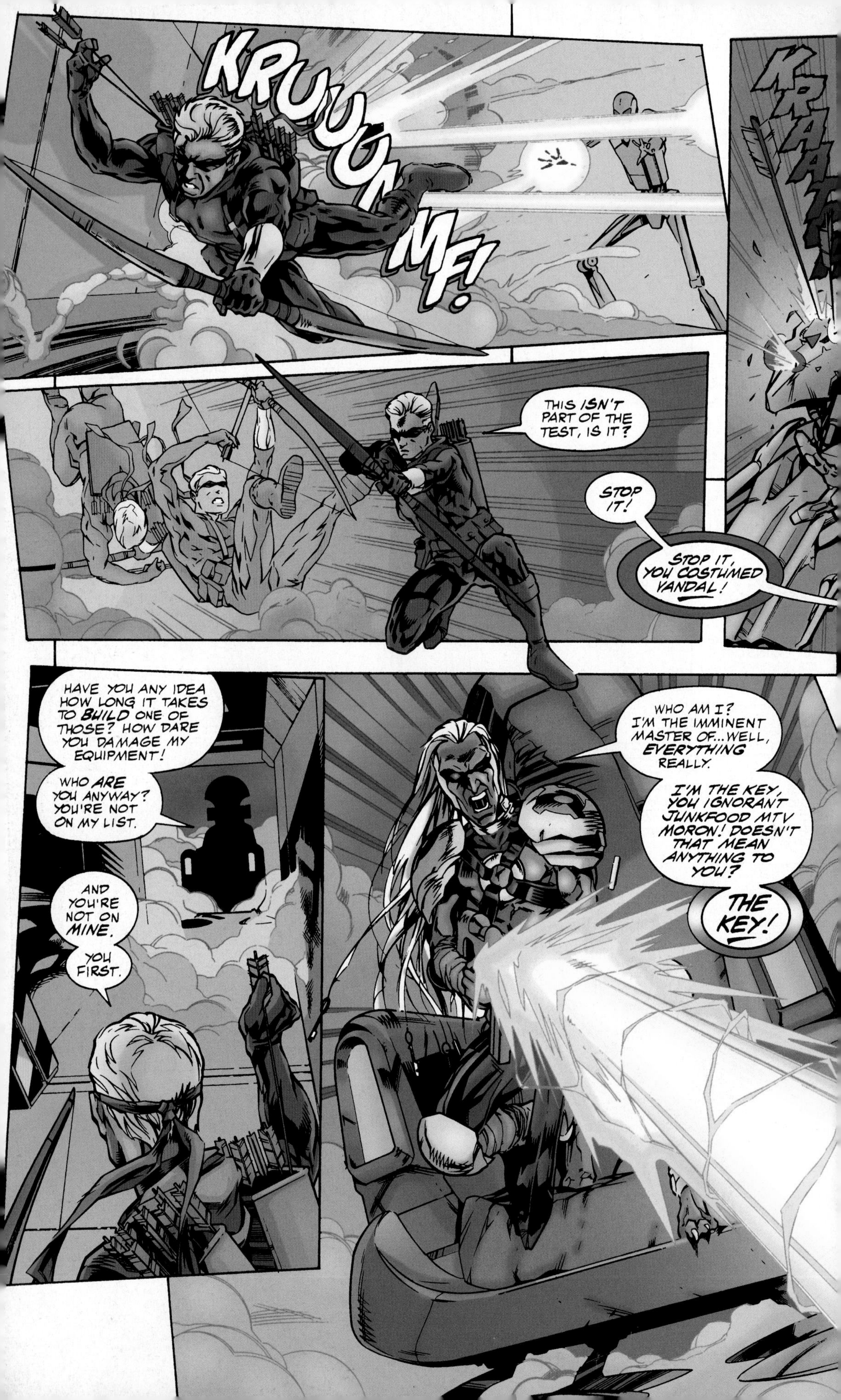
KRUUUMMF!
KRA
THIS ISN'T PART OF THE TEST, IS IT?
STOP IT!
STOP IT, YOU COSTUMED VANDAL!
HAVE YOU ANY IDEA HOW LONG IT TAKES TO BUILD ONE OF THOSE? HOW DARE YOU DAMAGE MY EQUIPMENT!
WHO ARE YOU ANYWAY? YOU'RE NOT ON MY LIST.
AND YOU'RE NOT ON MINE.
YOU FIRST.
WHO AM I? I'M THE IMMINENT MASTER OF...WELL, EVERYTHING REALLY.
I'M THE KEY, YOU IGNORANT JUNKFOOD MTV MORON! DOESN'T THAT MEAN ANYTHING TO YOU?
THE KEY!

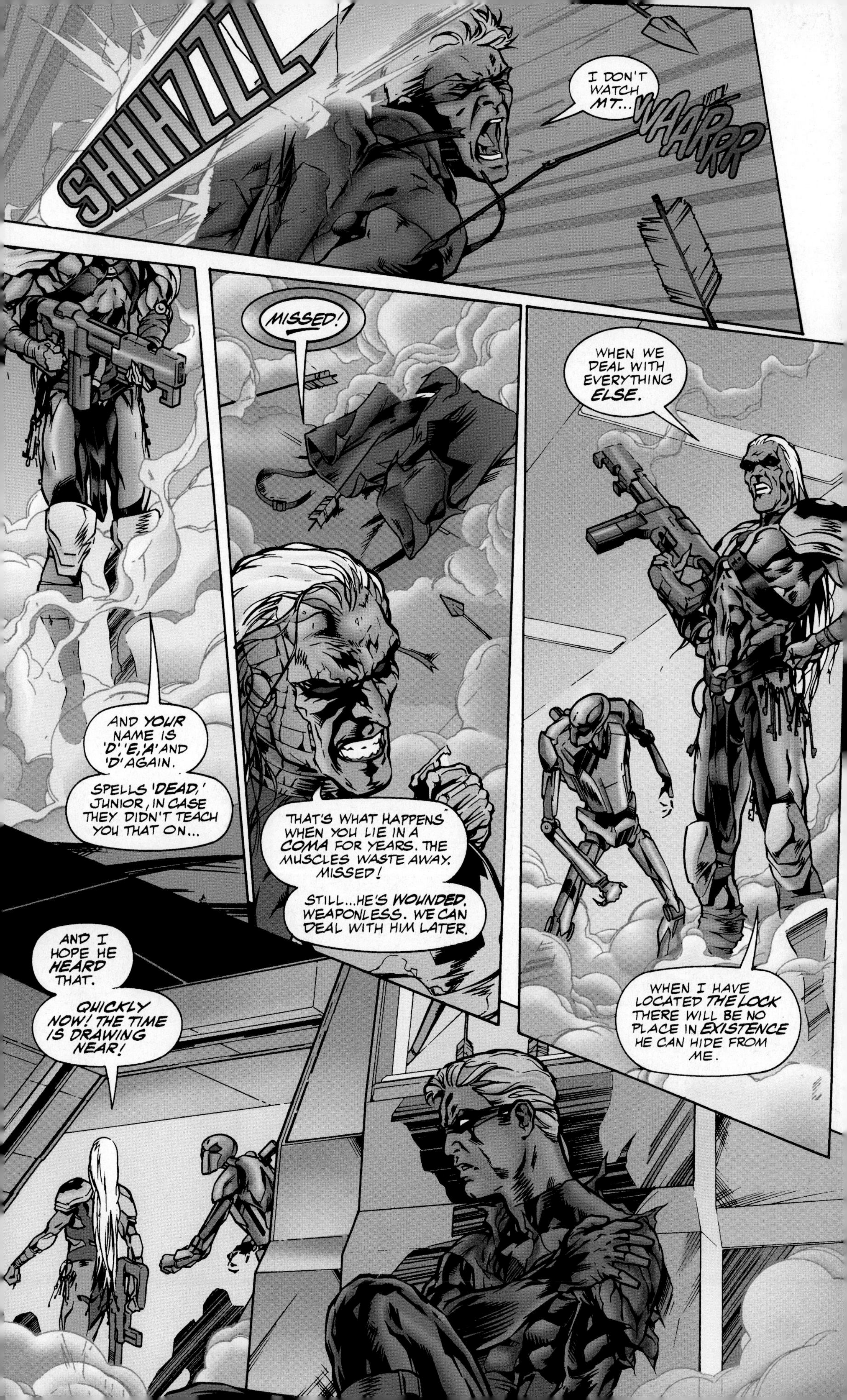
SHHHZZZL
I DON'T WATCH MT...
WAARRR
MISSED!
WHEN WE DEAL WITH EVERYTHING ELSE.
AND YOUR NAME IS 'D', 'E', 'A' AND 'D' AGAIN.
SPELLS 'DEAD,' JUNIOR, IN CASE THEY DIDN'T TEACH YOU THAT ON...
THAT'S WHAT HAPPENS WHEN YOU LIE IN A COMA FOR YEARS. THE MUSCLES WASTE AWAY. MISSED!
STILL...HE'S WOUNDED. WEAPONLESS. WE CAN DEAL WITH HIM LATER.
WHEN I HAVE LOCATED THE LOCK THERE WILL BE NO PLACE IN EXISTENCE HE CAN HIDE FROM ME.
AND I HOPE HE HEARD THAT.
QUICKLY NOW! THE TIME IS DRAWING NEAR!

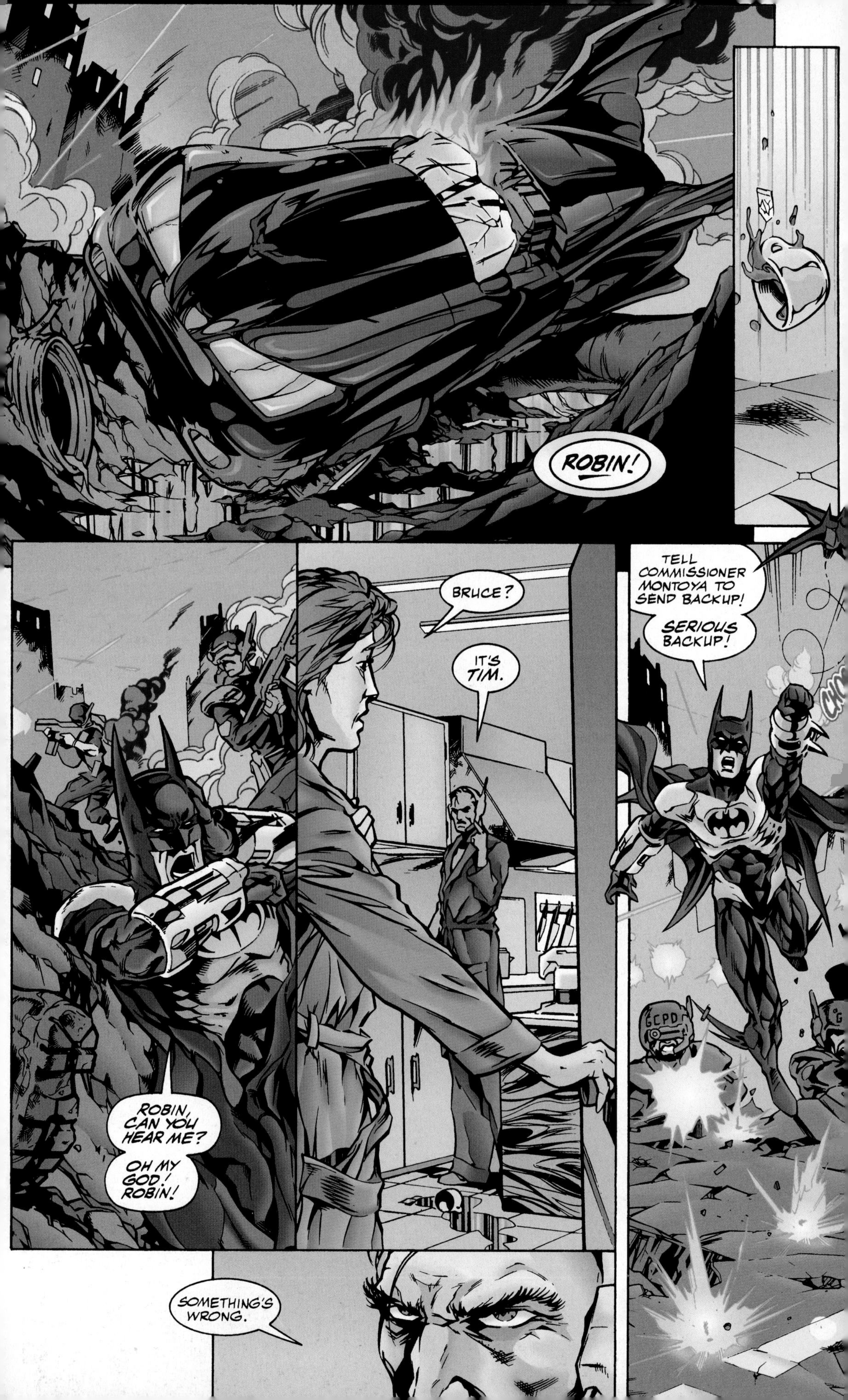

ROBIN!
BRUCE?
IT'S TIM.
TELL COMMISSIONER MONTOYA TO SEND BACKUP!
SERIOUS BACKUP!
ROBIN, CAN YOU HEAR ME?
OH MY GOD! ROBIN!
SOMETHING'S WRONG.

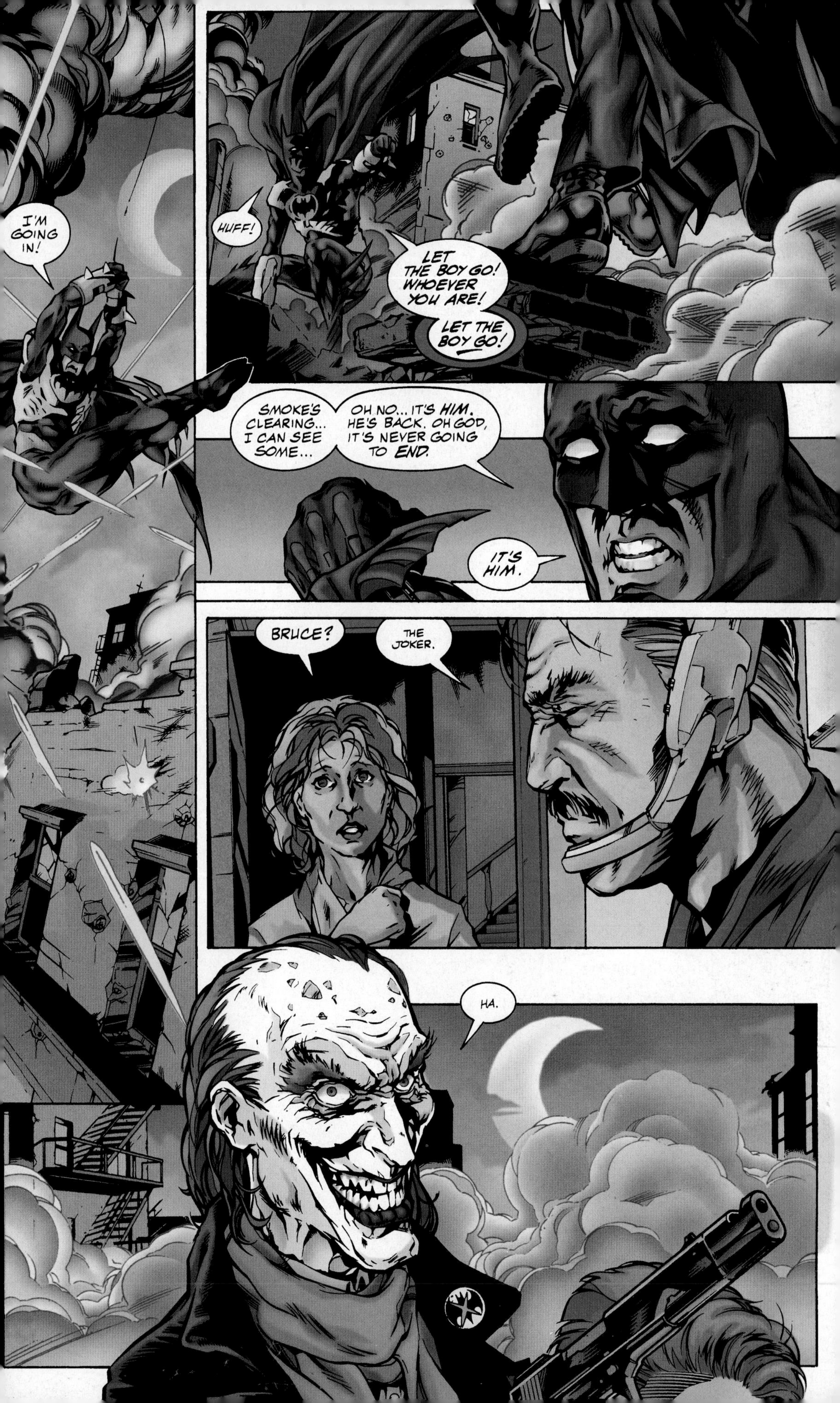

I'M GOING IN!
HUFF!
LET THE BOY GO! WHOEVER YOU ARE!
LET THE BOY GO!
SMOKE'S CLEARING... I CAN SEE SOME...
OH NO... IT'S HIM. HE'S BACK. OH GOD, IT'S NEVER GOING TO END.
IT'S HIM.
BRUCE?
THE JOKER.
HA.

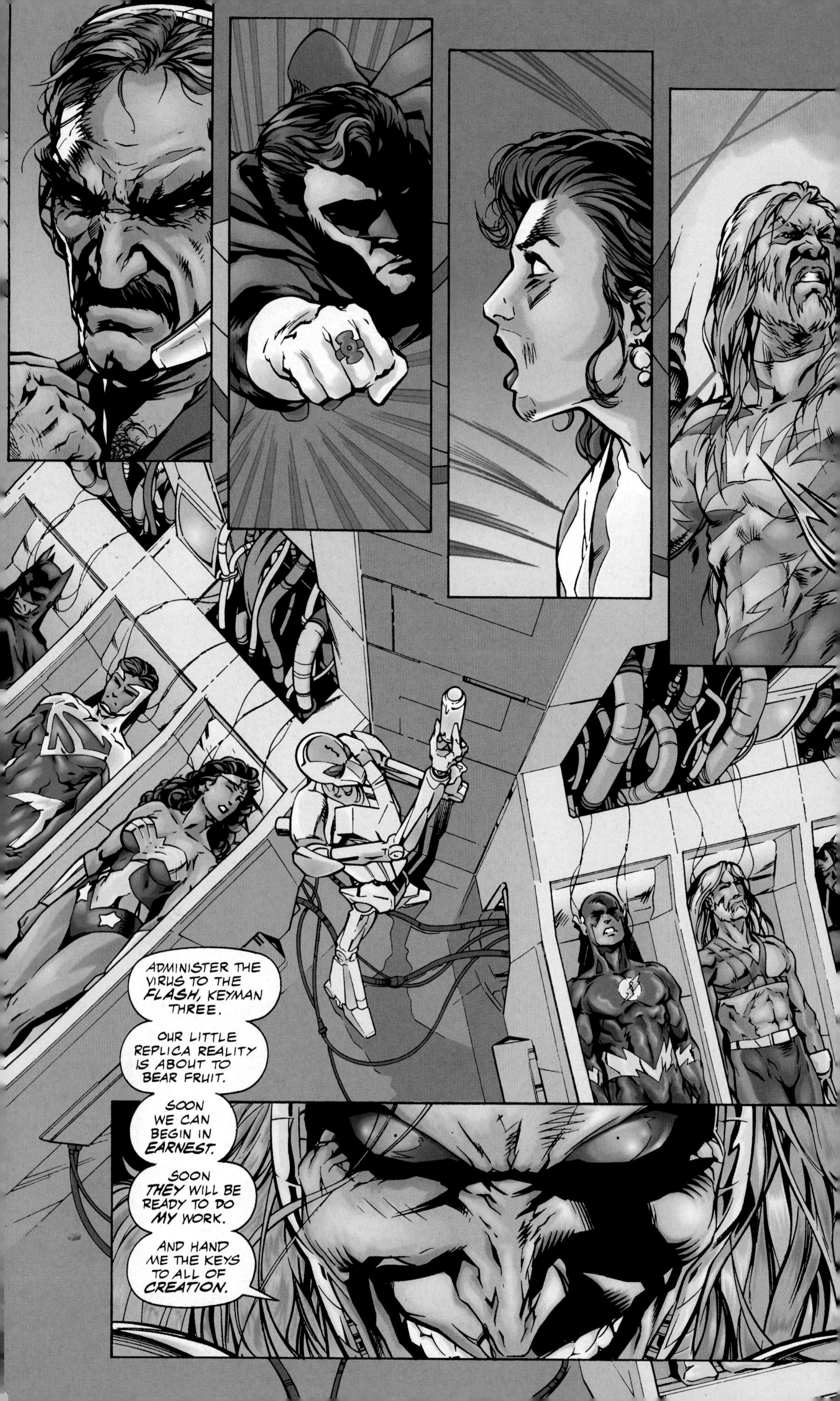
ADMINISTER THE VIRUS TO THE FLASH, KEYMAN THREE.
OUR LITTLE REPLICA REALITY IS ABOUT TO BEAR FRUIT.
SOON WE CAN BEGIN IN EARNEST.
SOON THEY WILL BE READY TO DO MY WORK.
AND HAND ME THE KEYS TO ALL OF CREATION.

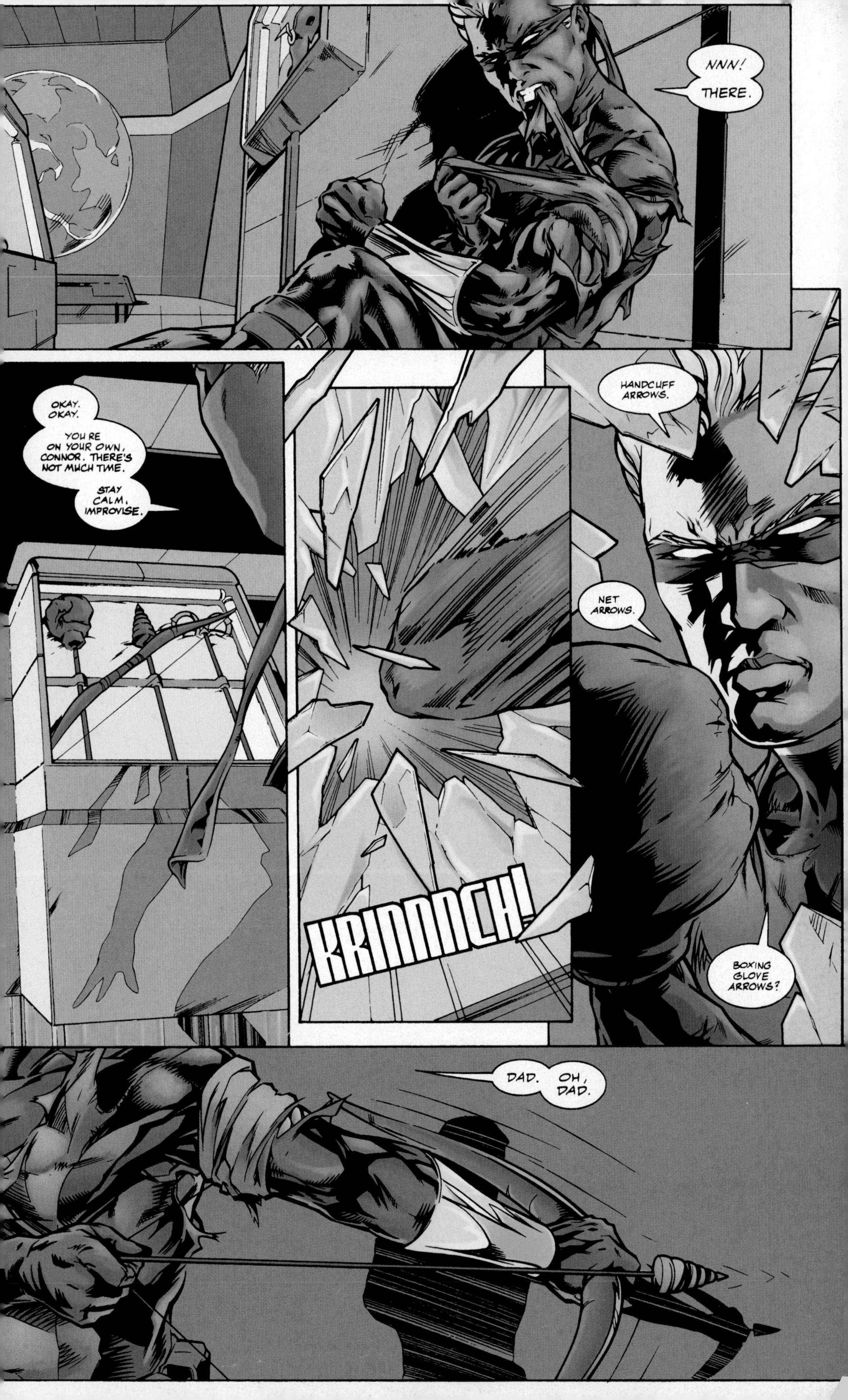
NNN!
THERE.
OKAY. OKAY.
YOU'RE ON YOUR OWN, CONNOR. THERE'S NOT MUCH TIME.
STAY CALM. IMPROVISE.
HANDCUFF ARROWS.
NET ARROWS.
KRINNNCH!
BOXING GLOVE ARROWS?
DAD. OH, DAD.

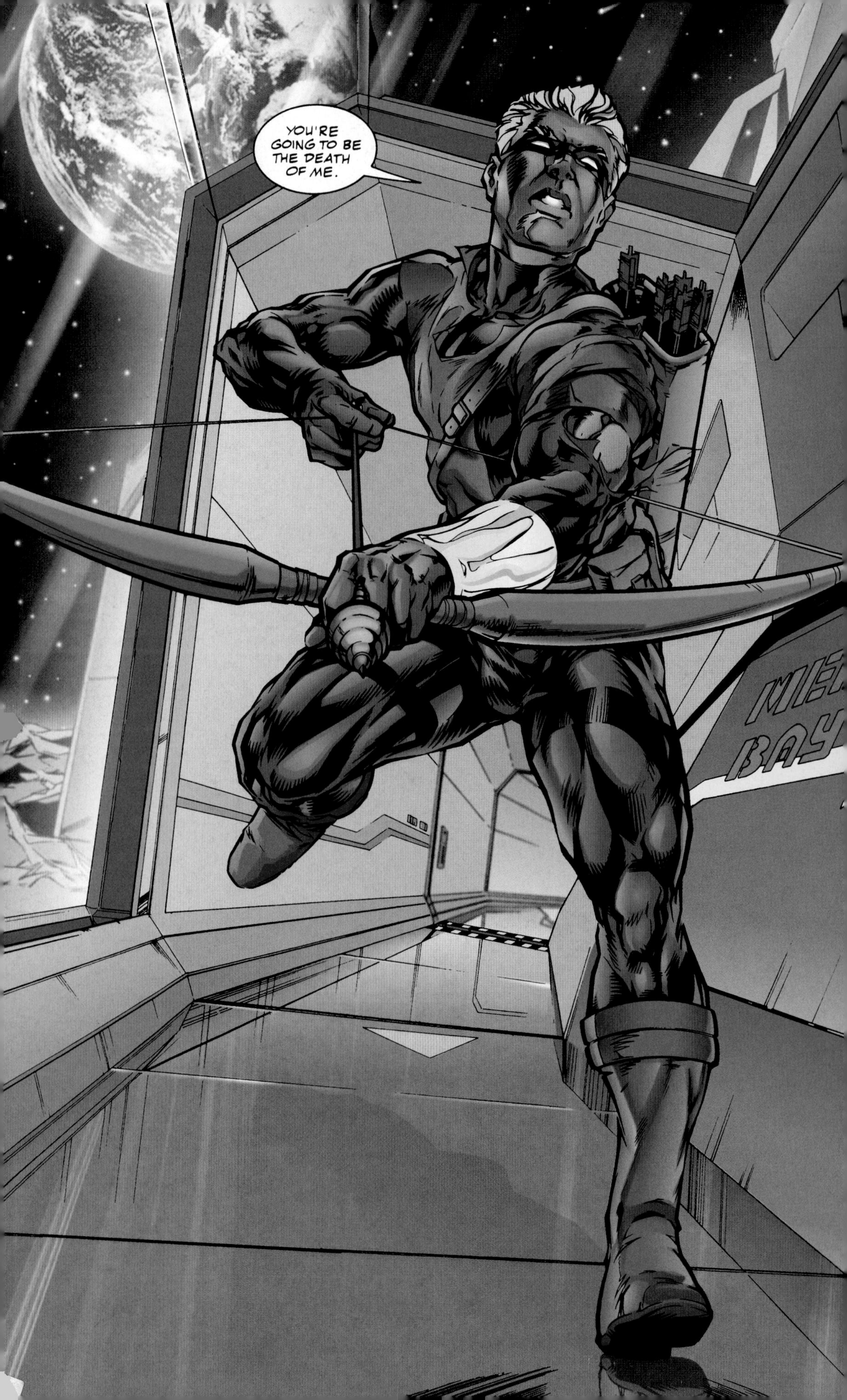
YOU'RE GOING TO BE THE DEATH OF ME.

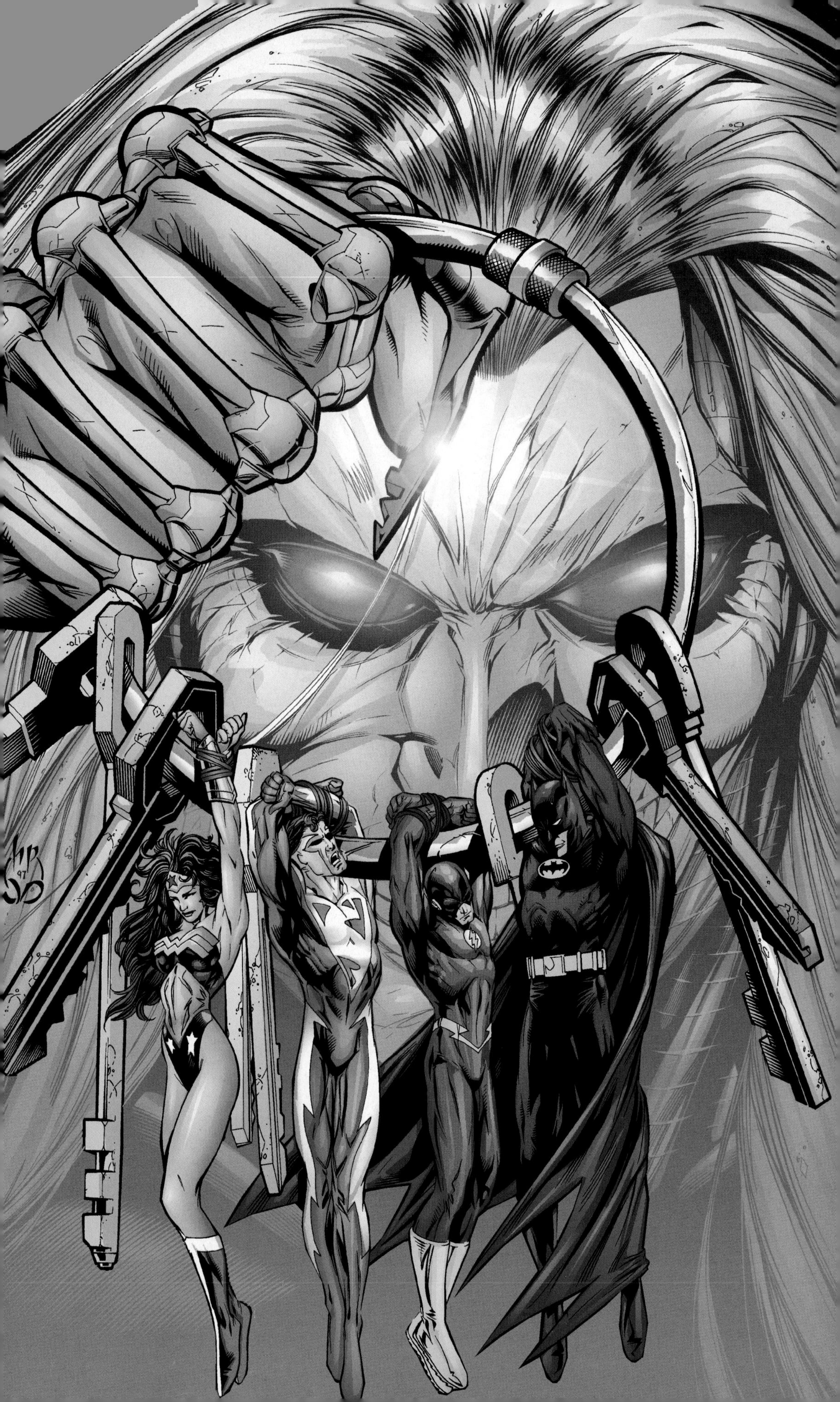

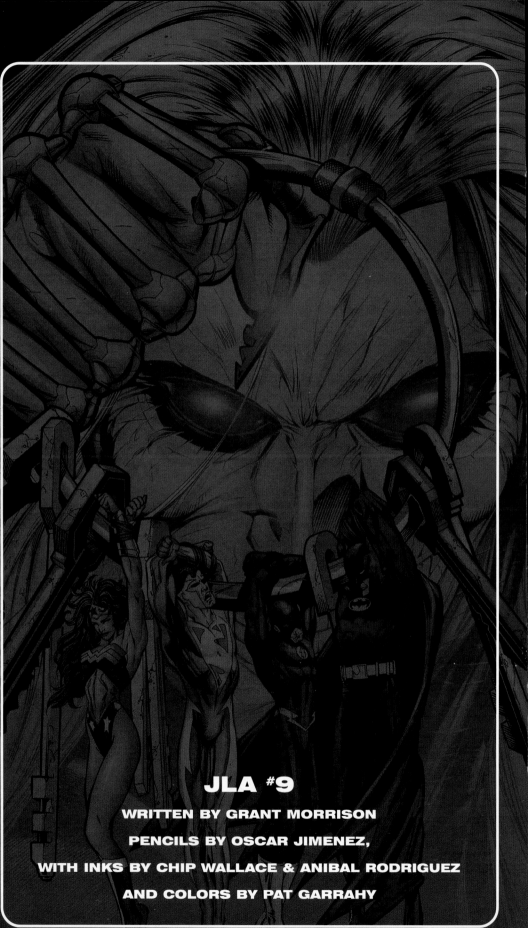

JLA #9

WRITTEN BY GRANT MORRISON

PENCILS BY OSCAR JIMENEZ,

WITH INKS BY CHIP WALLACE & ANIBAL RODRIGUEZ

AND COLORS BY PAT GARRAHY

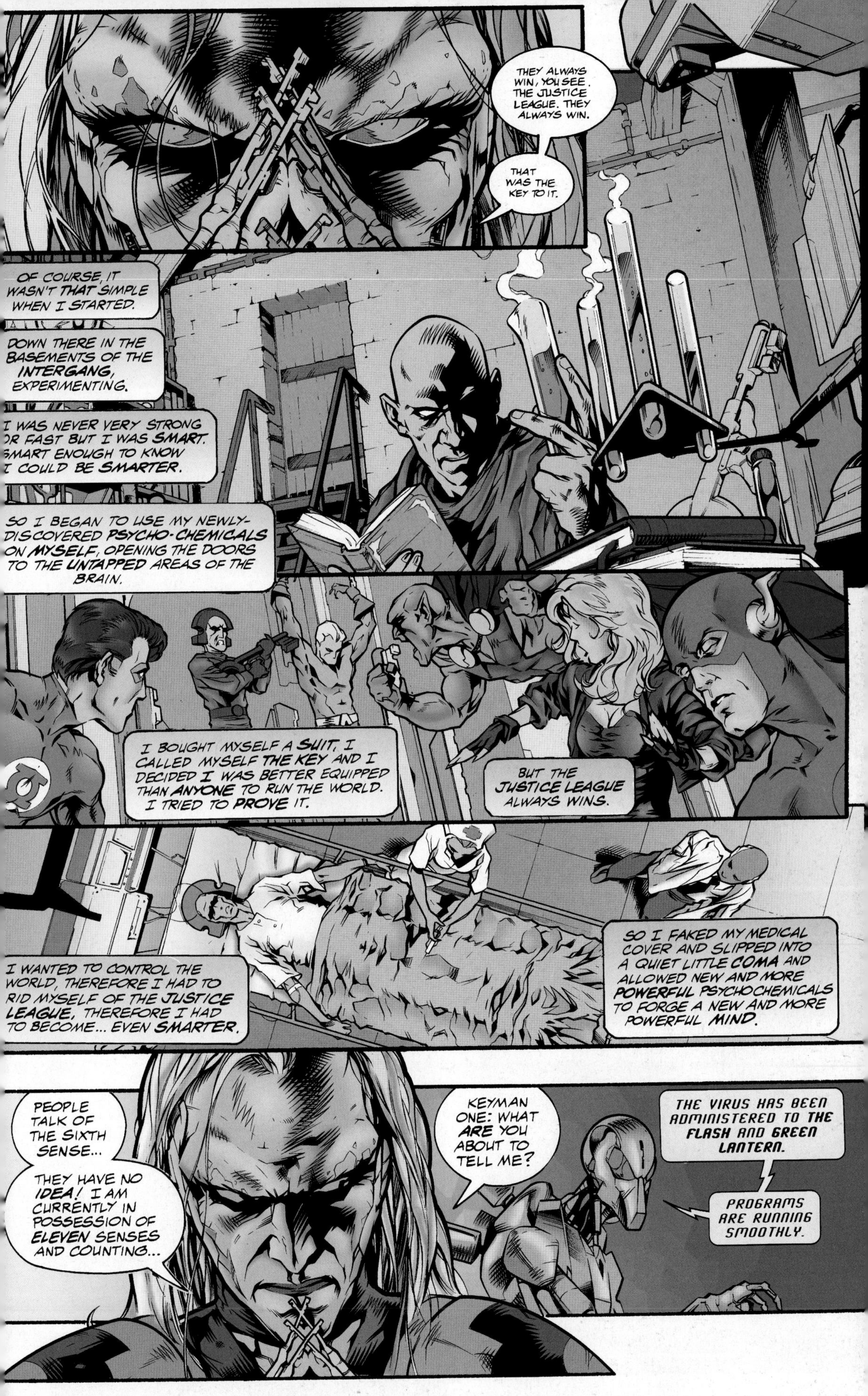

THEY ALWAYS WIN, YOU SEE. THE JUSTICE LEAGUE. THEY ALWAYS WIN.
THAT WAS THE KEY TO IT.
OF COURSE, IT WASN'T THAT SIMPLE WHEN I STARTED.
DOWN THERE IN THE BASEMENTS OF THE INTERGANG, EXPERIMENTING.
I WAS NEVER VERY STRONG OR FAST BUT I WAS SMART. SMART ENOUGH TO KNOW I COULD BE SMARTER.
SO I BEGAN TO USE MY NEWLY-DISCOVERED PSYCHO-CHEMICALS ON MYSELF, OPENING THE DOORS TO THE UNTAPPED AREAS OF THE BRAIN.
I BOUGHT MYSELF A SUIT, I CALLED MYSELF THE KEY AND I DECIDED I WAS BETTER EQUIPPED THAN ANYONE TO RUN THE WORLD. I TRIED TO PROVE IT.
BUT THE JUSTICE LEAGUE ALWAYS WINS.
I WANTED TO CONTROL THE WORLD, THEREFORE I HAD TO RID MYSELF OF THE JUSTICE LEAGUE, THEREFORE I HAD TO BECOME... EVEN SMARTER.
SO I FAKED MY MEDICAL COVER AND SLIPPED INTO A QUIET LITTLE COMA AND ALLOWED NEW AND MORE POWERFUL PSYCHOCHEMICALS TO FORGE A NEW AND MORE POWERFUL MIND.
PEOPLE TALK OF THE SIXTH SENSE...
THEY HAVE NO IDEA! I AM CURRENTLY IN POSSESSION OF ELEVEN SENSES AND COUNTING...
KEYMAN ONE: WHAT ARE YOU ABOUT TO TELL ME?
THE VIRUS HAS BEEN ADMINISTERED TO THE FLASH AND GREEN LANTERN.
PROGRAMS ARE RUNNING SMOOTHLY.

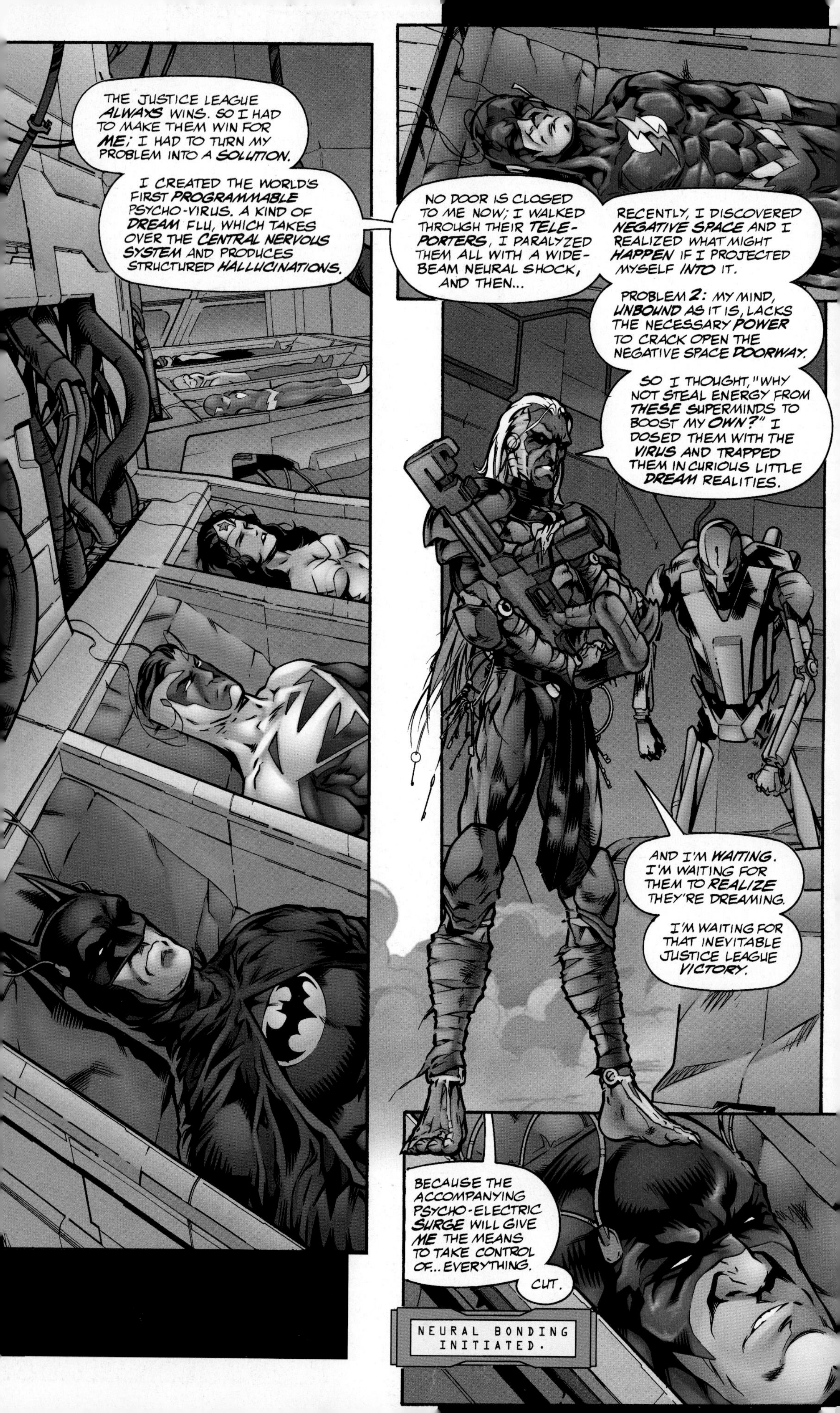
THE JUSTICE LEAGUE ALWAYS WINS. SO I HAD TO MAKE THEM WIN FOR ME; I HAD TO TURN MY PROBLEM INTO A SOLUTION.
I CREATED THE WORLD'S FIRST PROGRAMMABLE PSYCHO-VIRUS. A KIND OF DREAM FLU, WHICH TAKES OVER THE CENTRAL NERVOUS SYSTEM AND PRODUCES STRUCTURED HALLUCINATIONS.
NO DOOR IS CLOSED TO ME NOW; I WALKED THROUGH THEIR TELE-PORTERS, I PARALYZED THEM ALL WITH A WIDE-BEAM NEURAL SHOCK, AND THEN...
RECENTLY, I DISCOVERED NEGATIVE SPACE AND I REALIZED WHAT MIGHT HAPPEN IF I PROJECTED MYSELF INTO IT.
PROBLEM 2: MY MIND, UNBOUND AS IT IS, LACKS THE NECESSARY POWER TO CRACK OPEN THE NEGATIVE SPACE DOORWAY.
SO I THOUGHT, "WHY NOT STEAL ENERGY FROM THESE SUPERMINDS TO BOOST MY OWN?" I DOSED THEM WITH THE VIRUS AND TRAPPED THEM IN CURIOUS LITTLE DREAM REALITIES.
AND I'M WAITING. I'M WAITING FOR THEM TO REALIZE THEY'RE DREAMING.
I'M WAITING FOR THAT INEVITABLE JUSTICE LEAGUE VICTORY.
BECAUSE THE ACCOMPANYING PSYCHO-ELECTRIC SURGE WILL GIVE ME THE MEANS TO TAKE CONTROL OF... EVERYTHING.
CUT.
NEURAL BONDING INITIATED.

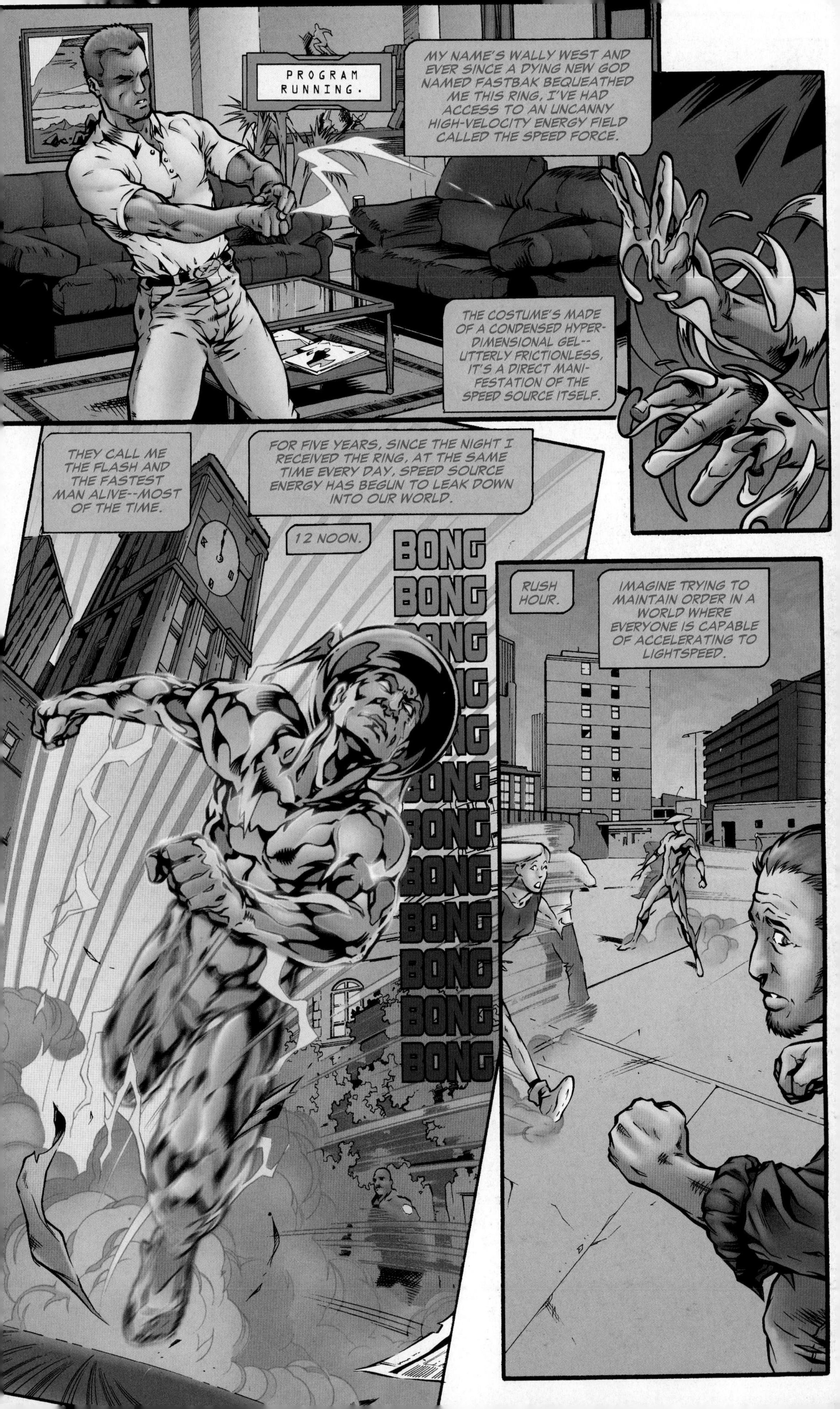
PROGRAM RUNNING.
MY NAME'S WALLY WEST AND EVER SINCE A DYING NEW GOD NAMED FASTBAK BEQUEATHED ME THIS RING, I'VE HAD ACCESS TO AN UNCANNY HIGH-VELOCITY ENERGY FIELD CALLED THE SPEED FORCE.
THE COSTUME'S MADE OF A CONDENSED HYPER-DIMENSIONAL GEL--UTTERLY FRICTIONLESS, IT'S A DIRECT MANI-FESTATION OF THE SPEED SOURCE ITSELF.
THEY CALL ME THE FLASH AND THE FASTEST MAN ALIVE--MOST OF THE TIME.
FOR FIVE YEARS, SINCE THE NIGHT I RECEIVED THE RING, AT THE SAME TIME EVERY DAY, SPEED SOURCE ENERGY HAS BEGUN TO LEAK DOWN INTO OUR WORLD.
12 NOON.
BONG
BONG
BONG
BONG
BONG
BONG
BONG
BONG
BONG
BONG
BONG
BONG
RUSH HOUR.
IMAGINE TRYING TO MAINTAIN ORDER IN A WORLD WHERE EVERYONE IS CAPABLE OF ACCELERATING TO LIGHTSPEED.

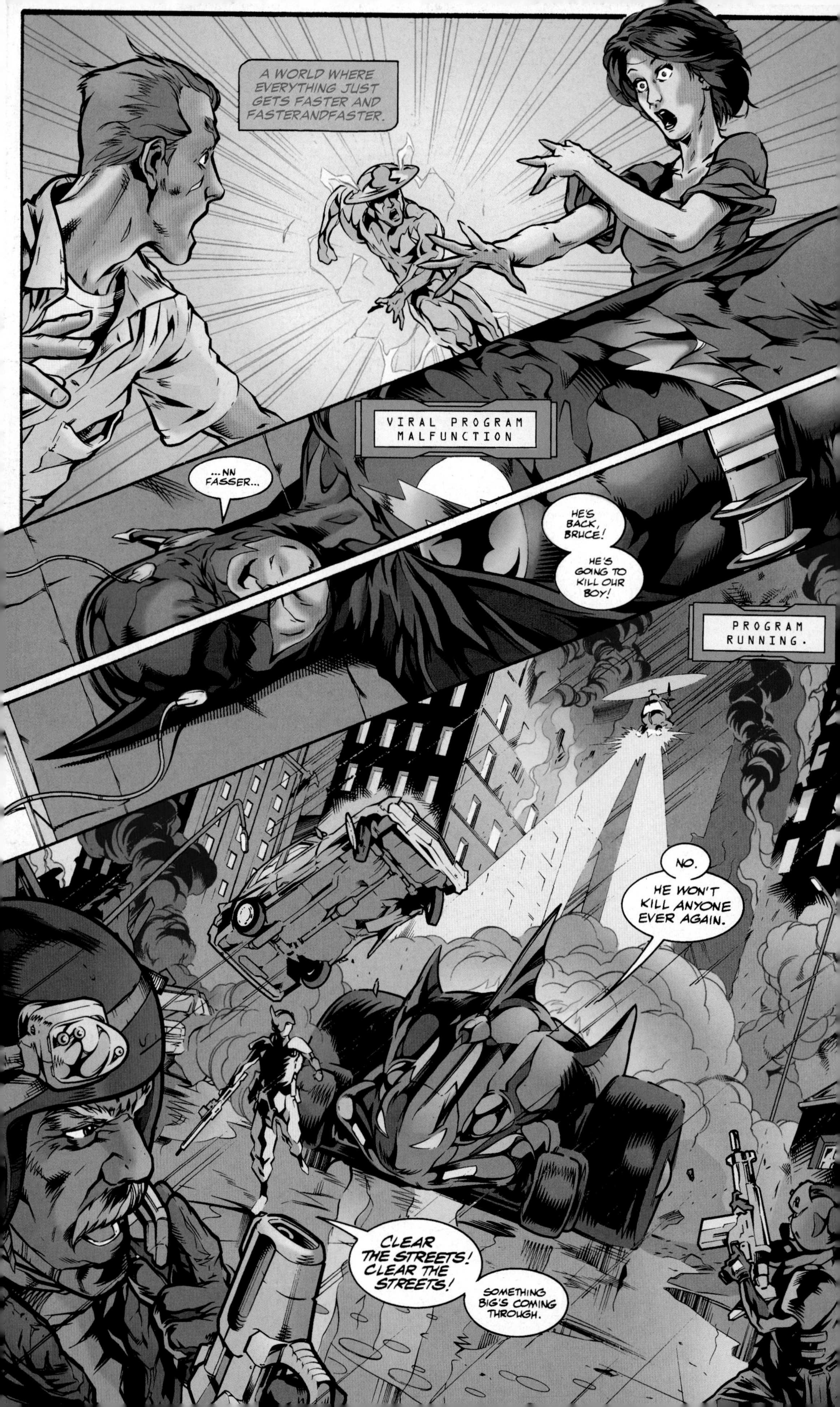
A WORLD WHERE EVERYTHING JUST GETS FASTER AND FASTERANDFASTER.
VIRAL PROGRAM MALFUNCTION
...NN FASSER...
HE'S BACK, BRUCE!
HE'S GOING TO KILL OUR BOY!
PROGRAM RUNNING.
NO.
HE WON'T KILL ANYONE EVER AGAIN.
CLEAR THE STREETS! CLEAR THE STREETS!
SOMETHING BIG'S COMING THROUGH.

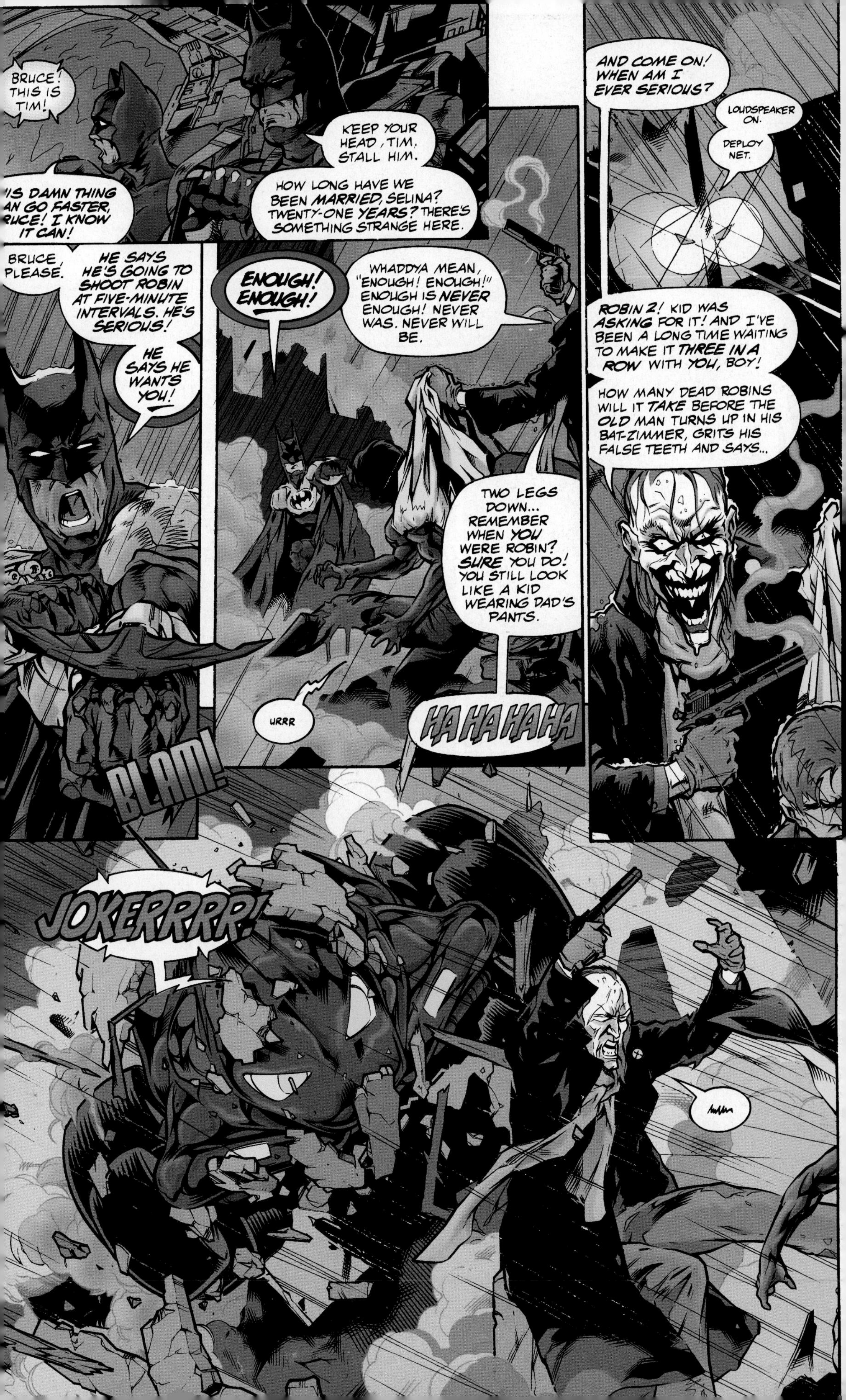
BRUCE! THIS IS TIM!
...IS DAMN THING ...AN GO FASTER, ...RUCE! I KNOW IT CAN!
KEEP YOUR HEAD, TIM. STALL HIM.
HOW LONG HAVE WE BEEN MARRIED, SELINA? TWENTY-ONE YEARS? THERE'S SOMETHING STRANGE HERE.
AND COME ON! WHEN AM I EVER SERIOUS?
LOUDSPEAKER ON.
DEPLOY NET.
BRUCE, PLEASE.
HE SAYS HE'S GOING TO SHOOT ROBIN AT FIVE-MINUTE INTERVALS. HE'S SERIOUS!
HE SAYS HE WANTS YOU!
ENOUGH! ENOUGH!
WHADDYA MEAN, "ENOUGH! ENOUGH!" ENOUGH IS NEVER ENOUGH! NEVER WAS. NEVER WILL BE.
TWO LEGS DOWN... REMEMBER WHEN YOU WERE ROBIN? SURE YOU DO! YOU STILL LOOK LIKE A KID WEARING DAD'S PANTS.
URRR
HA HA HA HA HA
ROBIN 2! KID WAS ASKING FOR IT! AND I'VE BEEN A LONG TIME WAITING TO MAKE IT THREE IN A ROW WITH YOU, BOY!
HOW MANY DEAD ROBINS WILL IT TAKE BEFORE THE OLD MAN TURNS UP IN HIS BAT-ZIMMER, GRITS HIS FALSE TEETH AND SAYS...
BLAM!
JOKERRRRR!

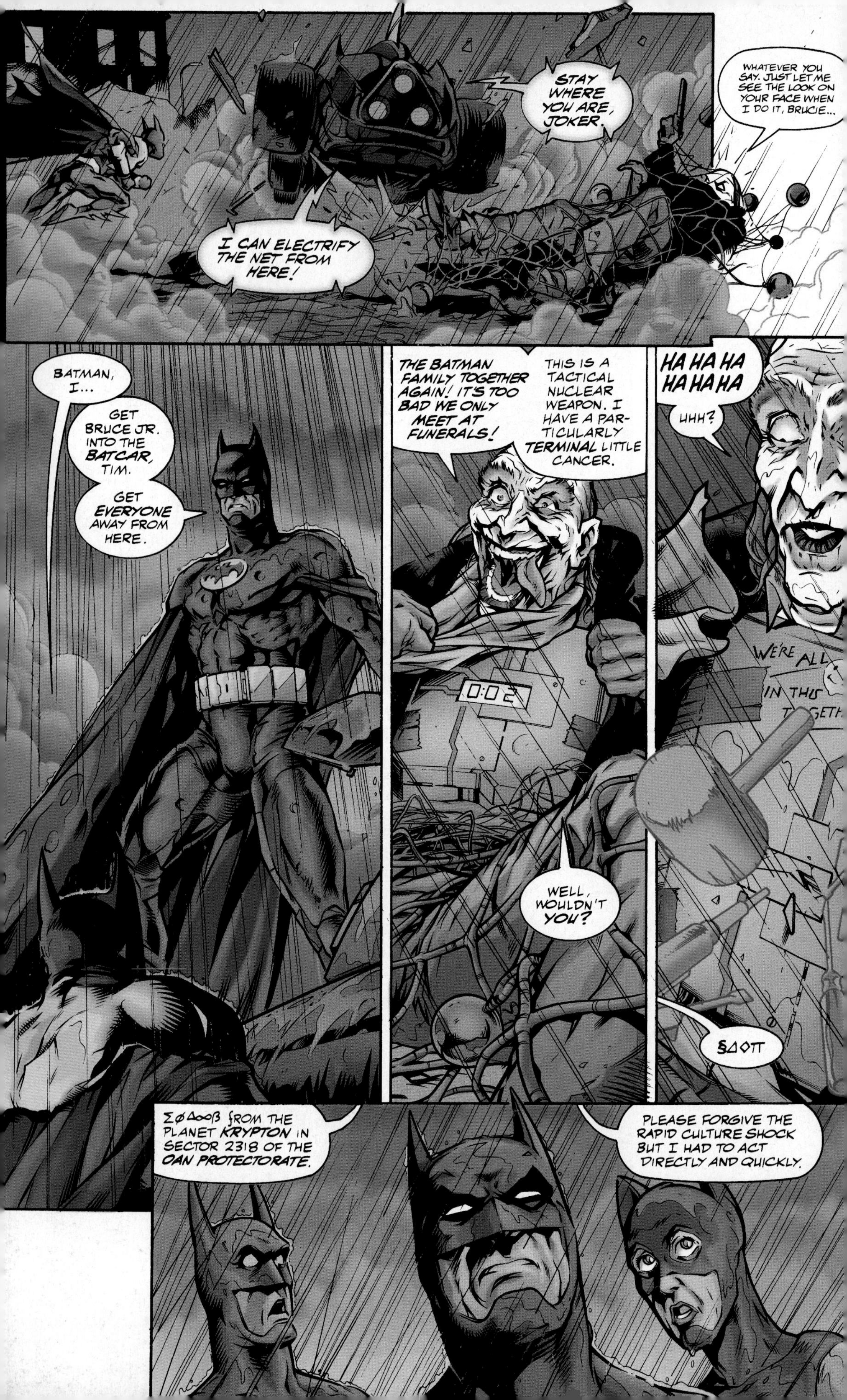
STAY WHERE YOU ARE, JOKER.
I CAN ELECTRIFY THE NET FROM HERE!
WHATEVER YOU SAY. JUST LET ME SEE THE LOOK ON YOUR FACE WHEN I DO IT, BRUCIE...
BATMAN, I...
GET BRUCE JR. INTO THE BATCAR, TIM.
GET EVERYONE AWAY FROM HERE.
THE BATMAN FAMILY TOGETHER AGAIN! IT'S TOO BAD WE ONLY MEET AT FUNERALS!
THIS IS A TACTICAL NUCLEAR WEAPON. I HAVE A PARTICULARLY TERMINAL LITTLE CANCER.
0:02
WELL, WOULDN'T YOU?
HA HA HA HA HA HA
UHH?
WE'RE ALL IN THIS TOGETH
§ΔΟΠ
ΣØΔ∞β FROM THE PLANET KRYPTON IN SECTOR 2318 OF THE OAN PROTECTORATE.
PLEASE FORGIVE THE RAPID CULTURE SHOCK BUT I HAD TO ACT DIRECTLY AND QUICKLY.

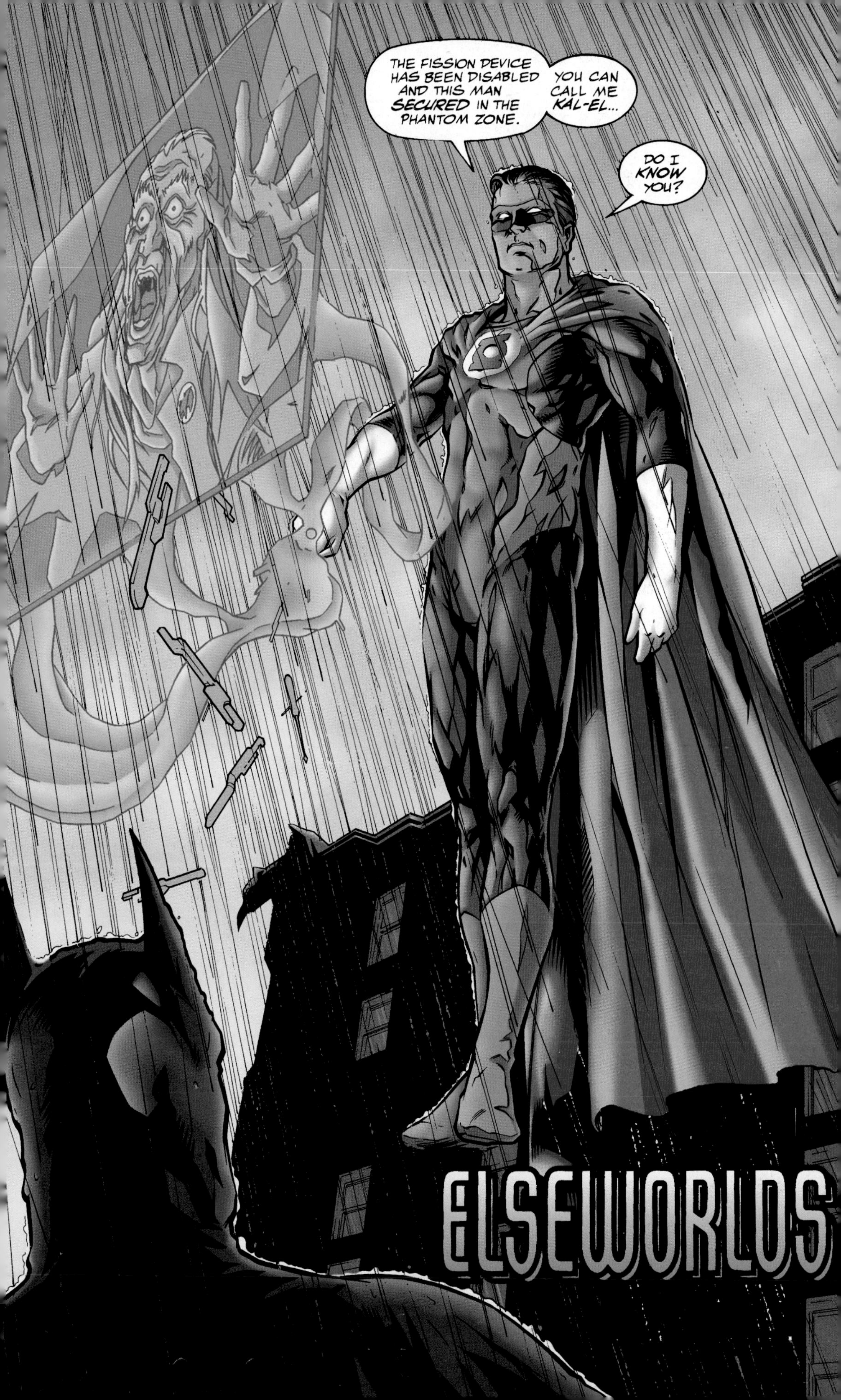
THE FISSION DEVICE HAS BEEN DISABLED AND THIS MAN SECURED IN THE PHANTOM ZONE.
YOU CAN CALL ME KAL-EL...
DO I KNOW YOU?
ELSEWORLDS

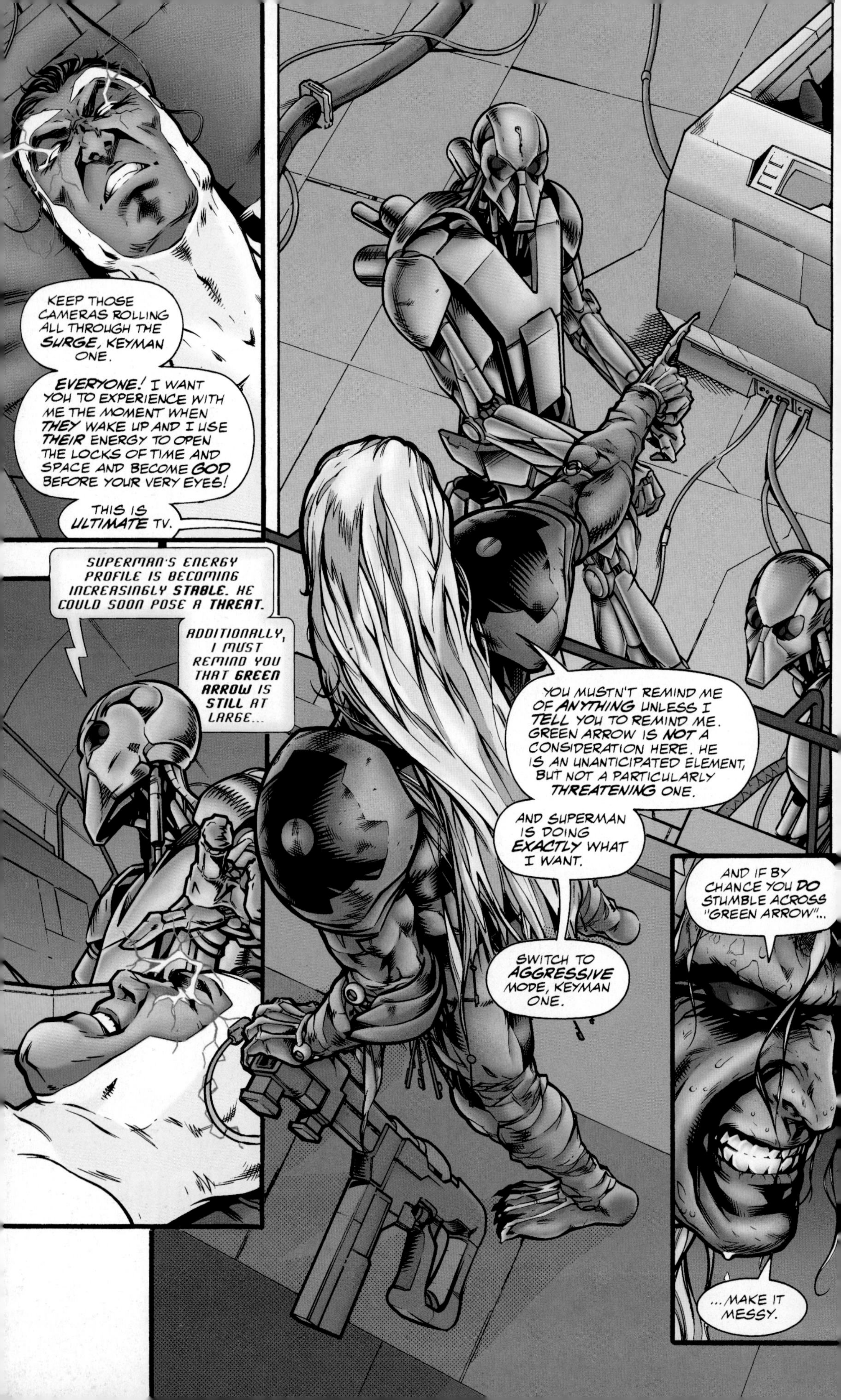
KEEP THOSE CAMERAS ROLLING ALL THROUGH THE SURGE, KEYMAN ONE.
EVERYONE! I WANT YOU TO EXPERIENCE WITH ME THE MOMENT WHEN THEY WAKE UP AND I USE THEIR ENERGY TO OPEN THE LOCKS OF TIME AND SPACE AND BECOME GOD BEFORE YOUR VERY EYES!
THIS IS ULTIMATE TV.
SUPERMAN'S ENERGY PROFILE IS BECOMING INCREASINGLY STABLE. HE COULD SOON POSE A THREAT.
ADDITIONALLY, I MUST REMIND YOU THAT GREEN ARROW IS STILL AT LARGE...
YOU MUSTN'T REMIND ME OF ANYTHING UNLESS I TELL YOU TO REMIND ME. GREEN ARROW IS NOT A CONSIDERATION HERE. HE IS AN UNANTICIPATED ELEMENT, BUT NOT A PARTICULARLY THREATENING ONE.
AND SUPERMAN IS DOING EXACTLY WHAT I WANT.
SWITCH TO AGGRESSIVE MODE, KEYMAN ONE.
AND IF BY CHANCE YOU DO STUMBLE ACROSS "GREEN ARROW"...
...MAKE IT MESSY.

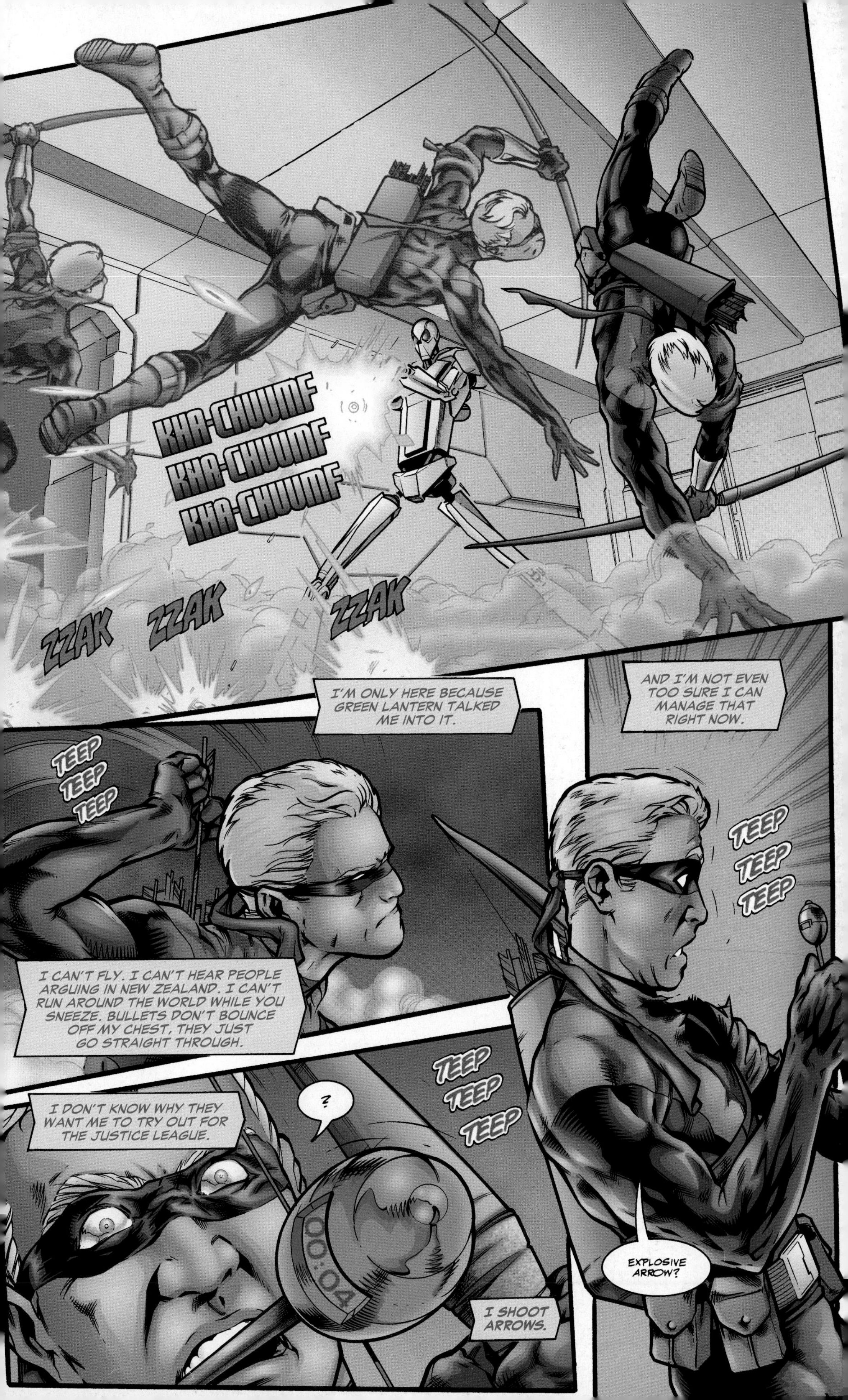
KHA-CHUUMF
KHA-CHUUMF
KHA-CHUUMF
ZZAK
ZZAK
ZZAK
I'M ONLY HERE BECAUSE GREEN LANTERN TALKED ME INTO IT.
AND I'M NOT EVEN TOO SURE I CAN MANAGE THAT RIGHT NOW.
TEEP
TEEP
TEEP
I CAN'T FLY. I CAN'T HEAR PEOPLE ARGUING IN NEW ZEALAND. I CAN'T RUN AROUND THE WORLD WHILE YOU SNEEZE. BULLETS DON'T BOUNCE OFF MY CHEST, THEY JUST GO STRAIGHT THROUGH.
TEEP
TEEP
TEEP
I DON'T KNOW WHY THEY WANT ME TO TRY OUT FOR THE JUSTICE LEAGUE.
?
TEEP
TEEP
TEEP
00:04
I SHOOT ARROWS.
EXPLOSIVE ARROW?

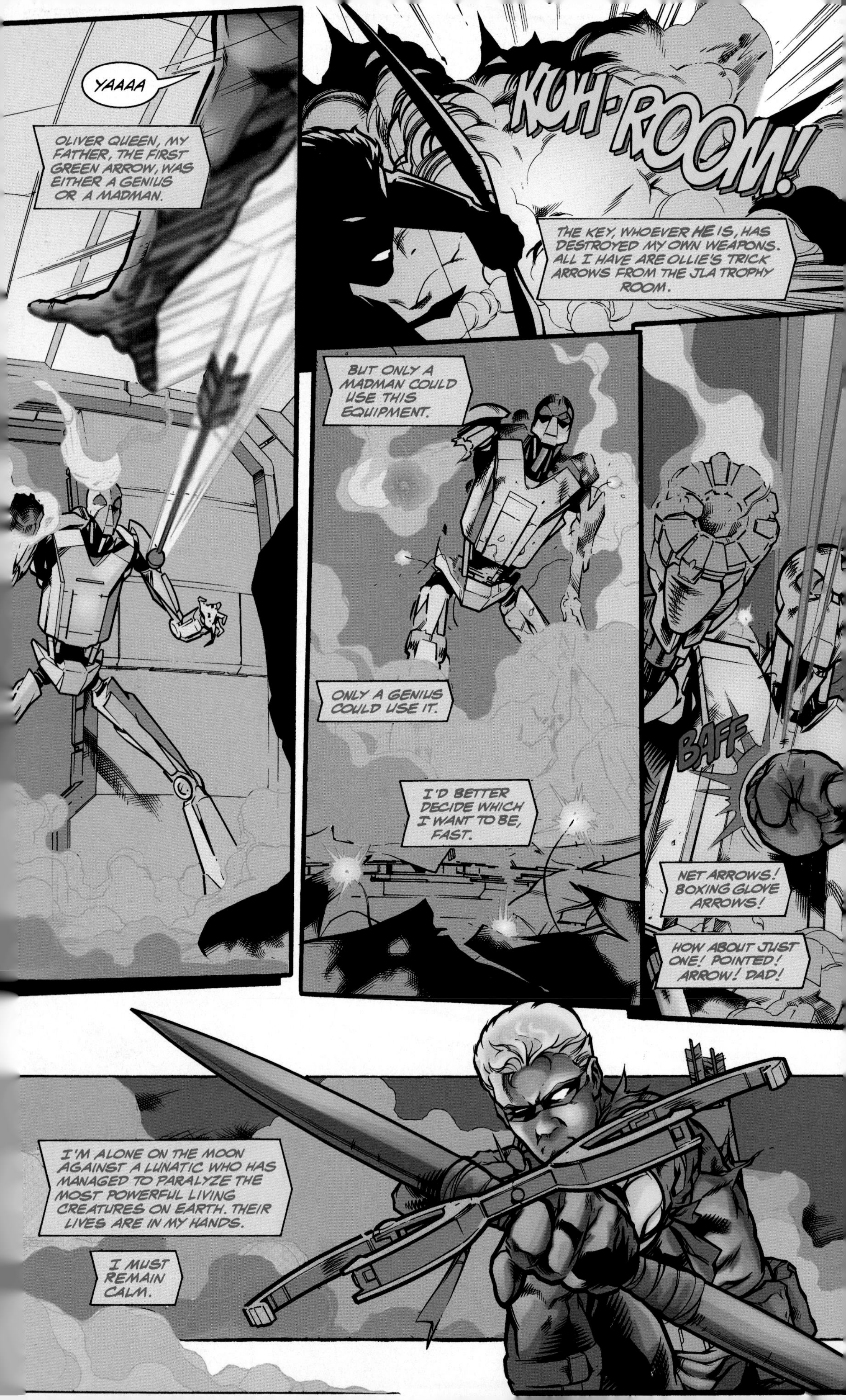
YAAAA
OLIVER QUEEN, MY FATHER, THE FIRST GREEN ARROW, WAS EITHER A GENIUS OR A MADMAN.
KUH-ROOM!
THE KEY, WHOEVER HE IS, HAS DESTROYED MY OWN WEAPONS. ALL I HAVE ARE OLLIE'S TRICK ARROWS FROM THE JLA TROPHY ROOM.
BUT ONLY A MADMAN COULD USE THIS EQUIPMENT.
ONLY A GENIUS COULD USE IT.
I'D BETTER DECIDE WHICH I WANT TO BE, FAST.
BAFF
NET ARROWS! BOXING GLOVE ARROWS!
HOW ABOUT JUST ONE! POINTED! ARROW! DAD!
I'M ALONE ON THE MOON AGAINST A LUNATIC WHO HAS MANAGED TO PARALYZE THE MOST POWERFUL LIVING CREATURES ON EARTH. THEIR LIVES ARE IN MY HANDS.
I MUST REMAIN CALM.

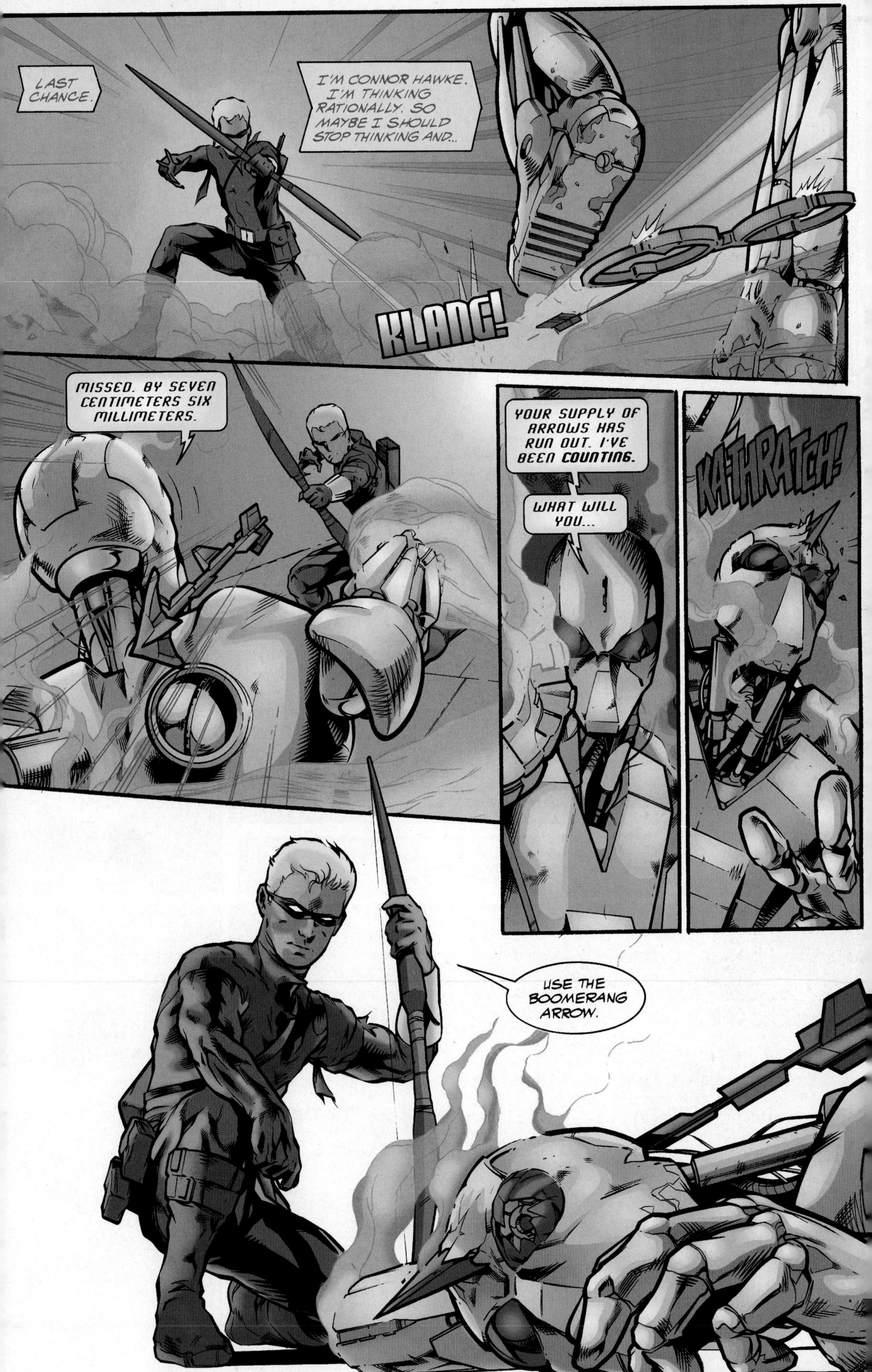
LAST CHANCE.
I'M CONNOR HAWKE. I'M THINKING RATIONALLY. SO MAYBE I SHOULD STOP THINKING AND...
KLANG!
MISSED. BY SEVEN CENTIMETERS SIX MILLIMETERS.
YOUR SUPPLY OF ARROWS HAS RUN OUT. I'VE BEEN COUNTING.
WHAT WILL YOU...
KA-THRATCH!
USE THE BOOMERANG ARROW.

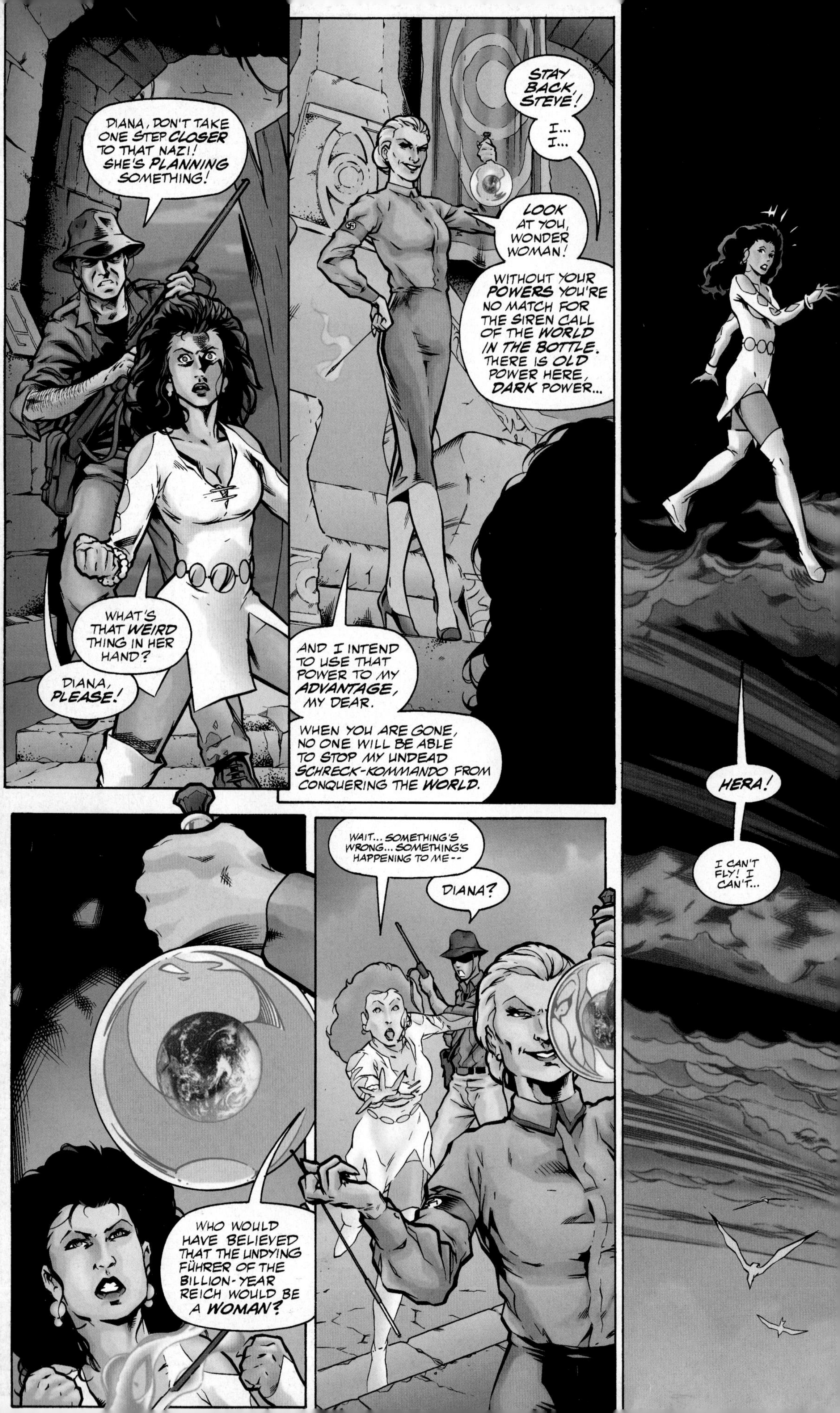

DIANA, DON'T TAKE ONE STEP CLOSER TO THAT NAZI! SHE'S PLANNING SOMETHING!
WHAT'S THAT WEIRD THING IN HER HAND?
DIANA, PLEASE!
STAY BACK, STEVE!
I... I...
LOOK AT YOU, WONDER WOMAN!
WITHOUT YOUR POWERS YOU'RE NO MATCH FOR THE SIREN CALL OF THE WORLD IN THE BOTTLE. THERE IS OLD POWER HERE, DARK POWER...
AND I INTEND TO USE THAT POWER TO MY ADVANTAGE, MY DEAR.
WHEN YOU ARE GONE, NO ONE WILL BE ABLE TO STOP MY UNDEAD SCHRECK-KOMMANDO FROM CONQUERING THE WORLD.
HERA!
I CAN'T FLY! I CAN'T...
WHO WOULD HAVE BELIEVED THAT THE UNDYING FÜHRER OF THE BILLION-YEAR REICH WOULD BE A WOMAN?
WAIT... SOMETHING'S WRONG... SOMETHING'S HAPPENING TO ME--
DIANA?

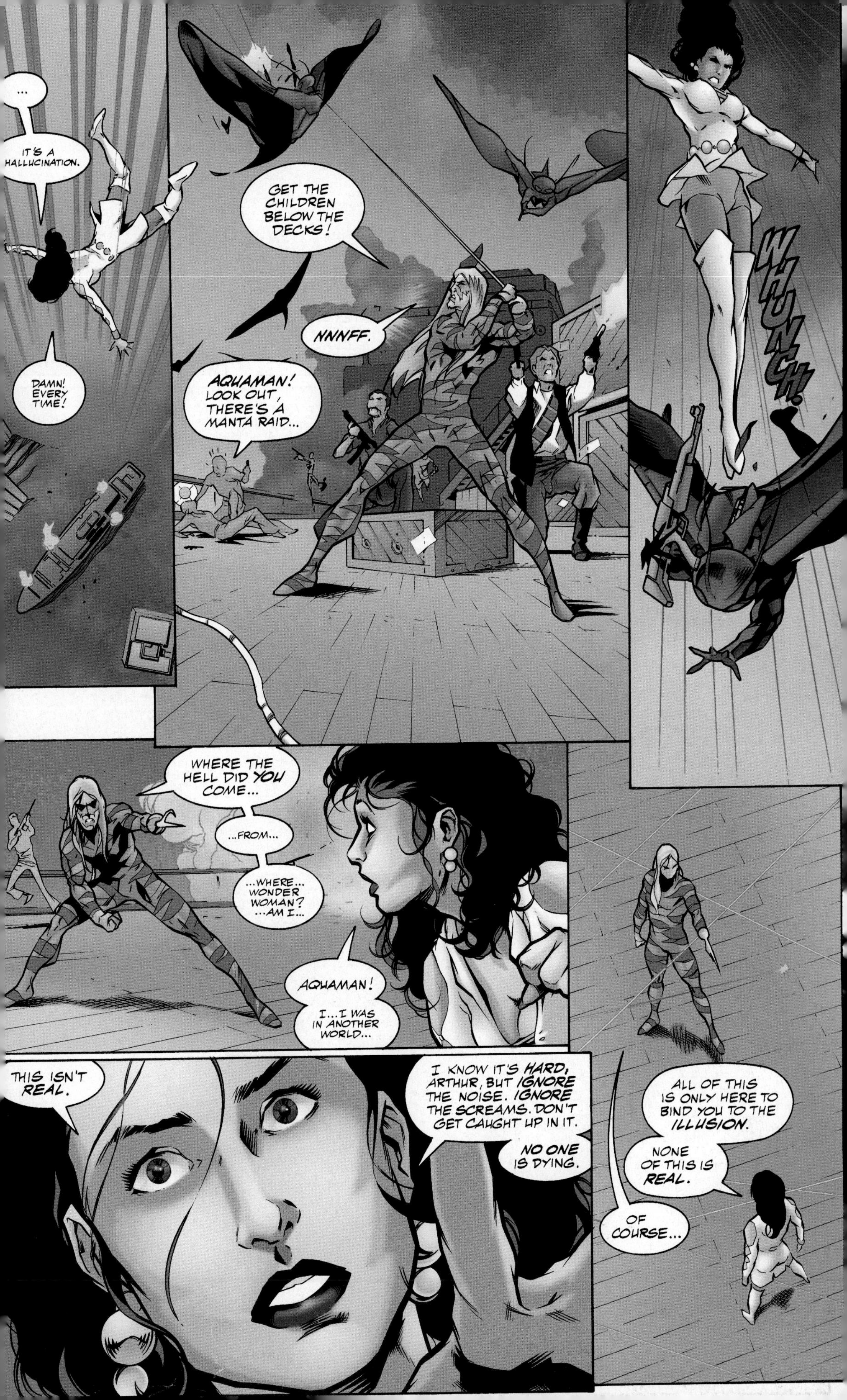
...
IT'S A HALLUCINATION.
DAMN! EVERY TIME!
GET THE CHILDREN BELOW THE DECKS!
NNNFF.
AQUAMAN! LOOK OUT, THERE'S A MANTA RAID...
WHUNCH!
WHERE THE HELL DID YOU COME...
...FROM...
...WHERE... WONDER WOMAN? ...AM I...
AQUAMAN!
I...I WAS IN ANOTHER WORLD...
THIS ISN'T REAL.
I KNOW IT'S HARD, ARTHUR, BUT IGNORE THE NOISE. IGNORE THE SCREAMS. DON'T GET CAUGHT UP IN IT.
NO ONE IS DYING.
ALL OF THIS IS ONLY HERE TO BIND YOU TO THE ILLUSION.
NONE OF THIS IS REAL.
OF COURSE...

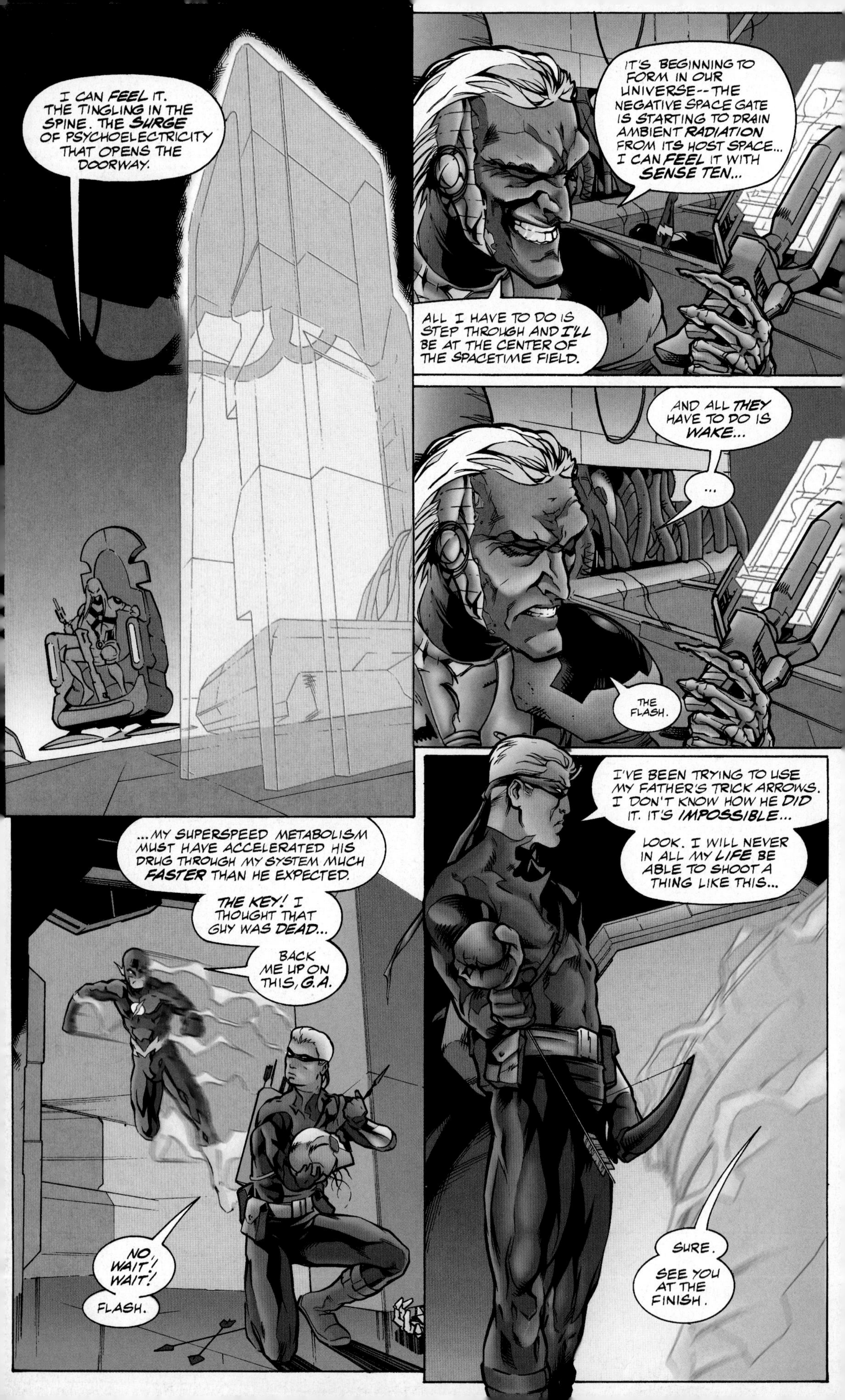
I CAN FEEL IT. THE TINGLING IN THE SPINE. THE SURGE OF PSYCHOELECTRICITY THAT OPENS THE DOORWAY.
IT'S BEGINNING TO FORM IN OUR UNIVERSE--THE NEGATIVE SPACE GATE IS STARTING TO DRAIN AMBIENT RADIATION FROM ITS HOST SPACE... I CAN FEEL IT WITH SENSE TEN...
ALL I HAVE TO DO IS STEP THROUGH AND I'LL BE AT THE CENTER OF THE SPACETIME FIELD.
AND ALL THEY HAVE TO DO IS WAKE...
...
THE FLASH.
...MY SUPERSPEED METABOLISM MUST HAVE ACCELERATED HIS DRUG THROUGH MY SYSTEM MUCH FASTER THAN HE EXPECTED.
THE KEY! I THOUGHT THAT GUY WAS DEAD...
BACK ME UP ON THIS, G.A.
NO! WAIT! WAIT!
FLASH.
I'VE BEEN TRYING TO USE MY FATHER'S TRICK ARROWS. I DON'T KNOW HOW HE DID IT. IT'S IMPOSSIBLE...
LOOK. I WILL NEVER IN ALL MY LIFE BE ABLE TO SHOOT A THING LIKE THIS...
SURE.
SEE YOU AT THE FINISH.

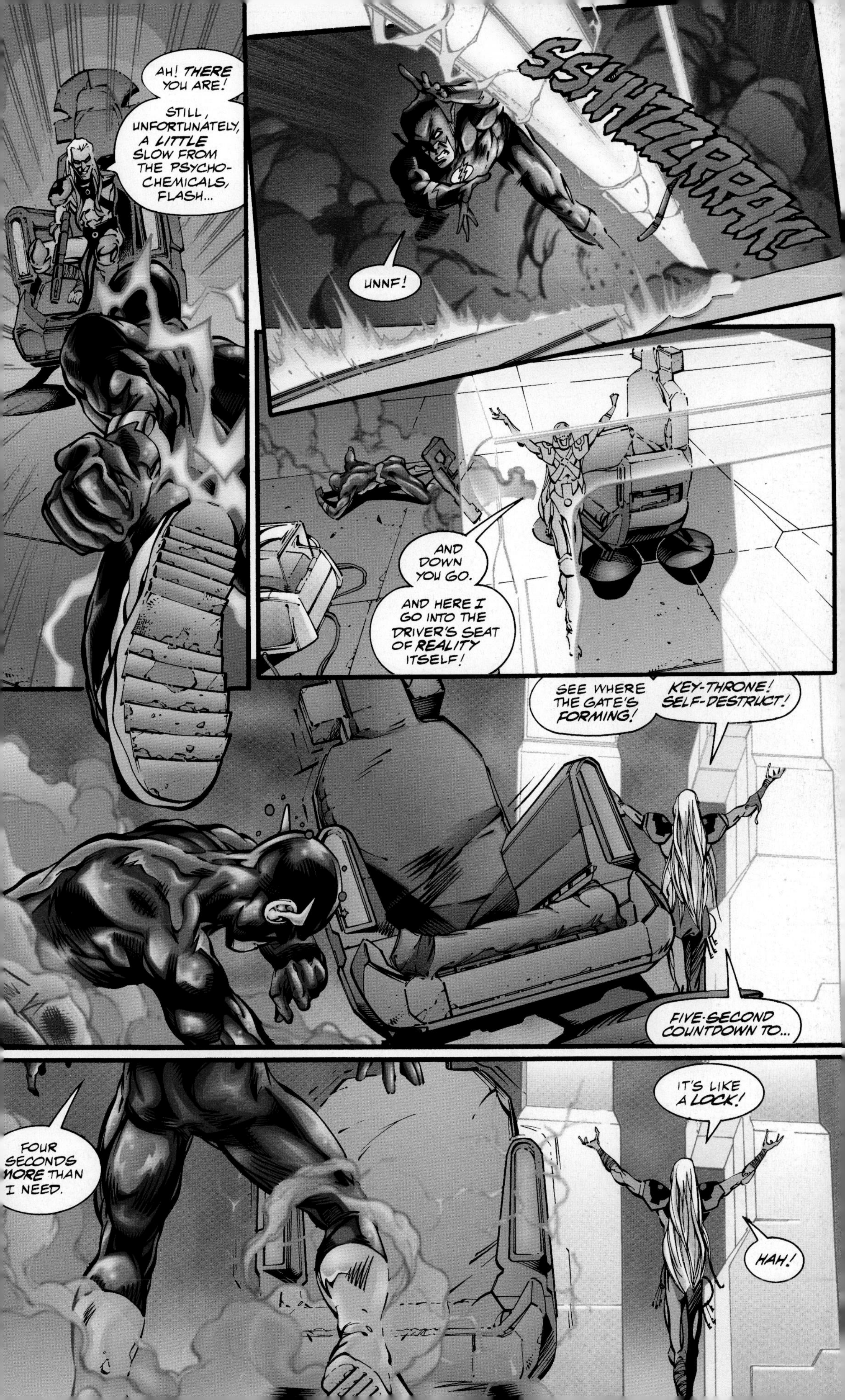
AH! THERE YOU ARE!
STILL, UNFORTUNATELY, A LITTLE SLOW FROM THE PSYCHO-CHEMICALS, FLASH...
SSHZZRRAK!!
UNNF!
AND DOWN YOU GO.
AND HERE I GO INTO THE DRIVER'S SEAT OF REALITY ITSELF!
SEE WHERE THE GATE'S FORMING!
KEY-THRONE! SELF-DESTRUCT!
FIVE-SECOND COUNTDOWN TO...
FOUR SECONDS MORE THAN I NEED.
IT'S LIKE A LOCK!
HAH!

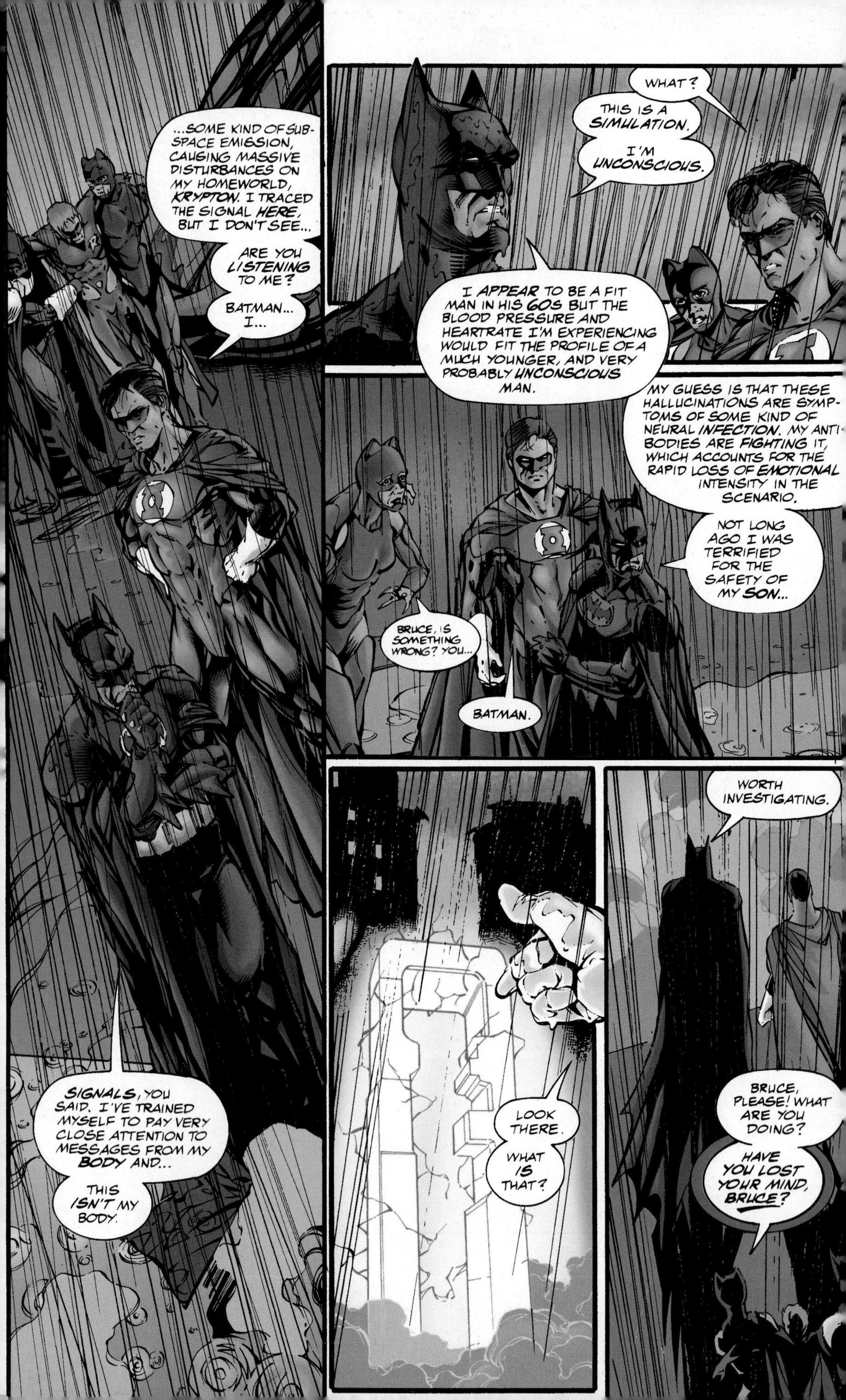

...SOME KIND OF SUB-SPACE EMISSION, CAUSING MASSIVE DISTURBANCES ON MY HOMEWORLD, KRYPTON. I TRACED THE SIGNAL HERE, BUT I DON'T SEE...
ARE YOU LISTENING TO ME?
BATMAN... I...
SIGNALS, YOU SAID. I'VE TRAINED MYSELF TO PAY VERY CLOSE ATTENTION TO MESSAGES FROM MY BODY AND...
THIS ISN'T MY BODY.
WHAT?
THIS IS A SIMULATION.
I'M UNCONSCIOUS.
I APPEAR TO BE A FIT MAN IN HIS 60S BUT THE BLOOD PRESSURE AND HEARTRATE I'M EXPERIENCING WOULD FIT THE PROFILE OF A MUCH YOUNGER, AND VERY PROBABLY UNCONSCIOUS MAN.
MY GUESS IS THAT THESE HALLUCINATIONS ARE SYMPTOMS OF SOME KIND OF NEURAL INFECTION. MY ANTIBODIES ARE FIGHTING IT, WHICH ACCOUNTS FOR THE RAPID LOSS OF EMOTIONAL INTENSITY IN THE SCENARIO.
NOT LONG AGO I WAS TERRIFIED FOR THE SAFETY OF MY SON...
BRUCE, IS SOMETHING WRONG? YOU...
BATMAN.
LOOK THERE.
WHAT IS THAT?
WORTH INVESTIGATING.
BRUCE, PLEASE! WHAT ARE YOU DOING?
HAVE YOU LOST YOUR MIND, BRUCE?

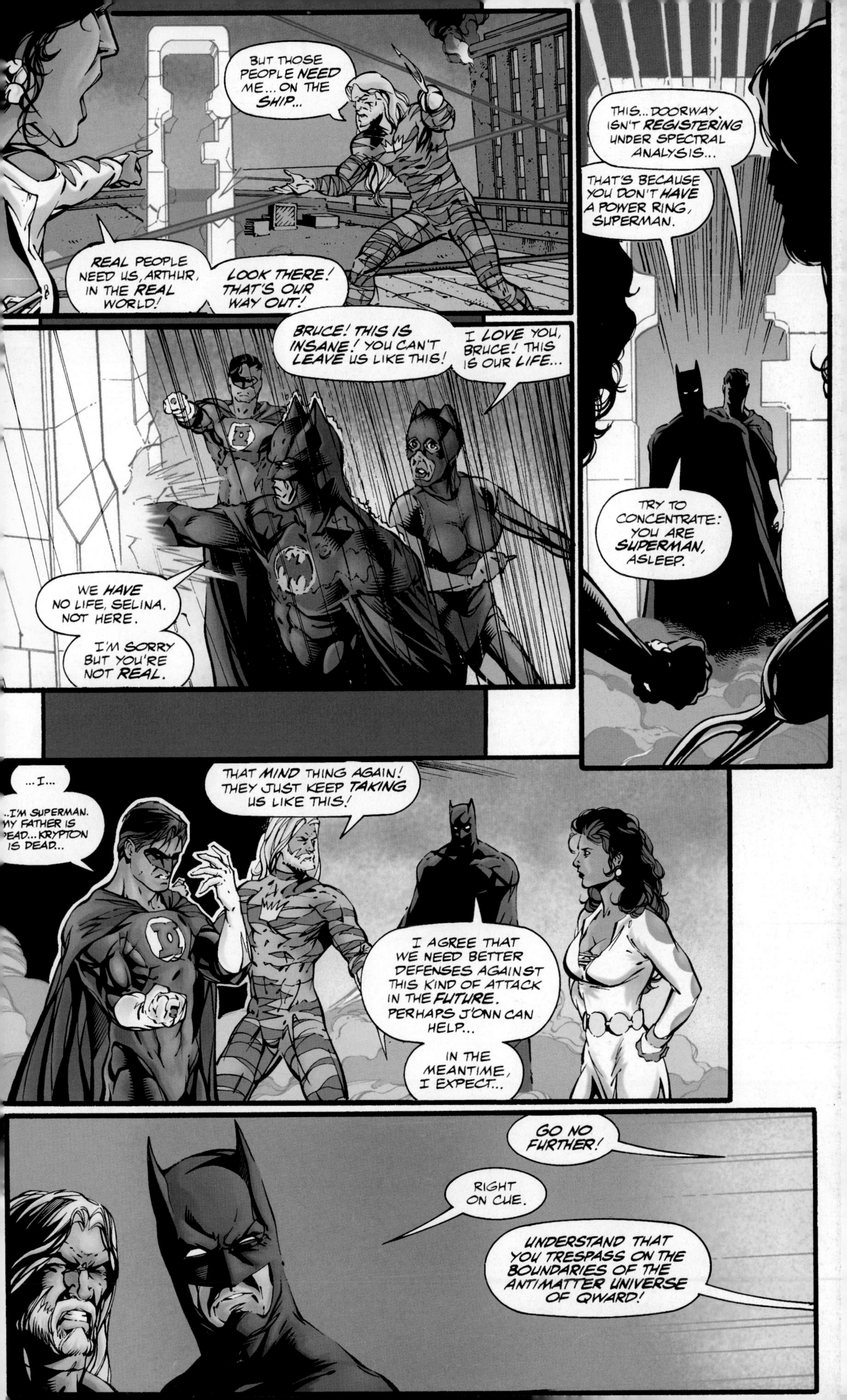
BUT THOSE PEOPLE NEED ME... ON THE SHIP...
REAL PEOPLE NEED US, ARTHUR, IN THE REAL WORLD!
LOOK THERE! THAT'S OUR WAY OUT!
THIS... DOORWAY ISN'T REGISTERING UNDER SPECTRAL ANALYSIS...
THAT'S BECAUSE YOU DON'T HAVE A POWER RING, SUPERMAN.
BRUCE! THIS IS INSANE! YOU CAN'T LEAVE US LIKE THIS!
I LOVE YOU, BRUCE! THIS IS OUR LIFE...
WE HAVE NO LIFE, SELINA. NOT HERE.
I'M SORRY BUT YOU'RE NOT REAL.
TRY TO CONCENTRATE: YOU ARE SUPERMAN, ASLEEP.
...I...
...I'M SUPERMAN. MY FATHER IS DEAD... KRYPTON IS DEAD...
THAT MIND THING AGAIN! THEY JUST KEEP TAKING US LIKE THIS!
I AGREE THAT WE NEED BETTER DEFENSES AGAINST THIS KIND OF ATTACK IN THE FUTURE. PERHAPS J'ONN CAN HELP...
IN THE MEANTIME, I EXPECT...
GO NO FURTHER!
RIGHT ON CUE.
UNDERSTAND THAT YOU TRESPASS ON THE BOUNDARIES OF THE ANTIMATTER UNIVERSE OF QWARD!

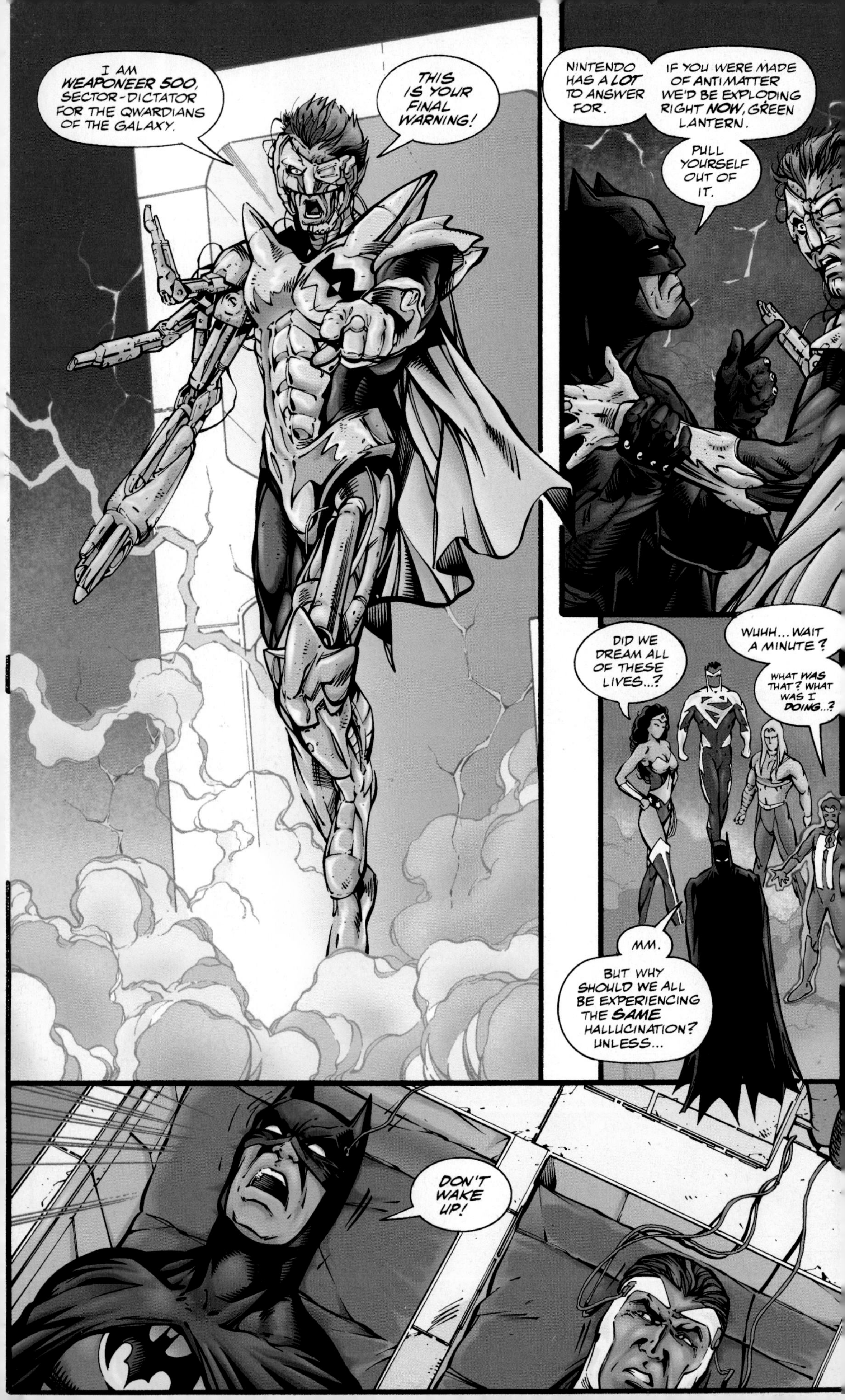
I AM WEAPONEER 500, SECTOR-DICTATOR FOR THE QWARDIANS OF THE GALAXY.
THIS IS YOUR FINAL WARNING!
NINTENDO HAS A LOT TO ANSWER FOR.
IF YOU WERE MADE OF ANTIMATTER WE'D BE EXPLODING RIGHT NOW, GREEN LANTERN.
PULL YOURSELF OUT OF IT.
DID WE DREAM ALL OF THESE LIVES...?
WUHH... WAIT A MINUTE?
WHAT WAS THAT? WHAT WAS I DOING...?
MM.
BUT WHY SHOULD WE ALL BE EXPERIENCING THE SAME HALLUCINATION? UNLESS...
DON'T WAKE UP!

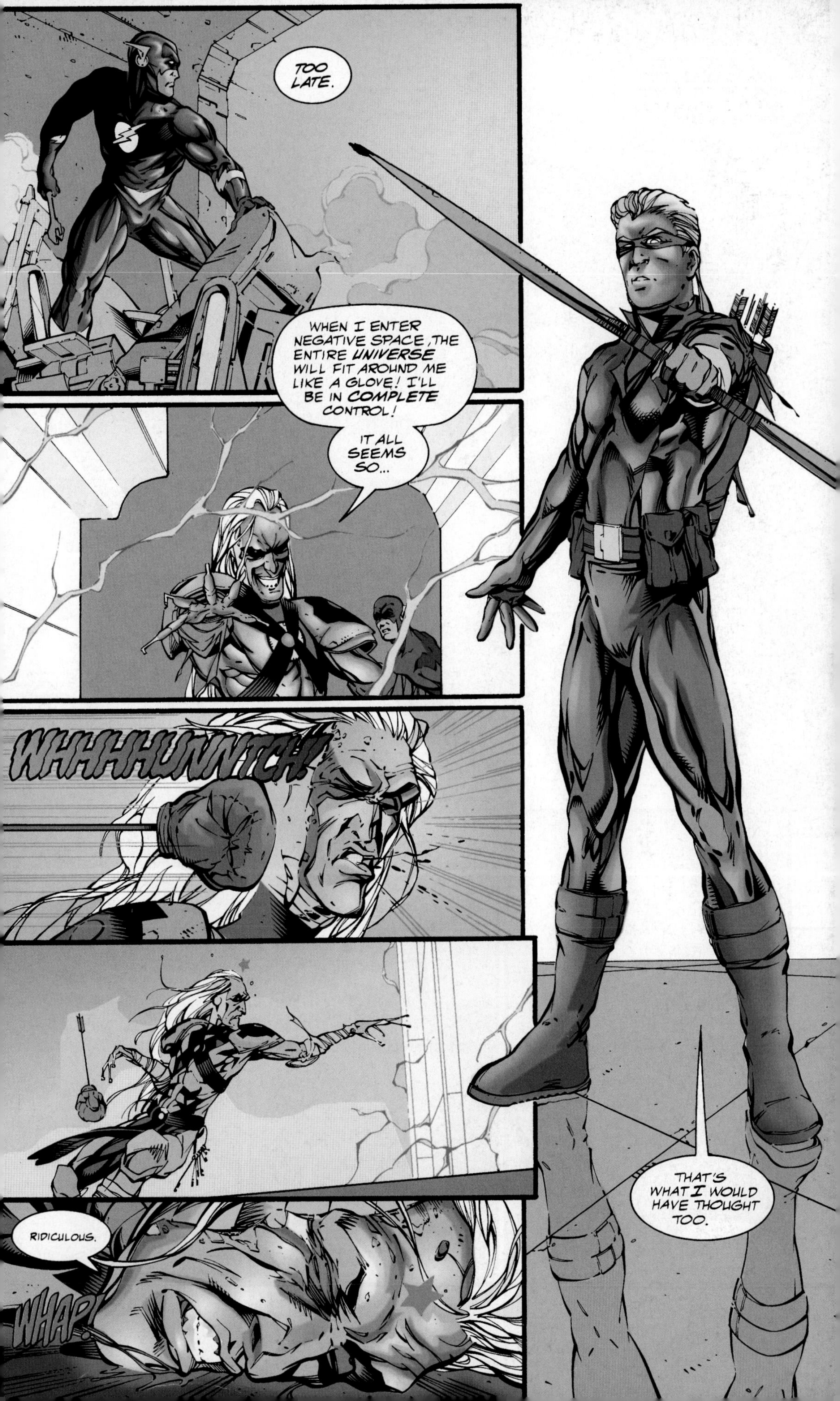
TOO LATE.
WHEN I ENTER NEGATIVE SPACE, THE ENTIRE UNIVERSE WILL FIT AROUND ME LIKE A GLOVE! I'LL BE IN COMPLETE CONTROL!
IT ALL SEEMS SO...
WHHHHUNNNTCH!
RIDICULOUS.
WHAP!
THAT'S WHAT I WOULD HAVE THOUGHT TOO.

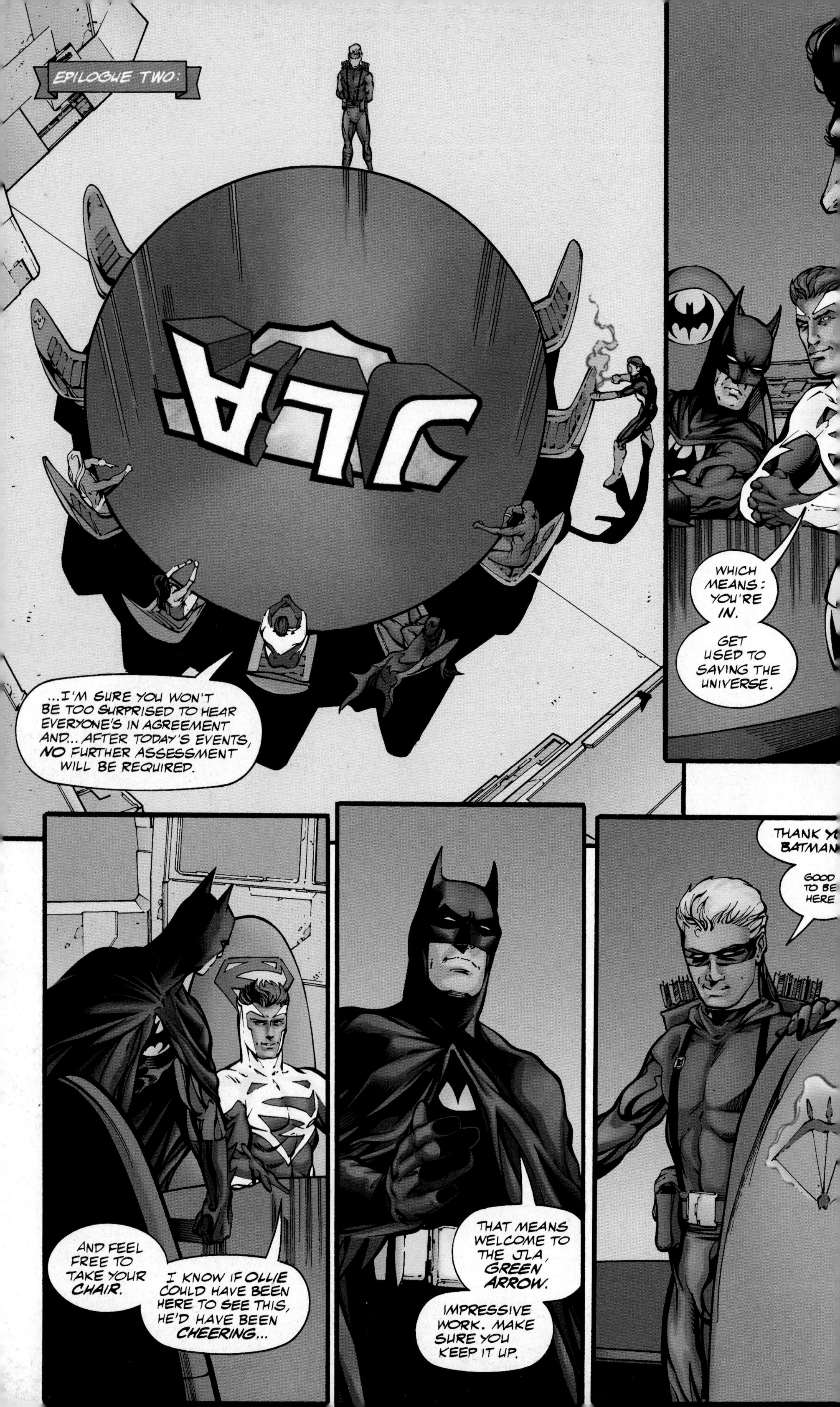
EPILOGUE TWO:
...I'M SURE YOU WON'T BE TOO SURPRISED TO HEAR EVERYONE'S IN AGREEMENT AND... AFTER TODAY'S EVENTS, NO FURTHER ASSESSMENT WILL BE REQUIRED.
WHICH MEANS: YOU'RE IN.
GET USED TO SAVING THE UNIVERSE.
AND FEEL FREE TO TAKE YOUR CHAIR.
I KNOW IF OLLIE COULD HAVE BEEN HERE TO SEE THIS, HE'D HAVE BEEN CHEERING...
THAT MEANS WELCOME TO THE JLA, GREEN ARROW.
IMPRESSIVE WORK. MAKE SURE YOU KEEP IT UP.
GOOD TO BE HERE

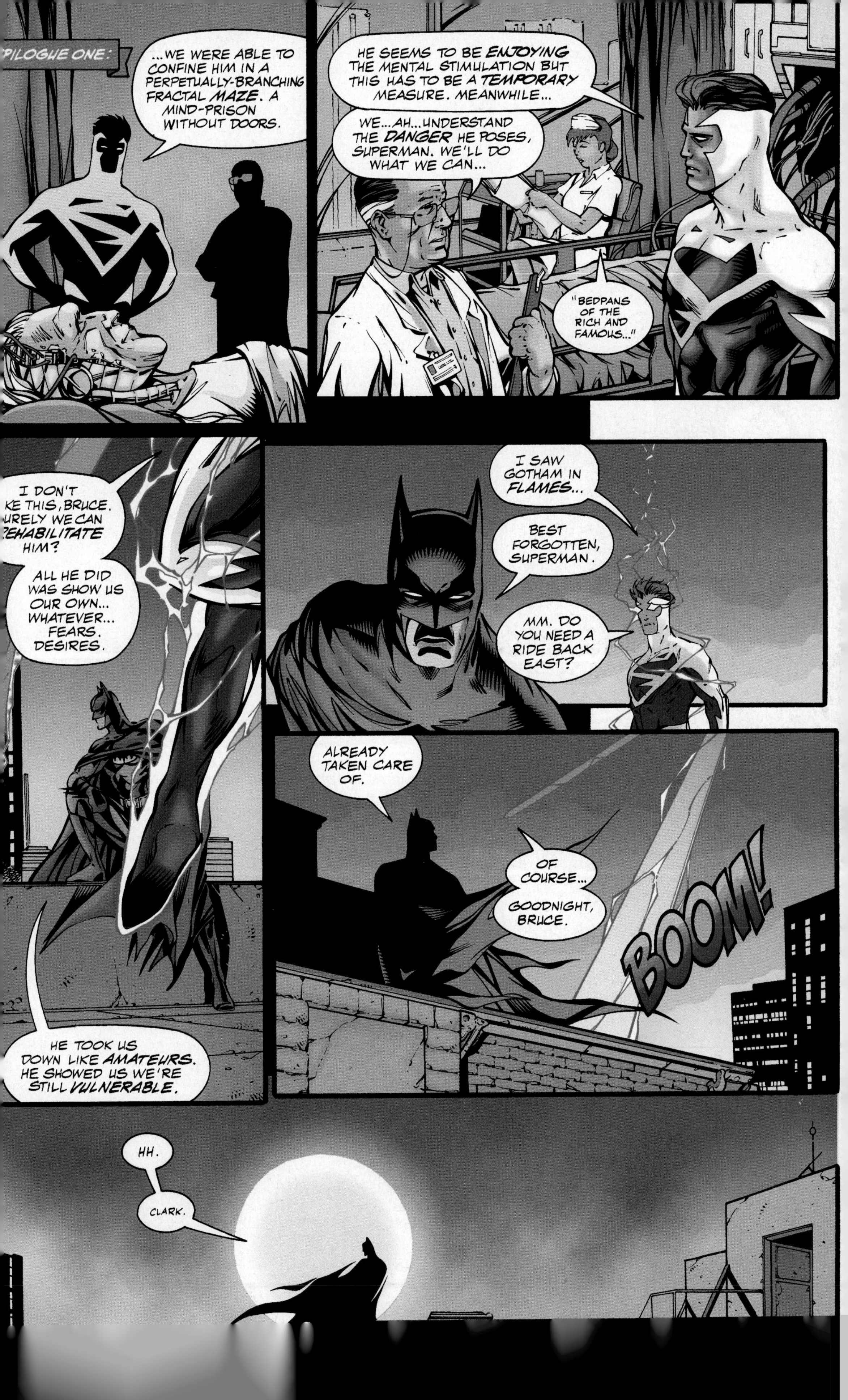
EPILOGUE ONE:
...WE WERE ABLE TO CONFINE HIM IN A PERPETUALLY-BRANCHING FRACTAL MAZE. A MIND-PRISON WITHOUT DOORS.
HE SEEMS TO BE ENJOYING THE MENTAL STIMULATION BUT THIS HAS TO BE A TEMPORARY MEASURE. MEANWHILE...
WE...AH...UNDERSTAND THE DANGER HE POSES, SUPERMAN. WE'LL DO WHAT WE CAN...
"BEDPANS OF THE RICH AND FAMOUS..."
I DON'T LIKE THIS, BRUCE. SURELY WE CAN REHABILITATE HIM?
ALL HE DID WAS SHOW US OUR OWN... WHATEVER... FEARS. DESIRES.
HE TOOK US DOWN LIKE AMATEURS. HE SHOWED US WE'RE STILL VULNERABLE.
I SAW GOTHAM IN FLAMES...
BEST FORGOTTEN, SUPERMAN.
MM. DO YOU NEED A RIDE BACK EAST?
ALREADY TAKEN CARE OF.
OF COURSE...
GOODNIGHT, BRUCE.
BOOM!
HH.
CLARK.

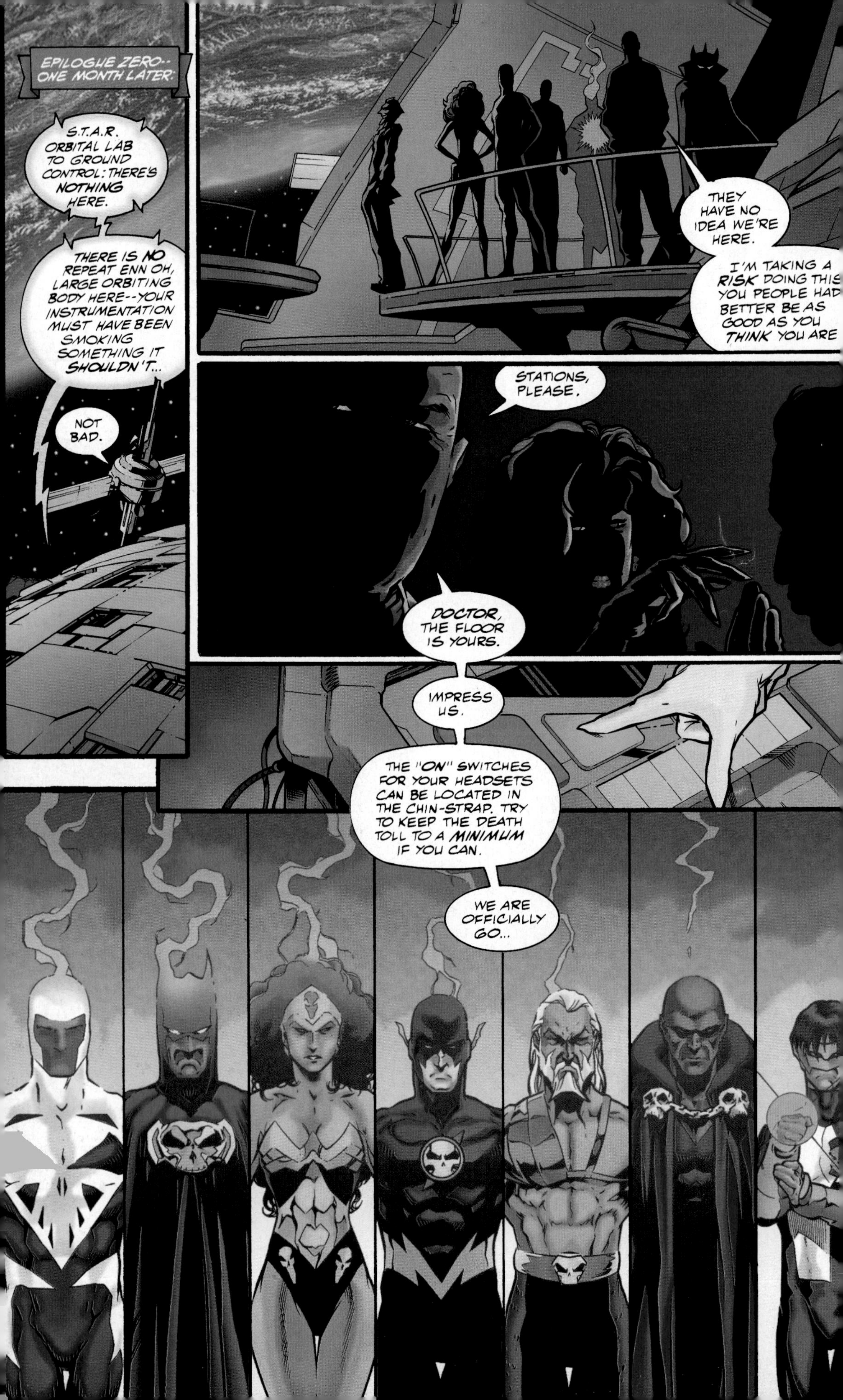
EPILOGUE ZERO-- ONE MONTH LATER:
S.T.A.R. ORBITAL LAB TO GROUND CONTROL: THERE'S NOTHING HERE.
THERE IS NO REPEAT ENN OH, LARGE ORBITING BODY HERE--YOUR INSTRUMENTATION MUST HAVE BEEN SMOKING SOMETHING IT SHOULDN'T...
NOT BAD.
THEY HAVE NO IDEA WE'RE HERE.
I'M TAKING A RISK DOING THIS. YOU PEOPLE HAD BETTER BE AS GOOD AS YOU THINK YOU ARE.
STATIONS, PLEASE.
DOCTOR, THE FLOOR IS YOURS.
IMPRESS US.
THE "ON" SWITCHES FOR YOUR HEADSETS CAN BE LOCATED IN THE CHIN-STRAP. TRY TO KEEP THE DEATH TOLL TO A MINIMUM IF YOU CAN.
WE ARE OFFICIALLY GO...

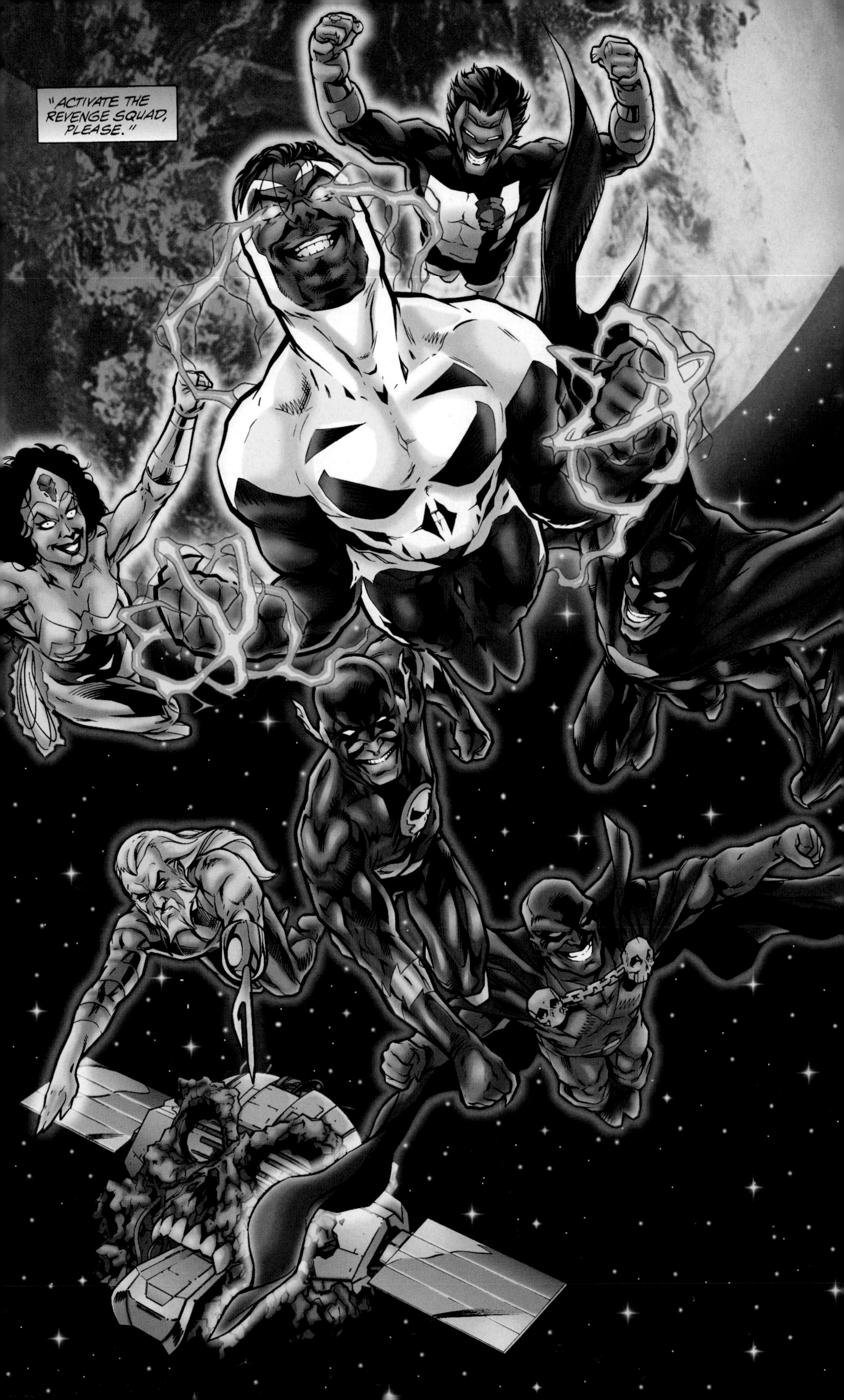
"ACTIVATE THE REVENGE SQUAD, PLEASE."

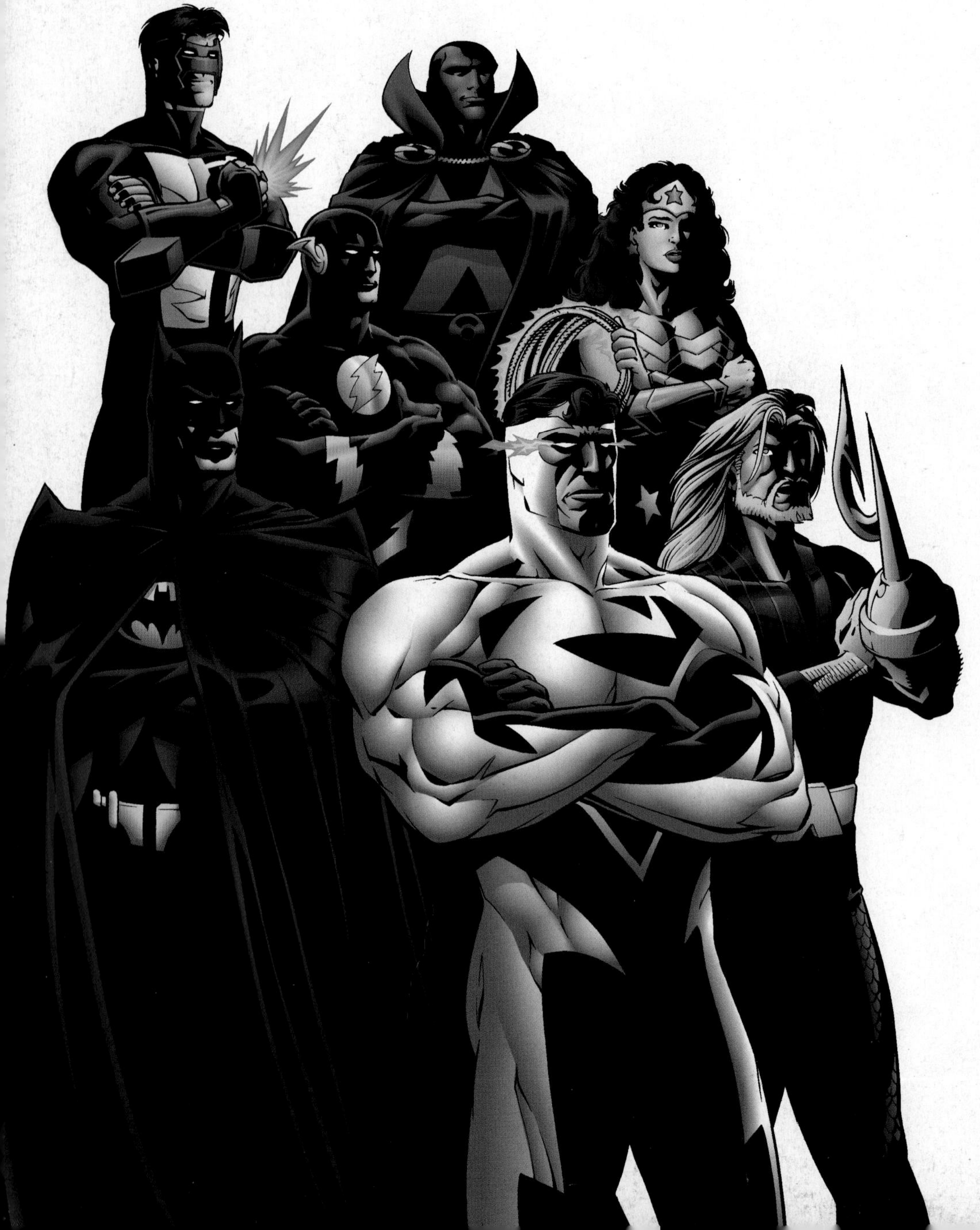

JLA SECRET FILES #1

WRITTEN BY GRANT MORRISON & MARK MILLAR

PENCILS BY HOWARD PORTER,

WITH INKS BY JOHN DELL AND COLORS BY JOHN KALISZ

NOTE: THIS STORY TAKES PLACE
BEFORE THE EVENTS IN JLA #1.

"THE LOST PAGES" AND "A DAY IN THE LIFE"

WRITTEN BY MARK MILLAR

ART BY DON HILLSMAN

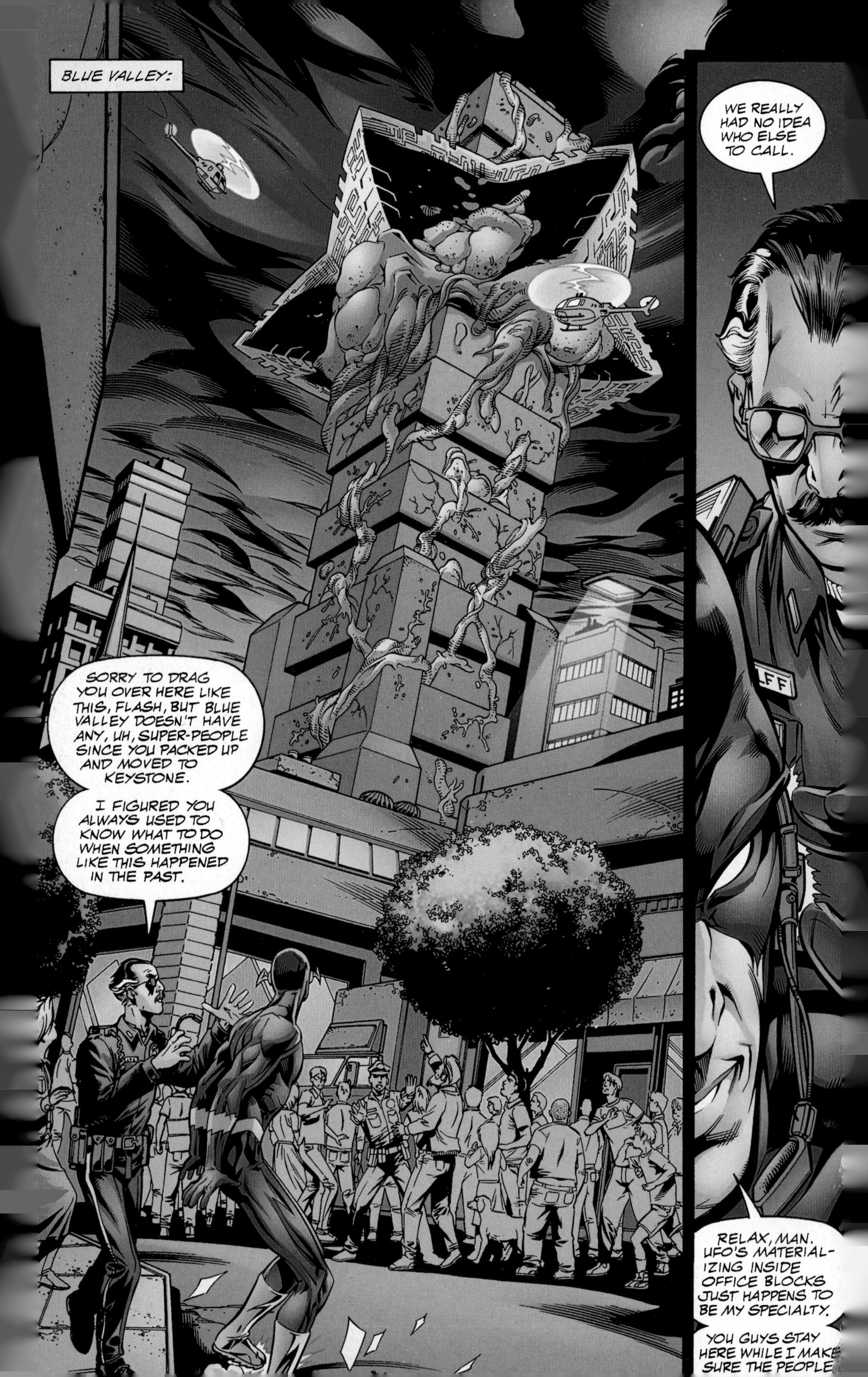
BLUE VALLEY:
SORRY TO DRAG YOU OVER HERE LIKE THIS, FLASH, BUT BLUE VALLEY DOESN'T HAVE ANY, UH, SUPER-PEOPLE SINCE YOU PACKED UP AND MOVED TO KEYSTONE.
I FIGURED YOU ALWAYS USED TO KNOW WHAT TO DO WHEN SOMETHING LIKE THIS HAPPENED IN THE PAST.
WE REALLY HAD NO IDEA WHO ELSE TO CALL.
RELAX, MAN. UFO'S MATERIAL-IZING INSIDE OFFICE BLOCKS JUST HAPPENS TO BE MY SPECIALTY.
YOU GUYS STAY HERE WHILE I MAKE SURE THE PEOPLE

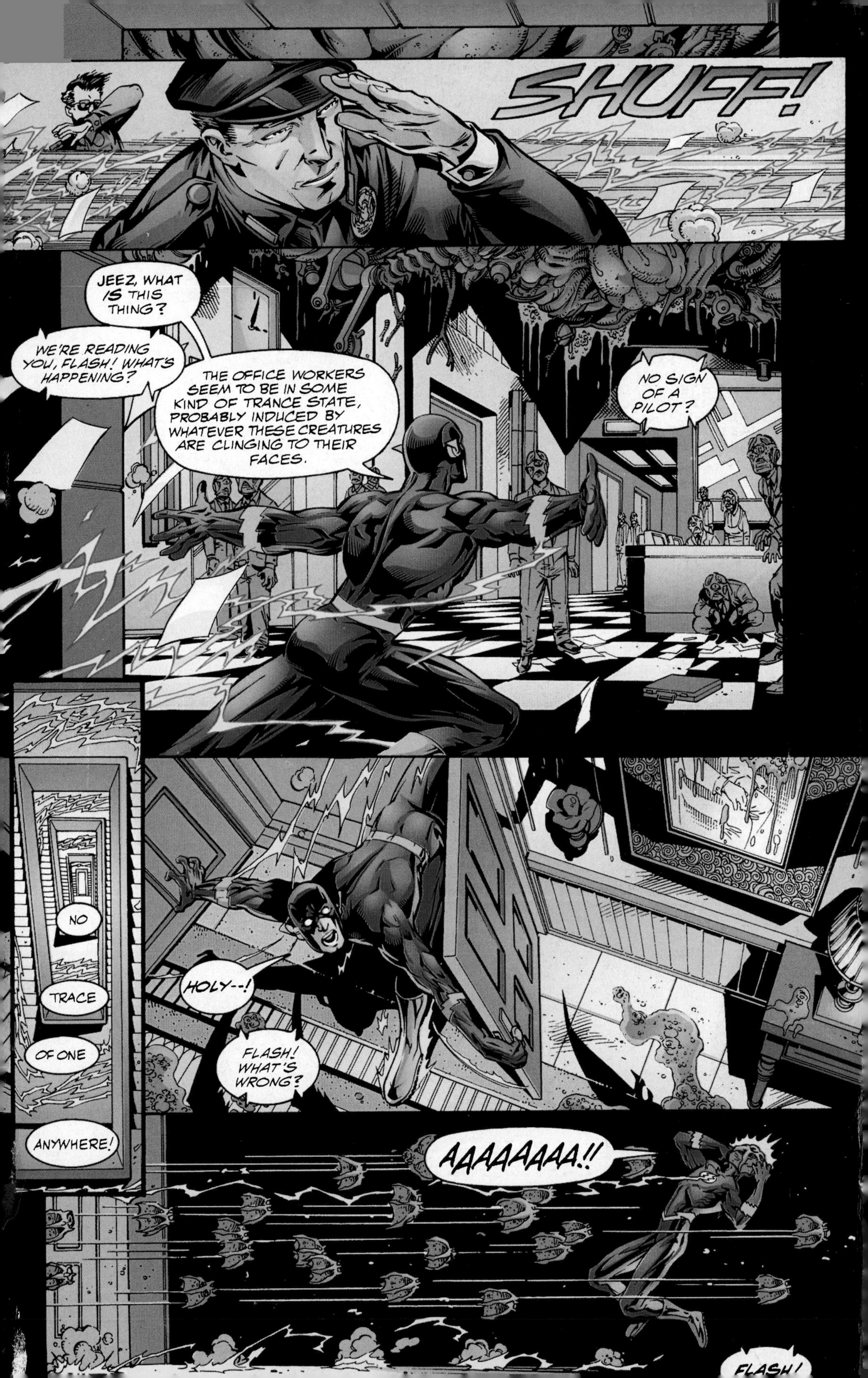
SHUFF!
JEEZ, WHAT IS THIS THING?
WE'RE READING YOU, FLASH! WHAT'S HAPPENING?
THE OFFICE WORKERS SEEM TO BE IN SOME KIND OF TRANCE STATE, PROBABLY INDUCED BY WHATEVER THESE CREATURES ARE CLINGING TO THEIR FACES.
NO SIGN OF A PILOT?
NO
TRACE
OF ONE
ANYWHERE!
HOLY--!
FLASH! WHAT'S WRONG?
AAAAAAAA!!
FLASH!

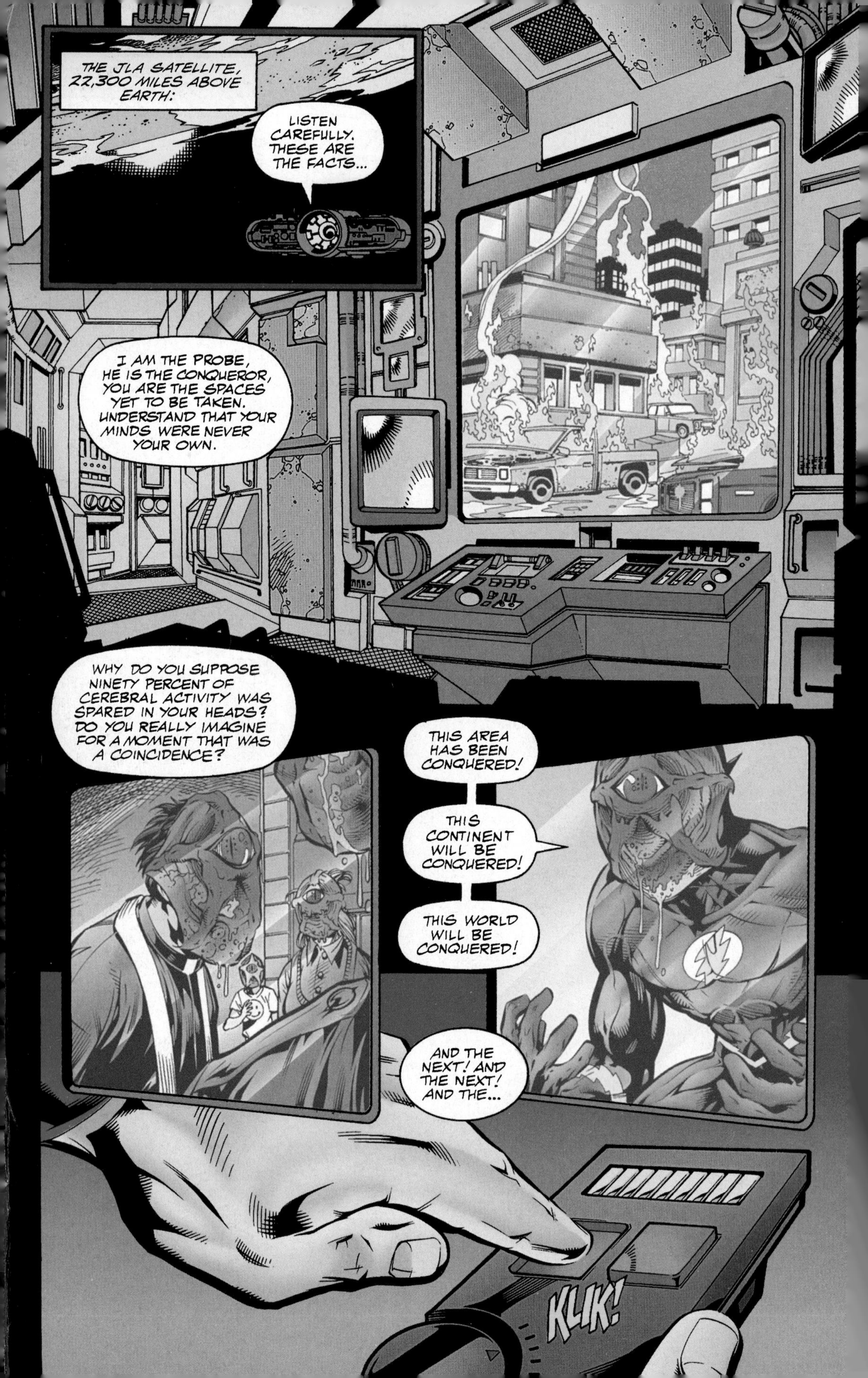
THE JLA SATELLITE, 22,300 MILES ABOVE EARTH:
LISTEN CAREFULLY. THESE ARE THE FACTS...
I AM THE PROBE, HE IS THE CONQUEROR, YOU ARE THE SPACES YET TO BE TAKEN. UNDERSTAND THAT YOUR MINDS WERE NEVER YOUR OWN.
WHY DO YOU SUPPOSE NINETY PERCENT OF CEREBRAL ACTIVITY WAS SPARED IN YOUR HEADS? DO YOU REALLY IMAGINE FOR A MOMENT THAT WAS A COINCIDENCE?
THIS AREA HAS BEEN CONQUERED!
THIS CONTINENT WILL BE CONQUERED!
THIS WORLD WILL BE CONQUERED!
AND THE NEXT! AND THE NEXT! AND THE...
KLIK!

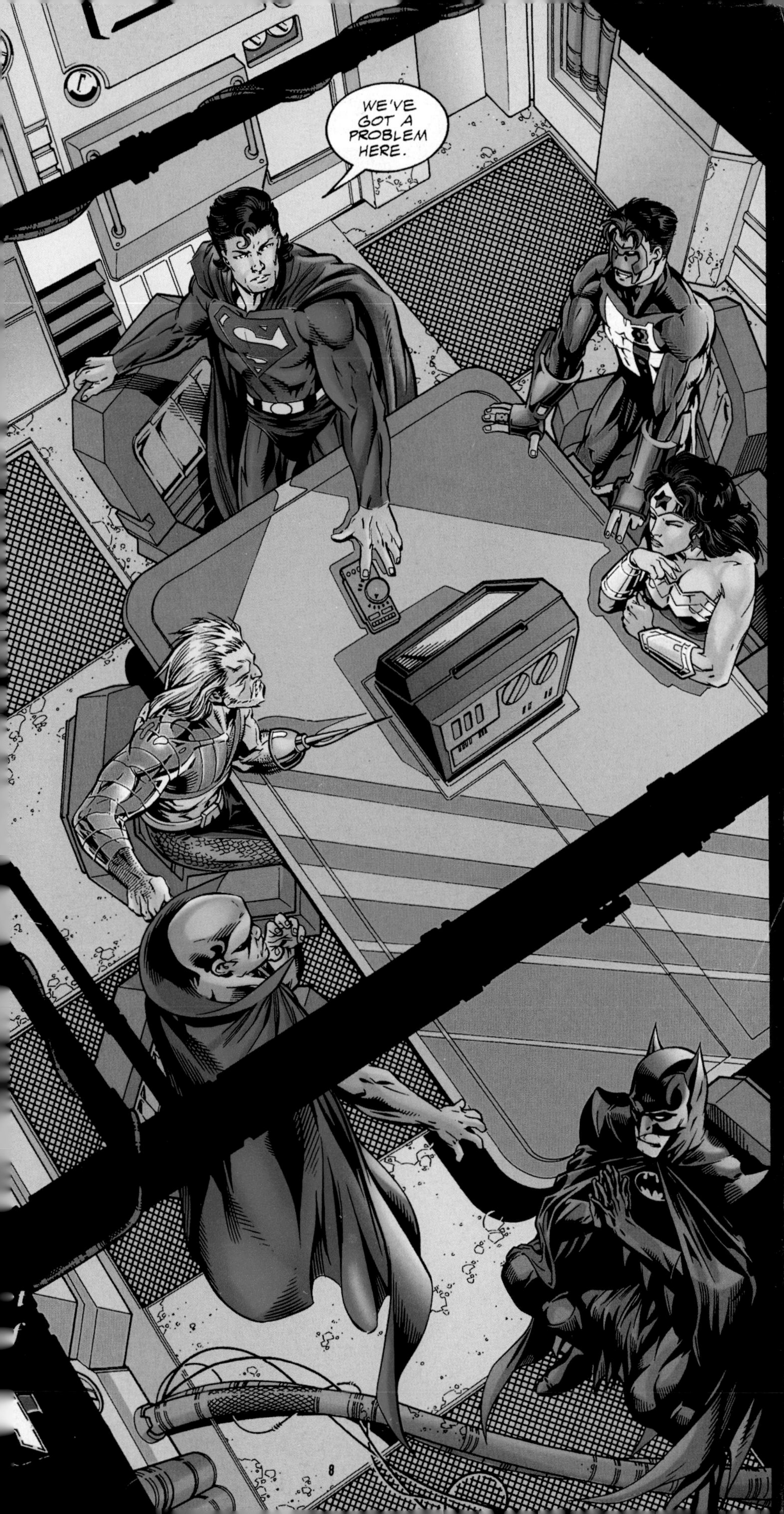
WE'VE GOT A PROBLEM HERE.

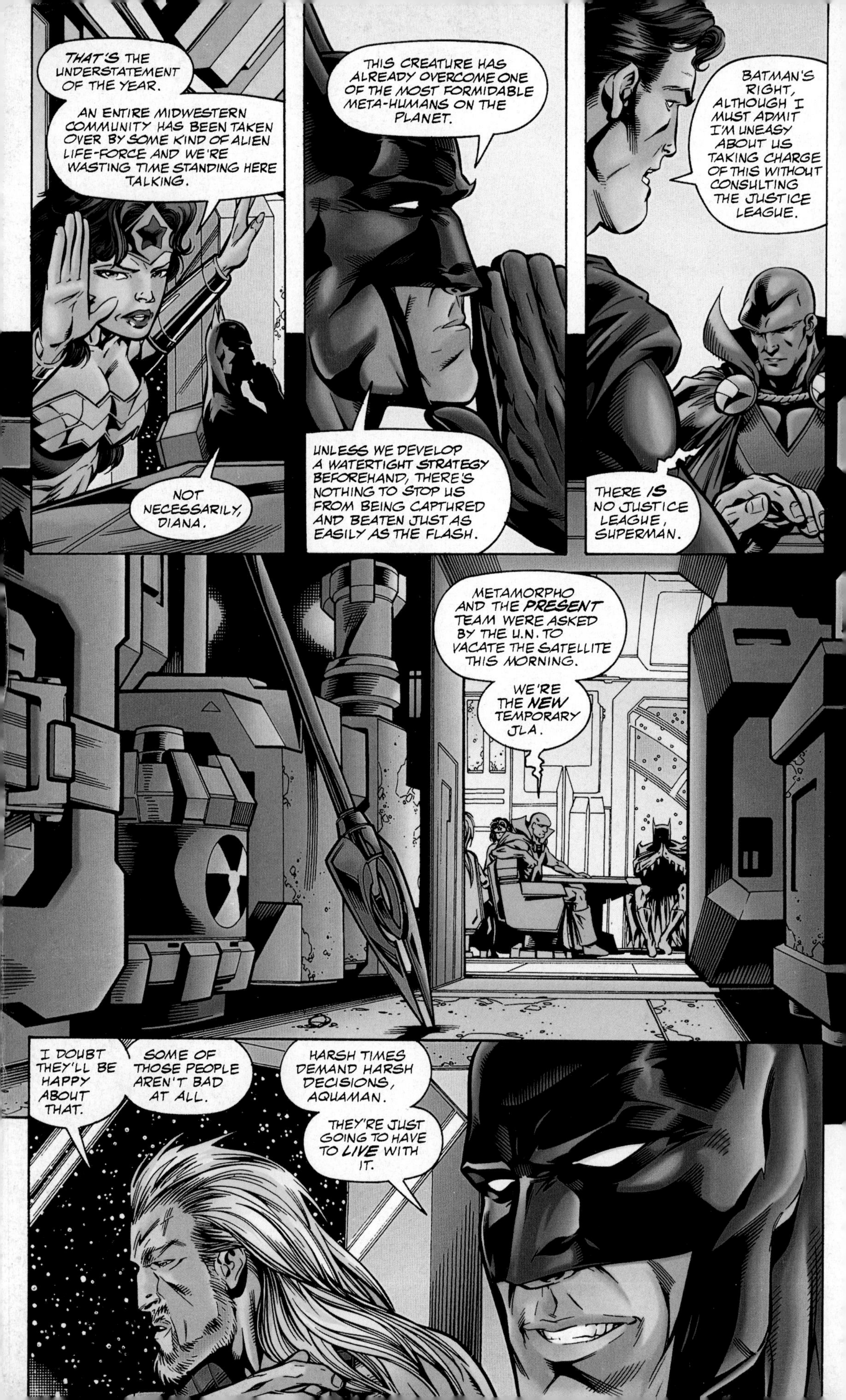
THAT'S THE UNDERSTATEMENT OF THE YEAR.
AN ENTIRE MIDWESTERN COMMUNITY HAS BEEN TAKEN OVER BY SOME KIND OF ALIEN LIFE-FORCE AND WE'RE WASTING TIME STANDING HERE TALKING.
NOT NECESSARILY, DIANA.
THIS CREATURE HAS ALREADY OVERCOME ONE OF THE MOST FORMIDABLE META-HUMANS ON THE PLANET.
UNLESS WE DEVELOP A WATERTIGHT STRATEGY BEFOREHAND, THERE'S NOTHING TO STOP US FROM BEING CAPTURED AND BEATEN JUST AS EASILY AS THE FLASH.
BATMAN'S RIGHT, ALTHOUGH I MUST ADMIT I'M UNEASY ABOUT US TAKING CHARGE OF THIS WITHOUT CONSULTING THE JUSTICE LEAGUE.
THERE IS NO JUSTICE LEAGUE, SUPERMAN.
METAMORPHO AND THE PRESENT TEAM WERE ASKED BY THE U.N. TO VACATE THE SATELLITE THIS MORNING.
WE'RE THE NEW TEMPORARY JLA.
I DOUBT THEY'LL BE HAPPY ABOUT THAT.
SOME OF THOSE PEOPLE AREN'T BAD AT ALL.
HARSH TIMES DEMAND HARSH DECISIONS, AQUAMAN.
THEY'RE JUST GOING TO HAVE TO LIVE WITH IT.

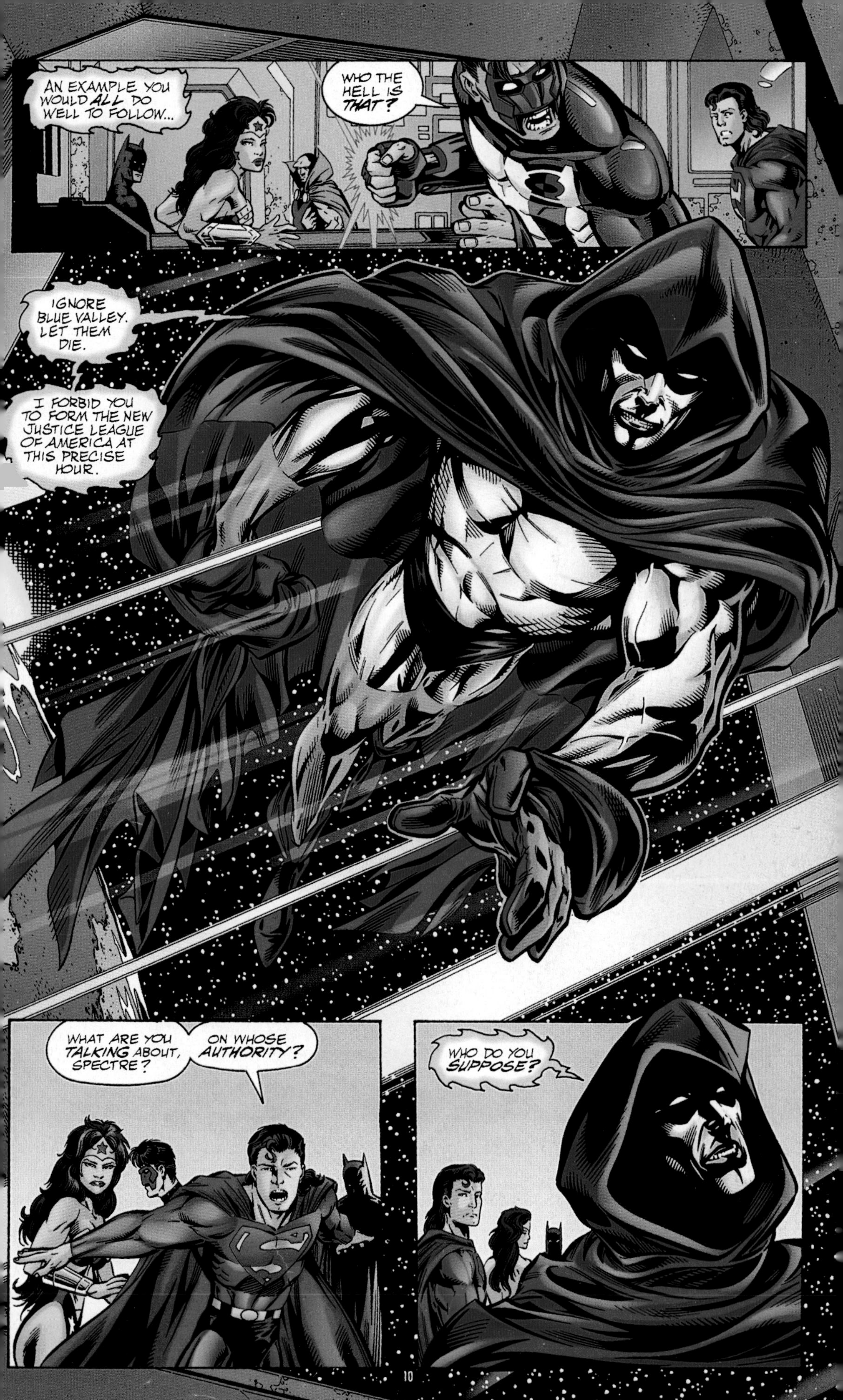

AN EXAMPLE YOU WOULD ALL DO WELL TO FOLLOW...
WHO THE HELL IS THAT?
IGNORE BLUE VALLEY. LET THEM DIE.
I FORBID YOU TO FORM THE NEW JUSTICE LEAGUE OF AMERICA AT THIS PRECISE HOUR.
WHAT ARE YOU TALKING ABOUT, SPECTRE?
ON WHOSE AUTHORITY?
WHO DO YOU SUPPOSE?

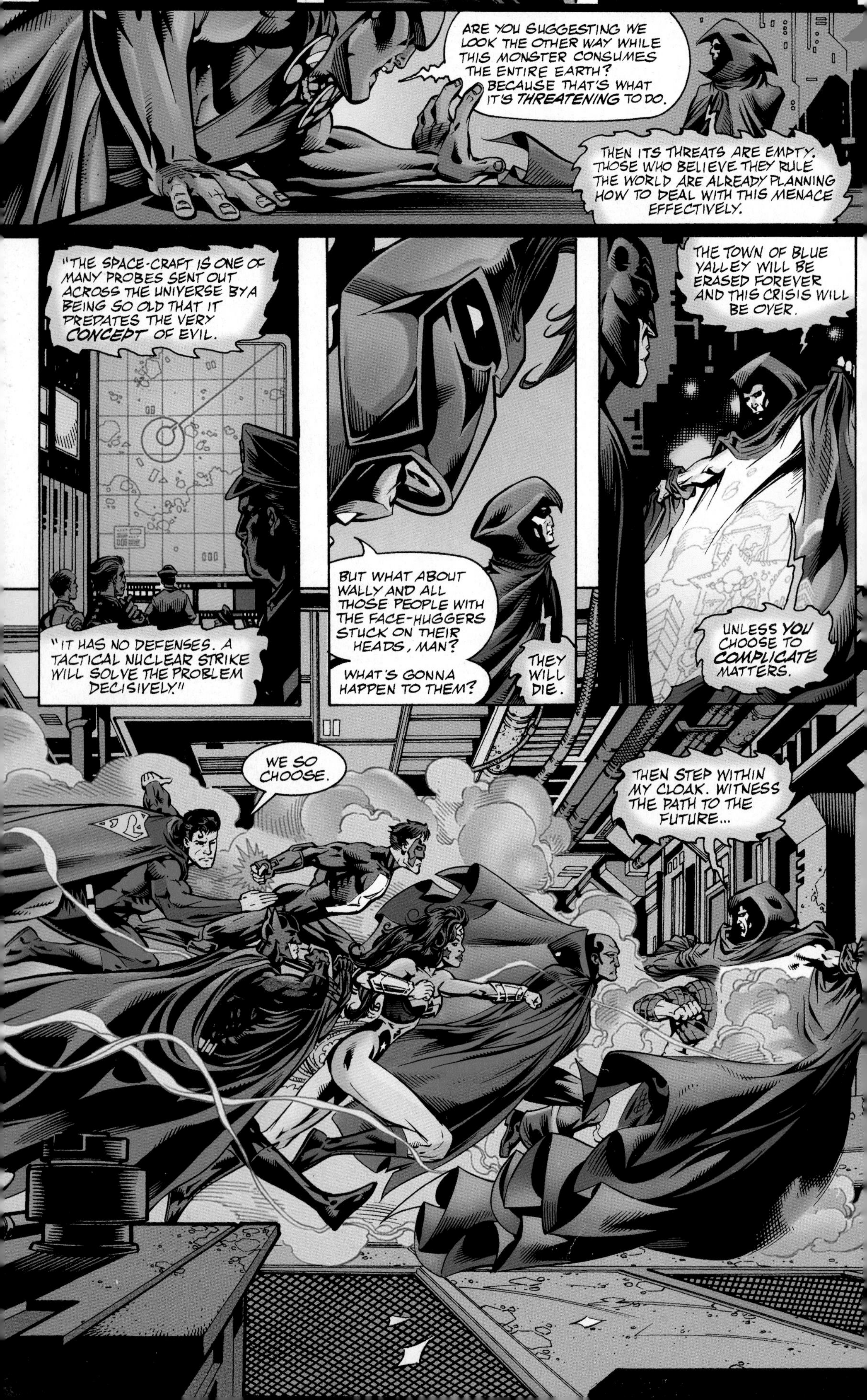
ARE YOU SUGGESTING WE LOOK THE OTHER WAY WHILE THIS MONSTER CONSUMES THE ENTIRE EARTH?
BECAUSE THAT'S WHAT IT'S THREATENING TO DO.
THEN ITS THREATS ARE EMPTY. THOSE WHO BELIEVE THEY RULE THE WORLD ARE ALREADY PLANNING HOW TO DEAL WITH THIS MENACE EFFECTIVELY.
"THE SPACE-CRAFT IS ONE OF MANY PROBES SENT OUT ACROSS THE UNIVERSE BY A BEING SO OLD THAT IT PREDATES THE VERY CONCEPT OF EVIL.
"IT HAS NO DEFENSES. A TACTICAL NUCLEAR STRIKE WILL SOLVE THE PROBLEM DECISIVELY."
BUT WHAT ABOUT WALLY AND ALL THOSE PEOPLE WITH THE FACE-HUGGERS STUCK ON THEIR HEADS, MAN?
WHAT'S GONNA HAPPEN TO THEM?
THEY WILL DIE.
THE TOWN OF BLUE VALLEY WILL BE ERASED FOREVER AND THIS CRISIS WILL BE OVER.
UNLESS YOU CHOOSE TO COMPLICATE MATTERS.
WE SO CHOOSE.
THEN STEP WITHIN MY CLOAK. WITNESS THE PATH TO THE FUTURE...

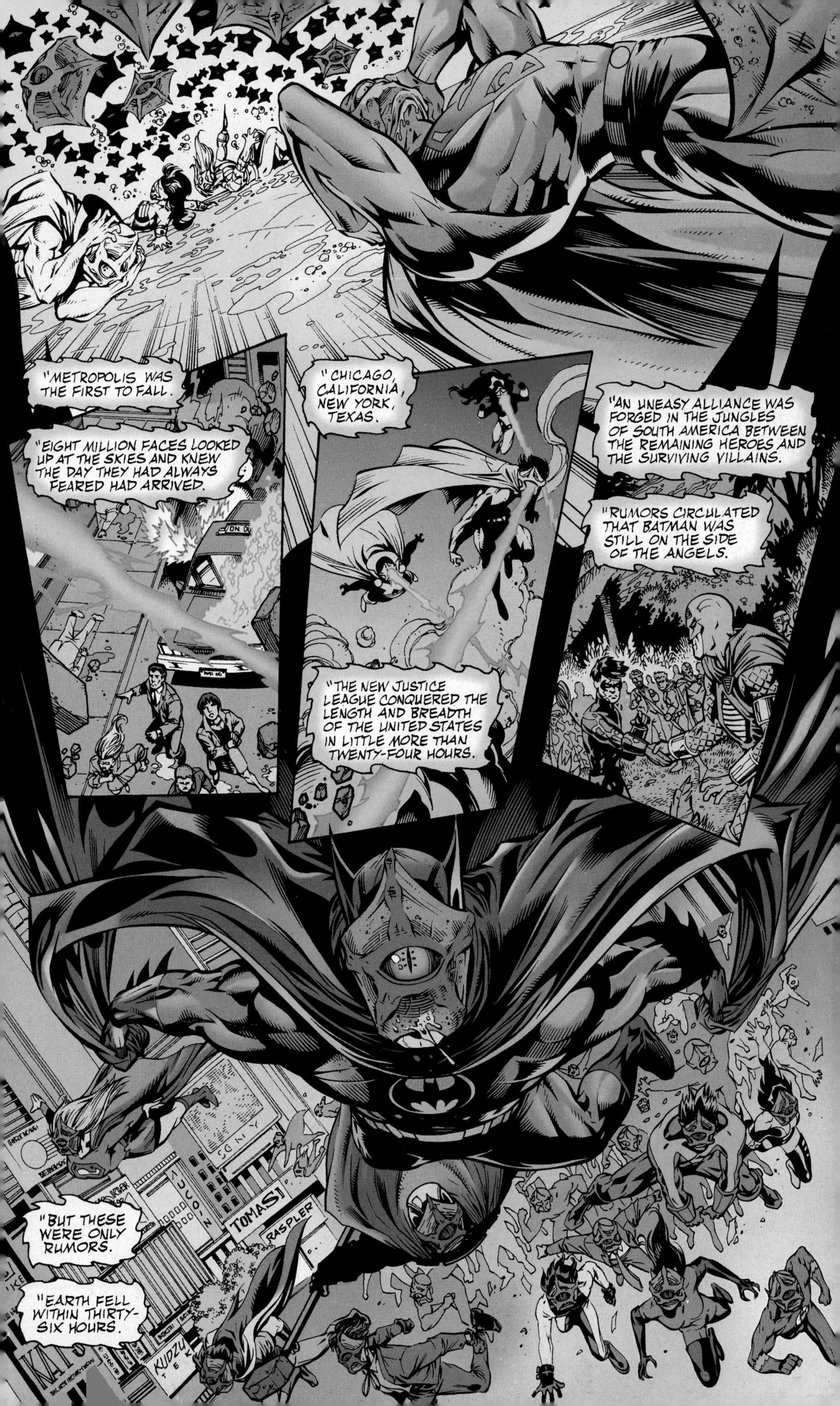

"METROPOLIS WAS THE FIRST TO FALL.
"EIGHT MILLION FACES LOOKED UP AT THE SKIES AND KNEW THE DAY THEY HAD ALWAYS FEARED HAD ARRIVED.
"CHICAGO, CALIFORNIA, NEW YORK, TEXAS.
"THE NEW JUSTICE LEAGUE CONQUERED THE LENGTH AND BREADTH OF THE UNITED STATES IN LITTLE MORE THAN TWENTY-FOUR HOURS.
"AN UNEASY ALLIANCE WAS FORGED IN THE JUNGLES OF SOUTH AMERICA BETWEEN THE REMAINING HEROES AND THE SURVIVING VILLAINS.
"RUMORS CIRCULATED THAT BATMAN WAS STILL ON THE SIDE OF THE ANGELS.
"BUT THESE WERE ONLY RUMORS.
"EARTH FELL WITHIN THIRTY-SIX HOURS.
AUCOIN
TOMASI
RASPLER
KUDZU

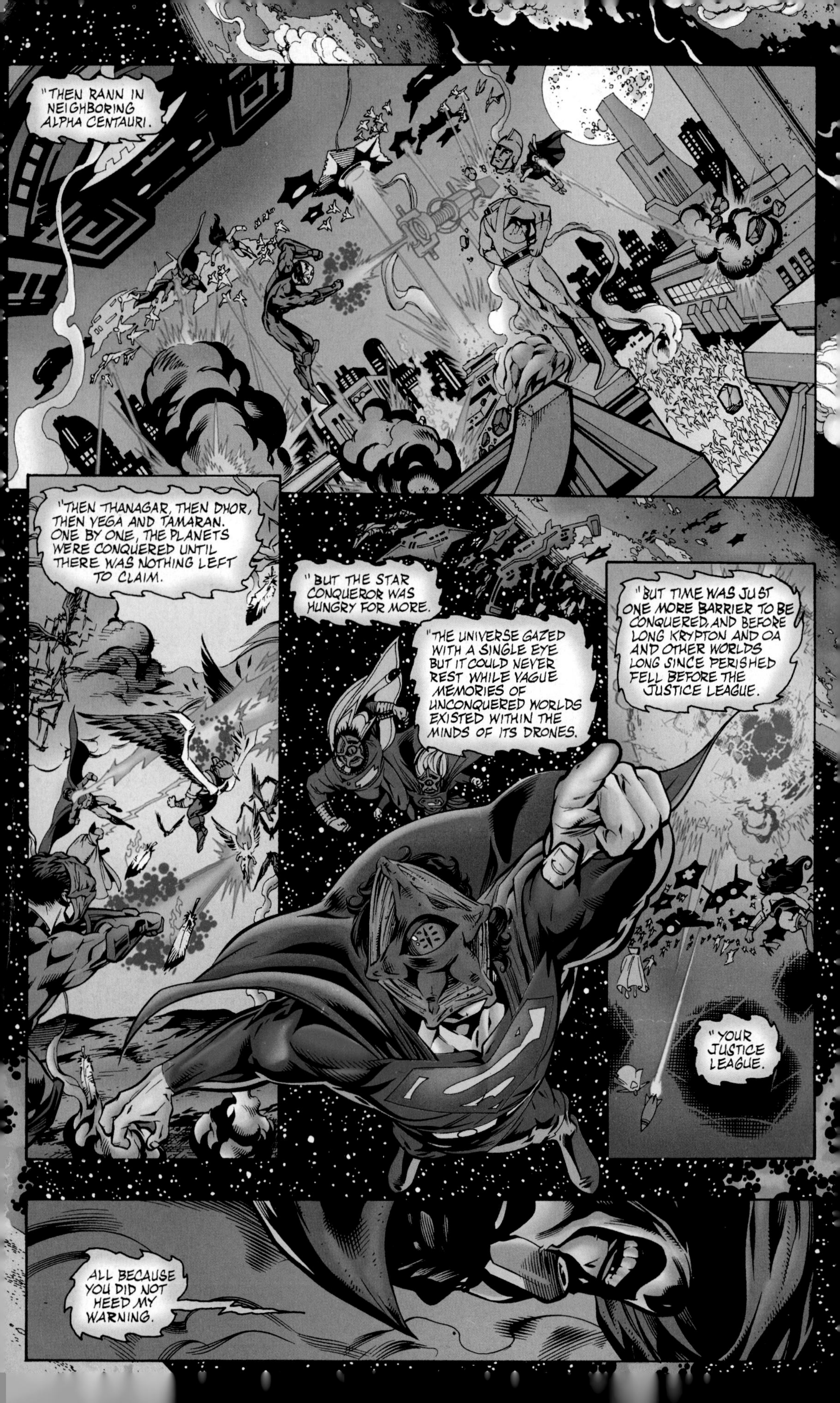
"THEN RANN IN NEIGHBORING ALPHA CENTAURI.
"THEN THANAGAR, THEN DHOR, THEN VEGA AND TAMARAN. ONE BY ONE, THE PLANETS WERE CONQUERED UNTIL THERE WAS NOTHING LEFT TO CLAIM.
"BUT THE STAR CONQUEROR WAS HUNGRY FOR MORE.
"THE UNIVERSE GAZED WITH A SINGLE EYE BUT IT COULD NEVER REST WHILE VAGUE MEMORIES OF UNCONQUERED WORLDS EXISTED WITHIN THE MINDS OF ITS DRONES.
"BUT TIME WAS JUST ONE MORE BARRIER TO BE CONQUERED, AND BEFORE LONG KRYPTON AND OA AND OTHER WORLDS LONG SINCE PERISHED FELL BEFORE THE JUSTICE LEAGUE.
"YOUR JUSTICE LEAGUE.
ALL BECAUSE YOU DID NOT HEED MY WARNING.

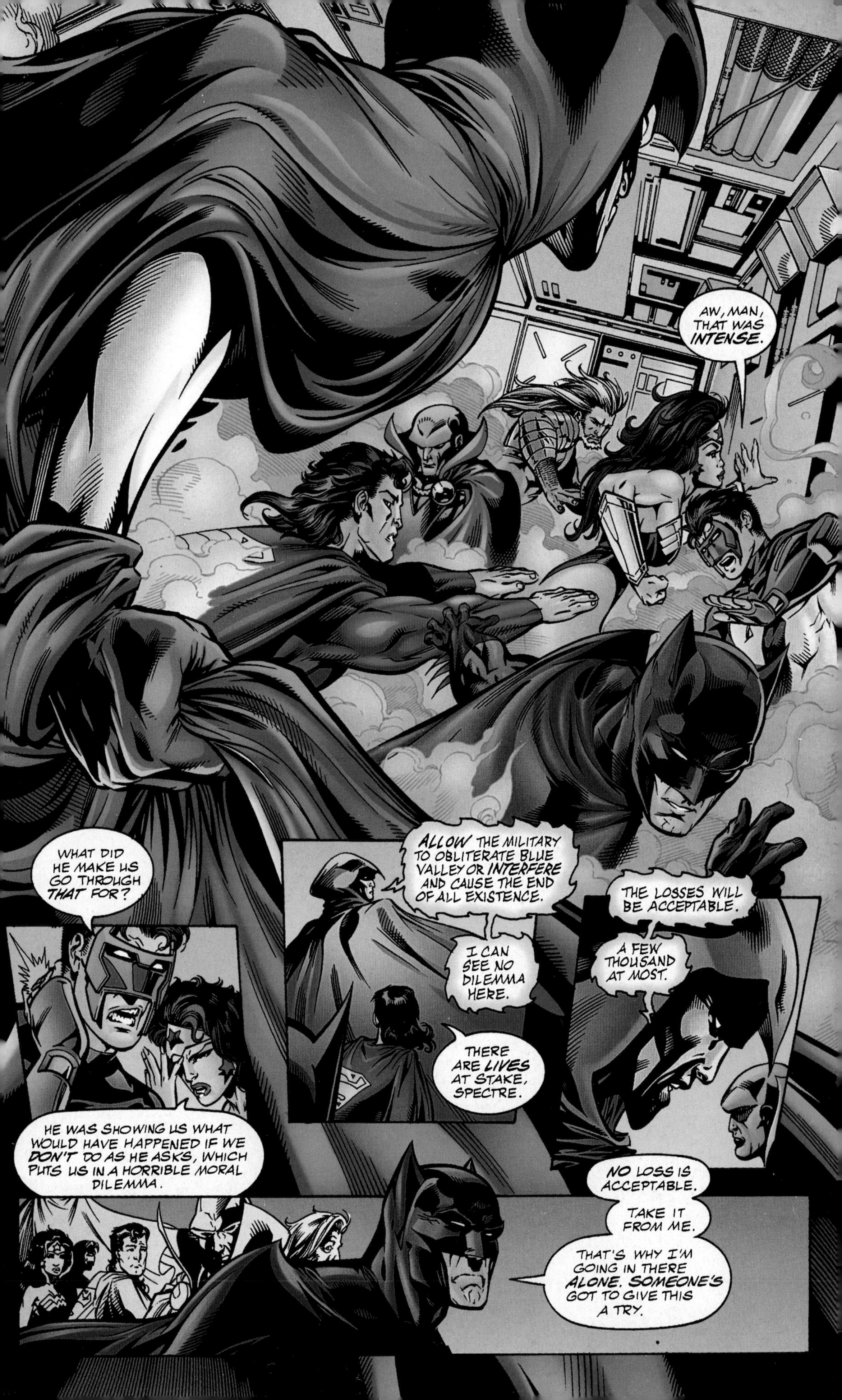

AW, MAN, THAT WAS INTENSE.
WHAT DID HE MAKE US GO THROUGH THAT FOR?
HE WAS SHOWING US WHAT WOULD HAVE HAPPENED IF WE DON'T DO AS HE ASKS, WHICH PUTS US IN A HORRIBLE MORAL DILEMMA.
ALLOW THE MILITARY TO OBLITERATE BLUE VALLEY OR INTERFERE AND CAUSE THE END OF ALL EXISTENCE.
I CAN SEE NO DILEMMA HERE.
THERE ARE LIVES AT STAKE, SPECTRE.
THE LOSSES WILL BE ACCEPTABLE.
A FEW THOUSAND AT MOST.
NO LOSS IS ACCEPTABLE.
TAKE IT FROM ME.
THAT'S WHY I'M GOING IN THERE ALONE. SOMEONE'S GOT TO GIVE THIS A TRY.

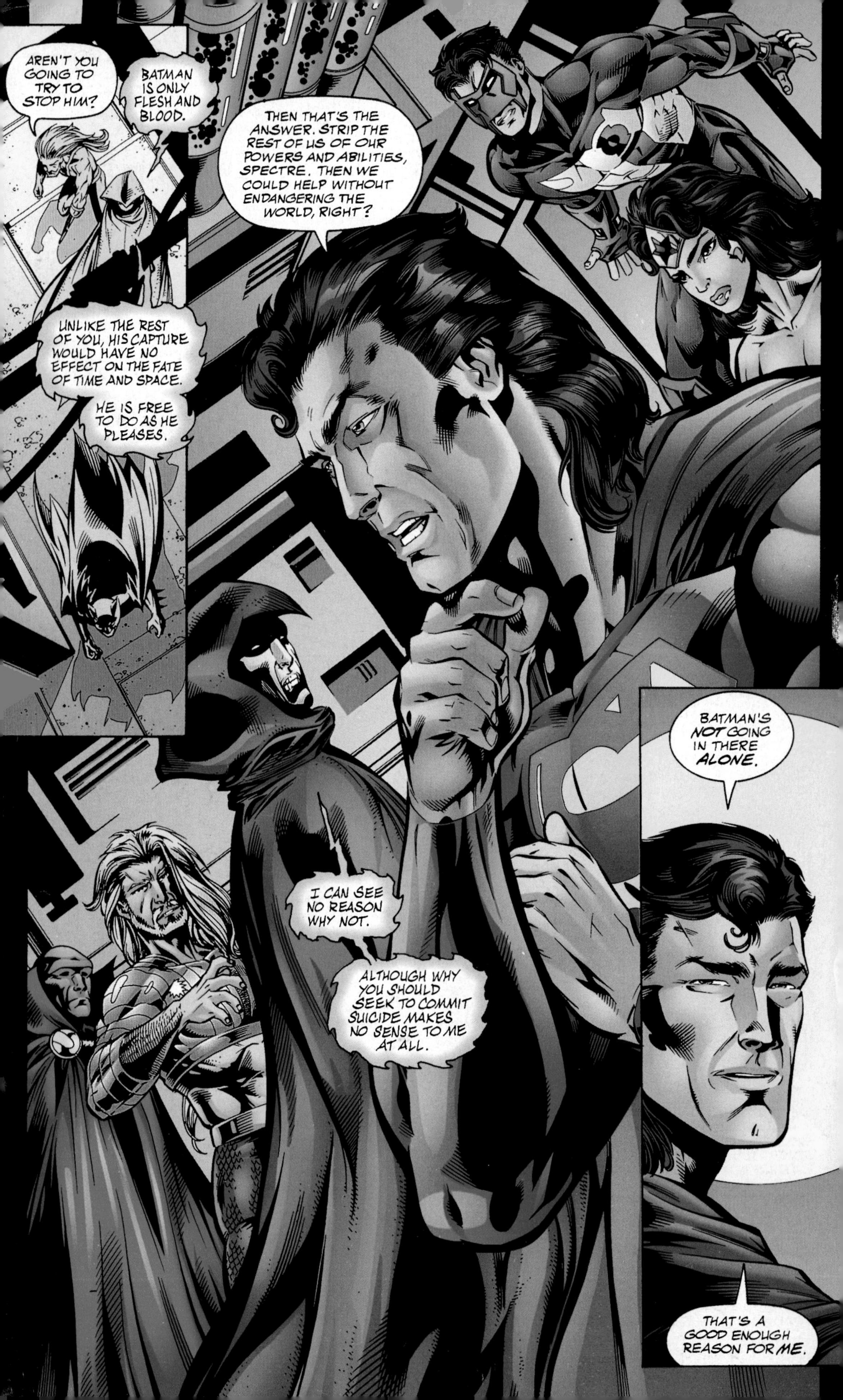
AREN'T YOU GOING TO TRY TO STOP HIM?
BATMAN IS ONLY FLESH AND BLOOD.
THEN THAT'S THE ANSWER. STRIP THE REST OF US OF OUR POWERS AND ABILITIES, SPECTRE. THEN WE COULD HELP WITHOUT ENDANGERING THE WORLD, RIGHT?
UNLIKE THE REST OF YOU, HIS CAPTURE WOULD HAVE NO EFFECT ON THE FATE OF TIME AND SPACE.
HE IS FREE TO DO AS HE PLEASES.
I CAN SEE NO REASON WHY NOT.
ALTHOUGH WHY YOU SHOULD SEEK TO COMMIT SUICIDE MAKES NO SENSE TO ME AT ALL.
BATMAN'S NOT GOING IN THERE ALONE.
THAT'S A GOOD ENOUGH REASON FOR ME.

I'VE GOT A BAD FEELING ABOUT THIS, SUPERMAN.

WHAT DO YOU THINK HE MEANT WHEN HE SAID WE SHOULDN'T GET OURSELVES INVOLVED IN THIS?

OBVIOUSLY, WE'RE AS MUCH AT RISK HERE AS THE FLASH WAS, BUT HOPEFULLY THE SIX OF US WORKING TOGETHER WILL PROVIDE THE NECESSARY EDGE.

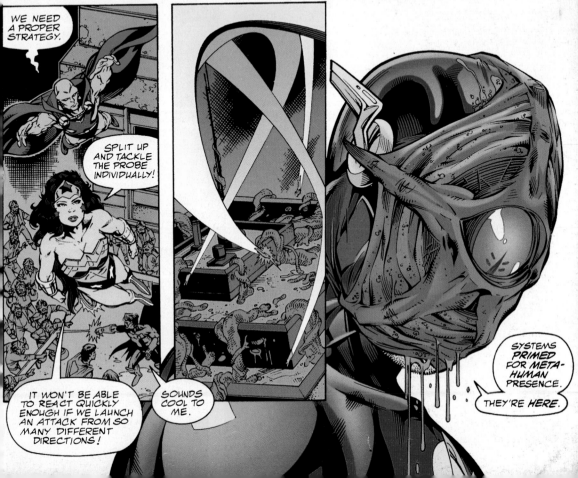

WE NEED A PROPER STRATEGY.

SPLIT UP AND TACKLE THE PROBE INDIVIDUALLY!

IT WON'T BE ABLE TO REACT QUICKLY ENOUGH IF WE LAUNCH AN ATTACK FROM SO MANY DIFFERENT DIRECTIONS!

SOUNDS COOL TO ME.

SYSTEMS PRIMED FOR META-HUMAN PRESENCE.

THEY'RE HERE.

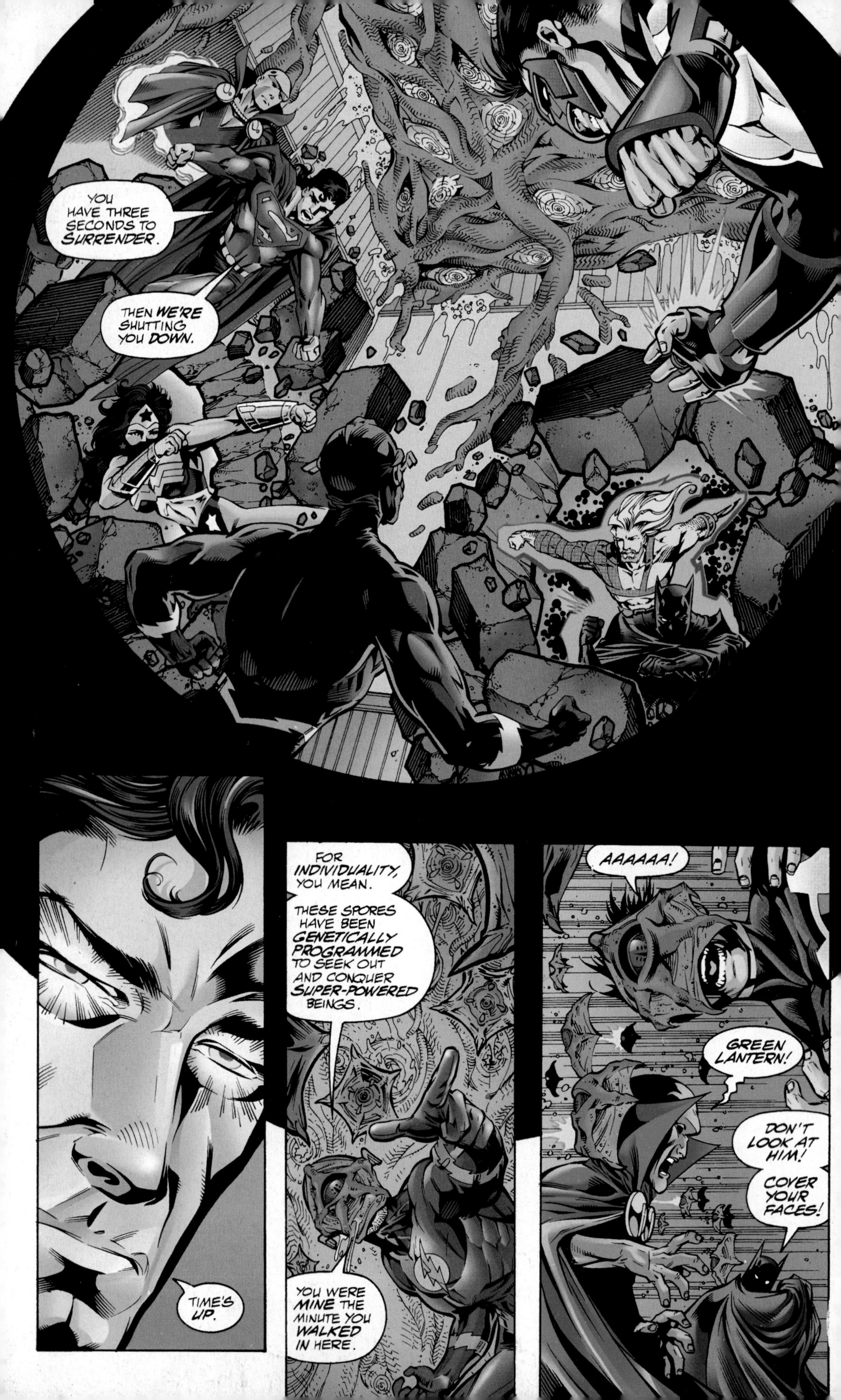
YOU HAVE THREE SECONDS TO SURRENDER.
THEN WE'RE SHUTTING YOU DOWN.
TIME'S UP.
FOR INDIVIDUALITY, YOU MEAN.
THESE SPORES HAVE BEEN GENETICALLY PROGRAMMED TO SEEK OUT AND CONQUER SUPER-POWERED BEINGS.
YOU WERE MINE THE MINUTE YOU WALKED IN HERE.
AAAAAA!
GREEN LANTERN!
DON'T LOOK AT HIM!
COVER YOUR FACES!

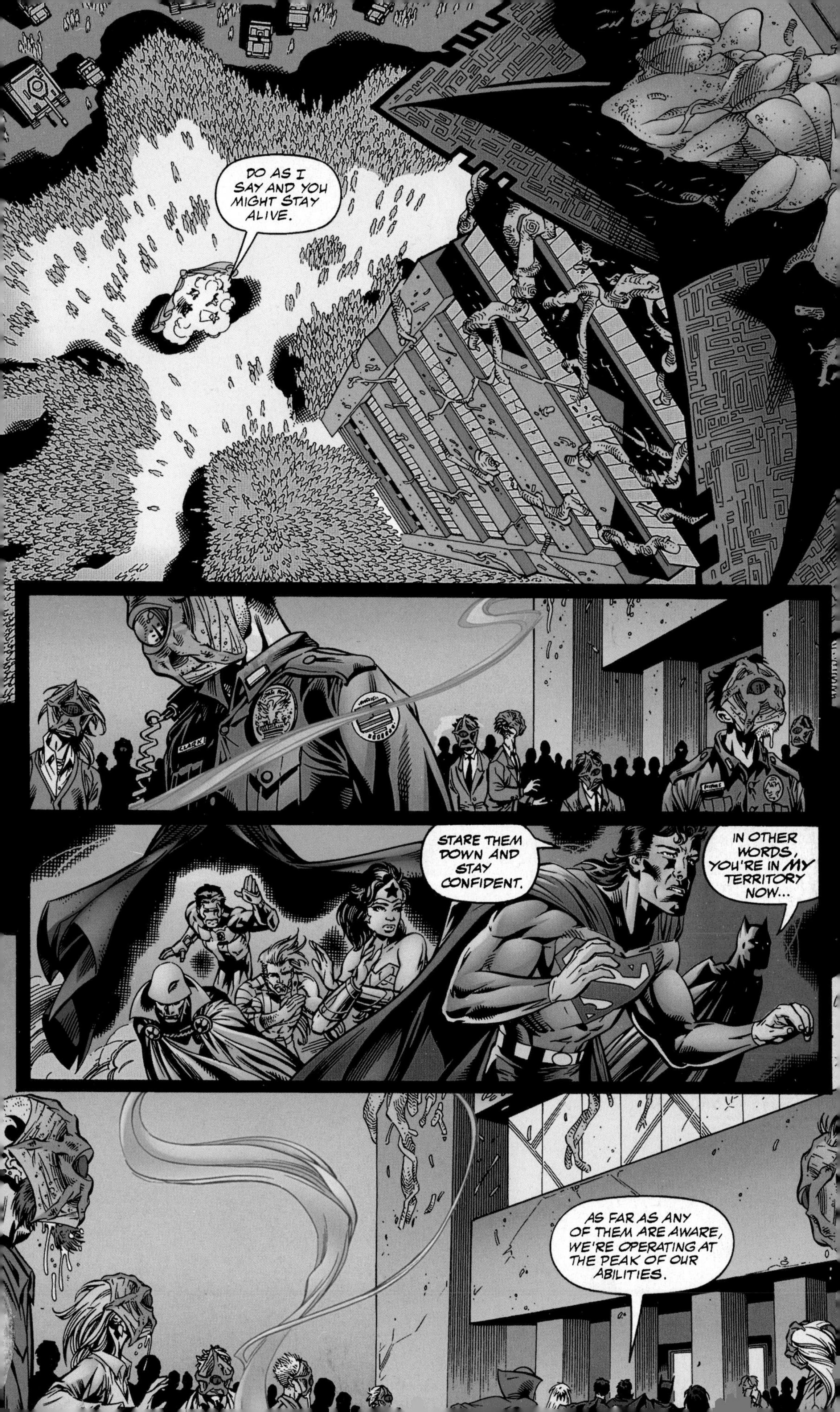
DO AS I SAY AND YOU MIGHT STAY ALIVE.
STARE THEM DOWN AND STAY CONFIDENT.
IN OTHER WORDS, YOU'RE IN MY TERRITORY NOW...
AS FAR AS ANY OF THEM ARE AWARE, WE'RE OPERATING AT THE PEAK OF OUR ABILITIES.

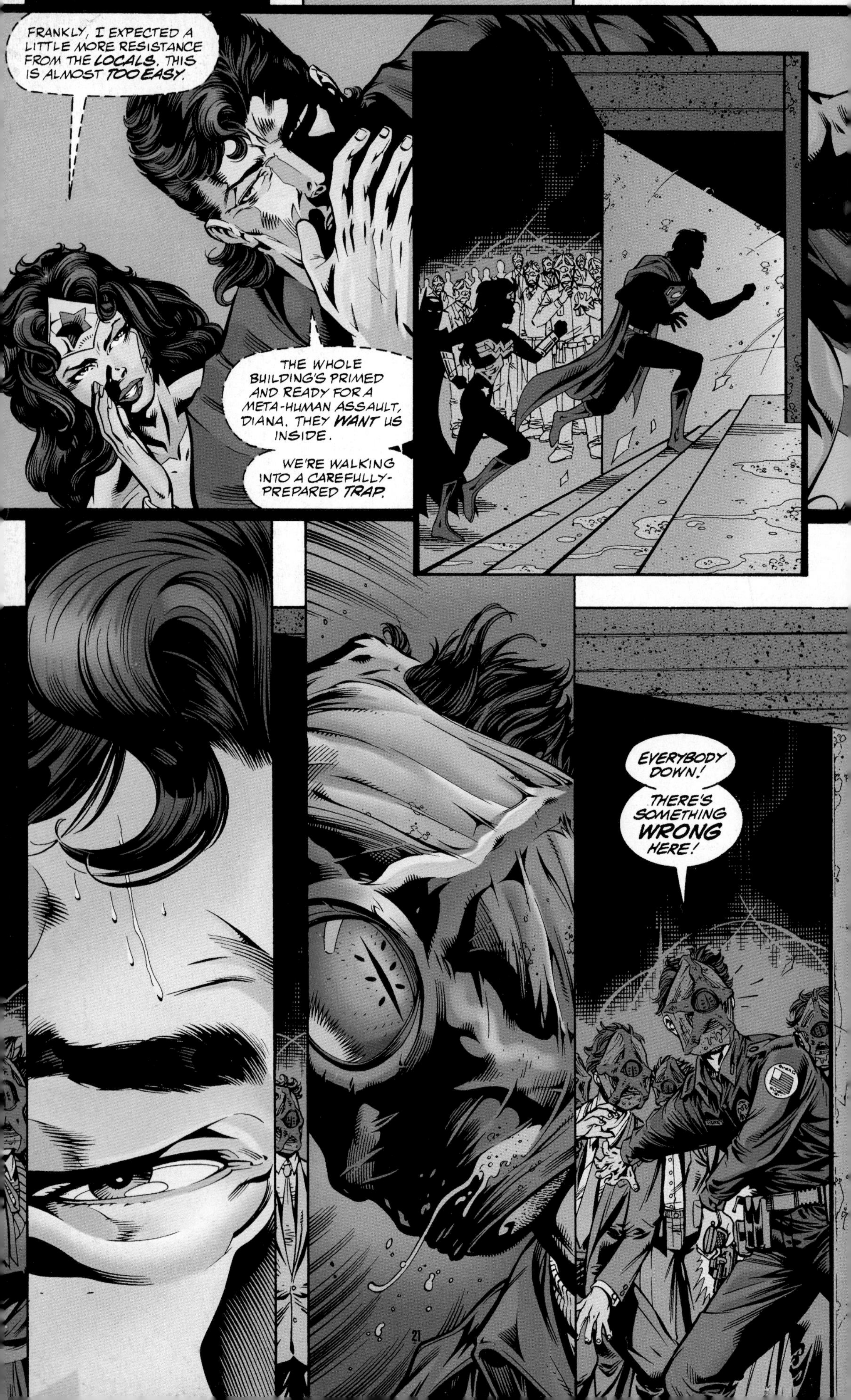

FRANKLY, I EXPECTED A LITTLE MORE RESISTANCE FROM THE LOCALS. THIS IS ALMOST TOO EASY.
THE WHOLE BUILDING'S PRIMED AND READY FOR A META-HUMAN ASSAULT, DIANA. THEY WANT US INSIDE.
WE'RE WALKING INTO A CAREFULLY-PREPARED TRAP.
EVERYBODY DOWN!
THERE'S SOMETHING WRONG HERE!

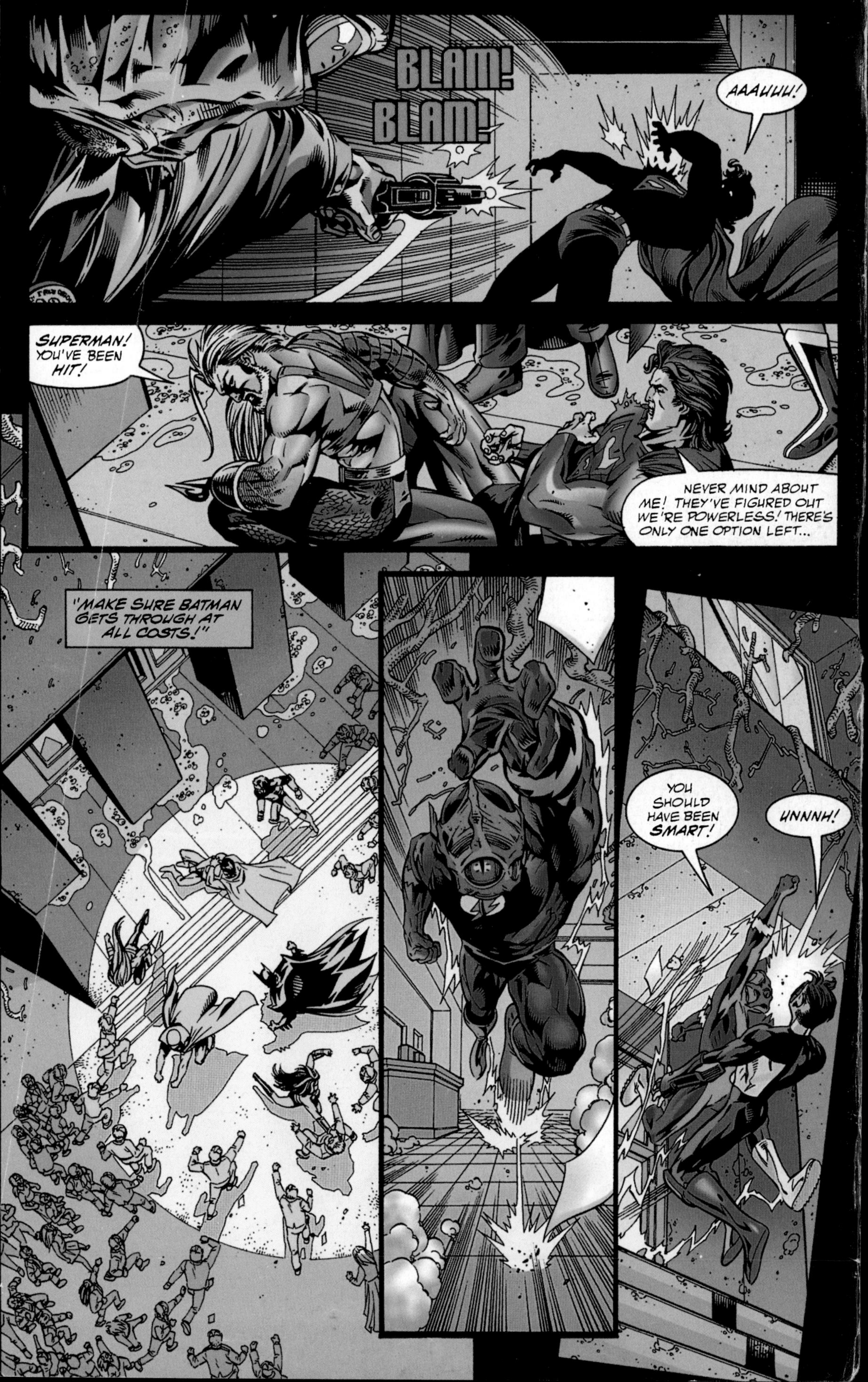
BLAM!
BLAM!
AAAUUU!
SUPERMAN! YOU'VE BEEN HIT!
NEVER MIND ABOUT ME! THEY'VE FIGURED OUT WE'RE POWERLESS! THERE'S ONLY ONE OPTION LEFT...
"MAKE SURE BATMAN GETS THROUGH AT ALL COSTS!"
YOU SHOULD HAVE BEEN SMART!
UNNNH!

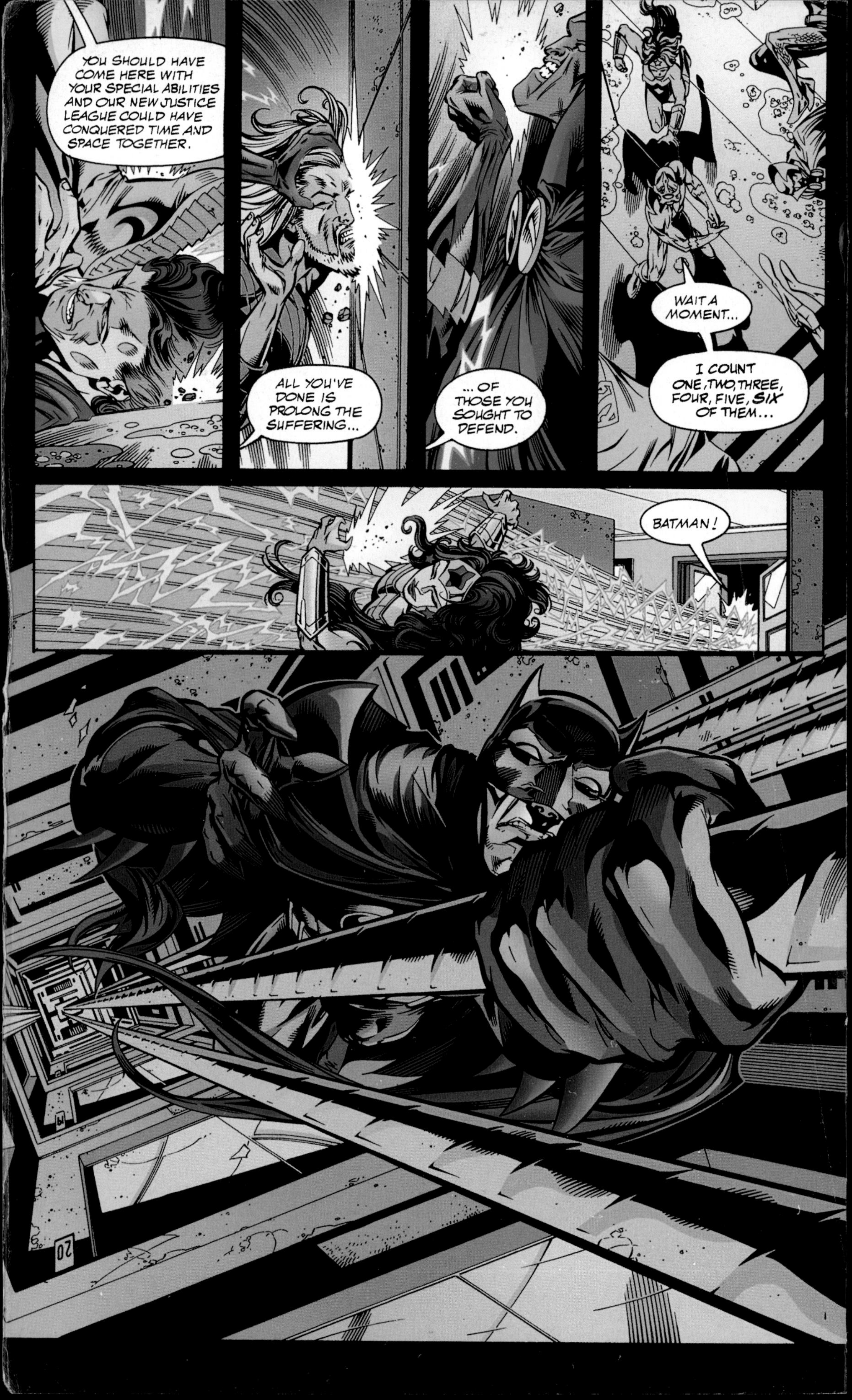
YOU SHOULD HAVE COME HERE WITH YOUR SPECIAL ABILITIES AND OUR NEW JUSTICE LEAGUE COULD HAVE CONQUERED TIME AND SPACE TOGETHER.
ALL YOU'VE DONE IS PROLONG THE SUFFERING...
...OF THOSE YOU SOUGHT TO DEFEND.
WAIT A MOMENT...
I COUNT ONE, TWO, THREE, FOUR, FIVE, SIX OF THEM...
BATMAN!

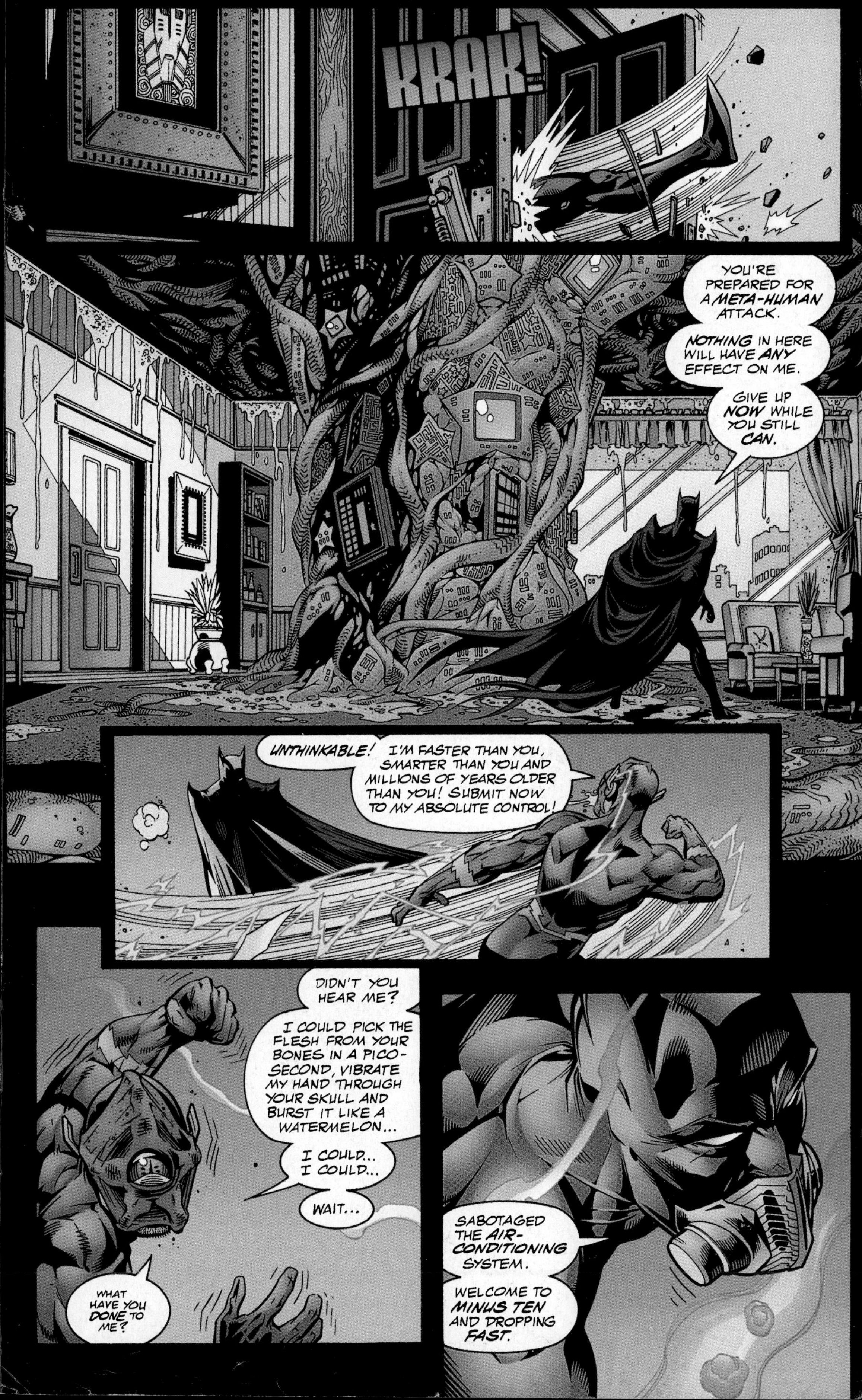
KRAK!
YOU'RE PREPARED FOR A META-HUMAN ATTACK.
NOTHING IN HERE WILL HAVE ANY EFFECT ON ME.
GIVE UP NOW WHILE YOU STILL CAN.
UNTHINKABLE! I'M FASTER THAN YOU, SMARTER THAN YOU AND MILLIONS OF YEARS OLDER THAN YOU! SUBMIT NOW TO MY ABSOLUTE CONTROL!
DIDN'T YOU HEAR ME?
I COULD PICK THE FLESH FROM YOUR BONES IN A PICO-SECOND, VIBRATE MY HAND THROUGH YOUR SKULL AND BURST IT LIKE A WATERMELON...
I COULD... I COULD...
WAIT...
WHAT HAVE YOU DONE TO ME?
SABOTAGED THE AIR-CONDITIONING SYSTEM.
WELCOME TO MINUS TEN AND DROPPING FAST.

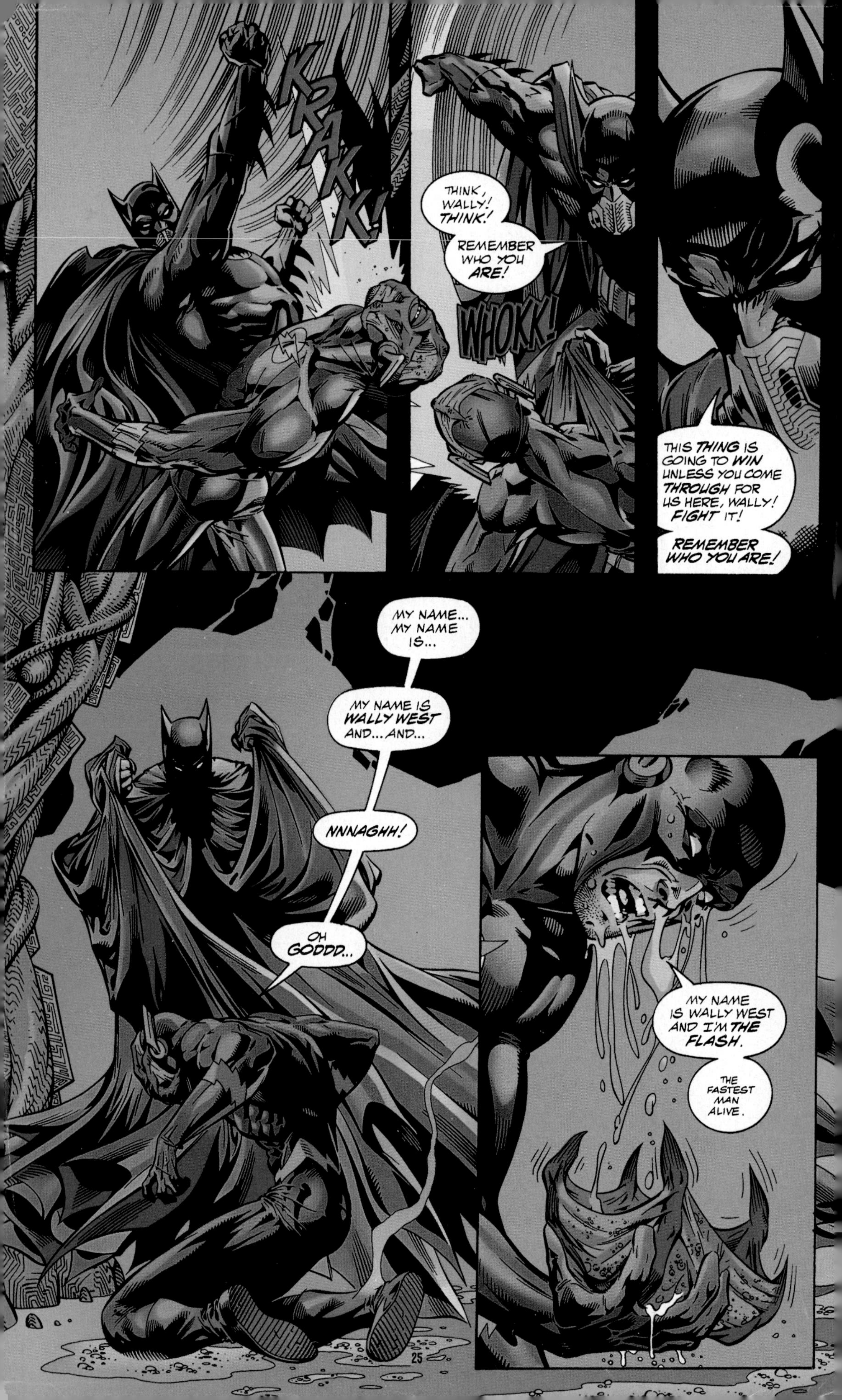
KRAKK!
THINK, WALLY! THINK!
REMEMBER WHO YOU ARE!
WHOKK!
THIS THING IS GOING TO WIN UNLESS YOU COME THROUGH FOR US HERE, WALLY! FIGHT IT!
REMEMBER WHO YOU ARE!
MY NAME... MY NAME IS...
MY NAME IS WALLY WEST AND... AND...
NNNAGHH!
OH GODDD...
MY NAME IS WALLY WEST AND I'M THE FLASH.
THE FASTEST MAN ALIVE.

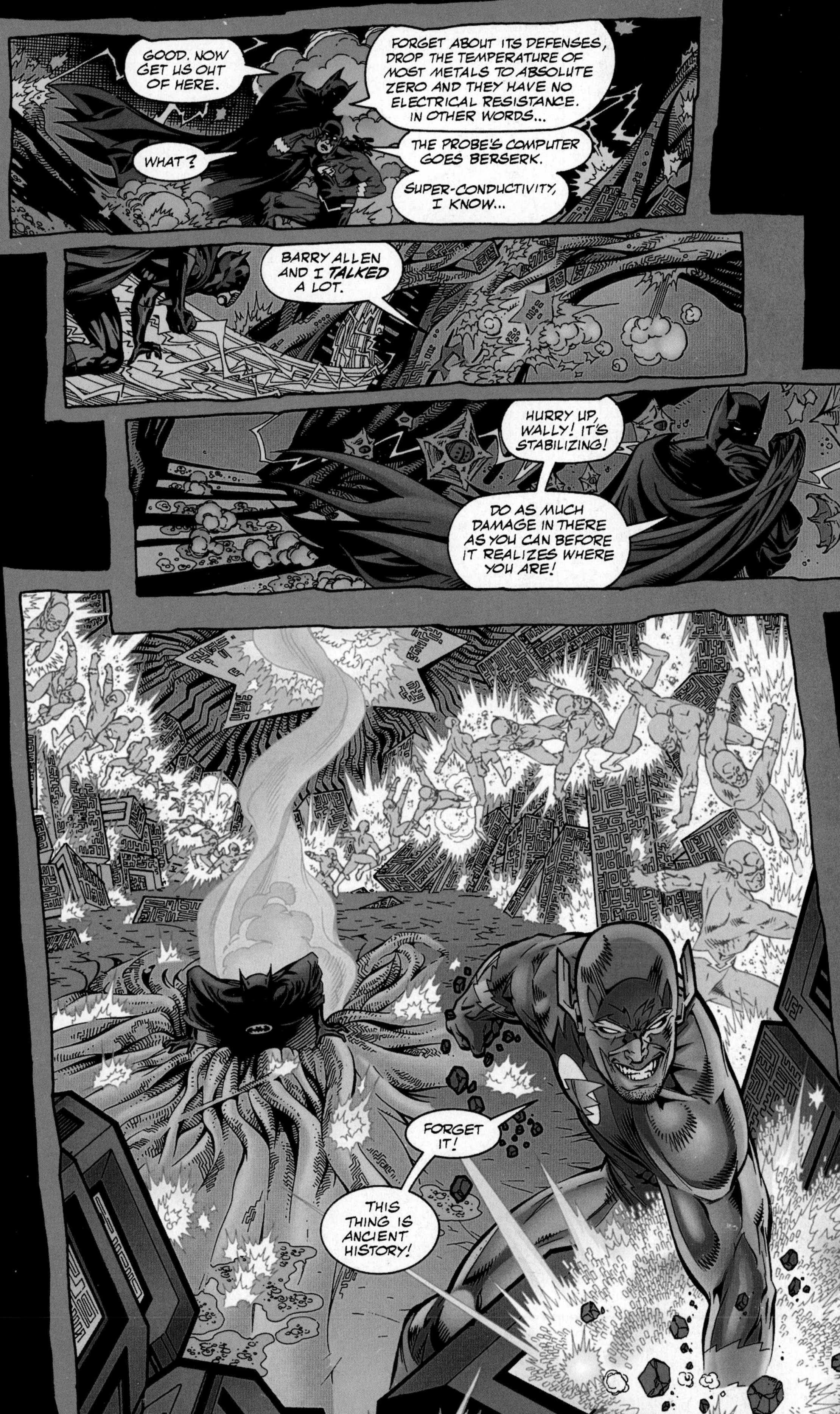
GOOD. NOW GET US OUT OF HERE.
FORGET ABOUT ITS DEFENSES, DROP THE TEMPERATURE OF MOST METALS TO ABSOLUTE ZERO AND THEY HAVE NO ELECTRICAL RESISTANCE. IN OTHER WORDS...
WHAT?
THE PROBE'S COMPUTER GOES BERSERK.
SUPER-CONDUCTIVITY, I KNOW...
BARRY ALLEN AND I TALKED A LOT.
HURRY UP, WALLY! IT'S STABILIZING!
DO AS MUCH DAMAGE IN THERE AS YOU CAN BEFORE IT REALIZES WHERE YOU ARE!
FORGET IT!
THIS THING IS ANCIENT HISTORY!

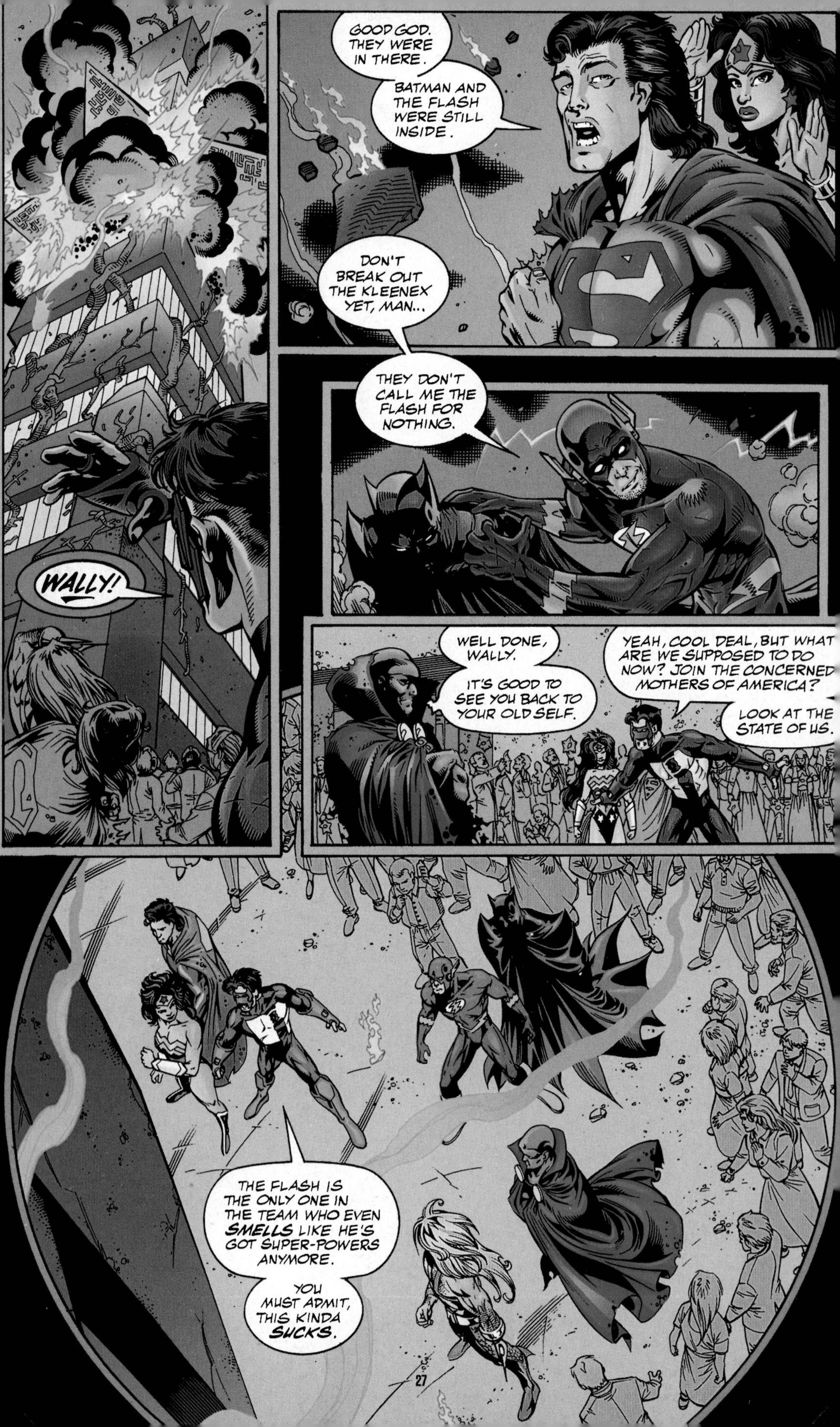
GOOD GOD. THEY WERE IN THERE.
BATMAN AND THE FLASH WERE STILL INSIDE.
DON'T BREAK OUT THE KLEENEX YET, MAN...
THEY DON'T CALL ME THE FLASH FOR NOTHING.
WALLY!
WELL DONE, WALLY.
IT'S GOOD TO SEE YOU BACK TO YOUR OLD SELF.
YEAH, COOL DEAL, BUT WHAT ARE WE SUPPOSED TO DO NOW? JOIN THE CONCERNED MOTHERS OF AMERICA?
LOOK AT THE STATE OF US.
THE FLASH IS THE ONLY ONE IN THE TEAM WHO EVEN SMELLS LIKE HE'S GOT SUPER-POWERS ANYMORE.
YOU MUST ADMIT, THIS KINDA SUCKS.

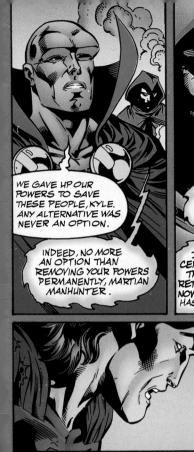

WE GAVE HP OUR POWERS TO SAVE THESE PEOPLE, KYLE. ANY ALTERNATIVE WAS NEVER AN OPTION.

INDEED, NO MORE AN OPTION THAN REMOVING YOUR POWERS PERMANENTLY, MARTIAN MANHUNTER.

THEY WERE NOT TAKEN AS A *PUNISHMENT*.

I CAN SEE NO CONCEIVABLE REASON WHY THEY SHOULD NOT BE RETURNED TO YOU IN FULL NOW THAT YOUR MISSION HAS BEEN ACCOMPLISHED.

ALL *RIGHT*!

GUESS THERE'S NO GETTING *RID* OF YOU, HUH?

SPECTRE?

I UNDERSTAND WHAT YOU DID FOR US TODAY AND WANT TO SAY HOW MUCH WE APPRECIATE YOUR INVOLVEMENT.

WHAT I DID WAS NOT FOR *YOU*, SUPERMAN.

THE FUTURE WAS MY ONLY CONCERN.

IT SHALL BE SAFE IN THE HANDS OF THE *JUSTICE LEAGUE*.

End

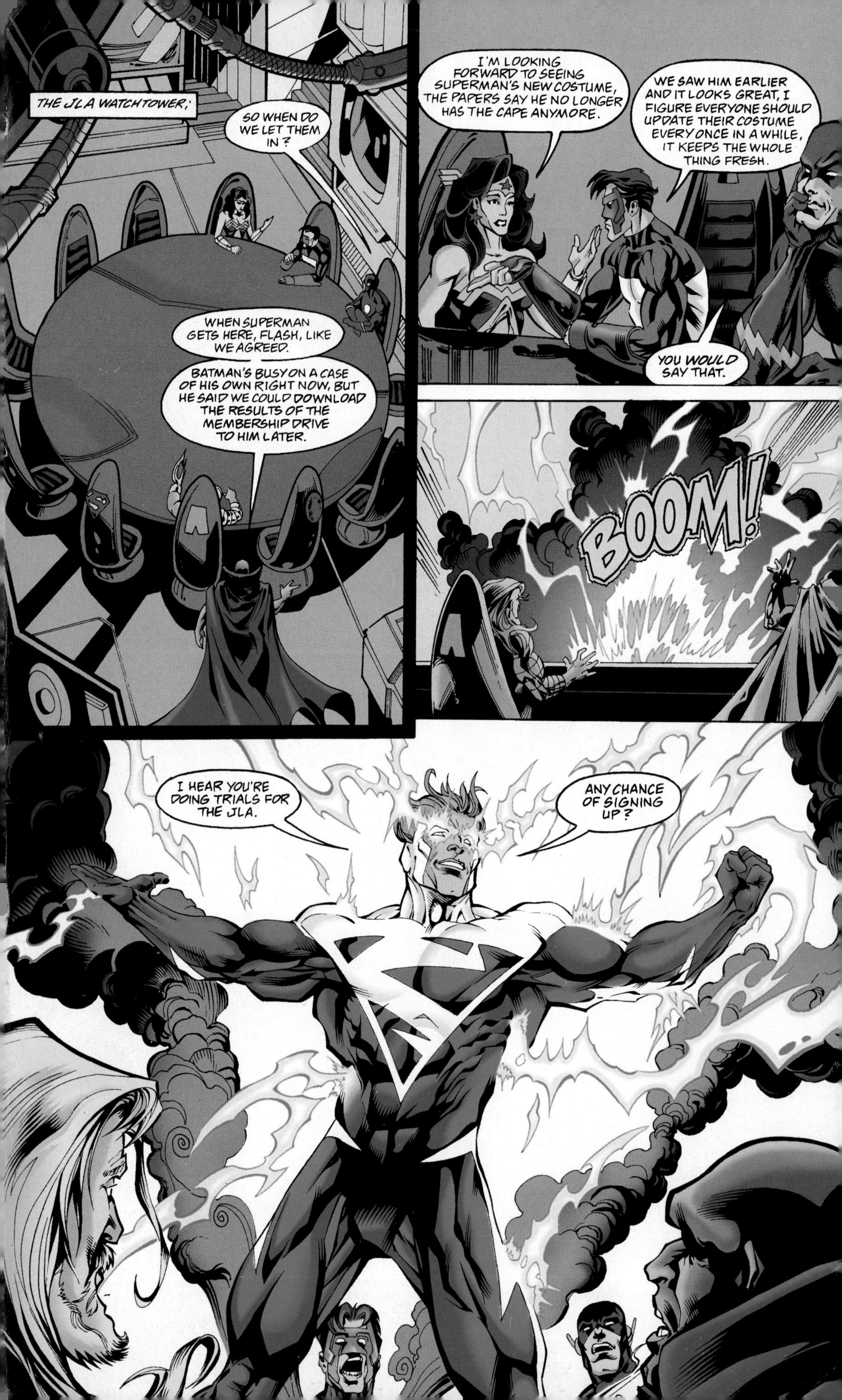
THE JLA WATCHTOWER;
SO WHEN DO WE LET THEM IN?
WHEN SUPERMAN GETS HERE, FLASH, LIKE WE AGREED.
BATMAN'S BUSY ON A CASE OF HIS OWN RIGHT NOW, BUT HE SAID WE COULD DOWNLOAD THE RESULTS OF THE MEMBERSHIP DRIVE TO HIM LATER.
I'M LOOKING FORWARD TO SEEING SUPERMAN'S NEW COSTUME, THE PAPERS SAY HE NO LONGER HAS THE CAPE ANYMORE.
WE SAW HIM EARLIER AND IT LOOKS GREAT, I FIGURE EVERYONE SHOULD UPDATE THEIR COSTUME EVERY ONCE IN A WHILE, IT KEEPS THE WHOLE THING FRESH.
YOU WOULD SAY THAT.
BOOM!
I HEAR YOU'RE DOING TRIALS FOR THE JLA.
ANY CHANCE OF SIGNING UP?

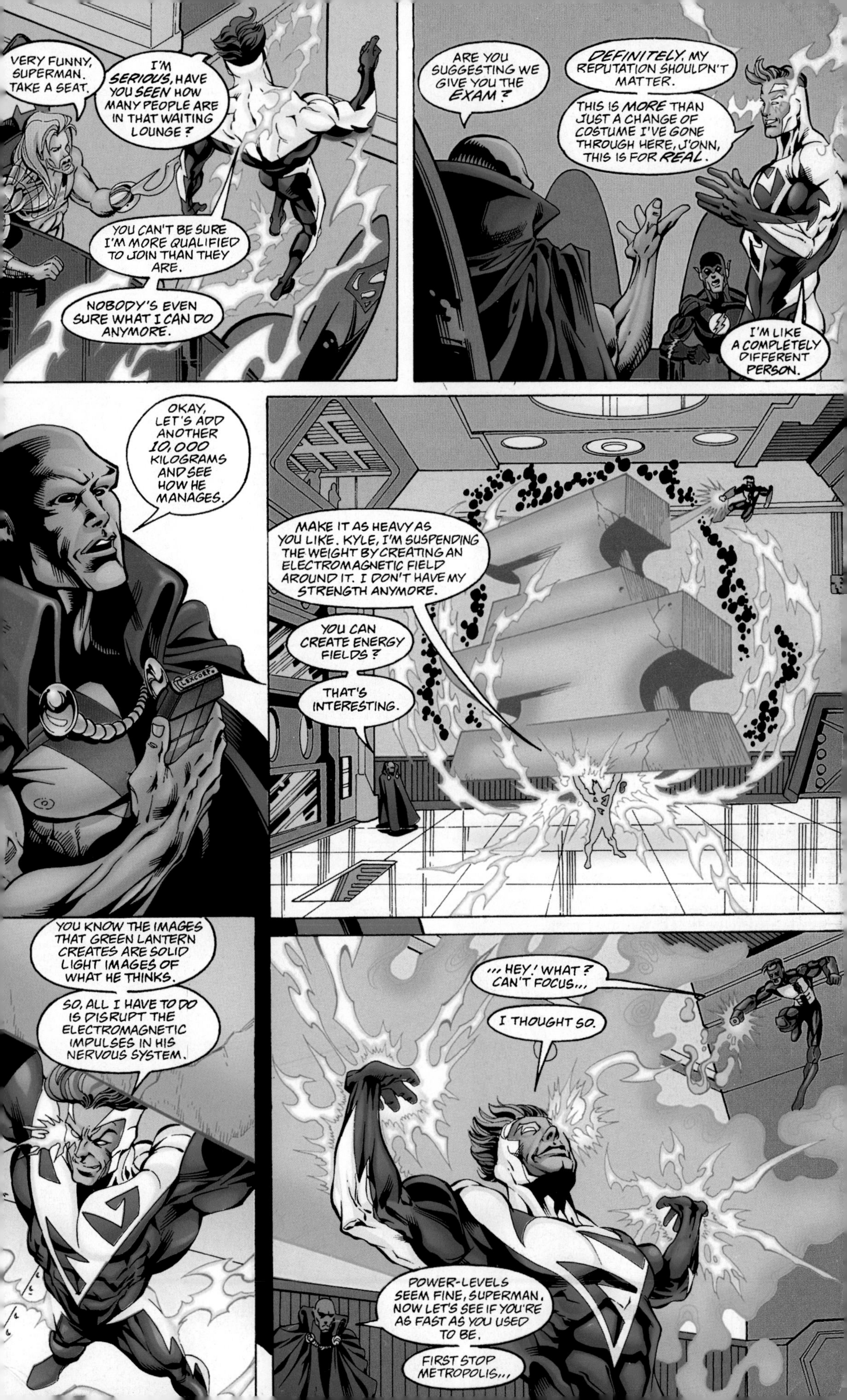
VERY FUNNY, SUPERMAN. TAKE A SEAT.
I'M SERIOUS, HAVE YOU SEEN HOW MANY PEOPLE ARE IN THAT WAITING LOUNGE?
YOU CAN'T BE SURE I'M MORE QUALIFIED TO JOIN THAN THEY ARE.
NOBODY'S EVEN SURE WHAT I CAN DO ANYMORE.
ARE YOU SUGGESTING WE GIVE YOU THE EXAM?
DEFINITELY. MY REPUTATION SHOULDN'T MATTER.
THIS IS MORE THAN JUST A CHANGE OF COSTUME I'VE GONE THROUGH HERE, J'ONN, THIS IS FOR REAL.
I'M LIKE A COMPLETELY DIFFERENT PERSON.
OKAY, LET'S ADD ANOTHER 10,000 KILOGRAMS AND SEE HOW HE MANAGES.
LEXCORP
MAKE IT AS HEAVY AS YOU LIKE. KYLE, I'M SUSPENDING THE WEIGHT BY CREATING AN ELECTROMAGNETIC FIELD AROUND IT. I DON'T HAVE MY STRENGTH ANYMORE.
YOU CAN CREATE ENERGY FIELDS?
THAT'S INTERESTING.
YOU KNOW THE IMAGES THAT GREEN LANTERN CREATES ARE SOLID LIGHT IMAGES OF WHAT HE THINKS.
SO, ALL I HAVE TO DO IS DISRUPT THE ELECTROMAGNETIC IMPULSES IN HIS NERVOUS SYSTEM.
...HEY! WHAT? CAN'T FOCUS...
I THOUGHT SO.
POWER-LEVELS SEEM FINE, SUPERMAN. NOW LET'S SEE IF YOU'RE AS FAST AS YOU USED TO BE.
FIRST STOP METROPOLIS...

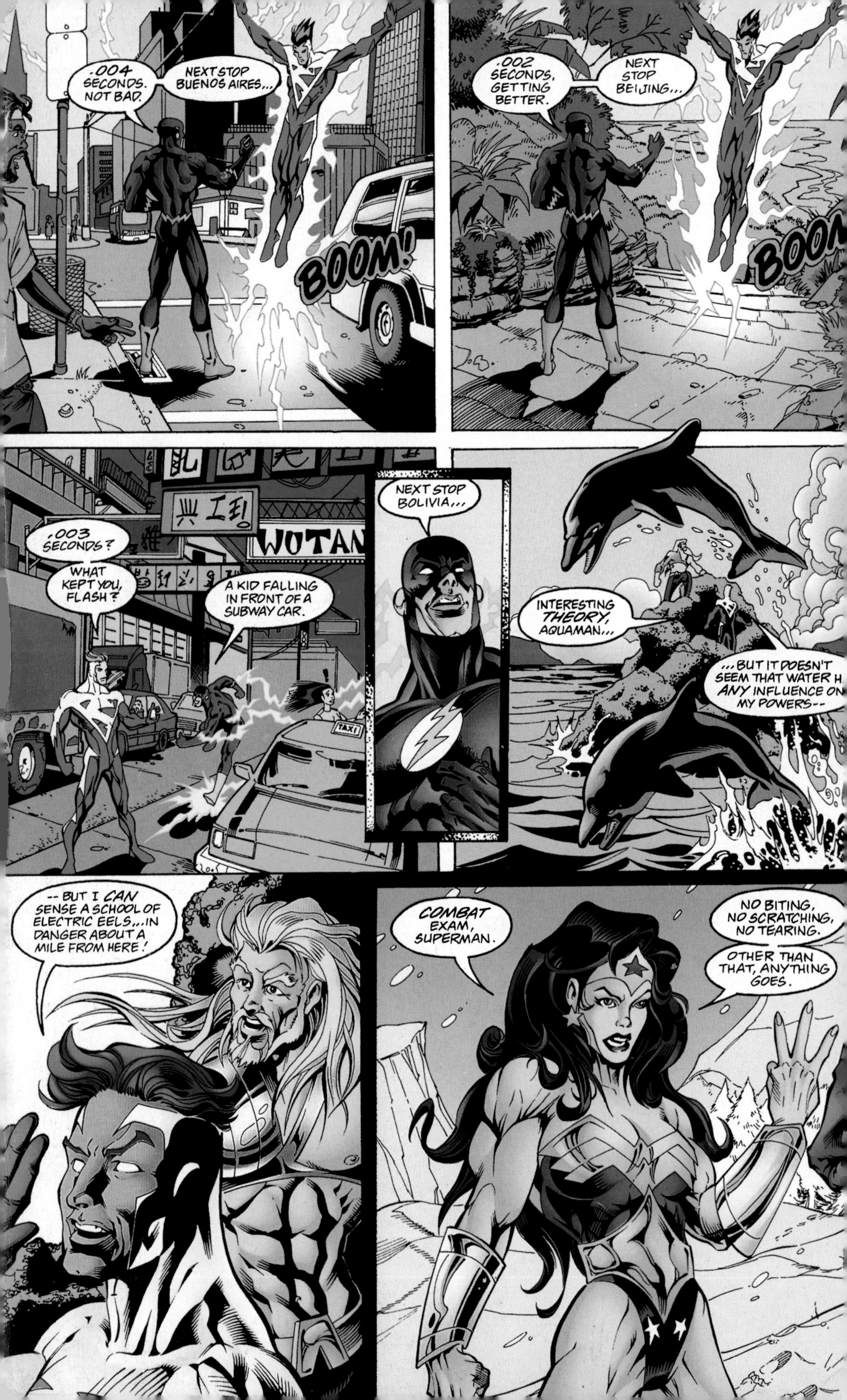
.004 SECONDS. NOT BAD.
NEXT STOP BUENOS AIRES...
BOOM!
.002 SECONDS, GETTING BETTER.
NEXT STOP BEIJING...
BOOM
.003 SECONDS?
WHAT KEPT YOU, FLASH?
A KID FALLING IN FRONT OF A SUBWAY CAR.
WOTAN
TAXI
NEXT STOP BOLIVIA...
INTERESTING THEORY, AQUAMAN...
...BUT IT DOESN'T SEEM THAT WATER H ANY INFLUENCE ON MY POWERS--
-- BUT I CAN SENSE A SCHOOL OF ELECTRIC EELS... IN DANGER ABOUT A MILE FROM HERE!
COMBAT EXAM, SUPERMAN.
NO BITING, NO SCRATCHING, NO TEARING.
OTHER THAN THAT, ANYTHING GOES.

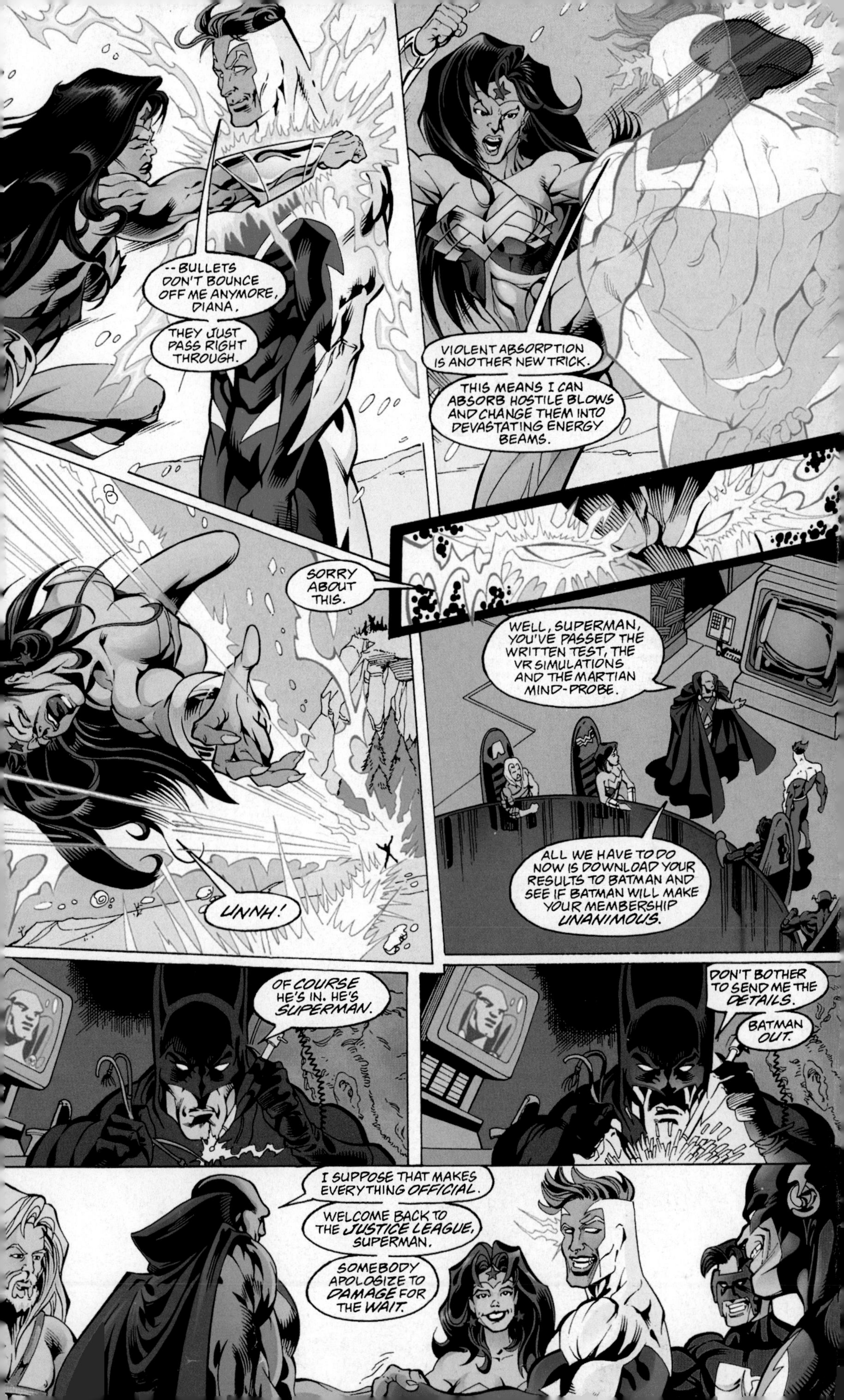
--BULLETS DON'T BOUNCE OFF ME ANYMORE, DIANA.
THEY JUST PASS RIGHT THROUGH.
VIOLENT ABSORPTION IS ANOTHER NEW TRICK.
THIS MEANS I CAN ABSORB HOSTILE BLOWS AND CHANGE THEM INTO DEVASTATING ENERGY BEAMS.
SORRY ABOUT THIS.
UNNH!
WELL, SUPERMAN, YOU'VE PASSED THE WRITTEN TEST, THE VR SIMULATIONS AND THE MARTIAN MIND-PROBE.
ALL WE HAVE TO DO NOW IS DOWNLOAD YOUR RESULTS TO BATMAN AND SEE IF BATMAN WILL MAKE YOUR MEMBERSHIP UNANIMOUS.
OF COURSE HE'S IN. HE'S SUPERMAN.
DON'T BOTHER TO SEND ME THE DETAILS.
BATMAN OUT.
I SUPPOSE THAT MAKES EVERYTHING OFFICIAL.
WELCOME BACK TO THE JUSTICE LEAGUE, SUPERMAN.
SOMEBODY APOLOGIZE TO DAMAGE FOR THE WAIT.

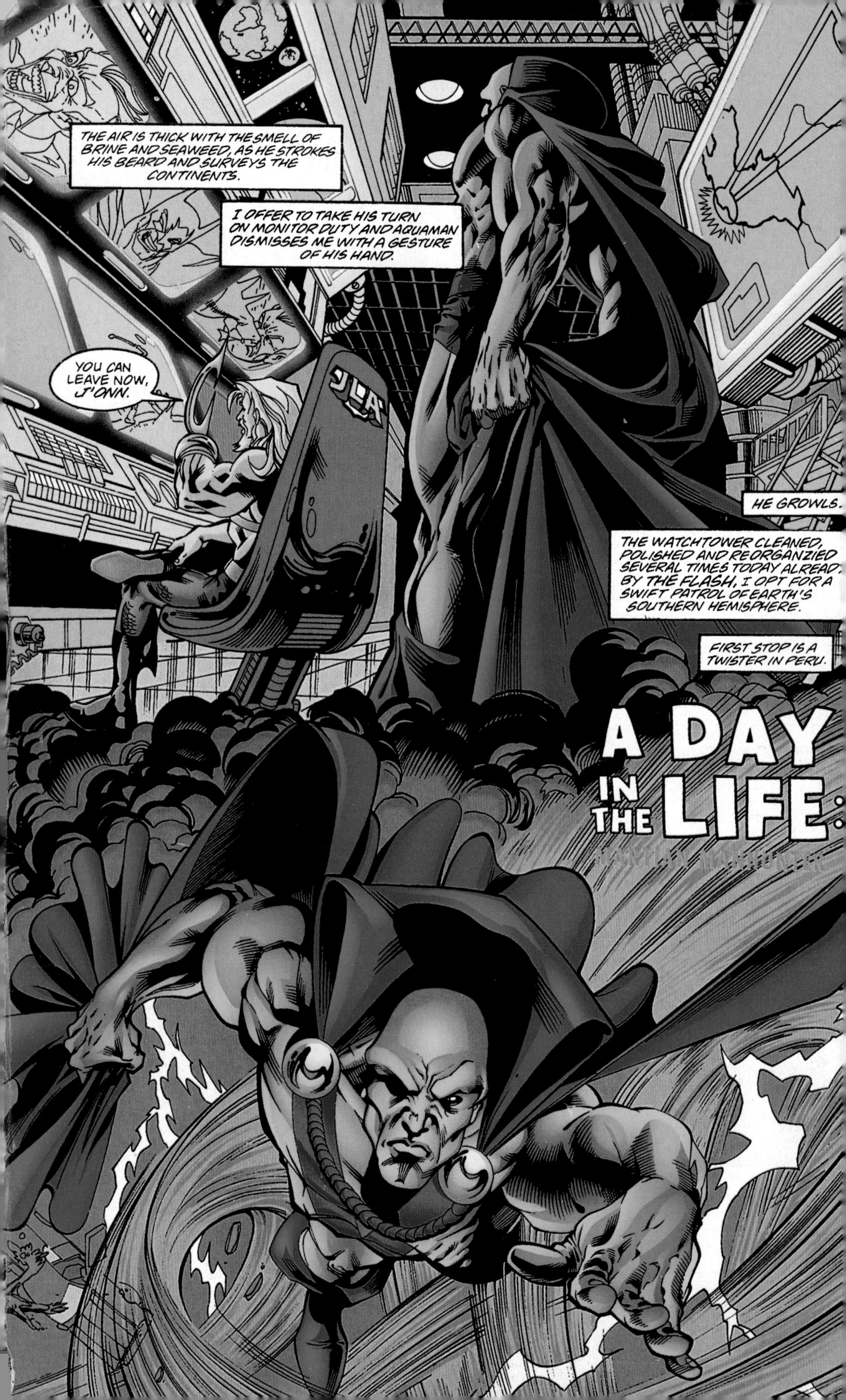
THE AIR IS THICK WITH THE SMELL OF BRINE AND SEAWEED, AS HE STROKES HIS BEARD AND SURVEYS THE CONTINENTS.
I OFFER TO TAKE HIS TURN ON MONITOR DUTY AND AQUAMAN DISMISSES ME WITH A GESTURE OF HIS HAND.
YOU CAN LEAVE NOW, J'ONN.
JLA
HE GROWLS.
THE WATCHTOWER CLEANED, POLISHED AND REORGANZIED SEVERAL TIMES TODAY ALREAD BY THE FLASH, I OPT FOR A SWIFT PATROL OF EARTH'S SOUTHERN HEMISPHERE.
FIRST STOP IS A TWISTER IN PERU.
A DAY IN THE LIFE:

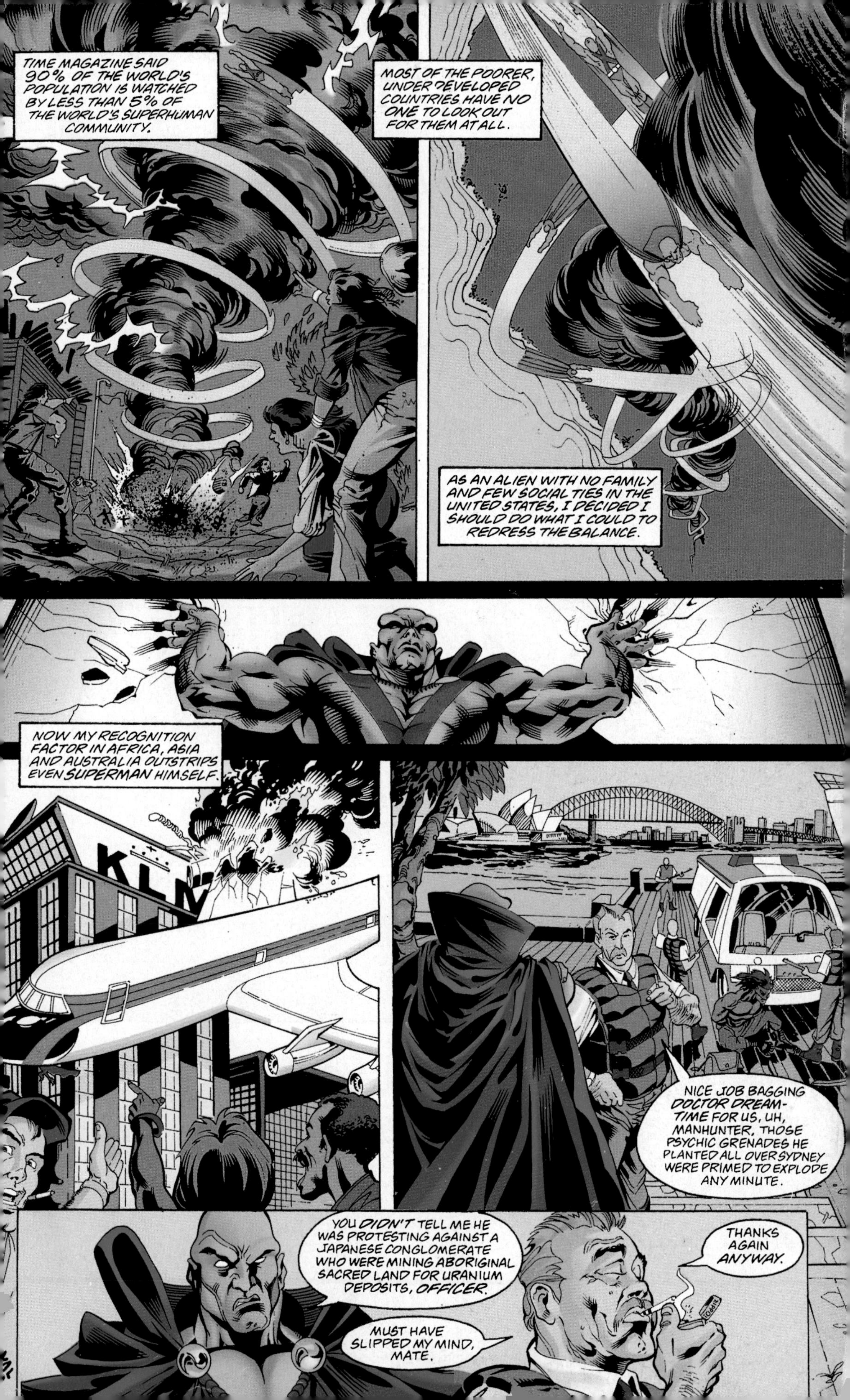
TIME MAGAZINE SAID 90% OF THE WORLD'S POPULATION IS WATCHED BY LESS THAN 5% OF THE WORLD'S SUPERHUMAN COMMUNITY.
MOST OF THE POORER, UNDERDEVELOPED COUNTRIES HAVE NO ONE TO LOOK OUT FOR THEM AT ALL.
AS AN ALIEN WITH NO FAMILY AND FEW SOCIAL TIES IN THE UNITED STATES, I DECIDED I SHOULD DO WHAT I COULD TO REDRESS THE BALANCE.
NOW MY RECOGNITION FACTOR IN AFRICA, ASIA AND AUSTRALIA OUTSTRIPS EVEN SUPERMAN HIMSELF.
NICE JOB BAGGING DOCTOR DREAMTIME FOR US, UH, MANHUNTER. THOSE PSYCHIC GRENADES HE PLANTED ALL OVER SYDNEY WERE PRIMED TO EXPLODE ANY MINUTE.
YOU DIDN'T TELL ME HE WAS PROTESTING AGAINST A JAPANESE CONGLOMERATE WHO WERE MINING ABORIGINAL SACRED LAND FOR URANIUM DEPOSITS, OFFICER.
MUST HAVE SLIPPED MY MIND, MATE.
THANKS AGAIN ANYWAY.

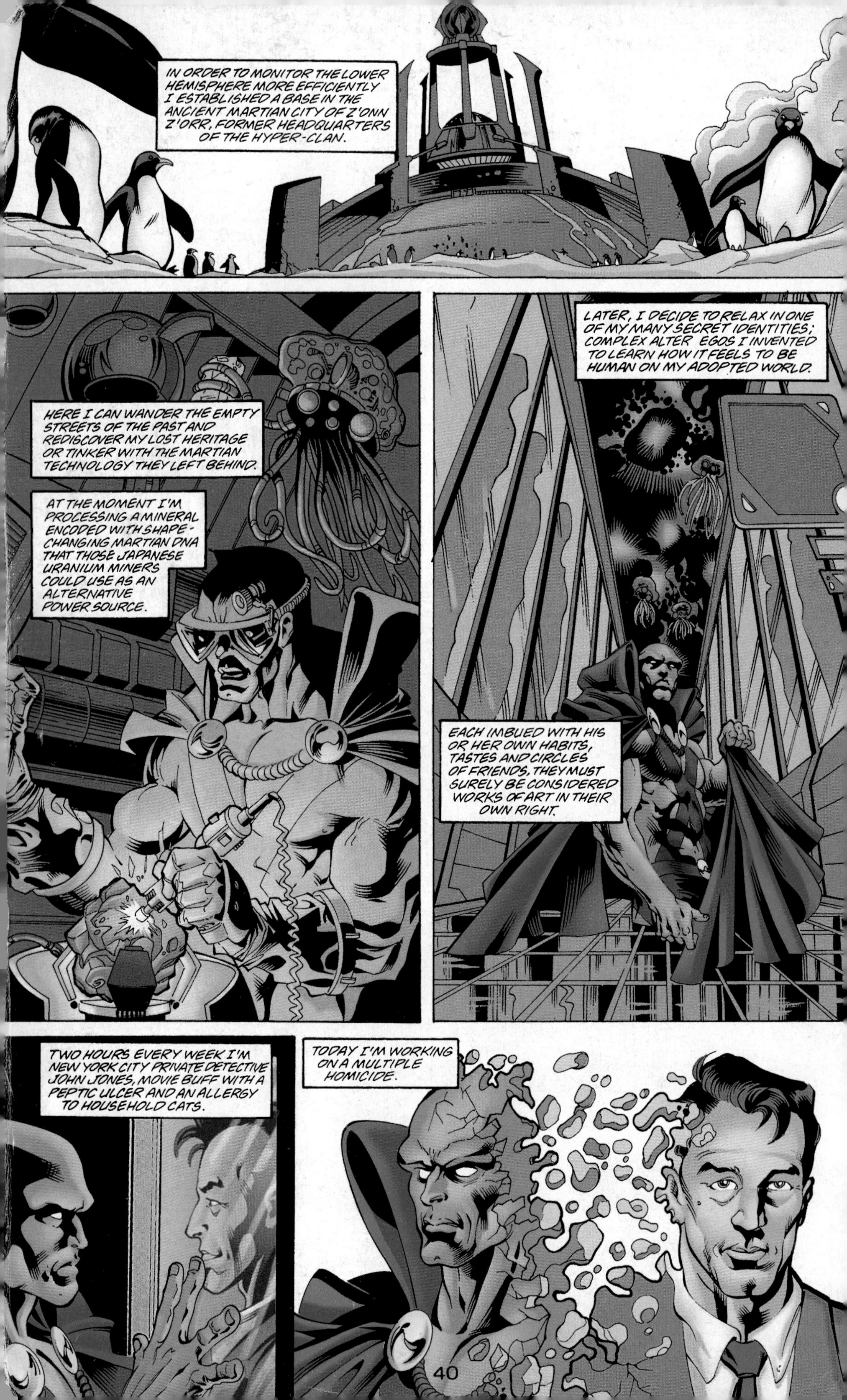
IN ORDER TO MONITOR THE LOWER HEMISPHERE MORE EFFICIENTLY I ESTABLISHED A BASE IN THE ANCIENT MARTIAN CITY OF Z'ONN Z'ORR, FORMER HEADQUARTERS OF THE HYPER-CLAN.
HERE I CAN WANDER THE EMPTY STREETS OF THE PAST AND REDISCOVER MY LOST HERITAGE OR TINKER WITH THE MARTIAN TECHNOLOGY THEY LEFT BEHIND.
AT THE MOMENT I'M PROCESSING A MINERAL ENCODED WITH SHAPE-CHANGING MARTIAN DNA THAT THOSE JAPANESE URANIUM MINERS COULD USE AS AN ALTERNATIVE POWER SOURCE.
LATER, I DECIDE TO RELAX IN ONE OF MY MANY SECRET IDENTITIES; COMPLEX ALTER EGOS I INVENTED TO LEARN HOW IT FEELS TO BE HUMAN ON MY ADOPTED WORLD.
EACH IMBUED WITH HIS OR HER OWN HABITS, TASTES AND CIRCLES OF FRIENDS, THEY MUST SURELY BE CONSIDERED WORKS OF ART IN THEIR OWN RIGHT.
TWO HOURS EVERY WEEK I'M NEW YORK CITY PRIVATE DETECTIVE JOHN JONES, MOVIE BUFF WITH A PEPTIC ULCER AND AN ALLERGY TO HOUSEHOLD CATS.
TODAY I'M WORKING ON A MULTIPLE HOMICIDE.

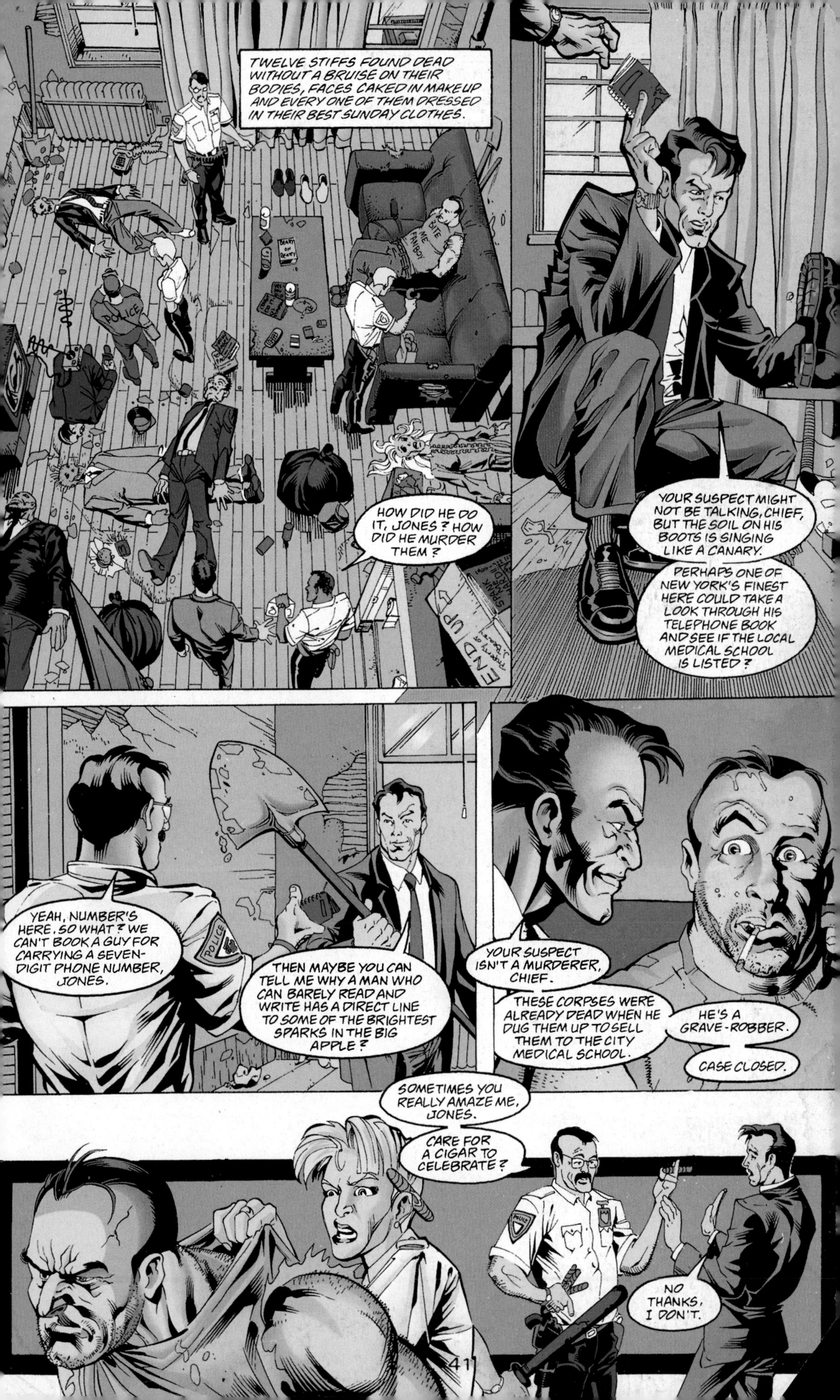
TWELVE STIFFS FOUND DEAD WITHOUT A BRUISE ON THEIR BODIES, FACES CAKED IN MAKEUP AND EVERY ONE OF THEM DRESSED IN THEIR BEST SUNDAY CLOTHES.
HOW DID HE DO IT, JONES? HOW DID HE MURDER THEM?
YOUR SUSPECT MIGHT NOT BE TALKING, CHIEF, BUT THE SOIL ON HIS BOOTS IS SINGING LIKE A CANARY.
PERHAPS ONE OF NEW YORK'S FINEST HERE COULD TAKE A LOOK THROUGH HIS TELEPHONE BOOK AND SEE IF THE LOCAL MEDICAL SCHOOL IS LISTED?
YEAH, NUMBER'S HERE. SO WHAT? WE CAN'T BOOK A GUY FOR CARRYING A SEVEN-DIGIT PHONE NUMBER, JONES.
THEN MAYBE YOU CAN TELL ME WHY A MAN WHO CAN BARELY READ AND WRITE HAS A DIRECT LINE TO SOME OF THE BRIGHTEST SPARKS IN THE BIG APPLE?
YOUR SUSPECT ISN'T A MURDERER, CHIEF.
THESE CORPSES WERE ALREADY DEAD WHEN HE DUG THEM UP TO SELL THEM TO THE CITY MEDICAL SCHOOL.
HE'S A GRAVE-ROBBER.
CASE CLOSED.
SOMETIMES YOU REALLY AMAZE ME, JONES.
CARE FOR A CIGAR TO CELEBRATE?
NO THANKS, I DON'T.

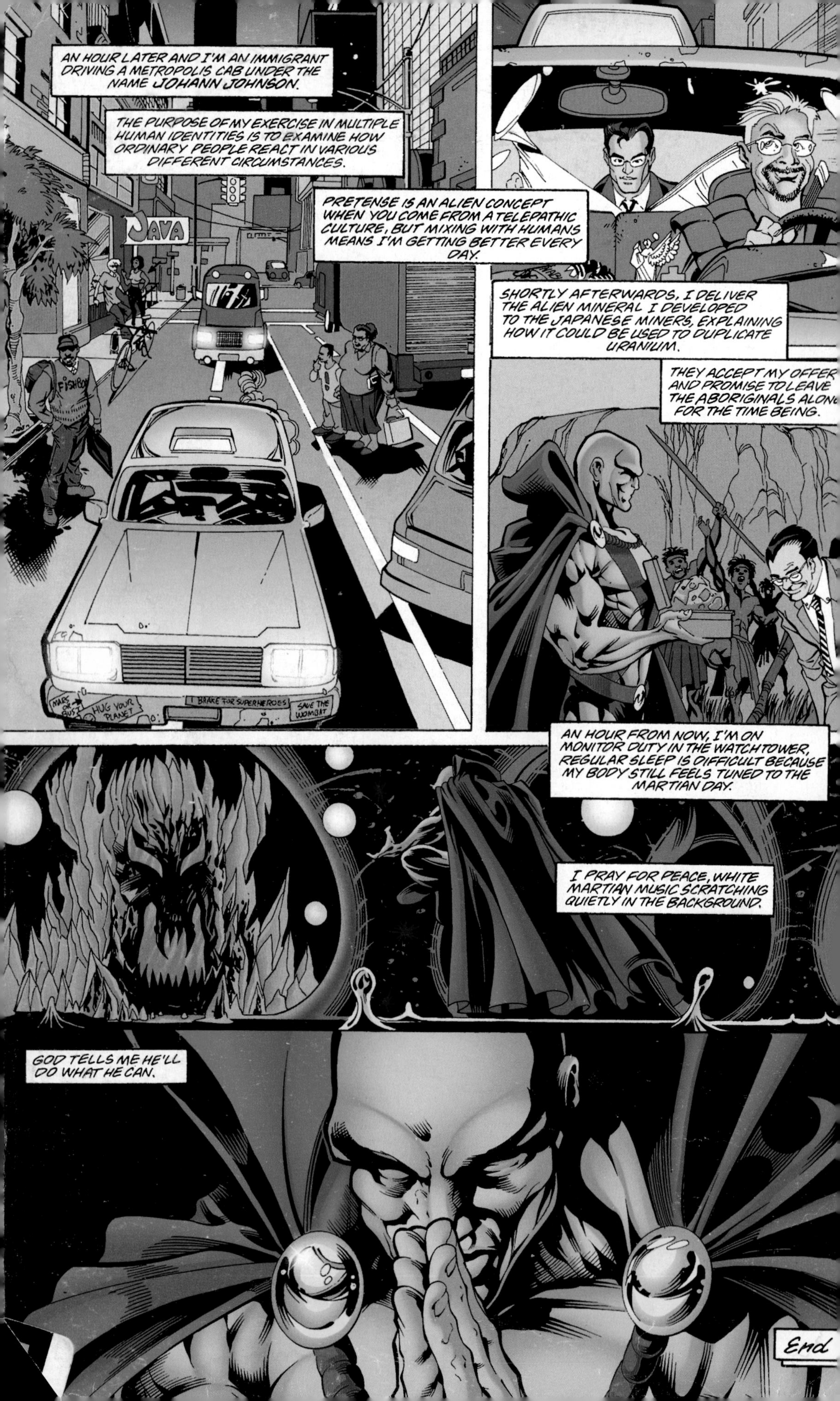
AN HOUR LATER AND I'M AN IMMIGRANT DRIVING A METROPOLIS CAB UNDER THE NAME JOHANN JOHNSON.
THE PURPOSE OF MY EXERCISE IN MULTIPLE HUMAN IDENTITIES IS TO EXAMINE HOW ORDINARY PEOPLE REACT IN VARIOUS DIFFERENT CIRCUMSTANCES.
PRETENSE IS AN ALIEN CONCEPT WHEN YOU COME FROM A TELEPATHIC CULTURE, BUT MIXING WITH HUMANS MEANS I'M GETTING BETTER EVERY DAY.
JAVA
FISHBOY
MARS OR BUST
HUG YOUR PLANET
I BRAKE FOR SUPERHEROES
SAVE THE WOMBAT
SHORTLY AFTERWARDS, I DELIVER THE ALIEN MINERAL I DEVELOPED TO THE JAPANESE MINERS, EXPLAINING HOW IT COULD BE USED TO DUPLICATE URANIUM.
THEY ACCEPT MY OFFER AND PROMISE TO LEAVE THE ABORIGINALS ALON FOR THE TIME BEING.
AN HOUR FROM NOW, I'M ON MONITOR DUTY IN THE WATCHTOWER. REGULAR SLEEP IS DIFFICULT BECAUSE MY BODY STILL FEELS TUNED TO THE MARTIAN DAY.
I PRAY FOR PEACE, WHITE MARTIAN MUSIC SCRATCHING QUIETLY IN THE BACKGROUND.
GOD TELLS ME HE'LL DO WHAT HE CAN.
End